Generis
PUBLISHING

AF842537

ADVANCED STATISTICS

GREEK ALPHABET					
Alpha	**Beta**	**Gamma**	**Delta**	**Epsilon**	**Phi**
$\mathrm{A}(\alpha)$	$\mathrm{B}(\beta)$	$\Gamma(\gamma)$	$\Delta(\delta)$	$E(\varepsilon)$	$\Phi(\varphi)$
Zeta	**Eta**	**Theta**	**Iota**	**Kappa**	**Chi**
$\mathrm{Z}(\zeta)$	$\mathrm{H}(\eta)$	$\Theta(\theta)$	$\mathrm{I}(\iota)$	$\mathrm{K}\ (\kappa)$	$\mathrm{X}(\chi)$
Lambda	**Mu**	**Nu**	**Xi**	**Omicron**	**Psi**
$\Lambda(\lambda)$	$M(\mu)$	$\mathrm{N}(\nu)$	$\Xi(\xi)$	$\mathrm{O}(o)$	$\Psi(\psi)$
Pi	**Rho**	**Sigma**	**Tau**	**Upsilon**	**Omega**
$\Pi(\pi)$	$\mathrm{P}(\rho)$	$\Sigma(\sigma)$	$\mathrm{T}(\tau)$	$\Upsilon(\upsilon)$	$\Omega(\omega)$

FIRST EDITION

MBOKA NYAMSI GEORGES BIENVENUE

University of Bamenda

mbokabienvenue@gmail.com

Title: Advanced statitics
ISBN: 978-1-63902-728-6
Author: MBOKA NYAMSI GEORGES BIENVENUE

Cover image: www.pixabay.com

Generis Publishing
Online orders: www.generis-publishing.com
Orders by email: info@generis-publishing.co

PREFACE

This book is conceived and written in a simple manner to provide mathematical analysis that uses quantified models, representations and synopses for a given set of experimental data or real-life situations. The author provides a thoughtful and practical guide to learners of advanced statistics in the area of linear correlation, time series analysis, probability analysis, sampling and estimation, hypotheses testing, project management, decision making, Chi-square test and control chart.

ACKNOWLEDGEMENT

This piece of work could not be completed without the support of some individual person, their contributions to this work is either direct or indirect.

I am sincerely grateful to the contribution of Mr. Vukenkeng Andrew Wujung (PhD), Mr. Saidou Baba Oumar (PhD) and Mr. Ngalim Valentine (PhD) and who out of their busy schedule and tied office duties, made critical comments which were considered in the realization of this work.

I am indebted to the following persons: Mrs. Azongwa Doris Ngeche, Mr. Chi Brandone, Mrs. Nfor Amalia, Mr. Derick Viban, Mr. Saidu Sali, Miss Fai Sairatu Miss Liybarfeh and Miss Tanfen Marinette, who took out time from the precious time to edit the work.

My particular thanks goes to the following persons: Mr. Wingo Kilian, Mrs. Ngoran Enerstine, Mrs. Fondzenyuy nee Anester Bonjeh, Mr. Anthony Lupiya. Mr. Tati Daniel for the moral contribution to the work.

Special thanks goes to the following friends and colleague: Mrs. Blandine Burinyuy, Mr. Mbinka Benoit Shalanyuy, Mrs Aghen Laura Endah epse Banseka, Mr. Sewoyehbaa Marcel, Mr. Shu Elvis, Mr. Eric Njong Seka, Mr. Akumbom Paul, Mr. Penanje Christain, Miss Emeniguene Balindi Laure, Mr. Wanda Njinkeu Bonaventure, Mr. Bonou Nkeh Blaise and Gola Kongnyuy Jean Claude for their moral and motivational support.

DEDICATION

To

The Family of Nyamsi Pierre

TABLE OF CONTENTS

CHAPTER 1

LINEAR CORRELATION

Statistically any elements (social economic, political and natural) under study are called variables. Variables can be independent variables (y) and dependent variables (x).

1.1 Meaning of Linear Correlation

Sir F. Galton

Linear correlation is a statistical tool that measures the direction and degree of relationship between variables. Note that correlation analysis does not measure variables cause-effect relationship or causality and its numerical value (nv) ranges from [$\pm 0 \leq nv \geq \pm 1$]

1.2 Types of Correlation

The different types of correlations are best understood under the following elements; the number of variables involved and the direction of variables numerical values.

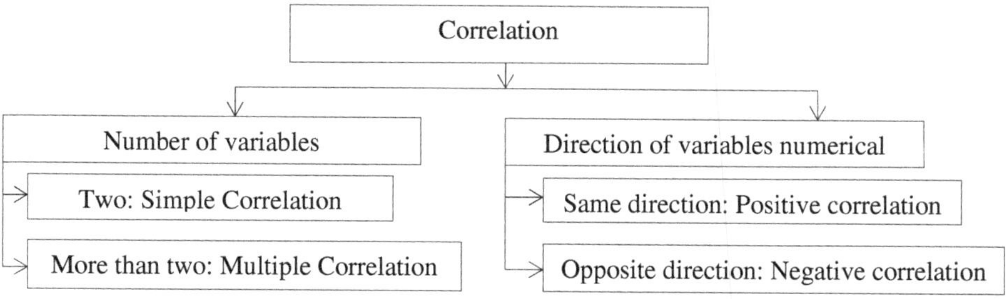

1.2.1 Positive Correlation and Negative Correlation

Correlation is positive when the numerical values of variables changes in the same direction. That is, a simultaneous increase or decrease of variables numerical values. Correlation is negative when variables numerical values changes in opposite direction. That is, when a variable numerical value increases (decreases), the numerical value of another variable decreases (increases).

Positive correlation					**Negative correlation**				
X	10	20	30	40	**X**	10	20	30	40
Y	5	10	15	20	**Y**	20	15	10	2
"**X**" is increasing and "**Y**" is also increasing"					"**X**" is increasing and "**Y**" is decreasing"				

Note: An alternative way to determine if a correlation is positive or negative is to compute the correlation value and identify its mathematical sign. For instance, $(+0.9)$ shows positive correlation and (-0.9) negative correlation.

1.2.2 Simple Correlation and Multiple Correlation

Correlation is simple when only two variables are compared. Correlation is multiple when more than two variables are compared.

Simple Correlation

Price [**X**]	10	20	30	40
Quantity [**Y**]	5	10	1	20

Multiple Correlation

Price [$\mathbf{X_1}$]	10	20	30	40
Income [$\mathbf{X_2}$]	15	20	25	30
Others [**X**]	20	25	30	35
Quantity [**Y**]	5	10	15	20

Note: The strength of correlation between variable is called the degree or magnitude of correlation (r) or correlation coefficient. The different sub-divided of the degree of correlations as seen below.

$r = \pm 1$ [That is exactly 1]	Positive or negative perfect Correlation
$\pm 1 > r \geq \pm 0.7$ [That is 0.9 to 0.7]	Positive or negative very Strong Correlation
$\pm 0.7 \geq r \geq 0.5$ [That is 0.6 to 0.5]	Positive or negative moderate Correlation
$\pm 0.5 \geq r \geq 0.3$ [That is 0.4 to 0.3]	Positive or negative weak Correlation
$\pm 0.3 \geq r > 0$ [That is 0.3 to 0.1]	Positive or negative very Weak Correlation
$r = 0$ [That is exactly 0]	No Correlation

1.3 Methods of Measuring Correlation

The direction and degree of correlation is computed using different graphical and algebraic methods as illustrated below.

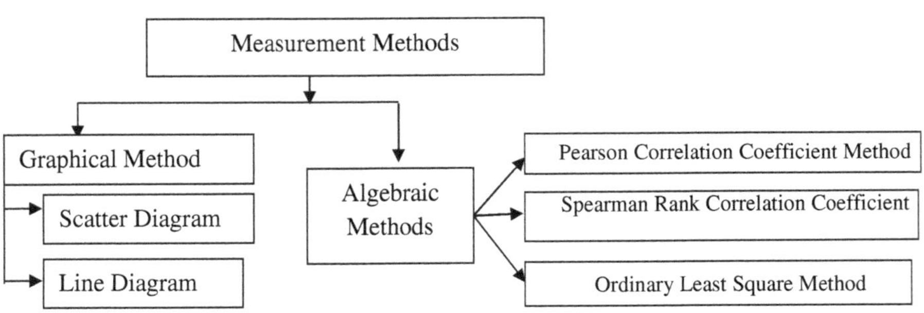

1.3.1 Graphical Methods of Measuring Linear Correlation

Here we are going to apply lines and dots to show how two or more set of measurement or variables are related to each other. Graphical methods are appropriate for two dimensional illustrations or two variables analysis and its complexity increases as the number of variable increase.

1) Scatter Diagram or Scatter plot

Scatter plot displays the relationship between variables using dots. It is a graph of observed plotted points where each point represents the coordinate values of variables. Scattered plot interpretation is based on the closeness of dots and direction of dots. The Closeness of dots shows the degree of correlation and the direction of dots shows the direction of correlation. Scatter plot is appropriate in determining the direction of correlation and more complex to use in determining the degree of correlation with accuracy.

Sir John Frederick

Example 1: The table below shows the production of cocoa measured in quantity for a given country over six years. What is the correlation between cocoa production and years using the scattered diagram method and justify your answer using the observation technique.

Years	2000	2001	2002	2003	2004	2005
Quantity	20	40	60	80	100	120

Solution

Step 1: Data Plotting. When plotting your data always remember to respect the concept of interval and all coordinate point must be identified by a dot. Lines linking the coordinate point should be slightly visible so that when erased, it should not dirty your illustration.

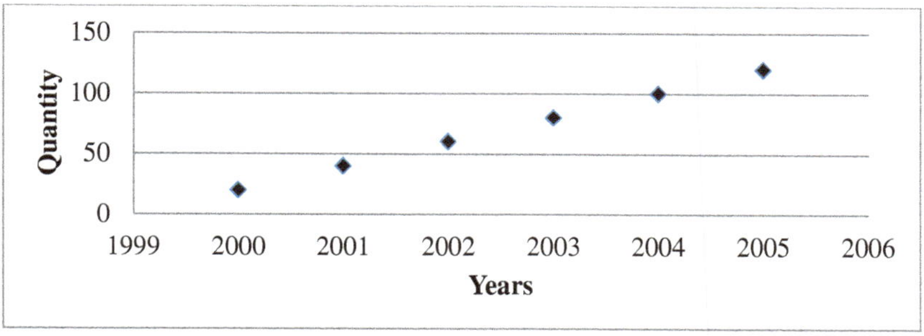

Step 2: Interpretation. The dot follows a perfectly straight line and is having a positive slope. The positive slope shows that the variable is positively related and the perfect lining of dots show perfect relationship. Therefore, our variables are perfectly and positively correlated.

Observation Justification: As the number of years increase, the quantity of production also increases. This shows that the variables are positively related.

Example 2: What is the correlation between the variables X and Y using information of the table below and justify your answer using observation.

X	2010	2011	2012	2013	2014
Y	1,000	800	600	400	200

Solution

Step 1: Data Plotting

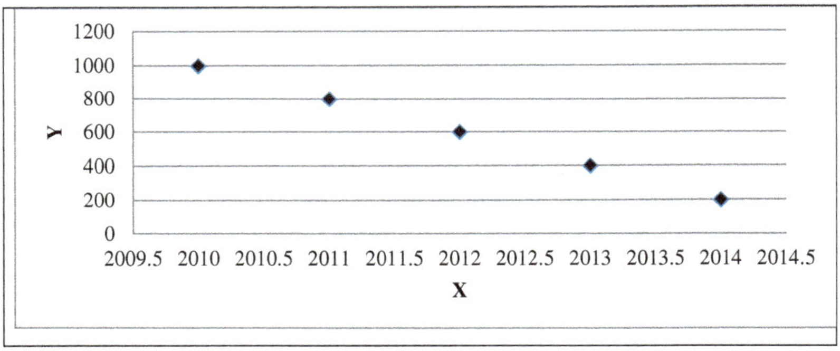

Step 2: Interpretation. The dot follows a perfectly straight line and is having a negative slope. The negative slope shows that the variable is negatively related and the perfect lining of dots show perfect relationship. Therefore, our variables are negatively and positively correlated.

Observation Justification: As numerical value of variable X increases, the numerical value of the variable Y decreases. This shows that our variables are negatively related.

2) Line (Chronological) Diagram Method

A line diagram is simply a scatter diagram in which dots are being connected by a line (usually a free hand line). Here, we are going to see just an example to avoid idea repetition.

Example 1: The table below shows a chronological series of Ndop rice production from 1990 to 1995 measured in quantity.

Years	1990	1991	1992	1993	1994	1995
Quantity	400	350	300	250	200	150

1) Draw a line or chronological diagram and interpret its meaning
2) What should be the government reaction based on your answer in 1 above.
3) Assume rice is the most consumed food and has no substitutes, what will be the effect on price and standard of living over time?

Solution

1) **Drawing of line or chronological diagram**

Step 1: Plotting of graph.

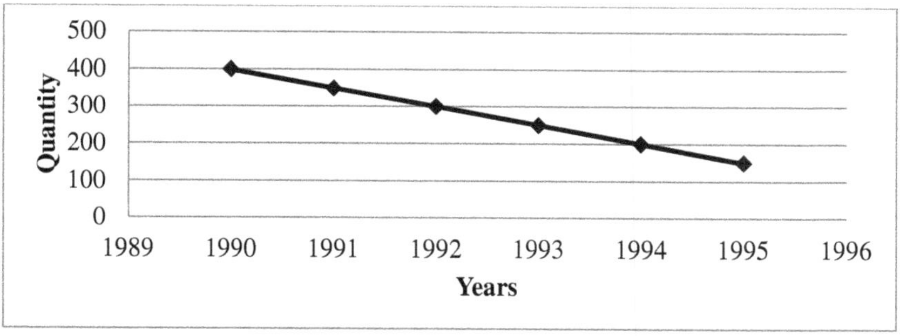

Step 2: Interpretation. There exists a perfectly and negative correlation between rice production and years. That is, the production of rice reduces as the years increases.

2) **What should be the government reaction based on your answer in 1 above.**

The government should put in place structural programs to help increase rice production. Such intervention is needed as rice production will continue to fall over the years if left on its own.

3) **Assume rice is the most consumed food and has no substitutes, what will be the effect on price and standard of living over time?**

The continuous reduction in rice production and continuous demand will leads to increase in the price of rice. The increase in the price will reduce consumer real income and hence reduces consumer standard of living.

Test Your Understanding

Exercise 1: The price and quantity supplied for a commodity for a period of 6 months is presented in the table below. What is the relationship between price and quantity supplied using the concept of scattered diagram

Price	12	12	16	15	18	19	19	14	15	10
Quantity	2	4	6	6	8	9	10	4	7	4

Exercise 2: The price and quantity demanded of bread is presented in the table below. Using the data in the table, determine the relationship between price and quantity demanded

Price	80	60	50	40	30	20
Quantity	40	70	60	100	80	140

Answers..[See appendix 1]

1.3.2 Algebraic Methods of Measuring Linear Correlation

The algebraic method is an alternative way of determining the direction and degree of correlation. Our analysis will be limited to four principal methods; Pearson moment correlation coefficient, spearman rank correlation coefficient, covariance method and ordinary least square method.

Karl Pearson

1) **Pearson Moment Correlation Coefficient**

Pearson product moment correlation coefficient can be obtained by using the actual values and/or variance values and values of standard deviation (SD).

$$r = \frac{n\sum XY - \sum X \sum Y}{\sqrt{[n\sum X^2 - (\sum X)^2][n\sum Y^2 - (\sum Y)^2]}} \text{.......[Actual Observation Values]}$$

Where: n = Number of observation(s) = 6,

$\sum X$ = Summation of the actual values of X,

$\sum Y$ = Summation of the actual values of Y ,

$\sum XY$ = Summation of the product of XY,

$(\sum X)^2$ = Square of the summation of X ,

$(\sum Y)^2$ = Square of the summation of Y,

$\sum X^2$ = Summation of the squares of X, $\sum Y^2$ = Summation of the squares of Y.

$r = \frac{\sum[(X-\bar{X})(Y-\bar{Y})]}{\sqrt{\sum(X-\bar{X})^2 \sum(Y-\bar{Y})^2}} \equiv r = \frac{\sum xy}{\sqrt{\sum x^2 \sum y^2}}$ ……………………………[Using Variance Values]

Where: $\bar{X} = \frac{\sum X}{N}$ is the mean of variable X numerical values

$\bar{Y} = \frac{\sum Y}{N}$ is the mean of variable Y numerical values

$\sum(X - \bar{X})^2 = \sum x^2$

$\sum(Y - \bar{Y})^2 = \sum y^2$

Example 1: The results of an inquiry realised in a shop to determine the number of potential buyers of a model of leather bags in function of its selling price are given in the following table. Determine the correlation between price and number of potential buyers.

Price (X)	350	400	450	500	550	600
Number of potential buyers (Y)	140	120	100	95	85	70

Solution

Step 1: Formula. $r = \frac{n\sum XY - \sum X \sum Y}{\sqrt{[n\sum X^2 - (\sum X)^2][n\sum Y^2 - (\sum Y)^2]}}$, where; n = 6

Step 2: Tabula calculation of formula components

Original Table		Working Table		
X	Y	**XY**	**X^2**	**Y^2**
350	140	$350 \times 140 = 49{,}000$	$350^2 = 122{,}500$	$140^2 = 19{,}600$
400	120	$400 \times 120 = 48{,}000$	$400^2 = 160{,}000$	$120^2 = 14{,}400$
450	100	$450 \times 100 = 45{,}000$	$450^2 = 202{,}500$	$100^2 = 10{,}000$
500	95	$500 \times 95 = 47{,}500$	$500^2 = 250{,}000$	$95^2 = 9{,}025$
550	85	$550 \times 85 = 46{,}750$	$550^2 = 302{,}500$	$85^2 = 7{,}225$
600	70	$600 \times 70 = 42{,}000$	$600^2 = 360{,}000$	$70^2 = 4{,}900$
$\sum = 2{,}850$	**$\sum = 610$**	**$\sum = 278{,}250$**	**$\sum = 1{,}397{,}500$**	**$\sum = 65{,}150$**
n = **6**	$(\sum X)^2 = (2{,}850)^2 = \mathbf{8{,}122{,}500}$ and $(\sum Y)^2 = (610)^2 = \mathbf{372{,}100}$			

Step 3: Data substitution and solving.

$r = \frac{n\sum XY - \sum X \sum Y}{\sqrt{[n\sum X^2 - (\sum X)^2][n\sum Y^2 - (\sum Y)^2]}}$ ……………[Substitute data values as derived in the table]

$r = \frac{6(278{,}250) - (2{,}850)(610)}{\sqrt{[6(1{,}397{,}500) - (8{,}122{,}500)][6(65{,}150) - (372{,}100)]}}$ …….[Simplify bracket by multiplication]

$r = \frac{1{,}669{,}500 - 1{,}738{,}500}{\sqrt{[8{,}385{,}000 - 8{,}122{,}500][390{,}900 - 372{,}100]}}$ …………..[Simplify numerator and denominator]

$r = \frac{-69{,}000}{\sqrt{[262{,}500][18{,}800]}}$ ……………………….[Simplify denominator and square root it value]

$r = \frac{-69{,}000}{70249.55516}$ ....[Simplify fraction by division]

$r = \mathbf{-0.98}$ ....[In two decimal place]

Step 4: Interpretation. The value (-0.98) shows that the variables are very strong and negatively related. An increase in price will lead to a very significant fall in the number of potential buyers.

Example 2: The price and quantity demanded schedule for Mr. John is presented below.

Price (X)	38	44	48	35	30	40	41	25
Quantity (Y)	60	67	75	58	55	70	71	50

Determine the degree and direction of relationship between price and quantity demanded using

a) The variables' actual values
b) The variables' deviational values

Solution

a) The variables actual values

Step 1: Formula. $r = \frac{n\sum XY - \sum X \sum Y}{\sqrt{[n\sum X^2 - (\sum X)^2][n\sum Y^2 - (\sum Y)^2]}}$, where; n = 8

Step 2: Tabular calculation of formula components

X	**Y**	$\sum$**XY**	$\sum$**X²**	$\sum$**Y²**
38	60	38 × 60 =2,280	38^2 =1,444	60^2 =3,600
44	67	44 × 67 =2,948	44^2 =1,936	67^2 =4,489
48	75	48 × 75 =3,600	48^2 =2,304	75^2 =5,625
35	58	35 × 58 =2,030	35^2 =1,225	58^2 =3,364
30	55	30 × 55 =1,650	30^2 =900	55^2 =3,025
40	70	40 × 70 =2,800	40^2 =1,600	70^2 =4,900
41	71	41 × 71 =2,911	41^2 =1,681	71^2 =5,041
25	50	25 × 50 =1,250	25^2 =625	50^2 =2,500
$\sum = \mathbf{301}$	$\sum = \mathbf{506}$	$\sum = \mathbf{19{,}469}$	$\sum = \mathbf{11{,}715}$	$\sum \mathbf{32{,}544}$
$(\sum X)^2 \rightarrow (301)^2 = \mathbf{90{,}601}$ and $(\sum Y)^2 \rightarrow (506)^2 = \mathbf{256{,}036}$				

Step 3: Data substitution and solving.

$r = \frac{n\sum XY - \sum X \sum Y}{\sqrt{[n\sum X^2 - (\sum X)^2][n\sum Y^2 - (\sum Y)^2]}}$ ....[Substitute data values into the equation]

$r = \frac{8(19469) - (301)(506)}{\sqrt{[8(11715) - (90601)][8(32544) - (256036)]}}$ ....[Simplify bracket of equation]

$r = \frac{155752 - 152306}{\sqrt{[93720 - 90601][260352 - 256036]}}$ ....[Simplify numerator and denominator]

$r = \frac{3446}{\sqrt{13461604}}$ ....[Square root denominator]

$r = \frac{3446}{3669.00586}$ ....[Simplify fraction of equation by division]

$\mathbf{r = 0.9}$ ....[In one decimal places]

b) The variables deviational values

Step 1: Formula. $r = \frac{\sum[(X - \bar{X})(Y - \bar{Y})]}{\sqrt{\sum(X - \bar{X})^2 \sum(Y - \bar{Y})^2}} \equiv r = \frac{\sum xy}{\sqrt{\sum x^2 \sum y^2}}$

Remember: $\sum x^2 = \sum(X - \bar{X})^2, \sum y^2 = \sum(Y - \bar{Y})^2$

$\sum xy = \sum[(X - \bar{X})(Y - \bar{Y})]$

$\sqrt{\sum x^2 \sum y^2} = \sqrt{\sum(X - \bar{X})^2 \sum(Y - \bar{Y})^2}$

Step 2: Tabular calculation of formula elements or components

X	Y	$X - \bar{X}$	$Y - \bar{Y}$	$(X - \bar{X})(Y - \bar{Y})$	$(X - \bar{X})^2$	$(Y - \bar{Y})^2$
38	60	0.375	−3.25	−1.21875	0.140625	10.5625
44	67	6.375	3.75	23.90625	40.640625	14.0625
48	75	10.375	11.75	121.90625	107.640625	138.0625
35	58	−2.625	−5.25	13.78125	6.890625	27.5625
30	55	−7.625	−8.25	62.90625	58.140625	68.0625
40	70	2.375	6.75	16.03125	5.640625	45.5625
41	71	3.375	7.75	26.15625	11.390625	60.0625
25	50	−12.625	−13.25	167.28125	159.390625	175.5625
$\sum = \mathbf{301}$	$\sum = \mathbf{506}$	$\sum = \mathbf{0}$	$\sum = \mathbf{0}$	$\sum = \mathbf{430.75}$	$\sum = \mathbf{389.875}$	$\sum = \mathbf{539.5}$
n = **8**	$\bar{Y} = \frac{\sum Y}{n} \rightarrow \bar{Y} = \frac{506}{8} \rightarrow \bar{Y} = \mathbf{63.25}$			$\bar{X} = \frac{\sum X}{n} \rightarrow \bar{X} = \frac{301}{8} \rightarrow \bar{X} = \mathbf{37.625}$		

Step 3: Data substitution and solving.

$$r = \frac{\sum[(X-\bar{X})(Y-\bar{Y})]}{\sqrt{\sum(X-\bar{X})^2 \sum(Y-\bar{Y})^2}}$$ ....[Substitute values into the equation]

$$r = \frac{430.75}{\sqrt{(389.875)(539.5)}}$$ ....[Simplify denominator by multiplication of bracket]

$$r = \frac{430.75}{\sqrt{210{,}337.5625}}$$ ....[Square denominator value]

$$r = \frac{430.75}{458.6257325}$$ ....[Simplify fraction by division]

$r = \mathbf{0.9}$ ....[In one decimal place]

Step 4: Interpretation. The value 0.9 shows that our variables are very strong and positively correlated. That is an increase in price will lead to a significant increase in quantity.

Note: Pearson moment correlation is also calculated as the covariance of two variables divided by the product of their standard deviation. The covariance and standard deviation of the variables are determined using the correlation matrix. The idea of linear algebra is of great importance here.

$$\text{Covariance Matrix} = \begin{bmatrix} Cov(X_1X_1) & Cov(X_1X_2) \\ Cov(X_2X_1) & Cov(X_2X_2) \end{bmatrix}$$ ....[Simple correlation]

$$\text{Covariance Matrix} = \begin{bmatrix} Cov(X_1X_1) & Cov(X_1X_2) & Cov(X_1X_3) \\ Cov(X_2X_1) & Cov(X_2X_2) & Cov(X_2X_3) \\ Cov(X_3X_1) & Cov(X_3X_2) & Cov(X_3X_3) \end{bmatrix}$$ ....[Multiple Correlation]

N/B: It is worth knowing that; $[Cov(X_1X_1)]$, $[Cov(X_2X_2)]$ and $[Cov(X_3X_3)]$ are the variance of variable (X_1), variable (X_2) and variable (X_3) respectively. The covariance between variable (X_m) and (X_n) is denoted $[Cov(X_mX_n)]$.The correlation of variable (X_m) and (X_n) is calculated using the formula below.

$$Correlation(r_{X_mX_n}) = \frac{Cov(X_mX_n)}{\sqrt{Var_{X_m}} \times \sqrt{Var_{X_n}}}$$ ....(1)

Example 1: Verify the existence of Multicolinearity using information in the table below

Y	4	7	5	2	9	6
X_1	3	5	8	13	16	15
X_2	6	12	9	14	15	13

Solution

1) **Determine the correlation matrix**.........[Note $\overline{X}_1 = 10,\ \overline{X}_2 = 11.5$ and $n = 6$]

Step 1: Determination of deviation matrix (A)

1) Formula. $A = B - \overline{B}$, where; $\overline{X}_1 = 10,\ \overline{X}_2 = 11.5$
2) Data substitution and solving

$$A = \begin{bmatrix} (3-10) & (6-11.5) \\ (5-10) & (12-11.5) \\ (8-10) & (9-11.5) \\ (13-10) & (14-11.5) \\ (16-10) & (15-11.5) \\ (15-10) & (13-11.5) \end{bmatrix} \Rightarrow A = \begin{bmatrix} -7 & -5.5 \\ -5 & 0.5 \\ -2 & -2.5 \\ 3 & 2.5 \\ 6 & 3.5 \\ 5 & 1.5 \end{bmatrix}$$ ....[Deviation matrix]

Step 2: Determination of covariance matrix (D)

1) Formula. $D = A^T \times A$, where; $A^T = \begin{bmatrix} -7 & -5 & -2 & 3 & 6 & 5 \\ -5.5 & 0.5 & -2.5 & 2.5 & 3.5 & 1.5 \end{bmatrix}$
2) Data substitution and solving

$$D = \begin{bmatrix} -7 & -5 & -2 & 3 & 6 & 5 \\ -5.5 & 0.5 & -2.5 & 2.5 & 3.5 & 1.5 \end{bmatrix} \begin{bmatrix} -7 & -5.5 \\ -5 & 0.5 \\ -2 & -2.5 \\ 3 & 2.5 \\ 6 & 3.5 \\ 5 & 1.5 \end{bmatrix}$$ ....[Multiply matrix]

$$D = \begin{bmatrix} 148 & 77 \\ 77 & 57.5 \end{bmatrix} = \begin{bmatrix} Cov(X_1X_1) & Cov(X_1X_2) \\ Cov(X_2X_1) & Cov(X_2X_2) \end{bmatrix}$$ ....[Covariance matrix]

Step 3: Determination of correlation matrix

$$\left[\text{Remember } Cov(X_nX_n) = Var(X_n) = \frac{Cov(X_nX_n)}{Cov(X_nX_n)}\right]$$

1) Formula. $Correlation(r_{X_1X_2}) = \frac{Cov(X_1X_2)}{\sqrt{Var_{X_1}} \times \sqrt{Var_{X_2}}}$

   Where; $Var_{X_1} = 148$, $Var_{X_2} = 57.5$ and $(r_{X_1X_2}) = (X_2X_1) = 77$

2) Data substitution and solving

$$Correlation(r_{X_1X_2}) = (X_2X_1) = \frac{77}{\sqrt{148} \times \sqrt{57.5}}$$ ....[Simplify denominator]

$$Correlation(r_{X_1X_2}) = (X_2X_1) = \frac{77}{92.24966125}$$ ....[Solve equation]

$$Correlation(r_{X_1X_2}) = (X_2X_1) = \mathbf{0.8347}$$

Note: The correlation matrix is given as; $\left\{\begin{bmatrix} Cov(X_1X_1) & Cov(X_1X_2) \\ Cov(X_2X_1) & Cov(X_2X_2) \end{bmatrix} = \begin{bmatrix} 1 & 0.8347 \\ 0.8347 & 1 \end{bmatrix}\right\}$

Example 2: Using the table below, determine the correlation between the variables

Y	10	20	30	40	50
X_1	40	44	46	48	52
X_2	6	10	12	14	16
X_3	4	4	5	7	9

Solution

a) **Method 1 [Using the matrix method]**

Step 1: Determination of Deviation matrix (A)........[Note $\overline{X}_1 = 46, \overline{X}_2 = 11.6$ and $\overline{X}_3 = 5.8$]

1) Formula. $A = B - \overline{B}$, where; $\overline{X}_1 = 46, \overline{X}_2 = 11.6$ and $\overline{X}_3 = 5.8$
2) Data substitution and solving

$$A = \begin{bmatrix} (40-46) & (6-11.6) & (4-5.8) \\ (44-46) & (10-11.6) & (4-5.8) \\ (46-46) & (12-11.6) & (5-5.8) \\ (48-46) & (14-11.6) & (7-5.8) \\ (52-46) & (16-11.6) & (9-5.8) \end{bmatrix} = \begin{bmatrix} -6 & -5.6 & -1.8 \\ -2 & -1.6 & -1.8 \\ 0 & 0.4 & -0.8 \\ 2 & 2.4 & 1.2 \\ 6 & 4.4 & 3.2 \end{bmatrix}$$

Step 2: Determination of covariance matrix (D)

1) Formula. $D = A^T \times A$, where; $A^T = \begin{bmatrix} -6 & -2 & 0 & 2 & 6 \\ -5.6 & -1.6 & 0.4 & 2.4 & 4.4 \\ -1.8 & -1.8 & -0.8 & 1.2 & 3.2 \end{bmatrix}$
2) Data substitution and solving

$$D = \begin{bmatrix} -6 & -2 & 0 & 2 & 6 \\ -5.6 & -1.6 & 0.4 & 2.4 & 4.4 \\ -1.8 & -1.8 & -0.8 & 1.2 & 3.2 \end{bmatrix} \begin{bmatrix} -6 & -5.6 & -1.8 \\ -2 & -1.6 & -1.8 \\ 0 & 0.4 & -0.8 \\ 2 & 2.4 & 1.2 \\ 6 & 4.4 & 3.2 \end{bmatrix} \text{..............[Multiply matrix]}$$

$$D = \begin{bmatrix} 80 & 68 & 36 \\ 68 & 59.2 & 29.6 \\ 36 & 29.6 & 18.8 \end{bmatrix} = D = \begin{bmatrix} Cov(X_1X_1) & Cov(X_1X_2) & Cov(X_1X_3) \\ Cov(X_2X_1) & Cov(X_2X_2) & Cov(X_2X_3) \\ Cov(X_3X_1) & Cov(X_3X_2) & Cov(X_3X_3) \end{bmatrix} \text{.........[Covariance matrix]}$$

Step 3: Determination of correlation matrix

$$\left[\text{Remember } Cov(X_nX_n) = Var(X_n) = \frac{Cov(X_nX_n)}{Cov(X_nX_n)}\right]$$

1) Formula. $Correlation(r_{X_2X_1}) = \frac{Cov(X_2X_1)}{\sqrt{Var_{X_2}} \times \sqrt{Var_{X_1}}}$ ....(1)

$Correlation(r_{X_3X_1}) = \frac{Cov(X_3X_1)}{\sqrt{Var_{X_3}} \times \sqrt{Var_{X_1}}}$ ....(2)

$Correlation(r_{X_2X_3}) = \frac{Cov(X_2X_3)}{\sqrt{Var_{X_2}} \times \sqrt{Var_{X_3}}}$ ....(3)

2) Data substitution and solving

Correlation$(r_{X_2X_1})$ = Correlation$(r_{X_1X_2})$	$(r_{X_2X_1}) = (r_{X_1X_2}) = \frac{68}{\sqrt{59.2}\times\sqrt{80}} = \frac{68}{68.81860214} = \mathbf{0.988}$
Correlation$(r_{X_3X_1})$ = Correlation$(r_{X_1X_3})$	$(r_{r_{X_3X_1}}) = (r_{X_1X_3}) = \frac{36}{\sqrt{18.8}\times\sqrt{80}} = \frac{36}{38.78143886} = \mathbf{0.928}$
Correlation$(r_{X_2X_3})$ = Correlation$(r_{X_3X_2})$	$(r_{X_2X_3}) = (r_{X_3X_2}) = \frac{29.6}{\sqrt{59.2}\times\sqrt{18.8}} = \frac{29.6}{33.36105514} = \mathbf{0.887}$
Note: $D = \begin{bmatrix} 1 & 0.988 & 0.928 \\ 0.988 & 1 & 0.887 \\ 0.928 & 0.887 & 1 \end{bmatrix} = \begin{bmatrix} \sigma_{X_1}{}^2 & r_{X_1X_2} & r_{X_1X_3} \\ r_{X_2X_1} & \sigma_{X_2}{}^2 & r_{X_2X_3} \\ r_{X_3X_2} & r_{X_3X_2} & \sigma_{X_3}{}^2 \end{bmatrix}$	

b) Method 2 [Using Pearson Moment Correlation Coefficient]

Step 1: Formula. Correlation$(r_{X_1X_2}) = \frac{n\sum X_1X_2 - \sum X_1 \sum X_2}{\sqrt{[n\sum X_2{}^2-(X_2)^2][n\sum X_1{}^2-(X_1)^2]}}$ ……………………………(1)

Correlation$(X_1X_3) = \frac{n\sum X_1X_3 - \sum X_1 \sum X_3}{\sqrt{[n\sum X_3{}^2-(X_3)^2][n\sum X_1{}^2-(X_1)^2]}}$ ……………………………………………(2)

Correlation$(X_2X_3) = \frac{n\sum X_2X_3 - \sum X_2 \sum X_3}{\sqrt{[n\sum X_3{}^2-(X_3)^2][n\sum X_2{}^2-(X_2)^2]}}$ ……………………………………………(3)

Step 2: Tabular determination of unknown

X_1X_2	X_1X_3	X_2X_3	$X^2{}_1$	$X^2{}_2$	$X^2{}_3$
240	160	24	1,600	36	16
440	176	40	1,936	100	16
552	230	60	2,116	144	25
672	336	98	2,304	196	49
832	468	144	2,704	256	81
$\sum = 2{,}736$	$\sum = 1{,}370$	$\sum = 366$	$\sum = 10{,}660$	$\sum = 732$	$\sum = 187$

Step 3: Data substitution and solving………[Note $\sum X_1 = 230, \sum X_2 = 58$ and $\sum X_3 = 29$]

$$\text{Correlation}(r_{X_1X_2}) = \frac{5(2{,}736)-(230)(58)}{\sqrt{[5(732)-(58)^2][5(10{,}660)-(230)^2]}} = \mathbf{0.988}$$

$$\text{Correlation}(X_1X_3) = \frac{5(1{,}370)-(230)(29)}{\sqrt{[5(187)-(29)^2][5(10{,}660)-(230)^2]}} = \mathbf{0.928}$$

$$\text{Correlation}(X_2X_3) = \frac{5(366)-(58)(29)}{\sqrt{[5(187)-(29)^2][5(732)-(58)^2]}} = \mathbf{0.887}$$

Test Your Understanding

Exercise 3: What is the correlation that exists between the variables in the tables below

Table 1

Independent variable [X]	1	2	3	4	5	6
Dependent variable [Y]	1	4	6	3	6	7

[Answer: r = 0.78. That is very strong positive correlation]

Table 2

Independent variable [X]	3	7	15	35	75
Dependent variable [Y]	40	35	30	25	18

[Answer: r = -0.95. That is very strong negative correlation]

Example 4: Use the table below and answer the questions that follows

Quantity of Rice [Y]	152	190	117	22	134	131
Quantity of fertilizer [X]	52	51	43	65	45	39

1) Calculate the value of correlation between quantity of rice and fertilizer used

   [Answer: r = 0.91. That is very strong positive correlation]

2) As a business math student, from your answer in one above, will you advice that farmer to use the fertilizer in future farming production of rice? Justify your answer

[Answer: Yes, this is because the positive relationship shows that the more of fertilizer used, the higher will be the production of rice]

Example 5: Given that; $\sum X = 210$, $\sum Y = 420$, $\sum Y^2 = 36{,}400$, $\sum X^2 = 9{,}100$, $n = 6$ and $\sum XY = 11{,}200$, determine the correlation value between the variable X and Y using Pearson moment correlation technique. ....**[Answer: r = -1. Perfect positive correlation]**

2) Spearman rank correlation coefficient

Spearman rank correlation coefficient is a non-parametric rank statistics. It is worth knowing that the formula used in calculating Spearman rank correlation coefficient depends on the nature of the observation

Charles E. Spearman

$R = 1 - \frac{6\sum D^2}{N(N^2-1)}$ or $R = 1 - \frac{6\sum D^2}{N^3-N}$..[Unpaired situation]

$R = 1 - \frac{6\left[\sum D^2 + \frac{1}{12}(m^3-m) + \frac{1}{12}(m^3-m) + \cdots \ldots \frac{1}{12}(m^3-m)\right]}{N^3-N}$ ....[Paired situation]

Where: $D = |R_2 - R_1|$. That is ignore any negative sign

$\mathbf{R_2}$ represent rank of dependent variable (X)

$\mathbf{R_1}$ represent rank of independent variable (Y)

m is the total frequency of observation repetition $[m = \sum m_\iota]$.

Note: Ranking in this situation means position numbers in ascending order. The highest number is rank 1, second highest 2, third highest 3 and n^{th} highest is rank n.

Example 1: Calculate rank correlation coefficient between two series X and Y given below

X	70	65	71	62	58	69	78	64
Y	91	76	65	83	90	64	55	48

Solution

Step 1: Formula and data. $R = 1 - \frac{6\sum D^2}{N(N^2-1)}$, where; $D = |R_2 - R_1| \equiv D = |R_1 - R_2|$

Step 2: Tabular calculation of formula components

Original Table [Ranking process]				**Working Table**			
Values	Rank	Values	Rank	**[Transfer and derivation process]**			
X	$\mathbf{R_1}$	Y	$\mathbf{R_2}$	R_1	$\mathbf{R_2}$	$D = \lvert R_2 - R_1 \rvert$	D^2
70	3	91	1	3	1	$D = \lvert 1-3 \rvert = 2$	$2^2 = 2 \times 2 = 4$
65	5	76	4	5	4	$D = \lvert 4-5 \rvert = 1$	$1^2 = 1 \times 1 = 1$
71	2	65	5	2	5	$D = \lvert 5-2 \rvert = 3$	$3^2 = 3 \times 3 = 9$
62	7	83	3	7	3	$D = \lvert 3-7 \rvert = 4$	$4^2 = 4 \times 4 = 16$
58	8	90	2	8	2	$D = \lvert 2-8 \rvert = 6$	$6^2 = 6 \times 6 = 36$
69	4	64	6	4	6	$D = \lvert 6-4 \rvert = 2$	$2^2 = 2 \times 2 = 4$
78	1	55	7	1	7	$D = \lvert 7-1 \rvert = 6$	$6^2 = 6 \times 6 = 36$
64	6	48	8	6	8	$D = \lvert 8-6 \rvert = 2$	$2^2 = 2 \times 2 = 4$
				$N = \mathbf{8}$ and $N^2 = 8^2 = 8 \times 8 = \mathbf{64}$			$\sum D^2 = \mathbf{110}$

Step 3: Data substitution and solving.

$R = 1 - \frac{6(110)}{8(64-1)}$.................................[Expand numerator and denominator bracket]

$R = 1 - \frac{660}{504}$ ....[Simplify fraction by division]

$R = 1 - 1.30952381$ ……...…..........…[Simplify right hand side of equation by subtraction]

$R = \mathbf{-0.31}$ …………………………...……………………………….[In two decimal places]

Step 4: Interpretation. The value (-0.31) shows that our variables are very weak and negatively related.

Example 2: Apply Spearman's rank correlation technique and determine the degree and direction of relationship between health expenditure and number of birth from the data given below.

Health Expenditure (X)	65	59	62	64	66	74	74	71	76	47
Number of birth (Y)	34	31	36	36	32	32	18	21	14	48

Solution

Step 1: Formula. $R = 1 - \frac{6\left[\sum D^2 + \frac{1}{12}(m^3-m) + \frac{1}{12}(m^3-m) + \cdots\cdots\frac{1}{12}(m^3-m)\right]}{N^3-N}$, where; $N = 10$

Step 2: Tabula calculation of formula components

Original Table/ Supposed Rank						**Working Table and transfer process**			
X	Rank $[R_1]$		Y	Rank $[R_2]$		R_1	R_2	$D = \lvert R_2 - R_1 \rvert$	D^2
65	6		34	4		6	4	$D = \lvert 4-6 \rvert = 2$	$2^2 = 4$
59	9		31	7		9	7	$D = \lvert 7-9 \rvert = 2$	$2^2 = 4$
62	8		36	**3**	$\bar{Y} = \frac{3+2}{2}$	8	**2.5**	$D = \lvert 2.5-8 \rvert = 5.5$	$5.5^2 = 30.25$
64	7		36	**2**	$\bar{Y} = \mathbf{2.5}$	7	**2.5**	$D = \lvert 2.5-7 \rvert = 4.5$	$4.5^2 = 20.25$
66	5		32	**5**	$\bar{Y} = \frac{5+6}{2}$	5	**5.5**	$D = \lvert 5.5-5 \rvert = 0.5$	$0.5^2 = 0.25$
74	**3**	$\bar{X} = \frac{3+2}{2}$	32	**6**	$\bar{Y} = \mathbf{5.5}$	**2.5**	**5.5**	$D = \lvert 5.5-2.5 \rvert = 3$	$3^2 = 9$
74	**2**	$\bar{X} = \mathbf{2.5}$	18	9		**2.5**	9	$D = \lvert 9-2.5 \rvert = 6.5$	$6.5^2 = 42.25$
71	4		21	8		4	8	$D = \lvert 8-4 \rvert = 4$	$4^2 = 16$
76	1		14	10		1	10	$D = \lvert 10-1 \rvert = 9$	$9^2 = 81$
47	10		48	1		10	1	$D = \lvert 1-10 \rvert = 9$	$9^2 = 81$
	55			**55**		**55**	**55**		$\sum D^2 = \mathbf{288}$

Where: m of variable x is 74 and repeat 2 times. therefore: $m_1 = \mathbf{2}$,

m of variable y is 36 and 32 repeat 2 times each, therefore: $m_2 = \mathbf{2}$ and $m_3 = \mathbf{2}$

$m = m_\iota = 2 + 2 + 2 = \mathbf{6}$

Step 3: Data substitution and solving.

$$R = 1 - \frac{6\left[288+\frac{1}{12}(2^3-2)+\frac{1}{12}(2^3-2)+\frac{1}{12}(2^3-2)\right]}{10^3-10}$$ ....[Solve exponents and simplify brackets]

$$R = 1 - \frac{6\left[288+\frac{1}{12}(6)+\frac{1}{12}(6)+\frac{1}{12}(6)\right]}{990}$$ .....[Reduce fraction and multiply brackets (Numerator)]

$$R = 1 - \frac{6[288+0.5+0.5+0.5]}{990}$$ ....[Simplify]

$$R = 1 - \frac{1{,}737}{990}$$ ....[Solve]

$$R = \mathbf{-0.75}$$ ....[In two decimal places]

Step 4: Interpretation. The value (-0.75) shows variables are very strong and negatively related.

Test Your Understanding

Exercise 6: Determine the correlation between the variable X and Y from the tables below.

Table 1

X	3		12	18	24
Y	60	95	140	170	185

[Answer: R = 1. That is perfect positive correlation]

Table 2

X	1	7	3	17	3	4
Y	16	50	22	59	63	40

[Answer: R = 0.54. That is moderately positively correlation]

3) Covariance Method of Calculating Linear Correlation

Covariance is defined as the expected value of the product of the deviation of two random variables from their respective means. Covariance measures how far two random variables vary together. The value of covariance between variables is calculated using the formula below.

$$\text{Cov(XY)} = \frac{\Sigma[(Y-\bar{Y})(X-\bar{X})]}{n-1}$$ ....[Unstandardized]

$$\text{Cov(XY)} = \frac{\Sigma[(Y-\bar{Y})(X-\bar{X})]}{\sqrt{\Sigma(Y-\bar{Y})^2\,\Sigma(X-\bar{X})^2}}$$ ....[Standardized]

Note: The unstandardized formula is often considered problematic as it provides values that are usually greater than 1, making it impossible to use the correlation coefficient limits for interpretation. Therefore, it is appropriate for the determination of direction of correlation. Standardized formula respects the correlation coefficient and can be used to determine both direction and degree of correlation.

Example 1: A manager wishes to re-structure the recruitment policy of his institution. The table below presents the average age of workers and their days of absence. Using the concept of covariance, should he employ more of young workers?

Age of workers (X)	10	20	30	40	50	60	70
Days of absence (Y)	5	7	10	15	25	13	30

<u>Solution</u>

Step 1: Formula. $\text{Cov(XY)} = \frac{\sum(\text{Y}-\bar{\text{Y}})(\text{X}-\bar{\text{X}})}{\sqrt{\sum(\text{Y}-\bar{\text{Y}})^2\sum(\text{X}-\bar{\text{X}})^2}} \equiv \text{Cov(XY)} = \frac{\sum xy}{\sqrt{\sum y^2 \sum x^2}}$

Step 2: Tabula calculation of formula components

Original Table		Working Table				
X	Y	**$\text{y} = (\text{Y} - \bar{\text{Y}})$**	**$\text{x} = (\text{X} - \bar{\text{X}})$**	**xy**	**y^2**	**x^2**
10	5	$5 - 15 = -10$	$10 - 40 = -30$	300	100	900
20	7	$7 - 15 = -8$	$20 - 40 = -20$	160	64	400
30	10	$10 - 15 = -5$	$30 - 40 = -10$	50	25	100
40	15	$15 - 15 = 0$	$40 - 40 = 0$	0	0	0
50	25	$25 - 15 = 10$	$50 - 40 = 10$	100	100	100
60	13	$13 - 15 = -2$	$60 - 40 = 20$	-40	4	400
70	30	$30 - 15 = 15$	$70 - 40 = 30$	450	225	900
$\sum = 280$	**$\sum = 105$**	**$\sum = 0$**	**$\sum = 0$**	**$\sum = 1{,}020$**	**$\sum = 518$**	**$\sum = 2{,}800$**

Step 3: Data substitution and solving.

$\text{Cov(XY)} = \frac{\sum xy}{\sqrt{\sum y^2 \sum x^2}}$ ....[Substitute data value into the equation]

$\text{Cov(XY)} = \frac{1{,}020}{\sqrt{(518)(2{,}800)}}$ ....[Simplify denominator by multiplying brackets]

$\text{Cov(XY)} = \frac{1{,}020}{\sqrt{1{,}450{,}400}}$ ....[Work denominator root]

$\text{Cov(XY)} = \frac{1{,}020}{1{,}204.325537}$ ....[Simplify fraction by division]

$\text{Cov(XY)} = \mathbf{0.85}$ ....[In two decimal places]

Step 4: The value [0.85]shows that our variables are very strong and positively related. Therefore, it's advisable for the manager to employ more of youth than age persons.

Example 2: The marks of 5 students in economics and business mathematics in the fifth sequences are presented below.

Marks in Economics (X)	70	68	67	55	60
Marks in Business Math's (Y)	65	70	80	85	98

Determine the correlation between Economics and Business Math marks of these students using the covariance technique. [Using both Non-standardized and standardized formula]

Solution

Step 1: Formulas. $Cov(XY) = \frac{\sum(Y-\bar{Y})(X-\bar{X})}{n-1}$ and $Cov(XY) = \frac{\sum(Y-\bar{Y})(X-\bar{X})}{\sqrt{\sum(Y-\bar{Y})^2 \sum(X-\bar{X})^2}}$, where; n = 5

Step 2: Tabula calculation of formulas components

Original Table		**Working Table**				
X	Y	$(Y_i - \bar{Y})$	$(X_i - \bar{X})$	$(Y_i - \bar{Y})(X_i - \bar{X})$	$(Y_i - \bar{Y})^2$	$(X_i - \bar{X})^2$
70	65	−14.6	6	−87.6	213.16	36
68	70	−9.6	4	−38.4	92.16	16
67	80	0.4	3	1.2	0.16	9
55	85	5.4	−9	−48.6	29.16	81
60	98	18.4	−4	−73.6	338.56	16
$\sum = \mathbf{320}$	$\sum = \mathbf{398}$	$\sum = \mathbf{0}$	$\sum = \mathbf{0}$	$\sum = \mathbf{-247}$	$\sum = \mathbf{673.2}$	$\sum = \mathbf{158}$

Step 3: Data substitution and solving.

1. **Using Non-standardized formula.**

$Cov(XY) = \frac{-247}{5-1}$ ....[Simplify denominator by subtraction]

$Cov(XY) = \frac{-247}{4}$ ....[Simplify fraction by division]

$Cov(XY) = \mathbf{-61.75}$

2. **Using standardized formula.**

$Cov(XY) = \frac{\sum(Y-\bar{Y})(X-\bar{X})}{\sqrt{\sum(Y-\bar{Y})^2 \sum(X-\bar{X})^2}}$..............................[Substitute data values into the equation]

$Cov(XY) = \frac{-247}{\sqrt{(673.2)(158)}}$ ....[Simplify denominator by expanding bracket]

$Cov(XY) = \frac{-247}{\sqrt{10,636.56}}$ ....[Work denominator root]

$Cov(XY) = \frac{-247}{326.1373944}$ ....[Simplify fraction of equation by division]

$Cov(XY) = \mathbf{-0.76}$ ....[In two decimal places]

Step 4: Interpretation. The value of covariance using the non-standardized formula $[-61.75]$ is less than zero $[-61.75 < 0]$ it shows that our variables are negatively related [direction of correlation only]. Covariance using the standardized formula value $[-0.76\,]$ shows that our variables are very strong and negatively related.

<u>Test Your Understanding</u>

Exercise 7: Determine the correlation between Variable X and Y using the standardized and non-standardized formula respectively from the table below.

Table 1

Independent variable [X]	3	5	0	2	1
Dependent variable [Y]	16	20	9	12	10

[Answer: $\mathbf{Cov(XY) = 0.99}$ and $\mathbf{Cov(XY) = 8.65}$ respectively]

Table 2

Land sizes X)	2	10	25	34	49
Quantity of Rice (Y)	100	85	20	15	10

[Answer: $\mathbf{Cov(XY) = -0.9}$ and $\mathbf{Cov(XY) = -742.5}$ respectively]

Exercise 8: Given that; $\sum xy = 54{,}736$, $x^2 = 12{,}324$, $y^2 = 307{,}892.8$ and $N = 5$, calculate the correlation value with the help of the covariance technique using;

1) Non-standardized formula. ..**[Answer: $\mathbf{Cov\ (XY) = 13{,}684}$. Positive correlation]**
2) Standardized formula. ....**[Answer: $\mathbf{Cov(XY) = 0.89}$. Very strong and positive]**

4) Least Square method

Least square method makes use of the regression equation or the regression line in explaining mainly the direction of relationship between variables. The regression equation based on simple correlation is given as seen below.

Car Frederick

$\hat{Y} = \hat{\beta}_0 \pm \hat{\beta}_1 X$ ....[Simple linear regression equation]

$$\hat{\beta}_1 = \frac{n\sum xy - \sum x \sum y}{n\sum x^2 - (\sum x)^2} \text{ OR } \hat{\beta}_1 = \frac{\sum XY - n\bar{X}\bar{Y}}{\sum X^2 - n\bar{X}^2} \quad \ldots\ldots(1)$$

$$\hat{\beta}_0 = \bar{Y} - \hat{\beta}_1 \bar{X} \text{ OR } \hat{\beta}_0 = \frac{\sum XY - \beta_1 \sum X^2}{\sum X} \quad \ldots\ldots(2)$$

$(\hat{Y})$ Represent the estimated value of the dependent variable [Y] as a result of changes in the independent variable[X].

$(\hat{\beta}_0$ and $\hat{\beta}_1)$Represent the estimated parameters independent variable towards the dependent variable. $(\hat{\beta}_0)$ Represents the amount by which dependent variable will change while holding independent variables in the model constant. $(\hat{\beta}_1)$ Represents the amount by which dependent variable will change when there is a unit change in the independent variable and it shows the correlation that exists between the dependent and independent variable. $(-\hat{\beta}_1)$ Shows negative relationship between variables and $(\hat{\beta}_1)$ shows positive relationship between variables.

Example 1: Determine the correlation that exists between price and supply and interpret your result using the least square method from the table below.

Price (X)	8	10	15	17	20	22	24	25
Supply (Y)	25	30	32	35	37	40	42	45

Solution

1) **Method 1**

Step 1: Formula and data. $\hat{Y} = \hat{\beta}_0 \pm \hat{\beta}_1 X$, where; $\hat{\beta}_1 = \frac{n\sum xy - \sum x \sum y}{n\sum x^2 - (\sum x)^2}$ and $\hat{\beta}_0 = \bar{Y} - \hat{\beta}_1 \bar{X}$

Step 2: Calculation of $\hat{\beta}_1$ and $\hat{\beta}_0$

1: Tabular derivation of $\hat{\beta}_1$ and $\hat{\beta}_0$ formula components

X	Y	$x = X - \bar{X}$	$y = Y - \bar{Y}$	xy	x^2
8	25	$8 - 17.625 = -9.625$	$25 - 35.75 = -10.75$	103.46875	92.641
10	30	$10 - 17.625 = -7.625$	$30 - 35.75 = -5.75$	43.84375	58.141
15	32	$15 - 17.625 = -2.625$	$32 - 35.75 = -3.75$	9.84375	6.891
17	35	$17 - 17.625 = -0.625$	$35 - 35.75 = -0.75$	0.46875	0.391
20	37	$20 - 17.625 = 2.375$	$37 - 35.75 = 1.25$	2.96875	5.641
22	40	$22 - 17.625 = 4.375$	$40 - 35.75 = 4.25$	18.59375	19.141
24	42	$24 - 17.625 = 6.375$	$42 - 35.75 = 6.25$	39.84375	40.641
25	45	$25 - 17.625 = 7.375$	$45 - 35.75 = 9.25$	68.21875	54.391
141	**286**	**0**	**0**	**287.25**	**277.88**

$n = \mathbf{8}$

$\bar{Y} = \frac{\sum Y_i}{n} \rightarrow \bar{Y} = \frac{286}{8} \rightarrow \bar{Y} = \mathbf{35.75}$, $\bar{X} = \frac{\sum X_i}{n} \rightarrow \bar{X} = \frac{141}{8} \rightarrow \bar{X} = \mathbf{17.625}$

Since $\sum x = 0$, then $(\sum x)^2 = (0)^2$. Therefore, $(\sum x)^2 = 0$

Value expressed in two decimal places

1 Data substitution and solving

a) Determination of $\hat{\beta}_1$

$\hat{\beta}_1 = \frac{n\sum xy - \sum x \sum y}{n\sum x^2 - (\sum x)^2}$..[Substitute data value into the formula]

$\hat{\beta}_1 = \frac{8(287.25)-(0)(0)}{8(277.88)-(0)}$..[Expand brackets]

$\hat{\beta}_1 = \frac{2,298-0}{2,223.04-0}$ ....[Simplify both numerator and denominator by subtraction]

$\hat{\beta}_1 = \frac{2,298}{2,223.04}$ ....[Simplify fraction by division]

$\hat{\beta}_1 = \mathbf{1.0337}$ ....[In four decimal places]

b) Determination of $\hat{\beta}_0$

$\hat{\beta}_0 = \overline{Y} - \hat{\beta}_1\overline{X}$ ....[Substitute data into the formula]

$\hat{\beta}_0 = 35.75 - (1.0337)17.625$ ....[Open bracket]

$\hat{\beta}_0 = 35.75 - 18.2189625$ ....[Solve equation]

$\hat{\beta}_0 = \mathbf{17.5310}$ ....[In four decimal places]

2) Method 2

Step 1: Formula. $\beta_1 = \frac{\sum XY - n\overline{X}\overline{Y}}{\sum X^2 - n\overline{X}^2}$ and $\hat{\beta}_0 = \overline{Y} - \hat{\beta}_1\overline{X}$, where; n = 8

Step 2: Tabular derivation of formula components

Y	X	$\sum XY$	$\sum X^2$
25	8	$25 \times 8 = 200$	$8^2 = 64$
30	10	$30 \times 10 = 300$	$10^2 = 100$
32	15	$32 \times 15 = 480$	$15^2 = 225$
35	17	$35 \times 17 = 595$	$17^2 = 289$
37	20	$37 \times 20 = 740$	$20^2 = 400$
40	22	$40 \times 22 = 880$	$22^2 = 484$
42	24	$42 \times 24 = 1,008$	$24^2 = 576$
45	25	$45 \times 25 = 1,125$	$25^2 = 625$
$\sum = \mathbf{286}$	$\sum = \mathbf{141}$	$\sum = \mathbf{5,328}$	$\sum = \mathbf{2,763}$
$\overline{X} = \frac{\sum X}{n}$, Where, $\sum X = 141$, n = 8 $\overline{X} = \frac{141}{8}$ =**17.625**		$\overline{Y} = \frac{\sum Y}{n}$, Where, $\sum Y = 286$, n = 8 $\overline{Y} = \frac{286}{8}$ =**35.75**	

Step 3: Data substitution and solving

a) Determination of β_1

$\beta_1 = \frac{\sum XY - n\bar{X}\bar{Y}}{\sum X^2 - n\bar{X}^2}$ ....[Substitute data values into the formula]

$\beta_1 = \frac{5{,}328-8(17.625)(35.75)}{2{,}763-8(17.625^2)}$ ....[Simplify brackets]

$\beta_1 = \frac{5{,}328-5{,}040.75}{2{,}763-2{,}485.125}$ ....[Simplify numerator and denominator]

$\beta_1 = \frac{287.25}{277.875}$ ....[Solve equation]

$\beta_1 = \mathbf{1.0337}$ ....[In four decimal places]

b) Determination of $\hat{\beta}_0$

$\hat{\beta}_0 = \bar{Y} - \hat{\beta}_1\bar{X}$ ....[Substitute data into the formula]

$\hat{\beta}_0 = 35.75 - (1.0337)(17.625)$ ....[Expand equation by multiplication]

$\hat{\beta}_0 = 35.75 - 18.2189625$ ....[Simplify equation by subtraction]

$\hat{\beta}_0 = \mathbf{17.5310}$ ....[In four decimal places]

Step 4: Determination of regression equation

$\hat{Y} = \hat{\beta}_0 \pm \hat{\beta}_1 X_1$ ....[Substitute data value into the equation]

$\hat{Y} = \mathbf{17.53 + 1.0337X}$ ....[Regression Line]

Step 5: Interpretation. $\hat{\beta}_1 = 1.033$ and positive, indicating that our variables are positively related. The result is economically logical as price motivate producers as it is a major element in the function of profit.

Example 2: The table below shows the statistics of monetary motivation and number of years workers put to work.

Motivation (in thousands of francs) (X)	64	65	66	67	68	69	70
Workers working hours (Y)	66	52	48	41	32	29	12

Using the least square technique, determine the relationship between motivation and workers working hours

Solution

Step 1: Formula and data. $\hat{Y} = \hat{\beta}_0 \pm \hat{\beta}_1 X$……………………………[Generalized regression line]

$\hat{\beta}_1 = \frac{n\sum xy - \sum x \sum y}{n\sum x^2 - (\sum x)^2}$ ……………………………………………[Independent variable parameter]

$\hat{\beta}_0 = \overline{Y} - \hat{\beta}_1 \overline{X}$………………………………[Intercept value or non-independent variable parameter]

Step 2: Calculation of $\hat{\beta}_1$ and $\hat{\beta}_0$

1: Tabular derivation of $\hat{\beta}_1$ and $\hat{\beta}_0$ formula components

X	Y	$x = X - \overline{X}$	$y = Y - \overline{Y}$	xy	x^2
64	66	-3	26	$(-3)(26) = -78$	$-3^2 = -3 \times -3 = 9$
65	52	-2	12	$(-2)(12) = -24$	$-2^2 = -2 \times -2 = 4$
66	48	-1	8	$(-1)(8) = -8$	$-1^2 = -1 \times -1 = 1$
67	41	0	1	$(0)(1) = 0$	$0^2 = 0 \times 0 = 0$
68	32	1	-8	$(1)(-8) = -8$	$1^2 = 1 \times 1 = 1$
69	29	2	-11	$(2)(-11) = -22$	$2^2 = 2 \times 2 = 4$
70	12	3	-28	$(3)(-28) = -84$	$3^2 = 3 \times 3 = 9$
$\sum = 469$	$\sum = 280$	$\sum = 0$	$\sum = 0$	$\sum = -224$	$\sum = 28$
n = **7**	$\overline{Y}$ = **40**	$\overline{X}$ = **67**	$\sum x = \mathbf{0}$	$(\sum x)^2 = (0)^2$	

2: Data substitution and solving

a) Calculation of $\hat{\beta}_1$

$\hat{\beta}_1 = \frac{n\sum xy - \sum x \sum y}{n\sum x^2 - (\sum x)^2}$ ……………………………………[Substitute data value into the equation]

$\hat{\beta}_1 = \frac{7(-224) - (0)(0)}{7(28) - (0)}$...[Simplify both numerator and denominator by expanding brackets]

$\hat{\beta}_1 = \frac{-1{,}568 - 0}{196 - 0}$ ……………………[Simplify both numerator and denominator by subtraction]

$\hat{\beta}_1 = \mathbf{-8}$

b) Calculation of $\hat{\beta}_0$

$\hat{\beta}_0 = \overline{Y} - \hat{\beta}_1 \overline{X}$ …………………………………………[Substitute data values into the equation]

$\hat{\beta}_0 = 40 — [(-8)(67)]$……………………………[Simplify equation by expanding bracket]

$\hat{\beta}_0 = 40 + 536$ ………………………………………………[Simplify equation by addition]

$\hat{\beta}_0 = \mathbf{576}$

Step 3: Data substitution and interpretation of regression line.

$\hat{Y} = \hat{\beta}_0 \pm \hat{\beta}_1 X_1$ …………………………………………[Substitute data values into the equation]

$\hat{Y} = \mathbf{576 - 8X}$ ………………………………………………………[Regression equation]

Step 4: Interpretation. $(\hat{\beta}_1 = -8)$ indicates that the variables are negatively related. The result is economically logical because as the rate of motivation increase, the number of hours put to work reduces [concept of abnormal supply curve].

Note: The values parameter of a regression line is also determined using the matrix method. The general formula of parameters is given as seen below.

$$\hat{\beta} = (X'X)^{-1}X'Y \text{ ....} (1)$$

The formula for the derivation of $(X'X)$ and $(X'Y)$, depends on the number of independent variables.

1) Simple regression situation..............................[One independent variable]

$$X'X = \begin{bmatrix} 1 & 1 & \cdots & 1 \\ X_{11} & X_{22} & \cdots & X_{1n} \end{bmatrix} \begin{bmatrix} 1 & X_{11} \\ 1 & X_{22} \\ \vdots & \vdots \\ 1 & X_{1n} \end{bmatrix} = \begin{bmatrix} n & \sum X_1 \\ \sum X_1 & \sum {X_1}^2 \end{bmatrix} \text{ ....} (1)$$

$$X'Y = \begin{bmatrix} 1 & 1 & \cdots & 1 \\ X_{11} & X_{22} & \cdots & X_{1n} \end{bmatrix} \begin{bmatrix} Y_1 \\ Y_2 \\ \vdots \\ Y_n \end{bmatrix} = \begin{bmatrix} \sum Y \\ \sum XY \end{bmatrix} \text{ ....} (2)$$

2) Multiple regression situation..................................[Two independent variables]

$$X'Y = \begin{bmatrix} \sum Y \\ \sum YX_1 \\ \sum YX_2 \end{bmatrix} \text{ ....} (3)$$

$$X'X = \begin{bmatrix} n & \sum X_1 & \sum X_2 \\ \sum X_1 & \sum {X_1}^2 & \sum X_1X_2 \\ \sum X_2 & \sum X_1X_2 & \sum {X_2}^2 \end{bmatrix} \text{ ....} (4)$$

Example 1: Determine the value of $(X'X)$ and $(X'Y)$ using information in the table below.

Y	2	4	12	16	26	36
X	43	50	75	100	150	200

Solution

1) Calculation of $(X'X)$

Step 1: Formula. $X'X = \begin{bmatrix} n & \sum X \\ \sum X & \sum X^2 \end{bmatrix}$, where; $n = 6$

Step 2: Determination of unknown and solving

Y	X	X^2	Solving
2	43	$43^2 = 1{,}849$	$X'X = \begin{bmatrix} n & \sum X \\ \sum X & \sum X^2 \end{bmatrix}$ ….[Substitute values]
4	50	$50^2 = 2{,}500$	Where; $n = 6$, $\sum X = 618$ and
12	75	$75^2 = 5{,}625$	$\sum X^2 = 82{,}474$
16	100	$100^2 = 10{,}000$	$X'X = \begin{bmatrix} \mathbf{6} & \mathbf{618} \\ \mathbf{618} & \mathbf{82,474} \end{bmatrix}$
26	150	$150^2 = 22{,}500$	
36	200	$200^2 = 40{,}000$	
	$\sum \mathbf{X} = \mathbf{618}$	$\sum \mathbf{X^2} = \mathbf{82,474}$	

2) Calculation of $(X'Y)$

Step 1: Formula. $X'Y = \begin{bmatrix} \sum Y \\ \sum XY \end{bmatrix}$

Step 2: Determination of unknown and solving

Y	X	XY	Solving
2	43	$2 \times 43 = 86$	Formula. $X'Y = \begin{bmatrix} \sum Y \\ \sum XY \end{bmatrix}$
4	50	$4 \times 50 = 200$	Where; $\sum Y = 96$ and $\sum XY = 13{,}886$
12	75	$12 \times 75 = 900$	$X'Y = \begin{bmatrix} \sum Y \\ \sum XY \end{bmatrix}$ …….[Substitute values]
16	100	$16 \times 100 = 1{,}600$	$X'Y = \begin{bmatrix} \mathbf{96} \\ \mathbf{13,886} \end{bmatrix}$
26	150	$26 \times 150 = 3{,}900$	
36	200	$36 \times 200 = 7{,}200$	
$\sum \mathbf{Y} = \mathbf{96}$		$\sum \mathbf{XY} = \mathbf{13,886}$	

Example 2: Determine the values of the parameter estimate using the table below

Y	2.8	3.4	3	3.5	3.6	3	2.7	3.7
X	21	24	26	27	29	25	25	30

Solution

Step 1: Formula. $\hat{\beta} = (X'X)^{-1}X'Y$, where; $X'X = \begin{bmatrix} 8 & 207 \\ 207 & 5{,}413 \end{bmatrix}$ and $X'Y = \begin{bmatrix} 25.7 \\ 670.8 \end{bmatrix}$

Step 2: Determination of $(X'X)^{-1}$

1) Formula. $(X'X)^{-1} = \frac{1}{\text{Matrix Determinant}}(X'X)' = \frac{1}{(ad)-(bc)}\begin{bmatrix} d & -b \\ -c & a \end{bmatrix}$

Where; $a = 8$, $b = 207$, $c = 207$ and $d = 5{,}413$

2) Data substitution and solving

$(X'X)^{-1} = \frac{1}{(8\times 5{,}413)-(207\times 207)}\begin{bmatrix} 5{,}413 & -207 \\ -207 & 8 \end{bmatrix}$ ....[Simplify denominator brackets]

$(X'X)^{-1} = \frac{1}{43{,}304-42{,}849}\begin{bmatrix} 5{,}413 & -207 \\ -207 & 8 \end{bmatrix}$ ....[Simplify denominator]

$(X'X)^{-1} = \frac{1}{455}\begin{bmatrix} 5{,}413 & -207 \\ -207 & 8 \end{bmatrix}$ ....[Multiply matrix by $\left(\frac{1}{455}\right)$]

$(X'X)^{-1} = \begin{bmatrix} 5{,}413/455 & -207/455 \\ -207/455 & 8/455 \end{bmatrix}$ ....[Simplify fractions]

$(X'X)^{-1} = \begin{bmatrix} 11.897 & -0.455 \\ -0.455 & 0.018 \end{bmatrix}$

Step 3: Data substitution and solving. $\hat{\beta} = \begin{bmatrix} 11.897 & -0.455 \\ -0.455 & 0.018 \end{bmatrix}\begin{bmatrix} 25.7 \\ 670.8 \end{bmatrix}$

1) **Calculation of $\hat{\beta}_0$**

$\hat{\beta}_0 = [11.897 \quad -0.455]\begin{bmatrix} 25.7 \\ 670.8 \end{bmatrix}$ ....[Multiply matrix]

$\hat{\beta}_0 = [11.897(25.7) + (-0.455)(670.8)]$ ....[Open inner brackets]

$\hat{\beta}_0 = 305.7529 - 305.214$ ....[Solve equation]

$\hat{\beta}_0 = \mathbf{0.5389}$

2) **Calculation of $\hat{\beta}_0$**

$\hat{\beta}_0 = [-0.455 \quad 0.018]\begin{bmatrix} 25.7 \\ 670.8 \end{bmatrix}$ ....[Multiply matrix]

$\hat{\beta}_0 = [-0.455(25.7) + (0.018)(670.8)]$ ....[Open inner brackets]

$\hat{\beta}_0 = -11.6935 + 12.0744$ ....[Solve equation]

$\hat{\beta}_0 = \mathbf{0.3809}$

Example 3: Determine the values of $(X'Y)$ and $(X'X)$ using the information in the table below.

Y	40	44	46	48	52
X_1	6	10	12	14	16
X_2	4	4	5	7	9

Solution

1) Calculation of (X′Y)

Step 1: Formula. $X'Y = \begin{bmatrix} \sum Y \\ \sum YX_1 \\ \sum YX_2 \end{bmatrix}$

Step 2: Determination of unknown

Y	X_1	X_2	YX_1	YX_2
40	6	4	240	160
44	10	4	440	176
46	12	5	552	230
48	14	7	672	336
52	16	9	832	468
$\sum Y = 230$			$\sum YX_1 = 2,736$	$\sum YX_2 = 1,370$

Step 3: Data substitution and solving. $X'Y = \begin{bmatrix} 230 \\ 2,736 \\ 1,370 \end{bmatrix}$

2) Calculation of (X′X)

Step 1: Formula. $X'X = \begin{bmatrix} n & \sum X_1 & \sum X_2 \\ \sum X_1 & \sum X_1^2 & \sum X_1X_2 \\ \sum X_2 & \sum X_1X_2 & \sum X_2^2 \end{bmatrix}$, where; n = 5

Step 2: Determination of unknown

Y	X_1	X_2	X_1X_2	X_1^2	X_2^2
40	6	4	24	36	16
44	10	4	40	100	16
46	12	5	60	144	25
48	14	7	98	196	49
52	16	9	144	256	81
	$\sum X_1 = 58$	$\sum X_2 = 29$	$\sum X_1X_2 = 366$	$\sum X_1^2 = 732$	$\sum X_2^2 = 187$

Step 3: Data substitution and solving. $X'X = \begin{bmatrix} 5 & 58 & 29 \\ 58 & 732 & 366 \\ 29 & 366 & 187 \end{bmatrix}$

Example 4: Given that $X = \begin{bmatrix} 1 & 3 & 5 \\ 1 & 1 & 4 \\ 1 & 5 & 6 \\ 1 & 2 & 4 \\ 1 & 4 & 6 \end{bmatrix}$ and $Y = \begin{bmatrix} 3 \\ 1 \\ 8 \\ 3 \\ 5 \end{bmatrix}$. Determine the value of $(X'X)$ and $(X'Y)$

Solution

1) **Calculation of (X′X)**

Step 1: Formula. $X'X = [X'][X]$, where; $X = \begin{bmatrix} 1 & 3 & 5 \\ 1 & 1 & 4 \\ 1 & 5 & 6 \\ 1 & 2 & 4 \\ 1 & 4 & 6 \end{bmatrix}$ and $X' = \begin{bmatrix} 1 & 1 & 1 & 1 & 1 \\ 3 & 1 & 5 & 2 & 4 \\ 5 & 4 & 6 & 4 & 6 \end{bmatrix}$

Step 2: Data substitution and solving

$$X'X = \begin{bmatrix} 1 & 1 & 1 & 1 & 1 \\ 3 & 1 & 5 & 2 & 4 \\ 5 & 4 & 6 & 4 & 6 \end{bmatrix} \begin{bmatrix} 1 & 3 & 5 \\ 1 & 1 & 4 \\ 1 & 5 & 6 \\ 1 & 2 & 4 \\ 1 & 4 & 6 \end{bmatrix}$$ ....[Apply multiplication of matrix principle]

$$X'X = \begin{bmatrix} \{1+1+1+1+1\} & \{3+1+5+2+4\} & \{5+4+6+4+6\} \\ \{3+1+5+2+4\} & \{9+1+25+4+16\} & \{15+4+30+8+24\} \\ \{5+4+6+4+6\} & \{15+4+30+8+24\} & \{25+16+36+16+36\} \end{bmatrix}$$

$$X'X = \begin{bmatrix} 5 & 15 & 25 \\ 15 & 55 & 81 \\ 25 & 81 & 129 \end{bmatrix}$$

2) **Calculation of (X′Y)**

Step 1: Formula. $X'Y = [X'][Y]$, where; $X' = \begin{bmatrix} 1 & 1 & 1 & 1 & 1 \\ 3 & 1 & 5 & 2 & 4 \\ 5 & 4 & 6 & 4 & 6 \end{bmatrix}$ and $Y = \begin{bmatrix} 3 \\ 1 \\ 8 \\ 3 \\ 5 \end{bmatrix}$

Step 2: Data substitution and solving

$$X'Y = \begin{bmatrix} 1 & 1 & 1 & 1 & 1 \\ 3 & 1 & 5 & 2 & 4 \\ 5 & 4 & 6 & 4 & 6 \end{bmatrix} \begin{bmatrix} 3 \\ 1 \\ 8 \\ 3 \\ 5 \end{bmatrix}$$ ....[Apply multiplication of matrix principles]

$$X'Y = \begin{bmatrix} \{1\times3\} + \{1\times1\} + \{1\times8\} + \{1\times3\} + \{1\times5\} \\ \{3\times3\} + \{1\times1\} + \{5\times8\} + \{2\times3\} + \{4\times5\} \\ \{5\times3\} + \{4\times1\} + \{6\times8\} + \{4\times3\} + \{6\times5\} \end{bmatrix}$$ ....[Open brackets]

$$X'Y = \begin{bmatrix} 3 + 1 + 8 + 3 + 5 \\ 9 + 1 + 40 + 6 + 20 \\ 15 + 4 + 48 + 12 + 30 \end{bmatrix} \Rightarrow X'Y = \begin{bmatrix} 20 \\ 76 \\ 109 \end{bmatrix}$$

Example 5: Given that; $X'X = \begin{bmatrix} 5 & 15 & 25 \\ 15 & 55 & 81 \\ 25 & 81 & 129 \end{bmatrix}$, determine the value of $(X'X)^{-1}$

Solution

Step 1: Formula. $(X'X)^{-1} = \frac{1}{\text{Matrix Determinant}}(X'X)'$

Where; $X'X = \begin{bmatrix} 5 & 15 & 25 \\ 15 & 55 & 81 \\ 25 & 81 & 129 \end{bmatrix}$

Where; $(X'X)' = \begin{bmatrix} 5 & -15 & -25 \\ -15 & 55 & -81 \\ -25 & -81 & 129 \end{bmatrix}$

Step 2: Determination of Determinant

$\text{Determinant} = +5\begin{vmatrix} 55 & 81 \\ 81 & 129 \end{vmatrix} - 15\begin{vmatrix} 15 & 81 \\ 25 & 129 \end{vmatrix} + 25\begin{vmatrix} 15 & 55 \\ 25 & 81 \end{vmatrix}$ ....[Work Sub-determinants]

$\text{Determinant} = +5|7{,}095 - 6{,}561| - 15|1{,}935 - 2{,}025| + 25|1{,}215 - 1{,}375|$ ....[Simplify]

$\text{Determinant} = +5|534| - 15|-90| + 25|-160|$ ....[Open brackets]

$\text{Determinant} = 2{,}670 + 1{,}350 - 4{,}000$ ....[Solve equation]

$\text{Determinant} = \mathbf{20}$ ....[Determinant of $(\mathbf{X'X})$]

Step 3: Determination of matrix transpose $(X'X)'$

$$(X'X)' = \begin{bmatrix} +\begin{vmatrix} 55 & 81 \\ 81 & 129 \end{vmatrix} & -\begin{vmatrix} 15 & 81 \\ 25 & 129 \end{vmatrix} & +\begin{vmatrix} 15 & 55 \\ 25 & 81 \end{vmatrix} \\ -\begin{vmatrix} 15 & 25 \\ 81 & 129 \end{vmatrix} & +\begin{vmatrix} 5 & 25 \\ 25 & 129 \end{vmatrix} & -\begin{vmatrix} 5 & 15 \\ 25 & 81 \end{vmatrix} \\ +\begin{vmatrix} 15 & 25 \\ 55 & 81 \end{vmatrix} & -\begin{vmatrix} 5 & 25 \\ 15 & 81 \end{vmatrix} & +\begin{vmatrix} 5 & 15 \\ 15 & 55 \end{vmatrix} \end{bmatrix}$$ ....[Work Sub-determinants]

$$(X'X)' = \begin{bmatrix} +|7{,}095 - 6{,}561| - |1{,}935 - 2{,}025| + |1{,}215 - 1{,}375| \\ -|1{,}935 - 2{,}025| + |645 - 625| - |405 - 375| \\ +|1{,}215 - 1{,}375| - |405 - 375| + |275 - 225| \end{bmatrix}$$ ......[Simplify brackets]

$$(X'X)' = \begin{bmatrix} +|534| - |-90| + |-160| \\ -|-90| + |20| - |30| \\ +|-160| - |30| + |50| \end{bmatrix}$$ ....[Open brackets]

$$(X'X)' = \begin{bmatrix} 534 & 90 & -160 \\ 90 & 20 & -30 \\ -160 & -30 & 50 \end{bmatrix}$$ ....[Perform reflection around the leading diagonal]

$$(X'X)' = \begin{bmatrix} 534 & 90 & -160 \\ 90 & 20 & -30 \\ -160 & -30 & 50 \end{bmatrix}$$ ....[Transpose of $(\mathbf{X'X})$]

Step 4: Data substitution and solving

$$(X'X)^{-1} = \frac{1}{20}\begin{bmatrix} 534 & 90 & -160 \\ 90 & 20 & -30 \\ -160 & -30 & 50 \end{bmatrix}$$ ....[Multiply matrix with $\left(\frac{1}{20}\right)$]

$$(X'X)^{-1} = \begin{bmatrix} 534/20 & 90/20 & -160/20 \\ 90/20 & 20/20 & -30/20 \\ -160/20 & -30/20 & 50/20 \end{bmatrix}$$ ....[Simplify fractions]

$$(X'X)^{-1} = \begin{bmatrix} \mathbf{26.7} & \mathbf{4.5} & \mathbf{-8} \\ \mathbf{4.5} & \mathbf{1} & \mathbf{-1.5} \\ \mathbf{-8} & \mathbf{-1.5} & \mathbf{2.5} \end{bmatrix}$$ ....[The inverse of matrix (X'X)]

Example 6: Determine the parameter estimate using the following information; $X'Y = \begin{bmatrix} 12 \\ 8 \\ 15 \end{bmatrix}$

and $(X'X)^{-1} = \begin{bmatrix} 0.1496 & -0.0641 & -0.0095 \\ -0.0641 & 0.1228 & -0.0435 \\ -0.0095 & -0.0435 & 0.0799 \end{bmatrix}$.

Solution

Step 1: Formula. $\hat{\beta} = (X'X)^{-1}X'Y$

Step 2: Data substitution and solving

1) **Calculation of $\hat{\beta}_0$**

$$\hat{\beta}_0 = \begin{bmatrix} 0.1496 & -0.0641 & -0.0095 \end{bmatrix}\begin{bmatrix} 12 \\ 8 \\ 15 \end{bmatrix}$$ ....[Perform matrix multiplication]

$\hat{\beta}_0 = 0.1496(12) + (-0.0641)(8) + (-0.0095)(15)$ ....[Open brackets]

$\hat{\beta}_0 = 1.7952 - 0.5128 - 0.1425$ ....[Solve equation]

$\hat{\beta}_0 = \mathbf{1.1399}$

2) **Calculation of $\hat{\beta}_1$**

$$\hat{\beta}_1 = \begin{bmatrix} -0.0641 & 0.1228 & -0.0435 \end{bmatrix}\begin{bmatrix} 12 \\ 8 \\ 15 \end{bmatrix}$$ ....[Perform matrix multiplication]

$\hat{\beta}_1 = -0.0641(12) + (0.1228)(8) + (-0.0435)(15)$ ....[Open brackets]

$\hat{\beta}_1 = -0.7692 + 0.9824 - 0.6525$ ....[Solve equation]

$\hat{\beta}_1 = \mathbf{-0.4393}$

3) **Calculation of $\hat{\beta}_2$**

$$\hat{\beta}_2 = \begin{bmatrix} -0.0095 & -0.0435 & 0.0799 \end{bmatrix}\begin{bmatrix} 12 \\ 8 \\ 15 \end{bmatrix}$$ ....[Perform matrix multiplication]

$\hat{\beta}_2 = -0.0095(12) + (-0.0435)(8) + (0.0799)(15)$ ....[Open brackets]

$\hat{\beta}_2 = -0.114 - 0.348 + 1.1985$ ....[Solve equation]

$\hat{\beta}_2 = \mathbf{0.7365}$

Note: The regression equation is therefore given as; $[\hat{Y}_i = 1.1399 - 0.4393X_1 + 0.7365X_2]$.

Test Your Understanding

Exercise 9: Determine the regression equation using information from the table below. Put answers in two decimal places

X	2	4	12	16	26	36
Y	43	50	75	100	150	200

[Answer: $\bar{Y} = 197.07 - 5.88X_i$. That is negative correlation]

Exercise 10: What is the relationship between quantity of yam and bags of fertilizer applied?

Quantity of Yam (Y)	152	190	11	222	134	131
Bags of fertilizer (X)	52	56	43	65	45	39

[Answer: $\bar{Y} = -40.91 + 3.98X_i$, that is positive relationship]

Exercise 11: Given that; $\sum xy = -297.76$, $\sum x^2 = 8.592$, $n = 5$, $\sum x = 0$ and $\sum y = 0$. Determine the relationship that exists between the variable X and Y.

[Answer: $\hat{\beta}_1 = -34.655$, showing a negative relationship]

Exercise 12: The average price and quantity demand of a commodity in Kumba from the years 2000 to the year 2004 are presented in the table below.

Years	2000	2001	2002	2003	2004
Price (in thousands of francs)	36	56	20	65	42
Quantity Demanded (Units)	50	35	70	25	58

1) Calculate the coefficient of correlation between price (X) and quantity demanded (Y) using spearman rank correlation technique

[Answer: -0.9, Very Strong and Negative relation]

2) Compare your result in 1 above using the Pearson correlation technique and covariance technique.

[Answer: Pearson Correlation (-0.9) and Covariance (-0.9)]

Exercise 13: The table below shows the salary of workers in a company from 1977 to 1981.

Years	1977	1978	1979	1980	1981
Salary (in thousands of francs)	95	80	75	60	55

1) Discuss the relationship that exists between years and salary of workers using the least square technique........................ **[Answer:$\hat{Y}_t = 103 - 10X_t$, Negative relation]**
2) Compare your result in 1 above using the Pearson coefficient correlation technique.

[Answer: -0.99, Very strong and negative correlation]

Exercise 14: Given that; $X'Y = \begin{bmatrix} 20 \\ 76 \\ 109 \end{bmatrix}$ and $(X'X)^{-1} = \begin{bmatrix} 26.7 & 4.5 & -8 \\ 4.5 & 1 & -1.5 \\ -8 & -1.5 & 2.5 \end{bmatrix}$. Compute the parameter estimates using the given data. **[Answer: $\hat{\beta}_0 = 4$, $\hat{\beta}_1 = 254.5$ and $\hat{\beta}_2 = -1.5$]**

CHAPTER TWO

TIME SERIES DATA

A time series data is a set of fixed interval observations (daily, weekly, monthly, quarterly, and annually) on the values of variables takes at different time period.

2.1 Time Series Components and Models

Time series data is made up of four components; trend(T_t), cyclical(C_t), seasonal (S_t) and irregular (R_t) components.

$$\text{Time Series Data} = f(\text{Trend}, \text{Cyclical}, \text{Seasonal}, \text{Irregular}) \quad \ldots\ldots(1)$$

$$Y_t = f(T_t, C_t, S_t, R_t) \quad \ldots\ldots(2)$$

1) **Trend (T):** It is the long term gradual increase or decrease of the variable under observation(Y_t). Time series trend pattern can be linear (straight line) or non-linear (curve).
2) **Cyclical (C):** It involves a gradual long term up and down rotation or oscillation of observation (Y_t) around the trend line.
3) **Seasonality (S):** Seasonality is a regular and relatively short-term (within a year) repetitive (repeated) up and down fluctuation (variation) of observation(Y_t). Seasonal variations are caused by natural factors (climate and weather) and human factors (customs and tradition). Seasonal components mostly measured in quarters as seen below.

   Note: Cyclical variation (C_t) and seasonal variation (S_t) differ in that cyclical variation (C_t) does not have a fixed frequency and seasonal variation (S_t) has a fixed frequency. Cyclical variation is a long term up and down movement and the seasonality is a short term up and down movement.
4) **Random or Irregular (R):** Irregular or remainder variations are caused by unpredictable influences, which are not regular and does not repeat in a particular pattern. Random or irregular component is also called noise. The three possible events with random component are given below.

Time series modeling is having as objective to carefully collect and thoroughly study the past observations in order to develop appropriate models which describe the structure of a time series data. Time series model can be additive and/or multiplicative

1) **Additive Model:** The additive model is based on the assumption that the four components of time series data are independent. The value of (Y_t) at time (t) is defined as the sum of the components.

$$Y_t = T_t + S_t + C_t + R_t \text{ ....(1)}$$

N/B: Applying the seasonality decomposition, we sum the trend (T_t) and the cyclical (C_t) components$(T_t + C_t)$ to obtain a new component called general movement component denoted(T_t).

$$Y_t = T_t + S_t + R_t \text{ ....(2)}$$

2) **Multiplicative Model:** The multiplicative model is based on the assumption that the four components of time series data are not necessarily independent and can influence each other. The value of (Y_t) at time (t) is defined as a product of the components.

$$Y_t = T_t \times S_t \times C_t \times I_t \text{ ....(1)}$$

N/B: Applying the seasonality decomposition, we multiply the trend (T_t) and the cyclical (C_t) components$(T_t \times C_t = T_tC_t)$.

$$Y_t = T_t \times S_t \times R_t \text{ ....(2)}$$

2.2 Linear Adjustment of a Time Series

Adjustment or smoothing of time series data is the process of removing fluctuations from a time series line chart in order to obtain a linear trend line. We are going to examine three major methods of adjustment; semi-average or Mayer method, moving average method and ordinary least squared method.

2.2.1 Semi-Average (Mayer) Adjustment Method

The Mayer method or semi average method of time series data adjustment depends on the nature of data. That is if the data is an even count in nature or odd count in nature.

a) **Even Count Time Series Data**

Even count time series data is one in which the time series observation duration is an even number. A 2years, 4years and 6years are examples of an even count time series data. To perform a time series adjustment using an even count time series data, we suggest the following procedures.

1) **Data Splitting:** Divide the data into two equal parts and see them as independent time series data. This division gives rise to two separate tables with one indicating the right hand count and the other the left hand count.

Original Table					**Divided Tables**			
					First Half		**Second Half**	
X	10	20	30	40	X_1	Y_1	X_2	Y_2
Y	5	15	25	30	10	5	30	25
					20	15	40	30

2) **Determine Individual Half's Average:** Determine the average value of independent variable and independent variable observations of each halves and formulate an average regression equation of the two halves. Doing this gives us a simultaneous equation as seen below.

$\overline{Y}_1 = \beta_0 \pm \beta\overline{X}_1$ ……………………………………………………………(1)

$\overline{Y}_2 = \beta_0 \pm \beta\overline{X}_2$ ……………………………………………………………(2)

First Half			**Second Half**		
X_1	Y_1	Note: n = 2	X_2	Y_2	Note: n = 2
10	5	$\overline{X} = \frac{30}{2} = 15$	30	25	$\overline{X} = \frac{70}{2} = 35$
20	15	$\overline{Y} = \frac{20}{2} = 10$	40	3	$\overline{Y} = \frac{55}{2} = 27.5$
$\boldsymbol{\Sigma = 30}$	$\boldsymbol{\Sigma = 20}$		$\Sigma = 70$	$\Sigma = 55$	
$\overline{Y}_1 = \beta_0 \pm \beta\overline{X}_1 \rightarrow \mathbf{10 = \beta_0 \pm 15\beta}$			$\overline{Y}_2 = \beta_0 \pm \beta\overline{X}_2 \rightarrow \mathbf{27.5 = \beta_0 \pm 35\beta}$		

$10 = \beta_0 \pm 15\beta_1$ ……………………………………………………………(1)

$27.5 = \beta_0 \pm 35\beta_2$ ……………………………………………………………(2)

3) **Determine the Regression Equation:** Solve the simultaneous equation and obtain the value of $[\beta_0 = \hat{\beta}_0]$ and $[\beta = \hat{\beta}_1]$. Re-write the adjusted regression equation $[\hat{Y} = \hat{\beta}_0 \pm \hat{\beta}_1 X_1]$ and substitute the numerical values of $[\hat{\beta}_0]$ and $[\hat{\beta}_1]$. Assuming that $[\beta_0 = \hat{\beta}_0 = 5]$ and $[\beta = \hat{\beta}_1 = 10]$, our final adjustment regression equation is given as $[\hat{Y} = 5 \pm 10X]$.

b) **Odd Count Time Series Data**

Odd count time series data is one in which the time series observation duration is an odd number. A 3years, 5years and 7years are examples of an odd count time series data. To perform a time series adjustment using an odd count time series data, we follow the same procedure as in the case of event counts seen above. The main and significant difference in the procedure is based on the procedure of data splitting.

To split an odd count time series data correctly, we do front-back counting and identify the middle observation which is called the omitted observation. The number of observations before the omitted observation is considered the first half and after the omitted observation is considered second half.

Original Table

X	10	20	**30**	40	50
Y	5	15	**25**	30	35

Omitted Observation here is $[X = 30, Y = 25]$

Divided Tables

First Half

X_1	Y_1
10	5
20	15

Second Half

X_2	Y_2
40	30
50	35

Example1: The table below summarizes the evolution of Bananas production in Cameroon measured in millions of tons.

Years	2003	2004	2005	2006	2007	2008
Quantity (Tons)	104	107	122	170	213	256

Work Required

1) Graphically represent the evolution of this production using a line diagram
2) Determine an equation of the trend line using the average point methods (Mayer) and draw the adjustment equation line on the graph above
3) What will be the quantity of Banana production in 2009?

Solution

1) Graphically represent the evolution of this production

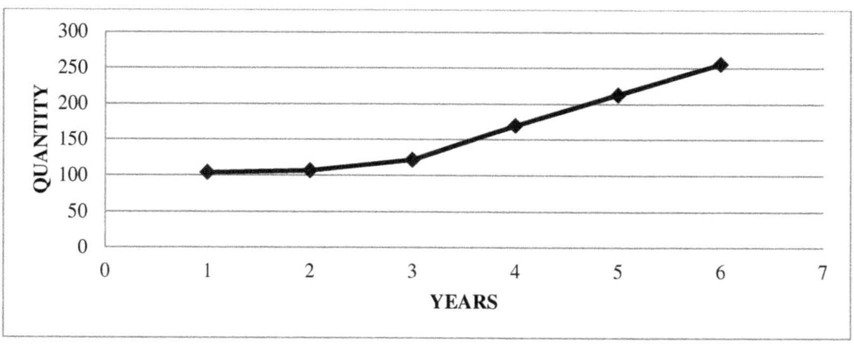

Supplementary Explanation: The almost perfect lining of dots shows the variables are strongly related and the positive slope line nature shows our variables are positively related. Therefore, as the years increase, the production of cocoa will also increase.

2) **Determine an equation of the trend line using the average point methods (Mayer) and draw the adjustment equation line on the graph above**

Hint: Counting the data trend period from 2003 to 2008 gives us duration of 6 years with 6 being an even number. Therefore, our table or situation is an even count time series data situation.

a) Determine an equation of the trend line using the average point methods (Mayer)

Step 1: Formula. $\hat{Y} = \hat{\beta}_0 \pm \hat{\beta}_1 X$

Step 2: Tabular determination of average regression equation.

First half of data $[\bar{Y}_1 = \beta_0 \pm \beta\bar{X}_1]$				Second half of data $[\bar{Y}_2 = \beta_0 \pm \beta\bar{X}_2]$			
Original Table		Working Table		Original Table		Working Table	
Years (x)	Quantity (Y)	X	Y	Years (X)	Quantity (Y)	X	Y
2003	104	1	104	2006	170	4	170
2004	107	2	107	2007	213	5	213
2005	122	3	122	2008	256	6	256
Summation (Σ)		**6**	**333**	Summation (Σ)		**15**	**639**
n = **3**				n = **3**			
$\bar{Y}_1 = \frac{\Sigma Y_i}{N} \rightarrow \bar{Y}_1 = \frac{333}{3} \rightarrow \bar{Y}_1 = \mathbf{111}$				$\bar{Y}_2 = \frac{\Sigma Y_i}{N} \rightarrow \bar{Y}_2 = \frac{639}{3} \rightarrow \bar{Y}_2 = \mathbf{213}$			
$\bar{X}_1 = \frac{\Sigma X_i}{N} \rightarrow \bar{X}_1 = \frac{6}{3} \rightarrow \bar{X}_1 = \mathbf{2}$				$\bar{X}_2 = \frac{\Sigma X_i}{N} \rightarrow \bar{X}_2 = \frac{15}{3} \rightarrow \bar{X}_2 = \mathbf{5}$			
$\bar{Y}_1 = \beta_0 \pm \beta\bar{X}_1 \rightarrow \mathbf{111 = \beta_0 + 2\beta}$ ....(1)				$\bar{Y}_2 = \beta_0 \pm \beta\bar{X}_1 \rightarrow \mathbf{213 = \beta_0 + 5\beta}$ ....(2)			

Step 3: Solving Simultaneous Equation

$111 = \beta_0 + 2\beta \equiv \beta_0 + 2\beta = 111$ ....(1)

$213 = \beta_0 + 5\beta \equiv \beta_0 + 5\beta = 213$ ....(2)

Subtract equation (1) from equation (2)

$\beta_0 + 5\beta - (\beta_0 + 2\beta) = 213 - 11$ ....[Expand bracket by multiplication]

$\beta_0 + 5\beta - \beta_0 - 2\beta = 213 - 111$ ....[Collect like items together and simplify]

$3\beta = 102$ ....[Divide both sides of equations by 3]

$\beta = \mathbf{34}$ ....[Value of $\hat{\beta}_1$]

Substitute the value of β (34) in any of the equation to obtain the value of $[\beta_0]$.

1) **Using equation (1)**

$\beta_0 + 2(34) = 111$ ....[Expand bracket and collect like terms together]

$\beta_0 = 111 - 68$ ....[Solve equation]

$\beta_0 = \mathbf{43}$ ....[Value of $\hat{\beta}_0$]

2) **Using equation (2).**

$\beta_0 + 5(34) = 213$ ....[Expand bracket and collect like terms together]

$\beta_0 = 213 - 170$ ....[Solve equation]

$\beta_0 = \mathbf{43}$ ....[Value of $\hat{\beta}_0$]

Substitute the values of $\hat{\beta}_0(43)$ and $\hat{\beta}_1(34)$ in the standard regression line equation. Therefore, our equation of the trend line is given as seen below

$\hat{Y} = \mathbf{43 + 34}X$...(1)

b) Drawing of equation of trend line on the graph above

Step 1: Determine the estimated values of the dependent variables $[\hat{Y}]$

Original Table		**Working**	
		Regression line equation	**Estimated value of Y**
Years (X)	Waste (Y)	$\hat{Y} = \mathbf{43 + 34X_i}$	$\hat{Y}$
1	104	$\hat{Y} = 43 + 34(1)$	77
2	107	$\hat{Y} = 43 + 34(2)$	111
3	122	$\hat{Y} = 43 + 34(3)$	145
4	170	$\hat{Y} = 43 + 34(4)$	179
5	213	$\hat{Y} = 43 + 34(5)$	213
6	256	$\hat{Y} = 43 + 34(6)$	247

Step 2: Plotting [Use the values of X and $\hat{Y}$]

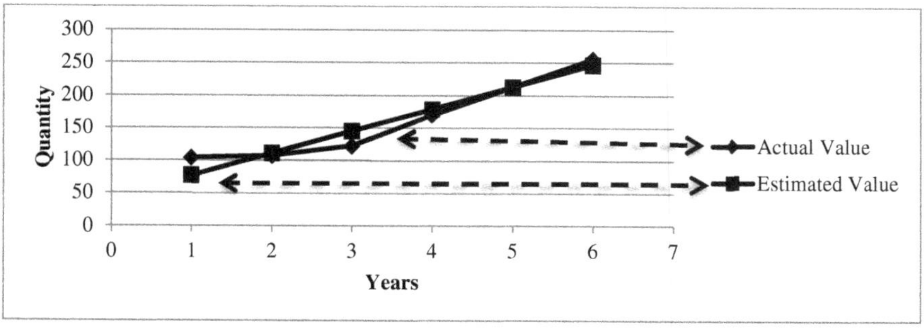

3) What will be the quantity of Banana production in 2009?

Step 1: Determine the Time Range

a) Formula. Time Range $= (T_n - T_0) + 1$, where; $T_n = 2009$ and $T_0 = 2003$

b) Data substitution and solving

$\text{Time Range} = (2009 - 2003) + 1$ ....[Simplify brackets]

$\text{Time Range} = 6 + 1$ ....[Solve equation]

$\text{Time Range} = \mathbf{7}$......[Value of independent variable to be substituted in the equation]

Step 2: Data substitution and solving.

$\hat{Y} = 43 + 34(7)$ ....[Expand equation bracket by multiplication]

$\hat{Y} = 43 + 238$ ....[Solve equation]

$\hat{Y} = \mathbf{281\ Tons\ of\ banana}$

Example 2: The sales information of Essombo Lid Company in Bare Bakem is presented in the table below.

Years	1990	1991	1992	1993	1994	1995	1996
Sales (Bags)	200	225	230	210	240	260	250

Work Required

a) Graphically represent these series using line graph technique

b) Determine the adjustment line equation using the double average of Mayer and draw the adjustment line equation on the graph above. [All values should be written into no decimal place]

Solution

a) Graphically represent these series using line graph technique

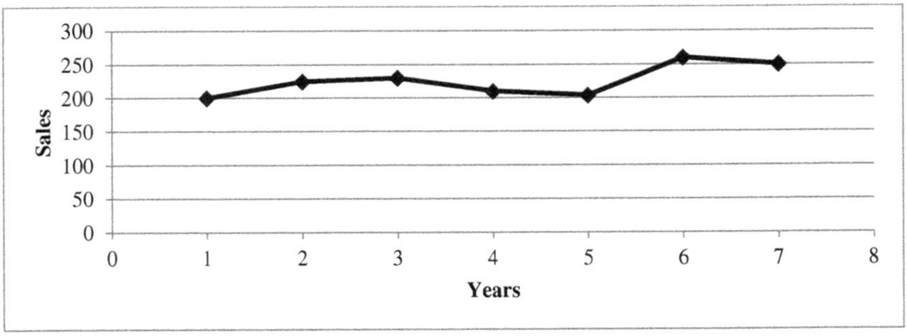

b) Determine the adjustment line equation using the double average of Mayer and draw the adjustment line equation on the graph above.

Step 1: Formula and data. $\hat{Y} = \hat{\beta}_0 \pm \hat{\beta}_1 X$

Step 2: Determine the estimated values of the dependent variables $[\hat{Y}]$

First half of data $[\overline{Y}_1 = \beta_0 \pm \beta\overline{X}_1]$				Second half of data $[\overline{Y}_2 = \beta_0 \pm \beta\overline{X}_1]$			
Original Table		Working Table		Original Table		Working Table	
Years (X)	Sales (Y)	X	Y	Years (X)	Sales (Y)	X	Y
1990	200	1	200	1994	240	5	240
1991	225	2	225	1995	260	6	260
1992	230	3	230	1996	250	7	250
n = **3**	Summation (Σ)	**6**	**655**	n = **3**	Summation (Σ)	**18**	**750**
$\overline{Y}_1 = \frac{\Sigma Y}{N} \rightarrow \overline{Y}_1 = \frac{655}{3} \rightarrow \overline{Y}_1 = \mathbf{218}$ $\overline{X}_1 = \frac{\Sigma X}{N} \rightarrow \overline{X}_1 = \frac{6}{3} \rightarrow \overline{X}_1 = \mathbf{2}$ $\overline{Y}_1 = \beta_0 \pm \beta\overline{X}_1 \rightarrow \mathbf{218 = \beta_0 + 2\beta}$ ....(1)				$\overline{Y}_2 = \frac{\Sigma Y}{N} \rightarrow \overline{Y}_2 = \frac{750}{3} \rightarrow \overline{Y}_2 = \mathbf{250}$ $\overline{X}_2 = \frac{\Sigma X}{N} \rightarrow \overline{X}_2 = \frac{18}{3} \rightarrow \overline{X}_2 = \mathbf{6}$ $\overline{Y}_2 = \beta_0 \pm \beta\overline{X}_2 \rightarrow \mathbf{250 = \beta_0 + 6\beta}$ ....(2)			

Step 2**:** Data substitution and solving [Algebraic calculation of $\hat{\beta}_1$ and $\hat{\beta}_0$]

$\beta_0 + 2\beta = 218$ ....(1)

$\beta_0 + 6\beta = 250$ ....(2)

Subtract equation 1 from equation 2. That is (2) − (1)

$\beta_0 + 6\beta - (\beta_0 + 2\beta) = 250 - 218$ ....[Expand bracket]

$\beta_0 + 6\beta - \beta_0 - 2\beta = 250 - 218$ ....[Collect like team together]

$4\beta = 32$ ....[Divide both sides of equation by 4]

$\beta = \mathbf{8}$ ....[Value of $\hat{\beta}_1$]

Substitute the value of β (8) in any of the equations

1) Using equation (1)

$B_0 + 2\beta_1 = 218$ ....[Substitute the value of β_1 into the equation]

$\beta_0 + 2(8) = 218$ ....[Expand equation bracket by multiplication]

$\beta_0 + 16 = 218$....................[Make β_0 subject of formula by collecting like terms together]

$\beta_0 = 218 - 16$ ....[Solve equation]

$\beta_0 = \mathbf{202}$ ....[Value of $\hat{\beta}_0$]

(Try to solve this by using equation 2 to verify the answer)

Substitute the values of $\hat{\beta}_0(202)$ and $\hat{\beta}_1(8)$ in the standard regression line equation. Therefore, our equation of the trend line is given as seen below

$\hat{Y} = 202 + 8X$..(1)

Step 3: Derivation of the estimated value of sales $(\hat{Y})$

Original Table		Working	
		Regression line equation	**Estimated value of Y**
Years (X)	Sales (Y)	$\hat{Y} = 202 + 8X$	$\hat{Y}$
1	200	$\hat{Y} = 202 + 8(1)$	210
2	225	$\hat{Y} = 202 + 8(2)$	218
3	230	$\hat{Y} = 202 + 8(3)$	226
4	210	$\hat{Y} = 202 + 8(4)$	234
5	240	$\hat{Y} = 202 + 8(5)$	242
6	260	$\hat{Y} = 202 + 8(6)$	250
7	250	$\hat{Y} = 202 + 8(7)$	258

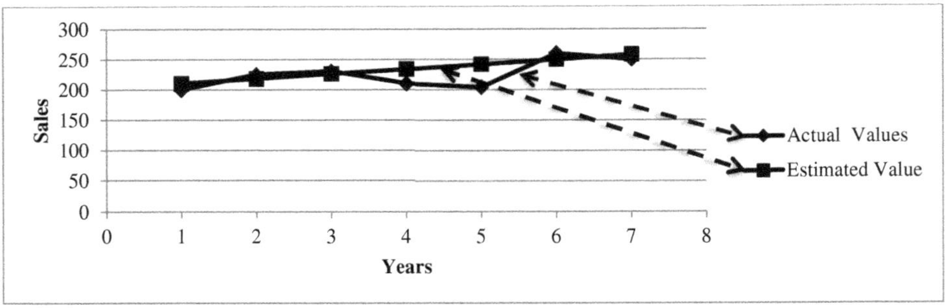

<u>Test Your Understanding</u>

Exercise 1: Use the table below and answer the questions that follow. Your answer should be put in one decimal place.

Bags of fertilizer (X)	19	31	34	35	40	39	44
Quantity of Beans (Y)	411	580	590	570	640	680	660

1) Calculate and present the adjustment equation. .... **[Answer: $\hat{Y} = 240.5 + 10.2X$]**
2) Estimate the beans produced if 35 bags of fertilizers are used.........**[Answer: 597.5 Bags]**
3) Forecast the bean produced if 50 bags of fertilizer are used...........**[Answer: 852.5 Bags]**

Exercise 2: The number of death rate and birth rate of a country from the year 2000 to the year 2002 is given below.

Years (X)	2000	2001	2002	2003
Birth rate (Y_1)	9.88	14.00	14.65	15.80
Death rate (Y_2)	19.77	15.88	14.50	12.92

1) Calculate and present the adjustment regression line using;
   a) Years and birth rate. ....**[Answer: $\hat{Y} = 9.47625 + 1.6425X$]**
   b) Years and death rate. ....**[Answer: $\hat{Y} = 20.91125 - 2.0575X$]**
2) What will be the death rate in 2008?... **[Answer: 2.39645]**
3) In which year will birth rate be 27.54375?........................... **[Answer: The year 2010]**

2.2.2 Moving Average Adjustment Method

As seen with the situation of Mayer method above, the methodology for deriving the adjustment line using the moving average also depends on the nature of data.

1) Even Count Time Series Data

Under the concept of moving average, even count time series data is based on the moving average period. Moving average period that are even numbers are considered even count time series data. For example 2 years moving average, 4years moving average, 6years moving average etc. To determine the regression equation, we are required to determine the allocation space and working table.

$$\text{Allocation Space(AS)} = \frac{\text{Giving moving average year}}{2} \quad \ldots\ldots\ldots\ldots\ldots\ldots\ldots\ldots\ldots\ldots(1)$$

$$\text{Working Table(WT)} = 2(\text{AS}) + 2[\text{Question Table Rows} - 2(\text{SA})] + 1 \ldots\ldots\ldots\ldots(2)$$

Note: Allocation space value direct us on how to fill the working table. An allocation space value of 2 means we should fill the first two and last two rows and from the first two rows skip a row after each row filling. After the determination of the allocation space and working table, the following concepts are worth knowing,

a) Period Grouping: It is the sequential segmentation of the working table. Given a data of; 2000, 2001, 2002, 2003, 2004 and 2005 and assuming a 2years moving average, period grouping will follow the pattern; segment 1 (2000 and 2001), segment 2 (2001 and 2002), segment 3 (2002 and 2003), segment 4 (2003 and 2004) and segment 5 (2004 and 2005).

b) Moving Total and Moving Total Average: Moving total is the sum of segment values and it value is filled in the segment middle row. Moving total average is the sequential average of moving total. Using the segments in (a) above, moving total average will be as follows;

$$\text{Moving Total Average 1} = \frac{\text{Segment 1 Moving Total+Segment 2 Moving Total}}{2} \quad \ldots\ldots\ldots\ldots(1)$$

$$\text{Moving Total Average 2} = \frac{\text{Segment 2 Moving Total+Segment 3 Moving Total}}{2} \quad \ldots\ldots\ldots\ldots(2)$$

$$\text{Moving Total Average 3} = \frac{\text{Segment 3 Moving Total+Segment 4 Moving Total}}{2} \quad \ldots\ldots\ldots\ldots(3)$$

$$\text{Moving Total Average 4} = \frac{\text{Segment 4 Moving Total+Segment 5 Moving Total}}{2} \quad \ldots\ldots\ldots\ldots(4)$$

Note: The value of moving total average is filled in the middle row of it corresponding moving totals

c) Centered Moving Average: The moving total average is often greater than the observed value. To solve this problem, we divide each moving total average by 2. The result obtained is called centered moving average.

Example 1: The wages of workers from the year 2005 to the year 2012 is presented in the table below.

Years	2005	2006	2007	2008	2009	2010	2011	2012
Wages (FRS)	1,150	1,250	1,320	1,400	1,300	1,320	1,500	1,700

1) Draw up the chronological curve of these series
2) Determine the adjustment trend of series using 4 years moving average method and draw adjustment trend on the curve above

Solution

1) Draw up the chronological curve of this series

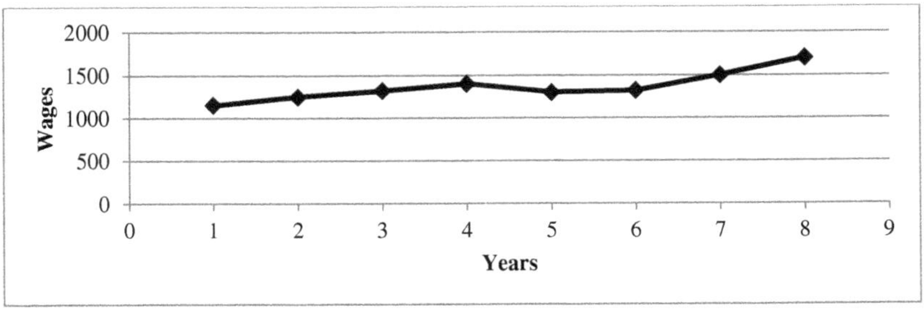

2) **Determine the adjustment trend of series using 4 years moving average method and draw adjustment trend on the curve above**

Step 1: Calculation of Space allocation and derivation of working table

$\text{Allocation Space(AS)} = \frac{\text{Giving moving average year}}{2}$ ....[Substitute data values]

$\text{SA} = \frac{4}{2}$ ....[Solve equation]

$\text{Allocation Space(AS)} = \mathbf{2}$

$\text{Working Table(WT)} = 2(\text{AS}) + 2[\text{Question Table Rows} - 2(\text{SA})] + 1$

$\text{WT} = 2(2) + 2[8 - 2(2)] + 1$ ....[Simplify brackets]

$\text{Working Table(WT)} = \mathbf{23}$

Interpretation: Working table values of 13 means our working table will be made up of 13 rows. The allocation space value of 2 means the first two and last two rows of the 13 rows should be filled first and from the first two filled rows, a row should be skipped before any further filling following a sequential manner.

Step 2: Establishment of working table [Grouping and averages calculations]

Years	Wages	4 years Moving Total	4 years Moving Average	**Centered Moving Average**
2005	1150			
2006	1250			
		5120		
2007	1320		$5120 + 5270/4 = \mathbf{2597.5}$	$2597.5/2 = \mathbf{1298.75}$
		5270		
2008	1400		$5270 + 5340/4 = \mathbf{2652.5}$	$2652.5/2 = \mathbf{1326.25}$
		5340		
2009	1300		$5340 + 5520/4 = \mathbf{2715}$	$2715/2 = \mathbf{1357.5}$
		5520		
2010	1320		$5520 + 5820/4 = \mathbf{2835}$	$2835/2 = \mathbf{1417.5}$
		5820		
2011	1500			
2012	1700			

Complementary Working

Segment 1 4years Moving Total $= 1150 + 1250 + 1320 + 1400 = \mathbf{5120}$

Segment 2 4years Moving Total $= 1250 + 1320 + 1400 + 1300 = \mathbf{5270}$

Segment 3 4years Moving Total $= 1320 + 1400 + 1300 + 1320 = \mathbf{5340}$

Segment 4 4years Moving Total $= 1400 + 1300 + 1320 + 1500 = \mathbf{5520}$

Segment 5 4years Moving Total] $= 1300 + 1320 + 1500 + 1700 = \mathbf{5820}$

Step 3: Drawing of adjustment trend on the curve above [Use4 year centered moving average and variable X (Years).

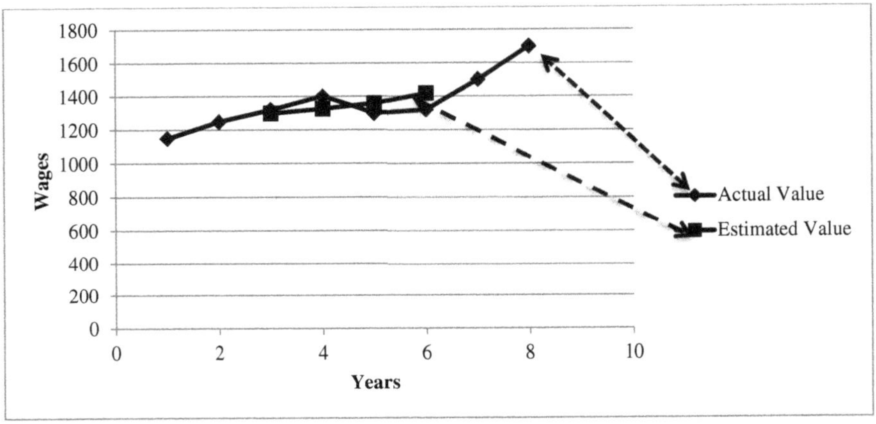

2) Odd Count Time Series Data

Moving average period that are odd numbers are considered odd count time series data. For example, 3years moves average, 5years moving average, 7years moving average etc. Here, the question table is considered the working table and the process of moving total and moving average calculation is the same as in even count time series data.

Example 1: A census statistics obtained from a period of 2000 to 2007 on the number of birth is presented in the table below.

Years	2000	2001	2002	2003	2004	2005	2006	2007
Number of Birth	1,200	1,500	1,400	1,750	1,800	1,700	1,600	1,500

Work Required

1) Draw up the chronological curve of these series
2) Determine the adjustment trend of series using 3 years moving average method and draw adjustment trend on the curve above

<u>**Solution**</u>

Remember: When dealing with odd situation, the table must remain the same. That is there should be no addition of rows or columns as the case with the even situation seen above.

1) Draw up the chronological curve of these series

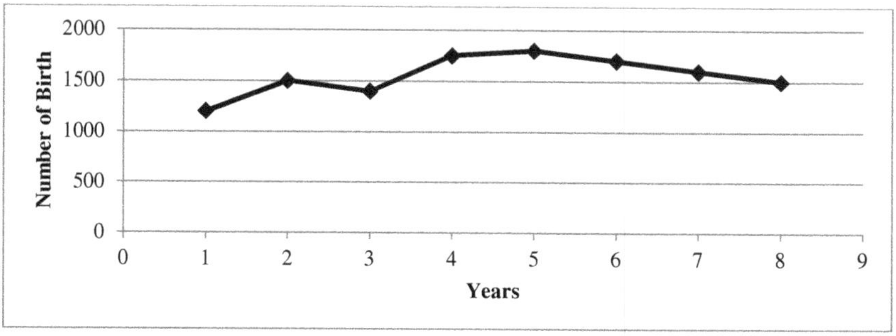

2) Determine the adjustment trend of series using 3 years moving average method and draw adjustment trend on the curve above

a) Determine the adjustment trend of series using 3 years moving average method

Step 1: Establishment of working table [Grouping and averages calculations]

Years	Number of Birth	3 Years Moving Total	3 Years Moving Average
2000	1200		
2001	1500	$1200 + 1500 + 1400 =$ **4100**	$4100/3 = \mathbf{1366.7}$
2002	1400	$1500 + 1400 + 1750 =$ **4650**	$4650/3 = \mathbf{1550}$
2003	1750	$1400 + 1750 + 1800 =$ **4950**	$4950/3 = \mathbf{1650}$
2004	1800	$1750 + 1800 + 1700 =$ **5250**	$5250/3 = \mathbf{1750}$
2005	1700	$1800 + 1700 + 1600 =$ **5100**	$5100/3 = \mathbf{1700}$
2006	1600	$1700 + 1600 + 1500 =$ **4800**	$4800/3 = \mathbf{1600}$
2007	1500		

Drawing of adjustment trend on the curve above

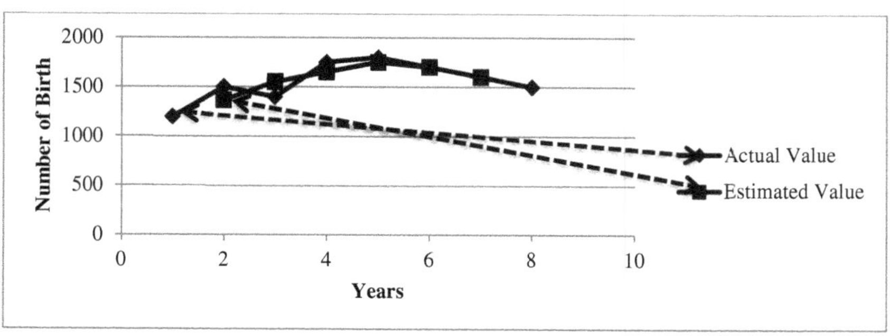

Test Your Understanding

Exercise 3: Use the statistics of workers' wages from 2000 to 2007 to determine the values of 5 years moving average.

Years	2000	2001	2002	2003	2 4	2005	2006	2007
Workers' wages	20	40	55	70	80	100	150	155

Exercise 4: From the given table, determine the value of 4 years moving average

Year (X)	2000	2001	2002	2003	2004	2005	2006
Salary (Y)	16	50	22	59	63	46	43

Exercise 5: Use the table below and answer the question that follows.

Years (X)	1	2	3	4	5	6	7
Quantity of cocoa (Y)	320	334	329	344	358	347	383

1) Determine the adjustment trend using 2 years moving average
2) Determine the adjustment trend using three years moving average

Answers..[Appendix 1]

2.2.3 Simple Least Square Adjustment Method

The estimated value of the dependent variable $[\hat{Y}]$ also called the adjustment time series value. In order to illustrate graphically the adjustment trend, the following steps are recommended.

1) Derivation of regression equation or line of best fit $[\hat{Y} = \hat{\beta}_0 \pm \hat{\beta}_1 X]$
2) Derivation of estimated value of the dependent variable $[\hat{Y}]$.
3) Plotting of estimated dependent variable $[\hat{Y}]$ values with the independent variables [X].

Example 1: The table below presents the data of workers salary from 2001 to 2005.

Years (X)	2001	2002	2003	2004	2005
Sales (Y) in bags	7	10	9	11	13

Work Required

1) Graphically produce a chronological curve
2) Determine an equation of the trend line using the least square method and draw the line on the graph above

3) Determine the forecasted sales for the year 2010

Solution

1) Graphically produce a chronological curve

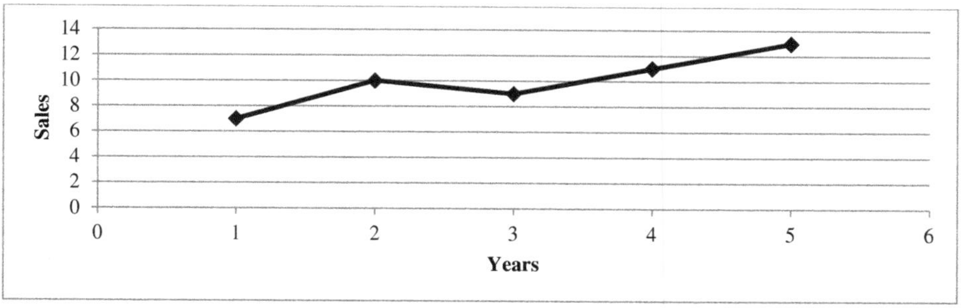

2) Determine an equation of the trend line using the least square method and draw the line on the graph above

Step 1: Formula. $\hat{Y} = \hat{\beta}_0 \pm \hat{\beta}_1 X$, where; n = 5, $\hat{\beta}_1 = \frac{n\sum xy - \sum x \sum y}{n\sum x^2 - (\sum x)^2}$ and $\hat{\beta}_0 = \bar{Y} - \hat{\beta}_1 \bar{X}$

Step 2: Tabula calculation of formula components

Original Table		Working Table			
X	Y	$x = \mathbf{X} - \bar{\mathbf{X}}$	$y = \mathbf{Y} - \bar{\mathbf{Y}}$	xy	x^2
1	7	$1 - 3 = -2$	$7 - 10 = -3$	6	4
2	10	$2 - 3 = -1$	$10 - 10 = 0$	0	1
3	9	$3 - 3 = 0$	$9 - 10 = -1$	0	0
4	11	$4 - 3 = 1$	$11 - 10 = 1$	1	1
5	13	$5 - 3 = 2$	$13 - 10 = 3$	6	4
$\sum = \mathbf{15}$	$\sum = \mathbf{50}$	$\sum = \mathbf{0}$	$\sum = \mathbf{0}$	$\sum = \mathbf{13}$	$\sum = \mathbf{10}$

Step 3: Data substitution and solving

a) Calculation of $[\hat{\beta}_1]$

$\hat{\beta}_1 = \frac{5(13)-(0)(0)}{5(10)-0}$ ....[Expand brackets by multiplication]

$\hat{\beta}_1 = \frac{65-0}{50-0}$ ....[Simplify both numerator and denominator by subtraction]

$\hat{\beta}_1 = \frac{65}{50}$ ....[Solve equation]

$\hat{\beta}_1 = \mathbf{1.3}$

b) Calculation of $[\hat{\beta}_0]$

$\hat{\beta}_0 = 10 - 1.3(3)$……………………..…………………[Expand bracket by multiplication]

$\hat{\beta}_0 = 10 - 3.9$ …………………...……………..….[Simplify equation by subtraction]

$\hat{\beta}_0 = \mathbf{6.1}$

Note: Regression line is given as $\hat{\mathbf{Y}} = \mathbf{6.1 + 1.3X}$

Step 4: Derivation of the estimated value of sales $[\hat{Y}]$

Original Table		**Working**	
		Regression line equation	**Estimated value of Y**
Years (X)	Sales (Y)	$\hat{\mathbf{Y}} = \mathbf{6.1 + 1.3X}$	$\hat{\mathbf{Y}}$
1	7	$\hat{Y} = 6.1 + 1.3(1)$	7.4
2	10	$\hat{Y} = 6.1 + 1.3(2)$	8.7
3	9	$\hat{Y} = 6.1 + 1.3(3)$	10
4	11	$\hat{Y} = 6.1 + 1.3(4)$	11.3
5	13	$\hat{Y} = 6.1 + 1.3(5)$	12.6

Step 5: Plotting of the estimated values of sales [Use X and $\hat{Y}$]

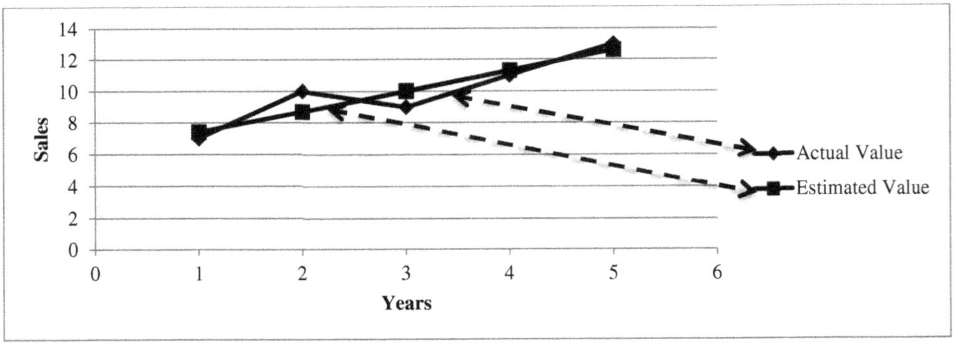

3) Determine the forecasted sales for the year 2010

Step 1: Formula. $\hat{Y} = 6.1 + 1.3X$, where; $X = [2010 - 2001] + 1 = 10$

Step 2: Value substitution and solving.

$\hat{Y} = 6.1 + 1.3X$ ……………………....…...[Substitute the value of (X) which in this case is 10]

$\hat{Y} = 6.1 + 1.3(10)$……...………...……….[Expand bracket of equation by multiplication]

$\hat{Y} = 6.1 + 13$ …………………………..……..………..[Simplify equation by addition]

$\hat{Y} = \mathbf{19.1\ Bags}$

Example 2: Use the table below and answer the questions that follow

X_i	5	6	7	8	9
Y_i	10	30	5	20	10

1) Determine the regression equation
2) Determine the estimated values of Y from the X values in the table

Solution

1) Determine the regression equation

Step 1: Formula and data. $\hat{Y} = \hat{\beta}_0 \pm \hat{\beta}_1 X$, where; $\hat{\beta}_1 = \frac{n\sum xy - \sum x \sum y}{n\sum x^2 - (\sum x)^2}$ and $\hat{\beta}_0 = \bar{Y} - \hat{\beta}_1 \bar{X}$

Step 2: Tabula calculation of formula components [n = 5]

X_i	Y_i	$x = X - \bar{X}$	$y = Y - \bar{Y}$	xy	X_i^2
5	10	-2	-5	$-2(-5) = 10$	$-2^2 = 4$
6	30	-1	15	$-1(15) = -15$	$-1^2 = 1$
7	5	0	-10	$0(-10) = 0$	$0^2 = 0$
8	20	1	5	$1(5) = 5$	$1^2 = 1$
9	10	2	-5	$2(-5) = -10$	$2^2 = 4$
$\boldsymbol{\sum = 35}$	$\boldsymbol{\sum = 75}$	$\boldsymbol{\sum = 0}$	$\boldsymbol{\sum = 0}$	$\sum = -10$	$\sum = 10$

Step 3: Data substitution and solving

a) Calculation of $\hat{\beta}_1$

$\hat{\beta}_1 = \frac{5(-10)-(0)(0)}{5(10)-0}$ ....[Solve]

$\hat{\beta}_1 = \mathbf{-1}$

b) Calculation of $\hat{\beta}_0$

$\hat{\beta}_0 = 15 - (-1)(7)$ ....[Solve]

$\hat{\beta}_0 = \mathbf{22}$

Step 4: Derivation of regression line

Step 1: Formula. $\hat{Y} = \hat{\beta}_0 \pm \hat{\beta}_1 X$, where; $\hat{\beta}_0 = 22$ and $\hat{\beta}_1 = -1$

Step 2: Data substitution

$\hat{Y} = \hat{\beta}_0 \pm \hat{\beta}_1 X$ ....[Substitute data values into the formula]

$\hat{Y} = \mathbf{22 - 1X}$ ....[Regression line equation]

2) Determine the estimated values of Y from the X values in the table

X_i	Y_i	$\hat{Y} = 22 - 1X$	$\hat{Y}$
5	10	$\hat{Y} = 22 - 1(5)$	17
6	30	$\hat{Y} = 22 - 1(6)$	16
7	5	$\hat{Y} = 22 - 1(7)$	15
8	20	$\hat{Y} = 22 - 1(8)$	14
9	10	$\hat{Y} = 22 - 1(9)$	13

Test Your Understanding

Exercise 6: The following table shows the statistics on the number of crime committed (X) and the amount of money spends on security (Y) by a local council. Put answer in two decimal places.

Number of crime committed (X_i)	1	3	3	5	8
Money spend on security (Y_i)	8	6	5	4	2

1) Determine the regression line. ....**[Answer: $\hat{Y} = 8.29 - 0.82X$]**
2) Calculate the values of $\hat{Y}$..**[Answer: See Appendix]**

Exercise 7: Using the data in the table below, [Put answer into two decimal places]

X_i	1	2	4	6	7	8	10	1
Y_i	11	14	12	13	15	12	13	20

1) Derive the straight line equation........................... **[Answer: $\hat{Y} = 10.76 + 0.48X$]**
2) Estimate the value of Y when X is 50............................... **[Answer: $\hat{Y} = 34.76$]**
3) What will be the value of X given that; $\hat{Y} = 58.76$. ....**[Answer: X = 100]**

Exercise 8: Given the following distribution. [Put answers into one decimal place]

Ye rs (X)	2000	2001	2002	2003	2004	2 05
Quantity of Irish (Y)	7	10	13	15	20	28

1) Determine the estimated quantities of Irish over the given years**[Answer: See Appendix]**
2) In which year will quantity of Irish amount to 40.8................ **[Answer: The year 2009]**
3) What will be the quantity of Irish in 2015? ....**[Answer: Irish quantity = 64.2]**

Exercise 9: The statistics of quantity demanded of rice registered by the national institute of statistics from the year 2000 to the year 2005 is presented in the table below.

Years (X)	2000	2001	2002	2003	2004	2005
Quantity Demanded (Y)	50	25	23	20	5	7

1) Draw a chronological diagram showing the relationship between years and quantity demand and interpret your diagram
2) Determine the adjustment equation of years and quantity demanded using
   a) Mayer method
   b) Moving Average method [3 years moving average]. Present the adjustment equation obtained using both methods in the same graph in 1 above

Exercise 10: The statistic below gives the evolution of the quantity of wastes rejected by HYSACAM in Edea town during the eight last years:

Years	2008	2009	2010	2011	2012	2013	2014	2015
Wastes	250	225	215	230	230	240	230	225

1) Present the evolution of wastes using line graph over the eight last years
2) Determine the adjustment regression equation using the least square method and plot the regression line in the line graph in 1 above.

Answers...[Appendix 1]

2.3 Seasonality Coefficient

Seasonality coefficient (S_t^*) is also called index of seasonality or seasonal index. It is derived using the formula below.

$$\text{Seasonality Coefficient}(S_i^*) = \text{Quarter Mean}(S_i) - \text{Total Mean }(\bar{S}_i) \text{ ...[Additive Model]}$$

$$\text{Seasonality Coefficient}(S_i^*) = \frac{\text{Quarter Mean}(S_i)}{\text{Total Mean }(\bar{S}_i)} \text{ ....[Multiplicative Model]}$$

$$\text{Where: Quarter Mean}(S_i) = \frac{\text{Sum of Quarter Observations }(Y_t)}{\text{Number of Quarter Observations (n)}} \text{ ....(1)}$$

$$\text{Total Mean }(\bar{S}_i) = \frac{\text{Sum of Quarter Mean}(\sum S_i)}{\text{Number of Quarter Mean (N)}} \text{ ....(2)}$$

N/B: The following verification checks are recommended. In an additive method, the sum of seasonality coefficient must be equal to zero ($\sum S_i^* = 0$) and in multiplicative method, the sum of seasonality coefficient must be equal to total number of quarters($\sum S_i^* = n$). After deriving the seasonality coefficient(S_t^*), we can then compute the deseasonalized time series data or observation without seasonal variations denoted(Y_t^*).

$$\text{Deseasonalized Value}(Y_t^*) = \text{Observed Values}(Y_t) - \text{Seasonality Index}(S_i^*).\text{[Additive.M]}$$

$$\text{Deseasonalized Value}(Y_t^*) = \frac{\text{Observed Values}(Y_t)}{\text{Seasonality Index}(S_i^*)} \ldots\ldots\ldots\ldots\ldots\ldots\ldots\text{[Multiplicative. M]}$$

Example 1: Determine the quarters mean and the total mean using the information in the table below.

Quarters	Periods (Years)		
	2015	2016	2017
Q_1	9.9	9.9	9.3
Q_2	9.5	8.8	7.5
Q_3	8.3	7.0	6.9
Q_4	8.7	7.9	6.9

Solution

Step 1: Formulas: $\text{Quarter Mean}(S_i) = \frac{\text{Sum of Quarter Observations }(Y_t)}{\text{Number of Quarter Observations (n)}} \ldots\ldots\ldots\ldots\ldots(1)$

$$\text{Total Mean }(\bar{S}_i) = \frac{\text{Sum of Quarter Mean}(\sum S_i)}{\text{Number of Quarter Mean (N)}} \ldots\ldots\ldots\ldots\ldots\ldots(2)$$

Step 2: Data substitution and solving

a) Calculation of quarter mean (S_i)

Original Table				Working Table
Quarters	Periods (Years)			$\left[\text{Quarter Mean}(S_i) = \frac{\text{Sum of Quarter Observations }(Y_t)}{\text{Number of Quarter Observations (n)}}\right], n = 3$
	2015	2016	2017	
Q_1	9.9	9.9	9.3	$\frac{1}{3}(9.9 + 9.9 + 9.3) = 29.1/3 = 9.7$
Q_2	9.5	8.8	7.5	$\frac{1}{3}(9.5 + 8.8 + 7.5) = 25.8/3 = 8.6$
Q_3	8.3	7.0	6.9	$\frac{1}{3}(8.3 + 7.0 + 6.9) = 22.2/3 = 7.4$
Q_4	8.7	7.9	6.9	$\frac{1}{3}(8.7 + 7.9 + 6.9) = 23.5/3 = 7.83$

b) Calculation of total mean ($\bar{S}_i$)…………………[Number of Quarter Mean (N) = 4]

$$\text{Total Mean }(\bar{S}_i) = \frac{9.7+8.6+7.4+7.83}{4} \ldots\ldots\ldots\ldots\text{[Simplify numerator]}$$

$$\text{Total Mean }(\bar{S}_i) = \frac{33.5}{4} \ldots\ldots\ldots\ldots\ldots\ldots\text{[Solve equation]}$$

$$\text{Total Mean }(\bar{S}_i) = \mathbf{8.375}$$

Note: The above observation table can be expressed vertically with quarters corresponding means as seen below.

Vertical Expression

Years/Quarters		Observed Values (Y_t)	Mean Values (S_i)
2015	Q_1	9.9	9.7
	Q_2	9.5	8.6
	Q_3	8.3	7.4
	Q_4	8.7	7.8
2016	Q_1	9.9	9.7
	Q_2	8.8	8.6
	Q_3	7.0	7.4
	Q_4	7.9	7.8
2017	Q_1	9.3	9.7
	Q_2	7.5	8.6
	Q_3	6.9	7.4
	Q_4	6.9	7.8

Horizontal Expression

Quarters	Periods (Years)			Mean (S_i)
	2015	2016	2017	
Q_1	9.9	9.9	9.3	9.7
Q_2	9.5	8.8	7.5	8.6
Q_3	8.3	7.0	6.9	7.4
Q_4	8.7	7.9	6.9	7.83

Example 2: Compute the quarters mean and the total mean using the information in the table below.

Years/Quarters		Observed Values (Y_t)
2009	Q_1	554
	Q_2	590
	Q_3	616
	Q_4	653
2010	Q_1	472
	Q_2	501
	Q_3	521
	Q_4	552

Solution

Step 1: Formulas: $\text{Quarter Mean}(S_i) = \frac{\text{Sum of Quarter Observations } (Y_t)}{\text{Number of Quarter Observations } (n)}$ ....(1)

$\text{Total Mean } (\bar{S}_i) = \frac{\text{Sum of Quarter Mean} (\sum S_i)}{\text{Number of Quarter Mean (N)}}$ ....(2)

Step 2: Data substitution and solving

a) Calculation of quarter mean (S_i)..............[$\text{Number of Quarter Observations (n)} = 2$]

Working

$$S_1 = \frac{2009(Q_1)+2010(Q_1)}{2} = \frac{554+472}{2} = \frac{1{,}026}{2} = 513$$

$$S_2 = \frac{2009(Q_2)+2010(Q_2)}{2} = \frac{590+501}{2} = \frac{1{,}091}{2} = 545.5$$

$$S_3 = \frac{2009(Q_3)+2010(Q_3)}{2} = \frac{616+521}{2} = \frac{1{,}137}{2} = 568.5$$

$$S_4 = \frac{2009(Q_4)+2010(Q_4)}{2} = \frac{653+552}{2} = \frac{1{,}205}{2} = 602.5$$

Tabula Presentation

Years/Quarters		(Y_t)	(S_i)
2009	Q_1	554	513
	Q_2	590	545.5
	Q_3	616	568.5
	Q_4	653	602.5
2010	Q_1	472	513
	Q_2	501	545.5
	Q_3	521	568.5
	Q_4	552	602.5

b) Calculation of total mean ($\bar{S}_i$)........................[Number of Quarter Mean (N) = 4]

$$\text{Total Mean } (\bar{S}_i) = \frac{513+545.5+568.5+602.5}{4} \text{ ....[Simplify numerator]}$$

$$\text{Total Mean } (\bar{S}_i) = \frac{2{,}229.5}{4} \text{ ....[Solve equation]}$$

$$\text{Total Mean } (\bar{S}_i) = \mathbf{557.375}$$

Example 3: Calculate the seasonality coefficient from the table below using the additive method and multiplicative method.

Years	Quarters (Q_i)			
	Q_1	Q_2	Q_3	Q_4
2003	289	241	273	232
2004	336	294	363	274
2005	297	270	263	198
2006	291	209	243	187

Solution

Step 1: Formula. $\text{Seasonality Coefficient}(S_i^*) = \text{Quarter Mean}(S_i) - \text{Total Mean } (\bar{S}_i)$

$$\text{Seasonality Coefficient}(S_i^*) = \frac{\text{Quarter Mean}(S_i)}{\text{Total Mean } (\bar{S}_i)}$$

Step 2: Determination of Quarter Mean(S_i) and Total Mean ($\bar{S}_i$)

Years	Quarters (Q_i)			
	Q_1	Q_2	Q_3	Q_4
2003	289	241	273	232
2004	336	294	363	274
2005	297	270	263	198
2006	291	209	243	187
SUM	1,213	1,014	1,142	891
Quarter Mean(S_i)	303.25	253.5	285.5	222.75
Total Mean ($\bar{S}_i$) = 266.25				

Step 3: Data substitution and solving

Years/Quarters		Observed Values (Y_t)	Mean Values (S_t)	Seasonality Coefficient	
				Additive Method	Multiplicative Method
2003	Q_1	289	303.25	$303.25 - 266.25 = 37$	$303.25/266.25 = 1.139$
	Q_2	241	253.5	$253.5 - 266.25 = -12.75$	$253.5/266.25 = 0.952$
	Q_3	273	285.5	$285.5 - 266.25 = 19.25$	$285.5/266.25 = 1.072$
	Q_4	232	222.75	$222.75 - 266.25 = -43.5$	$222.75/266.25 = 0.837$
2004	Q_1	336	303.25	$303.25 - 266.25 = 37$	$303.25/266.25 = 1.139$
	Q_2	294	253.5	$253.5 - 266.25 = -12.75$	$253.5/266.25 = 0.952$
	Q_3	363	285.5	$285.5 - 266.25 = 19.25$	$285.5/266.25 = 1.072$
	Q_4	274	222.75	$222.75 - 266.25 = -43.5$	$222.75/266.25 = 0.837$
2005	Q_1	297	303.25	$303.25 - 266.25 = 37$	$303.25/266.25 = 1.139$
	Q_2	270	253.5	$253.5 - 266.25 = -12.75$	$253.5/266.25 = 0.952$
	Q_3	263	285.5	$285.5 - 266.25 = 19.25$	$285.5/266.25 = 1.072$
	Q_4	198	222.75	$222.75 - 266.25 = -43.5$	$222.75/266.25 = 0.837$
2006	Q_1	291	303.25	$303.25 - 266.25 = 37$	$303.25/266.25 = 1.139$
	Q_2	209	253.5	$253.5 - 266.25 = -12.75$	$253.5/266.25 = 0.952$
	Q_3	243	285.5	$285.5 - 266.25 = 19.25$	$285.5/266.25 = 1.072$
	Q_4	187	222.75	$222.75 - 266.25 = -43.5$	$222.75/266.25 = 0.837$

N/B: The values of seasonality coefficient for both the additive method and multiplicative method are illustrated below.

Additive seasonality coefficient

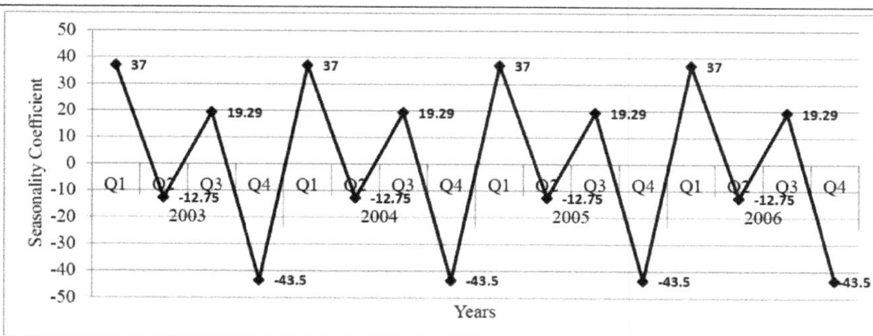

Multiplicative seasonality coefficient

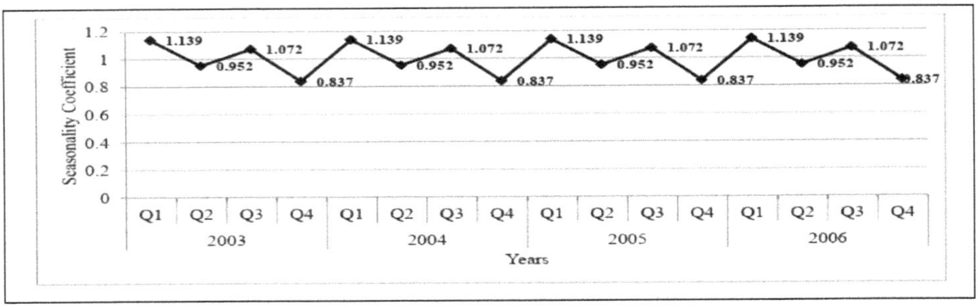

Example 4: Determine the deseasonalized value of the observations using the additive method and multiplicative method.

Years	Quarters			
	Q_1	Q_2	Q_3	Q_4
2018	480	410	600	650
2019	580	520	680	740
Quarter Mean(S_i)	530	465	640	695

<u>Solution</u>

Step 1: Formula.Deseasonalized Value(Y_t^*) = Observed Values(Y_t) − Seasonality Index(S_i^*)

$$\text{Deseasonalized Value}(Y_t^*) = \frac{\text{Observed Values}(Y_t)}{\text{Seasonality Index}(S_i^*)}$$

Step 2: Data substitution and solving

Original Table				Working Table			
				Seasonality Index (S_i^*)		Deseasonalized Value (Y_t^*)	
Years/Quarters		(Y_t)	(S_i)	Additive	Multiplicative	Additive	Multiplicative
2018	Q_1	480	530	−52.5	0.910	480 − (−52.5) = 532.5	480/0.910 = 527.5
	Q_2	410	465	−117.5	0.798	410 − (−117.5) = 527.5	410/0.798 = 513.8
	Q_3	600	640	57.5	1.099	600 − 57.5 = 542.5	600/1.099 = 545.9
	Q_4	650	695	112.5	1.193	650 − 112.5 = 537.5	650/1.193 = 544.8
2019	Q_1	580	530	−52.5	0.910	580 − (−52.5) = 632.5	580/0.910 = 637.4
	Q_2	520	465	−117.5	0.798	520 − (−117.5) = 637.5	520/0.798 = 651.6
	Q_3	680	640	57.5	1.099	680 − 57.5 = 622.5	680/1.099 = 618.7
	Q_4	740	695	112.5	1.193	740 − 112.5 = 627.5	740/1.193 = 620.3

N/B: The relationship between the observed values and deseasonalized value for both additive method and multiplicative method and the comparison of deseasonalized values for both additive and multiplicative method are illustrated below.

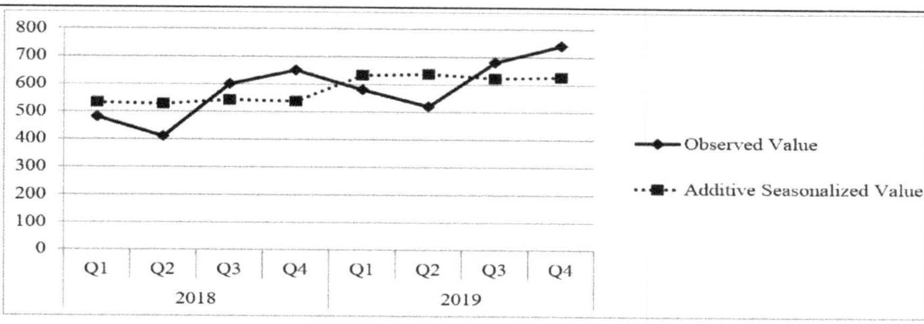

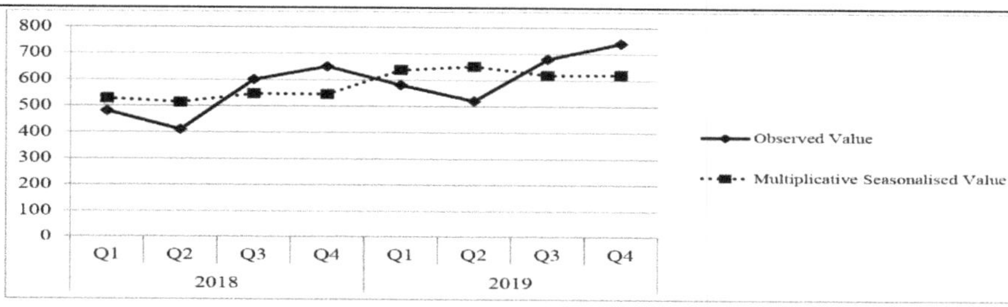

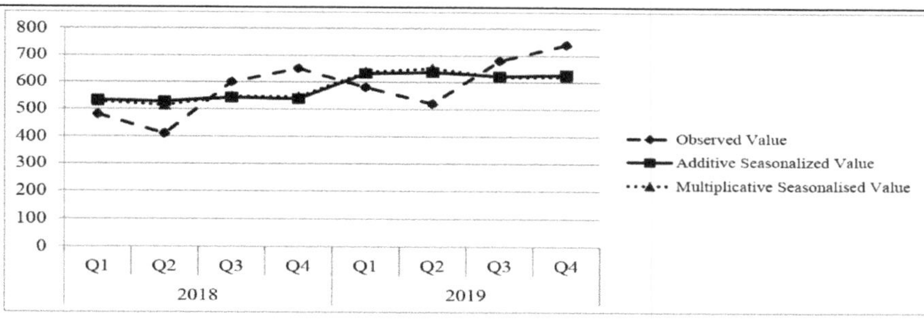

Test Your Understanding

Exercise 11: Fine the quarters mean and total mean using the table below

Years	Q_1	Q_2	Q_3	Q_4
2015	470	531	500	480
2016	340	450	410	380
2017	270	360	340	310
2018	240	330	320	290
2019	220	270	250	240

[Answer: ………………………………………………………………….See Appendix]

Exercise 12: Compute the seasonality coefficient using the additive method and multiplicative method.

	2001	2002
Q_1	240	470
Q_2	330	531
Q_3	320	500
Q_4	290	480

[Answer: ....See Appendix]

Exercise 13: Using the additive method and multiplicative method, determine the deseasonalized value of the observations.

		Observed Values (Y_t)
2009	Q_1	97.9
	Q_2	102.7
	Q_3	112.9
	Q_4	113.8
2010	Q_1	97.4
	Q_2	102.6
	Q_3	115.7
	Q_4	114.3

[Answer: ....See Appendix]

2.4 Time Series Prediction

Time series forecasting is the act of predicting the future by using past and current data. Our analysis will be limited to trend projection and exponential smoothing forecasting methods. The accuracy of forecasting is measured through the calculation of forecasting errors.

Forecasting error (e_t) is the difference between the actual data (Y_t) and the forecast data(F_t), that is($e_t = Y_t - F_t$). Major methods used and their formulas are given below.

$$\text{Mean Forecast Error (MFE)} = \frac{1}{n}\sum e_t \quad \text{.........(1)}$$

$$\text{Mean Absolute Error(MAE)} = \frac{1}{n}\sum|e_t| \quad \text{.........(2)}$$

$$\text{Mean Squared Error(MSE)} = \frac{1}{n}\sum e_t^2 \quad \text{.........(3)}$$

$$\text{Mean Absolute Percent Error(MAPE)} = \frac{1}{n}\sum\left|\frac{e_t}{Y_t}\right| \times 100 \quad \ldots\ldots(4)$$

$$\text{Mean Percentage Error(MPE)} = \frac{1}{n}\sum\left(\frac{e_t}{Y_t}\right) \times 100 \quad \ldots\ldots(5)$$

$$\text{Signed Mean Squared Error(SMSE)} = \frac{1}{n}\sum\left(\frac{e_t}{|e_t|}\right) e_t^2 \quad \ldots\ldots(6)$$

$$\text{Root Mean Squared Error(RMSE)} = \sqrt{\frac{1}{n}\sum e_t^2} \quad \ldots\ldots(7)$$

2.4.1 Moving Average Method

Using the moving average, the next forecast is the average of the most recent (n) data from the time series.

$$F_{t+1} = \frac{Y_t + Y_{t-1} + Y_{t-n+1}}{n} \quad \ldots\ldots(1)$$

$$F_{t+1} = \frac{w_t Y_t + w_2 Y_{t-1} + w_n Y_{t-n+1}}{w_1 + w_2 + w_n} \quad \ldots\ldots(2)$$

Where; (F_{t+1}) represent forecast for time period $(t + 1)$

(Y_t) represent actual value in time (t)

(n) represent the number of period to average

N/B: Equation (1) is used when dealing with simple moving average and equation (2) when dealing with weighted moving average.

Example 1: Determine the forecast value using 3 years moving average and the forecast errors.

Years	1	2	3	4	5	6	7	8	9	10	11	12
Quantity	240	350	230	260	280	320	220	310	240	310	240	230

Solution

Step 1: Formula. $F_{t+1} = \frac{Y_t + Y_{t-1} + Y_{t-n+1}}{n}$, where; n = 3

Step 2: Data substitution and solving

Years		Quantity	3-Years Moving Average Forecast	
			Formula	Working
1	Y_1	80		
2	Y_2	82		
3	Y_3	84		
4	Y_4	83	$F_4 = (Y_1 + Y_2 + Y_3)/n$	$(80 + 82 + 84)/3 = 82.00$
5	Y_5	83	$F_5 = (Y_2 + Y_3 + Y_4)/n$	$(82 + 84 + 83)/3 = 83.00$
6	Y_6	84	$F_6 = (Y_3 + Y_4 + Y_5)/n$	$(84 + 83 + 83)/3 = 83.33$
7	Y_7	85	$F_7 = (Y_4 + Y_5 + Y_6)/n$	$(83 + 83 + 84)/3 = 83.33$
8	Y_8	84	$F_8 = (Y_5 + Y_6 + Y_7)/n$	$(83 + 84 + 85)/3 = 84.00$
9	Y_9	93	$F_9 = (Y_6 + Y_7 + Y_8)/n$	$(84 + 85 + 84)/3 = 84.33$
10	Y_{10}		$F_{10} = (Y_7 + Y_8 + Y_9)/n$	$(85 + 84 + 93)/3 = 87.33$

Example 2: Compute the forecast value and the forecast errors using 4 years moving average.

Years	1	2	3	4	5	6	7	8	9	10	11	12
Quantity	240	350	230	260	280	320	220	310	240	310	240	230

Solution

Step 1: Formula. $F_{t+1} = \frac{Y_t + Y_{t-1} + Y_{t-n+1}}{n}$, where; $n = 4$

Step 2: Data substitution and solving

Years		Quantity	4-Years Moving Average Forecast		Forecast Error
			Formula	Working	$[e_t = Y_t - F_t]$
1	Y_1	240			
2	Y_2	350			
3	Y_3	230			
4	Y_4	260			
5	Y_5	280	$F_5 = (Y_1 + Y_2 + Y_3 + Y_4)/n$	$F_5 = (240 + 350 + 230 + 260)/4 = 270$	$280 - 270 = 10$
6	Y_6	320	$F_6 = (Y_2 + Y_3 + Y_4 + Y_5)/n$	$F_6 = (350 + 230 + 260 + 280)/4 = 280$	$320 - 280 = 40$
7	Y_7	220	$F_7 = (Y_3 + Y_4 + Y_5 + Y_6)/n$	$F_7 = (230 + 260 + 280 + 320)/4 = 272.5$	$220 - 272.5 = -52.5$
8	Y_8	310	$F_8 = (Y_4 + Y_5 + Y_6 + Y_7)/n$	$F_8 = (260 + 280 + 320 + 220)/4 = 270$	$310 - 270 = 40$
9	Y_9	240	$F_9 = (Y_5 + Y_6 + Y_7 + Y_8)/n$	$F_9 = (280 + 320 + 220 + 310)/4 = 282.5$	$240 - 282.5 = -42.5$
10	Y_{10}	310	$F_{10} = (Y_6 + Y_7 + Y_8 + Y_9)/n$	$F_{10} = (320 + 220 + 310 + 240)/4 = 272.5$	$310 - 272.5 = 37.5$
11	Y_{11}	240	$F_{11} = (Y_7 + Y_8 + Y_9 + Y_{10})/n$	$F_{11} = (220 + 310 + 240 + 310)/4 = 270$	$240 - 270 = -30$
12	Y_{12}	230	$F_{12} = (Y_8 + Y_9 + Y_{10} + Y_{11})/n$	$F_{12} = (310 + 240 + 310 + 240)/4 = 275$	$230 - 275 = -45$

Example 3: Compute the forecast value and the forecast errors using 4 years weighted moving average.

Years	1	2	3	4	5	6	7	8	9	10	11	12
Quantity	10	12	13	16	19	23	26	30	28	18	16	14

Solution

Step 1: Formula. $F_{t+1} = \frac{w_t Y_t + w_2 Y_{t-1} + w_n Y_{t-n+1}}{w_1 + w_2 + w_n}$

Step 2: Data substitution and solving

Years		Quantity	3-Years Moving Average Forecast
Expression	Representation		
1	Y_1	10	
2	Y_2	12	
3	Y_3	13	
4	Y_4	16	$F_4 = \frac{[(1\times10)+(2\times12)+(3\times13)]}{1+2+3} = 12.167$
5	Y_5	19	$F_5 = \frac{[(1\times12)+(2\times13)+(3\times16)]}{1+2+3} = 14.333$
6	Y_6	23	$F_6 = \frac{[(1\times13)+(2\times16)+(3\times19)]}{1+2+3} = 17$
7	Y_7	26	$F_7 = \frac{[(1\times16)+(2\times19)+(3\times23)]}{1+2+3} = 20.5$
8	Y_8	30	$F_8 = \frac{[(1\times19)+(2\times23)+(3\times26)]}{1+2+3} = 23.833$
9	Y_9	28	$F_9 = \frac{[(1\times23)+(2\times26)+(3\times30)]}{1+2+3} = 27.5$
10	Y_{10}	18	$F_{10} = \frac{[(1\times26)+(2\times30)+(3\times28)]}{1+2+3} = 28.333$
11	Y_{11}	16	$F_{11} = \frac{[(1\times30)+(2\times28)+(3\times18)]}{1+2+3} = 23.333$
12	Y_{12}	14	$F_{12} = \frac{[(1\times28)+(2\times18)+(3\times16)]}{1+2+3} = 18.667$

Test Your Understanding

Exercise 14: Compute the forecast value using 2 years moving average

Years	2000	2001	2002	2003	200	2005
Sales (Quantity)	18	13	16	11	17	

[Answer: ....See Appendix]

Exercise 15: Compute the forecast value and the forecast errors using 3 years moving average.

Years	1	2	3	4	5	6
Demand	24	13	20	12	19	23

Exercise 16: Compute the forecast value and the forecast errors using 2 years weighted moving average.

Years	2010	2011	2012	2013	2014	2015
Quantity	17	21	19	23	18	16

[Answer: ....See Appendix]

2.4.2 Trend Projection Method

The trend projection method uses the regression line to determine the forecast value. The regression equation can be annual or quarter.

$$Y_t = \beta_0 + \beta_1 X_t \quad \text{...}(1)$$

Example 1: The sale regression equation of sale is given as $[Y_t = 2.69 + 1.55X_t]$. Compute the value of sale when $[X_t = 25]$.

Solution

Step 1: Regression Equation. $Y_t = 2.69 + 1.55X_t$. where; $X_t = 25$

Step 2: Data substitution and solving

$Y_t = 2.69 + 1.55(25)$ ....[Open bracket]

$Y_t = 2.69 + 38.75$ ....[Solve equation]

$Y_t = \mathbf{41.44\ Units}$

Example 2: The hypothetical quarter regression line of production is given as $[Q_1 = 59 + 6X_t]$, $[Q_2 = 89 + 9X_t]$, $[Q_3 = 108 + 10X_t]$ and $[Q_4 = 39 + 5X_t]$. What will be the production in 2019?

Years	Q_1	Q_2	Q_3	Q_4
2016	62	94	113	41
2017	73	110	130	52
2018	79	118	140	58

Solution

Step 1: Formula. Annual Production Forecast $= \sum$ of Quarter Production Forecast

Step 2: Determination of quarter forecast

Quarters	Q_1	Q_2	Q_3	Q_4
Regression line	$[Q_1 = 59 + 6X_t]$	$[Q_2 = 89 + 9X_t]$	$[Q_3 = 108 + 10X_t]$	$[Q_4 = 39 + 5X_t]$
Data	Where: $X_t = 2019$ which is year 4. Therefore, $X_t = 4$			
Working	$\hat{Q}_1 = 59 + 6(4) = 83$	$\hat{Q}_2 = 89 + 9(4) = 125$	$\hat{Q}_3 = 108 + 10(4) = 148$	$\hat{Q}_4 = 39 + 5(4) = 59$
Quarter Forecast $(\hat{Q}_i)$	**83**	**125**	**148**	**59**

Step 3: Data substitution and solving

Annual Production Forecast(2019) $= 83 + 125 + 148 + 59$ ....[Solve equation]

Annual Production Forecast(2019) $= \mathbf{415\ Units}$

Example 3: The quarter production of rice in Bamenda is given in the table below

Years	Q_1	Q_2	Q_3	Q_4
2016	62	94	113	41
2017	73	110	130	52
2018	79	118	140	58
2019	83	124	146	62

1) The quarter regression line
2) The production in 2010

Solution

1) The quarter regression line

Step 1: Formula. $\widehat{Y}_i = \widehat{\beta}_0 \pm \widehat{\beta}_1$, where; $\widehat{\beta}_1 = \frac{n\sum x_i y_i - \sum x_i \sum y_i}{n\sum x_i^2 - (\sum x_i)^2}$ and $\widehat{\beta}_0 = \overline{Y} - \widehat{\beta}_1\overline{X}$

Step 2: Data substitution and solving

a) Quarter 1 regression line

Original Table		Transform Table		Working			
Years	Q_1	(X)	(Y)	x_i	y_i	$x_i y_i$	x_i^2
2016	62	1	62	−1.5	−12.25	18.375	2.25
2017	73	2	73	−0.5	−1.25	0.625	0.25
2018	79	3	79	0.5	4.75	2.375	0.25
2019	83	4	83	1.5	8.75	13.125	2.25
		$\Sigma = 10$	$\Sigma = 297$	$\Sigma = 0$	$\Sigma = 0$	$\Sigma = 16.125$	$\Sigma = 5$
$[\overline{X} = 10/4 = 2.5]$ and $[\overline{Y} = 297/4 = 74.25]$							

$\widehat{\beta}_1 = \frac{64.5}{20}$

$\widehat{\beta}_1 = \mathbf{3.225}$

$\widehat{\beta}_0 = 74.25 - 8.0625$

$\widehat{\beta}_0 = \mathbf{66.1875}$

Quarter 1 regression line$(Q_1) = Y_t = 66.1875 + 3.225X_t$

b) Quarter 2 regression line

Original Table		Transform Table		Working			
Years	Q_2	(X)	(Y)	x_i	y_i	$x_i y_i$	x_i^2
2016	94	1	94	−1.5	−17.5	26.25	2.25
2017	110	2	110	−0.5	−1.5	0.75	0.25
2018	118	3	118	0.5	6.5	3.25	0.25
2019	124	4	124	1.5	12.5	18.75	2.25
		$\Sigma = 10$	$\Sigma = 446$	$\Sigma = 0$	$\Sigma = 0$	$\Sigma = 49$	$\Sigma = 5$
$[\overline{X} = 10/4 = 2.5]$ and $[\overline{Y} = 446/4 = 111.5]$							

$\widehat{\beta}_1 = \frac{196}{20}$

$\widehat{\beta}_1 = \mathbf{9.8}$

$\widehat{\beta}_0 = 111.5 - 24.5$

$\widehat{\beta}_0 = \mathbf{87}$

Quarter 2 regression line$(Q_2) = Y_t = 87 + 9.8X_t$

c) Quarter 3 regression line

Original Table		Transform Table		Working			
Years	Q_3	(X)	(Y)	x_i	y_i	$x_i y_i$	x_i^2
2016	113	1	113	−1.5	−19.25	28.875	2.25
2017	130	2	130	−0.5	−2.25	1.125	0.25
2018	140	3	140	0.5	7.75	3.875	0.25
2019	146	4	146	1.5	13.75	20.625	2.25
		$\sum = 10$	$\sum = 529$	$\sum = 0$	$\sum = 0$	$\sum = 54.5$	$\sum = 5$
$[\bar{X} = 10/4 = 2.5]$ and $[\bar{Y} = 529/4 = 132.25]$							

$\hat{\beta}_1 = \frac{218}{20}$

$\hat{\beta}_1 = \mathbf{10.9}$

$\hat{\beta}_0 = 132.25 - 27.25$

$\hat{\beta}_0 = \mathbf{105}$

Quarter 3 regression line$(Q_3) = Y_t = 105 + 10.9X_t$

d) Quarter 4 regression line

Original Table		Transform Table		Working			
Years	Q_4	(X)	(Y)	x_i	y_i	$x_i y_i$	x_i^2
2016	41	1	41	−1.5	−12.25	18.375	2.25
2017	52	2	52	−0.5	−1.25	0.625	0.25
2018	58	3	58	0.5	4.75	2.375	0.25
2019	62	4	62	1.5	8.75	13.125	2.25
		$\sum = 10$	$\sum = 213$	$\sum = 0$	$\sum = 0$	$\sum = 34.5$	$\sum = 5$
$[\bar{X} = 10/4 = 2.5]$ and $[\bar{Y} = 213/4 = 53.25]$							

$\hat{\beta}_1 = \frac{138}{20}$

$\hat{\beta}_1 = \mathbf{6.9}$

$\hat{\beta}_0 = 53.25 - 17.25$

$\hat{\beta}_0 = \mathbf{36}$

Quarter 4 regression line$(Q_4) = Y_t = 36 + 6.9X_t$

2) The production in 2010

Step 1: Formula. Annual Production Forecast $= \sum$ of Quarter Production Forecast

Step 2: Determination of quarter forecast

Regression line	$[Q_1 = 66.1875 + 3.225X_t]$	$[Q_2 = 87 + 9.8X_t]$	$[Q_3 = 105 + 10.9X_t]$	$[Q_4 = 36 + 6.9X_t]$
Data	Where: $X_t = 2020$ which is year 5. Therefore, $X_t = 5$			
Working	$66.1875 + 3.225(5)$	$\hat{Q}_2 = 87 + 9.8(5)$	$\hat{Q}_3 = 105 + 10.9(5)$	$\hat{Q}_4 = 36 + 6.9(5)$
Quarter Forecast $(\hat{Q}_i)$	**82.3125**	**136**	**159.5**	**70.5**

Step 3: Data substitution and solving

Annual Production Forecast$(2020) = 82.3125 + 136 + 159.5 + 70.5$...........[Solve]

Annual Production Forecast$(2020) =$ **448 Units**

Test Your Understanding

Exercise 17: The demand regression line is given as$[Y_t = 295 + 30X_t]$. Compute the value of demand when$[X_t = 8]$. ....**[Answer: 535 Units]**

Exercise 18: Determine the annual quantity demand when $(X_t = 30)$ using quarter information in the table below.

Quarter	Q_1	Q_2	Q_3	Q_4
Regression Line	$[25 + 5.4X_t]$	$[15 + 3.0X_t]$	$[10 + 3.9X_t]$	$[40 + 6X_t]$

[Answer: 639 Units]

Exercise 19: Using the cocoa quarter information in the table below, determine the annual production in 2025.

Years	Q_1	Q_2	Q_3	Q_4
2016	62	94	113	41
2017	73	110	130	52
2018	79	118	140	58

[Answer: ....See Appendix]

2.4.3 Exponential Smoothing Methods

The three main exponential smoothing method of interest includes simple exponential smoothing, double exponential smoothing and triple exponential smoothing. We are going to examine the simple and double exponential smoothing method

1) **Simple Exponential Smoothing:** It is used when the time series data is having no trend and no seasonality. Simple exponential smoothing is based only on the level smoothing parameter (α) and the level smoothing parameter ranges between 1 and 0 $(0 \leq \alpha \leq 1)$. The smoothing equation is given as seen below.

   $$L_t = \alpha Y_t + (1 - \alpha)L_{t-1} \quad \text{.........................(1)}$$

   Since there is no trend and no seasonality, the prediction or forecasting equation is there same as the smoothing equation.

   $$F_{t+1} = L_t = \alpha Y_t + (1 - \alpha)L_{t-1} \quad \text{.........................(2)}$$

Example 1: Assume the level coefficient (α) is 0.2, calculate the following.

Periods	1	2	3	4	5	6
Demand (Y_t)	446.7	454.5	455.7	423.6	456.3	440.6

1) The demand level values
2) The mean forecast error (MFE) method

Solution

1) **The demand level values**

Step 1: Formula. $L_t = \alpha Y_t + (1-\alpha)L_{t-1}$, where; $\alpha = 0.2$

Step 2: Data substitution and solving

$L_1 = Y_1 = 446.7$

$L_2 = 0.2(454.5) + (1-0.2)446.7 = 90.9 + 357.36 = 448.26$

$L_3 = 0.2(455.7) + (1-0.2)448.26 = 91.14 + 358.608 = 449.748$

$L_4 = 0.2(423.6) + (1-0.2)449.748 = 84.72 + 359.7984 = 444.5184$

$L_5 = 0.2(456.3) + (1-0.2)444.5184 = 91.26 + 355.61472 = 446.87472$

$L_6 = 0.2(440.6) + (1-0.2)446.87472 = 88.12 + 357.499776 = 445.619776$

N/B: The smoothing values calculated above are included in the original table as seen below in one decimal place.

Periods	1	2	3	4	5	6
Demand (Y_t)	446.7	454.5	455.7	423.6	456.3	440.6
Level (L_t)	446.7	448.3	449.7	444.5	446.9	445.6

2) **The mean forecast error (MFE) method**

Step 1: Formula. Mean Forecast Error (MFE) $= \frac{1}{n}\sum e_t$

Step 2: Determination of unknown [e_t]

1) Formula. Forecast Error(e_t) = Actual Value(Y_t) − Forecast Value(F_t)
2) Data substitution and solving……………………………[Forecast Value(F_{t+1}) = L_t]

Periods	Demand (Y_t)	Level (L_t)	Forecast(F_{t+1})	Forecast Error(e_t)
1	446.7	446.7		
2	454.5	448.3	446.7	$448.3 - 446.7 = 1.6$
3	455.7	449.7	448.3	$449.7 - 448.3 = 1.4$
4	423.6	444.5	449.7	$444.5 - 449.7 = -5.2$
5	456.3	446.9	444.5	$446.9 - 444.5 = 2.4$
6	440.6	445.6	446.9	$445.6 - 446.9 = -1.3$
				$\sum = -1.1$

Step 3: Data substitution and solving...[where; n = 5]

Mean Forecast Error (MFE) $= \frac{1}{5}(-1.1)$ ....[Solve equation]

Mean Forecast Error (MFE) $= \mathbf{-0.22}$

N/B: The mean forecast error is limited in that positive errors cancel the negative errors. This problem is solved by the mean absolute error (MAE) and mean squared error (MSE).

2) Double Exponential Smoothing Method: It is also called Holt's exponential smoothing method and is used when the time series data has trend but not seasonality. This method is based on the level (α) and trend (β) parameters, with their values ranging between 1 and 0 $[(0 \le \alpha \le 1)$ and $(0 \le \beta \le 1)]$. The smoothing equations and forecasting equation depends on the type of model (additive or multiplicative).

Type of Model	Smoothing Equations	Forecasting Equation
Additive	$L_t = \alpha Y_t + (1-\alpha)(L_{t-1} + T_{t-1})$	$F_{t+m} = L_t + m(T_t)$
	$T_t = \beta(L_t - L_{t-1}) + (1-\beta)T_{t-1}$	
Multiplicative	$L_t = \alpha Y_t + (1-\alpha)(L_{t-1}T_{t-1})$	$F_{t+m} = L_t T_t{}^m$
	$T_t = \beta(L_t/L_{t-1}) + (1-\beta)T_{t-1}$	

Example 1: Determine the level and trend of the sales realized by a business man presented in the table below. Assume level parameter (α) is 0.1 and trend parameter (β) is 0.2. Use the additive model principle and given that the first level and trend are 1,010 and 10 respectively.

Years	2001	2002	2003	2004	2005
Sales	1,010	1,020	1,220	1,340	1,360

Solution

Step 1: Formula. $L_t = \alpha Y_t + (1-\alpha)(L_{t-1} + T_{t-1})$ and $T_t = \beta(L_t - L_{t-1}) + (1-\beta)T_{t-1}$

Where; $\alpha = 0.1$ and $\beta = 0.2$

Step 2: Data substitution and solving

Years	Working
2001	$L_1 = Y_1 = 1{,}010$ ....[Given]
	$T_1 = 10$ ....[Given]
2002	$L_2 = 0.1\,(1{,}020) + (1 - 0.1)(1{,}010 + 10) = 102 + 910 = 1{,}020$
	$T_t = 0.2(1{,}020 - 1{,}010) + (1 - 0.2)10 = 2 + 8 = 10$
2003	$L_t = 0.1\,(1{,}220) + (1 - 0.1)(1{,}020 + 10) = 122 + 927 = 1{,}049$
	$T_t = 0.2(1{,}049 - 1{,}020) + (1 - 0.2)10 = 5.8 + 8 = 13.8$
2004	$L_t = 0.1\,(1{,}340) + (1 - 0.1)(1{,}049 + 13.8) = 134 + 956.52 = 1{,}090.52$
	$T_t = 0.2(1{,}090.52 - 1{,}049) + (1 - 0.2)13.8 = 8.304 + 11.04 = 19.344$
2005	$L_t = 0.1\,(1{,}360) + (1 - 0.1)(1{,}090.52 + 19.344) = 136 + 998.8776 = 1{,}134.8776$
	$T_t = 0.2(1{,}134.8776 - 1{,}090.52) + (1 - 0.2)19.344 = 8.87152 + 15.4752 = 24.34672$

N/B: The calculated level and trend can be represented in zero decimal place as seen below

Years	Sales	Level ($\alpha = 0.1$)	Trend ($\beta = 0.2$)
2001	1,010	1,010	10
2002	1,020	1,020	10
2003	1,220	1,049	14
2004	1,340	1,091	19
2005	1,360	1,135	24

Example 2: Determine the forecast quantity of rice production from the year 2000 to 2004. Assume the level smoothing coefficient (α) is 0.3 and the trend smoothing coefficient (β) is 0.5 and the trend for the year 2000 is 5.

Years	2000	2001	2002	2003
Quantity	6	11	9	14

Solution

Step 1: Formulas. $F_{t+m} = L_t + m(T_t)$ ....(1)

$L_t = \alpha Y_t + (1 - \alpha)(L_{t-1} + T_{t-1})$ ....(2)

$T_t = \beta(L_t - L_{t-1}) + (1 - \beta)T_{t-1}$ ....(3)

Step 2: Data substitution and solving...**[m = 1]**

Years	Quantity (Y_t)	Level ($\alpha = 0.3$) $[L_t = \alpha Y_t + (1-\alpha)(L_{t-1} + T_{t-1})]$	Trend ($\beta = 0.5$) $[T_t = \beta(L_t - L_{t-1}) + (1-\beta)T_{t-1}]$	Forecast $[F_{t+m} = L_t + m(T_t)]$
2000	6	$L_1 = Y_1 = 6$	$T_1 = 5$	
2001	11	$L_2 = 0.3(11) + (1-0.3)(6+5) = 11$	$T_2 = 0.5(11-6) + (1-0.5)5 = 5$	$6 + 5 = 11.00$
2002	9	$L_3 = 0.3(9) + (1-0.3)(11+5) = 13.9$	$T_3 = 0.5(13.9-11) + (1-0.5)5 = 3.95$	$11 + 5 = 16.00$
2003	14	$L_4 = 0.3(14) + (1-0.3)(13.9+3.95) = 16.695$	$T_4 = 0.5(16.695-13.9) + (1-0.5)3.95 = 3.3725$	$13.9 + 3.95 = 17.85$
2004				$16.695 + 3.3725 = 20.07$

Example 3: Given that; $e_{t+1} = 37.2450$, $L_t = 193.4016$ and $T_t = -0.6466$, determine the value of Y_{t+1}.

Solution

Step 1: Formula. $Y_{t+1} = e_{t+1} + F_{t+1}$, where; $e_{t+1} = 37.2450$

Step 2: Determination of unknown $[F_{t+1}]$

1) Formula. $F_{t+1} = L_t + T_t$, where; $L_t = 193.4016$ and $T_t = -0.6466$
2) Data substitution and solving

$F_{t+1} = 193.4016 + (-0.6466)$ ....[Solve equation]

$F_{t+1} = 192.755$

Step 3: Data substitution and solving

$Y_{t+1} = 37.2450 + 192.755$ ....[Solve equation]

$Y_{t+1} = \mathbf{230\ Units}$ ....[In no decimal place]

Example 4: The level and trend of sale in December 2003 is 4,616 and 106 respectively. Compute the sale in April 2004 using the additive model.

Solution

Step 1: Formula. $F_{t+m} = L_t + m(T_t)$, where; $m =$ 4 [4 months from Dec 2003 to April 2004],

$L_t = 4{,}616$ and $T_t = 106$

Step 2: Data substitution and solving

$F_{(Apr/04)} = 4{,}616 + 4(106)$ ....[Open bracket]

$F_{(Apr/04)} = 4{,}616 + 424$ ....[Solve equation]

$F_{(Apr/04)} = \mathbf{5{,}040\ Units}$

Example 5: Determine the 2001 level ($\alpha = 0.6$) and trend ($\beta = 0.4$) values using the 2002 table below. Assume the model is additive.

Year	Sales	Level	Trend
2002	246	245.89	7.13

Solution

Step 1: Formula. $L_t = \alpha Y_t + (1-\alpha)(L_{t-1} + T_{t-1})$ and $T_t = \beta(L_t - L_{t-1}) + (1-\beta)T_{t-1}$

Step 2: Determine the working equation

Equation 1	$L_t = \alpha Y_t + (1-\alpha)(L_{t-1} + T_{t-1})$ ....[Open bracket] $L_t = \alpha Y_t + (1-\alpha)L_{t-1} + (1-\alpha)T_{t-1}$ ....[Derive equation] $\mathbf{(1-\alpha)L_{t-1} + (1-\alpha)T_{t-1} = L_t - \alpha Y_t}$ **........................(1)**
Equation 2	$T_t = \beta(L_t - L_{t-1}) + (1-\beta)T_{t-1}$ ....[Open bracket] $T_t = \beta L_t - \beta L_{t-1} + (1-\beta)T_{t-1}$ ....[Derive equation] $\mathbf{-\beta L_{t-1} + (1-\beta)T_{t-1} = T_t - \beta L_t}$ **..............................(2)**

Step 3: Data substitution and solving....[Let $L_{t-1} = X$ and $T_{t-1} = V$]

$$\left.\begin{array}{l}(1-\alpha)X + (1-\alpha)V = L_t - \alpha Y_t \ldots\ldots(1)\\ -\beta X + (1-\beta)V = T_t - \beta L_t \ldots\ldots\ldots(2)\end{array}\right\}$$ ....[Substitute data]

$$\left.\begin{array}{l}(1-0.6)X + (1-0.6)V = 245.89 - 0.6(246) \ldots\ldots(1)\\ -(0.4)X + (1-0.4)V = 7.13 - 0.4(245.89) \ldots\ldots\ldots(2)\end{array}\right\}$$ ....[Simplify equations]

$$\left.\begin{array}{l}0.4X + 0.4V = 98.29 \ldots\ldots(1)\\ -0.4X + 0.6V = -91.226 \ldots(2)\end{array}\right\}$$ ....[Add equation (1) to equation (2)]

$-0.4X + 0.4X + 0.6V + 0.4V = -91.226 + 98.29$ ....[Collect like terms together]

$V = T_{t-1} = \mathbf{7.064}$

N/B: To derive the value of X, we substitute the value of V in any of the equation. Let use equation (1).

$(1-0.6)X + (1-0.6)7.064 = 245.89 - 0.6(246)$ ....[Simplify equation]

$0.4X + 2.8256 = 98.29$ ....[Collect like terms together]

$0.4X = 95.4644$ ....[Divide both sides of equation by (0.4)]

$X = L_{t-1} = \mathbf{238.661}$

Note: The calculated level and trend values of 2001 are represented in the table with that of 2002 is given below.

Year	Sales	Level	Trend
2001		238.661	7.064
2002	246	245.89	7.13

Test Your Understanding

Exercise 20: Compute the demand level using the simple exponential smoothing method. Assume the level parameter (α) is 0.29.

Years	2012	2013	2014	2015	2016	2017
Demand	17,496	18,965	12,535	14,781	16,722	15,858

[Answer: ....See Appendix]

Exercise 21: calculate the forecast supply from the year 2013 to 2018 using the simple exponential smoothing method. Assume the level parameter (α) is 0.2.

Years	2013	2014	2015	2016	2017
Supply	80	82	84	83	83

[Answer: ....See Appendix]

Exercise 22: Given that $L_t = 445.6$, $L_{t-1} = 446.9$ and $Y_t = 440.6$, Determine the level parameter (α) value...**[Answer: 0.2 or 20%]**

Exercise 23: Fill the empty spaces in the table below. Assume the mean forecast error (MFE) is -1.278.

Years	Sales	or cast	Forecast Error
2001	18		
2002	**13**	18.00	−5.00
2003	16	15.50	**0.50**
004	11	**16.67**	−4.67
2005	17	14.50	2.50
2006	14	**14.998**	**−0.998**

[Answer: ....See Appendix]

Exercise 24: Determine forecast production from the year 2015 to 2018 using information in the table below. Assume $\alpha = 0.6$, $\beta = 0.4$ and $L_1 = 7$

Years	2015	2016	2017	2018	2019
Production	205	212	218	224	

[Answer: ....See Appendix]

Exercise 25: Assume $e_t = 24.7943$ and $F_t = 182.2057$, calculate Y_t...**[Answer: 207 Units]**

Exercise 26: Given that $L_{t-1} = 193.4016$, $T_{t-1} = -0.6466$ and $e_t = 37.2450$. Compute the value of Y_t..**[Answer: 230 Units]**

Exercise 27: Determine the level parameter (α) and trend parameter (β) using information in the table below.

Year	Sales	Level	Trend
2018		218.40	6.76
201	22	224.46	6.48

[Answer: $\alpha = 0.6$ and $\beta = 0.4$]

Note: Triple exponential smoothing method is also called Holt-winter exponential smoothing method and is used when the time series data have both trend and seasonality. It is based on the level (α), trend (β) and seasonality (γ) parameters, with their values ranging between 1 and 0 $[(0 \leq \alpha \leq 1)$, $(0 \leq \beta \leq 1)$ and $(0 \leq \gamma \leq 1)]$. The smoothing equations and forecasting equation depends on the type of model (additive or multiplicative).

Type of Model	Smoothing Equations	Forecasting Equation
Additive	$L_t = \alpha(Y_t - S_{t-m}) + (1-\alpha)(L_{t-1} + T_{t-1})$	$F_{t+m} = L_t = m(T_t) + S_{t-m}$
	$T_t = \beta(L_t - L_{t-1}) + (1-\beta)T_{t-1}$	
	$S_t = \gamma(Y_t - L_{t-1} - T_{t-1}) + (1-\gamma)S_{t-m}$	
Multiplicative	$L_t = \alpha(Y_t/S_{t-m}) + (1-\alpha)(L_{t-1} + T_{t-1})$	$F_{t+m} = [L_t + m(T_t)]S_{t-m}$
	$T_t = \beta(L_t - L_{t-1}) + (1-\beta)T_{t-1}$	
	$S_t = \gamma(Y_t/L_{t-1} + T_{t-1}) + (1-\gamma)S_{t-m}$	

CHAPTER THREE

PROBABILITY THEORY

3.1 Meaning of Probability

Girolamo Cardano

Probability theory originated from the game of chance and is used to determine possibilities of events occurrence. An event is defined as something that occurs or happens. The probability of an event (X) is denoted (P_X) and probability value ranges from zero (0) to one (1) expressing the certainty and uncertainty of an event occurrence.

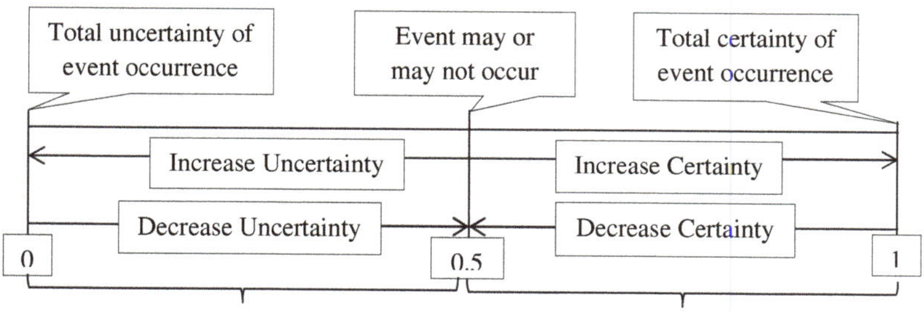

Note: The probability of an event can be expressed in fraction [20/100], decimal [0.2] and percentage [20%]. To determine the probability of an event, we are required to know the event outcome and sample space. Mathematically events are sub-divided into the following types;

1) Independent Events: Events which the outcome of one does not influence the outcome of another. The multiplication law is used when determining independent event probability.

$$\mathbf{P(A\ and\ B) = P(A) \times P(B)} \quad \text{.......(1)}$$

2) Dependent Events: Events which the outcome of one influences the outcome of another. It is expressed mathematically as:

$$\mathbf{P(A\ and\ B) = P(A) \times P(B/A)} \quad \text{.......(2)}$$

3) Mutually Exclusive Events: Events that cannot occur at the same time. The addition law is used when determining mutually exclusive event probability.

$$\mathbf{P(A\ or\ B) = P(A) + P(B)} \quad \text{.......(3)}$$

4) Mutually Inclusive Event: Events that can occur at the same time. Mathematically, it is expressed as;

$$\mathbf{P(A\ and\ B) = P(A) + P(B) - P(A\ and\ B)} \text{.......................................(4)}$$

5) Complement Events($\bar{A}$): It consists of all events that are not the occurring event. It is the mathematical expression is given as;

$$\mathbf{P(\bar{A}) = 1 - P(A)} \text{...(5)}$$

3.2 Types of Probability

There exist different types of probability. Our analysis will be focused on three major types; theoretical probability, experimental probability and conditional probability.

3.2.1 Theoretical Probability

It is the name given to probability that is calculated without any experiment (uses only information). The formula used is given as;

$$\mathbf{P(A)} = \frac{\textbf{Number of Favourable Outcome}}{\textbf{Total Number of Possible Outcome}} \text{..(1)}$$

Example 1: A dice is made of 8 equally likely outcomes. What is the probability of having?

1) The number 4
2) Numbers greater than 4
3) Number less than 5
4) An even number
5) An odd number

<u>**Solution**</u>

Note: The formula applicable is given as; $P(A) = \frac{\text{Number of Favourable Outcome}}{\text{Total Number of Possible Outcome}}$

1) The number 4

Hint: The required event is the number **4**. The number of favourable outcome (the number of time 4 can occur in the total outcome) is **1**. The total number of possible outcome is **8**.

$$P(A) = \frac{\text{Number of Favourable Outcome}}{\text{Total Number of Possible Outcome}} = \frac{1}{8} \text{.............................[Simplify fraction]}$$

$$P(A) = \mathbf{0.125} \text{..[0.125 or 12.5\%]}$$

2) Numbers greater than 4

Hint: The required event are numbers greater than 4 (that is 5, 6, 7 and 8). The number of time this event can occur in the total outcome is 4 and the total number of outcomes is 8.

$$P(A) = \frac{\text{Number of Favourable Outcome}}{\text{Total Number of Possible Outcome}} = \frac{4}{8} \text{ ....[Simplify fraction]}$$

$$P(A) = \mathbf{0.5} \text{ ....[0.5, or 50\%]}$$

3) **Numbers less than 5**

Hint: The required events are numbers less than 5 (that is 4, 3, 2 and 1). The number of time this event can occur in the total outcome is 4 and the total number of outcomes is 8.

$$P(A) = \frac{\text{Number of Favourable Outcome}}{\text{Total Number of Possible Outcome}} = \frac{4}{8} \text{ ....[Simplify fraction]}$$

$$P(A) = \mathbf{0.5} \text{ ....[0.5, or 50\%]}$$

4) **An even number**

Hint: The required events are even numbers (that is 2, 4, 6, and 8). The number of time this event can occur in the total outcome is 4 and the total number of outcomes is 8.

$$P(A) = \frac{\text{Number of Favourable Outcome}}{\text{Total Number of Possible Outcome}} = \frac{4}{8} \text{ ....[Simplify fraction]}$$

$$P(A) = \mathbf{0.5} \text{ ....[0.5, or 50\%]}$$

5) **An odd number**

Hint: The required events are odd numbers (that is 1, 3, 5, and 7). The number of time this event can occur in the total outcome is 4 and the total number of outcomes is 8.

$$P(A) = \frac{\text{Number of Favourable Outcome}}{\text{Total Number of Possible Outcome}} = \frac{4}{8} \text{ ....[Simplify fraction]}$$

$$P(A) = \mathbf{0.5} \text{ ....[0.5, or 50\%]}$$

Example 2: There are 7 balls in a bag in which; 2 are red, 3 are green and the remaining are yellow. Assume random drawing of balls is done with replacement, find the probability that the draw is:

1) Green
2) Yellow
3) Not red

<u>Solution</u>

Note: Replacement means a draw is re-introduced into the total outcome. Total outcome is unchanged or remain constant no matter the degree of drawing. The total number of possible outcome is 7 and formula applied is given as; $\left[P(A) = \frac{\text{Number of Favourable Outcome}}{\text{Total Number of Possible Outcome}}\right]$

1) Green

Hint: The required event is green balls occurrence and the number of favourable outcome is 3 (since there are three green balls).

$$P(A) = \frac{\text{Number of Favourable Outcome}}{\text{Total Number of Possible Outcome}} = \frac{3}{7}$$ ....[Simplify fraction]

$$P(A) = \mathbf{0.43} = \mathbf{43\%}$$ ....[In two decimal places]

2) Yellow

Hint: The required event is yellow balls occurrence and the number of favourable outcome is unknown. We are required to determine the unknown value before probability determination.

Step 1: Calculation of unknown number of favourable outcome of yellow balls.

a) Formula: $\text{Unknown outcome} = \text{Total possible otcome} - \sum(\text{Alternative outcomes})$

Where; total possible outcome is 7 and $\sum(\text{Alternative outcomes})$ is 5 [That is $2 + 3 = 5$].

b) Data substitution and solving.

$$\text{Unknown outcome(Yellow)} = 7 - 5$$ ....[Simplify equation]

$$\text{Unknown outcome(Yellow)} = \mathbf{2}$$ ....[Yellow outcome is 2]

Step 2: Data substitution and solving.

$$P(A) = \frac{\text{Number of Favourable Outcome}}{\text{Total Number of Possible Outcome}} = \frac{2}{7}$$ ....[Simplify fraction]

$$P(A) = \mathbf{0.29} = \mathbf{29\%}$$ ....[In two decimal places]

3) Not red

Hint: The event is not drawing red balls. Not drawing red balls means red ball is a complement event.

Step 1: Formula. $P(\bar{A}) = 1 - P(A)$, where; $P(A)$ is the probability of drawing being red.

Step 2: Calculation of the probability of red [$P(A)$]

$$P(A) = \frac{\text{Number of Favourable Outcome}}{\text{Total Number of Possible Outcome}} = \frac{2}{7}$$ ....[Simplify fraction]

$$P(A) = \mathbf{0.29} = \mathbf{29\%}$$ ....[In two decimal places]

Step 3: Data substitution and solving

$$P(\bar{A}) = 1 - 0.29$$ ....[Simplify equation]

$$P(\bar{A}) = \mathbf{0.71}$$ ....[71%]

Example 3: A lecture on a topic of public health is held and 300 people attend. They are classified in the following ways;

Gender	Doctors	Nurses	Total
Female	90	90	180
Male	100	20	120
Total	190	110	300

If one person is selected at random, fine the following probability

1) Selecting a doctor
2) Selecting a female
3) Selecting a female nurse
4) Selection a male doctor

Solution

1) **Selecting a doctor**

Hint: The event required is doctor. The gender is not specified, therefore the number of favourable outcome is the sum of male and female doctors [190]. Total number of possible outcome is 300.

$$P(A) = \frac{\text{Number of Favourable Outcome}}{\text{Total Number of Possible Outcome}} = \frac{190}{300}$$ ....[Simplify fraction]

$$P(A) = \mathbf{0.63} = \mathbf{63\%}$$ ....[In two decimal places]

2) **Selecting a female**

Hint: The event required is female. The occupation/function is not specified, therefore the number of favourable outcome is the sum of female doctor and female nurses [180]. Total number of possible outcome is 300.

$$P(A) = \frac{\text{Number of Favourable Outcome}}{\text{Total Number of Possible Outcome}} = \frac{180}{300}$$ ....[Simplify fraction]

$$P(A) = \mathbf{0.6} = \mathbf{60\%}$$

3) **Selecting a female nurse**

Hint: The event required is female nurses. Both occupation and gender is specified, therefore the number of favourable outcome is limited only to the number of female nurses [90]. Total number of possible outcome is 300.

$$P(A) = \frac{\text{Number of Favourable Outcome}}{\text{Total Number of Possible Outcome}} = \frac{90}{300}$$ ....[Simplify fraction]

$$P(A) = \mathbf{0.3} = \mathbf{30\%}$$

4) **Selection a male doctor**

Hint: The event required is male doctor. Both occupation and gender is specified, therefore the number of favourable outcome is limited only to the number of male doctor [100]. Total number of possible outcome is 300.

$$P(A) = \frac{\text{Number of Favourable Outcome}}{\text{Total Number of Possible Outcome}} = \frac{100}{300}$$ ....[Simplify fraction]

$P(A) = \mathbf{0.33} = \mathbf{33\%}$ ....[In two decimal places]

Example 4: A container is loaded with different coloured shapes as follows; Triangles (3 reds, 2 green, 1 yellow), Rectangles (4 red, 1 green, 5 yellow, 2 blue) and circles (2 red, 2 green, 1 yellow, 4 blue). What is the probability that a shaped drawn at random is:

1) Red
2) A rectangle
3) A green circle
4) A circle or a yellow triangle

Solution

1) **Red**

Hint: The required event is the coloured red. Since no specific shape (triangle, rectangle and circle) is mentioned, number of favourable outcome of red colour is the combination of red colours of all shapes. Total number of possible outcome is the sum of all shapes

$$[\text{Traingles}(6) + \text{Rectangles}(12) + \text{Circles}(9) = 27].$$

Step 1: Formula and data. $P(A) = \frac{\text{Number of Favourable Outcome of event red}}{\text{Total Number of Possible Outcome}}$

Where; $\text{Total Number of Possible Outcome} = 27$

Step 2: Calculation of Number of favourable outcome

Number of reds in all shapes				
Shapes	Triangle	Rectangle	Circle	Total
Number	3	4	5	9

Step 3: Data substitution and solving.

$$P(A) = \frac{\text{Number of Favourable Outcome of event red}}{\text{Total Number of Possible Outcome}} = \frac{9}{27}$$ ....[Simplify fraction]

$P(A) = \mathbf{0.33} = \mathbf{33\%}$ ....[In two decimal places]

2) A rectangle

Hint: The required event is the shape rectangle. Since no specific colour is specified, the number of favourable outcome is the sum of all rectangles (2) and total number of possible outcome is the sum of all shapes since the shape rectangle contains colours that are found in the other shapes.

Step 1: Formula. $P(A) = \frac{\text{Number of Favourable Outcome of event rentangles}}{\text{Total Number of Possible Outcome}}$

Where; $\text{Total Number of Possible Outcome} = 27$

Step 2: Data substitution and solving.

$P(A) = \frac{\text{Number of Favourable Outcome of event rentangles}}{\text{Total Number of Possible Outcome}} = \frac{12}{27}$ ....[Simplify fraction]

$P(A) = \mathbf{0.44} = \mathbf{44\%}$ ....[In two decimal places]

3) A green circle

Hint: The required event is green circle. The shape and colour is specified. Our analysis is therefore limited to the shape circle. Number of favourable outcome of green circle is (2) and number of possible outcome is (27) since the colour green is found in other shapes.

$P(A) = \frac{\text{Number of Favourable Outcome of event rentangles}}{\text{Total Number of Possible Outcome}} = \frac{2}{27}$ ....[Simplify fraction]

$P(A) = \mathbf{0.07} = \mathbf{7\%}$ ....[In two decimal places]

4) A circle or a yellow triangle

a) Method 1

Hint: The required event is the shape circle (9 since no colour is specified) and yellow triangle (1).

Step 1: Formula. $P(A \text{ or } B) = \frac{\sum(\text{of occurance of shape cricle and yellow triangle})}{\sum f\,(\text{Total number of occurance irresoective of shapes or colours})}$

Where; $\sum(\text{of occurance of shape cricle and yellow triangle}) = 9 + 1 = 10$

$\sum f\,(\text{Total number of occurance irresoective of shapes or colours}) = 27$

Step 2: Data substitution and solving.

$P(A \text{ or } B) = \frac{\sum(\text{of occurance of shape cricle and yellow triangle})}{\sum f\,(\text{Total number of occurance irresoective of shapes or colours})} = \frac{10}{27}$ ....[Simplify]

$P(A \text{ or } B) = \mathbf{0.37} = \mathbf{37\%}$ ....[In two decimal places]

b) Method 2

Hint: The events (circle) and (yellow triangle) are mutually exclusive. This is because no circle can be a yellow triangle.

Step 1: Formula. $P(A \text{ or } B) = P(A) + P(B)$. Let event circle be (A) and yellow triangle be (B)

Step 2: Data substitution and solving

$P(A \text{ or } B) = \frac{9}{27} + \frac{1}{27}$ ....[Simplify equation]

$P(A \text{ or } B) = \frac{10}{27}$ ....[Simplify fraction]

$P(A \text{ or } B) = \mathbf{0.37} = \mathbf{37\%}$ ....[In two decimal places]

Note: The above problem can be solved using the contingency table. A contingency table is a table that shows the one quality of a variable in the row and another quality in the column. Let assume shape quality takes the row and colour quality takes the column, our problem representation is seen below. This formula used still remains the same

$$\left[P(A) = \frac{\text{Number of Favourable Outcome of event red}}{\text{Total Number of Possible Outcome}}\right]$$

	Red	Green	Yellow	Blue	Total
Triangle	3	2	1	0	6
Rectangle	4	1	5	2	12
Circle	2	2	1	4	9
Total	9	5	7	6	27

What is the probability that a shaped drawn at random is:

1) Red $\left[P(\text{Red}) = \frac{9}{27} = \mathbf{0.33} = \mathbf{33\%}\right]$
2) A rectangle $\left[P(\text{A rectangle}) = \frac{12}{27} = \mathbf{0.44} = \mathbf{44\%}\right]$
3) A green circle $\left[P(\text{A green circle}) = \frac{2}{27} = 0.07 = 7\%\right]$
4) A circle or a yellow triangle $\left[P(\text{A circle or a yellow triangle}) = \frac{9}{27} + \frac{1}{27} = \frac{10}{27} = 0.37\right]$

Test Your Understanding

Exercise 1: A box contains the number 2 to 11. What is the probability that a random draw is;

1) An even number is drawn................ **[Answer: $\mathbf{0.5} = \mathbf{50\%}$ chance or possibility]**
2) An odd number is drawn................. **[Answer: $\mathbf{0.5} = \mathbf{50\%}$ chance or possibility]**
3) An even number lesser than 8 is drawn................. **[Answer: $\mathbf{0.3} = \mathbf{30\%}$ chance]**
4) An odd number greater than 3...........**[Answer: $\mathbf{0.4} = \mathbf{40\%}$ chance or possibility]**
5) A number greater than 8................. **[Answer: $\mathbf{0.3} = \mathbf{30\%}$ chance or possibility]**

Exercise 2: A bag contains 20 balls from which 12 are white, 6 are green and the remainder black. What is the probability that a random draw is;

1) Not Green................................. **[Answer: 0.7 = 70% chance or possibility]**
2) Not black.................................. **[Answer: 0.9 = 90% chance or possibility]**
3) Not white.................................. **[Answer: 0.4 = 40% chance or possibility]**

Exercise 3: The contain of a bag is given as follows;

	White	Red	Brown	Yellow
Square	10	5	11	4
Rectangle	15	5	5	5
Ci cle	12	2	2	4

What is the probability that;

1) A square shape is drawn.......... [**Answer**: **0.375 = 37.5% chance or possibility**]
2) A red shape is drawn................. [**Answer**: **0.15 = 15% chance or possibility**]
3) White circle shape is drawn........... [**Answer: 0.15 = 15% chance or possibility**]
4) Not a rectangle shape is drawn..................... [**Answer: 0.625 = 62.5% chance**]
5) Circle or square is drawn......... [**Answer: 0.625 = 62.5% chance or possibility**]
6) Brown rectangle or yellow circle..............[**Answer: 0.1125 = 11.25% chance**]
7) Not a brown rectangle is drawn................ [**Answer: 0.9375 = 93.75% chance**]
8) Circle or rectangle or square shape is drawn ....[**Answer: 1 = 100% chance**]
9) White or brown or red or yellow shape is drawn. ....[**Answer: 1 = 100% chance**]

3.2.2 Experimental Probability

It is the probability that is calculated using the result of an experiment that has been performed a number of times. Probability in this case is calculated using the formula;

$$\mathbf{P(A)} = \frac{\textbf{Number of Time the event (A) occurred}}{\textbf{Total number of time the experiment was performed}} \quad \ldots\ldots\ldots\ldots\ldots\ldots\ldots\ldots(1)$$

Example 1: The statistics of the number of days of work by school personnel is given in the table below.

Personnel	Teacher	Discipline master	Principal	Vice Principal	HOD
Days of work	42	10	18	31	23

Determine the relative frequency of the following personnel with respect to their days of work.

1) Teachers
2) Discipline master or HOD [Assuming no discipline master is an HOD]

Solution

1) **Teachers**

Step 1: Formula. $P(A) = \frac{\text{Number of Time the event (A) occurred}}{\text{Total number of time the experiment was performed}} = \frac{f(A)}{\sum f}$

Where; $f(A) = 42$ and $\sum f = 42 + 10 + 18 + 31 + 23 = \mathbf{124}$

Step 2: Data substitution and solving.

$P(A) = \frac{24}{124}$ ……………………………………………………………..[Simplify fraction]

$P(A) = \mathbf{0.34} = \mathbf{34\%}$ ………………………………………………[In two decimal places]

2) **Discipline master or HOD [Let discipline master be (A) and HOD be (B)]**

Method 1: Mutual Exclusive Concept	**Method 2:** Relative Frequency Concept
Formula: $P(A \text{ or } B) = P(A) + P(B)$	**Formula**: $P(A \text{ or } B) = \frac{\sum f(A \text{ and } B)}{\sum f}$
Where: A=10, B = 23, $\sum f\,(A \text{ and } B) = 33$(that is $10 + 23$) and $\sum f = 124$	
$P(A \text{ or } B) = \frac{10}{124} + \frac{23}{124}$ $P(A \text{ or } B) = 33/124$ $P(A \text{ or } B) = \mathbf{0.27} = \mathbf{27\%}$	$P(A \text{ or } B) = \frac{33}{124}$ $P(A \text{ or } B) = \mathbf{0.27} = \mathbf{27\%}$

Example 2: A bag contains balls of the following colours; red, blue, green and yellow

Colour	Red	Blue	Green	Yellow
Number of balls	20	15Y	Y − 10	40Y

The probability of chosen a red ball is $20/850$, fine the probability that a ball drawn at random is the following;

1) Green
2) Yellow
3) Green

Solution

Hint: The probability of chosen a red ball helps us identify the total number of outcome. Therefore, the total number of balls is 850. To determine the probabilities of other balls, we are required to determine the valued of "Y" to have a definite value of each ball.

Step 1: Determination of value of "Y"

a) Formula. $\text{Total Outcome} = \text{Sum of Balls, where; Total Outcome} = 850$

b) Data substitution and solving

$850 = 20 + 15\text{Y} + (\text{Y} - 10) + 40\text{Y}$................[Simplify bracket and collect like terms]

$15\text{Y} + \text{Y} + 40\text{Y} = 850 - 10$ ....[Simplify both sides of the equation]

$56\text{Y} = 840$ ....[Divide both sides of equation by (56)]

$\text{Y} = \mathbf{15}$

Colour	Red	Blue	Green	Yellow	Total
Number of balls	20	225	5	600	850

Step 2: Determination of probabilities

a) Formula. $\text{Probability} = \frac{\text{Number of favourable outcome}}{\text{Total number of outcome}}$

b) Data substitution and solving

Colour	Blue	Green	Yellow	Total
Number of balls	225	5	600	
Probabilities	$225/850 = \mathbf{0.265}$	$5/850 = \mathbf{0.006}$	$600/850 = \mathbf{0.706}$	1

Example 3: Use the table below and answer the following

	Red	White	Green	Blue
Number of Balls	a	c	19	d

Given the probability of selecting a green ball is $[19/250]$ and that $[a = 2c]$ and $[d = 4a]$ fine the probability that a ball chosen at random is;

1) Red
2) White
3) Blue

Solution

Step 1: Formula. $\text{Probability} = \frac{\text{Number of favourable outcome}}{\text{Total number of outcome}}$

Where; $\text{Total Number of Outcome} = 250$

Step 2: Determination of Unknown [a, c and d]

a) Formula. $\text{Total Number of Outcome} = \text{Sum of Balls}$

b) Data substitution and solving

$250 = a + c + 19 + d$ ....[Substitute variables equivalent to harmonize equation]

$a + \frac{a}{2} + 19 + 4a = 250$ ....[Linearized the equation]

$2a + a + 38 + 8a = 500$ ....[Collect like terms together]

$11a = 462$ ....[Divide both sides by (11)]

$a = \mathbf{42}$

	Red	White	Green	Blue	Total
Number of Balls	42	21	19	168	250

Step 2: Determination of probabilities

	Red	White	Blue
Number of Balls	42	21	168
Probability	$42/250 = \mathbf{0.168}$	$21/250 = \mathbf{0.084}$	$168/250 = \mathbf{0.672}$

Example 4: A number of families of a particular type were measured by the number of children they contain to give the following frequency distribution table.

Number of children	2	3	4	5	6	7	8
Number of family	6	10	14	20	9	6	5

Calculate the relative probability that another family will have;

1) 5 children
2) 7 children
3) More than 6 children
4) 4 children or less

<u>**Solution**</u>

1) 5 bags

Step 1: Formula and data. $P(A) = \frac{\text{Number of Time the event (A) occurred}}{\text{Total number of time the experiment was performed}} = \frac{f(A)}{\sum f}$

Where; $f(A) = 20$ and $\sum f = 70$

Step 2: Data substitution and solving.

$P(A) = \frac{20}{70}$ ....[Simplify fraction]

$P(A) = \mathbf{0.29} = \mathbf{29\%}$ ....[In two decimal places]

Step 3: Interpretation. There is 29% chance for the farm to produce 5 bags of rice.

2) 7 bags

Step 1: Formula and data. $P(A) = \frac{\text{Number of Time the event (A) occurred}}{\text{Total number of time the experiment was performed}} = \frac{f(A)}{\sum f}$

Where; $f(A) = 6$ and $\sum f = 70$

Step 2: Data substitution and solving.

$P(A) = \frac{6}{70}$ ....[Simplify fraction]

$P(A) = \mathbf{0.09} = \mathbf{9\%}$ ....[In two decimal places]

Step 3: Interpretation. There is 9% chance of producing 7 bags of rice.

3) More than 6 bags

Hint: More than 6 bags is there same as 7 bags or 8 bags. The additive law is applied to calculate this probability. [$f(\text{bags} > 6) \equiv \text{frequency of 7 bags} + \text{frequency of 8 bags} = 6 + 5 = 11$].

Step 1: Formula. $P(A) = \frac{\text{Number of Time the event (A) occurred}}{\text{Total number of time the experiment was performed}} = \frac{f(A)}{\sum f}$

Where; $f(A) = 11$ and $\sum f = 70$

Step 2: Data substitution and solving.

$P(A) = \frac{11}{70}$ ....[Simplify fraction]

$P(A) = \mathbf{0.16} = \mathbf{16}\ \%$ ....[In two decimal places]

4) 4 bags or less

Hint: 4bags or less is there same as sum of frequency of 4 bags, 3 bags and 2 bags. That is 30.

Step 1: Formula. $P(A) = \frac{\text{Number of Time the event (A) occurred}}{\text{Total number of time the experiment was performed}} = \frac{f(A)}{\sum f}$

Where; $f(A) = 30$ and $\sum f = 70$

Step 2: Data substitution and solving.

$P(A) = \frac{30}{70}$ ....[Simplify fraction]

$P(A) = \mathbf{0.43} = \mathbf{43\%}$ ....[In two decimal places]

Example 4: The histogram below shows the statistics of student's marks in business mathematics examination and the number of students.

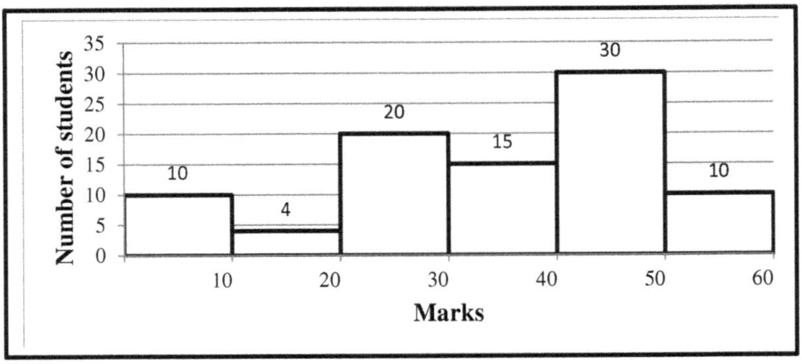

Find the experimental probability that a randomly selected student score;

1) Is 18 marks
2) At least 30 marks
3) At most 40 marks
4) 10 marks or 55 marks

Solution

1) Is 18 marks

Step 1: Formula and data. $P(A) = \frac{\text{Number of Time the event (A) occurred}}{\text{Total number of time the experiment was performed}} = \frac{f(A)}{\sum f}$

Where; $f(A) = f(18) = 4$ and $\sum f = 89$

Step 2: Data substitution and solving.

$P(A) = \frac{4}{89}$ ....[Simplify fraction]

$P(A) = \mathbf{0.045 = 4.5\%}$ ....[In three decimal places]

2) At least 30 marks

Hint: At least 30 marks can be represented as $[\text{Marks} \geq 30]$ which equals $[15 + 30 + 10 = 55]$

Step 1: Formula. $P(\text{Score at least } 30) = \frac{\sum f(\text{Score at least } 30)}{\sum f}$, where; $\sum f = 89$

Step 2: Data substitution and solving.

$P(\text{Score at least } 30) = \frac{55}{89}$ ....[Simplify fraction]

$P(\text{Score at least } 30) = \mathbf{0.62 = 62\%}$ ....[In two decimal places]

3) At most 40 marks

Hint: The word at most 40 means we are required to sum the frequencies of all events from 40 to the lowest event (which in this case is 0).

Step 1: Formula and data. $P(\text{Score at most } 40) = \frac{\sum f(\text{Score at most } 40)}{\sum f}$

Where; $\sum f = 89$ and $\sum f(\text{Score at most } 40) = 30 + 15 + 20 + 4 + 10 = \mathbf{79.}$

Step 2: Data substitution and solving.

$P(\text{Score at most } 40) = \frac{79}{89}$ ....[Simplify fraction]

$P(\text{Score at most } 40) = \mathbf{0.89 = 89\%}$ ....[In two decimal places]

4) 10 marks or 55 marks

Hint: Here, we are required to solve individual probabilities of events and sum their probability or sum the events frequencies and solve their probability in a single working.

$P(\text{Score } 10 \text{ or } 55) = \frac{14}{89}$ ....[Simplify] $P(\text{Score } 10 \text{ or } 55) = \mathbf{0.16 = 16\%}$	$P(\text{Score } 10 \text{ or } 55) = \frac{4}{89} + \frac{10}{89}$ $P(\text{Score } 10 \text{ or } 55) = \frac{14}{89}$ ....[Simplify] $P(\text{Score } 10 \text{ or } 55) = \mathbf{0.16 = 16\%}$

<u>Test Your Understanding</u>

Exercise 4: In a medical examination of students of a class, the following blood groups are recorded

Blood group	A	AB	B	O
Number of students	5X	13	6 – X	5

Considering that the probability of choosing a student at random with blood group "O" is $5/40$, fine the probability that a student drawn at random is having;

1) A blood group ....[**Answer:** $\mathbf{0.5 = 50\%}$]
2) B blood group..[**Answer:** $\mathbf{0.05 = 5\%}$]
3) AB blood group...[**Answer:** $\mathbf{0.325 = 32.5\%}$]

Exercise 5: Use the table below and answer the following

	Black	White	Green
Number of Balls	10	a	c

Assume the probability of selecting a black ball is $[10/100]$ and that [a = 2c], fine the probability that a ball chosen at random is;

1) White ……………………………………………………[Answer: $0.6 = 60\%$]
2) Green ……………………………………………………[Answer: $0.3 = 30\%$]

Exercise 6: Bulbs are packed in cartons each containing 40 bulbs. Seven hundred cartons were examined for defective bulbs and the results are given in the table below;

Number of defective goods	0	1	2	3	4	5	6	< 6
Frequency	400	180	48	41	18	8	3	2

One carton was selected at random. What is the probability that it has; [Leave answer in two decimal places]

1) No defective bulb……………………………………[Answer: $0.57 = 57\%$]
2) Defective bulbs from 2 to 6……………………………[Answer: $0.17 = 17\%$]
3) Defective bulbs less than 4……………………………[Answer: $0.96 = 96\%$]

3.2.3 Conditional Probability/Tree Diagram

Conditional probability is the probability that event "A" will occur given that or on the condition that, event "B" has already occurred. The idea of conditional probability is best explained using the tree diagram. Probability tree diagram is a tree-like illustration of events probabilities. Probability tree diagram can be expressed in it generalized or summarized form. The following ideas are worth knowing when drawing a probability tree diagram.

Thomas Bayes

1) The number of branches: The number of events involved determines the number of branches to be drawn to make up the tree diagram. Two events situation means two branches and n^{th} events means n^{th} branches.

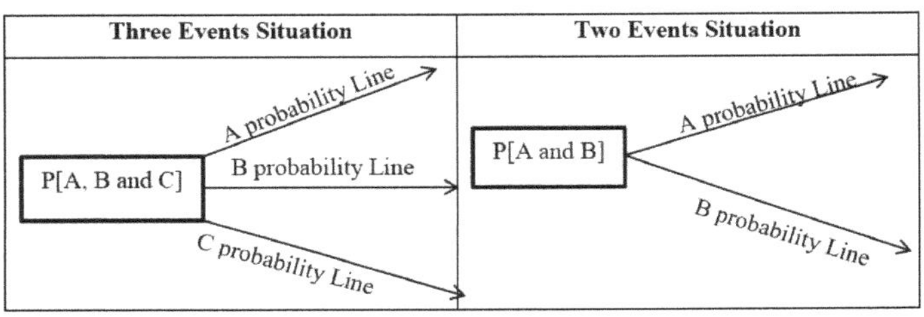

2) Number of stages/segment: The numbers of stages are determined from the number of draws or happening of events.

Two Draws Situation with three events

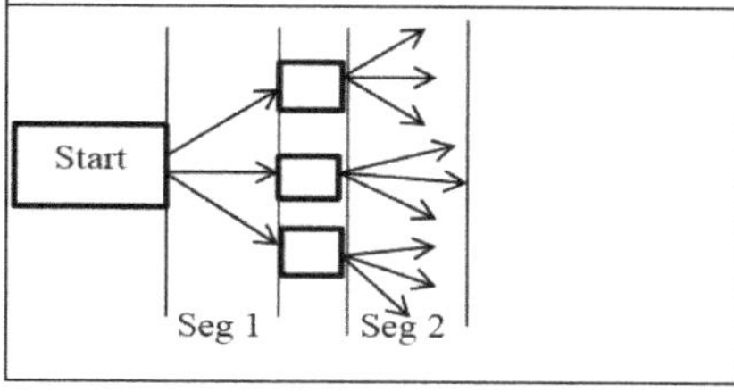

Three Draws Situation with two events

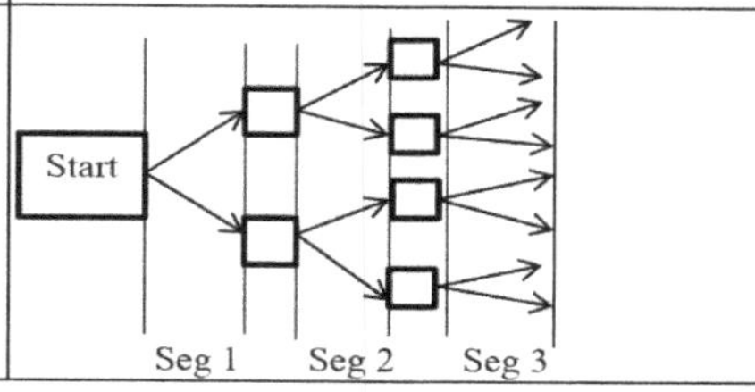

3) Main branch and the complement branch: Main branch is the branch of the draw being performed. Complement branch represent the other events sub-branches along the events or main branch. The probability of the main branch and complement branches must be equal to one in any stage.

Two Draws Situation with Two Events [Red Balls And Blue Balls]

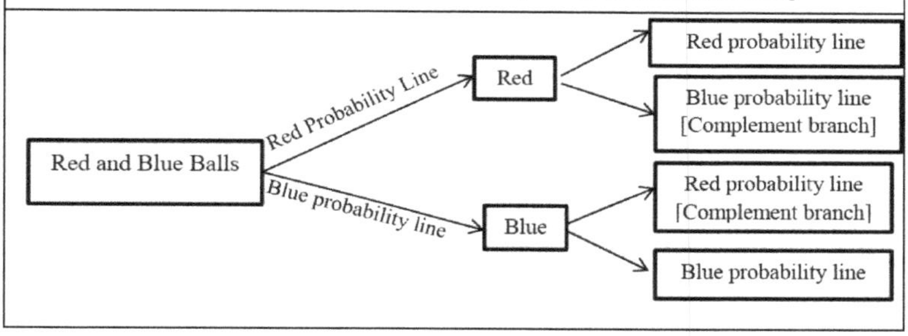

Note: The sum of the complement branches probabilities equals the probability of the main event not occurring. The numerator of a complement branch does not change from it pre-probability situation and it denominator will change if and only if the drawing is non-replaceable.

Example 1: A bag contains 4 green balls and 6 red balls. Assuming that after a draw, the drawn ball is not replaced. Draw a probability tree diagram under the following three drawing situations

1) Green first and red second balls drawing
2) Red, green and red balls drawing respectively

Solution

Note: drawing being not replaced means the number of favourable outcome of the event and the total number of possible outcome reduces after each segment.

1) Green and Red balls drawing

Hint: The two events [green balls and red balls] indicate two branches in the probability tree diagram. Two draws [green draw and red draw] indicate two segments.

Step 1: Drawing of probability tree diagram

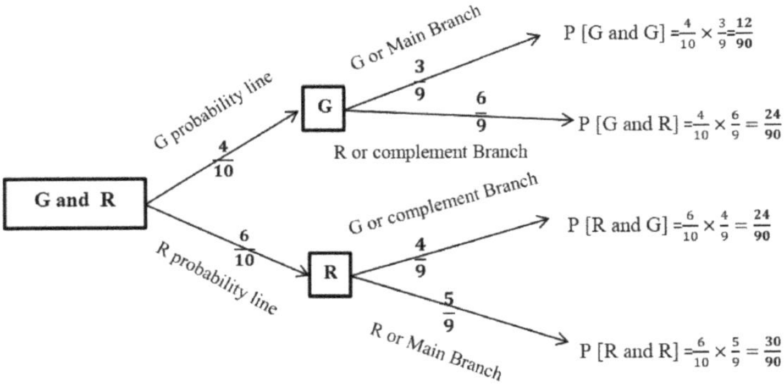

Validity Test [Σ of all probability = 1] $=\frac{12}{90}+\frac{24}{90}+\frac{24}{90}+\frac{30}{90}=\frac{90}{90}=\mathbf{1}$. Therefore the tree is valid

Step 2: Determination of probability

Note: $\mathrm{P(Green\ First\ and\ Red\ Second)} = \mathrm{P(Green)}$ and $\mathrm{P(Red|Green)} = \mathrm{P[G \times (R|G)]}$. The First draw being green indicates our focus should be on the green branch.

a) Formula. $\mathrm{P(Green\ First\ and\ Red\ Second)} = \mathrm{P(G)} \times \mathrm{P(R|G)}$

Where; $\mathrm{P(G)} = \frac{4}{10}$ and $\mathrm{P(R|G)} = \frac{6}{9}$

b) Data substitution and solving

$\mathrm{P(Green\ First\ and\ Red\ Second)} = \frac{4}{10} \times \frac{6}{9}$ ……………………[Perform direct multiplication]

$\mathrm{P(Green\ First\ and\ Red\ Second)} = \frac{24}{90}$ ………………………………..[Simplify fraction]

$\mathrm{P(Green\ First\ and\ Red\ Second)} = \mathbf{0.27} = \mathbf{27\%}$ ………………..[In two decimal places]

2) Red, green and red balls drawing respectively

Hint: Two events (green balls and red balls) indicate two branches. Three draws (red, green and red) indicate three segments.

Step 1: Drawing of probability tree diagram

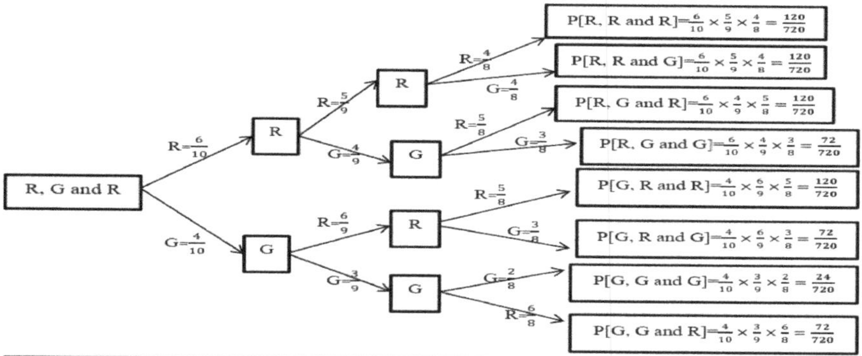

Validity Test [Σ of all probability = 1] $= \frac{120}{720} + \frac{120}{720} + \frac{120}{720} + \frac{72}{720} + \frac{120}{720} + \frac{72}{720} + \frac{24}{720} + \frac{72}{720} = \frac{720}{720} = \mathbf{1}$.

Tabular Technique	Draws	First Draw	Second Draw	Third Draw
Events	Green	4/10	4/9	3/8
	Red	6/10	5/9	5/8
Description		−1 Red	−1 Green	−1 Red
Total Probability		1	1	1

Step 3: Determination of probability

Note: $\text{P(Red, Green and Red)} = \text{P(Red)}, \text{P(Green|Red)and P(Red|Greed, Red)}$. The First draw being red, indicate our focus should be on the red branch.

a) Formula. $\text{P(Green First and Red Second)} = \text{P(G)} \times \text{P(G|R)} \times \text{P(R|GR)}$

Where; $\text{P(R)} = \frac{6}{10}$, $\text{P(G|R)} = \frac{4}{9}$ and $\text{P(R|GR)} = \frac{5}{8}$

b) Data substitution and solving

$\text{P(Red, Green and Red)} = \frac{6}{10} \times \frac{4}{9} \times \frac{5}{8}$ ....[Perform direct multiplication]

$\text{P(Green First and Red Second)} = \frac{120}{720}$ ....[Simplify fraction]

$\text{P(Green First and Red Second)} = \mathbf{0.17 = 17\%}$ ....[In two decimal places]

Example 2: A box contains six red pens and three blue pens. A pen is selected at random, the colour is noted and the pen is returned to the box. This procedure is performed a second, then a third time. Find the probability of obtaining using the tree diagram technique;

1) Three red pens
2) Two red pens and one blue pen, in any order
3) More than one blue pen

Solution

Step 1: Drawing of probability tree diagram

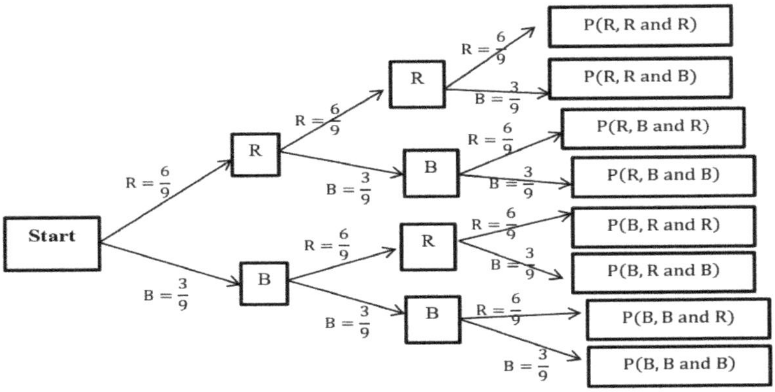

Step 3: Determination of general probability value.

1) **Three red pens**

Hint: Three red pens mean the first, second and third selections are all red. That is, P(R, R and R).

Step 1: Formula. P[R, R and R]

Step 2: Data substitution and solving

$P = \frac{6}{9} \times \frac{6}{9} \times \frac{6}{9}$ ....[Perform direct multiplication]

$P = \frac{216}{729}$ ....[Simplify fraction]

$P = \mathbf{0.30} = \mathbf{30\%}$ ....[In two decimal places]

Step 3: Interpretation: We have 30% chance of selecting three red pens in three draws.

2) **Two red pens and one blue pen, in any order**

Hint: This means that the selection can be in the following ways; [P(R, R and B)], [P(R, B and R)] and [P(B, R and R)] since order of event occurrence is not considered.

a) Specific probability occurrence

$P(R, R \text{ and } B) = \frac{6}{9} \times \frac{6}{9} \times \frac{3}{9} = \frac{108}{729}$ ....[Experiment 1]

$P(R, B \text{ and } R) = \frac{6}{9} \times \frac{3}{9} \times \frac{6}{9} = \frac{108}{729}$ ....[Experiment 2]

$P(R, R \text{ and } R) = \frac{3}{9} \times \frac{6}{9} \times \frac{6}{9} = \frac{108}{729}$ ....[Experiment 3]

b) General probability occurrence

Note: Since this situation is made up of three different experiment occurrences, it therefore, means that the events are mutually exclusive as all three experiments cannot occur at the same time. Note, E represent equipment.

a) Formula. $P(E_1, E_2, \text{and } E_3) = P(E_1) + P(E_2) + P(E_3)$

Where; $E_1 = \frac{108}{729}$, $E_2 = \frac{108}{729}$ and $E_3 = \frac{108}{729}$

b) Data substitution and solving

$P(E_1, E_2, \text{and } E_3) = \frac{108}{729} + \frac{108}{729} + \frac{108}{729}$ ....[Sum numerator and maintain denominator]

$P(E_1, E_2, \text{and } E_3) = \frac{324}{729}$ ....[Simplify fraction by division]

$P(E_1, E_2, \text{and } E_3) = \mathbf{0.44 = 44\%}$ ....[In two decimal places]

c) Interpretation: There is 44% chance of selecting two red pens and one blue pen, in any order in three draws.

3) More than one blue pen

Hint: More than one blue pen means two blues pens of any order or three blues pens. That is[P(R, B and B)], P(B, R and B) , P(B, B and R) and [P(B, B and B)].

a) Specific probability occurrence

$P(R, B \text{ and } B) = \frac{6}{9} \times \frac{3}{9} \times \frac{3}{9} = \frac{54}{729}$ ....[Experiment 1]

$P(B, R \text{ and } B) = \frac{3}{9} \times \frac{6}{9} \times \frac{3}{9} = \frac{54}{729}$ ....[Experiment 2]

$P(B, B \text{ and } R) = \frac{3}{9} \times \frac{3}{9} \times \frac{6}{9} = \frac{54}{729}$ ....[Experiment 3]

$P(B, B \text{ and } B) = \frac{3}{9} \times \frac{3}{9} \times \frac{3}{9} = \frac{27}{729}$ ....[Experiment 4]

b) General probability occurrence [**Note**: events are mutually exclusive. E represent experiment]

1) Formula. $P(E_1, E_2, E_3 \text{ and } E_4) = P(E_1) + P(E_2) + P(E_3) + P(E_4)$.

Where; $E_1 = \frac{54}{729}$, $E_2 = \frac{54}{729}$, $E_3 = \frac{54}{729}$ and $E_4 = \frac{27}{729}$

2) Data substitution and solving

$P(E_1, E_2, E_3 \text{ and } E_4) = \frac{54}{729} + \frac{54}{729} + \frac{54}{729} + \frac{27}{729}$

$P(E_1, E_2, E_3 \text{ and } E_4) = \frac{189}{729}$ ....[Simplify fraction]

$P(E_1, E_2, E_3 \text{ and } E_4) = \mathbf{0.26 = 26\%}$ ....[In two decimal places]

c) Interpretation: There is 26% chance of selecting more than one blue pen in three draws.

Example 3: A bag contains 8 red balls, 12 blue balls, 9 yellow balls and 11 green balls. Three balls are randomly drawn from the bag one at a time and not replaced. Find the probability respecting the order of random drawing below:

1) red, blue and green
2) yellow, yellow and not green

Solution

1) **red, blue and green**

a) **Using a Formula Method**

Note: $n(Z)$ = Number of Z before any draw and u = Total number of outcomes before any draw

Step 1: Formula. $P(R, B \text{ and } G) = \frac{n(R)}{u} \times \frac{n(B)}{u-1} \times \frac{n(G)}{u-2}$

Where; $n(R) = 8$, $n(B) = 12$, $n(G) = 11$ and $u = 40$,

Step 2: Data substitution and solving.

$P(R, B \text{ and } G) = \frac{8}{40} \times \frac{12}{39} \times \frac{11}{38}$ ....[Perform direct multiplication]

$P(R, B \text{ and } G) = \frac{1056}{59{,}280}$ ....[Simplify fraction]

$P(R, B \text{ and } G) = \mathbf{0.02 = 2\%}$ ....[In two decimal places]

b) **Using the Tree Diagram Method**

i. **Using the Summarized Technique of Tree Diagram**

Hint: Concentrate only on the first draw tree branch (red draw) and continue till last draw. This method is used to manage time and reduce over crowd when dealing with more than two events.

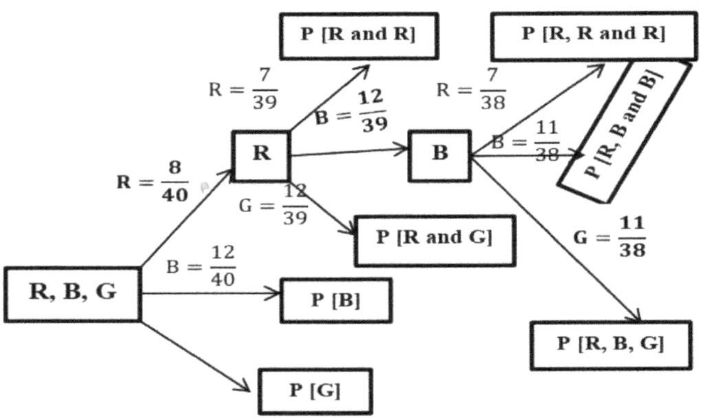

2) **yellow, yellow and not green**

a) **Formula Method**

Step 1: Formula. $P(Y, Y \text{ and not } G) = \frac{Y}{u} \times \frac{Y-1}{u-1} \times \left[1 - \frac{G}{u-2}\right]$

Where; $Y = 9$, $G = 11$ and $u = 40$

Step 2: Data substitution and solving.

$P(Y, Y \text{ and not } G) = \frac{9}{40} \times \frac{9-1}{40-1} \times \left[1 - \frac{11}{40-2}\right]$ ....[Simplify equation]

$P(Y, Y \text{ and not } G) = \frac{9}{40} \times \frac{8}{39} \times \frac{27}{38}$ ....[Perform direct multiplication]

$P(Y, Y \text{ and not } G) = \frac{1{,}944}{59{,}280}$ ....[Simplify fraction]

$P(Y, Y \text{ and not } G) = \mathbf{0.03} = \mathbf{3\%}$ ....[In two decimal places]

b) Tree Diagram Method

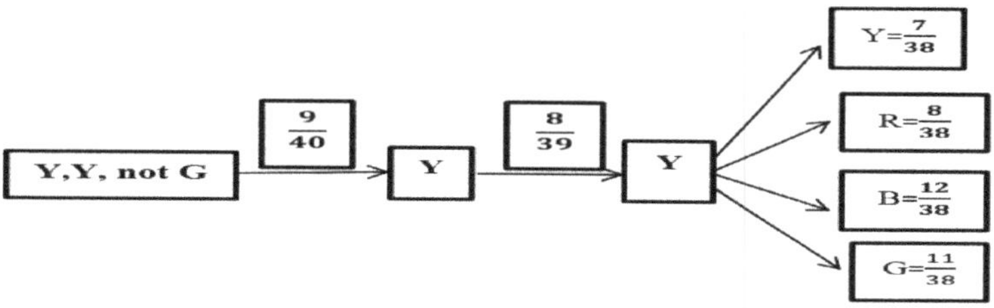

Step 1: Formula. $P(Y, Y \text{ and } \overline{G})$

Step 2: Data substitution and solving.

$P(Y, Y \text{ and } \overline{G}) = \frac{9}{40} \times \frac{8}{39} \times \left[\frac{7}{38} + \frac{8}{38} + \frac{12}{38}\right]$ ....[Simplify bracket]

$P(Y, Y \text{ and } \overline{G}) = \frac{9}{40} \times \frac{8}{39} \times \frac{27}{38}$ ....[Perform direct multiplication]

$P(Y, Y \text{ and } \overline{G}) = \frac{1{,}944}{59{,}280}$ ....[Simplify fraction]

$P(Y, Y \text{ and } \overline{G}) = \mathbf{0.03} = \mathbf{3\%}$ ....[In two decimal places]

Example 4: A box contains 3 red, 4 black and 3 white balls. Two balls are drawn with replacement. What is the probability of selecting?

1) A red ball in the first and second draw
2) A black ball in the first drawn and a white or red ball in the second drawn.

Solution

Hint: Since drawn balls are replaced, it means the outcome of an event will not affect the occurrence of other events as the total possible occurrence remains unchanged.

1) A red ball in the first and second draw

a) Formula Method

Step 1: Formula. $P(R \text{ and } R) = \frac{R}{u} \times \frac{R}{u}$, where; $R = 3$ and $u = 10$

Step 2: Data substitution and solving.

$P(\text{R and R}) = \frac{3}{10} \times \frac{3}{10}$ ....[Perform direct multiplication]

$P(\text{R and R}) = \frac{\mathbf{9}}{\mathbf{100}}$ ....[Simplify fraction]

$P(\text{R and R}) = \mathbf{0.09} = \mathbf{9\%}$

Step 3: Interpretation: There is 9% chance that the two draws will be red balls

b) Summarized Probability Tree Diagram Technique

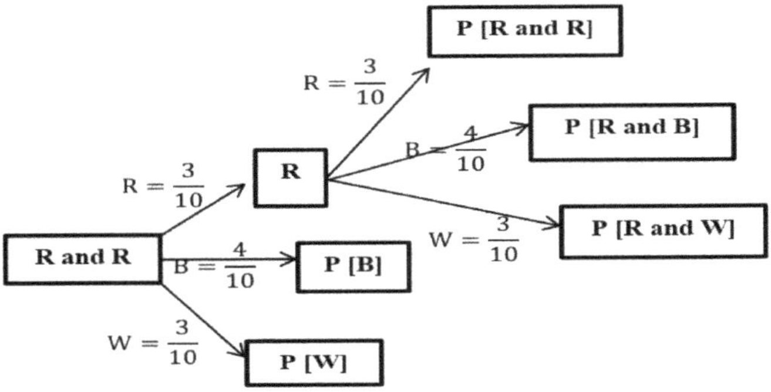

Probability Determination

$P(\text{R and R}) = \frac{3}{10} \times \frac{3}{10}$ ....[Perform direct multiplication]

$P(\text{R and R}) = \frac{9}{100}$ ....[Simplify fraction]

$P(\text{R and R}) = \mathbf{0.09} = \mathbf{9\%}$

2) A black ball in the first drawn and a white or red ball in the second drawn.

a) Using the General Formula Method

1) Using mutually exclusive events technique

Step 1: Formula. $P[\text{B and (W or R)}] = \frac{B}{u} \times \left[\frac{W}{u} + \frac{R}{u}\right]$

Where; $B = 4, R = 3, W = 3 = \frac{6}{10}$ and $u = 10$.

Step 2: Data substitution and solving.

$P[\text{B and (W or R)}] = \frac{4}{10} \times \left[\frac{3}{10} + \frac{3}{10}\right]$ ....[Simplify bracket]

$P[\text{B and (W or R)}] = \frac{4}{10} \times \frac{6}{10}$ ....[Perform direct multiplication]

$P[\text{B and (W or R)}] = \frac{24}{100}$ ....[Simplify fraction]

$P[\text{B and (W or R)}] = \mathbf{0.24} = \mathbf{24\%}$

2) Using complementary event technique

Step 1: Formula. $P[B \text{ and } (\bar{B})] = \frac{B}{u} \times \left[1 - \frac{B}{u}\right]$, where; B = 4 and u = 10.

Step 2: Data substitution and solving.

$P[B \text{ and } (\bar{B})] = \frac{4}{10} \times \left[1 - \frac{4}{10}\right]$ ……………………………………………[Simplify bracket]

$P[B \text{ and } (\bar{B})] = \frac{4}{10} \times \frac{6}{10}$ ……………………………………[Perform direct multiplication]

$P[B \text{ and } (\bar{B})] = \frac{24}{100}$ ……………………………………………………[Simplify fraction]

$P[B \text{ and } (\bar{B})] = \mathbf{0.24 = 24\%}$

b) Using the Summarized Formula Method

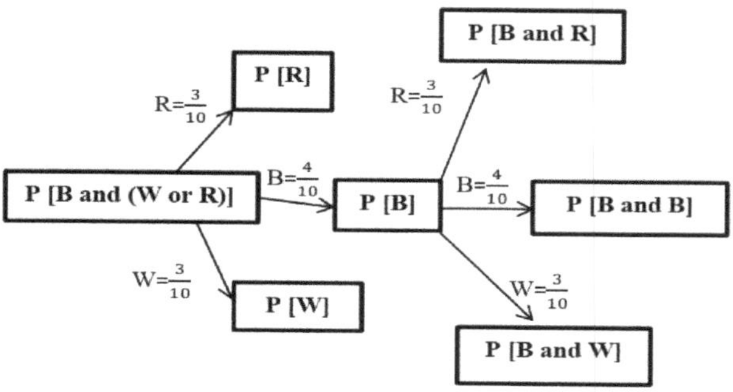

Step 2: Data substitution and solving.

$P[B \text{ and } (W \text{ or } R)] = \frac{4}{10} \times \left[\frac{3}{10} + \frac{3}{10}\right]$ …………………………………[Simplify bracket]

$P[B \text{ and } (W \text{ or } R)] = \frac{4}{10} \times \frac{6}{10}$ …………………………………[Perform direct multiplication]

$P[B \text{ and } (W \text{ or } R)] = \frac{24}{100}$ ……………………………………………[Simplify fraction]

$P[B \text{ and } (W \text{ or } R)] = \mathbf{0.24 = 24\%}$

Example 5: A bag contains three red balls and seven white balls. A ball is drawn from the bag, its colour noted and it is replaced by a ball of the other colour. A second ball is then drawn from the bag. Draw a probability tree diagram showing all possibilities and fine the probability that,

1) The first and second balls drawn are red
2) Both balls are of the same colour
3) At least a ball of each colour is drawn

Solution

Step 1: Drawing probability tree diagram of all possibilities

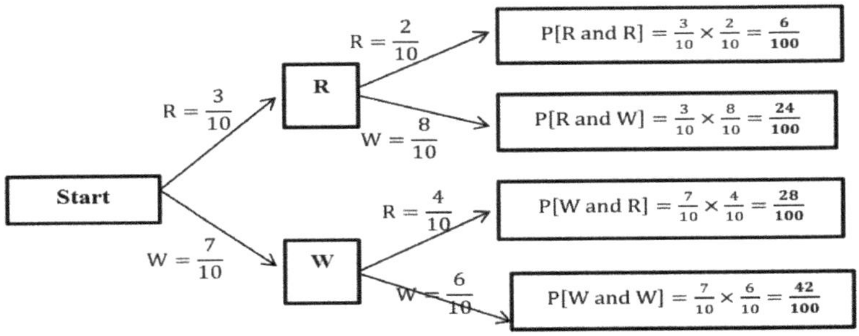

Validation of tree diagram: $\frac{6}{100}+\frac{24}{100}+\frac{28}{100}+\frac{42}{100}=\frac{100}{100}=\mathbf{1}$. Valid since sum equals 1

Step 2: Calculating of probabilities values

1) The first and second balls drawn are red

Probability of $P[\text{R and R}] = \frac{3}{10} \times \frac{2}{10}$ ....[Perform direct multiplication]

Probability of $P[\text{R and R}] = \frac{6}{100}$ ....[Simplify fraction]

Probability of $P[\text{R and R}] = \mathbf{0.06 = 6\%}$

2) Both balls are of the same colour

Hint: That is both drawn can be red balls [R and R] or both drawn can be while balls [W and W].

Step 2: Data substitution and solving

Probability $P[(\text{R and R}) \text{ or } (\text{W and W})] = \frac{6}{100} + \frac{42}{100}$ ....[Sum numerator]

Probability $P[(\text{R and R}) \text{ or } (\text{W and W})] = \frac{48}{100}$ ....[Simplify fraction]

Probability $P[(\text{R and R}) \text{ or } (\text{W and W})] = \mathbf{0.48 = 48\%}$

3) At least a ball of each colour is drawn

Hint: That is the draws can be (R and W) or (R and W).

Probability $P[(\text{R and W}) \text{ or } (\text{W and R})] = \frac{24}{100} + \frac{28}{100}$ ....[Sum numerator]

Probability $P[(\text{R and R}) \text{ or } (\text{W and W})] = \frac{52}{100}$ ....[Simplify fraction]

Probability $P[(\text{R and R}) \text{ or } (\text{W and W})] = \mathbf{0.52 = 52\%}$

Example 6: A box contains seven green balls and four yellow balls. Two balls are selected at random from the bad without replacement. Find the probability that:

1) They are both yellow
2) They are of different colours
3) They are of the same colour

Solution

1) **They are both yellow**

Step 1: Formula. $P(\text{Y and Y}) = \frac{Y}{u} \times \frac{Y-1}{u-1}$, where; $Y = 4$ and $u = 11$.

Step 3: Data substitution and solving.

$P(\text{Y and Y}) = \frac{4}{11} \times \frac{4-1}{11-1}$ ....[Simplify equation]

$P(\text{Y and Y}) = \frac{4}{11} \times \frac{3}{10}$ ....[Perform direct multiplication]

$P(\text{Y and Y}) = \frac{12}{110}$ ....[Simplify fraction]

$P(\text{Y and Y}) = \mathbf{0.11} = \mathbf{11\%}$ ....[In two decimal places]

2) **They are of different colours**

Step 1: Formula. $P[(\text{G and Y}) \text{ or } (\text{Y and G})] = \left(\frac{G}{u} \times \frac{Y}{u-1}\right) + \left(\frac{Y}{u} \times \frac{G}{u-1}\right)$

Where; $G = 7, Y = 4, u = 11$

Step 2: Data substitution and solving.

$P[(\text{A and B}) \text{ or } (\text{B and A})] = \left(\frac{7}{11} \times \frac{4}{11-1}\right) + \left(\frac{4}{11} \times \frac{7}{11-1}\right)$ ....[Simplify denominators]

$P[(\text{A and B}) \text{ or } (\text{B and A})] = \left(\frac{7}{11} \times \frac{4}{10}\right) + \left(\frac{4}{11} \times \frac{7}{10}\right)$..............[Perform direct multiplication]

$P[(\text{A and B}) \text{ or } (\text{B and A})] = \frac{28}{110} + \frac{28}{110}$ ....[Simplify equation]

$P[(\text{A and B}) \text{ or } (\text{B and A})] = \frac{\mathbf{56}}{\mathbf{110}}$ ....[Simplify fraction]

$P[(\text{A and B}) \text{ or } (\text{B and A})] = \mathbf{0.51} = \mathbf{51\%}$ ....[In two decimal places]

3) **They are of the same colour**

Step 1: Formula. $P[(\text{G and G}) \text{ or } (\text{Y and Y})\ ] = \left(\frac{G}{u} \times \frac{G-1}{u-1}\right) + \left(\frac{Y}{u} \times \frac{Y-1}{u-1}\right)$

Where; $G = 7, Y = 4, u = 11$.

Step 2: Data substitution and solving.

$P[(\text{A and A}) \text{ or } (\text{B and B})\ ] = \left(\frac{7}{11} \times \frac{7-1}{11-1}\right) + \left(\frac{4}{11} \times \frac{4-1}{11-1}\right)$ ....[Simplify equation]

$P[(\text{A and A}) \text{ or } (\text{B and B})\ ] = \left(\frac{7}{11} \times \frac{6}{10}\right) + \left(\frac{4}{11} \times \frac{3}{10}\right)$ ....[Perform direct multiplication]

$P[(\text{A and A}) \text{ or } (\text{B and B})\ ] = \frac{42}{110} + \frac{12}{110}$..[Simplify equation]

$P[(A \text{ and } A) \text{ or } (B \text{ and } B)\,] = \frac{54}{110}$ ....[Simplify fraction]

$P[(A \text{ and } A) \text{ or } (B \text{ and } B)\,] = \mathbf{0.50} = \mathbf{50\%}$ ....[In two decimal places]

Example 7: A box contains 5 red balls and 7 blue balls. Two balls are selected at random, one after the other. When the first ball is selected, its colour is noted and it is replaced to the box together with another ball of the same colour. Find the probability that:

1) They are all red
2) They are of the same colour
3) They are of different colour

Solution

1) They are all red

Step 1: Formula. $P(R \text{ and } R) = \frac{R}{u} \times \frac{R+1}{u+1}$, where: $R = 5$ and $u = 12$

Step 2: Data substitution and solving.

$P(R \text{ and } R) = \frac{5}{12} \times \frac{5+1}{12+1}$ ....[Simplify equation]

$P(R \text{ and } R) = \frac{5}{12} \times \frac{6}{13}$ ....[Perform direct multiplication]

$P(R \text{ and } R) = \frac{\mathbf{30}}{\mathbf{156}}$ ....[Simplify fraction]

$P(R \text{ and } R) = \mathbf{0.19} = \mathbf{19\%}$ ....[In two decimal places]

2) They are of the same colour

Step 1: Formula. $P[(R \text{ and } R) \text{ or } (B \text{ and } B)] = \left(\frac{R}{u} \times \frac{R+1}{u+1}\right) + \left(\frac{B}{u} \times \frac{B+1}{u+1}\right)$

Where; $R = 5$, $B = 7$, $u = 12$.

Step 2: Data substitution and solving.

$P[(R \text{ and } R) \text{ or } (B \text{ and } B)] = \left(\frac{5}{12} \times \frac{5+1}{12+1}\right) + \left(\frac{7}{12} \times \frac{7+1}{12+1}\right)$ ....[Simplify equation]

$P[(R \text{ and } R) \text{ or } (B \text{ and } B)] = \left(\frac{5}{12} \times \frac{6}{13}\right) + \left(\frac{7}{12} \times \frac{8}{13}\right)$ ....[Perform direct multiplication]

$P[(R \text{ and } R) \text{ or } (B \text{ and } B)] = \frac{30}{156} + \frac{56}{156}$ ....[Simplify equation]

$P[(R \text{ and } R) \text{ or } (B \text{ and } B)] = \frac{86}{156}$ ....[Simplify fraction]

$P[(R \text{ and } R) \text{ or } (B \text{ and } B)] = \mathbf{0.55} = \mathbf{55\%}$ ....[In two decimal places]

3) They are of different colour

Step 1: Formula. $P[(R \text{ and } B) \text{ or } (B \text{ and } R)] = \left(\frac{R}{u} \times \frac{B}{u+1}\right) + \left(\frac{B}{u} \times \frac{R}{u+1}\right)$

Where; $R = 5$, $B = 7$, $u = 12$.

Step 3: Data substitution and solving.

$P[(R \text{ and } B) \text{ or } (B \text{ and } R)] = \left(\frac{5}{12} \times \frac{7}{12+1}\right) + \left(\frac{7}{12} \times \frac{5}{12+1}\right)$ ....[Simplify equation]

$P[(A \text{ and } B) \text{ or } (B \text{ and } A)] = \left(\frac{5}{12} \times \frac{7}{13}\right) + \left(\frac{7}{12} \times \frac{5}{13}\right)$ ....[Perform direct multiplication]

$P[(A \text{ and } B) \text{ or } (B \text{ and } A)] = \frac{35}{156} + \frac{35}{156}$ ....[Simplify equation]

$P[(A \text{ and } B) \text{ or } (B \text{ and } A)] = \frac{70}{156}$ ....[Simplify fraction]

$P[(A \text{ and } B) \text{ or } (B \text{ and } A)] = \mathbf{0.45} = \mathbf{45\%}$ ....[In two decimal places]

Example 8: A bag contains 4 red balls and 6 white balls. A ball is drawn from the urn and a ball of the other colour is then put into the urn. A second ball is then drawn from the bag.

1) Find the probability that the second ball is red.
2) Fined the probability that both balls drawn are of the same colour
3) If both balls were of the same colour, what is the probability that they were both red?

Solution

1) **Find the probability that the second ball is red.**

Hint: Since the first ball drawn is not specified, it can be red or white. The second ball drawn is specified (red). Therefore, in the two draws, we can have; red and red balls $[P(\text{Red and Red})]$ or white and red balls $[P(\text{White and Red})]$. The draws can be seen below

$[P(\text{Red and Red})]$					$[P(\text{White and Red})]$				
Balls	Draw 1		Draw 2		Balls	Draw 1		Draw 2	
	Before	After	Before	After		Before	After	Before	After
Red	**4**	4 − 1	**3**	3 − 1	Red	**4**	4 + 1	**5**	5 − 1
White	**6**	6 + 1	**7**	7 + 1	White	**6**	6 − 1	**5**	5 + 1
Total	**10**	10	**10**	10	Total	**10**	10	**10**	10

Step 1: Formula. $\text{Probability} = P(\text{Red and Red}) + P(\text{White and Red})$

Step 2: Data substitution and solving

$\text{Probability} = \left(\frac{4}{10} \times \frac{3}{10}\right) + \left(\frac{6}{10} \times \frac{5}{10}\right)$ ....[Simplify brackets]

$\text{Probability} = \frac{12}{100} + \frac{30}{100}$ ....[Solve equation]

$\text{Probability} = \mathbf{0.42} = \mathbf{42\%}$

2) **Find the probability that both balls drawn are of the same colour**

[P(Red and Red)]					[P(White and White)]				
Balls	Draw 1		Draw 2		Balls	Draw 1		Draw 2	
	Before	After	Before	After		Before	After	Before	After
Red	**4**	$4-1$	**3**	$3-1$	Red	**4**	$4+1$	**5**	$5+1$
White	**6**	$6+1$	**7**	$7+1$	White	**6**	$6-1$	**5**	$5-1$
Total	**10**	10	**10**	10	Total	**10**	10	**10**	10

Step 1: Formula. $\text{Probability} = \text{P(Red and Red)} + \text{P(White and White)}$

Step 2: Data substitution and solving

$\text{Probability} = \left(\frac{4}{10} \times \frac{3}{10}\right) + \left(\frac{6}{10} \times \frac{5}{10}\right)$ ....[Simplify brackets]

$\text{Probability} = \frac{12}{100} + \frac{30}{100}$ ....[Solve equation]

$\text{Probability} = \mathbf{0.42} = \mathbf{42\%}$

3) **If both balls were of the same colour, what is the probability that they were both red?**

Hint: Here, total outcome is the number of favourable outcome when both balls drawn are of the same colour [$12 + 30 = 42$] and the number of favourable outcome is the number of favourable outcome when both balls drawn are red [12].

Step 1: Formula. $\text{Probability} = \frac{\text{Number of favourable outcome when both balls drawn are red}}{\text{Number of favourable outcome when both balls drawn are of the same colour}}$

Step 2: Data substitution and solving

$\text{Probability} = \frac{12}{12+30}$ ....[Simplify denominator]

$\text{Probability} = \frac{12}{42}$ ....[Solve fraction]

$\text{Probability} = \mathbf{0.29} = \mathbf{29\%}$ ....[In two decimal places]

Test Your Understanding

Exercise 7: A box contains 4 red balls and 5 white balls. Three balls are drawn at random, successively and without replacement from the box. Draw a probability tree diagram illustrating the various possibilities.

a) Draw the probability tree diagram of three draws.....................**[Answer: See Appendix 1]**

b) Find the probability that; [Leave answers in two decimal places]

1) Exactly one white ball is drawn...................................**[Answer: $0.36 = 36\%$]**

2) No white ball is drawn..**[Answer: $0.05 = 5\%$]**

3) At least one white ball is drawn.................................**[Answer: $0.95 = 95\%$]**

Exercise 8: A bag contains seven black and three white marbles. Three marbles are chosen at random and in succession, each marble being replaced after it has been taken out of the bag. Draw a probability tree diagram to show all possible selections. From your tree diagram, calculate to two significant figure the probability of choosing,

a) Three black marbles...**[Answer: $0.34 = 34\%$]**

b) A white marble, a black marble and a white marble in that order..........**[Answer: $0.06 = 6\%$]**

c) Two white marble and a black marble in any order..............**[Answer: $0.19 = 19\%$]**

d) At least one black marble...**[Answer: $0.97 = 97\%$]**

Exercise 9: A bag initially contains 1 red ball and 2 blue balls. A trail consists of selecting a ball at random, noting its colour and replacing it together with an additional ball of the same colour. Given that three trials are made, draw a probability tree diagram illustrating the various possibilities and hence find the probability that;

a) At least one blue ball is drawn.....................................**[Answer: $0.9 = 90\%$]**

b) Exactly one blue ball is drawn......................................**[Answer: $0.2 = 20\%$]**

c) Given that all three balls are of the same colour, fine the probability that they are all red...**[Answer: $0.1 = 10\%$]**

CHAPTER FOUR

FURTHER ANALYSIS OF PROBABILITY

The concept of probability is not only limited with the calculation of events probability or event occurrence.

4.1 Probability distribution and shapes

Probability distribution is a table that shows the probability of individual item in which the sum of probabilities equal one (1). Probability distribution as calculated using the formula below;

$$P(X_i) = P(X = x) = \frac{F(X_i)}{\sum f_i} \quad \dots\dots(1)$$

Where: $P(X_i) = P(X = x)$ is the probability of individual item,

$F(X_i)$ is the frequency of individual item,

$\sum f_i$ is the sum of frequencies of all items.

Example 1: Derive the probability distribution using the frequency distribution table below.

Marks	1	2	3	4	5	6
Frequencies	10	15	25	25	15	10

<u>Solution</u>

Step 1: Formula. $F(X_i) = P(X = x) = \frac{F(X_i)}{\sum f_i}$, where; $\sum f_i = 100$

Step 2: Data substitution and solving

Marks	1	2	3	4	5	6
Frequencies	10	15	25	25	15	10
$P(X = x) = \frac{F(X_i)}{\sum f_i}$	$\frac{10}{100} = 0.1$	$\frac{15}{100} = 0.15$	$\frac{25}{100} = 0.25$	$\frac{25}{100} = 0.25$	$\frac{15}{100} = 0.15$	$\frac{10}{100} = 0.1$

Step 3: Justification. $\sum P(X_i) = 1$. That is $[0.1 + 0.15 + 0.25 + 0.25 + 0.15 + 0.1 = 1]$.

Example 2: The probability model below gives the probabilities of the maximum number of laps completed by people who play the video game.

Lap	1	2	3	4	5
Probabilities	0.29	0.38	0.17	0.11	0.05

Determine the value of the following

1) The mode
2) Probability of Lap greater than four [P(Lap > 4)]
3) Probability of Lap greater or equal to four [P(Lap ≥ 4)]
4) P(1 ≤ Lap < 4)

Solution

1) The mode

Hint: Using the concept of probability distribution, the mode is any value with the highest probability.

Lap	1	**2**	3	4	5	Total
Probabilities (P_i)	0.29	**0.38**	0.17	0.11	0.05	1
Whole Number = $P_i \times 100$	29	**38**	17	11	5	100

From the table, the 0.38 or 38% is the highest probability. Therefore, 2 is the mode as it is the value with the highest probability.

2) Probability of Lap less than four [$\mathbf{P(Lap < 4)}$]

Hint: $P(Lap < 4)$ means we should sum the probability of values greater than 4 [from 1 to 3].

Step 1: $P(Lap < 4) = P(Lap = 1) + P(Lap = 2) + P(Lap = 3)$

Where: $P(Lap = 1) = 0.29,\ \ P(Lap = 2) = 0.38\quad P(Lap = 3) = 0.17$

Step 2: Data substitution and solving

$P(Lap < 4) = P(Lap = 1) + P(Lap = 2) + P(Lap = 3)$ ……………..[Substitute data value]

$P(Lap < 4) = 0.29 + 0.38 + 0.17$ ……………...………….......………...[Simplify equation]

$P(Lap < 4) = \mathbf{0.84}$

3) Probability of Lap less than or equal to four [$\mathbf{P(Lap \leq 4)}$]

Hint: $P(Lap \leq 4)$ means we should sum the probability of values from 1 to 4.

Step 1: $P(Lap \leq 4) = P(Lap = 1) + P(Lap = 2) + P(Lap = 3) + P(Lap = 4)$

Where: $P(Lap = 1) = 0.29,\quad P(Lap = 2) = 0.38\quad P(Lap = 3) = 0.17,$ $P(Lap = 4) = 0.11$

Step 2: Data substitution and solving

$P(Lap \leq 4) = P(Lap = 1) + P(Lap = 2) + P(Lap = 3) + P(Lap = 4)$……[Substitute data]

$P(Lap \leq 4) = 0.29 + 0.38 + 0.17 + 0.11$ …………………......[Simplify equation by addition]

$P(Lap \leq 4) = \mathbf{0.95}$

4) $\mathbf{P(1 \leq Lap < 3)}$

Hint: $P(1 \leq Lap < 3)$ means we should sum the probability from value range of 1 to 2.

Step 1: $P(1 \leq Lap < 3) = P(Lap = 1) + P(Lap = 2)$

Where: $P(Lap = 1) = 0.29$, $P(Lap = 2) = 0.38$,

Step 2: Data substitution and solving

$P(1 \leq Lap < 3) = P(Lap = 1) + P(Lap = 2)$ ……………………………[Substitute data value]

$P(1 \leq Lap < 3) = 0.29 + 0.38$ ……………………………….[Simplify equation by addition]

$P(1 \leq Lap < 3) = \mathbf{0.67}$

Example 3: The table below represents the number of vehicles and the associated probability of having that number of vehicles in an individual household. Find the value of the unknown (k).

Vehicles	1	2	3	4	5
Probability	28k	k	19k	12k	4k

Solution

Hint: Sum of all probabilities in a probability distribution table must be equal to one.

Step 1: Formula. $\sum P(X_i) = 1$

Step 2: Data substitution and solving for K

$\sum P(X_i) = 1$ ……………………………………….[Substitute data values into the formula]

$28k + k + 19k + 12k + 4k = 1$ ………………..[Factorized K from the left side of equation]

$k(28 + 1 + 19 + 12 + 4) = 1$ ……………………………[Simplify bracket by addition]

$k(64) = 1$ ……………………………………………[Divide both sides of equation by 64]

$k = \frac{1}{64}$

Step 3: Justification: Substitute the value of K into the probability distribution and verify if the sum of probabilities equal 1

Vehicles	1	2	3	4	5	Total
Probability	$28\left(\frac{1}{64}\right) = \frac{28}{64}$	$\frac{1}{64}$	$119\left(\frac{1}{64}\right) = \frac{19}{64}$	$12\left(\frac{1}{64}\right) = \frac{12}{64}$	$4\left(\frac{1}{64}\right) = \frac{4}{64}$	$\frac{64}{64} = 1$

Test Your Understanding

Exercise 1: Derive the probability distribution of the following tables below.

Table 1

Scores	5	10	15	20	25	30	35	40	45	50
frequency	20	10	8	12	15	3	7	5	4	16

Table 2

Marks	1	2	3	4	5	Total
Frequency	30	X	20	10	25	100

Table 3 [Assume Y = 1.5X]

Scores	1	2	3	4	5	Total
Number of student	25	10	X	15	Y	100
Probability	0.25	K	0.2	0.15	0.3	1

Answer……………………………………………………………………………**[See Appendix]**

Exercise 2: The probability model below gives the probabilities of student marks in an examination.

Mark	1	2	3	4	5	6	Total
Probability	0.35	0.10	0.02	0.40	0.05	0.08	1

From the table above, determine the probability that a student is having the following marks;

1) Less than 4……………………………………………**[Answer: $\mathbf{0.45 = 45\%}$]**
2) More than 4……………………………………………**[Answer: $\mathbf{0.13 = 13\%}$]**
3) $P(2 \leq X < 4)$……………………………………………**[Answer: $\mathbf{0.12 = 12\%}$]**
4) $P(3 \leq X \leq 6)$……………………………………………**[Answer: $\mathbf{0.55 = 55\%}$]**

4.2 Probability expectation

Probability expectation is denoted E(X) or μ. Probability expectation is also known as the expected value or the mean value of a probability distribution. Probability expectation is calculated using the formula seen below.

$$\mathbf{E(X) = \sum[X_i(P_i)]} \quad \text{………………………………(1)}$$

Where; $\mathbf{E(X)}$ represents the expectation value of the probability

$\mathbf{X_i}$ Represents the actual value of the probability distribution

$\mathbf{P_i}$ Represents the probability distribution value

Example 1: A random variable X has probability distribution as shown on the table below. Use the table and find the expectation value of the variable X.

Actual Value (X)	−2	−1	0	1	2
Probability distribution value [P(X=x)]	0.3	0.1	0.15	0.4	0.05

Solution

Step 1: Formula. $E(X) = \sum[X_i(P_i)]$

Step 2: Data substitution and solving.

$E(X) = \sum[X_i(P_i)]$ ……………………………………………[Substitute data into the formula]

$E(X) = [-2(0.3)] + [-1(0.1)] + [0(0.15)] + [1(0.4)] + [2(0.05)]$ ……….[Simplify bracket]

$E(X) = [-0.6] + [-0.1] + [0] + [0.4] + [0.1]$ ………………[Remove bracket from equation]

$E(X) = -0.6 - 0.1 + 0 + 0.4 + 0.1$ ……………………………………………[Simplify equation]

$E(X) = \mathbf{-0.2}$

Example 2: The probability distribution of a random variable X is shown on the table below. With the help of this table, determine the expected value of the variable X.

X_i	1	2	3	4	5
$P_i(X=x)$	0.1	0.3	y	0.2	0.1

Solution

Step 1: Formula. $E(X) = \sum[X_i(P_i)]$

Step 2: Determine the value of the unknown. That is the value of (y).

a) State Formula. $\sum P_i = 1$, where; P_i ranges from P_1 to P_5.

b) Data substitution and solving

$\sum P_i = 1$ ……………………………………………………[Substitute data into the formula]

$0.1 + 0.3 + y + 0.2 + 0.1 = 1$ …………………………………[Simplify equation by addition]

$0.7 + y = 1$ ……………………………………………………[Collect like terms together]

$y = 1 - 0.7$ ……………………………………………[Simplify equation by subtraction]

$y = \mathbf{0.3}$ …………………………………………………………[Value of the unknown (y)]

Step 3: Data substitution and solving of expectation value of variable (X)

$E(X) = [1(0.1)] + [2(0.3)] + [3(0.3)] + [4(0.2)] + [5(0.1)]$ ………………[Simplify bracket]

$E(X) = [0.1] + [0.6] + [0.9] + [0.8] + [0.5]$ ……………………………………[Remove bracket]

$E(X) = 0.1 + 0.6 + 0.9 + 0.8 + 0.5$ …………………………[Simplify equation by addition]

$E(X) = \mathbf{2.9}$

Example 3: The probability distribution table of a given variable X is given below. Considering that the expected value is given to be 0.61, determine the value of the unknown given as z.

X	0	1	z	3
P(X=x)	0.51	0.38	0.10	0.01

Solution

Step 1: Formula. $E(X) = \sum[X_i(P_i)]$, where; $E(X) = 0.61$

Step 2: Data substitution and solving of unknown (z)

$E(X) = \sum[X_i(P_i)]$ ....[Substitute data values into formula]

$0.61 = [0(0.51)] + [1(0.38)] + [z(0.10)] + [3(0.01)]$ ....[Simplify bracket]

$0.61 = [0] + [0.38] + [0.10z] + [0.03]$ ....[Remove bracket]

$0.61 = 0 + 0.38 + 0.10z + 0.03$ ....[Simplify equation]

$0.61 = 0.41 + 0.10z$ ....[Collect like terms together]

$0.10z = 0.61 - 0.41$ ....[Simplify right side of equation by subtraction]

$0.10z = 0.2$ ....[Divide both sides by 0.10]

$z = \frac{0.2}{0.10}$ ....[Simplify fraction by division]

$z = \mathbf{2}$ ....[The value of the unknown (z)]

Example 4: Determine the probability mean from the frequency distribution table below

Amount [in dollar]	1	5	10	Total
Number of Students [X_i]	80	25	20	125

Solution

Step 1: Formula. $E(X) = \sum[X_i(P_i)]$, where; P_i = Unknown

Step 2: Determination of probability distribution table [P_i]

Amount [in dollar]	1	5	10	Total
Number of Students [X_i]	80	25	20	125
Probability distribution [P_i]	$\frac{80}{125} = \mathbf{0.64}$	$\frac{25}{125} = \mathbf{0.2}$	$\frac{20}{125} = \mathbf{0.16}$	1

Step 3: Data substitution and solving of average donation per student

$E(X) = \sum[X_i(P_i)]$ ....[Substitute data values into the equation]

$E(X) = [1(0.64)] + [5(0.2)] + [10(0.16)]$ ....[Simplify brackets]

$E(X) = \mathbf{3.24\ dollar}$

Note: It is worth knowing that the general formula of probability expectation seen above can be modified by adding values or exponents as seen below. Here, "n" will be representing a counting number.

$E\left(\frac{n}{X}\right) = \sum\left[\frac{n}{X_i}(P_i)\right]$ ....(1.1)

$E(X^n) = \sum[X_i{}^n(P_i)]$ ....(1.2)

$E(nX) = \sum[nX_i(P_i)]$ ....(1.3)

$E(n) = \sum[n(P_i)]$ ....(1.4)

$E(nX_i \pm nY_i) = E(nX_i) \pm E(nY_i)$ ....(1.5)

Note: $E(XY) \neq E(X)E(Y)$

Example 5: Use the probability distribution table below and answer the questions that follow.

Hours	1	2	3	4
Probabilities	0.2	0.3	0.2	0.3

Determine the values of the following;

1) $E\left(\frac{1}{X}\right)$ 2) $E(X^2)$ 3) $E(2X)$ 4) $E(4)$

Solution

1) $\mathbf{E\left(\frac{1}{X}\right)}$ ....[Probability expectation fraction situation]

Step 1: Formula. $E\left(\frac{n}{X}\right) \equiv E\left(\frac{1}{X}\right) = \sum\left[\frac{1}{X_1}(P_i)\right]$

Step 2: Data substitution and solving

$E\left(\frac{1}{X}\right) = \left[\frac{1}{1}(0.2)\right] + \left[\frac{1}{2}(0.3)\right] + \left[\frac{1}{3}(0.2)\right] + \left[\frac{1}{4}(0.3)\right]$ ....[Simplify fractions]

$E\left(\frac{1}{X}\right) = [1(0.2)] + [0.5(0.3)] + [0.333^+(0.2)] + [0.25(0.3)]$ ....[Simplify brackets]

$E\left(\frac{1}{X}\right) = [0.2] + [0.15] + [0.666^+] + [0.075]$ ....[Remove brackets]

$E\left(\frac{1}{X}\right) = 0.2 + 0.15 + 0.066666666 + 0.075$ ....[Simplify equation by addition]

$E\left(\frac{1}{X}\right) = \mathbf{0.49}$ ....[In two decimal places]

2) $\mathbf{E(X^2)}$ ....[Probability expectation exponent situation]

Step 1: Formula. $E(X^n) \equiv E(X^2) = \sum[X_i^2(P_i)]$

Step 2: Data substitution and solving

$E(X^2) = [1^2(0.2)] + [2^2(0.3)] + [3^2(0.2)] + [4^2(0.3)]$ ....[Simplify exponents]

$E(X^2) = [1(0.2)] + [4(0.3)] + [9(0.2)] + [16(0.3)]$ ....[Simplify bracket]

$E(X^2) = [0.2] + [1.2] + [1.8] + [4.8]$ ....[Remove bracket]

$E(X^2) = 0.2 + 1.2 + 1.8 + 4.8$ ....[Simplify equation by addition]

$E(X^2) = \mathbf{8}$

3) $\mathbf{E(2X)}$ ....[Probability expectation multiplication situation]

Step 1: Formula. $E(nX) \equiv E(2X) = \sum[2X_i(P_i)]$

Step 2: Data substitution and solving

$E(2X) = [2(1)(0.2)] + [2(2)(0.3)] + [2(3)(0.2)] + [2(4)(0.3)]$ ....[Simplify first brackets]

$E(2X) = [2(0.2)] + [2(0.3)] + [6(0.2)] + [8(0.3)]$ ....[Simplify second brackets]

$E(2X) = [0.4] + [0.6] + [1.2] + [2.4]$ ....[Remove brackets]

$E(2X) = 0.4 + 0.6 + 1.2 + 2.4$ ....[Simplify equation by addition]

$E(2X) = \mathbf{4.6}$

4) $\mathbf{E(4)}$ ....[Probability expectation only constant situation]

Step 1: Formula. $E(n) \equiv E(4) = \sum[4(P_i)]$

Step 2: Data substitution and solving

$E(4) = [4(0.2)] + [4(0.3)] + [4(0.2)] + [4(0.3)]$ ....[Simplify brackets]

$E(4) = [0.8] + [1.2] + [0.8] + [1.2]$ ....[Remove brackets]

$E(4) = 0.8 + 1.2 + 0.8 + 1.2$ ....[Simplify equation by addition]

$E(4) = \mathbf{4}$

Example 6: Use the probability distribution table below and answer the following questions

X_i	0	1	2
P(X= x)	0.3	0.3	0.4

Determine the values of the following:

1) $E(2X + 5)$ 2) $E(4 + X^2)$

Solution

1) (2X + 5)

Step 1: Formula. $E(nX + n) = E(nX) + E(n) = E(2X) + E(5) = \sum[2X_i(P_i)] + \sum[5(P_i)]$

Step 2: Data substitution and solving

$$E(2X) + E(5) = \{[2(0)(0.3)] + [2(1)(0.3)] + [2(2)(0.4)]\} + \{[5(0.3)] + [5(0.3)] + [5(0.4)]\}$$

$$E(2X) + E(5) = \{[0(0.3)] + [2(0.3)] + [4(0.4)]\} + \{[5(0.3)] + [5(0.3)] + [5(0.4)]\}$$

$$E(2X) + E(5) = \{[0] + [0.6] + [1.6]\} + \{[1.5] + [1.5] + [2]\}$$

$$E(2X) + E(5) = \{0 + 0.6 + 1.6\} + \{1.5 + 1.5 + 2\}$$

$$E(2X) + E(5) = \{2.2\} + \{5\}$$

$$E(2X) + E(5) = \mathbf{7.2}$$

2) $E(4 + X^2)$

Step 1: Formula. $E(4 + X^2) = E(4) + E(X^2) = \sum[4(P_i)] + \sum[X^2(P_i)]$

Step 1: Data substitution and solving

$$E(4) + E(X^2) = \{[4(0.3)] + [4(0.3)] + [4(0.4)]\} + \{[0^2(0.3)] + [1^2(0.3)] + [2^2(0.4)]\}$$

$$E(4) + E(X^2) = \{[4(0.3)] + [4(0.3)] + [4(0.4)]\} + \{[0(0.3)] + [1(0.3)] + [4(0.4)]\}$$

$$E(4) + E(X^2) = \{[1.2] + [1.2] + [1.6]\} + \{[0] + [0.3] + [1.6]\}$$

$$E(4) + E(X^2) = \{1.2 + 1.2 + 1.6\} + \{0 + 0.3 + 1.6\}$$

$$E(4) + E(X^2) = \{4\} + \{1.9\}$$

$$E(4) + E(X^2) = \mathbf{5.9}$$

Example 7: Given that the probability distribution below in which a = 2b, determine $E(X^2)$

X	5	11	19	21	24
P(x)	a	b	42/100	0.1	0.18

Solution

Hint: Since a = 2b, the above table can still be expressed as seen below.

X	5	11	19	21	24
P(x)	2b	b	$\frac{42}{100} = 0.42$	0.1	0.18

Step 1: Formula. $E(X^2) = \sum[X_i^{\,2}(P_i)]$. Note that not all values of $[(P_i) = (P(x))]$ are known

Step 2: Determination of the unknown. That is the values of "a" and "b"

a) Formula. $\sum P_i = 1$

b) Data substitution and solving

$1 = 2b + b + 0.42 + 0.1 + 0.18$ ....[Simplify right side of equation]

$1 = 3b + 0.7$ ....[Collect like terms together]

$3b = 1 - 0.7$ ....[Simplify right side of equation]

$3b = 0.3$ ....[Divide both sides of equation by 3]

$b = \frac{0.3}{3} = \mathbf{0.1}$ ....[Value of b]

$\text{if } a = 2b, \text{there } a = 2(0.1)$ ....[Simplify bracket by multiplication]

$a = \mathbf{0.2}$ ....[Value of a]

Note: The new working probability distribution table is now given as follows;

X	5	11	19	21	24	**Total**
P(x)	0.2	0.1	0.42	0.1	0.18	**1**

Step 3: Data substitution and solving

$$E(X^2) = [5^2(0.2)] + [11^2(0.1)] + [19^2(0.42)] + [21^2(0.1)] + [24^2(0.18)]$$

$$E(X^2) = [25(0.2)] + [121(0.1)] + [361(0.42)] + [441(0.1)] + [576(0.18)]$$

$$E(X^2) = [5] + [12.1] + [151.62] + [44.1] + [103.68]$$

$$E(X^2) = 5 + 12.1 + 151.62 + 44.1 + 103.68$$

$$E(X^2) = \mathbf{316.5}$$

<u>Test Your Understanding</u>

Exercise 3: Use the table below and answer the following questions

Values [Y]	0	1	2	3	4	5
Probabilities [P_i (Y = y)]	0.02	0.26	0.37	0.19	0.12	0.04

a) Justify if the table is a probability distribution table

[**Answer: Sum of probability is 1**]

b) Determine the expected value from the data in the table......................[**Answer: 2.25**]

Exercise 4: From the table below answer the questions that follows

X_i	30	20	10	1
$P_i(X=x)$	0.01	0.03	z	0.9

a) Determine the value of the missing probability (z). ....**[Answer: z = 0.06]**

b) Determine the value of E(X). ....**[Answer: 2.4]**

Exercise 5: Considering that the expected value is 1, from the table below, determine the value of z

X_i	0	1	3	Z **[Answer: 4]**
$P_i(X=x)$	0.45	0.35	0.15	0.05

Exercise 6: A college statistics class has 20 students. The ages of these students are as follows; one student is 16 years old, four students are 18 years old, nine students are 19 years old, three students are 20 years old, two students are 21 years old and one student is 30 years old. Let x represent the age of any student,

1) Construct the probability distribution of x. ....**[See appendix]**
2) Determine the average age of students. ....**[See appendix]**

4.3 Probability variance and standard deviation

Apart of probability expectation, the concept of probability variance and standard deviation is also worth examining. The formula used for the calculation of probability variance and standard deviation is given as;

$$\text{Variance } (\sigma^2) = \sum[(X-\mu)^2 P_i] \quad \ldots\ldots(1)$$

$$\text{Standard Deviation } (\sigma) = \sqrt{\sum[(X-\mu)^2 P_i]} \text{ or Standard deviation}(\sigma) = \sqrt{\sigma^2} \quad \ldots(2)$$

Example 1: Assuming the expected value of the probability distribution table of variable x below is given as 1.5; determine the value of Var (X) and standard deviation of X.

X	0	1	2	3
P(X=x)	0.125	0.375	0.375	0.125

Solution

a) Calculation of variance value of X

Step 1: Formula. Variance $(\sigma^2) = \sum[(X-\mu)^2 P_i]$, Where; $\mu = 1.5$

Step 2: Data substitution and solving

Variance $(\sigma^2) = \sum[(X-\mu)^2 P_i]$ ....[Substitute data values into the formula]

$\sigma^2 = [(0-1.5)^2 0.125] + [(1-1.5)^2 0.375] + [(2-1.5)^2 0.375] + [(3-1.5)^2 0.125]$

$\sigma^2 = [(-1.5)^2 0.125] + [(-0.5)^2 0.375] + [(0.5)^2 0.375] + [(1.5)^2 0.125]$

$\sigma^2 = [(2.25)0.125] + [(0.25)0.375] + [(0.25)0.375] + [(2.25)0.125]$

$\sigma^2 = [0.28125] + [0.09375] + [0.09375] + [0.28125]$

$\sigma^2 = \mathbf{0.75}$

b) Calculation of standard deviation value of X

Step 1: Standard Deviation $(\sigma) = \sqrt{\sum[(X-\mu)^2 P_i]}$ or $= \sqrt{\sigma^2}$, where; $\sigma^2 = 0.75$

Step 2: Data substitution and solving

$\sigma = \sqrt{0.75}$ ....[Simplify equation by square root]

$\sigma = \mathbf{0.87}$ ....[In two decimal places]

Example 2: Determine the probability variance and probability standard deviation using the probability distribution table below.

Values (X)	0	1	2	3	4	5
Probabilities [P(X=x)]	0.002	0.029	0.132	0.309	0.360	0.168

Solution

a) Calculation of variance value of X

Step 1: Formula. Variance $(\sigma^2) = \sum[(X-\mu)^2 P_i]$, Where; $\mu =$ Unknown

Step 2: Determination of expected value (μ)

a) Formula. $E(X) = \sum[X_i(P_i)]$

b) Data substitution and solving

$E(X) = [0(0.002)] + [1(0.029)] + [2(0.132)] + [3(0.309)] + [4(0.360)] + [5(0.168)]$

$E(X) = 0 + 0.029 + 0.264 + 0.927 + 1.44 + 0.84$

$E(X) = \mathbf{3.5}$ ....[The value of μ]

Step 3: Data substitution and solving

$$\left.\begin{array}{l}\sigma^2 = [(0-3.5)^2 0.002] + [(1-3.5)^2 0.029] + [(2-3.5)^5 0.132] \\ +[(3-3.5)^2 0.309] + [(4-3.5)^2 0.360] + [(5-3.5)^5 0.168]\end{array}\right\}$$

$\sigma^2 = 0.0245 + 0.18125 + 0.297 + 0.07725 + 0.09 + 0.378$

$\sigma^2 = \mathbf{1.048}$

b) Calculation of standard deviation value of X

Step 1: Standard Deviation $(\sigma) = \sqrt{\Sigma[(X-\mu)^2 P_i]}$ or $= \sqrt{\sigma^2}$, where; $\sigma^2 = 1.048$

Step 2: Data substitution and solving

$(\sigma) = \sqrt{\sigma^2}$ ....[Substitute data value into the formula]

$\sigma = \sqrt{1.048}$ ....[Simplify equation by square root]

$\sigma = \mathbf{1.02}$ ....[In two decimal places]

Test Your Understanding

Exercise 7: The probability distribution table of a discrete variable is given below

X	0	1	2	3	4
P [X=x]	0.1	0.4	0.2	0.1	0.2

Determine the value of the following

a) Var (X).. **[Answer: 1.69]**

b) Standard deviation of variable X ....**[Answer: 1.3]**

Example 8: Use the probability distribution table below and answer the question that follows. Leave answers in two decimal places.

Y	0	1	2	3
P [Y = y]	1/8	3/8	2/8	z

1) What is the value of Z? ....**[Answer: Z = 0.25]**

2) Calculate the variance of Y $[\sigma^2(Y)]$ ....**[Answer: 0.98]**

3) Determine the standard deviation of Y $[\sigma(Y)]$ ....**[Answer: 0.99]**

4.4 Permutation and Combination

4.4.1 The Concept of Factorial

Christian Kramp

The determination of permutation and combination of items or events can be done with the application of the idea of factorial [!]. Factorial is the multiplied value from the factorial number (that is the number or coefficient in front of the factorial sign) to the factorial smallest value (1). Factorial elements are those items or events that are between the factorial number and factorial smallest value.

The general elements of a factorial are the sum of the elements of the factorial number, factorial element and factorial smallest number.

Example 1: Identify the factorial number, factorial smallest value and factorial element of 4-factorial.

Solution

Hint. 4-factorial can also be written as 4!.

1) Factorial number: The coefficient in front of the factorial sign is 4. Therefore, the factorial number is 4.
2) Factorial smallest value: It is worth knowing that by default, the factorial smallest value is 1.
3) Factorial element: The number between the factorial number (4) and the factorial smallest number (1) are 3 and 2.

Therefore, the general element of a 4-factorial are; 4 (from the factorial number), 3, 2 (from the factorial element) and 1 (from factorial smallest number).

Example 2: Expand the expression 8!.

Solution

Step 1: Derivation of factorial general element.

1) Factorial number: 8
2) Factorial smallest value: 1
3) Factorial element: 7, 6, 5, 4, 3 and 2

.[Factorial general elements are; 8,7,6,4,3,2, 1]

Step 2: Derivation of expand form of factorial.

Expand form of 8! $= \mathbf{8 \times 7 \times 6 \times 5 \times 4 \times 3 \times 2 \times 1}$

Example 3: Determine the value of 5-factorial [5!]

Solution

Step 1: Derivation of factorial general element.

1) Factorial number: 5
2) Factorial smallest value: 1
3) Factorial element: 4, 3 and 2

Therefore, factorial general element are; **5, 4, 3, 2 and 1.**

Step 2: Derivation of factorial value.

$5! = 5 \times 4 \times 3 \times 2 \times 1$ ....[Simplify equation]

$5! = \mathbf{120}$

Example 4: Determine the value of $\frac{6!}{4!}$

<u>**Solution**</u>

$\frac{6!}{4!} = \frac{6\times5\times4\times3\times2\times1}{4\times3\times2\times1}$ ....[Simplify numerator and denominator]

$\frac{6!}{4!} = \frac{720}{24}$ ....[Simplify fraction]

$\frac{6!}{4!} = \mathbf{30}$

Example 5: Determine the value of $\frac{5!4!}{5!}$

<u>**Solution**</u>

a) Method 1

$\frac{5!4!}{5!} \equiv \left\{\frac{[5\times4\times3\times2\times1][4\times3\times2\times1]}{5\times4\times3\times2\times1}\right\}$ ....[Simplify brackets and denominator]

$\frac{5!4!}{5!} \equiv \left\{\frac{[120][24]}{120}\right\}$ ....[Expand bracket of numerator]

$\frac{5!4!}{5!} \equiv \frac{2,880}{120}$ ....[Simplify fraction by division]

$\frac{5!4!}{5!} = \mathbf{24}$

Method 2:

Using large factorial	**Using small factorial**
$\frac{5!4!}{5!} \equiv \frac{4!}{1}$ ....[Expand and solve problem]	$\frac{5!4!}{5!} \equiv \frac{5!}{5}$ ....[Expand and solve problem]
$\frac{4\times3\times2\times1}{1}$ ....[Simplify numerator]	$\frac{5!4!}{5!} = \frac{5\times4\times3\times2\times1}{5}$ ....[Simplify numerator]
$\frac{5!4!}{5!} = \mathbf{24}$	$\frac{5!4!}{5!} = \frac{120}{5}$ ....[Simplify fraction]
	$\frac{5!4!}{5!} = \mathbf{24}$

4.4.2 The concept of permutation

Permutation problems are those who made use of the word orderly in the arrangement of items. The general formula used to determine the number of possible arrangement using the idea of permutation is given as;

$$\mathbf{nPr} = \frac{n!}{[n-r]!} \quad \text{...(1)}$$

Where: **nPr** represent the number of possible arrangment

n represents the total number of possible items

r represents the given number of items from the entire possible items.

Note: The value of **r** must be greater or equal to zero and lesser or equal to **n**.

Example 1: A computer requires 3 letters orderly password. Determine how many 10 letters passwords can be made considering that no word is used twice.

Solution

Hint: The nature of item here is letters, in which the total number of letters is 26 [that is from A to Z] and the given number of item here is 3 letters.

Step 1: Formula. Number of Possible Arrangment $= \frac{n!}{[n-r]!}$, where; n = 26 and r = 3

Step 2: Data substitution and solving.

Number of Possible Arrangment $= \frac{26!}{[26-3]!}$ ....[Simplify denominator by subtraction]

Number of Possible Arrangment $= \frac{26!}{[23]!}$ ....[Expand denominator]

Number of Possible Arrangment $= \frac{26!}{23!}$ ....[Work factorial of numerator and denominator]

Number of Possible Arrangment $= \frac{26!}{23!} = \frac{26\times25\times24}{1}$.....................,[Simplify numerator]

Number of Possible Arrangment $= \mathbf{15.600}$

Step 3: Interpretation: There are 15,600 possible arrangement of 3 letter password from the entire letter without any usage twice of any letter.

Example 2: How many arrangements can be made using 4 letters from the word CAMEROON if no letter is used more than once?

Solution

Hint: Even though the nature of item here are letters, the total possible occurrence of the letters in this case is limited to the word CAMEROON and not the entire letters from A to Z. Therefore, the total possible items occurrence here is 8 (as there are 8 letters in the word CAMEROON).

Step 1: Formula and data. Number of Possible Arrangment $= \frac{n!}{[n-r]!}$, where; n = 8 and r = 4

Step 2: Data substitution and solving.

Number of Possible Arrangment $= \frac{8!}{[8-4]!}$ .... [Simplify denominator by subtraction]

Number of Possible Arrangment $= \frac{8!}{4!}$ .....[Work factorial of numerator and denominator]

Number of Possible Arrangment $= \frac{40,320}{24}$ ....[Simplify fraction by division]

Number of Possible Arrangment $= \mathbf{1,680}$

Step 3: Interpretation: There are 1,680 four letters possible arrangements from the word CAMEROON without any use more than once.

4.4.3 The concept of combination

Combination problems ignore the idea or orderliness in arrangement. The general formula used for the determination of number of possible arrangement using the idea of combination is given as;

$\mathbf{nPr} = \frac{n!}{r![n-r]!}$ ....(2)

Where: **nPr** represent the number of possible arrangment

n represents the total number of possible items

r represents the given number of items from the entire possible items.

Note: The value of **r** must be greater or equal to zero and lesser or equal to **n**.

Example 1: A DJ in Jakiri wishes to select 6 songs from an album containing 16 songs. How many 6-song selections can he possibly made?

Solution

Step 1: Formula. Number of Possible Arrangment $= \frac{n!}{r![n-r]!}$, where; n = 16 and r = 6

Step 2: Data substitution and solving

Number of Possible Arrangment $= \frac{16!}{6![16-6]!}$ ....[Simplify denominator bracket]

Number of Possible Arrangment $= \frac{16!}{6![10]!}$ ....[Multiply denominator bracket factorial sign]

Number of Possible Arrangment $= \frac{16\times15\times14\times13\times12\times11}{6!} = \frac{5,765,760}{720}$ ....[Simplify fraction]

Number of Possible Arrangment $= \mathbf{8,008}$ ....[8,008 possible 6 song selection]

Example 2: How many different arrangements can be made using 4 letters from the word AMERICA?

Solution

Step 1: Number of Possible Arrangment $= \frac{n!}{r![n-r]!}$, where; n = 7 and r = 4

Step 2: Data substitution and solving

Number of Possible Arrangment $= \frac{7!}{4![7-4]!}$ ....[Simplify denominator bracket by subtraction]

Number of Possible Arrangment $= \frac{7!}{4![3]!}$ ....[Multiply denominator bracket factorial sign]

$\text{Number of Possible Arrangment} = \frac{7!}{4!3!}$ ....[Solve factorial of numerator and denominator]

$\text{Number of Possible Arrangment} = \frac{7 \times 6 \times 5}{3!} \equiv \frac{210}{6}$ ....[Simplify fraction]

$\text{Number of Possible Arrangment} = \mathbf{35}$

Step 3: Interpretation: There are 35 possible 4 letters arrangements from the word AMERICA.

Test Your Understanding

Exercise 9: Determine the value of the following factorial problem;

a) $\frac{10!}{6!}$. .... **[Answer: 5,040]**	c) $\frac{10!}{6!4!}$ .... **[Answer: 210]**
b) $\frac{20!2!}{15!}$. ....**[Answer: 3,720,960]**	d) $\frac{8!2!}{5!1!}$. ....**[Answer: 672]**

Exercise 10: A diplomatic document safe requires 4 numbers passwords. Considering that the producer of this safe is given numbers from 1 to 15, determine how many 4 number password can be arranged if no two numbers are used more than one time

[Answer: 32,760 arrangements]

Exercise 11: How many different arrangements can be made using 6 if no letter is used more than once? ....**[Answer: 165,765,600 arrangements]**

Exercise 12: Using the concept of combination, determine how many 3 students selection can be made from a class of 30 students? .... **[Answer: 4,060 arrangements]**

Exercise 13: How many different arrangements can be made using 2 letters from the word "BIENVENUE" assuming no word is used twice using the following concept?

1) Permutation.. **[Answer: 72 arrangements]**
2) Combination ....**[Answer: 36 arrangements]**

CHAPTER FIVE

SPECIAL PROBABILITY DISTRIBUTIONS

Here, we are going to the examine major types of discrete and continuous probability distributions such as; binomial distribution, Poisson distribution and normal distribution respectively

5.1 Binomial distribution

A binomial distribution is a discrete probability distribution that satisfies the following conditions or requirements;

Jacob Bernoulli

1) It is made up of a countable or finite set of experiments or trials (n).
2) Each trial (n) results in either a success (p) or a failure (q), such that their sum equal one$[p + q = 1]$. Note that the value for p and q are the same for all trials or experiments.
3) The outcomes or results of the different trials are independent and interest is in the number of successes in the total number of trials (n).

In summary, it is a type of probability which involves a given (fixed) number of independent trials with only two possible outcomes (success or failure which is the same for each trial).

5.1.1 Binomial Probability

Binomial probability is denoted as; Bin or Simply as B. The probability of a discrete random variable (X), is modeled in binomial probability distribution as; $X \sim Bin(np)$ or $X \sim B(np)$. The probability of an exactly (r) success from a given set of independent trials (n) is calculated using the formula;

$$P(X = r) = \frac{n!}{r!(n-r)!}(p^r \times q^{n-r}) \quad \text{...(1)}$$

Where; $r = \text{Exact trial}$

$n = \text{Total number of trials}$

$P = \text{The probability of success}$

$q = \text{The probability of failure} = 1 - P$

Example 1: A bag contains balls of which 40% are red and the rest yellow. A ball is taken from the bag, its colour noted and replaced. Considering that this activity is performed nine times, calculate the probability that;

1) Exactly three will be red [P (x = 3)]
2) At least one will be red [P(x ≥ 1)]
3) More than seven will be yellow [P(x > 7)]

Solution

1) **Exactly three will be red [P (x = 3)]**

Step 1: Formula. $P(X = 3) = \frac{n!}{r!(n-r)!}(p^r \times q^{n-r})$, where; n = 9, r = 3, p = 0.4 and q = 0.6

Step 2: Data substitution and solving

$P(X = 3) = \frac{9!}{3!(9-3)!}(0.4^3 \times 0.6^{9-3})$ ....[Simplify bracket and exponent]

$P(X = 3) = \frac{9!}{3!6!}(0.4^3 \times 0.6^6)$ ....[Work exponent and factorial]

$P(X = 3) = \frac{362{,}880}{6 \times 720}(0.064 \times 0.046656)$ ....[Simplify fraction and bracket]

$P(X = 3) = 84(0.002985984)$ ....[Solve equation]

$P(X = 3) = \mathbf{0.25} = \mathbf{25\%}$ ....[In two decimal places]

2) **At least one will be red [P(x ≥ 1)]**

Step 1: Formula. $P(x \geq 1) = 1 - P(x < 1) \equiv P(x \geq 1) = 1 - P(X = 0)$

Where; n = 9, r = 0, p = 0.4 and q = 0.6

Step 2: Data substitution and solving

$P(x \geq 1) = 1 - \frac{9!}{0!(9-0)!}(0.4^0 \times 0.6^{9-0})$ ....[Simplify fraction and exponent]

$P(x \geq 1) = 1 - \frac{9!}{0!9!}(0.4^0 \times 0.6^9)$ ....[Work exponent and factorial]

$P(x \geq 1) = 1 - \frac{362{,}880}{1 \times 362{,}880}(1 \times 0.010077696)$ ....[Simplify fraction and bracket]

$P(x \geq 1) = 1 - 1(0.010077696)$ ....[Solve equation]

$P(x \geq 1) = \mathbf{0.99} = \mathbf{99\%}$ ....[In two decimal places]

3) **More than seven will be yellow [P(x > 7)]**

Step 1: Formula. $P(x > 7) = P(x = 8) + P(x = 9)$...............................**[Progressive method]**

Step 2: Calculation of individual probabilities

a) Calculating $P(x = 8)$

i) Formula. $P(x = 8) = \frac{n!}{r!(n-r)!}(p^r \times q^{n-r})$, where; n = 9, r = 8, p = 0.6 and q = 0.4

ii) Data substitution and solving

$P(x = 8) = \frac{9!}{8!(9-8)!}(0.6^8 \times 0.4^{9-8})$ ....[Simplify bracket and exponent]

$P(x = 8) = \frac{9!}{8!1!}(0.6^8 \times 0.4^1)$ ....[Work exponent and factorial]

$P(x = 8) = \frac{362{,}880}{40{,}320 \times 1}(0.01679616 \times 0.4)$ ....[Simplify fraction and bracket]

$P(x = 8) = 9(0.006718464)$ ....[Solve equation]

$P(x = 8) = \mathbf{0.06} = \mathbf{6\%}$ ....[Two decimal places]

b) Calculating $P(X = 9)$

i) Formula. $P(x = 9) = \frac{n!}{r!(n-r)!}(p^r \times q^{n-r})$, where; n = 9, r = 9, p = 0.6 and q = 0.4

ii) Data substitution and solving

$P(x = 9) = \frac{9!}{9!(9-9)!}(0.6^9 \times 0.4^{9-9})$ ....[Simplify bracket and exponent]

$P(x = 9) = \frac{9!}{9!0!}(0.6^9 \times 0.4^0)$ ....[Work exponent and factorial]

$P(x = 9) = \frac{362{,}880}{362{,}880 \times 1}(0.010077696 \times 1)$ ....[Simplify fraction and bracket]

$P(x = 9) = 1(0.010077696)$ ....[Solve equation]

$P(x = 9) = \mathbf{0.01} = \mathbf{1\%}$ ....[In two decimal places]

Step 3: Data substitution and solving

$P(x > 7) = 6\% + 1\%$ ....[Solve equation]

$P(x > 7) = \mathbf{7\%}$

Example 2: The random variable X is $Bin(6, 0.42)$. Fine the following probabilities;

1) $P(x = 6)$ 2) $P(x \leq 1)$ 3) $P(x \leq 4)$

Solution

1) P(x = 6)

Step 1: Formula. $P(x = 6) = \frac{n!}{r!(n-r)!}(p^r \times q^{n-r})$, where; n = 6, r = 6, p = 0.42 and q = 0.58

Step 2: Data substitution and solving

$P(x = 6) = \frac{6!}{6!(6-6)!}(0.42^6 \times 0.58^{6-6})$ ....[Simplify bracket and exponent]

$P(x = 6) = \frac{6!}{6!1!}(0.42^6 \times 0.58^0)$ ....[Work exponent and factorial]

$P(x = 6) = \frac{720}{702 \times 1}(0.005489031 \times 1)$ ....[Simplify fraction and brackets]

$P(x = 6) = 1(0.005489031)$ ....[Solve equation]

$P(x = 6) = \mathbf{0.01} = \mathbf{1\%}$ ....[In two decimal places]

2) $\mathbf{P(x \leq 1)}$

Step 1: Formula. $P(x \leq 1) = P(x = 0) + P(x = 1)$, where; p = 0.42 and q = 0.58

Step 2: Data substitution and solving

$P(x \leq 1) = \frac{6!}{0!(6-0)!}(0.42^0 \times 0.58^{6-0}) + \frac{6!}{1!(6-1)!}(0.42^1 \times 0.58^{6-1})$ ....[Simplify equation]

$P(x \leq 1) = \frac{6!}{0!6!}(0.42^0 \times 0.58^6) + \frac{6!}{1!5!}(0.42^1 \times 0.58^5)$ ....[Work exponent and factorial]

$P(x \leq 1) = \frac{720}{1\times720}(1 \times 0.038068692) + \frac{720}{1\times120}(0.42 \times 0.065635676)$...[Simplify equation]

$P(x \leq 1) = 1(0.038068692) + 6(0.027566984)$ ....,,,,,.........[Solve equation]

$P(x \leq 1) = \mathbf{0.55} = \mathbf{55\%}$ ....[In two decimal places]

3) $\mathbf{P(x \leq 4)}$

Step 1: Formula. $P(x \leq 4) = 1 - P(x > 4) = 1 - [P(x = 5) + P(x = 6)]$

Where; p = 0.42, q = 0.58

Step 2: Data substitution and solving

$P(x \leq 4) = 1 - \left[\frac{6!}{5!(6-5)!}(0.42^5 \times 0.58^{6-5}) + \frac{6!}{6!(6-6)!}(0.42^6 \times 0.58^{6-6})\right]$ ....[Simplify]

$P(x \leq 4) = 1 - \left[\frac{6!}{5!1!}(0.42^5 \times 0.58^1) + \frac{6!}{6!0!}(0.42^6 \times 0.58^0)\right]$.[Work power and factorial]

$P(x \leq 4) = 1 - \left[\frac{720}{120\times1}(0.013069123 \times 0.58) + \frac{720}{720\times1}(0.005489031 \times 1)\right]$...[Simplify]

$P(x \leq 4) = 1 - [6(0.007580091) + 1(0.005489031)]$ ....[Simplify bracket]

$P(x \leq 4) = 1 - 0.050969579$ ....[Solve equation]

$P(x \leq 4) = \mathbf{0.95} = \mathbf{95\%}$ ....[In two decimal places]

Example 3: The probability that a match stick will break on being stuck is 0.04. What is the probability that out of a box of 50 sticks,

1) None will break
2) More than 2 will break

Solution

1) None will break

a) Method 1[Using none will break idea]. That is $P(x = 0)$

Step1: Formula. $P(x = 0) = \frac{n!}{r!(n-r)!}(p^r \times q^{n-r})$, where; $n = 50, r = 0, p = 0.04, q = 0.96$

Step 2: Data substitution and solving. Note that $[0! = 1]$

$P(x = 0) = \frac{50!}{0!(50-0)!}(0.04^0 \times 0.96^{50-0})$.....................[Simplify bracket and exponent]

$P(x = 0) = \frac{\cancel{50!}}{0!\cancel{50}!}(0.04^0 \times 0.96^{50})$ ....[Work exponent and factorial]

$P(x = 0) = \frac{1}{1}(1 \times 0.129885793)$ ....[Solve equation]

$P(x = 0) = \mathbf{0.13 = 13\%}$ ....[In two decimal places]

b) Method 2 [Using all will not break]. That is $P(x = 50)$

Step 1: Formula. $P(x = 50) = \frac{n!}{r!(n-r)!}(p^r \times q^{n-r})$,where; $n = 50, r = 0, p = 0.96, q = 0.04$

Step 2: Data substitution and solving

$P(x = 50) = \frac{50!}{50!(50-50)!}(0.96^{50} \times 0.04^{50-50})$ ....[Simplify bracket and exponent]

$P(x = 50) = \frac{\cancel{50}!}{\cancel{50}!0!}(0.96^{50} \times 0.04^0)$ ....[Work exponent and factorial]

$P(x = 50) = \frac{1}{1}(0.129885793 \times 1)$ ....[Solve equation]

$P(x = 50) = \mathbf{0.13 = 13\%}$

2) More than 2 will break

Step 1: Formula. $P(x > 2) = 1 - P(x \leq 2) = 1 - [P(x = 0) + P(x = 1) + P(x = 2)]$

Step 2: Calculation of individual probabilities. $\mathbf{P(x = 0)} = 0.13$.[Already calculated in a above]

$\mathbf{P(x = 1)}$

a) Formula. $P(x = 1) = \frac{n!}{r!(n-r)!}(p^r \times q^{n-r})$, where; $n = 50, r = 1, p = 0.04, q = 0.96$

b) Data substitution and solving

$P(x = 1) = \frac{50!}{1!(50-1)!}(0.04^1 \times 0.96^{50-1})$..................[Simplify bracket and exponent]

$P(x = 1) = \frac{50!}{1!49!}(0.04^1 \times 0.96^{49}) == \frac{50 \times 49!}{1!49!}(0.04^1 \times 0.96^{49})$.........[Work exponent]

$P(x = 1) = \frac{50}{1}(0.04 \times 0.135297701)$ ....[Solve equation]

$P(x = 1) = \mathbf{0.27 = 27\%}$ ....[In two decimal places]

$\mathbf{P(x = 2)}$

a) Formula. $P(x = 2) = \frac{n!}{r!(n-r)!}(p^r \times q^{n-r})$, where; $n = 50, r = 2, p = 0.04, q = 0.96$

b) Data substitution and solving

$P(x = 2) = \frac{50!}{2!(50-2)!}(0.04^2 \times 0.96^{50-2})$..............[Simplify bracket and exponent]

$P(x = 2) = \frac{50!}{2!48!}(0.04^2 \times 0.96^{48}) = \frac{50\times49\times48!}{1!48!}(0.04^2 \times 0.96^{48})$

$P(x = 2) = \mathbf{0.28} = \mathbf{28\%}$ ....[In two decimal places]

Step 3: Data substitution and solving

$P(x > 2) = 1 - [0.13 + 0.27 + 0.28]$ ....[Simplify bracket]

$P(x > 2) = 1 - 0.68$ ....[Solve equation]

$P(x > 2) = 0.32 = 32\%$ ....[In two decimal places]

Example 4: An exam consist of 6 questions, each question having 4 possible answers or choices with only one choice being the correct answer. Considering that choosing the correct answer is the success event, calculate the following probabilities;

1) That the student will answer 4 questions correctly
2) That the student will have above average
3) That the student will fail the exam

Solution

Hint: When the probability of success is not given directly, we note the event of success and calculate the probability of success using the experimental probability formula $\left[P = \frac{\text{Number of success event}}{\text{Total number of events}}\right]$. Therefore, the probability of success equals $P(\text{Success}) = \frac{1}{4} = 0.25$.

1) That the student will answer 4 questions correctly

Step 1: Formula. $P(x = r) = \frac{n!}{r!(n-r)!}(p^r \times q^{n-r})$, where; $n = 6, r = 4, p = 0.25, q = 0.75$

Step 2: Data substitution and solving

$P(x = 4) = \frac{6!}{4!(6-4)!}(0.25^4 \times 0.75^{6-4})$ ....[Work exponent and factorial]

$P(x = 4) = \frac{720}{24\times2}(0.00390625 \times 0.5625)$ ....[Simplify fraction and bracket]

$P(x = 4) = \mathbf{0.014} = \mathbf{1.4\%}$ ....[In three decimal place]

2) That the student will have above average

Step 1: Formula. $P(x \geq 4) = P(x = 4) + P(x = 5) + P(x = 6)$, where; $p = 0.25, q = 0.75$

Step 2: Calculation of individual probabilities

$$P(x = 4) = \frac{6!}{4!(6-4)!}(0.25^4 \times 0.75^{6-4}) = 0.032958984$$

$$P(x = 5) = \frac{6!}{5!(6-5)!}(0.25^5 \times 0.75^{6-5}) = 0.004394531$$

$$P(x = 6) = \frac{6!}{6!(6-6)!}(0.25^6 \times 0.75^{6-6}) = 0.00024414$$

Step 3: Data substitution and solving

$$P(x \geq 4) = 0.032958984 + 0.004394531 + 0.00024414$$

$P(x \geq 4) = \mathbf{0.038} = \mathbf{3.8\%}$ ……………………………………[In three decimal places]

3) That the student will fail the exam

a) Method 1: The student will fail if he/she pass at most two questions $[P(X \leq 2)]$

Step 1: Formula. $P(X \leq 2) = P(x = 0) + P(x = 1) + P(x = 2)$, where; $p = 0.25$, $q = 0.75$

Step 2: Data substitution and solving

$$P(x \leq 2) = \frac{6!}{0!(6-0)!}(0.25^0 \times 0.75^{6-0}) + \frac{6!}{1!(6-1)!}(0.25^1 \times 0.75^{6-1}) + \frac{6!}{2!(6-2)!}(0.25^2 \times 0.75^{6-2})$$

$$P(x \leq 2) = \frac{6!}{0!6!}(0.25^0 \times 0.75^6) + \frac{6!}{1!5!}(0.25^1 \times 0.75^5) + \frac{6!}{2!4!}(0.25^2 \times 0.75^6)$$

$$P(x \leq 2) = 1(0.177978515) + 6(0.059326171) + 15(0.01977539)$$

$P(x \leq 2) = \mathbf{0.83} = \mathbf{83\%}$ ……………………………………[In two decimal places]

b) Method 2: The student will fail if he/she fails at least 4 question $[P(X \geq 4)]$

$$P(X \geq 4) = \frac{6!}{4!(6-4)!}(0.75^4 \times 0.25^{6-4}) + \frac{6!}{5!(6-5)!}(0.75^5 \times 0.25^{6-5}) + \frac{6!}{6!(6-6)!}(0.75^6 \times 0.25^{6-6})$$

$$P(X \geq 4) = \frac{6!}{4!2!}(0.75^4 \times 0.25^2) + \frac{6!}{5!1!}(0.75^5 \times 0.25^1) + \frac{6!}{6!0!}(0.75^6 \times 0.25^0)$$

$$P(X \geq 4) = 15(0.01977539) + 6(0.059326171) + 1(0.177978515)$$

$P(x \leq 2) = \mathbf{0.83} = \mathbf{83\%}$ ……………………………………[In two decimal places]

<u>Test Your Understanding</u>

Exercise 1: A study shows that 80% of students speak pidgin language in school. Considering that five students are selected at random, calculate the probability that;

1) Exactly three student speak pidgin language …………[**Answer: $\mathbf{0.2048 = 20.48\%}$**]
2) At most four student speak pidgin language ………[**Answer: $\mathbf{0.67232 = 67.232\%}$**]
3) No student speak pidgin language……………………[**Answer: $\mathbf{0.00032 = 0.032\%}$**]

Exercise 2: The random variable X is $B(15, 0.7)$. Fine the following probabilities; [Leave answer in three decimal places]

1) $P(x = 10)$. ....[Answer: $\mathbf{0.206 = 20.6\%}$]
2) $P(x \geq 14)$. ....[Answer: $\mathbf{0.025 = 2.5\%}$]
3) $P(x \leq 14)$. ....[Answer: $\mathbf{0.995 = 99.5\%}$]

Exercise 3: A coin with two sides (head and tail) is tossed 6 times. Considering that the experiment follows a binomial distribution, calculate the following probabilities; [Leave answer in 3 decimal]

1) That exactly 5 heads will be seen.................................... [Answer: $\mathbf{0.094 = 9.4\%}$]
2) More than 3 and less than and equal to 5 heads will be seen............[Answer: $\mathbf{32.8\%}$]
3) That no heads will be seen. ....[Answer: $\mathbf{0.016 = 1.6\%}$]

5.1.2 Probability Distribution table

The simple probability of a given trial is calculated using the exact trial probability formula given above. When calculating the cumulative probability of a given trial, we calculate the given trail simple probability and add to the sum of the trial previous simple probabilities. The cumulative probability of a given trial (r) from a set of independent trials (n) is calculated using the formula;

$$P(X = r) = \frac{n!}{r!(n-r)!}(p^r \times q^{n-r}) + \frac{n!}{(r-1)!(n-r-1)!}(p^{r-1} \times q^{n-r-1}) \quad \text{.....................................(1)}$$

Where; $\frac{n!}{r!(n-r)!}(p^r \times q^{n-r})$ ....[Probability of the said or given period]

$\frac{n!}{(r-1)!(n-r-1)!}(p^{r-1} \times q^{n-r-1})$ ....[Probability of the previous period]

Note: The first simple probability equals the first cumulative probability.

Example 1: The probability of customers paying with credit card in a shop is 0.5. Considering that 4 customers are selected at random, construct the following;

1) A simple binomial probability distribution table
2) Cumulative binomial probability distribution table

Solution

1) A simple binomial probability distribution table

Step 1: Calculation of individual probabilities

$$P(x = 0) = \frac{4!}{0!(4-0)!}(0.5^0 \times 0.5^{4-0}) = 0.0625$$

$$P(x = 1) = \frac{4!}{1!(4-1)!}(0.5^1 \times 0.5^{4-1}) = 0.25$$

$$P(x = 2) = \frac{4!}{2!(4-2)!}(0.5^2 \times 0.5^{4-2}) = 0.375$$

$$P(x = 3) = \frac{4!}{3!(4-3)!}(0.5^3 \times 0.5^{4-3}) = 0.25$$

$$P(x = 4) = \frac{4!}{4!(4-4)!}(0.5^4 \times 0.5^{4-4}) = 0.0625$$

Step 2: Presentation of probability distribution

X	0	1	2	3	4	Total
P(x = r)	0.0625	0.25	0.375	0.25	0.0625	1

2) Cumulative binomial probability distribution table

Step 1: Calculation of individual probabilities

$$P(x = 0) = \frac{4!}{0!(4-0)!}(0.5^0 \times 0.5^{4-0}) = 0.0625$$

$$P(x = 1) = P(x = 1) + P(x = 0) = \frac{4!}{1!(4-1)!}(0.5^1 \times 0.5^{4-1}) = 0.25 + 0.0625 = 0.3125$$

$$P(x = 2) = P(x = 2) + P(x = 1) = \frac{4!}{2!(4-2)!}(0.5^2 \times 0.5^{4-2}) = 0.375 + 0.3125 = 0.6875$$

$$P(x = 3) = P(x = 3) + P(x = 2) = \frac{4!}{3!(4-3)!}(0.5^3 \times 0.5^{4-3}) = 0.25 + 0.6875 = 0.9375$$

$$P(x = 4) = P(x = 4) + P(x = 3) = \frac{4!}{4!(4-4)!}(0.5^4 \times 0.5^{4-4}) = 0.0625 + 0.9375 = 1$$

Step 2: Presentation of probability distribution

X	0	1	2	3	4
P(x = n)	0.0625	0.3125	0.6875	0.9375	1

Example 2: The random variable X is $B(6, 0.8)$. Derive a binomial probability distribution for X.

Solution

Step 1: Calculation of individual probabilities

$P(x=0) = \frac{6!}{0!(6-0)!}(0.8^0 \times 0.2^{6-0}) = 0.000064$	$P(x=4) = \frac{6!}{4!(6-4)!}(0.8^4 \times 0.2^{6-4}) = 0.24576$
$P(x=1) = \frac{6!}{1!(6-1)!}(0.8^1 \times 0.2^{6-1}) = 0.001536$	$P(x=5) = \frac{6!}{5!(6-5)!}(0.8^5 \times 0.2^{6-5}) = 0.393216$
$P(x=2) = \frac{6!}{2!(6-2)!}(0.8^2 \times 0.2^{6-2}) = 0.01536$	$P(x=6) = \frac{6!}{6!(6-6)!}(0.8^6 \times 0.2^{6-6}) = 0.262144$
$P(x=3) = \frac{6!}{3!(6-3)!}(0.8^3 \times 0.2^{6-3}) = 0.08192$	

Step 2: Presentation of probability distribution

X	0	1	2	3	4	5	6
$P(x=n)$	0.000064	0.001536	0.01536	0.08192	0.24576	0.393216	0.262144

Example 3: Use the extract of the cumulative binomial probability distribution table for $X \sim B(4, 0.8)$ and find the following;

X	0	1	2	3	4
$P(x=n)$	0.0016	0.0272	0.1808	0.5904	1

1) $P(X=2)$, 2) $P(X \geq 3)$, 3) $P(X \leq 1)$, 4) $P(X \geq 1)$

Solution

1) $P(X=2)$

Hint: The cumulative probability value of $[P(X=2)$, that is $0.1808]$ given in the table above is a combination of the real value of $[P(X=2)]$ and the sum of previous probabilities$[P(X < 2)]$ which is the same as$[P(X \leq 1)]$. Therefore, the value 0.1808 is the value of the probability of$[P(X \leq 2)]$.

Step 1: Formula. $P(X=2) = P(X \leq 2) - P(X \leq 1)$

Where; $P(X \leq 2) = 0.1808$, $P(X \leq 1) = 0.0272$

Step 2: Data substitution and solving

$P(X=2) = 0.1808 - 0.0272$ ....[Solve equation]

$P(X=2) = \mathbf{0.1536 = 15.36\%}$

2) $P(X \geq 3)$

Step 1: Formula. $P(X \geq 3) = P(X=3) + P(X=4)$

Step 2: Calculation of individual probabilities

$\mathbf{P(X = 3)}$

1) Formula. $P(X = 3) = P(X \leq 3) - P(X \leq 2)$

   Where; $P(X \leq 3) = 0.5904$, $P(X \leq 2) = 0.1808$

2) Data substitution and solving

   $P(X = 3) = 0.5904 - 0.1808$ ……………………………………[Solve equation]

   $P(X = 3) = \mathbf{0.4096}$

$\mathbf{P(X = 4)}$

1) Formula. $P(X = 4) = P(X \leq 4) - P(X \leq 3)$

   Where; $P(X \leq 4) = 1$, $P(X \leq 3) = 0.5904$

2) Data substitution and solving

   $P(X = 4) = 1 - 0.5904$ ……………………………………[Solve equation]

   $P(X = 4) = \mathbf{0.4096}$

Step 3: Data substitution and solving

$P(X \geq 3) = 0.4096 + 0.4096$ ……………………………………[Solve equation]

$P(X \geq 3) = \mathbf{0.8192 = 81.92}\%$

3) $\mathbf{P(X \leq 1)}$

Step 1: Formula. $P(X \leq 1) = P(X = 0) + P(X = 1)$

Step 2: Calculation of individual probabilities

$P(X = 0) = 0.0016$......[Remember the first cumulative probability equal simple probability]

$\mathbf{P(X = 1)}$

1) Formula. $P(X = 1) = P(X \leq 1) - P(X < 1)$

   Where; $P(X \leq 1) = 0.0272$, $P(X < 1) = 0.0016$

2) Data substitution and solving

   $P(X = 1) = 0.0272 - 0.0016$ ……………………………………[Solve equation]

   $P(X = 1) = \mathbf{0.0256}$

Step 3: Data substitution and solving

$P(X \leq 1) = 0.0016 + 0.0256$ ……………………………………[Solve equation]

$P(X \leq 1) = \mathbf{0.0272 = 2.72}\%$

4) $\mathbf{P(X \geq 1)}$

Step 1: Formula. $P(X \geq 1) = 1 - P(X < 1) = 1 - P(X = 0)$, where; $P(X = 0) = 0.0016$

Step 2: Data substitution and solving

$P(X \geq 1) = 1 - 0.0016$ ……………………………………[Solve equation]

$P(X \geq 1) = \mathbf{0.9984 = 99.84}\%$

5.1.3 Expectation, Variance and Standard Deviation

1) **Expectation**

The term expectation or expected value is the mean value or average. The method and formula used in calculating expected value depends on the data given. That is;

Expected value$[E(X)] = np$ ....[When a success probability is given]

Expected value$[E(X)] = \sum[r \times P(X = r)]$...[When a probability distribution table is given]

Where: **n** is the total number of independent trials,

p is the given success probability

r is the individual trials values

$\mathbf{P(X = r)}$ is the probability of individual trials

Example 1: The probability that a driver must stop at any one traffic light along Yaoundé University is 40 percent. Considering that 15 set of traffic light are selected at random on the journey, determine the expected number of stops effectuated by the driver.

Solution

Step 1: Formula. Expected value$[E(X)] = np$, where; n = 15 and p = 0.4

Step 2: Data substitution and solving

Expected value$[E(X)] = 15 \times 0.4$ ....[Solve equation]

Expected value$[E(X)] = \mathbf{6}$ ....[He will make averagely 6 stops on the journey]

Example 2: The random variable X can be modeled by a binomial distribution with n = 3 and p = 0.5. Using this giving data,

1) Construct a binomial probability distribution table
2) From the table, determine the mean value

Solution

1) **Construct a binomial probability distribution table**

Step 1: Formula. $P(X = r) = \frac{n!}{r!(n-r)!}(p^r \times q^{n-1})$, where: p = 0.5 and r ranges from 0 to 3

Step 2: Calculation of individual trial probability

$$P(X = 0) = \frac{3!}{0!(3-0)!}(0.5^0 \times 0.5^{3-0}) = 0.125$$

$$P(X = 1) = \frac{3!}{1!(3-1)!}(0.5^1 \times 0.5^{3-1}) = 0.375$$

$$P(X = 2) = \frac{3!}{2!(3-2)!}(0.5^2 \times 0.5^{3-2}) = 0.375$$

$$P(X = 3) = \frac{3!}{3!(3-3)!}(0.5^3 \times 0.5^{3-3}) = 0.125$$

Step 3: Drawing of binomial probability distribution table

Variable (r)	0	1	2	3	Total
Probability [P(X = r)]	0.125	0.375	0.375	0.125	1

2) From the table, determine the mean value

Step 1: Formula. $\text{Expected value}[E(X)] = \sum[r \times P(X = r)]$

Step 2: Data substitution and solving

$\text{Expected value}[E(X)] = (0 \times 0.125) + (1 \times 0.375) + (2 \times 0.375) + (3 \times 0.125)$

$\text{Expected value}[E(X)] = (0) + (0.375) + (0.75) + (0.375)$ ....[Expand bracket]

$\text{Expected value}[E(X)] = 0 + 0.375 + 0.75 + 0.375$ ....[Solve equation]

$\text{Expected value}[E(X)] = \mathbf{1.5}$

Example 3: A random variable X can be modeled by a binomial distribution as $X \sim B(4, 0.6)$. The cumulative probability distribution table derived from this function is seen below. Use the table and compute the average value.

Variable (r)	0	1	2	3	4
Probability [P(X = r)]	0.0256	0.1792	0.5248	0.8704	1

Solution

Step 1: Change the cumulative table to simple table

a) Converting cumulative probabilities to simple probabilities

$P(X = 0) = \mathbf{0.0256}$

$P(X = 1) = P(\leq 1) - P(X = 0) = 0.1792 - 0.0256 = \mathbf{0.1536}$

$P(X = 2) = P(X \leq 2) - P(X \leq 1) = 0.5248 - 0.1792 = \mathbf{0.3456}$

$P(X = 3) = P(X \leq 3) - P(X \leq 2) = 0.8704 - 0.5248 = \mathbf{0.3456}$

$P(X = 4) = P(X \leq 4) - P(X \leq 3) = 1 - 0.8704 = \mathbf{0.1296}$

b) Construction of simple binomial probability distribution table

Variable (r)	0	1	2	3	4	Total
Probability [P(X = r)]	0.0256	0.1536	0.3456	0.3456	0.1296	1

Step 2: Calculation of average value

a) Formula. $\text{Expected value}[E(X)] = \sum[r \times P(X = r)]$

b) Data substitution and solving

$E(X) = (0 \times 0.0256) + (1 \times 0.1536) + (2 \times 0.3456) + (3 \times 0.3456) + (4 \times 0.1296)$

$E(X) = (0) + (0.1536) + (0.6912) + (1.0368) + (0.5184)$ ………[Expand bracket]

$E(X) = 0 + 0.1536 + 0.6912 + 1.0368 + 0.5184$ ……………………[Solve equation]

$E(X) = \mathbf{2.4}$

Example 4: The table below is the binomial probability distribution of a random variable X modeled as $X \sim \text{Bin}(4, 0.7)$. Find the value of the missing probability (x and y) considering that the mean value is 2.8 and that $y - x = 0.336$.

Variable	0	1	2	3	4	Total
P(X = r)	0.0081	0.0756 (x)	0.2646	0.4116 (y)	0.2401	1

Solution

Step 1: Formula. Expected value$[E(X)] = \sum[r \times P(X = r)]$

Where; $E(X) = 2.8$, $y = 0{,}336 + x$ and $x = -0.336 + y$

Step 2: Data substitution and solving

a) **Method 1: Solving for y**

$2.8 = (0 \times 0.0081) + (1 \times [-0.336 + y]) + (2 \times 0.2646) + (3 \times y) + (4 \times 0.2401)$

$2.8 = (0) + (-0.336 + y) + (0.5292) + (3y) + (0.9604)$ ……………[Expand bracket]

$2.8 = 0 - 0.336 + y + 0.5292 + 3y + 0.9604$ ………………[Collect like terms together]

$2.8 - 0 + 0.336 - 0.5292 - 0.9604 = y + 3y$ ………………………[Simplify equation]

$4y = 1.6464$ …………………………………………[Divide both sides of equation by 4]

$y = \mathbf{0.4116}$

b) **Method 2: solving for x**

$2.8 = (0 \times 0.0081) + (1 \times x) + (2 \times 0.2646) + (3 \times [0.336 + x]) + (4 \times 0.2401)$

$2.8 = (0) + (x) + (0.5292) + (1.008 + 3x) + (0.9604)$ ………………[Expand brackets]

$2.8 = 0 + x + 0.5292 + 1.008 + 3x + 0.9604$ ………………[Collect like terms together]

$2.8 - 0 - 0.5292 - 1.008 - 0.9604 = x + 3x$ ………………………[Simplify equation]

$4x = 0.3024$ …………………………………………[Divide both sides of equation by 4]

$x = \mathbf{0.0756}$

Step 3: Probability distribution table filling and justification

Variable	0	1	2	3	4	Total
P(X = r)	0.0081	0.0756	0.2646	0.4116	0.2401	1

Note: The binomial probability distribution table above is justified as the sum of the entire individual trial probabilities equal 1.

2) Variance and Standard Deviation

The formula used for the calculation of variance $[\mathrm{Var(X)}]$ and standard deviation $[\mathrm{SD(X)}]$ is;

$\text{Variance } [\mathrm{Var(X)}] = \mathrm{np}(1-\mathrm{p}) \text{ or } \mathrm{npq}$ ....(1)

$\text{Standard deviation} = \sqrt{\mathrm{np}(1-\mathrm{p})} \text{ or} \sqrt{\mathrm{Var(X)}}$ ....(2)

Example 1: A random variable X follows a binomial probability distribution and is modeled as $\mathrm{X} \sim \mathrm{B}(10, 0.65)$. Determine the following;

1) Variance value
2) Standard deviation value

Solution

1) Variance value

Step 1: Formula. $\text{Variance } [\mathrm{Var(X)}] = \mathrm{np}(1-\mathrm{p})$, where; n = 10 and p = 0.65

Step 2: Data substitution and solving

$\text{Variance } [\mathrm{Var(X)}] = 10 \times 0.65(1-0.65)$ ....[Simplify and expand bracket]

$\text{Variance } [\mathrm{Var(X)}] = 6.5(0.35)$ ....[Solve equation]

$\text{Variance } [\mathrm{Var(X)}] = \mathbf{2.275}$

2) Standard deviation value

Step 1: Formula. $\text{Standard deviation} = \sqrt{\mathrm{np}(1-\mathrm{p})}$, where; n = 10 and p = 0.65

Step 2: Data substitution and solving

$\text{Standard deviation} = \sqrt{10 \times 0.65(1-0.65)}$ ....[Simplify equation]

$\text{Standard deviation} = \sqrt{6.5(0.35)}$ ....[Expand bracket and work root]

$\text{Standard deviation} = \mathbf{1.508}$ ....[In three decimal places]

Example 2: A survey from the national institute of statistics shows that 10% of teachers received their spending money from part-time schools. The binomial probability distribution table showing this survey is illustrated below

Variable	0	1	2	3	4
Probabilities	0.6561	0.2916	0.0486	0.0036	0.0001

1) Determine the variance
2) Compute the value of standard deviation

Solution

1) Determine the variance

Method 1: Tabula technique

a) Formula. $Var(X) = E(X^2) - E(X)^2$, where; $E(X^2) = r^2 \times P(r)$, $E(X) = r \times P(r)$

b) Tabular determination of formula components

Variable (r)	Probability [P(r)]	$r \times P(r)$	r^2	$r^2 \times P(r)$
0	0.6561	$0 \times 0.6561 = 0$	$0^2 = 0$	$0 \times 0.6561 = 0$
1	0.2916	$1 \times 0.2916 = 0.2916$	$1^2 = 1$	$1 \times 0.2916 = 0.2916$
2	0.0486	$2 \times 0.0486 = 0.0972$	$2^2 = 4$	$4 \times 0.0486 = 0.1944$
3	0.0036	$3 \times 0.0036 = 0.0108$	$3^2 = 9$	$9 \times 0.0036 = 0.0324$
4	0.0001	$4 \times 0.0001 = 0.0004$	$4^2 = 16$	$16 \times 0.0001 = 0.0016$
		$\mathbf{E(X) = 0.4}$		$\mathbf{E(X^2) = 0.52}$

c) Data substitution and solving

$Var(X) = 0.52 - 0.4^2$ ....[Work exponent]

$Var(X) = 0.52 - 0.16$ ....[Solve equation]

$Var(X) = \mathbf{0.36}$

Method 2: Algebraic technique

Step 1: Formula. $Var(X) = E(X^2) - E(X)^2$, where; $E(X^2) = r^2 \times P(r)$, $E(X) = r \times P(r)$

Step 2: Calculation of formula components ($E(X^2)$ and $E(X)^2$)

a) Derivation of $E(X^2)$

$$E(X^2) = (0^2 \times 0.6561) + (1^2 \times 0.2916) + (2^2 \times 0.0486) + (3^2 \times 0.0036) + (4^2 \times 0.0001)$$

$$E(X^2) = (0 \times 0.6561) + (1 \times 0.2916) + (4 \times 0.0486) + (9 \times 0.0036) + (16 \times 0.0001)$$

$$E(X^2) = (0) + (0.2916) + (0.1944) + (0.0324) + (0.0016)$$

$$E(X^2) = \mathbf{0.52}$$

b) Derivation of $E(X)^2$

$$E(X)^2 = \{(0 \times 0.6561) + (1 \times 0.2916) + (2 \times 0.0486) + (3 \times 0.0036) + (4 \times 0.0001)\}^2$$

$$E(X)^2 = \{(0) + (0.2916) + (0.0972) + (0.0108) + (0.0004)\}^2$$

$E(X)^2 = \{0.4\}^2$ ....[Work exponent]

$E(X)^2 = \mathbf{0.16}$

Step 3: Data substitution and solving

$\text{Var}(X) = 0.52 - 0.16$ ....[Solve equation]

$\text{Var}(X) = \mathbf{0.36}$

2) Compute the value of standard deviation

Step 1: Formula. Standard deviation $= \sqrt{\text{Var}(X)}$, where; $\text{Var}(X) = 0.36$

Step 2: Data substitution and solving

$\text{Standard deviation} = \sqrt{0.36}$ ....[Square root value]

$\text{Standard deviation} = \mathbf{0.6}$

<u>Test Your Understanding</u>

Exercise 4: The probability of police receiving calls in a given random selected hour is 0.2. Considering that 5 calls are made in a given hour, construct the following;

1) Simple binomial probability distribution table ....**[Answer (See appendix)]**
2) Cumulative binomial probability distribution table ....**[Answer (See appendix)]**

Exercise 5: A random variable X is modeled by binomial probability distribution as; $X \sim \text{Bin}(15{,}0.45)$. Calculate the following

1) $\text{E}(X)$. ....**[Answer: 6.75]**
2) $\text{Var}(X)$ [Answer: **3.7125**] and Standard deviation............. **[Answer: 1.926784887]**

Exercise 6: The probability of accident in Limbe-Douala road is 40 percent per month. Giving that in a given month there are 60 accidents, calculate the following;

1) The expected number of accident.. **[Answer: 24]**
2) The variance.. **[Answer: 14.4]**
3) Standard deviation... **[Answer: 3.794733192]**

Exercise 7: The simple probability distribution table below represents that of a random variable X modeled by a binomial distribution.

Variable (r)	0	1	2	(y)	4	5
Probability [P(X = r)]	0.07776	0.2592	0.3456	(z)	0.0768	0.01024

1) Considering that mean is 2, determine the value of z and y

[Answer: z = $\mathbf{0.2304}$ and y = 3]

2) Calculate the value of standard deviation. ....**[Answer: 1.095445115]**

5.2 Poisson Distribution

Poisson distribution is also called distribution of rare events. Poisson is seen as event that occurs in a continuous process but in a finite interval of time and/or space. Poisson probability is a discrete probability for the count of event (X) that occurs singly and randomly in a given interval of time and space (place). A Poisson random variable can take any positive integer value and Poisson distribution is unimodal in nature.

Simeon D. Poisson

The probability of observing an event (X) in a given interval following a poison distribution is modeled as; $[X \sim Po(\lambda)]$ and is calculated using the formula;

$$P(X = x) = e^{-\lambda}\left(\frac{\lambda^x}{x!}\right) \quad \text{...(1)}$$

Where; λ represents the mean or average of an event or of event per interval

X represents the number of event interval

Note: Poisson distribution can also be used as an approximation for binomial distribution if and only if the given trial is large $[n > 50]$ and the probability rate is small$[P < 0.1]$. Since binomial probability does not make use of average, the average is derived using the following; $\lambda = E(X) = np$.

Example 1: The number of accident along Bamenda-Limbe high way follows a Poisson distribution with a mean of 2 per day. What is the probability that on a certain day, there was no accident?

Solution

Step 1: Formula. $P(X = x) = e^{-\lambda}\left(\frac{\lambda^x}{x!}\right)$, where; $\lambda = 2$, $x = 0$ and $e = e^1 = 2.718281828$

Step 2: Data substitution and solving

$P(X = 0) = 2.718281828^{-2}\left(\frac{2^0}{0!}\right)$ ....[Work exponent and factorial]

$P(X = 0) = 0.135335283\left(\frac{1}{1}\right)$ ....[Simplify fraction]

$P(X = 0) = 0.135335283(1)$ ....[Solve equation]

$P(X = 0) = \mathbf{0.135 = 13.5\%}$ ....[In three decimal places]

Example 2: Death in a particular village in Cameroon occurs randomly at an average rate of 1.9 deaths per day.

1) What is the probability of observing 3 deaths in a given day?
2) What is the probability of observing more than or equal to 2 death in a given day

Solution

1) What is the probability of observing 3 deaths in a given day?

Step 1: Formula. $P(X = x) = e^{-\lambda}\left(\frac{\lambda^x}{x!}\right)$, where; $\lambda = 1.9$, x = 3 and $e = e^1 = 2.718281828$

Step 2: Data substitution and solving

$P(X = 3) = 2.718281828^{-1.9}\left(\frac{1.9^3}{3!}\right)$ ....[Work exponent and factorial]

$P(X = 3) = 0.149568619\left(\frac{6.859}{6}\right)$ ....[Simplify fraction]

$P(X = 3) = 0.149568619(1.143166667)$ ....[Solve equation]

$P(X = 3) = \mathbf{0.171} = \mathbf{17.1\%}$ ....[In three decimal places]

2) What is the probability of observing more than or equal to 2 death in a given day

Hint. Since there is not finite number of total death, we are required to transform all greater than and greater than or equal to less than or less than or equal.

a) Method 1

Step 1: $P(X \geq 2) = 1 - P(X > 2) = 1 - [P(X = 0) + P(X = 1)]$, where; $\lambda = 1.9$

Step 2: Calculation of individual probabilities

$\mathbf{P(X = 0)}$

i. Formula. $P(X = 0) = e^{-\lambda}\left(\frac{\lambda^x}{x!}\right)$, where; $\lambda = 1.9$, x = 0 and $e = e^1 = 2.718281828$

ii. Data substitution and solving

$P(X = 0) = e^{-1.9}\left(\frac{1.9^0}{0!}\right)$ ....[Work exponent and factorial]

$P(X = 0) = 0.149568619\left(\frac{1}{1}\right)$ ....[Simplify fraction and solve equation]

$P(X = 0) = 0.15$ ....[In two decimal places]

$\mathbf{P(X = 1)}$

i. Formula. $P(X = 0) = e^{-\lambda}\left(\frac{\lambda^x}{x!}\right)$, where; $\lambda = 1.9$, x = 1 and $e = e^1 = 2.718281828$

ii. Data substitution and solving

$P(X = 1) = e^{-1.9}\left(\frac{1.9^1}{1!}\right)$ ....[Work exponent and factorial]

$P(X = 1) = 0.149568619\left(\frac{1.9}{1}\right)$ ....[Simplify fraction and solve equation]

$P(X = 1) = 0.28$ ....[In two decimal places]

Step 3: Data substitution and solving

$P(X \geq 2) = 1 - [0.15 + 0.28]$ ....[Simplify bracket]

$P(X \geq 2) = 1 - 0.43$ ....[Solve equation]

$P(X \geq 2) = \mathbf{0.57} = \mathbf{57\%}$ ....[In two decimal places]

b) **Method 2**

Step 1: Formula. $P(X \geq 2) = 1 - P(X > 2) = 1 - [P(X = 0) + P(X = 1)]$, where; $\lambda = 1.9$

Step 2: Data substitution and solving

$P(X \geq 2) = 1 - \left[e^{-1.9}\left(\frac{1.9^0}{0!}\right) + e^{-1.9}\left(\frac{1.9^1}{1!}\right)\right]$ ....[Work exponent and factorial]

$P(X \geq 2) = 1 - \left[0.149568619\left(\frac{1}{1}\right) + 0.149568619\left(\frac{1.9}{1}\right)\right]$ ....[Simplify fractions]

$P(X \geq 2) = 1 - [0.149568619(1) + 0.149568619(1.9)]$ ....[Simplify bracket]

$P(X \geq 2) = 1 - 0.433748995$ ....[Solve equation]

$P(X \geq 2) = \mathbf{0.57} = \mathbf{57\%}$ ....[In two decimal places]

c) **Method 3**

Step 1: Formula. $P(X \geq 2) = 1 - P(X > 2) = 1 - [P(X = 0) + P(X = 1)]$, where; $\lambda = 1.9$

Step 2: Data substitution and solving

$P(X \geq 2) = 1 - e^{-1.9}\left[\left(\frac{1.9^0}{0!}\right) + \left(\frac{1.9^1}{1!}\right)\right]$................................[Work exponent and factorial]

$P(X \geq 2) = 1 - 0.149568619\left[\left(\frac{1}{1}\right) + \left(\frac{1.9}{1}\right)\right]$ ......[Simplify fractions and simplify bracket]

$P(X \geq 2) = 1 - 0.149568619[2.9]$ ....[Expand bracket]

$P(X \geq 2) = 1 - 0.433748995$ ....[Solve equation]

$P(X \geq 2) = \mathbf{0.57} = \mathbf{57\%}$ ....[In two decimal places]

Example 3: The number of students absenting from school follows a Poisson distribution with an average of 1.5 per day. What is the probability of seeing 3 students absent from school in 2 days?

Solution

Hint: The given average (1.5) is for a day but we are required to calculate the probability in two days (change in interval time). Therefore, we are required to change the day average to two days average and use the value obtain as the real or true average in two days.

Step 1: Formula. $P(X = x) = e^{-\lambda}\left(\frac{\lambda^x}{x!}\right)$

Where; $x = 3$, $e = 2.718281828$ and $\lambda = (2 \times 1.5) = 3$

Step 2: Data substitution and solving

$P(X = 3) = e^{-3}\left(\frac{3^3}{3!}\right)$ ....[Work exponent and factorial]

$P(X = 3) = 0.049787068\left(\frac{27}{6}\right)$ ....[Simplify fraction]

$P(X = 3) = 0.049787068(4.5)$ ....[Solve equation]

$P(X = 3) = \mathbf{0.22} = \mathbf{22\%}$ ....[In two decimal places]

Example 4: The average number of birth in hospital X per day is 1.9 and in hospital Y per day is 1.5. What is the probability that there will be in total 5 births in both hospitals in a given day.

Solution

Hint: The time interval is given in days but there are two space intervals (hospital X and hospital Y). Since the probability to be calculated is for both spaces and the time interval is constant or unchanged, we simply sum their averages to obtain the true average to be used.

Step 1: Formula. $P(X + Y = 5) = e^{-\lambda}\left(\frac{\lambda^x}{x!}\right)$

Where; $x = 5$, $e = 2.718281828$, $\lambda = (1.9 + 1.5) = 3.4$

Step 2: Data substitution and solving

$P(X + Y = 5) = e^{-3.4}\left(\frac{3.4^5}{5!}\right)$ ....[Work exponent and factorial]

$P(X + Y = 5) = 0.033373269\left(\frac{454.35424}{120}\right)$ ....[Simplify fraction]

$P(X + Y = 5) = 0.033373269(3.786285333)$ ....[Solve equation]

$P(X + Y = 5) = \mathbf{0.13} = \mathbf{13\%}$ ....[In two decimal places]

Example 5: The probability that a computer is defective equals 0.05. Use the Poisson distribution to estimate the probability that from a random sample of 100 computers four are defective.

Solution

Hint. The question is asked in binomial probability with probability (0.05) and a definite number of trials (100). Probability to be calculated is asked in Poisson distribution, therefore, we are required to use the given data [p(0.03) and n(100)]to derive the average[λ].

Step 1: Formula. $P(X = x) = e^{-\lambda}\left(\frac{\lambda^x}{x!}\right)$

Where; $x = 4$, $e = 2.718281828$ and $\lambda = (0.05 \times 100) = 5$

Step 2: Data substitution and solving

$P(X = 4) = e^{-5}\left(\frac{5^4}{4!}\right)$ ....[Work exponent and factorial]

$P(X = 4) = 0.006737946\left(\frac{625}{24}\right)$ ....[Simplify fraction]

$P(X = 4) = 0.006737946(26.04166667)$ ....[Solve equation]

$P(X = 4) = \mathbf{0.16} = \mathbf{16\%}$ ....[In two decimal places]

Example 6: On average one in 200 cars break down on a certain stretch of rood per day. Find the probability that, on a randomly chosen day,

1) None of a sample of 250 cars break down
2) More than two of a sample of 300 cars break down

Solution

Hint: The total number of trial given (200) changes (250 and 300). Therefore, since these total numbers of trials is greater than 50$[n > 50]$, it means we can apply binomial probability in solving giving that the probability of success is less than 0.1$[p < 0.1]$.

Step 1: Preliminary calculation [Calculation of probability of success]

a) Formula. Success Probability $(p) = \frac{\lambda}{n}$, where; $\lambda = 1$ and $n = 200$
b) Data substitution and solving

$\text{Success Probability } (p) = \frac{1}{200}$ ....[Solve equation]

$\text{Success Probability } (p) = \mathbf{0.005}$ ....[Note that $(p < 0.1)$]

Step 2: Calculation of given trials number probabilities

1) **None of a sample of 250 cars breaks down. That is, $\mathbf{P(X = 0)}$**
   a) Formula. $P(X = r) = \frac{n!}{r!(n-r)!}(p^r \times q^{n-r})$

      Where: n = 250, r = 0, p = 0.005, q = 0.995
   b) Data substitution and solving

      $P(X = 0) = \frac{250!}{0!(250-0)!}(0.005^0 \times 0.995^{250-0})$ ....[work exponents and factorials]

      $P(X = 0) = 1(1 \times 0.28560788)$ ....[Solve equation]

      $P(X = 0) = \mathbf{0.29} = \mathbf{29\%}$ ....[In two decimal places]
2) **More than two of a sample of 300 cars breaks down. That is, $\mathbf{P(X > 2)}$**
   a) Formula. $P(X > 2) = 1 - P(X \leq 2) = 1 - [P(X = 0) + P(X = 1) + P(X = 2)]$

      Note: $P(X = r) = \frac{n!}{r!(n-r)!}(p^r \times q^{n-r})$

      Where: n = 300, r = 0, p = 0.005, q = 0.995
   b) Calculation of individual probabilities

      i. $P(X = 0) = \frac{300!}{0!(300-0)!}(0.005^0 \times 0.995^{300}) = 0.222292199$

      ii. $P(X = 1) = \frac{300!}{1!(300-1)!}(0.005^1 \times 0.995^{299}) = 0.335113869$

      iii. $P(X = 2) = \frac{300!}{2!(300-2)!}(0.005^2 \times 0.995^{298}) = 0.251756399$

c) Data substitution and solving

$P(X > 2) = 1 - [0.222292199 + 0.335113869 + 0.251756399]$ ....[Sum values]

$P(X > 2) = 1 - 0.809162467$ ....[Solve equation]

$P(X > 2) = \mathbf{0.19 = 19\%}$ ....[In two decimal places]

Test Your Understanding

Exercise 8: A study gives a statistics that on average 6 girls a married per month in Bakem village. In a randomly selected month, calculate the following probabilities; [Leave answer in four decimal places]

1) No girl is married in Bakem village...............................**[Answer: $0.0025 = 0.25\%$]**
2) More than 4 girls are married in Bakem village. ....**[Answer: $0.8488 = 84.88\%$]**
3) At most 2 girls are married in Bakem village................ **[Answer: $0.0620 = 6.20\%$]**

Exercise 9: A random variable X is modeled by Poisson distribution as $X \sim Po(2.5)$ per hour. In a randomly selected hour, fine the following probabilities; [Leave answer in four decimal places]

1) $P(X = 0)$. ....**[Answer: $0.0821 = 8.21\%$]**
2) $P(X \geq 2)$. ....**[Answer: $0.7127 = 71.27\%$]**
3) $P(X < 1)$.. **[Answer: $0.0821 = 8.21\%$]**

Exercise 10: A survey shows that on average 3 cars passes through street A daily and on average 2 car passes through street B daily. [Leave answer in four decimal places]

a) Find the following probabilities;
   i. No car will pass through street A in three days. ....**[Answer: $0.0001 = 0.01\%$]**
   ii. More than three cars will pass through street A and street B daily

[Answer: $0.735 = 73.5\%$]

b) Assume that an average, 4 in 100 cars pass through street C per week. In a given randomly selected week, find the probability that more than a car from a sample of 400 cars will pass the street C....................................... **[Answer: $0.9999 = 99.99\%$]**

5.3 Normal distribution

Normal distribution or Gaussian distribution is the most important distribution. Generally, normal distribution has the following properties;

Carl F. Gauss

1) The shape of the normal distribution curve depends on the mean and variance$[X \sim N(\mu, \sigma^2)]$. Normal distribution curve is unimodal in nature.
2) The normal distribution curve is bell-shaped (mean, median and mode) and symmetrical in nature (equal opposite sides from the center).
3) The total area under the normal distribution curve equals 1. The curve is continuous and never touches the x-axis.

5.3.1 Probability of Normal Distribution

The probability of normal distribution also called the P-Value is calculated with the help of the Z-value and the standard normal distribution function table. The computed Z-values or standard normal variable must be expressed in three decimal places in order to fit the normal distribution function table values. Z-Value is calculated as;

$$\text{Standardised Normal Variable (Z)} = \frac{\text{Value} - \text{Mean}}{\text{Standard Deviation}} = Z = \frac{X - \mu}{\sigma} \quad \text{..........................(1)}$$

Where; μ represents the mean of the normal distribution

σ represent the standard deviation of the normal distribution

X represent the given value of the continuous variable

The standard normal table value of a given value of Z is expressed as $[\Phi(z)]$. The probability of the computed Z value is expressed as $[P(Z < z)]$ or $[P(Z > z)]$ for single problem and $[a < Z < b]$ for double problem. The following expressions are worth knowing in order to write the probability value of a given Z-value(s).

$P(Z < a) = \Phi(a)$ ....(1)

$P(Z > a) = 1 - \Phi(a)$ ....(2)

$P(Z < -a) = P(Z > a) = 1 - \Phi(a)$ ....(3)

$P(Z > -a) = P(Z < a) = \Phi(a)$ ....(4)

In situation of both greater and lesser than inequality sign, the mathematical sign (+ or −) of the limits "a" (lower limit) and "b" (upper limit) determines the formula to be applied. The value of probability is the simply the range of the limits.

$P(a < Z < b)$ ....[Both limits being positive]

Where; $a = \Phi(a)$ and $b = \Phi(b)$

$\mathbf{P = \Phi(b) - \Phi(a)}$ ....(1)

$P(-a < Z < b)$ ....[When lower limit is negative]

Where; $-a = 1 - \Phi(a)$ and $b = \Phi(b)$

$P = \Phi(b) - [1 - \Phi(a)]$ ....[Expand bracket]

$P = \Phi(b) - 1 + \Phi(a)$ ....[Adjust equation]

$\mathbf{P = \Phi(a) + \Phi(b) - 1}$ **or** $\mathbf{\Phi(b) + \Phi(a) - 1}$ ....(2)

$P(-a < Z < -b)$ ....[When both limits are negative]

Where; $-a = 1 - \Phi(a)$ and $-b = 1 - \Phi(b)$

$P = 1 - \Phi(b) - [1 - \Phi(a)]$ ....[Expand bracket]

$P = 1 - \Phi(b) - 1 + \Phi(a)$ ....[Simplify equation]

$\mathbf{P = \Phi(a) - \Phi(b)}$ ....(3)

Example 1: The life of a electric light bulb is known to be normally distributed with a mean life of 2,000 hours and a standard deviation of 120 hours. Estimate the probability that the life of such a bulb will be;

1) Greater than 2,150 hours
2) lesser than 1,910 hours

Solution

1) Greater than 2,150 hours. That is $\mathbf{P(X > 2,150)}$

Step 1: Calculation of standardized normal variable value (Z)

a) Formula. Standardised Normal Variable $(Z) = \frac{X-\mu}{\sigma}$

Where; $X = 2150$, $\mu = 2000$, $\sigma = 120$

b) Data substitution and solving

Standardised Normal Variable $(Z) = \frac{2,150-2.000}{120}$ ....[Simplify numerator]

Standardised Normal Variable $(Z) = \frac{150}{120}$ ....[Solve equation]

Standardised Normal Variable $(Z) = 1.25$ ....[That is $P(Z > 1.25)$]

Step 2: Determination of probability value

a) Formula. $P(Z > a) = 1 - \Phi(a)$, where; a = 1.25.

b) Reading the $[\Phi(a) = 1.25]$ from the standard normal distribution table

z	0	1	2	3	4	5	6	7	8	9	1	2	3	4	5	6	7	8	9
															ADD				
0.0	0.5000	0.5040	0.5080	0.5120	0.5160	0.5199	0.5239	0.5279	0.5319	0.5359	4	8	12	16	20	24	28	32	36
1.0	0.8413	0.8438	0.8461	0.8485	0.8508	0.8531	0.8554	0.8577	0.8599	0.8621	2	5	7	9	12	14	16	19	21
1.1	0.8643	0.8665	0.8686	0.8708	0.8729	0.8749	0.8770	0.8790	0.8810	0.8830	2	4	6	8	10	12	14	16	18
1.2 →	0.8849	0.8869	0.8888	0.8907	0.8925	0.8944	0.8962	0.8980	0.8997	0.9015	2	4	6	7	9	11	13	15	17
1.3	0.9032	0.9049	0.9066	0.9082	0.9099	0.9115	0.9131	0.9147	0.9162	0.9177	2	3	5	6	8	10	11	13	14
1.4	0.9192	0.9207	0.9222	0.9236	0.9251	0.9265	0.9279	0.9292	0.9306	0.9319	1	3	4	6	7	8	10	11	13

$$\boldsymbol{\Phi(1.25) = 0.8944}$$

c) Data substitution and solving

$P(X > 2{,}150) = 1 - 0.8944$ ....[Solve equation]

$P(X > 2{,}150) = \mathbf{0.1056 = 10.56\%}$

2) Lesser than 1,910 hours. That is $P(X < 1{,}910)$

Step 1: Calculation of standardized normal variable value (Z)

a) Formula. Standardised Normal Variable $(Z) = \frac{X-\mu}{\sigma}$

Where; $X = 1{,}910$, $\mu = 2000$, $\sigma = 120$

b) Data substitution and solving

Standardised Normal Variable $(Z) = \frac{1{,}910-2{,}000}{120}$ ....[Solve]

Standardised Normal Variable $(Z) = -0.75$ ....[That is $\mathbf{P(Z < -0.75)}$]

Step 2: Derivation of probability using the standardized normal distribution table

a) Formula. $P(Z < -a) = P(Z > a) = 1 - \Phi(a)$, where; a = 0.75.

b) Reading the $[\Phi(a) = 0.75]$ from the standard normal distribution table

z	0	1	2	3	4	5	6	7	8	9	1	2	3	4	5	6	7	8	9
															ADD				
0.0	0.5000	0.5040	0.5080	0.5120	0.5160	0.5199	0.5239	0.5279	0.5319	0.5359	4	8	12	16	20	24	28	32	36
0.5	0.6915	0.6950	0.6985	0.7019	0.7054	0.7088	0.7123	0.7157	0.7190	0.7224	3	7	10	14	17	20	24	27	31
0.6	0.7257	0.7291	0.7324	0.7357	0.7389	0.7422	0.7454	0.7486	0.7517	0.7549	3	7	10	13	16	19	23	26	29
0.7	0.7580 →	0.7611	0.7642	0.7673	0.7704	0.7734	0.7764	0.7794	0.7823	0.7852	3	6	9	12	15	18	21	24	27
0.8	0.7881	0.7910	0.7939	0.7967	0.7995	0.8023	0.8051	0.8078	0.8106	0.8133	3	5	8	11	14	16	19	22	25
0.9	0.8159	0.8186	0.8212	0.8238	0.8264	0.8289	0.8315	0.8340	0.8365	0.8389	3	5	8	10	13	15	18	20	23

$$\boldsymbol{\Phi(0.75) = 0.7734}$$

c) Data substitution and solving

$P(X < 1{,}910) = 1 - 0.7734$ ....[Solve equation]

$P(X < 1{,}910) = \mathbf{0.2266 = 22.66\%}$

Example 2: The weight of vegetable marrows supplied to retailers by a wholesaler has a normal distribution with mean 32.4 kg and a standard deviation of 2 kg. Fine the probability that a randomly vegetable marrow supplied weight;

1) Less than 33.09 kg
2) More than 31.51 kg

Solution

1) Less than 33.09 kg. That is $P(X < 33.09)$

Step 1: Calculation of standardized normal variable value (Z)

a) Formula. Standardised Normal Variable $(Z) = \frac{X-\mu}{\sigma}$

Where; $X = 33.09$, $\mu = 32.4$ and $\sigma = 2$

b) Data substitution and solving

Standardised Normal Variable $(Z) = \frac{33.09-32.4}{2}$ ....[Simplify numerator]

Standardised Normal Variable $(Z) = \frac{0.69}{2}$ ....[Solve equation]

Standardised Normal Variable $(Z) = 0.345$ ....[That is $\mathbf{P(Z < 0.345)}$]

Step 2: Derivation of probability using the standardized normal distribution table

a) Formula. $P(Z < a) = \Phi(a)$

Where; a = 0.345 [0.34 + column 5 value in the ADD sector]

b) Reading the $[\Phi(a) = 0.345]$ from the standard normal distribution table

z	0	1	2	3	4	5	6	7	8	9	1	2	3	4	5	6	7	8	9
															ADD				
0.0	0.5000	0.5040	0.5080	0.5120	0.5160	0.5199	0.5239	0.5279	0.5319	0.5359	4	8	12	16	20	24	28	32	36
0.1	0.5398	0.5438	0.5478	0.5517	0.5557	0.5596	0.5636	0.5675	0.5714	0.5753	4	8	12	16	20	24	28	32	36
0.2	0.5793	0.5832	0.5871	0.5910	0.5948	0.5987	0.6026	0.6064	0.6103	0.6141	4	8	12	15	19	23	27	31	35
0.3 →	0.6179	0.6217	0.6255	0.6293	0.6331	0.6368	0.6406	0.6443	0.6480	0.6517	4	7	11	15	19	22	26	30	34
0.4	0.6554	0.6591	0.6628	0.6664	0.6700	0.6736	0.6772	0.6808	0.6844	0.6879	4	7	11	14	18	22	25	29	32

$\Phi(0.345) = 0.6331 + [19/10{,}000]$ ....[Simplify fraction]

$\Phi(0.345) = 0.6331 + 0.0019$ ....[Sum values]

$\Phi(0.345) = \mathbf{0.635}$

c) Derivation of probability value: $P(X < 33.09) = \mathbf{0.635} \equiv \mathbf{63.5\%}$

2) More than 31.51 kg. That is $P(X > 31.51)$

Step 1: Calculation of standardized normal variable value (Z)

a) Formula. Standardised Normal Variable $(Z) = \frac{X-\mu}{\sigma}$

Where; $X = 31.51$, $\mu = 32.4$ and $\sigma = 2$

b) Data substitution and solving

Standardised Normal Variable $(Z) = \frac{31.51-32.4}{2}$ ....[Solve]

Standardised Normal Variable $(Z) = -0.445$ ....[That is $\mathbf{P(Z > -0.445)}$]

Step 2: Derivation of probability using the standardized normal distribution table

a) Formula. $P(Z > -a) = P(Z < a) = \Phi(a)$

Where; a = 0.445 [0.44 + column 5 value in the ADD sector].

b) Reading the $[\Phi(a) = 0.445]$ from the standard normal distribution table

z	0	1	2	3	4	5	6	7	8	9	1	2	3	4	5	6	7	8	9
															ADD				
0.0	0.5000	0.5040	0.5080	0.5120	0.5160	0.5199	0.5239	0.5279	0.5319	0.5359	4	8	12	16	20	24	28	32	36
0.1	0.5398	0.5438	0.5478	0.5517	0.5557	0.5596	0.5636	0.5675	0.5714	0.5753	4	8	12	16	20	24	28	32	36
0.2	0.5793	0.5832	0.5871	0.5910	0.5948	0.5987	0.6026	0.6064	0.6103	0.6141	4	8	12	15	19	23	27	31	35
0.3	0.6179	0.6217	0.6255	0.6293	0.6331	0.6368	0.6406	0.6443	0.6480	0.6517	4	7	11	15	19	22	26	30	34
0.4	0.6554	0.6591	0.6628	0.6664	0.6700	0.6736	0.6772	0.6808	0.6844	0.6879	4	7	11	14	18	22	25	29	32

$\Phi(0.345) = 0.6700 + [18/10{,}000]$ ....[Simplify fraction]

$\Phi(0.345) = 0.6700 + 0.0018$ ....[Sum values]

$\Phi(0.345) = \mathbf{0.6718}$

c) Derivation of probability value: $P(X > 31.51) = \mathbf{0.6718} \equiv \mathbf{67.18}\%$

Example 3: Giving that a normal random variable is model as $X \sim N(50, 8^2)$, calculate the following;

1) $P(X < 56)$
2) $P(X > 45)$
3) $P(50 < X < 60)$

<u>Solution</u>

1) $P(X < 56)$

Step 1: Calculation of standardized normal variable value (Z)

a) Formula. Standardised Normal Variable $(Z) = \frac{X-\mu}{\sigma}$, where; $X = 56$, $\mu = 50$ and $\sigma = 8$

b) Data substitution and solving

Standardised Normal Variable $(Z) = \frac{56-50}{8}$ ....[Simplify numerator]

Standardised Normal Variable $(Z) = \frac{6}{8}$ ....[Solve equation]

Standardised Normal Variable $(Z) = 0.75$ ....[That is $\mathbf{P(Z < 0.75)}$]

Step 2: Derivation of probability using the standardized normal distribution table

a) Formula. $P(Z < a) = \Phi(a)$, where; a = 0.75 and $\Phi(0.75) = 0.7734$

b) Probability value. $P(X < 56) = \mathbf{0.7734} = \mathbf{77.34}\%$

2) $P(X > 45)$

Step 1: Calculation of standardized normal variable value (Z)

a) Formula. Standardised Normal Variable (Z) $= \frac{X-\mu}{\sigma}$

Where; $X = 45$, $\mu = 50$ and $\sigma = 8$

b) Data substitution and solving

Standardised Normal Variable (Z) $= \frac{45-50}{8}$ ....[Simplify numerator]

Standardised Normal Variable (Z) $= \frac{-5}{8}$ ....[Solve equation]

Standardised Normal Variable (Z) $= -0.625$ ....[That is $\mathbf{P(Z > -0.625)}$]

Step 2: Derivation of probability using the standardized normal distribution table

a) Formula. $P(Z > -a) = P(Z < a) = \Phi(a)$

Where; a = 0.625 [0.62 + column 5 value in the ADD sector]

b) Reading the $[\Phi(a) = 0.625]$ from the standard normal distribution table

z	0	1	2	3	4	5	6	7	8	9	1	2	3	4	5 (ADD)	6	7	8	9
0.0	0.5000	0.5040	0.5080	0.5120	0.5160	0.5199	0.5239	0.5279	0.5319	0.5359	4	8	12	16	20	24	28	32	36
0.5	0.6915	0.6950	0.6985	0.7019	0.7054	0.7088	0.7123	0.7157	0.7190	0.7224	3	7	10	14	17	20	24	27	31
0.6 →	0.7257	0.7291	0.7324	0.7357	0.7389	0.7422	0.7454	0.7486	0.7517	0.7549	3	7	10	13	16	19	23	26	29
0.7	0.7580	0.7611	0.7642	0.7673	0.7704	0.7734	0.7764	0.7794	0.7823	0.7852	3	6	9	12	15	18	21	24	27
0.8	0.7881	0.7910	0.7939	0.7967	0.7995	0.8023	0.8051	0.8078	0.8106	0.8133	3	5	8	11	14	16	19	22	25
0.9	0.8159	0.8186	0.8212	0.8238	0.8264	0.8289	0.8315	0.8340	0.8365	0.8389	3	5	8	10	13	15	18	20	23

$[\Phi(0.625) = 0.7341]$. Therefore, $P(X > 45) = 0.7341 = 73.41\%$

c) $P(50 < X < 60)$

Step 1: Calculation of standardized normal variable value (Z)

a) Formula. $Z = \left[\frac{X_1-\mu}{\sigma} < Z < \frac{X_2-\mu}{\sigma}\right]$, where; $X_1 = 50$, $X_2 = 60$ $\mu = 50$ and $\sigma = 8$

b) Data substitution and solving

Standardised Normal Variable (Z) $= \left[\frac{50-50}{8} < Z < \frac{60-50}{8}\right]$ .....[Simplify numerator]

Standardised Normal Variable (Z) $= \left[\frac{0}{8} < Z < \frac{10}{8}\right]$ ....[Solve equation]

Standardised Normal Variable (Z) $= [0 < Z < 1.25]$**....[where a = 0 and b = 1.25]**

Step 2: Derivation of probability using the standardized normal distribution table

a) Formula. $P(a < Z < b) = \Phi(b) - \Phi(a)$, where; $a = 0 \equiv 0.000$, $b = 1.25$

b) Reading the [$\Phi(a) = 0$ and $\Phi = 1.25$] from the standard normal distribution table

z	0	1	2	3	4	5	6	7	8	9	1	2	3	4	5	6	7	8	9
															ADD				
0.0	0.5000	0.5040	0.5080	0.5120	0.5160	0.5199	0.5239	0.5279	0.5319	0.5359	4	8	12	16	20	24	28	32	36
1.0	0.8413	0.8438	0.8461	0.8485	0.8508	0.8531	0.8554	0.8577	0.8599	0.8621	2	5	7	9	12	14	16	19	21
1.1	0.8643	0.8665	0.8686	0.8708	0.8729	0.8749	0.8770	0.8790	0.8810	0.8830	2	4	6	8	10	12	14	16	18
1.2	0.8849	0.8869	0.8888	0.8907	0.8925	0.8944	0.8962	0.8980	0.8997	0.9015	2	4	6	7	9	11	13	15	17
1.3	0.9032	0.9049	0.9066	0.9082	0.9099	0.9115	0.9131	0.9147	0.9162	0.9177	2	3	5	6	8	10	11	13	14
1.4	0.9192	0.9207	0.9222	0.9236	0.9251	0.9265	0.9279	0.9292	0.9306	0.9319	1	3	4	6	7	8	10	11	13

$\mathbf{\Phi(a) = 0.5000}$ **and** $\mathbf{\Phi(b) = 0.8944}$

c) Data substitution and solving

$P(a < Z < b) = \Phi(b) - \Phi(a)$ ....[Substitute component numerical value]

$P(50 < X < 60) = 0.8944 - 0.5000$ ....[Solve equation]

$P(50 < X < 60) = \mathbf{0.3944 = 39.44\%}$

Example 5: The masses of packages produced by a particular machine are normally distributed with a mean of 200 grams and a variance of 4 grams squared. Find the probability that a randomly selected package from the machine weights

1) Less than 197 grams
2) More than 200 grams
3) Between 150 grams and 200 grams

Solution

1) Less than 197 grams. That is $\mathbf{P(X < 197)}$

Step 1: Calculation of standardized normal variable value (Z)

a) Formula. Standardised Normal Variable $(Z) = \frac{X-\mu}{\sigma}$

Where; $X = 197$, $\mu = 200$ and $\sigma = 2$

b) Data substitution and solving

Standardised Normal Variable $(Z) = \frac{197-200}{2}$ ....[Simplify numerator]

Standardised Normal Variable $(Z) = \frac{-3}{2}$ ....[Solve equation]

Standardised Normal Variable $(Z) = -1.5$ ...[That is $\mathbf{P(Z < -1.5)}$=$\mathbf{P(Z > 1.5)}$]

Step 2: Derivation of probability using the standardized normal distribution table

a) Formula. $P(Z > 1.5) = 1 - \Phi(1.5)$, where; $\Phi(1.5) = 0.9332$

b) Data substitution and solving

$P(Z > 1.5) = 1 - 0.9332$ ....[Solve equation]

$P(Z > 1.5) = \mathbf{0.0668 = 6.68\%}$

2) More than 200 grams. That is $\mathbf{P(X > 200)}$

Step 1: Calculation of standardized normal variable value (Z)

a) Formula. Standardised Normal Variable $(Z) = \frac{X-\mu}{\sigma}$

Where; $X = 200$, $\mu = 200$ and $\sigma = 2$

b) Data substitution and solving

Standardised Normal Variable $(Z) = \frac{200-200}{2}$ ………………..….[Simplify numerator]

Standardised Normal Variable $(Z) = \frac{0}{2}$ ……………..………..…………[Solve equation]

Standardised Normal Variable $(Z) = 0$ ……………………….......[That is $\mathbf{P(Z > 0)}$]

Step 2: Derivation of probability using the standardized normal distribution table

a) Formula. $P(Z > 0) = 1 - \Phi(0)$, where; $\Phi(0) = 0.5000$

b) Data substitution and solving

$P(Z > 1.5) = 1 - 0.5000$ …………………………………..…..…..[Solve equation]

$P(Z > 1.5) = \mathbf{0.5} = \mathbf{50\%}$

3) Between 199 grams and 200 grams. That is $\mathbf{P(150 < X < 200)}$

Step 1: Calculation of standardized normal variable value (Z)

The Z value of 150	The Z value of 200
Formula. $Z = \frac{X-\mu}{\sigma}$, where; $X = 199$, $\mu = 200$, $\sigma = 2$	Formula. $Z = \frac{X-\mu}{\sigma}$, where; $X = 200$, $\mu = 200$, $\sigma = 2$
$Z = \frac{199-200}{2}$ ………[Simplify numerator] $Z = \frac{-1}{2}$ ……………...…[Solve equation] $Z = -0.5$ …[$P(X > -0.5) = P(X < 0.5)$]	$Z = \frac{200-200}{2}$ …………[Simplify numerator] $Z = \frac{0}{2}$ ……………….……[Solve equation] $Z = 0$ ………………..…[That is $P(Z < 0)$]
It should be noted here that $a = -0.5$ and $b = 0$, since it is considered that $a < b$	

Step 2: Derivation of probability using the standardized normal distribution table

a) Formula. $P(-a < Z < b) = \Phi(b) + \Phi(a) - 1$

Where; $a = 0.5$, $b = 0$, $\Phi(b) = 0.5000$ and $\Phi(a) = 0.6915$

b) Data substitution and solving

$P(-0.5 < Z < 0) = 0.5000 + 0.6915 - 1$ ……………...……..………..[Add values]

$P(-0.5 < Z < 0) = 0.5000 + (-0.3085)$ ……………..…………..[Solve equation]

$P(-0.5 < Z < 0) = \mathbf{0.1915} = \mathbf{19.15\%}$

Example 6: The heights of boys at a particular age follow a normal distribution with a mean 200 cm and standard deviation of 2 cm. Find the probability that a boy picked at random from this age group has height;

1) Less than 198 cm
2) More than 201 cm
3) Between 198.5 cm and 199.5 cm

<u>**Solution**</u>

1) Less than 198 cm. That is $P(X < 198)$

Step 1: Calculation of standardized normal variable value (Z)

a) Formula. Standardised Normal Variable $(Z) = \frac{X-\mu}{\sigma}$

   Where; $X = 198$, $\mu = 200$ and $\sigma = 2$

b) Data substitution and solving

   Standardised Normal Variable $(Z) = \frac{198-200}{2}$ ....[Simplify numerator]

   Standardised Normal Variable $(Z) = \frac{-2}{2}$ ....[Solve equation]

   Standardised Normal Variable $(Z) = -1$ ....[That is $\mathbf{P(Z < -1) = P(Z > 1)}$]

Step 2: Derivation of probability using the standardized normal distribution table

a) Formula. $P(Z > a) = 1 - \Phi(a)$, where; a = 1 and $\Phi(1) = 0.8413$

b) Data substitution and solving

   $P(Z > 1) = 1 - 0.8413$ ....[Solve equation]

   $P(Z > 1) = \mathbf{0.1587 = 15.87\%}$

2) More than 201 cm. That is $P(X > 201)$

Step 1: Calculation of standardized normal variable value (Z)

a) Formula. Standardised Normal Variable $(Z) = \frac{X-\mu}{\sigma}$

   Where; $X = 201$, $\mu = 200$ and $\sigma = 2$

b) Data substitution and solving

   Standardised Normal Variable $(Z) = \frac{201-200}{2}$ ....[Simplify numerator]

   Standardised Normal Variable $(Z) = \frac{1}{2}$ ....[Solve equation]

   Standardised Normal Variable $(Z) = 0.5$ ....[That is $\mathbf{P(Z > 0.5)}$]

Step 2: Derivation of probability using the standardized normal distribution table

a) Formula. $P(Z > a) = 1 - \Phi(a)$, where; a = 0.5 and $\Phi(1.5) = 0.6915$

b) Data substitution and solving

$P(Z > 0.5) = 1 - 0.6915$ ....[Solve equation]

$P(Z > 0.5) = \mathbf{0.3085 = 30.85\%}$

c) Between 198 cm and 199 cm. That is $\mathbf{P(198 < X < 199)}$

Step 1: Calculation of standardized normal variable value (Z)

a) Formula. $Z(a, b) = P\left[\frac{X_1-\mu}{\sigma} < Z < \frac{X_2-\mu}{\sigma}\right]$

Where; $X_1 = 198$, $X_b = 199$, $\mu = 200$ and $\sigma = 2$

b) Data substitution and solving

$P(198 < Z < 199) = P\left[\frac{198-200}{2} < Z < \frac{199-200}{2}\right]$ ....[Simplify numerator]

$P(198 < Z < 199) = P\left[\frac{-2}{2} < Z < \frac{-1}{2}\right]$ ....[Solve equations]

$P(198 < Z < 199) = P[-1 < Z < -0.5]$....[Note; $\mathbf{a = -1}$, $\mathbf{b = -0.5}$, since $a < b$]

Step 2: Derivation of probability using the standardized normal distribution table

a) Formula. $P(-a < Z < -b) = \Phi(a) - \Phi(b)$

Where; a = 1, b = 0.5, $\Phi(a) = 0.8413$ and $\Phi(b) = 0.6915$

b) Data substitution and solving

$P(198 < Z < 199) = 0.8413 - 0.6915$ ....[Solve equation]

$P(198 < Z < 199) = \mathbf{0.1498 = 14.98\%}$

Test Your Understanding

Exercise 11: The distance in kilometer travelled to work by the employee of a city council may be modeled by a normal distribution with a mean 7.5 and standard deviation 2.5. Find the probability that the distance travelled to work by a randomly selected employee of the city council is;

1) Less than 11.0 km ....**[Answer: $\mathbf{0.9192 = 91.92\%}$]**
2) Greater than 10.5 km ....**[Answer: $\mathbf{0.1151 = 11.51\%}$]**
3) Between 5.5 km and 10.5 km.................................. **[Answer: $\mathbf{0.673 = 67.3\%}$]**

Example 12: The scores of a match are normally distributed with a mean of 35 and a standard deviation of 10. What percent of the scores is

1) $P(X > 34)$... **[Answer: $\mathbf{0.5398 = 53.98\%}$]**
2) $P(X < 42)$.. **[Answer: $\mathbf{0.7580 = 75.8\%}$]**
3) $P(28 < X < 34)$.. **[Answer: $\mathbf{0.0119 = 1.19\%}$]**

Example 13: If $X \sim N(80, 30^2)$ fine the following probability

1) $P(X > 125)$..**[Answer: $0.0668 = 6.68\%$]**
2) $P(65 < X < 95)$.......................................**[Answer: $0.383 = 38.3\%$]**
3) $P(X < 115)$..**[Answer: $0.8784 = 87.84\%$]**

5.3.2 Continuity Correction

Continuity correction is a technique applied to change a discrete distribution (outcome with finite values) to continuous distribution (outcome with infinite values). The concept of continuity correction is used when discrete values are given to determine the probability of normal distribution.

a) When dealing with [≤] and [≥] inequality sign

The equality signs [≤] and [≥] is discrete or non-continuous due to the equality sign in the inequality sign. to make the inequality sign continuous, we are required to remove the equality sign in the inequality sign by adding and subtracting 0.5 from the lower and upper limits respectively.

$P(X \geq \pm a) = P(X > \pm a - 0.5)$ ....(1)

$P(X \leq \pm a) = P(X < \pm a + 0.5)$ ....(2)

$P(X = a) = P(\pm a - 0.5 < X < \pm a + 0.5)$ ....(3)

Example 1: Perform the continuity correction of the following probability expressions;

1) $P(X \geq 255)$
2) $P(X \leq 215)$
3) $P(X = 260)$

<u>**Solution**</u>

1) $\mathbf{P(X \geq 255)}$...[Lower Limit Re-adjustment]

Step 1: Formula. $P(X \geq \pm a) = P(X > \pm a - 0.5)$, where; $a = 255$

Step 2: Data substitution and solving

$P(X > a - 0.5)$ ....[Substitute component numerical value]

$P(X > 255 - 0.5)$ ....[Simplify equation]

$P(X > 245.5)$ ....[Continuity correction from]

2) $\mathbf{P(X \leq 215)}$...[Upper Limit Re-adjustment]

Step 1: Formula. $P(X \leq \pm a) = P(X < \pm a + 0.5)$, where; $a = 215$

Step 2: Data substitution and solving

$P(X < a + 0.5)$ ....[Substitute component numerical value]

$P(X < 215 + 0.5)$ ....[Simplify equation]

$P(X < 215.5)$ ....[Continuity correction from]

3) $P(X = 260)$..[Lower and Upper Limit Re-adjustment]

Step 1: Formula. $P(X = a) = P(\pm a - 0.5 < X < \pm a + 0.5)$, where; $a = 260$

Step 2: Data substitution and solving

$P(a - 0.5 < X < a + 0.5)$ ....[Substitute component numerical value]

$P(260 - 0.5 < X < 260 + 0.5)$ ....[Simplify equation]

$P(259.5 < X < 260.5)$ ....[Continuity correction from]

b) When dealing with [<] and [>] inequality sign

In situation of [<] and [>] inequality signs, we apply two steps to perform continuity correction. Step one is the determination of [<] and [>] equivalent form $[(\leq)$ and $(\geq)]$ and the second step is to add and subtract 0.5 from the lower and upper limit respectively.

$P(X < a) = P(X \leq a - 1)$ ....(4)

$P(X > a) = P(X \geq a + 1)$ ....(5)

Example 1: Perform the continuity correction of the following probability expressions;

1) $P(X < 4)$
2) $P(X > 4)$

Solution

1) $P(X < 4)$..[Upper Limit Re-adjustment]

Step 1: Formula. $P(X < \pm a) = P(X < \pm a^{*} + 0.5)$, where; $a^{*} =$ Unknown

Step 2: Determination of unknown $[a^{*}]$ or equivalent forn.

a) Formula. $P(X < a) = P(X \leq a - 1)$, where; $a = 4$
b) Data substitution and solving

$P(X < a) = P(X \leq a - 1)$ ....[Substitute component numerical value]

$P(X < 4) = P(X \leq 4 - 1)$ ....[Simplify bracket]

$P(X < 4) = P(X \leq 3)$ ....[Equivalent Form]

Step 3: Data substitution and solving

$P(X < 4) = P(X < a^{*} + 0.5)$ ....[Substitute component numerical value]

$P(X < 4) = P(X < 3 + 0.5)$ ....[Simplify bracket]

$P(X < 4) = \mathbf{P(X < 3.5)}$ ....[Continuity Correction Form]

2) $P(X > 4)$……………………………………………[Lower Limit Re-adjustment]

Step 1: Formula. $P(X > \pm a) = P(X > \pm a^* - 0.5)$, where; $a^* = \text{Unknown}$

Step 2: Determination of unknown [a^*]

a) Formula. $P(X > a) = P(X \geq a + 1)$, where; $a = 4$

b) Data substitution and solving

$P(X > a) = P(X \geq a + 1)$ ……………[Substitute component numerical value]

$P(X > 4) = P(X \geq 4 + 1)$ ……………………………[Simplify bracket]

$P(X > 4) = P(X \geq 5)$ ……………………………[Equivalent Form]

Step 3: Data substitution and solving

$P(X > \pm a) = P(X > \pm a^* - 0.5)$ ……………[Substitute component numerical values]

$P(X > 4) = P(X > 5 - 0.5)$ ……………………………[Simplify bracket]

$P(X > 4) = \mathbf{P(X > 4.5)}$ ……………………………[Continuity Correction Form]

c) When dealing with [$<$ or $>$] and [$\leq$ or $\geq$] inequality sign

In situation of a [$\leq$ and $<$] and [$<$ and $\leq$], we are required to perform two steps. In step one, we change the [$<$] inequality sign to [$\leq$] and the second step is to transform the equation to continuity form. That is [$\leq$ and $<$] is changed to [$\leq$ *and* $\leq$] and [$<$ and $\leq$] is changed to [$\leq$ and $\leq$]. The formula of transforming the equivalent form is given as seen below,

$P(a < X \leq b) = P(a + 1 - 0.5 < X < b + 0.5) = P(a + 0.5 < X < b + 0.5)$ ……………(6)

$P(a \leq X < b) = P(a - 0.5 < X < b - 1 + 0.5) = P(a - 0.5 < X < b - 0.5)$ ……………(7)

Example 1: Perform the continuity correction of the following probability expressions;

1) $P(5 < X \leq 8)$
2) $P(5 \leq X < 8)$
3) $P(X = 0)$

Solution

1) **$P(5 < X \leq 8)$**……………………………………………Lower Limit Re-adjustment

Step 1: Formula. $P(\pm a \leq X \leq \pm b) = P(\pm a - 0.5 < X < \pm b + 0.5)$, where; $b = 8$

Step 2: Equivalence of upper limit

a) Formula. $P(a < X) \equiv P(a + 1 \leq X)$, where; $a = 5$

b) Data substitution and solving

$P(a < X) \equiv P(a + 1 \leq X)$ ……………[Substitute component numerical value]

$P(5 < X) \equiv P(5 + 1 \leq X)$ ……………………………[Simplify bracket]

$P(5 < X) \equiv P(6 \leq X)$ ……………………[Lower Limit Equivalent Form]

Step 3: Data substitution and solving

$P(a - 0.5 < X < b + 0.5)$ ……………………[Substitute component numerical value]

$P(6 - 0.5 < X < 8 + 0.5)$ ……………………………………[Simplify equation]

$P(5 < X \leq 8) \equiv \mathbf{P(5.5 < X < 8.5)}$ ……………………[Continuity Correction Form]

2) $\mathbf{P(5 \leq X < 8)}$……………………………………[Upper Limit Re-adjustment]

Step 1: Formula. $P(\pm a \leq X \leq \pm b) = P(\pm a - 0.5 < X < \pm b + 0.5)$, where; $a = 5$

Step 2: Equivalence of upper limit

a) Formula. $P(X < b) \equiv P(X \leq b - 1)$, where; $b = 8$

b) Data substitution and solving

$P(X < 8) \equiv P(X \leq 8 - 1)$ ……………………………[Simplify bracket]

$P(X < 8) \equiv P(X \leq 7)$ …………………………[Upper Limit Equivalent Form]

Step 3: Data substitution and solving

$P(\pm a - 0.5 < X < \pm b + 0.5)$ ……………[Substitute component numerical value]

$P(5 - 0.5 < X < 7 + 0.5)$ ……………………………………[Simplify equation]

$P(5 \leq X < 8) \equiv P(4.5 < X < 7.5)$ ……………………[Continuity Correction Form]

3) $\mathbf{P(X = 0)}$

Step 1: Formula. $P(X = a) = P(\pm a - 0.5 < X < \pm a + 0.5)$, where; $a = 0$

Step 2: Data substitution and solving

$P(a - 0.5 < X < a + 0.5)$ ……………………[Substitute component numerical value]

$P(0 - 0.5 < X < 0 + 0.5)$ ……………………………………[Simplify equation]

$P(-0.5 < X < 0.5)$ ……………………………………[Continuity correction from]

<u>Test Your Understanding</u>

Exercise 14: Perform the continuity correction of the following probability expressions;

1) $P(X < 63)$……………………………………………**[Answer:** $\mathbf{P(X < 62.5)}$**]**
2) $P(X > 70)$……………………………………………**[Answer:** $\mathbf{P(X > 70.5)}$**]**
3) $P(4 < X < 7)$………………………………………**[Answer:** $\mathbf{P(4.5 < X < 6.5)}$**]**

Exercise 15: Perform the continuity correction of the following probability expressions;

1) $P(20 \leq X \leq 25)$……………………………………**[Answer:** $\mathbf{P(19.5 < X < 25.5)}$**]**
2) $P(X \geq 10)$……………………………………………**[Answer:** $\mathbf{P(X > 9.5)}$**]**
3) $P(X \leq 25)$……………………………………………**[Answer:** $\mathbf{P(X < 25.5)}$**]**
4) $P(X = 96)$……………………………………**[Answer:** $\mathbf{P(95.5 < X < 96.5)}$**]**

Exercise 16: Perform the continuity correction of the following probability expressions;

1) $P(9 < X \leq 30)$..[Answer: $\mathbf{P(9.5 < X < 30.5)}$]
2) $P(10 \leq X < 15)$..[Answer: $\mathbf{P(9.5 < X < 14.5)}$]

5.3.3 Normal Approximation to the Binomial Distribution

Normal distribution is considered a close approximation to the binomial distribution when the product of the probability of success [P] and number of trial [n] is greater than or equal to five. That is$[np \geq 5 \text{ and } n(1-p) \text{ or } nq \geq 5]$. The binomial distribution mean is given as $[np]$ and the binomial standards deviation is given as $[\sqrt{np(1-p)}]$. the formula for standardized normal variable is given as;

$$\text{Standardised Normal Variable (Z)} = \frac{X_n - np}{\sqrt{np(1-p)}} \qquad \text{(1)}$$

Note: To perform the approximation; verify the approximation condition, perform the continuity correction and use the normal distribution to approximate binomial probability.

Example 1: The random variable X is distributed $[Bin(200, 0.7)]$. Use the normal approximation to the binomial distribution to fine the following

1) $P(X \geq 130)$
2) $P(136 \leq X < 148)$
3) $P(X < 142)$
4) $P(X = 152)$

Solution

1) $\mathbf{P(X \geq 130)}$.......[After performing continuity correction, we obtain $\mathbf{P(X > 129.5)}$]

Step 1: Determination of Z-Value

a) Formula. $\text{Standardised Normal Variable (Z)} = \frac{X_n - np}{\sqrt{np(1-p)}}$

Where; $n = 200$, $p = 0.7$,$X = 129.5$

b) Data substitution and solving

$\text{Standardised Normal Variable (Z)} = \frac{129.5 - 200(0.7)}{\sqrt{200 \times 0.7(1-0.7)}}$ ....[Simplify brackets]

$\text{Standardised Normal Variable (Z)} = \frac{129.5 - 140}{\sqrt{42}}$ ....[Simplify numerator and work root]

$\text{Standardised Normal Variable (Z)} = \frac{-10.5}{6.480740698}$ ....[Solve equation]

$\text{Standardised Normal Variable (Z)} = \mathbf{-1.620}$ ....[$P(Z > -1.620)$]

Step 2: Determination of probability value

a) Formula. $P(Z > -a) = P(Z < a) = \Phi(a)$, where; $\Phi(1.620) = 0.9474$

b) Data substitution and solving: $P(X \geq 130) = \mathbf{0.9474 = 94.74\%}$

2) $\mathbf{P(136 \leq X < 148)}$................[Continuity correction, give us $\mathbf{P(135.5 < X < 147.5)}$]

Step 1: Determination of Z-Value

a) Formula. $P(a < X < b) = P\left(\frac{X_a - np}{\sqrt{np(1-p)}} < Z < \frac{X_b - np}{\sqrt{np(1-p)}}\right)$

Where; $X_a = 135.5$, $X_b = 147.5$, $np = 140$ and $np(1-p) = 42$

b) Data substitution and solving

$$P(136 \leq X < 148) = P\left(\frac{135.5-140}{\sqrt{42}} < Z < \frac{147.5-140}{\sqrt{42}}\right)$$ ....[Simplify and work root]

$$P(136 \leq X < 148) = P\left(\frac{-4.5}{6.480740698} < Z < \frac{7.5}{6.480740698}\right)$$ ....[Simplify fraction]

$$P(136 \leq X < 148) = P(-0.694 < Z < 1.157)$$ ....[That is, $\mathbf{P(-a < Z < b)}$]

Step 2: Determination of probability value

a) Formula. $P(-a < Z < b) = \Phi(a) + \Phi(b) - 1$

Where; $\Phi(a) = 0.7562$ and $\Phi(b) = 0.8763$

b) Data substitution and solving

$$P(136 \leq X < 148) = 0.7562 + 0.8763 - 1$$ ....[Solve equation]

$$P(136 \leq X < 148) = \mathbf{0.6325 = 63.25\%}$$

3) $\mathbf{P(X = 152)}$ ....[Continuity correction gives us $\mathbf{P(151.5 < X < 152.5)}$]

Step 1: Determination of Z-Value

a) Formula. $P(a < X < b) = P\left(\frac{X_a - np}{\sqrt{np(1-p)}} < Z < \frac{X_b - np}{\sqrt{np(1-p)}}\right)$

Where; $X_a = 151.5$, $X_b = 152.5$, $np = 140$ and $np(1-p) = 42$

b) Data substitution and solving

$$P(X = 152) = P\left(\frac{151.5-140}{\sqrt{42}} < Z < \frac{152.5-140}{\sqrt{42}}\right)$$ ....[Simplify and work root]

$$P(X = 152) = P\left(\frac{11.5}{6.480740698} < Z < \frac{12.5}{6.480740698}\right)$$ ....[Simplify fraction]

$$P(X = 152) = P(1.774 < Z < 1.929)$$ ....[That is, $\mathbf{P(a < Z < b)}$]

Step 2: Determination of probability value

a) Formula. $P(a < Z < b) = \Phi(b) - \Phi(a)$, where; $\Phi(a) = 0.962$ and $\Phi(b) = 0.9731$

b) Data substitution and solving

$$P(X = 152) = 0.9731 - 0.962$$ ....[Solve equation]

$$P(X = 152) = \mathbf{0.0111 = 1.11\%}$$

4) $\mathbf{P(X < 142)}$ ………………………..…..Continuity correction gives us $\mathbf{P(X < 141.5)}$]

Step 1: Determination of Z-Value

a) Formula. $\text{Standardised Normal Variable (Z)} = \frac{X_n - np}{\sqrt{np(1-p)}}$

Where;$n = 200,\ p = 0.7, X_n = 141.5$

b) Data substitution and solving

$\text{Standardised Normal Variable (Z)} = \frac{141.5 - 200(0.7)}{\sqrt{200 \times 0.7(1-0.7)}}$ …………..[Simplify equation]

$\text{Standardised Normal Variable (Z)} = \frac{1.5}{\sqrt{42}}$ ………..[Work root and simplify fraction]

$\text{Standardised Normal Variable (Z)} = \mathbf{0.231}$ ………….………[That is, $\mathbf{P(Z < a)}$]

Step 2: Determination of probability value

a) Formula. $P(Z < a) = \Phi(a)$, where; $\Phi(0.231) = 0.5914$

b) Data substitution and solving. $P(X < 142) = \mathbf{0.5914} = \mathbf{59.14}$

Example 2: A study shows that 10% of the chocolates produced in a factory are badly shaped. Considering that a random selected sample of 1000 chocolates, fine the probability that;

1) Exactly 100 are badly shaped
2) Less than 80 are badly shaped
3) Between 90 and 115 (both inclusive) are badly shaped
4) 120 or more are badly shaped

Solution

Hint: The question provides a probability percentage ($10\% = 0.1 = p$) of event of interest and a finite total number of trails or experiments($n = 1{,}000$). Using the data, [$np = 100 \times 0.1 = 100$] and [$nq = 1000 \times 0.9 = 900$], showing that both values are greater than 5.

1) Exactly 100 are badly shaped………………………[$P(X = 100) = P(99.5 < Z < 100.5)$]

Step 1: Derivation of standardized normal variable

a) Formula. $P(a < X < b) = P\left(\frac{X_a - np}{\sqrt{np(1-p)}} < Z < \frac{X_b - np}{\sqrt{np(1-p)}}\right)$,

Where; $X_a = 99.5,\ X_b = 100.5,\ np = 100,\ np(1-p) = 90$

b) Data substitution and solving

$P(X = 100) = P\left(\frac{99.5 - 100}{\sqrt{90}} < Z < \frac{100.5 - 100}{\sqrt{90}}\right)$ ………………..[Simplify numerator]

$P(X = 100) = P\left(\frac{-0.5}{\sqrt{90}} < Z < \frac{0.5}{\sqrt{90}}\right)$ ………..…….[Work denominator square root]

$P(X = 100) = P\left(\frac{-0.5}{9.486832981} < Z < \frac{0.5}{9.486832981}\right)$ ………………..[Solve equation]

$P(X = 100) = P(\mathbf{-0.053 < Z < 0.053})$ ……………………..[$P(-a < Z < b)$]

Step 2: Derivation of required probability

a) Formula. $P(-a < Z < b) = \Phi(a) + \Phi(b) - 1$

Where; $\Phi(a) = 0.5211$, and $\Phi(b) = 0.5211$

b) Data substitution and solving

$P(X = 100) = 0.5211 + 0.5211 - 1$ ....[Solve equation]

$P(X = 100) = \mathbf{0.0422 = 4.22\%}$

2) Less than 80 are badly shaped..............................[$P(X < 80) = P(X < 79.5)$]

Step 1: Derivation of standardized normal variable

a) Formula. $Z = \frac{X_n - np}{\sqrt{np(1-p)}}$, where; $X_n = 79.5$, $np = 100$ and $np(1-p) = 90$

b) Data substitution and solving

Standardized normal variable $(Z) = \frac{79.5 - 100}{\sqrt{100(0.9)}}$ ....[Simplify equation]

Standardized normal variable $(Z) = \frac{-20.5}{\sqrt{90}}$ ....[Work denominator square]

Standardized normal variable $(Z) = \frac{-20.5}{9.486832981}$ ....[Solve equation]

Standardized normal variable $(Z) = \mathbf{-2.161}$ ....[$P(Z < -a)$]

Step 2: Derivation of required probability

a) Formula. $P(Z < -a) = P(Z > a) = 1 - \Phi(a)$, where; a = 2.161 and $\Phi(a) = 0.9846$

b) Data substitution and solving

$P(X < 80) = 1 - 0.9846$ ....[Solve equation]

$P(X < 80) = \mathbf{0.0154 = 1.54\%}$

3) Between 90 and 115 (both inclusive) are badly shaped...........[$P(89.5 < X < 115.5)$]

Step 1: Derivation of standardized normal variable

a) Formula. $P(a < X \leq b) = P\left(\frac{X_a - np}{\sqrt{np(1-p)}} < Z < \frac{X_b - np}{\sqrt{np(1-p)}}\right)$

Where; $X_a = 89.5$, $X_b = 115.5$, $np = 100$, and $np(1-p) = 90$

b) Data substitution and solving

$P(90 < X \leq 115) = P\left(\frac{89.5 - 100}{\sqrt{90}} < Z < \frac{115.5 - 100}{\sqrt{90}}\right)$ ....[Simplify numerator]

$P(90 < X \leq 115) = P\left(\frac{-10.5}{\sqrt{90}} < Z < \frac{15.5}{\sqrt{90}}\right)$ ....[Work square root of values]

$P(90 < X \leq 115) = P\left(\frac{-10.5}{9.486832981} < Z < \frac{15.5}{9.486832981}\right)$ ....[Solve equation]

$P(90 < X \leq 115) = \mathbf{P(-1.107 < Z < 1.634)}$ ....[$P(-a < Z < b)$]

Step 2: Derivation of required probability

a) Formula. $P(-a < Z < b) = \Phi(a) + \Phi(b) - 1$

Where; $\Phi(a) = 0.8657$ and $\Phi(a) = 0.9488$

b) Data substitution and solving

$P(90 \leq X \leq 115) = 0.8657 + 0.9488 - 1$ ....[Solve equation]

$P(90 \leq X \leq 115) = \mathbf{0.8145 = 81.45\%}$

4) 120 or more are badly shaped................................[$P(X \geq 120) = P(X > 119.5)$]

Step 1: Derivation of standardized normal variable

a) Formula. $Z = \frac{X_n - np}{\sqrt{np(1-p)}}$, where; $X_n = 119.5$, $np = 100$ and $np(1-p) = 90$

b) Data substitution and solving

$\text{Standardized normal variable (Z)} = \frac{119.5-100}{\sqrt{100(0.9)}}$ ....[Simplify equation]

$\text{Standardized normal variable (Z)} = \frac{19.5}{\sqrt{90}}$ ....[Solve]

$\text{Standardized normal variable (Z)} = \mathbf{2.055}$................................[$P(Z > a)$]

Step 2: Derivation of required probability

a) Formula. $P(Z > a) = 1 - \Phi(a)$, where; $\mathbf{\Phi(a) = 0.98}$

b) Data substitution and solving

$P(X \geq 120) = 1 - 0.98$ ....[Solve equation]

$P(X \geq 120) = \mathbf{0.02 = 2\%}$

<u>Test Your Understanding</u>

Exercise 17: Based upon past experience, 40% of all customers at Millers Automotive service station pay their purchases with a credit card. If a random sample of 200 customers is selected, what is the approximate probability that;

1) At least 75 pay with a credit card......................... **[Answer: $\mathbf{0.7864 = 78.64\%}$]**
2) Not more than 70 pay with a credit card.................. **[Answer: $\mathbf{0.0648 = 6.48\%}$]**
3) Between 70 and 75 customers, inclusive, pay with a credit card

[Answer: $\mathbf{0.193 = 19.3\%}$]

Exercise 18: Given that $n = 1{,}000$ and $p = 0.5$, use the normal distribution to calculate the following;

1) $P(X \leq 510)$..**[Answer: $\mathbf{0.7467 = 74.67\%}$]**
2) $P(X > 495)$..**[Answer: $\mathbf{0.6122 = 61.22\%}$]**
3) $P(X = 495)$..**[Answer: $\mathbf{0.0239 = 2.39\%}$]**

Exercise 19: The probability that a female student will pass the math test is 2%. If 400 female students are sampled, use the normal approximation to calculate the probability that more than or equal to 15 out of the 400 passed.................................. **[Answer: $0.0102 = 1.02\%$]**

5.3.4 Normal Approximation to the Poisson Distribution

The approximation is possible when the mean (λ) equals or exceed 5, that is [$\lambda \geq 5$]. Remember that in Poisson distribution, the average [λ] equals the variance [λ]. Therefore, the standard deviation is the square root of the variance [$\sqrt{\lambda}$]. The formula for standardized normal variable is given as;

$$\text{Standardized Normal Variable (Z)} = \frac{X_n - \lambda}{\sqrt{\lambda}} \quad \ldots\ldots\ldots\ldots\ldots\ldots\ldots\ldots(1)$$

Note: To perform the approximation; verify the approximation condition, perform the continuity correction and use the normal distribution to approximate poisson probability.

Example 1: The number of calls per hour received by an office follows a Poisson distribution with parameter 30. Using the normal approximation to the Poisson distribution, find the probability that in one hour;

1) There are more than 33 calls
2) There are between 25 and 28 calls (inclusive)
3) There are 34 calls

Solution

1) **There are more than 33 calls**.......[Continuity correction $P(X > 33) = P(X > 33.5)$]

Step 1: Derivation of standardized normal variable

a) Formula. Standardized Normal Variable (Z) $= \frac{X_n - \lambda}{\sqrt{\lambda}}$, where; $\lambda = 30$ and $X_n = 33.5$
b) Data substitution and solving

$$\text{Standardized Normal Variable (Z)} = \frac{33.5 - 30}{\sqrt{30}} \quad \ldots\ldots\ldots\text{[Simplify numerator]}$$

$$\text{Standardized Normal Variable (Z)} = \frac{3.5}{\sqrt{30}} \quad \ldots\ldots\ldots\text{[Work square root]}$$

$$\text{Standardized Normal Variable (Z)} = \frac{3.5}{5.477225575} \quad \ldots\ldots\ldots\text{[Solve equation]}$$

$$\text{Standardized Normal Variable (Z)} = \mathbf{0.639} \quad \ldots\ldots\ldots[\mathbf{P(Z > a)}]$$

Step 2: Derivation of required probability

c) Formula. $P(Z > a) = 1 - \Phi(a)$, where; $\Phi(a) = 0.7386$
d) Data substitution and solving

$$P(X < 33) = 1 - 0.7386 \quad \ldots\ldots\ldots\text{[Solve equation]}$$

$$P(X < 33) = \mathbf{0.2614 = 26.14\%}$$

2) **There are between 25 and 28 calls (inclusive)**....[$P(25 \leq X \leq 28) = P(24.5 < X < 28.5)$]

Step 1: Derivation of standardized normal variable

a) Formula. $P(a < X \leq b) = P\left(\frac{X_a - \lambda}{\sqrt{\lambda}} < Z < \frac{X_b - \lambda}{\sqrt{\lambda}}\right)$

Where; $X_a = 24.5, X_b = 28.5, \lambda = 30$

b) Data substitution and solving

$P(25 \leq X \leq 28) = P\left(\frac{24.5-30}{\sqrt{30}} < Z < \frac{28.5-30}{\sqrt{30}}\right)$ ....[Simplify numerator]

$P(25 \leq X \leq 28) = P\left(\frac{-5.5}{\sqrt{30}} < Z < \frac{-1.5}{\sqrt{30}}\right)$ ....[Work square root]

$P(25 \leq X \leq 28) = P\left(\frac{-5.5}{5.477225575} < Z < \frac{-1.5}{5.477225575}\right)$ ....[Solve equation]

$P(25 \leq X \leq 28) = \mathbf{P(-1.004 < Z < -0.274)}$ ....[$P(-a < Z < -b)$]

Step 2: Derivation of required probability

a) Formula. $P(-a < Z > -b) = \Phi(a) - \Phi(b)$, where; $\Phi(a) = 0.8422$, $\Phi(b) = 0.6079$

b) Data substitution and solving

$P(X < 33) = 0.8422 - 0.6079$ ....[Solve equation]

$P(X < 33) = \mathbf{0.2343 = 23.43\%}$

3) There are 34 calls..................[Continuity correction $P(X = 34) = P(33.5 < X < 34.5)$]

Step 1: Derivation of standardized normal variable

a) Formula. $P(X = x) = P\left(\frac{X_a - \lambda}{\sqrt{\lambda}} < Z < \frac{X_b - \lambda}{\sqrt{\lambda}}\right)$, where; $X_a = 33.5, X_b = 34.5, \lambda = 30$

b) Data substitution and solving

$P(X = 34) = P\left(\frac{33.5-30}{\sqrt{30}} < Z < \frac{34.5-30}{\sqrt{30}}\right)$ ....[Simplify numerator and work root]

$P(X = 34) = P\left(\frac{3.5}{5.477225575} < Z < \frac{4.5}{5.477225575}\right)$ ....[Solve fraction]

$P(X = 34) = \mathbf{P(0.639 < Z < 0.822)}$ ....[$P(a < Z < b)$]

Step 2: Derivation of required probability

a) Formula. $P(a < Z > b) = \Phi(b) - \Phi(a)$, where; $\Phi(a) = 0.7386$ and $\Phi(b) = 0.7944$

b) Data substitution and solving

$P(X < 33) = 0.7944 - 0.7386$ ....[Solve equation]

$P(X < 33) = \mathbf{0.0558 = 5.58\%}$

Example 2: Considering that $X \sim Po(60)$, use the normal approximation to find the following

1) $P(50 < X \leq 58)$
2) $P(57 \leq X < 68)$
3) $P(X > 52)$
4) $P(X \geq 70)$

Solution

1) $P(50 < X \leq 58)$.....................................[Continuity correction $P(50.5 < X < 58.5)$]

Step 1: Derivation of standardized normal variable

a) Formula. $P(a < X \leq b) = P\left(\frac{X_a - \lambda}{\sqrt{\lambda}} < Z < \frac{X_b - \lambda}{\sqrt{\lambda}}\right)$

Where; $X_a = 50.5, X_b = 58.5, \lambda = 60$

b) Data substitution and solving

$P(a < X \leq b) = P\left(\frac{X_a - \lambda}{\sqrt{\lambda}} < Z < \frac{X_b - \lambda}{\sqrt{\lambda}}\right)$ ....[Substitute component numerical data]

$P(50 < X \leq 58) = P\left(\frac{50.5-60}{\sqrt{60}} < Z < \frac{58.5-60}{\sqrt{60}}\right)$ ......[Simplify numerator and work root]

$P(50 < X \leq 58) = P\left(\frac{-9.5}{7.745966692} < Z < \frac{-1.5}{7.745966692}\right)$ ....[Simplify fraction]

$P(50 < X \leq 58) = \mathbf{P(-1.226 < Z < -0.194)}$ ....[$P(-a < Z < -b)$]

Step 2: Derivation of required probability

a) Formula. $P(-a < Z > -b) = \Phi(a) - \Phi(b)$,where; $\Phi(a) = 0.8899, \Phi(b) = 0.5769$

b) Data substitution and solving

$P(50 < X \leq 58) = 0.8899 - 0.5769$ ....[Solve equation]

$P(50 < X \leq 58) = \mathbf{0.313 = 31.3\%}$

2) $\mathbf{P(57 \leq X < 68)}$......................................[Continuity correction $P(56.5 < X < 67.5)$]

Step 1: Derivation of standardized normal variable

a) Formula. $P(a < X \leq b) = P\left(\frac{X_a - \lambda}{\sqrt{\lambda}} < Z < \frac{X_b - \lambda}{\sqrt{\lambda}}\right)$

Where; $X_a = 56.5, X_b = 67.5, \lambda = 60$

b) Data substitution and solving

$P(a < X \leq b) = P\left(\frac{X_a - \lambda}{\sqrt{\lambda}} < Z < \frac{X_b - \lambda}{\sqrt{\lambda}}\right)$ ....[Substitute component numerical data]

$P(57 \leq X < 68) = P\left(\frac{56.5-60}{\sqrt{60}} < Z < \frac{67.5-60}{\sqrt{60}}\right)$ ......[Simplify numerator and work root]

$P(57 \leq X < 68) = P\left(\frac{-3.5}{7.745966692} < Z < \frac{7.5}{7.745966692}\right)$ ....[Simplify fraction]

$P(57 \leq X < 68) = \mathbf{P(-0.452 < Z < 0.968)}$ ....[$P(-a < Z < b)$]

Step 2: Derivation of required probability

a) Formula. $P(-a < Z < b) = \Phi(a) + \Phi(b) - 1$

Where; $\Phi(a) = 0.6743$ and $\Phi(b) = 0.8335$

b) Data substitution and solving

$P(57 \leq X < 68) = 0.6743 + 0.8335 - 1$ ....[Solve equation]

$P(57 \leq X < 68) = \mathbf{0.5078 = 50.78\%}$

3) $\mathbf{P(X > 52)}$..[Continuity correction $P(X > 52.5)$]

Step 1: Derivation of standardized normal variable

a) Formula. Standardized Normal Variable $(Z) = \frac{X_n - \lambda}{\sqrt{\lambda}}$, where; $\lambda = 60$ and $X_n = 52.5$

b) Data substitution and solving

Standardized Normal Variable $(Z) = \frac{52.5-60}{\sqrt{60}}$ .....[Simplify numerator and work root]

Standardized Normal Variable $(Z) = \frac{-7.5}{7.745966692}$ ....[Simplify fraction]

Standardized Normal Variable $(\mathbf{Z}) = \mathbf{-0.968}$ ....[$P(Z > -a)$]

Step 2: Derivation of required probability

a) Formula. $P(Z > -a) = P(Z < a) = \Phi(a)$, where; $\Phi(a) = 0.8335$

b) Data substitution and solving. $P(X > 52) = \mathbf{0.8335 = 83.35\%}$

4) $P(X \geq 70)$...[Continuity correction $P(X > 69.5)$]

Step 1: Derivation of standardized normal variable

a) Formula. Standardized Normal Variable $(Z) = \frac{X_n - \lambda}{\sqrt{\lambda}}$, where; $\lambda = 60$ and $X_n = 69.5$

b) Data substitution and solving

Standardized Normal Variable $(Z) = \frac{69.5-60}{\sqrt{60}}$......[Simplify numerator and work root]

Standardized Normal Variable $(Z) = \frac{9.5}{7.745966692}$ ....[Simplify fraction]

Standardized Normal Variable $(Z) = \mathbf{1.226}$ ....[$P(Z > a)$]

Step 2: Derivation of required probability

a) Formula. $P(Z > a) = 1 - \Phi(a)$, where; $\Phi(a) = 0.8899$

b) Data substitution and solving.

$P(X \geq 70) = 1 - 0.8899$ ....[Solve equation]

$P(X \geq 70) = \mathbf{0.1101 = 11.01\%}$

<u>**Test Your Understanding**</u>

Exercise 20: The mean number of typing errors in a document is 12 per page. Use the normal approximation, find the probability that on a page chosen at random there are;

1) Exactly 10 mistakes..**[Answer: $\mathbf{0.0973 = 9.73\%}$]**
2) More than 2 mistakes.......................................**[Answer: $\mathbf{0.9969 = 99.69\%}$]**
3) Exactly 15 mistakes...**[Answer: $\mathbf{0.079 = 7.9\%}$]**

Example 21: Considering that $X \sim Po(22)$, use the normal approximation to find

1) $P(X < 22)$..**[Answer: $\mathbf{0.4574 = 45.74\%}$]**
2) $P(25 < X < 30)$.......................................**[Answer: $\mathbf{0.173 = 17.3\%}$]**

3) $P(X \geq 18)$...[**Answer: $0.8312 = 83.12\%$**]

Example 22: If $X \sim Po(25)$, what is the approximate probability that in any given ten-minute period;

1) Exactly 20 cars arrive.. [**Answer: $0.0484 = 4.84\%$**]
2) Not more than 20 cars arrive................................. [**Answer: $0.1357 = 13.57\%$**]
3) Between 20 and 30 cars arrive............................ [**Answer: $0.6318 = 63.18\%$**]

CHAPTER SIX

SAMPLING AND ESTIMATION

Information is essential for the understanding of economic phenomena, establishment of data base and development of models, theories and laws. Such information is obtained from the entire or fraction of the element of study or element of interest.

6.1 The Concept of Population

Statistically, a population (denoted N) is defined as the entire elements of interest from which a researcher collects information from or about. Population also called universe can be living things (humans and animals) or non-living things (cars and stars). The major terms about population are;

a) Finite Population: A population is finite when it consists of a fixed number of elements such that it is possible to enumerate or count it totality. Finite population is usually any population confined in specific geographical area, occupation and social class. For example, the population of students in a given educational institution or town, the population of doctors in a given hospital or region, the population of rich and poor in a given area.

b) Infinite Population: A population is infinite when it is impossible to observe or enumerate all the elements of the population. For example, the population of stars in a galaxy, the population of fishes in an ocean. Practically and scientifically, an infinite population is defined as a very large finite population that is impossible to enumerate all its elements in a given research period.

c) Homogeneous Population: A homogenous population is any population in which all it elements are similar to each other in all aspects of interest. Considering a class room to be our population, the population elements are homogenous in that they are all students.

d) Heterogeneous Population: A heterogeneous population is any population in which all it elements differs from each other in all or majority aspects of interest. For example, a population of students in a given class room may differ from each other in terms of their gender, age, ethnicity, religion and socio-economic status.

Note: The notion of homogeneity and heterogeneity of population depends on the objective and nature of the research or study being carried out.

6.2 The Concept of Sampling

Practically, getting information from a large population is possible but at times very difficult due to natural barriers (rivers and mountains) and human constraints (time, finance and intellectual capability). Therefore, the researcher is required to select from a complete list of population elements a pre-determined number of elements smaller than the population to be used as the study population.

The complete list of population elements is called a sampling frame or sampling list. Sampling frame can be in three forms; adopted form, adapted or modified form and developed form. For analytical and statistical precision, it is advisable that the sampling frame should be recent (reflect existing situation) and exhaustive (representative).

The pre-determined number of selected elements smaller than the population is called sample. Statistically, a sample is defined as a fraction selected from a given sampling frame from which information collected is analysis and result derived is generalized to the population. Sample elements are called sample units and the sum of the sample units is called sample size (n). The sample size must be greater than zero and lesser than the population size ($0 < n < N$).

The process of selecting the appropriate sample units from a given population to obtain the required sample size is called sampling. In summary, sampling is also defined as the process of selecting sample from a given population. Sampling should not be seen as a means to an end and is recommended only when restrictions to collect information from the entire population are enough to influence significant and negatively the result. Therefore sample must be statistical and logical justifications.

6.2.1Sampling Techniques

The required sample size can be derived using several sampling techniques in a separated and/or combined manner. Sampling methods or techniques are sub-divided into two main groups; the probabilistic and non-probabilistic methods.

6.2.1.1 Probabilistic Sampling Method

It is a sampling method in which all elements of the sampling frame have the same opportunity (greater than zero) of being included in the sample and in which the mathematical probability of their selection can be calculated with accuracy. Here, all sampling frame elements are given the same weight or importance, making this method to also be called self-weighting method.

1) Simple Random Sampling

It is a probability sampling method in which each and every element of the population has an equal chance of being selected in the sample. It is the probability sampling method mostly used in both finite and non-finite population. Simple random sampling selection styles includes; lottery technique, blind folded technique, using random number table and using computer programs.

2) Stratified Random Sampling

It is a method applicable mostly in heterogeneous population, as it sub-divides the heterogeneous population into homogenous sub-populations or group called strata. The number of strata (L) depends on number of sub-categories in each factor that causes the heterogeneity in the population and the degree of stratification depends on the number of factor that causes the heterogeneity. The sum of strata $[N_1, N_2, \ldots\ldots N_L]$ must be equal to the population (N). It is worth knowing that strata must be homogenous within and heterogeneous between themselves and the quality of result in stratified random sampling is directly related to the homogeneity of strata and indirectly related to the heterogeneity of strata.

Example 1: From a population of 25 students below, stratify the population based on the criterion or factor gender.

Solution

Hint: The factor that causes the heterogeneity is gender and is made up of two categories (male and female). Therefore, the number of strata is 2 $[N_1$ and $N_2]$. Since there is only a (one) factor that causes the heterogeneity, the degree or level of stratification is 1.

Male (Stratum 1) $[\mathbf{N_1 = 12}]$	**Female (Stratum 2)** $[\mathbf{N_2 = 13}]$
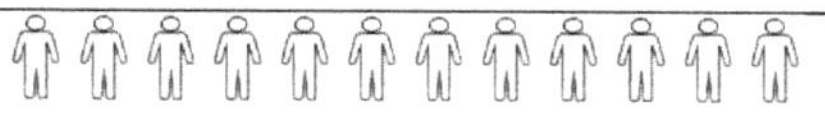	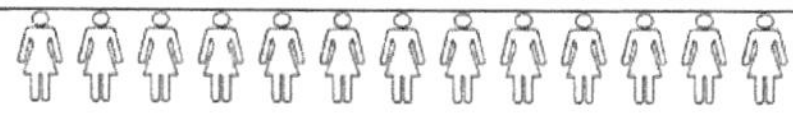
Note: Sum of strata must equal population. $[N_1 + N_2 = N \therefore 12 + 13 = 25]$	

Note: Stratum 1 and 2 are homogenous within in that all their elements are males and female respectively. Stratum 1 is heterogeneous from stratum 2 as it is made up of males while stratum 2 is made up of females which are mutually exclusive or completely opposite attributes.

Example 2: In a class of 36 students of males and females given below, stratify the population based on the criterion gender and race.

Solution

Hint: There are two factors that cause the heterogeneity of population indicating two levels of stratification. The population is having four categories; male and female for gender and white and black for race, indicating four strata $[N_1, N_2, N_3 \text{ and } N_4]$. Possible stratifications are illustrated below.

<table>
<tr><td colspan="4">Stratification based on gender [partial stratification]</td></tr>
<tr><td colspan="2">Male $[N_1 = 16]$</td><td colspan="2">Female $[N_2 = 20]$</td></tr>
<tr><td colspan="2">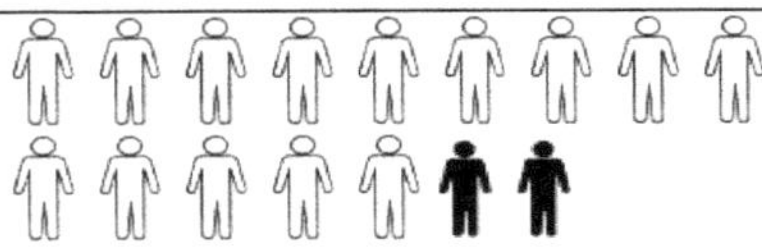</td><td colspan="2"></td></tr>
<tr><td colspan="4">Stratification based on race [partial stratification]</td></tr>
<tr><td colspan="2">Married $[N_1 = 22]$</td><td colspan="2">Single $[N_2 = 14]$</td></tr>
<tr><td colspan="2">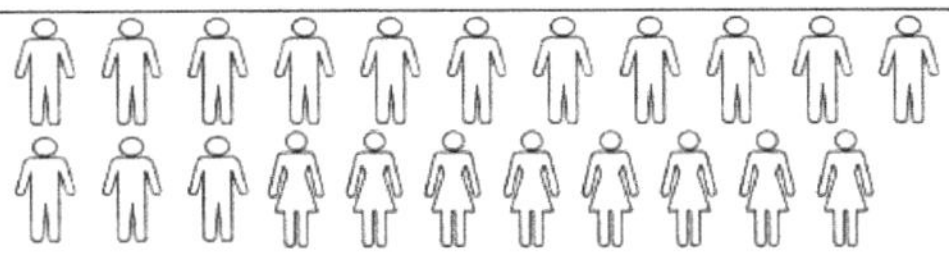</td><td colspan="2"></td></tr>
<tr><td colspan="4">Stratification based on gender and race [Complete stratification]</td></tr>
<tr><td>Single Males</td><td>Married Males</td><td>Single Females</td><td>Married Females</td></tr>
<tr><td></td><td>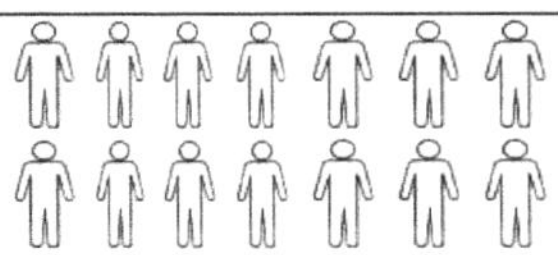</td><td></td><td>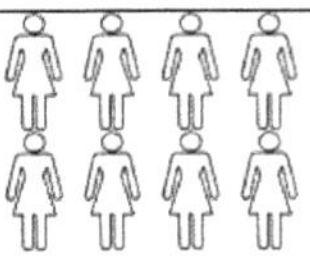</td></tr>
<tr><td>$[N_1 = 2]$</td><td>$[N_2 = 14]$</td><td>$[N_3 = 12]$</td><td>$[N_4 = 8]$</td></tr>
</table>

Note: The first two stratifications fail to respect the condition of homogenous with strata. First stratification is homogenous in gender but heterogeneous in race and the second stratification is homogenous in race but heterogeneous in gender. The third stratification is complete or ideal as strata are homogenous in both gender and race.

The development of strata is a step and the manner of sample selection from strata is another. The two main sample selection styles are; proportionate and non-proportionate. In order to obtain stratum sample, one is required to determine the value of sampling fraction, which is the ratio between the sample size and the population size. The sum of stratum sample must equal the required sample size.

a) **Proportionate Selection Technique**: In proportionate sample selection technique, the same sampling fraction is applied to all the strata. Here, the stratum sample selected is directly related to the stratum size. That is, the higher the stratum size, the higher the sample elements selected from the stratum.

Example 1: The table below represents four strata of a population of 40 students. Select a sample of 10 students using the proportionate selection technique.

Black Males	White Males	Black Females	White Females
	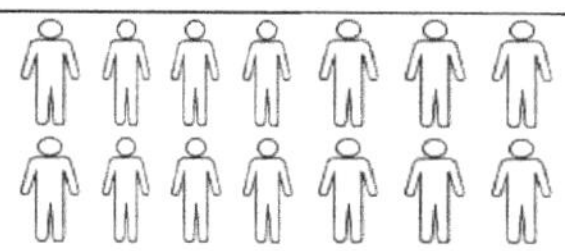		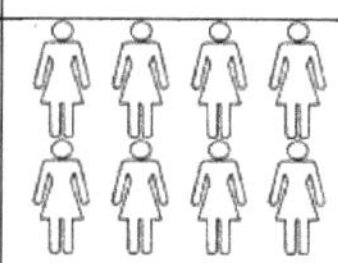

Solution

Step 1: Calculation of the sampling fraction

a) Formula. Sampling fraction $= \frac{\text{Required sample size(n)}}{\text{Total population size(N)}}$, where; n = 10 and N = 40

b) Data substitution and solving

$$\text{Sampling Fraction} = \frac{\text{Required sample size(n)}}{\text{Total population size(N)}} \text{ ....[Substitute data values]}$$

$$\text{Sampling Fraction} = \frac{10}{40} \text{ ....[Simplify fraction]}$$

$$\text{Sampling Fraction} = \frac{1}{4} = \mathbf{25\%}$$

c) Interpretation: Sampling fraction value in fraction indicates that 4 units in each stratum are represented by 1 unit in the stratum sample. Sampling fraction in percentage indicates that 25% of the each stratum population will be included in the sample.

Step 2: Determination of stratum samples (S_n) and required sample size (n):

Hint: To determine the stratum sample (S_n), we simply multiple the sampling fraction by the stratum size. In case of a fraction, the value is being rounded up or down. The sum of stratum sample must be equal to the required sample.

a) Formula: $\text{Stratum Size}(S_n) = \frac{\text{Required Sample Size(n)}}{\text{Population Size(N)}} \times \text{Stratum Size}(N_L)$

Where; $\frac{\text{Required Sample Size(n)}}{\text{Population Size(N)}}$ represents the sampling fraction and equals $\frac{1}{4} = 25\%$

b) Tabular determination of stratum sample and required sample size

STRATA	Formula. Sample fraction × Stratum size	
	Using Fraction	Using Percentage [25% = 0.25]
Black Males [4 Units]	$\frac{1}{4} \times 4 = \mathbf{1}$	$0.25 \times 4 = \mathbf{1}$
White Males [14 Units]	$\frac{1}{4} \times 14 = 3.4 \cong \mathbf{4}$	$0.25 \times 14 = 3.5 \cong \mathbf{4}$
Black Females [12 Units]	$\frac{1}{4} \times 12 = \mathbf{3}$	$0.25 \times 12 = \mathbf{3}$
White Females [8 Units]	$\frac{1}{4} \times 8 = \mathbf{2}$	$0.25 \times 8 = \mathbf{2}$
Interpretation: The required sample is therefore a combination of the following; 1 black male, 4 white males, 3 black females and 2 white females.		

b) **Non-Proportionate Technique**: Here, the sampling fractions is sub-divided into unequal fractions and applied to the different strata in a manner in which the sum of the unequal sampling fraction must be equal to 100 in percentage or 1 in fraction. This method is less utilized as the sampling fraction distribution amongst strata is not statistically justifiable and leads to over-sampling and under-sampling of strata, which in tend reduces accuracy and reliability.

Example 1: The total population of a University is 10,000 students, with 6,000 female students and 4,000 male students. Draw a sample of 1,000 students from the University using the non-proportionate technique.

Solution

Step 1: Determination of sampling fraction

a) Formula. $\text{Sampling fraction} = \frac{\text{Required sample size(n)}}{\text{Total population size(N)}}$, where; $n = 1{,}000,\ N = 10{,}000$

b) Data substitution and solving

$\text{Sampling Fraction} = \frac{\text{Required sample size(n)}}{\text{Total population size(N)}}$ ....[Substitute data values]

$\text{Sampling Fraction} = \frac{1{,}000}{10{,}000}$ ....[Simplify fraction]

$\text{Sampling Fraction} = \frac{\mathbf{1}}{\mathbf{10}} \cong \mathbf{10\%}$

c) Interpretation: The sampling fraction value shows that the sample is 10% of the total population size.

Step 2: Sampling fraction discriminatory allocation and determination of stratum sample

Hint: To obtain the stratum sample, we decide on the unequal sampling fraction distribution and multiply the unequal sampling fraction by the stratum size.

Favor of Males [Over-Sampling Males]			Favor of Females [Over-Sampling Females]		
[80% For Male and 20% For Females]			[80% For Female and 20% For Males]		
Gender	Working	Sample proportion	Gender	Working	Sample proportion
Males	0.8 × 1,000	800 Males	Males	0.2 × 1,000	200 Males
Females	0.2 × 1,000	200 Females	Females	0.8 × 1,000	800 Females
Note: Sample is made up of 800 males and 200 females			**Note**: Sample is made up of 200 males and 800 females		

3) Systematic Random Sampling

To perform systematic sampling, we are required number all sampling frame units. The number assigned to a given unit is considered the unit serial number. Systematic sampling is applicable when the population is small and homogenous and the sampling frame units are having unequal probability of being included in the sample. The two types of systematic random sampling includes; linear systematic random sampling and circular systematic random sampling.

a) **Linear Systematic Random Sampling**: It is applicable when the total population size value (N) is a multiple of the sample size value (n) or when the product of the sample size (n) and sampling interval (K) equals the total population size (N), [N = nK].

Example 1: Considering that the table below represents the total number of population and their respective serial number. From the population, draw a sample size of 5 individuals.

1	2	3	4	5	6	7	8	9	10
				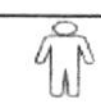	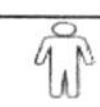	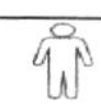	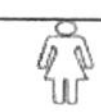	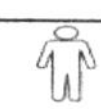	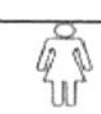
11	12	13	14	15	16	17	18	19	20
	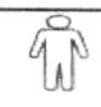		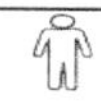	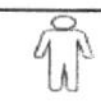			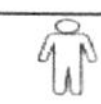		
Note: Total population size (N) equals 20. Number of males equal 8 (40%) and number of females equal 12 (60%). The percentage difference is 20%.									

Solution

Step 1: Determination of sampling interval(K) and verification [nK = N].

a) Formula: Sampling Interval (K) $= \frac{\text{Population Size(N)}}{\text{Sample Size (n)}}$, where; N = 20 and n = 5

b) Data substitution and solving

Sampling Interval (K) $= \frac{\text{Population Size(N)}}{\text{Sample Size (n)}}$ ....[Substitute data into the formula]

Sampling Interval (K) $= \frac{20}{5}$ ....[Work fraction]

Sampling Interval (K) = **4**

c) Interpretation: The sampling interval value (4) indicates that we skip 4 possible sample units after each selection.

d) Verification: $N = nK \rightarrow 5 \times 4 = 20$ and K is not negative $[K = 4 \therefore K > 0]$

Step 2: Determination of first sample serial number (λ_1): The sampling interval value also means we select a random number between 1 and 4 (inclusive) and considered it as the first sample unit serial number. Assuming that the number 2 is selected, therefore $[\lambda_1 = 2]$.

Step 3: Derivation of remaindering sample units serial numbers ($\lambda_2 \rightarrow \lambda_5$):

a) Formula. $\lambda_m = \lambda_{m-1} + K$

Where; K = 4, m is current serial number and m − 1 is the preceding serial number

b) Tabular determination of remainder serial numbers. [Remember $\lambda_1 = 2$]

units to be drawn	Formula $[\lambda_m = \lambda_{m-1} + K]$	Serial Numbers
λ_2	$\lambda_2 = \lambda_{2-1} + K \Rightarrow \boldsymbol{\lambda_2 = \lambda_1 + K}$, where; $\boldsymbol{\lambda_1 = 2}$	$\lambda_2 = 2 + 4 = \mathbf{6}$
λ_3	$\lambda_3 = \lambda_{3-1} + K \Rightarrow \boldsymbol{\lambda_3 = \lambda_2 + K}$, where; $\boldsymbol{\lambda_2 = 6}$	$\lambda_3 = 6 + 4 = \mathbf{10}$
λ_4	$\lambda_4 = \lambda_{4-1} + K \Rightarrow \boldsymbol{\lambda_4 = \lambda_3 + K}$, where; $\boldsymbol{\lambda_3 = 10}$	$\lambda_4 = 10 + 4 = \mathbf{14}$
λ_5	$\lambda_5 = \lambda_{5-1} + K \Rightarrow \boldsymbol{\lambda_5 = \lambda_4 + K}$, where; $\boldsymbol{\lambda_4 = 14}$	$\lambda_5 = 14 + 4 = \mathbf{18}$

Step 4: Identification of sample units: Consider only the sampling frame units corresponding to the calculated serial numbers (2, 6, 10, 14 and 18).

b) **Circular Systematic Random Sampling:** It is applicable when the product of the sample size (n) and the sampling interval (K) is not equal the total population size (N). The value of sampling interval should be rounded up or down. When rounded down, the product of the sampling interval and the sample size is lesser than the population and when rounded up, the product is greater than the population size. It is advisable to always round down the value of sample interval before usage.

Example 1: Draw a sample of 5 units from a population of 12 individuals, using the systematic sampling method.

Solution

Step 1: Determination of sampling interval.

a) Formula: $\text{Sampling Interval (K)} = \frac{\text{Population Size(N)}}{\text{Sample Size (n)}}$, where; $N = 12$ and $n = 5$

b) Data substitution and solving

$\text{Sampling Interval (K)} = \frac{\text{Population Size(N)}}{\text{Sample Size (n)}}$ ....[Substitute data into the formula]

$\text{Sampling Interval (K)} = \frac{12}{5}$ ....[Work fraction]

$\text{Sampling Interval (K)} = \mathbf{2.4 \cong 2}$

c) Verification: $N = N \neq nK \rightarrow 5 \times 2 = 10 \therefore$ and K is not negative $[K = 2 \therefore K > 0]$

Step 2: Determination of first sample unit serial number (r): The first sample unit serial number is any randomly selected number between one (1) and the population size (12). Assume we select 4, therefore$[r = 4]$.

Step 3: Determination of other sample unit's serial numbers:

a) Formula. $\lambda_m = r + (m - 1)K$, where; $K = 2$, $r = 4$ and m current serial number.

b) Tabular determination of other serial units numbers

Number of draws	Formula. $\lambda_m = r + (m - 1)K$	Working
First draw $[m = 1]$	$r = 4$ [Determined in step 2]	$\lambda_1 = r = 4$
Second draw $[m = 2]$	$\lambda_2 = r + (2 - 1)K \Rightarrow \boldsymbol{\lambda_2 = r + (1)K}$	$\lambda_2 = 4 + (1)2 = 6$
Third draw $[m = 3]$	$\lambda_3 = r + (3 - 1)K \Rightarrow \boldsymbol{\lambda_3 = r + (2)K}$	$\lambda_3 = 4 + (2)2 = 8$
Fourth draw $[m = 4]$	$\lambda_4 = r + (4 - 1)K \Rightarrow \boldsymbol{\lambda_4 = r + (3)K}$	$\lambda_4 = 4 + (3)2 = 10$
Fifth draw $[m = 5]$	$\lambda_5 = r + (5 - 1)K \Rightarrow \boldsymbol{\lambda_5 = r + (4)K}$	$\lambda_5 = 4 + (4)2 = 12$

Step 4: Derivation of sample units: Simply identify units in the population corresponding to the calculated serial numbers. Therefore, the sample units will be population units corresponding to the serial numbers 4, 6, 8, 10 and 12.

4) Cluster Random Sampling

In cluster sampling, the study population is sub-divided into groups called clusters and in which each cluster is considered a sample unit. The clusters must be heterogeneous within and homogeneous without and should also be representative.

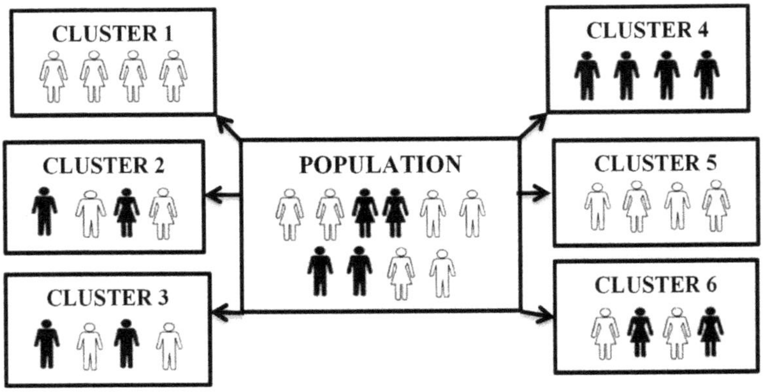

Cluster 1 and 4 are not heterogeneous with respect to gender and race and is not representative. Cluster 3 and 6 are not heterogeneous with respect to gender and are also not representative. Cluster 5 is not heterogeneous with respect to race and is not representative. Cluster 2 is heterogeneous with respect to gender and race and is representative. Therefore, with respect to the given population, cluster 2 is the ideal cluster amongst the alternative clusters.

Cluster random sampling method is generally sub-divided into three groups; one-stage cluster sampling, two-stage cluster random sampling and multi-stage cluster random sampling. Our analysis will be limited to the first two types of cluster random sampling.

1) **One-Stage Cluster Sampling:** Here, all elements in the selected clusters are included in the sample. Therefore, one-stage cluster sampling can be considered a census of a miniature population. A major limitation of one-stage cluster sampling is that the cluster elements maybe greater or lesser than the required sample size.

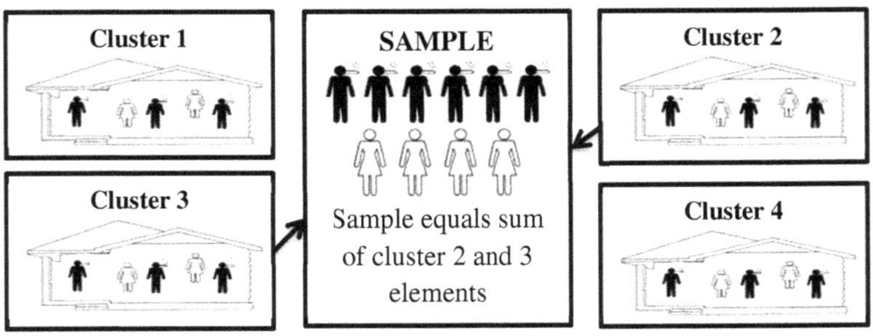

2) **Two-Stage Cluster Sampling:** Here, all elements in the pre-selected clusters are not included in the sample. A fraction of cluster elements are randomly selected to from each pre-selected cluster separately to obtain the required sample. The selected sample is therefore a sub-set of the selected clusters.

Chosen Clusters		Selected Cluster Elements	Sample
Cluster 2			 Therefore, the sample is the combination of selected elements from both clusters.
Cluster 3			

Note: Although stratified and cluster sampling may seem similar, the main difference between them includes the following;

i) In stratified sampling, all strata must be homogenous within and heterogeneous between themselves. In cluster sampling, clusters must be heterogeneous within and homogenous between themselves.

ii) In stratified sampling method, all strata are included into the final sample. In cluster sampling, only selected clusters are included into the final sample.

5) Multi-Stage Sampling Method

It is a sampling method that uses or combines variety or several sampling methods in drawing the required sample size. Practically, it is the most used sampling method as a given sampling method limitations is been covered by another method.

6.2.1.2 Non-Probabilistic Sampling Method

In non-sampling probability method, all elements in the study population or sampling frame are not having equal opportunity or probability of being included in the sample and there exist not pre-determine sample selection procedure. This is because elements or sample units are selected on the basis of availability, personal judgment (interest) and in which the probability of selection can't be accurately calculated. Here, selection of elements is non-random. Major examples includes; accidental (accidental) sampling, quota sampling and purposive (judgmental) sampling.

1) Convenience Sampling Method

It is a sampling method in which sample units are selected based on ease of accessibility, proximity and volunteerism. It is mostly used when the available resources allocated for the study is insufficient and when a researcher is unwilling to accept research stress and difficulties. The final sample is usually made up of easily accessible, proximity and volunteers sample units rather than representative units. Convenience sampling is also called available sampling, grab (selfishly) or opportunity sampling and accidental or haphazard (without order or plan) sampling method.

2) Snowball Sampling Method

It is a sampling method in which selected participants helps in the selection of other potential participants of the study. It is made up of two stages; identifying potential participants from the population and asking the identified participants other potential participants. Snowball sampling in used mostly in study that deals with; illegal activities (drugs dealing, human trafficking), social stigma population (prostitutes, gays, transgender) and population difficult to identify or locate (homeless). Snowball sampling is sub-divided into two types; linear snowball sampling (subjects identify only one other potential participant) and exponential snowball sampling (Subjects identify multiple potential participants). Snowball sampling is also called chain sampling.

3) Judgmental Sampling

It is a sampling method in which the research sample is drawn from the study population units that are appropriate or suitable for the study. Here, the researcher uses the pre-determined objective or purpose of the study to properly choose and approach qualified or eligible participants. Purposive sampling is sub-divided into two mean types; heterogeneous purposive (maximum variation) and homogeneous purposive sampling. Judgmental sampling is also called selective sampling, subjective sampling and deliberate sampling.

6.2.2 Sampling Units Selection Methods

Understanding the various sampling methods is a significant step in the concept of sampling. The next major question asked is; how should a researcher select the required sample size from the sampling frame? The two main sampling units selection methods includes; sampling without replacement and sampling with replacement.

1) Sampling without Replacement

In this sampling unit selection method, once a sampling unit is selected from the sampling frame to be part of the sample, the selected sampling unit is not replaced or put back in the sampling frame.

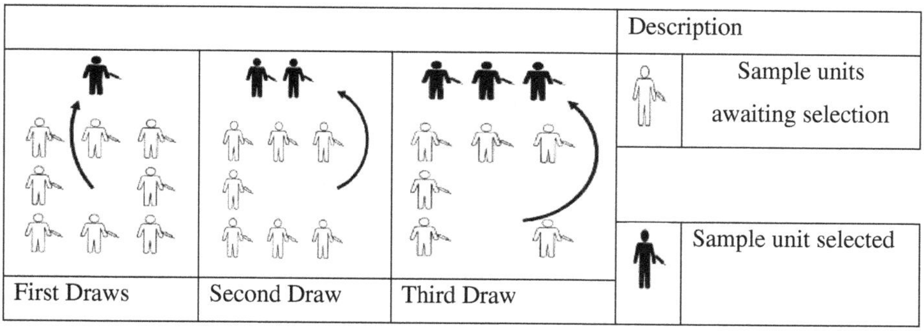

Here, there is no possibility for a given sampling unit to be selected more than a time. The number of possible sample formation from the sampling frame can be calculated using the following formula;

$$\text{Possible Sample Combination} = \frac{N!}{n!(N-n)!} \quad \ldots\ldots\ldots\ldots\ldots\ldots\ldots\ldots\ldots\ldots\ldots\ldots(1)$$

Where; (N) represents the number of units in the population (population size).

(n) represents the number of units in the sample (sampling size).

(!) represents the factorial notation.

Example 1: Determine the number of possible sample that can be drawn from; 3, 6, 9, 12 and 15 given that the sample size is 2 using sampling without replacement method.

<u>Solution</u>

Step 1: Possible Sample Combination $= \frac{N!}{n!(N-n)!}$, where; N = 5 and n = 2

Step 2: Data substitution and solving

$\text{Possible Sample Combination} = \frac{N!}{n!(N-n)!}$ ......[Substitute formula components values]

$\text{Possible Sample Combination} = \frac{5!}{2!(5-2)!}$ ....[Simplify denominator bracket]

$\text{Possible Sample Combination} = \frac{5!}{2!3!}$ ....[Work factorial]

$\text{Possible Sample Combination} = \frac{120}{2(6)}$ ....[Expand bracket and simplify fraction]

$\text{Possible Sample Combination} = \mathbf{10}$

Step 3: Derivation of possible combinations. The possible sample combinations are; (3,6), (3,9), (3,12), (3,15), (6,9), (6,12), (6,15), (9,12), (9,15) and (12,15). From these combinations, we see that no number repeats itself in any combination, showing that that with sampling without replacement, it is practically impossible to select a given unit more than once.

Example 2: Determine the probability of drawing each of the following numbers; 3, 6, 9, 12 and 15, considering that the sample size is 3 and sampling is done without replacement.

Solution

Step 1: Formula: $\text{Probability} = \frac{\text{Unit number of occurence in population}}{\text{Total Population size after each draw}}$

Where: Unit number of occurence in population = 1

Total Population size after each draw = Reduces by 1 after each draw

Step 2: Determination of probability after each draw

	Total Population	Values in decimal	Values in percent
First draw	5	0.2	20%
Second draw	4	0.25	25%
Third draw	3	0.33	33%

Step 3: Interpretation: From the table above, we realized that the probability of selecting a sampling unit increases after each draw when sampling is done without replacement. This is due to the fact that total population size reduced after each draw.

2) **Sampling with Replacement**

Here, after the selection of a sampling unit is from the sampling frame to be in a sample unit, the selected sampling unit is replaced into the sampling frame before the next selection.

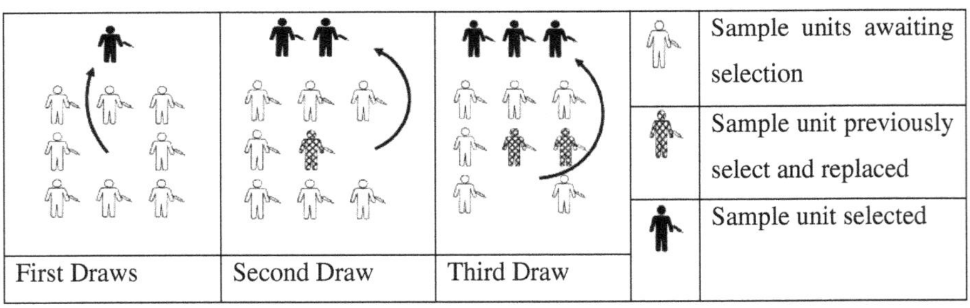

In such a situation, there is a possibility for a sampling unit to be selected more than a time. The possible number of sample drawn from a given population with replacement is determined using the following formula.

$$\text{Possible Sample Combination} = N^n \quad \text{..........(2)}$$

Where; (N) represents the number of units in the population (population size).

(n) represents the number of units in the sample (sampling size).

Example 1: Determine the number of possible sample that can be drawn from; 3, 6, 9, 12 and 15 given that the sample size is 2 using sampling with replacement method.

Solution

Step 1: Possible Sample Combination $= N^n$, where; N = 5 and n = 2

Step 2: Data substitution and solving

Possible Sample Combination $= N^n$ ....[Substitute formula components values]

Possible Sample Combination $= 5^2$ ....[Work power]

Possible Sample Combination $= \mathbf{25}$

Step 3: Derivation of possible sample combination

(3, 3), (3, 6), (3, 9), (3, 12) and (3, 15).............[Assuming first draw is always 3]

(6, 3), (6, 6), (6, 9), (6, 12) and (6, 15) ....[Assuming first draw is always 6]

(9, 3), (9, 6), (9, 9), (9, 12) and (9, 15) ....[Assuming first draw is always 9]

(12, 3), (12, 6), (12, 9), (12, 12) and (12, 15) ....[Assuming first draw is always 12]

(15, 3), (15, 6), (15, 9), (15, 12) and (15, 15) ....[Assuming first draw is always 15]

Note: Using the same population size of 5 and sample size of 2 as in the case of sampling without replacement, we realized that the number of possible sample combination has increase significantly. Under sampling without replacement, the possible combination is 10 while in sampling with replacement, the possible combination is 25. Looking at the combinations, we also released that sample units can be selected more than one time [(3, 3), (6, 6), (9, 9), (12, 12) and (15, 15)]. Therefore, there is possibility that the sample size is made up of only a particular sample unit.

Example 2: Determine the probability of drawing each of the following numbers; 3, 6, 9, 12 and 15, considering that the sample size is 3 and sampling is done with replacement.

Solution

Step 1: Formula: $\text{Probability} = \frac{\text{Unit number of occurence in population(1)}}{\text{Total Population size after each draw(N)}}$

Where: $\text{Unit number of occurence in population} = 1$

$\text{Total Population size after each draw} = \text{Remain constant}$

Step 2: Determination of probability after each draw

	Total Population	Values in decimal	Values in percent
First draw	5	0.2	20%
Second draw	5	0.2	20%
Third draw	5	0.2	20%

Step 3: Interpretation: The probability of selecting a sampling unit is constant or the same when sampling is done with replacement. This is because total population size remains the same after each draw.

Test Your Understanding

Exercise 1: Determine the possible sample that can be drawn from; 4, 5, 8 and 12 given that the sample size is 3 using with replacement method

[Answer: (4,5,8), (4,5,12), (4,8,12) and (5,8,12)]

Exercise 2: Determine the number of possible sample that can be drawn from a population size of 9 given that the sample size is 3 using;

1) Sampling with replacement method.........[**Answer: 729 Possible combinations**]
2) Sampling without replacement method. ....[**Answer: 84 Possible combination**]

6.2.3 Complementary Concepts of Sampling

Here, we are going to see concepts such as; variable, types of data and instrument of data collection. A variable is defined as any characteristics, number or quantity that can be counted or measured and whose value varies over time. The major type of variables include; dependent variable, independent variable, endogenous variable and exogenous variable.

A) Types of Statistical Data

Data is defined as measured observations obtained from officially or privately collected statistics. Data also considered as the actual values of the variable and can be numbers or words. Statistically, the different types of data can be viewed through major headings such as; the nature of data, the collector of data and the base of data as illustrated below.

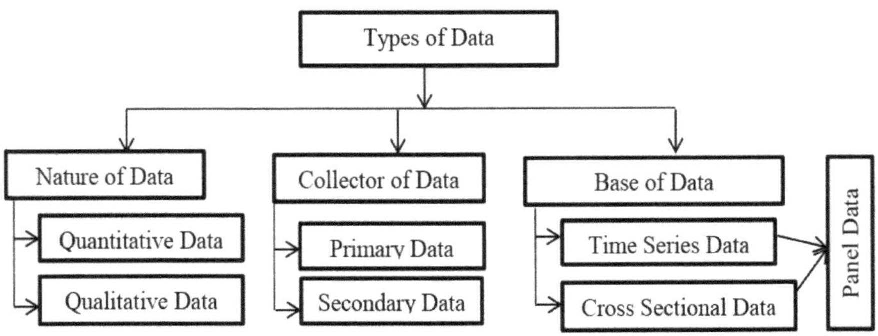

1) Quantitative Data

It is defined as any quantifiable or measurable information that can be used for mathematical calculations and statistical analysis. Quantitative data are numerical in nature, easily mathematically computed and produce results that are easy to summarize, compare and generalize. It is used to answer questions such as; how many, how often and how much and can be counts (discrete) and/or measured (continuous) in nature. It is also called measurement or numerical data.

2) Qualitative Data

It is defined as any information collected from the studied population that cannot be quantified or measureable without the application of coding. Qualitative data are mostly non-numerical (words and sentences) and usually descriptive or nominal in nature (explains how and why). It measures feelings, emotions and subjective perceptions as well as describes character and qualities and can be nominal and ordinal in nature.

Note: It is worth that most study makes use of both qualitative and quantitative data as such combination reduces the weaknesses stem from using a single data type and increases the validity and reliability of the study.

3) Primary Data

It is first-hand information collected directly from the studied population by the researcher performing the research or study. Primary data is considered more reliable, authentic and objective since it is a data not yet being changed and/or altered by humans and economic phenomena over time from the time of research. Since primary data are unpublished data, major sources of primary data includes; experiments, survey, questionnaire, interview (face-to-face) and observations.

4) Secondary Data

It is defined as data collected from an already published source (government agencies, public international organizations, and independent research organizations) of any form. It is used in situations where primary data is difficult or worst impossible to get. Major sources of secondary data includes; books, records, newspapers, published censuses, data archives, internet articles, research articles by other researchers (journals) and databases. It is worth knowing that a research can be conducted without secondary data but a research based on only secondary data is least reliable (misleading and biased) due to economic situation and human modifications.

5) Time Series Data

It is defined as the collection of quantitative observation or information at a fixed or regular and successively time interval (daily, weekly, monthly, and yearly) over a period of time (usually years). Time series data allows one to identify changes within a given variable over time and are usually plotted via line chart and scatter plots. Examples of time series data include; Gross Domestic Product (GDP), export index, prices of product and produce over time.

6) Cross Sectional Data

It is defined as a set of observation or data (information) which is collected from one or more variables or statistical unit (participants, subjects) at the same point in time or single point in time. Here, we are not interested in the changes of data over time but in current (study) time period.

B) Level of Measurement of Data

Stanley S. Steven

Measurement is the foundation of any scientific investigation or study. Measurement is defined as the assignment of numerals (a symbol or labels used to denote a number) and numbers (numerals that have quantitative meaning and can be analyzed) to objects or events or observations according to rules. The level of measurement or scale of measure is defined as a classification that describes the nature of information.

It can also be seen as the manner in which a set of data or information is measured. According to psychologist Stanley Smith Stevens there exist four levels of data measurement (Steven's taxonomy); nominal, ordinal, interval, and ratio.

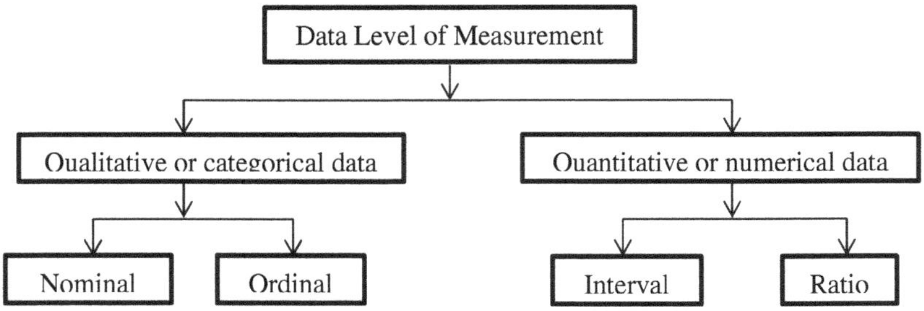

1) Nominal Measurement Level or Scale

The term nominal is derived from a Latin word "Nomen", meaning name or label. Nominal level measurement is defined as the utilization of symbols (names or labels) to classify observations into mutually exclusive and exhaustive categories. Mutually exclusive means the categories must be distinct so that no observation falls into more than one category and exhaustiveness means sufficient categories must exist so that all observations fall into some category. Gender (male and female), nationality (Cameroonian, Nigerian), religion (Christian, Muslim, Jew, Hindu), location (rural, urban), and race (white, black) are common classic nominal scales used in the behavioral sciences and nominal measurements are usually represented in bar charts and pie charts.

2) Ordinal Measurement Level or Scale

It is the next level of measurement in terms of complexity. It respects the assumptions of mutual exclusivity and exhaustiveness but in which the categories follows a strict natural order. Ordinal measurement is used for measure variables that tend to vary in degree between observations or individuals such as; attitudes, intentions, opinions or judgments (strongly agree, agree, neutral, disagree and strongly disagree), personality (excellent, good, average, poor, appallingly bad), well-being and depression (very high, high, indifference, low and very low).

3) Interval Measurement Level or Scale

Interval measurement is defined as the splitting of quantitative variables in to equal (known and exact) dimension or distance. Interval measurement respects the idea of mutually exclusive and exhaustiveness and follows a definite ordering. Age, weight and height are common variable of interval measurement. Using variable age as an example, interval measurement can be expressed as seen below; (10 to 20), (20 to 30), (30 to 40), (40 to 50) etc. interval measurements are appropriately represented using histogram.

4) Ratio Measurement Level or Scale

Ratio scale measurement is similar to interval measurement but differs only in that it implies the existence of a potential absolute zero value. Length, area, speed and time are common examples of ratio measurements scales.

C) Instruments of Data Collection

Data collection is the process of using appropriate instruments in gathering and measuring information in a systematic and scientific manner that enables one to answer stated research questions, test hypotheses and monitoring and evaluates outcomes. Instruments or tools of data collection on the other hand are defined as are measurement devices or ways designed to obtain data on a topic of interest. Major examples of instruments of data collection include;

1) **Questionnaire:** It is defined as a form consisting of printed or written questions with and without stated answers from which participants are to choose amongst. Questionnaire was invented by Sir Francis Galton and is usually divided into sections consisting of both open and close questions. A questionnaire can be structured or unstructured

2) **Interview:** It is defined as a form consisting of printed questions or guides without stated answers from which participants gives their opinion related to the question. The response of participants is strictly restricted by the questions. Interview can take the following form; face to face interview, telephone interview and email interview. Interview can be structured or unstructured.
3) **Observation:** It is defined as a careful planning and selective application of human senses (sight, hearing, smell, taste and touch) to examine participants in their natural setting and obtaining the needed data. Observation can be structured or unstructured and controlled or uncontrolled observation.
4) **Focus Group Discussion:** It is defined as an in-depth field method that brings together a small homogeneous group in a relaxed atmosphere to reveal their; opinions, perceptions, feelings, attitudes and reasoning to a given topic with the help of pre-established guides and trained moderator or facilitator. Here, the researcher or moderator observes and take notes or tape recording information.
5) **Debates**: It is a discussion secession in which each participant is asked to take a position either for or against a certain idea of interest. These tasks help to draw out data such as the expression of opinions, arguments and discussions that can often get out of control. A moderator is needed to control participants in case of disputes between participants.

6.3 The Concept of Statistical Estimation

Estimation is defined as a statistical process that provides the mathematical means and procedures for determining properties of a population (parameter) through information collected from a sample. The two mean types of estimation include; point estimation and interval estimation. It is worth knowing that estimation is a part of statistical inference with the other being hypothesis testing.

6.3.1 Estimation Terminologies

In order to understand the concept of estimation, we are required to know (define, calculate and interpret) the following terms or terminologies seen below.

1) Parameter

It is defined as any numerical value that describes a population in a specified domain. It is also seen as a descriptor of a population. Major examples of parameters includes; population size (N), population mean (μ), population variance (σ^2) and population standard deviation (σ).

a) **Population Mean (μ):** Consider a population made up of N observations ranging from; X_1 , X_2, X_3 .. X_N. These observations can be written or summarized in the form; X_ι where ι ranges from 1 to N. population mean is therefore, the sum of observations divided by the total number of observations. Algebraically, it is written as seen below.

$$\text{Population Mean}(\mu) = \frac{X_1+X_2+X_3+\cdots+X_N}{N} \quad \text{.......................................(1)}$$

b) **Population Variance (σ^2):** Variance is defined as the average of the sum of the squares of deviations of data from their mean. Generally, the population variance is calculated using any of the following formulas;

$$\text{Population Variance }(\sigma^2) = \frac{\sum(X-\mu)^2}{N} = \frac{1}{N}\sum(X-\mu)^2 \quad \text{..........................(2)}$$

$$\text{Population Variance }(\sigma^2) = \frac{\sum X^2}{N} - \mu^2 = \frac{1}{N}\sum X^2 - \mu^2 \quad \text{..........................(3)}$$

$$\text{Population Variance }(\sigma^2) = \frac{N(\sum X^2)-(\sum X)^2}{N^2} = \frac{\sum X^2}{N} - \frac{(\sum X)^2}{N^2} \quad \text{.......................(4)}$$

Mathematical Illustration [Changing equation (2) to equation (3) and (4)]

$$\sigma^2 = \frac{\sum(X-\mu)^2}{N} \quad \text{.......[Expand numerator]}$$

$$\sigma^2 = \frac{\sum[(X-\mu)(X-\mu)]}{N} \quad \text{.......[Expand numerator bracket]}$$

$$\sigma^2 = \frac{\sum[X^2-\mu X-\mu X+\mu^2]}{N} \quad \text{.......[Simplify numerator bracket]}$$

$$\sigma^2 = \frac{\sum[X^2-2\mu X+\mu^2]}{N} \quad \text{.......[Multiply numerator bracket by summation sign]}$$

$$\sigma^2 = \frac{\sum X^2-2\mu(\sum X)+\mu^2(\sum 1)}{N} \quad \text{.......[Remember } \textstyle\sum X = \mu N \text{ and } \mu(\sum 1) = \mu N]$$

$$\sigma^2 = \frac{\sum X^2-2\mu(\mu N)+\mu^2 N}{N} \rightarrow \sigma^2 = \frac{\sum X^2-2\mu^2 N+\mu^2 N}{N} \quad \text{.......[Simplify numerator]}$$

$$\sigma^2 = \frac{\sum X_\iota^2-\mu^2 N}{N} \quad \text{.......[Formula]}$$

$\sigma^2 = \frac{\sum X^2-\mu^2 N}{N}$ ....[Segment equation]	$\sigma^2 = \frac{\sum X^2-\mu^2 N}{N}$ [Multiply equation fraction by N]
$\sigma^2 = \frac{\sum X^2}{N} - \frac{-\mu^2 N}{N}$ ......[Simplify fractions]	$\sigma^2 = \frac{N(\sum X^2-\mu^2 N)}{N(N)} = \frac{N(\sum X^2)-\mu^2 N^2}{N^2} = \frac{N(\sum X^2)-(\mu N)^2}{N^2}$
$\sigma^2 = \frac{\sum X^2}{N} - \mu^2$ ....[Formula]	$\sigma^2 = \frac{N(\sum X^2)-(\mu N)^2}{N^2}$ ....[Change $\mu N = \sum X$]
	$\sigma^2 = \frac{N(\sum X^2)-(\sum X)^2}{N^2} = \frac{\sum X^2}{N} - \frac{(\sum X)^2}{N^2}$ ....[Formula]

c) **Population Standard Deviation (σ):** Standard deviation is defined as the positive square root of the variance. A Population standard deviation is calculated using the following formula;

$$\text{Population Standard Deviation}(\sigma) = \sqrt{\frac{\Sigma(X_\iota-\mu)^2}{N}} \quad \text{.....................................(5)}$$

$$\text{Population Standard Deviation}(\sigma) = \sqrt{\frac{\Sigma X_\iota^{\,2}}{N} - \mu^2} \quad \text{.....................................(6)}$$

$$\text{Population Standard Deviation}(\sigma) = \sqrt{\frac{\Sigma X_\iota^{\,2}}{N} - \frac{(\Sigma X_\iota)^2}{N^2}} \quad \text{...........................(7)}$$

Mathematical Illustration Standard Deviation Formula (5) Using Equation (2)

$$\sigma^2 = \frac{\Sigma(X-\bar{X})^2}{N} \quad \text{..........................[Multiply both sides by } 2^{-1} \text{ or } \tfrac{1}{2} \text{ exponent]}$$

$$(\sigma^2)^{\frac{1}{2}} = \left(\frac{\Sigma(X-\bar{X})^2}{N}\right)^{\frac{1}{2}} \quad \text{..........................[Remember } (M^a)^{\frac{1}{a}} = M^{\frac{a}{a}} = M^1 = M\text{]}$$

$$\sigma = \left(\frac{\Sigma(X-\bar{X})^2}{N}\right)^{\frac{1}{2}} \quad \text{..[Remember } (X)^{\frac{1}{2}} = \sqrt{X}\text{]}$$

$$\sigma = \sqrt{\frac{\Sigma(X-\bar{X})^2}{N}} \quad \text{......................................[Population standard deviation]}$$

2) Statistics

It is defined as any measurable quantity (numerical value) calculated from a sample. It can also be seen as numerical values that describes a given sample properties, such as; sample size (n), sample variance (S^2) and sample standard deviation (S). The formulas of the following statistics are given below;

a) **Sample Mean ($\bar{X}$)**

Sample mean is defined as the sum of sample units divided by the number of sample units. It is calculated using the following formula,

$$\text{Sample mean}(\bar{X}) = \frac{\Sigma X_\iota}{n} \quad \text{...(8)}$$

Example 1: Determine the sample mean of the following sample information; 32, 30, 25, 28, 40 and 42.

Solution

Step 1: Formula. Sample mean$(\overline{X}) = \frac{\sum X}{n}$, where; $n = 6$

Step 2: Data substitution and solving

Sample mean$(\overline{X}) = \frac{32+30+25+28+40+42}{6}$ ....[Sum numerator values]

Sample mean$(\overline{X}) = \frac{197}{6}$ ....[Simplify fraction]

Sample mean$(\overline{X}) = \mathbf{32.8333}$

Example 2: A sample of 10 students drew from a population of 40 students yield a total score of 56. Determine the value of the sample mean.

Solution

Step 1: Formula. Sample mean$(\overline{X}) = \frac{\sum X_i}{n}$, where; $\sum X_i = 56$ and $n = 10$

Step 2: Data substitution and solving

Sample mean$(\overline{X}) = \frac{56}{10}$ ....[Simplify fraction]

Sample mean$(\overline{X}) = \mathbf{5.6}$

Test Your Understanding

Exercise 3: Determine the sample mean of the following sample information; 170, 300, 430, 470 and 600.. **[Answer: Sample Mean$(\overline{X}) = 394$]**

Exercise 4: Determine the sample mean from the following data; $\sum X = 195$ and $n = 10$

[Answer: Sample Mean$(\overline{X}) = 19.5$]

Exercise 5: Determine the sample size (n) that will yield the sample mean of 10, assuming the sum of sample units is given as 80. ....**[Answer: Sample Size$(n) = 8$]**

b) Sample Variance(S^2)

As seen above, variance is defined as the average of the sum of the squares of deviations of data from their mean. Here, the sum of the squares of deviations is divided by $(n - 1)$ and not (N) as the case of population variance. Population variance is calculated using any of the following formulas:

Sample variance $(S^2) = \frac{\sum(X-\bar{X})^2}{n-1}$ ....(9)

Sample variance $(S^2) = \frac{\sum X^2 - n\bar{X}^2}{n-1}$ ....(10)

Sample variance $(S^2) = \frac{n}{n(n-1)}[\sum X^2 - n\bar{X}^2]$ ....(11)

Sample variance $(S^2) = \frac{1}{n-1}\left[\sum X^2 - \frac{(\sum X)^2}{n}\right]$ ....(12)

Mathematical Illustration Sampling Variance Formulas

$S^2 = \frac{\sum(X-\bar{X})^2}{n-1}$ ....[Work out the square of the numerator]

$S^2 = \frac{\sum[(X-\bar{X})(X-\bar{X})]}{n-1}$ ....[Expand bracket]

$S^2 = \frac{\sum[X^2 - \bar{X}X - \bar{X}X + \bar{X}^2]}{n-1}$ ....[Simplify numerator bracket]

$S^2 = \frac{\sum[X^2 - 2\bar{X}X + \bar{X}^2]}{n-1}$ ....[Multiply numerator by summation sign]

$S^2 = \frac{\sum X^2 - 2\bar{X}(\sum X) + \bar{X}^2(\sum 1)}{n-1}$ ....[Remember $(\sum X = \bar{X}n)$ and $(\sum 1 = n)$]

$S^2 = \frac{\sum X^2 - 2\bar{X}(\bar{X}n) + \bar{X}^2(n)}{n-1} = \frac{\sum X^2 - 2\bar{X}^2 n + \bar{X}^2 n}{n-1}$ ....[Simplify numerator]

$\mathbf{S^2} = \frac{\sum \mathbf{X^2 - \bar{X}^2 n}}{\mathbf{n-1}} = \frac{\sum \mathbf{X^2 - n\bar{X}^2}}{\mathbf{n-1}}$ ....[Formula]

$S^2 = \frac{\sum X^2 - n\bar{X}^2}{n-1}$ ..[Multiply fraction by n]

$S^2 = \frac{n(\sum X^2) - n(n\bar{X}^2)}{n(n-1)}$ [Factorize equation]

$S^2 = \frac{n}{\mathbf{n(n-1)}}[\sum X^2 - \mathbf{n\bar{X}^2}]$ ..[Formula]

$S^2 = \frac{n}{\mathbf{n(n-1)}}\left[\sum X^2 - \frac{(\sum \mathbf{X_i})^2}{\mathbf{n}}\right]$.[Formula]

$S^2 = \frac{\sum X^2 - n\bar{X}^2}{n-1}$ ....[Change $\bar{X}^2 = \frac{(\sum \mathbf{X})^2}{n^2}$]

$S^2 = \frac{\sum X^2 - n\left[\frac{(\sum X)^2}{n^2}\right]}{n-1}$ ....[Rem. $n\left[\frac{(X)^2}{n^2}\right] = \frac{(X)^2}{n}$]

$S^2 = \frac{\sum X^2 - \frac{(\sum X)^2}{n}}{n-1}$ ....[Factorize $(n-1)$]

$S^2 = \frac{\mathbf{1}}{\mathbf{n-1}}\left[\sum X^2 - \frac{(\sum \mathbf{X})^2}{\mathbf{n}}\right]$ ....[Formula]

Example 1: The marks of a sample of 5 students in applied math are given as follows; 65, 70, 71, 63 and 69. Calculate the Sample variance

Solution

Step 1: Formula. Sample Variance $(S^2) = \frac{\sum(X-\bar{X})^2}{n-1}$, where; $\bar{X} = 67.6$, $n = 5$ and $\sum(X-\bar{X})^2 = ?$

Step 2: Tabular derivation of unknown component [$\sum(X-\bar{X})^2$]

X	X^2	$(X-\bar{X})^2$	Sample Mean ($\bar{X}$)
65	$65^2 = 4{,}225$	$(65-67.6)^2 = 6.76$	Sample mean$(\bar{X}) = \frac{\sum X}{n}$
70	$70^2 = 4{,}900$	$(70-67.6)^2 = 5.76$	Sample mean$(\bar{X}) = \frac{65+70+71+63+69}{5}$
71	$71^2 = 5{,}041$	$(71-67.6)^2 = 11.56$	Sample mean$(\bar{X}) = \frac{338}{5}$
63	$63^2 = 3{,}969$	$(63-67.6)^2 = 21.16$	Sample mean$(\bar{X}) = \mathbf{67.6}$
69	$69^2 = 4{,}761$	$(69-67.6)^2 = 1.96$	
$\sum = \mathbf{338}$	$\sum = \mathbf{22,896}$	$\sum = \mathbf{47.2}$	

Step 3: Data substitution and solving

Formula 1: $S^2 = \frac{\sum(X-\bar{X})^2}{n-1}$, where; $\sum(X-\bar{X})^2 = 47.2$ and n

$S^2 = \frac{47.2}{5-1}$ ....[Simplify denominator]

$S^2 = \frac{47.2}{4}$ ....[Solve fraction]

$S^2 = \mathbf{11.8}$ ....[Sample variance]

Formula 2: $S^2 = \frac{\sum X^2 - n\bar{X}^2}{n-1}$, where; $\sum X^2 = 22{,}896$, $\bar{X} = 67.6$ and $n = 5$

$S^2 = \frac{22{,}896-5(67.6)^2}{5-1}$ ....[Work exponent and simplify denominator]

$S^2 = \frac{22{,}896-5(4{,}569.76)}{4}$ ....[Expand bracket and simplify numerator]

$S^2 = \frac{47.2}{4}$ ....[Simplify fraction]

$S^2 = \mathbf{11.8}$ ....[Sample variance]

Formula 3: $S^2 = \frac{n}{n(n-1)}[\sum X^2 - n\bar{X}^2]$, where; $\sum X^2 = 22{,}896$, $\bar{X} = 67.6$ and $n = 5$

$S^2 = \frac{5}{5(5-1)}[22{,}896 - 5(67.6)^2]$ ....[Work exponent and simplify bracket]

$S^2 = \frac{5}{5(4)}[22{,}896 - 5(4{,}569.76)]$ ....[Expand bracket and simplify fraction]

$S^2 = 0.25[22{,}896 - 22{,}848.8]$........[Simplify equation bracket and solve equation]

$S^2 = \mathbf{11.8}$ ....[Sampling variance]

Formula 4: $S^2 = \frac{1}{n-1}\left[\sum X^2 - \frac{(\sum X)^2}{n}\right]$, where; $\sum X^2 = 22{,}896$, $\sum X = 338$ and $n = 5$

$S^2 = \frac{1}{5-1}\left[22{,}896 - \frac{(338)^2}{5}\right]$ ....[Work exponent and simplify fractions]

$S^2 = 0.25[22{,}896 - 22{,}848.8]$ ....[Simplify bracket]

$S^2 = 0.25[47.2]$ ....[Solve equation]

$S^2 = \mathbf{11.8}$ ....[Sample variance]

Example 2: The sample score of 4 students yields the following information; $\sum X^2 = 152{,}154$, and $\sum X = 778$. Determine the sample variance score/value.

Solution

Step 1: Formula: $S^2 = \frac{1}{n-1}\left[\sum X^2 - \frac{(\sum X)^2}{n}\right]$, where; $\sum X^2 = 152{,}154$, $\sum X = 778$ and $n = 4$

Step 2: Data substitution and solving

$S^2 = \frac{1}{4-1}\left[152{,}154 - \frac{(778)^2}{4}\right]$ ....[Work exponent and simplify fractions]

$S^2 = \frac{1}{3}[152{,}154 - 151{,}321]$ ....[Simplify bracket]

$S^2 = \mathbf{277.667}$ ....[Sample variance in three decimal places]

Test Your Understanding

Exercise 6: The marks of a sample of 5 students in applied math are given as follows; 74, 67, 69, 77 and 84. Calculate the sample variance ...**[Answer: Sample variance $(S^2) = 45.7$]**

Exercise 7: Determine the sample variance from the following information; $\sum X^2 = 51{,}633$, $\sum X = 351$ and $n = 6$.........................**[Answer: Sample variance $(S^2) = 6{,}219.9$]**

Exercise 8: Determine the sample variance from the following data; $\sum X^2 = 884{,}700$, $\bar{X} = 394$ and $n = 5$. ....**[Answer: Sample variance $(S^2) = 6{,}219.9$]**

c) **Sample Standard Deviation(S)**

Remember standard deviation is defined as the positive square root of the variance. Therefore, to get the sample standard deviation, we simply root the sample variance as seen below.

$$\text{Sample Standard Deviation } (S) = \sqrt{\frac{\sum(X-\bar{X})^2}{n-1}} \quad \text{.........(13)}$$

$$\text{Sample Standard Deviation } (S) = \sqrt{\frac{\sum X^2 - n\bar{X}^2}{n-1}} \quad \text{.........(14)}$$

$$\text{Sample Standard Deviation } (S) = \sqrt{\frac{n}{n(n-1)}\left[\sum X^2 - n\bar{X}^2\right]} \quad \text{.........(15)}$$

$$\text{Sample Standard Deviation } (S) = \sqrt{\frac{1}{n-1}\left[\sum X^2 - \frac{(\sum X_i)^2}{n}\right]} \quad \text{.........(16)}$$

Example 1: Determine the sample standard deviation from the following sample data; $\sum X^2 = 3{,}863$, $\sum X = 135$ and $n = 6$.

Solution

Step 1: Formula. $S = \sqrt{\frac{1}{n-1}\left[\sum X^2 - \frac{(\sum X)^2}{n}\right]}$, where; $\sum X^2 = 3,863$, $\sum X = 135$ and $n = 6$.

Step 2: Data substitution and solving

Sample Standard Deviation (S) = $\sqrt{\frac{1}{5-1}\left[3,863 - \frac{(135)^2}{6}\right]}$........[Work power and fraction]

Sample Standard Deviation (S) = $\sqrt{0.2[3,863 - 3,037.5]}$ ....[Simplify bracket]

Sample Standard Deviation (S) = $\sqrt{0.2[825.5]}$ ....[Solve]

Sample Standard Deviation (S) = $\mathbf{12.849}$

Example 2: Determine the sample standard deviation from the following sample data; $\sum X^2 = 40,777$, $\bar{X} = 79.83$ and $n = 6$.

Solution

Step 1: Formula. $S = \sqrt{\frac{\sum X^2 - n\bar{X}^2}{n-1}}$, where; $\sum X^2 = 40,777$, $\bar{X} = 79.83$ and $n = 6$.

Step 2: Data substitution and solving

Sample Standard Deviation (S) = $\sqrt{\frac{40,777-6(79.83)^2}{6-1}}$ ....[Work exponent]

Sample Standard Deviation (S) = $\sqrt{\frac{40,777-6(6,372.8289)}{6-1}}$ ....[Simplify equation]

Sample Standard Deviation (S) = $\sqrt{\frac{2,540.0266}{5}}$ ....[Work fraction]

Sample Standard Deviation (S) = $\sqrt{508.00532}$ ....[Work root]

Sample Standard Deviation (S) = $\mathbf{22.54}$

Test Your Understanding

Example 9: Determine the sample standard deviation from the following sample information; $\sum X^2 = 1,365,625$, $\sum X = 2,725$ and $n = 6$. ....**[Answer: $S = 160$]**

Example 10: Determine the sample standard deviation from the following sample data; $\sum X^2 = 6,697$, $\bar{X} = 32.8333$ and $n = 6$. ....**[Answer: $S = 6.765$]**

Example 11: From the table below, calculate the mean, variance and standard deviation.

Samp e 1	134	139	17	52	122	166	129	161
Sample 2	128	136	163	153	157	154	125	124

[Answer: $\bar{X}_1 = 147.4$, $S_1{}^2 = 371.98$, $S_1 = 19.27$,

$\bar{X}_2 = 142.5$, $S_2{}^2 = 253.43$, $S_2 = 15.92$]

3) Estimator

It is defined as a rule, method or criterion for arriving at an estimate of the value of a parameter. Estimator numerical value is considered as the estimated value of the unknown population property (parameter). The sample mean ($\overline{X}$) is the estimator of the population mean (μ), the sample variance (S^2) is an estimator of the population variance (σ^2) and the sample standard deviation (S) is an estimator of the population standard deviation (σ). Statistically, an estimator must be; unbiased, consistent and efficient. Our analysis will be limited to sample mean and population mean.

a) Unbiasedness

Unbiasedness literally means impartial which means equality. An estimator ($\hat{\theta}$) of a parameter (θ) is said to be unbiased if the expected value of the estimator $[E(\hat{\theta})]$ equals the observed or real value of the population (θ). That is, $\{[E(\hat{\theta})] = \theta\}$.

<u>**Mathematical Illustration of sample mean**</u>

Considering a sample elements; $X_1, X_2, X_3 \cdots X_n$, where (n) represents the sample size. The sample mean is derived by dividing the sum of the sample elements ($X_1, X_2, X_3 \cdots X_n$) by the number of element in the sample (n).

$$\overline{X} = \frac{X_1+X_2+X_3+\cdots\cdots+X_n}{n} \quad \text{..[Segmentation of fraction]}$$

$$\overline{X} = \frac{X_1}{n} + \frac{X_2}{n} + \frac{X_3}{n} + \cdots + \frac{X_n}{n} \quad \text{...[Factories n in each term in the right hand side of equation]}$$

$$\overline{X} = \frac{1}{n}X_1 + \frac{1}{n}X_2 + \frac{1}{n}X_3 + \cdots\cdots + \frac{1}{n}X_n \quad \text{....[Attached expectation on both sides of equation]}$$

<u>**Mathematical Illustration of Unbiasedness of an estimator**</u>

$$E(\overline{X}) = E\left[\frac{1}{n}X_1 + \frac{1}{n}X_2 + \frac{1}{n}X_3 + \cdots\cdots + \frac{1}{n}X_n\right] \quad \text{[Multiply bracket by expectation sign]}$$

$$E(\overline{X}) = E\left(\frac{1}{n}X_1\right) + E\left(\frac{1}{n}X_2\right) + E\left(\frac{1}{n}X_3\right) + \cdots\cdots + E\left(\frac{1}{n}X_n\right) \quad \text{..[Remember } E(aX) = aE(X)\text{]}$$

$$E(\overline{X}) = \frac{1}{n}E(X_1) + \frac{1}{n}E(X_2) + \frac{1}{n}E(X_3) + \cdots\cdots + \frac{1}{n}E(X_n) \quad \text{.........[Remember } E(X) = \mu\text{]}$$

$$E(\overline{X}) = \frac{1}{n}\mu + \frac{1}{n}\mu + \frac{1}{n}\mu \cdots + \frac{1}{n}\mu$$ .....[Since all terms are identical, reduce equation by taking a term $\left(\frac{1}{n}\mu\right)$ and multiply by the total number of terms(n)]

$$E(\overline{X}) = \frac{1}{n}\mu n = \frac{\mu n}{n} = \frac{\mu}{1} \quad \text{...[Work fraction]}$$

$$E(\overline{X}) = \mu \quad \text{...[1]}$$

Note: From equation (1) we can also conclude that an unbiased estimator is one in which the difference between the expectation of the estimator and the parameter is zero. $[E(\bar{X}) - \mu = 0]$.

b) Consistency

Consistency literally means conforming to a regular pattern. Statistically, the regular pattern of an estimator is that its expected value $[E(\hat{\theta})]$ should be equal to the observed value (θ). An estimator $(\hat{\theta})$ is a consistent estimator of a parameter (θ) if as the sample size (n) tend to infinity (∞), the expected value of the estimator $[E(\hat{\theta})]$ moves towards the observed of the population (θ) and the variance of the estimator $[Var(\hat{\theta})]$ tend to zero (0).

Mathematical Illustration of Variance Sample Mean ($Var_{\bar{X}}$)

Given that sample mean is $\left[\bar{X} = \frac{1}{n}X_1 + \frac{1}{n}X_2 + \cdots\cdots + \frac{1}{n}X_n\right]$, sample mean variance formula is derived as seen below (assuming sample is done with replacement).

$Var_{\bar{X}} = Var\left[\frac{1}{n}X_1 + \frac{1}{n}X_2 + \cdots\cdots + \frac{1}{n}X_n\right]$ ....[Expand bracket with Var]

$Var_{\bar{X}} = Var\left(\frac{1}{n}X_1\right) + Var\left(\frac{1}{n}X_2\right) + \cdots + Var\left(\frac{1}{n}X_n\right)$ ......[Remember $Var(aX) = a^2Var(X)$]

$Var_{\bar{X}} = \left(\frac{1}{n}\right)^2 Var(X_1) + \left(\frac{1}{n}\right)^2 Var(X_2) + \cdots + \left(\frac{1}{n}\right)^2 Var(X_n)$ ....[Remember $\left(\frac{a}{b}\right)^2 = \frac{a^2}{b^2}$]

$Var_{\bar{X}} = \frac{1^2}{n^2}Var(X_1) + \frac{1^2}{n^2}Var(X_2) + \cdots + \frac{1^2}{n^2}Var(X_n)$ ....[Remember $Var(X) = \sigma^2$]

$Var_{\bar{X}} = \frac{1}{n^2}\sigma^2 + \frac{1}{n^2}\sigma^2 + \cdots + \frac{1}{n^2}\sigma^2$ ....[Reduce equation by multiplying a term by n]

$Var_{\bar{X}} = \frac{1}{n^2}\sigma^2 n = \frac{\sigma^2 n}{n^2} = \sigma^2(n^{1-2}) = \sigma^2 n^{-1}$ ....[Remember $a^{-n} = \frac{1}{a^n}$]

Variance Sample Mean $(Var_{\bar{X}}) = \frac{\sigma^2}{n}$ ....(1)

Note: The population variance is always greater than the sample mean variance. This is because we divide the population variance by the sample size in order to derive the sample mean variance. When dealing with sampling without replacement, the formula of sample mean variance is given as seen below,

Variance Sample Mean $(Var_{\bar{X}}) = \frac{\sigma^2}{n}\left(\frac{N-n}{N-1}\right)$ ....(2)

Example 1: Considering that the population variance is 144, determine the sample mean variance when the sample size is 36.

Solution

Step 1: Formula. Variance Sample Mean $(Var_{\bar{X}}) = \frac{\sigma^2}{n}$, where; $\sigma^2 = 144$ and $n = 36$

Step 2: Data substitution and solving

$$Variance\ Sample\ Mean\ (Var_{\bar{X}}) = \frac{\sigma^2}{n}$$ ....[Substitute component numerical value]

$$Variance\ Sample\ Mean\ (Var_{\bar{X}}) = \frac{144}{36}$$ ....[Simplify fraction]

$$Variance\ Sample\ Mean\ (Var_{\bar{X}}) = \mathbf{4}$$

Note: From the calculation, the population variance (144) is greater than the sample mean variance (4)

Example 2: Determine the variance of the sampling distribution of the sample mean using the following information; $\sum X = 3{,}744$, $\bar{X} = 144$ and $\sigma^2 = 40$.

Solution

Step 1: Formula. Variance Sample Mean $(Var_{\bar{X}})$, where; $\sigma^2 = 40$ and $n = ?$

Step 2: Determination of sample size (n). Remember $\bar{X} = \frac{\sum X}{n}$, therefore $n = \frac{\sum X}{\bar{X}}$

a) Formula. Sample size $(n) = \frac{\sum X}{\bar{X}}$, where; $\sum X = 3{,}744$ and $\bar{X} = 144$

b) Data substitution and solving

$$Sample\ size\ (n) = \frac{\sum X}{\bar{X}}$$ ....[Substitute components numerical values]

$$Sample\ size\ (n) = \frac{3{,}744}{144}$$ ....[Simplify fraction]

$$Sample\ size\ (n) = \mathbf{26}$$

Step 3: Data substitution and solving

$$Variance\ Sample\ Mean (Var_{\bar{X}}) = \frac{40}{26}$$ ....[Simplify fraction]

$$Variance\ Sample\ Mean\ (Var_{\bar{X}}) = \mathbf{1.538}$$ ....[In three decimal places]

Test Your Understanding

Exercise 12: Determine the variance of the sample mean using the following information; $n = 19$ and $\sigma^2 = 68.4$. ....**[Answer: $(Var_{\bar{X}}) = 3.6$]**

Exercise 13: Given that the population variance is 162.5, determine the variance of the sample mean when the sample size is 25. .... **[Answer: $(Var_{\bar{X}}) = 6.5$]**

Exercise 14: Determine the variance of the sample mean using the following inform; $\sum X = 900$, $\bar{X} = 25$ and $\sigma^2 = 424.8$. ....**[Answer: $(Var_{\bar{X}}) = 11.8$]**

Mathematical Illustration of Consistency of Estimator

1) First condition: The first condition states that as the sample size (n) increases to infinite ($n \to \infty$), the expected value of an estimator $[E(\overline{X})]$ moves towards the parameter (μ). Remember all parameters (μ) are constant. Here, we make use of the idea of limit to prove this claim.

$$E(\overline{X}) = \mu \text{ ....[Apply the idea of limit into the equation]}$$

$$\lim_{n\to\infty} E(\overline{X}) = \lim_{n\to\infty} \mu \text{ .... [Applying the constant law of limit]}$$

$$\lim_{n\to\infty} E(\overline{X}) = \mu \text{ ....[1]}$$

2) Second condition: The second condition states that as the sample size (n) increases to infinity ($n \to \infty$), the variance of the estimator $\left[Var(\hat{\theta})\right]$ moves towards zero.

$$\lim_{n\to\infty} Var(\overline{X}) = \lim_{n\to\infty} \frac{\sigma^2}{n} \text{ ....[Applying the concept of limit at infinity]}$$

$$\lim_{n\to\infty} Var(\overline{X}) = 0 \text{ ....[2]}$$

c) Efficiency

Efficiency means the capability of an estimator to produce accuracy result (minimal or zero error). Efficiency measures the precision and reliability of an estimator and is measurable using the concept of standard error (SE). An estimator is efficient if the expected value of the parameter equals the estimator value$\left[E(\theta) = \hat{\theta}\right]$. When comparing two estimator say ($\hat{\theta}_1$) and ($\hat{\theta}_2$), estimator $\hat{\theta}_1$ is efficient than $\hat{\theta}_2$ if the standard error of ($\hat{\theta}_1$) is smaller than the standard error of ($\hat{\theta}_2$). That is $\left[SE(\hat{\theta}_1) < SE(\hat{\theta}_2)\right]$.

Mathematical Illustration Standard Deviation of Sample Mean($\sigma_{\overline{X}}$)

Remember, standard deviation is the square root of variance and variance of an estimator is $\left[Var(\overline{X}) = \frac{\sigma^2}{n}\right]$ and $\left[Var(\overline{X}) = \frac{\sigma^2}{n}\left(\frac{N-n}{N-1}\right)\right]$ for sampling with replacement and sampling without replacement respectively.

$$\text{Standard Deviation of Sample Mean } (\sigma_{\overline{X}}) = \sqrt{\frac{\sigma^2}{n}} \text{ ....[Remember } \sqrt{\frac{a}{b}} = \frac{\sqrt{a}}{\sqrt{b}}\text{]}$$

$$\text{Standard Deviation of Sample Mean } (\sigma_{\overline{X}}) = \frac{\sqrt{\sigma^2}}{\sqrt{n}} \text{ .....[Remember } \sqrt{a^m} = (a^m)^{\frac{1}{2}} = a^{\frac{m}{2}}\text{]}$$

$$\text{Standard Deviation of Sample Mean } (\sigma_{\overline{X}}) = \frac{(\sigma^2)^{\frac{1}{2}}}{\sqrt{n}} = \frac{(\sigma)^{\frac{2}{2}}}{\sqrt{n}} \text{ ....[Simplify exponent]}$$

$$\text{Standard Deviation of Sample Mean } (\sigma_{\overline{X}}) = \frac{\sigma}{\sqrt{n}} \text{ ....(3)}$$

Note: Standard deviation is also called standard error. The sample mean standard deviation is smaller than the population standard deviation, as it is divided by the root of the sample size (n). Standard error is used as a measure of efficiency because of their inverse relationship. That is, the larger the value of standard error, the low efficiency of an estimator and the smaller the value of standard error, the high the efficiency of the estimator. When dealing with sampling without replacement, the sample mean standard error is calculated using the formula

$$\text{Standard Deviation of Sample Mean } (\sigma_{\bar{X}}) = \frac{\sigma}{\sqrt{n}}\left[\sqrt{\frac{N-n}{N-1}}\right] \text{..............................(4)}$$

Example 1: Given that the population standard deviation (σ) is 10, determine the value of the standard deviation sample mean when the sample size is 30.

Solution

Step 1: Formula. Standard Deviation of Sample Mean $(\sigma_{\bar{X}}) = \frac{\sigma}{\sqrt{n}}$, where; $\sigma = 10$, $n = 30$

Step 2: Data substitution and solving

$$\text{Standard Deviation of Sample Mean } (\sigma_{\bar{X}}) = \frac{10}{\sqrt{30}} \text{ ....[Simplify denominator]}$$

$$\text{Standard Deviation of Sample Mean } (\sigma_{\bar{X}}) = \frac{10}{5.477225575} \text{ ....[Work fraction]}$$

$$\text{Standard Deviation of Sample Mean } (\sigma_{\bar{X}}) = \mathbf{2} \text{ ....[In no decimal place]}$$

Step 3: Interpretation: The sample mean standard deviation or standard error value of 2 shows that our sample mean estimate value differ from true value of the population mean by 2 points. We can also realize that the sample mean standard error (2) is smaller than the population standard error (10).

Example 2: Suppose the population standard deviation (σ) is 50, determine the value of standard error of the sample mean when;

1) The sample size (n) is 100
2) The sample size (n) is 400

Solution

1) The sample size is 100

Step 1: Formula. Standard Deviation of Sample Mean $(\sigma_{\bar{X}}) = \frac{\sigma}{\sqrt{n}}$, where; $\sigma = 50$, $n = 100$

Step 1: Data substitution and solving

$$\text{Standard Deviation of Sample Mean } (\sigma_{\bar{X}}) = \frac{50}{\sqrt{100}} \text{ ....[Simplify numerator]}$$

Standard Deviation of Sample Mean $(\sigma_{\bar{X}}) = \frac{50}{10}$ ....[Work fraction]

Standard Deviation of Sample Mean $(\sigma_{\bar{X}}) = \mathbf{5}$

2) **The sample size is 400**

Step 1: Formula. Standard Deviation of Sample Mean $(\sigma_{\bar{X}}) = \frac{\sigma}{\sqrt{n}}$, where; $\sigma = 50,\ n = 400$

Step 1: Data substitution and solving

Standard Deviation of Sample Mean $(\sigma_{\bar{X}}) = \frac{50}{\sqrt{400}}$ ....[Simplify numerator]

Standard Deviation of Sample Mean $(\sigma_{\bar{X}}) = \frac{50}{20}$ ....[Work fraction]

Standard Deviation of Sample Mean $(\sigma_{\bar{X}}) = \mathbf{2.5}$

Note: The sample mean standard deviation reduces as the sample size increases (inverse relationship) at a given population standard deviation. When the sample size is 100, the standard error is 5 and when the sample size is 400, the standard error is 2,5. Secondly, we also realize that a small change in sample mean standard deviation (5 to 2.5 showing 50% reduction) requires a significant change in sample size (100 to 400 showing 300% increase). This is because it is the root value of the sample size that is used and not the sample size actual value.

Example 3: The heights of 3000 people are normally distributed with a mean of 175 cm, and a standard deviation of 8 cm. Considering that a random samples of 40 people is taken, determine the standard deviation of the sampling distribution of means under the following heading;

1) Sampling with replacement
2) Sampling without replacement

Solution

1) **Sampling with replacement**

Step 1: Formula. Standard Deviation of Sample Mean $(\sigma_{\bar{X}}) = \frac{\sigma}{\sqrt{n}}$, where; $\sigma = 8$ and $n = 40$

Step 2: Data substitution and solving

Standard Deviation of Sample Mean $(\sigma_{\bar{X}}) = \frac{8}{\sqrt{40}}$ ....[Simplify the denominator]

Standard Deviation of Sample Mean $(\sigma_{\bar{X}}) = \frac{8}{6.32455532}$ ....[Simplify fraction]

Standard Deviation of Sample Mean $(\sigma_{\bar{X}}) = \mathbf{1.265}$ ....[In three decimal places]

2) **Sampling without replacement**

Step 1: Formula. Standard Deviation of Sample Mean $(\sigma_{\bar{X}}) = \frac{\sigma}{\sqrt{n}}\left[\sqrt{\frac{N-n}{N-1}}\right]$

Where; $\sigma = 8, n = 40, N = 3{,}000$

Step 2: Data substitution and solving

$$\text{Standard Deviation of Sample Mean } (\sigma_{\bar{X}}) = \frac{8}{\sqrt{40}}\left[\sqrt{\frac{3{,}000-40}{3{,}000-1}}\right] \text{..............[Simplify fraction]}$$

$$\text{Standard Deviation of Sample Mean } (\sigma_{\bar{X}}) = \frac{8}{\sqrt{40}}\left[\sqrt{\frac{2{,}960}{2{,}999}}\right] \text{..............[Work square roots]}$$

$$\text{Standard Deviation of Sample Mean } (\sigma_{\bar{X}}) = \frac{8}{6.32455532}[0.993476554] \text{......[Solve equation]}$$

$$\text{Standard Deviation of Sample Mean } (\sigma_{\bar{X}}) = \mathbf{1.257} \text{..............[In three decimal places]}$$

Test Your Understanding
Exercise 15: Determine the value of standard deviation of sample mean using the following data; $\sigma = 20.6107$ and $n = 36$. ....**[Answer: $(\sigma_{\bar{X}}) = 3.435$]**
Exercise 16: The population variance is 50, what is the value of the standard deviation sample mean when the sample size is 25..............................**[Answer: $(\sigma_{\bar{X}}) = 1.414$]**
Exercise 17: Determine the standard error of the sampling distribution of the sample mean using the following information; $\sum X_i = 1{,}800$, $\bar{X} = 72$ and $\sigma^2 = 64$
[Answer: $(\sigma_{\bar{X}}) = 1.6$]

Mathematical Illustration of Efficiency of Estimator

a) Non-relative measure: In a non-relative sense, an estimator is efficient if the expected standard error of the estimator is equal to zero $\{E[SE(\hat{\theta}) = 0]\}$

b) Relative measure: Relative measure talks about the comparison of two estimators. Using the mean concept, the difference between estimators will be seen in terms of the sample size (n). Let assume two different sample sizes $(n_1 = 25)$ and $(n_2 = 16)$.

Sample size $(n_1 = 25)$	Sample size $(n_2 = 16)$
Note: Substitute the value of n in the standard error formula	
Standard error $= \frac{\sigma}{\sqrt{25}}$ ....[Simplify] Standard error $= \frac{\sigma}{5}$ ....[1]	Standard error $= \frac{\sigma}{\sqrt{16}}$ ....[Simplify] Standard error $= \frac{\sigma}{4}$ ....[2]
Interpretation: Since the value of (σ) is the same on both estimator, we can conclude that estimator of equation (1) is more efficient than estimator of equation (2) since it is having a higher denominator. From this, we can conclude that, the higher the sample size, the more efficient an estimator.	

6.3.2 Types of Estimation

An estimate is defined as the numerical value of an estimator calculated from a sample and used to indicate or, make known the value of a parameter. When an estimate is a single digit it is called point estimate and when it is an interval, it is called interval estimate. The concept of sample statistic seen above is considered point estimate since we are limiting our analysis to population mean. Our focus here will be on interval estimation.

Interval estimation is defined as the process of using the sample data to calculate an interval from which the unknown population parameter is expected to be within. Interval estimation is an alternative method to point estimation and major types includes; confidence interval, credible interval, likelihood interval, fiducial interval, tolerance interval and prediction interval. Our analysis will be limited to confidence interval.

1) Confidence Interval of Population mean

Jerzy S. Neyman

Confidence interval is the process of using sample data to obtain an estimated interval at a given confidence level and/or significance level that the unknown population parameter value is likely to lie within. The calculation of confidence interval depend the population variance. The summarized formula of confidence interval is given as seen below,

$$\textbf{Confidence Interval(CI)} = \textbf{Estimate } (\bar{\mathbf{X}}) \pm \textbf{Margin of Error} \quad \ldots\ldots\ldots\ldots(1)$$

Note: To determine the confidence interval of population mean, the following concepts below are worth knowing.

a) Confidence Level

It is the probability that the value of a parameter falls within a specific range of value or interval. It is also known as the probability of sureness or the probability of no doubt/certainty. Confidence level can be expressed in percentage (90%, 95%, 99%) or decimal (0.9, 0.95, 0.99). When not given directly, confidence level is calculated as;

$$\text{Confidence Level(CL)} = 1 - \alpha \quad \ldots\ldots\ldots\ldots\text{[In decimal]}$$

$$\text{Confidence Level(CL)} = (1 - \alpha)100 \quad \ldots\ldots\ldots\ldots\text{[In percentage]}$$

Note: Confidence level is inversely related to significance level (α). A 95% confidence level means we are 95% (0.95) confidence or certain or 5% (0.05) uncertain that our parameter falls within the computed confidence interval.

Example 1: Determine the confidence level considering that the significance level (α) is 5%. Express answer in percentage.

Solution

Step 1: Formula. $\text{Confidence Level(CL)} = (1 - \alpha)100$, where; $\alpha = 5\% \equiv 0.05$

Step 2: Data substitution and solving

$\text{Confidence Level(CL)} = (1 - \alpha)100$ ....[Substitute component numerical value]

$\text{Confidence Level(CL)} = (1 - 0.05)100$ ....[Simplify bracket]

$\text{Confidence Level(CL)} = (0.95)100$ ....[Expand bracket]

$\text{Confidence Level(CL)} = \mathbf{95\%}$

Example 2: Assume a significance level of 0.01, determine the confidence level in percentage.

Solution

Step 1: Formula. $\text{Confidence Level(CL)} = (1 - \alpha)100$, where; $\alpha = 0.01$

Step 2: Data substitution and solving

$\text{Confidence Level(CL)} = (1 - \alpha)100$ ....[Substitute component numerical value]

$\text{Confidence Level(CL)} = (1 - 0.01)100$ ....[Simplify bracket]

$\text{Confidence Level(CL)} = (0.99)100$ ....[Expand bracket]

$\text{Confidence Level(CL)} = 99\%$

Example 3: Determine the significance level when the confidence level is 90%.

Solution

Step 1: Formula. $\text{Confidence Level(CL)} = (1 - \alpha)100$

Where; $\text{Confidence Level} = 90\% = 0.9$

Step 2: Data substitution and solving

$90 = (1 - \alpha)100$ ....[Divide both sides of equation by 100]

$0.9 = 1 - \alpha$ ....[Make (α) subject of the formula and simplify equation]

$\text{Significance Level } (\alpha) = \mathbf{0.1} = \mathbf{10\%}$

b) Critical value

It is the limit of confidence or boundary of certainty and uncertainty. The critical value can be derived using the critical value for the normal distribution table with the help of the probability (P) component when the population variance is known. The probability component is calculated using the following formula;

$\text{Probability (P)} = 1 - \alpha/2$ ....[In decimal]

Probability $(P) = (1 - \alpha/2)100$ ....[In percentage]

Note: The significance level (α) is divided by two due the symmetric nature of confidence interval. When the population variance is unknown, we use the t-distribution with the help of the degree of freedom to determine the critical value.

Example 1: The confidence level is 90%, what is the value of the confidence coefficient assuming the population variance is known.

Solution

Hint: Since the population variance is known, it shows that the Z-distribution is the appropriate distribution table to read the critical value.

Step 1: Determine the value of P

1) Formula. $P = 1 - \frac{\text{significance level}(\alpha)}{2}$, where; $\alpha = 10\% = 0.1$
2) Data substitution and solving

$P = 1 - 0.1/2$ ....[Solve equation]

$P = \mathbf{0.95}$ ....[P value at 10% significance level]

Step 2: Reading of critical value

Critical Values For The Normal Distribution									
P	0.75	0.90	0.95	0.975	0.99	0.995	0.9975	0.999	0.9995
Z	0.674	1.282	1.645	1.960	2.326	2.576	2.807	3.090	3.291
Note: The critical value at 10% significance level is $\pm\mathbf{1.645}$									

Example 2: Given that the significance level is 5%, determine the critical value assuming that the population variance is known.

Solution

Step 1: Determine the value of P

1) Formula. $P = 1 - \frac{\text{significance level}(\alpha)}{2}$, where; $\alpha = 5\% \equiv 0.05$
2) Data substitution and solving

$P = 1 - 0.05/2$ ....[Solve equation]

$P = \mathbf{0.975}$ ....[P value at 5% significance level]

Step 2: Reading of critical value

Critical Values For The Normal Distribution									
P	0.75	0.90	0.95	0.975	0.99	0.995	0.9975	0.999	0.9995
Z	0.674	1.282	1.645	1.960	2.326	2.576	2.807	3.090	3.291
Note: The critical value at 5% significance level is $\pm\mathbf{1.960}$									

Example 3: The sample size of a study is given as 30. Determine the critical value considering that the significance level is 5% and the population variance is unknown.

Solution

Hint: Since the population variance is unknown, it shows that the t-distribution is the appropriate distribution table to read the critical value.

Step 1: Determination of probability (P)

1) Formula. $P = 1 - \frac{\text{significance level}(\alpha)}{2}$, where; $\alpha = 5\% \equiv 0.05$
2) Data substitution and solving

   $P = 1 - 0.05/2$ ....[Solve equation]

   $P = \mathbf{0.975}$ ....[P value at 5% significance level]

Step 2: Determination of degree of freedom (ν)

1) Formula. $df = \nu = n - 1$, where; $\text{Sample size } (n) = 30$
2) Data substitution and solving. $df = \nu = 30 - 1 = \mathbf{29}$

Step 3: Determination of critical value

p	0.75	0.90	0.95	0.975	0.99	0.995	0.9975	0.999	0.9995
$\nu = 1$	1.000	3.078	6.314	12.71	31.82	63.66	127.3	318.3	636.6
2	0.816	1.886	2.920	4.303	6.965	9.925	14.09	22.33	31.60
25	0.684	1.316	1.708	2.060	2.485	2.787	3.078	3.450	3.725
26	0.684	1.315	1.706	2.056	2.479	2.779	3.067	3.435	3.707
27	0.684	1.314	1.703	2.052	2.473	2.771	3.057	3.421	3.689
28	0.683	1.313	1.701	2.048	2.467	2.763	3.047	3.408	3.674
29	0.683	1.311	1.699	2.045	2.462	2.756	3.038	3.396	3.660

Note: The critical value at 5% significance level is $\pm\mathbf{2.045}$

c) **Margin of Error**

It is the degree of error resulted from the usage of sample data in estimating a population parameter. It is the range of values below and above the sample statistic of a confidence interval. Mathematically, margin of error is the amount added to (+) and subtracted (−) from the point estimation to formulate the confidence interval. The margin of error is calculated using the following formulas;

$\text{Margin of Error(ME)} = \pm(\text{Standard Error} \times \text{Critical Value})$ ....(1)

$$\text{Margin of Error(ME)} = \frac{\text{Upper Confidence Limit} - \text{Lower Confidence Limit}}{2} \quad \ldots\ldots\ldots\ldots\ldots\ldots\ldots(2)$$

Note: Margin of error is affected by the following factors; variance, sample size and confidence level. Practical examples of the determination of margin of error will be illustrated below.

d) Confidence Limits

It is the end-points of the confidence interval. That is the lower confidence limit/boundary and upper confidence limit/boundary. Their respective formulas are given as seen below;

$$\text{Lower Confidence Limit(LCL)} = \text{Estimate } (\overline{X}) - \text{Margin of Error} \quad \ldots\ldots\ldots\ldots\ldots(1)$$

$$\text{Upper Confidence Limit(UCL)} = \text{Estimate } (\overline{X}) + \text{Margin of Error} \quad \ldots\ldots\ldots\ldots\ldots(2)$$

Note: The lower confidence limit is less than the estimate $(\text{LCL} < \overline{X})$ and the upper confidence limit is greater than the estimate$(\text{UCL} > \overline{X})$. The upper confidence limit is always greater than the lower confidence limit $(\text{UCL} > \text{LCL})$.

e) Confidence Interval Length

It is the difference between the upper confidence limit and the lower confidence limit. Confidence interval length is positively related to the confidence level and indirectly related to the significance level. Mathematically, confidence interval length is calculated using the following formula,

$$\text{Confidence Interval Length} = \text{Upper Limit} - \text{Lower Limit} \quad \ldots\ldots\ldots\ldots\ldots\ldots(1)$$

$$\text{Confidence Interval Length} = 2 \times \text{Margin of Error} \quad \ldots\ldots\ldots\ldots\ldots\ldots\ldots(2)$$

1.1 Calculation of population mean Confidence Interval

The understanding of the above concepts makes the calculation of population mean confidence interval easier. The manner of determining the confidence interval depends on whether the population variance is known or unknown.

a) When the Population Variance is Known

When the population variance is known or given, the Z-statistics is applied. The Z-statistics of a normal distribution is expressed in a summarized form as $[Z_{\alpha/2} < Z < Z_{\alpha/2}]$. Applying the symmetric concept of the confidence interval, the left side is negative and right side positive $[-Z_{\alpha/2} < Z < Z_{\alpha/2}]$. From this new equation, the formula of confidence interval can be derived as seen below.

$-Z_{\alpha/2} < Z < Z_{\alpha/2}$ ……………………[Substitute the formula for Z. that is $\left(Z = \frac{\overline{X}-\mu}{\sigma/\sqrt{n}}\right)$]

$$-Z_{\alpha/2} < \frac{\bar{X}-\mu}{\sigma/\sqrt{n}} < Z_{\alpha/2}$$ ....[Multiply all terms of equation by $\left(\sigma/\sqrt{n}\right)$]

$$-Z_{\alpha/2}\frac{\sigma}{\sqrt{n}} < \bar{X} - \mu < Z_{\alpha/2}\frac{\sigma}{\sqrt{n}}$$ ....[Multiply all three terms by $(-\bar{X})$]

$$-\bar{X} - Z_{\alpha/2}\frac{\sigma}{\sqrt{n}} < -\mu < -\bar{X} + Z_{\alpha/2}\frac{\sigma}{\sqrt{n}}$$ ....[Multiply all terms by (-1)]

$$\bar{X} + Z_{\alpha/2}\frac{\sigma}{\sqrt{n}} > \mu > \bar{X} - Z_{\alpha/2}\frac{\sigma}{\sqrt{n}}$$ ....[Re-write equation]

$$\bar{X} - Z_{\alpha/2}\frac{\sigma}{\sqrt{n}} < \mu < \bar{X} + Z_{\alpha/2}\frac{\sigma}{\sqrt{n}}$$ ....**[Confidence interval]**

Note: The estimated true values of the population mean is given as (μ). From the confidence interval, the confidence limits formulas are seen below.

$$\text{Lower Confidence Limit (LCL)} = \bar{X} - Z_{\alpha/2}\left(\frac{\sigma}{\sqrt{n}}\right)$$ ....(1)

$$\text{Upper Confidence Limit (UCL)} = \bar{X} + Z_{\alpha/2}\left(\frac{\sigma}{\sqrt{n}}\right)$$ ....(2)

Where; $\left(\frac{\sigma}{\sqrt{n}}\right)$ Represent the standard error using population standard deviation

$Z_{\alpha/2}$ Represent the critical value using Z-distribution table

$Z_{\alpha/2}\left(\frac{\sigma}{\sqrt{n}}\right)$ Represent the margin of error

$\bar{X}$ Represent the estimate (Sample mean)

Example 1: Determine the value of margin of error from the following results; sample size (10), sample mean (29), population standard deviation (4.30) and confidence level (90%).

Solution

Step 1: Formula. Margin of Error $= \pm Z_{\alpha/2}\left(\frac{\sigma}{\sqrt{n}}\right)$, where; $Z_{\alpha/2} = 1.645$, $\sigma = 4.30$ and $n = 29$

Step 2: Data substitution and solving

$$\text{Margin of Error} = \pm 1.645\left(\frac{4.30}{\sqrt{29}}\right)$$ ....[Work root]

$$\text{Margin of Error} = \pm 1.645\left(\frac{4.30}{5.385164807}\right)$$ ....[Simplify fraction]

$$\text{Margin of Error} = \pm 1.645(0.798489954)$$ ....[Expand bracket]

$$\text{Margin of Error} = \pm 1.314$$ ....**[In four decimal places]**

Example 2: The mean mark of a sample of 64 students is 70.6. Considering that the standard deviation marks of the student population is 2.5, find the 95% confidence interval of the population mean mark.

Solution

a) Method 1 [Expanded Form]

Step 1: Formula. Confidence Interval $= \overline{X} - Z_{\alpha/2}\left(\frac{\sigma}{\sqrt{n}}\right) < \mu < \overline{X} + Z_{\alpha/2}\left(\frac{\sigma}{\sqrt{n}}\right)$

Where; $\overline{X} = 70.6,\ \sigma = 2.5,\ n = 64,\ Z_{\alpha/2} = 1.960$

Step 2: Data substitution and solving

Confidence Interval $= 70.6 - 1.960\left(\frac{2.5}{\sqrt{64}}\right) < \mu < 70.6 + 1.960\left(\frac{2.5}{\sqrt{64}}\right)$ ....[Work root]

Confidence Interval $= 70.6 - 1.960\left(\frac{2.5}{8}\right) < \mu < 70.6 + 1.960\left(\frac{2.5}{8}\right)$.......[Simplify fraction]

Confidence Interval $= 70.6 - 1.960(0.3125) < \mu < 70.6 + 1.960(0.3125)$

Confidence Interval $= 70.6 - 0.6125 < \mu < 70.6 + 0.6125$ ....[Solve both sides]

Confidence Interval $= \mathbf{69.9875 < \mu < 71.2125}$

b) Method 2 [Summarized Form]

Step 1: Formula. Confidence Interval $= \overline{X} \pm Z_{\alpha/2}\left(\frac{\sigma}{\sqrt{n}}\right)$

Where; $\overline{X} = 70.6,\ \sigma = 2.5,\ n = 64,\ Z_{\alpha/2} = 1.960$ [Already calculated above]

Step 2: Data substitution and solving

Confidence Interval $= 70.6 \pm 1.960\left(\frac{2.5}{\sqrt{64}}\right)$ ....[Work root and simplify fraction]

Confidence Interval $= 70.6 \pm 1.960(0.3125)$ ....[Expand bracket]

Confidence Interval $= 70.6 \pm 0.6125$

Step 3: Determination of individual confidence limits

$$\left.\begin{array}{l}\text{Lower Confidence Limit} = 70.6 - 0.6125 = 69.9875 \\ \text{Upper Confidence Limit} = 70.6 + 0.6125 = 71.2125\end{array}\right\} \ \mathbf{CI = 69.9875 < \mu < 71.2125}$$

Step 3: Interpretation: We are 95% confident/certain that the population mean mark is between 69.9875 and 71.2125. The confidence interval length is 1.225 [71.2125 – 69.9875 = 1.225].

Example 3: A randomly selected sample of 30 students yields a sample mean score of 375. Assume the population variance is 656.1, determine the confidence limits at;

1) 99% confidence level
2) 95% confidence level

Solution

1) 99% confidence level

Step 1: Formula. Confidence Interval Length = Upper Limit − Lower Limit

Step 2: Calculation of confidence limits

a) Formula: Lower Confidence Limit (LCL) $= \overline{X} - Z_{\alpha/2}\left(\frac{\sigma}{\sqrt{n}}\right)$

Upper Confidence Limit (UCL) $= \overline{X} + Z_{\alpha/2}\left(\frac{\sigma}{\sqrt{n}}\right)$

Where; $\overline{X} = 375$, $\sigma = \sqrt{656.1} = 81$, $n = 30$, $Z_{\alpha/2} = 2.576$

b) Determination of margin of error

1) Margin of Error $= \pm Z_{\alpha/2}\left(\frac{\sigma}{\sqrt{n}}\right)$, Where; $\sigma = \sqrt{656.1} = 81$, $n = 30$, $Z_{\alpha/2} = 2.576$

2) Data substitution and solving

Margin of Error $= \pm 2.576\left(\frac{81}{\sqrt{30}}\right)$ ....[Work root and simplify fraction]

Margin of Error $= \pm 2.576(14.78850905)$ ....[Expand bracket]

Margin of Error $= \pm \mathbf{38.0952}$ ....[In four decimal places]

c) Data substitution and solving

Lower Confidence Limit $= 375 - 38.0952 = \mathbf{336.9048}$

Upper Confidence Limit $= 375 + 38.0952 = \mathbf{413.0952}$

Note: From the above value, the confidence interval length is given as;

a) Formula 1: Confidence Interval Length = Upper Limit − Lower Limit

Confidence Interval Length $= 413.0952 - 336.9048$ ....[Solve equation]

Confidence Interval Length $= \mathbf{79.1904}$

b) Formula 2: Confidence Interval Length = 2 × Margin of Error

Confidence Interval Length $= 2 \times 38.0952$ ....[Solve equation]

Confidence Interval Length $= \mathbf{76.1904}$

2) 95% confidence level

a) Method 1

Step 1: Formula. Confidence Interval Length = Upper Limit − Lower Limit

Step 2: Determination of confidence interval

a) Formula: Confidence Interval $= \overline{X} - Z_{\alpha/2}\left(\frac{\sigma}{\sqrt{n}}\right) < \mu < \overline{X} + Z_{\alpha/2}\left(\frac{\sigma}{\sqrt{n}}\right)$

Where; $\overline{X} = 375$, $\sigma = 81$, $n = 30$, $Z_{\alpha/2} = 1.960$

b) Data substitution and solving

$CI = 375 - 1.960\left(\frac{81}{\sqrt{30}}\right) < \mu < 375 + 1.960\left(\frac{81}{\sqrt{30}}\right)$ ....[Work root]

$CI = 375 - 1.960\left(\frac{81}{5.477225575}\right) < \mu < 375 + 1.960\left(\frac{81}{5.477225575}\right)$ ....[Simplify]

$CI = 375 - 1.960(14.78850905) < \mu < 375 + 1.960(14.78850905)$

$CI = 375 - 28.98547774 < \mu < 375 + 28.98547774$ ....[Solve both sides]

$\text{Confidence Interval} = 346.0145 < \mu < 403.9855$ ....[In four decimal places]

Step 3: Data substitution and solving

$\text{Confidence Interval Length} = \text{Upper Limit} - \text{Lower Limit}$............Substitute values]

$\text{Confidence Interval Length} = 403.9855 - 346.0145$ ....[Solve equation]

$\text{Confidence Interval Length} = \mathbf{57.971}$

b) Method 2

Step 1: Formula. $\text{Confidence Interval Length} = 2\left[Z_{\alpha/2}\left(\frac{\sigma}{\sqrt{n}}\right)\right]$

Where; $\sigma = 81$, $n = 30$, $Z_{\alpha/2} = 1.960$

Step 2: Data substitution and solving

$\text{Confidence Interval Length} = 2\left[1.960\left(\frac{81}{\sqrt{30}}\right)\right]$ ....[Work root and simplify fraction]

$\text{Confidence Interval Length} = 2[1.960(14.78850905)]$ ....[Expand internal bracket]

$\text{Confidence Interval Length} = \mathbf{57.971}$ ....[In three decimal places]

Complementary Explanation: From the above calculations, the higher the confidence level (95% to 99%), the higher the length of the confidence interval (57.971 to 79.190). The higher the significance level (1% to 5%), the lower the length of the confidence interval (79.190 to 57.971).

Test Your Understanding

Exercise 18: A sample of 25 students yield a mean score of 10.38, assuming that the population standard deviation score is 5.74, at 95% confidence level determine the following;

1) Critical Value... **[Answer: 1.960]**
2) Margin of Error. ....**[Answer: $\pm\mathbf{2.2501}$]**

Exercise 19: The population variance (σ^2) from a normally distributed population is 100. A sample of 1000 students selected at random yields a sample mean ($\overline{X}$) of 498. Calculate a 95% and 99% confidence interval for the population mean.

[Answer: ($497.38 < \mu < 498.62$) **and** ($497.19 < \mu < 498.81$) **respectively]**

Exercise 20: The mean mark of a sample of 25 students is 6.2. Considering that the standard deviation marks of the student population is 2, using a 90% confidence level, determine the following;

1) Upper limit confidence interval ....**[Answer: 6.858]**
2) Lower limit confidence interval ....**[Answer: 5.542]**
3) The length of confidence interval ....**[Answer: 1.316]**

b) When the Population Variance is Unknown

When the population variance is unknown, the t-statistics following the concept of symmetric distribution is given as; $\left[t_{n-1:\alpha/2} < T < t_{n-1:\alpha/2}\right]$. Applying the concept of the confidence interval, the left hand side is negative and right hand side positive $\left[-t_{n-1:\alpha/2} < T < t_{n-1:\alpha/2}\right]$. The formula of confidence interval can be derived as seen below.

$-t_{n-1:\alpha/2} < T < t_{n-1:\alpha/2}$ ....[Substitute the formula for T. that is $\left(T = \frac{\bar{X}-\mu}{S/\sqrt{n}}\right)$]

$-t_{n-1:\alpha/2} < \frac{\bar{X}-\mu}{S/\sqrt{n}} < t_{n-1:\alpha/2}$ ....[Multiply all terms of equation by $\left(\frac{S}{\sqrt{n}}\right)$]

$-\frac{S}{\sqrt{n}}t_{n-1:\alpha/2} < \bar{X} - \mu < \frac{S}{\sqrt{n}}t_{n-1:\alpha/2}$ ....[Multiply all three terms by $(-\bar{X})$]

$-\bar{X} - \frac{S}{\sqrt{n}}t_{n-1:\alpha/2} < -\mu < -\bar{X} + \frac{S}{\sqrt{n}}t_{n-1:\alpha/2}$ ....[Multiply all terms by (-1)]

$\bar{X} + \frac{S}{\sqrt{n}}t_{n-1:\alpha/2} > \mu > \bar{X} - \frac{S}{\sqrt{n}}t_{n-1:\alpha/2}$ ....[Re-write equation]

$\bar{X} - \frac{S}{\sqrt{n}}t_{n-1:\alpha/2} < \mu < \bar{X} + \frac{S}{\sqrt{n}}t_{n-1:\alpha/2}$ ....**[Confidence interval]**

Note: The estimated true values of the population mean is (μ). The confidence limits formulas are seen below.

$$\text{Upper Confidence Limit(UCL)} = \bar{X} + \left(\frac{S}{\sqrt{n}}\right)t_{n-1:\alpha/2} \quad \text{.........................(1)}$$

$$\text{Lower Confidence Limit(LCL)} = \bar{X} - \left(\frac{S}{\sqrt{n}}\right)t_{n-1:\alpha/2} \quad \text{.........................(2)}$$

Where; $\left(\frac{S}{\sqrt{n}}\right)$ Represent the standard error using sample standard deviation

$t_{n-1:\alpha/2}$ Represent the critical value using t-distribution table

$\left(\frac{S}{\sqrt{n}}\right)t_{n-1:\alpha/2}$ Represent the margin of error

$\bar{X}$ Represent the estimate (Sample mean)

Example 1: Determine the margin of error using the following data; $n = 41, \overline{X} = 66, S = 1.9$ and 95% confidence level.

Solution

Step 1: Formula. $\text{Margin of Error} = \pm\left(\frac{S}{\sqrt{n}}\right)t_{n-1:\alpha/2}$

Where; $n = 41, S = 1.9$ and $t_{n-1:\alpha/2} = 2.021$

Step 2: Data substitution and solving

$\text{Margin of Error} = \pm\frac{1.9}{\sqrt{41}}(2.021)$ ....[Work root and simplify fraction]

$\text{Margin of Error} = \pm 0.296730147(2.021)$ ....[Expand bracket]

$\text{Margin of Error} = \pm 0.5997$ ....**[In four decimal places]**

Example 2: The sample marks of 7 students is 10 and sample standard deviation is 0.283. Calculate a 95% confidence interval for the population mean.

Solution

a) **Method 1 [Expanded Technique]**

Step 1: Formula. $\text{Confidence Interval} = \overline{X} - \frac{S}{\sqrt{n}}t_{n-1:\alpha/2} < \mu < \overline{X} + \frac{S}{\sqrt{n}}t_{n-1:\alpha/2}$

Where; $\overline{X} = 10, S = 0.283, n - 1 = 7 - 1 = 6$ and $t_{n-1:\alpha/2} = 1.237$

Step 2: Data substitution and solving

$\text{Confidence Interval} = 10 - \frac{0.283}{\sqrt{7}}(1.237) < \mu < 10 + \frac{0.283}{\sqrt{7}}(1.237)$......[Simplify fractions]

$CI = 10 - 0.106963945(1.237) < \mu < 10 + 0.106963945(1.237)$ ....[Expand bracket]

$Cl = 10 - 0.132314401 < \mu < 10 + 0.132314401$ ....[Simplify both sides]

$\text{Confidence Interval} = 9.8677 < \mu < 10.1323$

b) **Method 2 [Summarized Technique]**

Step 1: Formula. $\text{Confidence Interval} = \overline{X} \pm \frac{S}{\sqrt{n}}t_{n-1:\alpha/2}$

Where; $\overline{X} = 10, S = 0.283, n - 1 = 7 - 1 = 6$ and $t_{n-1:\alpha/2} = 1.237$

Step 2: Data substitution and solving

$\text{Confidence Interval} = 10 \pm \frac{0.283}{\sqrt{7}}(1.237)$ ....[Simplify fraction]

$\text{Confidence Interval} = 10 \pm 0.106963945(1.237)$ ....[Expand bracket]

$\text{Confidence Interval} = 10 \pm 0.1323$ ....[In three decimal places]

Step 3: Determination of confidence limits

$\text{Upper Confidence Limit(UCL)} = 10 + 0.1323 = 10.1323$

$\text{Lower Confidence Limit(LCL)} = 10 - 0.1323 = 9.8677$

$\mathbf{CI = 9.8677 < \mu < 10.1323}$

Example 3: Determine the confidence interval and confidence interval length given that; $n = 100$, $S^2 = 16$, $\overline{X} = 23.5$ and 95% confidence level.

Solution

1) Determination of confidence interval

Step 1: Formula. Confidence Interval $= \overline{X} - \frac{S}{\sqrt{n}} t_{n-1:\alpha/2} < \mu < \overline{X} + \frac{S}{\sqrt{n}} t_{n-1:\alpha/2}$

Where; $\overline{X} = 23.5$, $S = \sqrt{16} = 4$, $n = 100$ and $t_{n-1:\alpha/2} = 1.980$

Step 2: Data substitution and solving

Confidence Interval $= 23.5 - \frac{4}{\sqrt{100}}(1.980) < \mu < 23.5 + \frac{4}{\sqrt{100}}(1.980)$ .....[Work root]

Confidence Interval $= 23.5 - \frac{4}{10}(1.980) < \mu < 23.5 + \frac{4}{10}(1.980)$...[Simplify fraction]

Confidence Interval $= 23.5 - 0.4(1.980) < \mu < 23.5 + 0.4(1.980)$.[Expand brackets]

Confidence Interval $= 23.5 - 0.792 < \mu < 23.5 + 0.792$ ....[Simplify equation]

Confidence Interval $= \mathbf{22.708} < \boldsymbol{\mu} < \mathbf{24.292}$

2) Determination of confidence Interval Length

a) Method 1

Step 1: Formula. Confidence Interval Length $=$ UCL $-$ LCL

Where; Upper Confidence Limit $= 24.292$ and Lower Confidence Limit $= 22.708$

Step 2: Data substitution and solving

Confidence Interval Length $=$ UCL $-$ LCL .....[Substitute components numerical values]

Confidence Interval Length $= 24.292 - 22.708$ ....[Solve equation]

Confidence Interval Length $= \mathbf{1.584}$

b) Method 2

Step 1: Formula. Confidence Interval Length $= 2\left[\frac{S}{\sqrt{n}}\left(t_{n-1:\alpha/2}\right)\right]$

Where; $S = \sqrt{16} = 4$, $n = 100$ and $t_{n-1:\alpha/2} = 1.980$

Step 2: Data substitution and solving

Confidence Interval Length $= 2\left[\frac{4}{\sqrt{100}}(1.980)\right]$ ....[Work root and simplify fraction]

Confidence Interval Length $= 2[0.4(1.980)]$ ....[Expand internal bracket]

Confidence Interval Length $= 2[0.792]$ ....[Solve equation]

Confidence Interval Length $= \mathbf{1.584}$

Example 4: A random sample of 100 observations from a normal population with mean (μ) gave the following data; $\sum X = 8{,}200$ and $\sum X^2 = 686{,}800$. Find a 99% confidence interval for the population mean(μ).

Solution

Step 1: Formula. Confidence Interval $= \overline{X} \pm \frac{S}{\sqrt{n}} t_{n-1:\alpha/2}$

Where; $\overline{X} = \frac{8{,}200}{100} = 82 =$, $n - 1 = 100 - 1 = 99$ and $t_{n-1:\alpha/2} = 2.617$

Step 2: Determination of sample variance (S^2)

1) Formula. Sample Variance$(S^2) = \frac{1}{n-1}\left(\sum X_\iota{}^2 - \frac{(\sum X_\iota)^2}{n}\right)$

Where; $n = 100$, $\sum X = 8{,}200$ and $\sum X^2 = 686{,}800$

2) Data substitution and solving

Sample Variance$(S^2) = \frac{1}{100-1}\left(686{,}800 - \frac{(8{,}200)^2}{100}\right)$ ....[Work exponent]

Sample Variance$(S^2) = \frac{1}{99}\left(686{,}800 - \frac{67{,}240{,}000}{100}\right)$ ....[Simplify bracket fraction]

Sample Variance$(S^2) = \frac{1}{99}(686{,}800 - 672{,}400)$ ....[Simplify bracket]

Sample Variance$(S^2) = \frac{1}{99}(14{,}400)$ ....[Solve equation]

Sample Variance$(S^2) = \mathbf{145.4545}$ ....[In four decimal places]

Step 3: Data substitution and solving. $S^2 = 145.4545 \rightarrow S = 12.0605$

Confidence Interval $= 82 \pm \frac{12.0605}{\sqrt{100}}(2.617)$ ....[Work root and simplify fraction]

Confidence Interval $= 82 \pm 1.20605(2.617)$ ....[Expand bracket]

Confidence Interval $= 82 \pm 3.15623285$ ....[Derive confidence limits]

Confidence Interval $= \mathbf{78.84 < \mu < 85.16}$

Example 5: A random sample of 10 items is observed from a normal population with the following values: 27, 25, 31, 23, 27, 37, 28, 30, 24 and 29. What is the 95% confidence interval estimate of the population mean? Can you conclude that the population mean is greater than 25?

Solution

Step 1: Formula. Confidence Interval $= \overline{X} \pm \frac{S}{\sqrt{n}} t_{n-1:\alpha/2}$

Where; $n = 10$ and $t_{n-1:\alpha/2} = 2.262$

Step 2: Determination of unknown components [$\overline{X}$ and S]

a) Formulas: $\overline{X} = \frac{\sum X_\iota}{n}$ and $S = \sqrt{\frac{1}{n-1}\left[\sum X^2 - \frac{(\sum X)^2}{n}\right]}$, where; $\sum X_\iota$ and $\sum X^2{}_\iota$ are unknown

b) Tabular determination of formula unknown components

X	27	25	31	23	27	37	28	30	24	29	$\sum X = 281$
X^2	729	625	961	529	729	1,369	784	900	576	841	$\sum X^2 = 8{,}043$

c) Data substitution and solving

$\text{Sample mean}(\overline{X}) = \frac{281}{10}$ ……………………………………………………[Solve equation]

$\text{Sample mean}(\overline{X}) = \mathbf{28.1}$

$\text{Sample standard deviation}(S) = \sqrt{\frac{1}{n-1}\left[\sum X^2 - \frac{(\sum X)^2}{n}\right]}$……..[Substitute numerical values]

$S = \sqrt{\frac{1}{10-1}\left[8{,}043 - \frac{(281)^2}{10}\right]}$ ……………………………[Work exponent and simplify bracket]

$S = \sqrt{\frac{1}{9}[146.9]}$ …………………………………………[Expand bracket and work root]

$\text{Sample Standard Deviation } (S) = \mathbf{4.0401}$ ……………………………[In four decimal places]

Step 3: Data substitution and solving

$\text{Confidence Interval} = \overline{X} \pm \frac{S}{\sqrt{n}} t_{n-1:\alpha/2}$ ……………[Substitute components numerical values]

$\text{Confidence Interval} = 28.1 + \frac{4.0401}{\sqrt{10}}(2.262)$ …………………[Work root and simplify fraction]

$\text{Confidence Interval} = 28.1 + 1.277591797(2.262)$ ……………………………[Expand bracket]

$\text{Confidence Interval} = 28.1 + 2.889912646$ ……………………………………[Work out limits]

$\text{Confidence Interval} = 25.21 < \mu < 30.99$ ……………………………**[In two decimal places]**

Note: The population mean is greater than 25 because the upper confidence limit is 30.99 and is greater than 25.

Test Your Understanding

Exercise 21: An educational inspector intends to use the mean of a random sample size of 81 students to estimate the mean mark of the entire class. Considering that the sample mean mark is 50 and sample standard deviation mark is 27, determine a 95% confidence interval for the class mean. ……………………………………………………**[Answer: $44.06 < \mu < 55.94$]**

Exercise 22: Determine the confidence interval of a population mean using the following information; $\overline{X} = 17.25$, $n = 20$, $S = 3.3$ and a confidence level of 90%

[Answer: $15.97 < \mu < 18.53$]

Exercise 23: A random sample of 25 was found to have a mean of 23.4 with an estimated standard deviation of 8.50. Determine the confidence interval length, assuming that the confidence level is 90%......................**[Answer: Confidence Interval Length = 5.8174]**

Exercise 24: A random sample of 50 from a normal population with mean yield the following data; $\sum X = 1{,}200$ and $\sum X^2 = 37{,}000$. Fine a 95% confidence interval for the population mean(μ)...**[Answer: $20.3411 < \mu < 27.6589$]**

1.2 Determination of Sample Size

When using sampling to estimate the value of a population parameter, the major problem is to know the appropriate sample size. A large sample size is costly and time consuming and a small sample size may produce unreliable result. To solve this problem, we can pre-determine the required sample size based on our desired margin of error and confidence level.

a) When the population variance is known

The sample size can be derived from the margin of error formula by making the sample size (n) subject of formulas as illustrated below. Remember the margin of error when the population variance is known is given as $\left[\text{Margin of Error(ME)} = \pm Z_{\alpha/2}\left(\frac{\sigma}{\sqrt{n}}\right)\right]$

$\text{ME} = \pm Z_{\alpha/2}\left(\frac{\sigma}{\sqrt{n}}\right)$ ....[Divide both sides of equation by $(\pm Z_{\alpha/2})$]

$\frac{\text{ME}}{\pm Z_{\alpha/2}} = \frac{\sigma}{\sqrt{n}}$ ....[Perform cross multiplication]

$\sqrt{n}(\text{ME}) = \pm\sigma(Z_{\alpha/2})$ ....[Divide both sides of equation by (ME)]

$\sqrt{n} = \frac{\sigma(Z_{\alpha/2})}{\text{ME}} \equiv (n)^{\frac{1}{2}} = \frac{\sigma(Z_{\alpha/2})}{\text{ME}}$ ....[Square both sides of the equation]

$\text{Sample Size (n)} = \frac{[\sigma(Z_{\alpha/2})]^2}{(\text{ME})^2} \equiv \frac{\sigma^2}{(\text{ME})^2}(Z_{\alpha/2})^2$ ....**[Expressed in no decimal place]**

Example 1: Suppose that the population standard deviation (σ) is 15, calculate the required sample size that will yield a margin of error is 6.44, at 99% confidence level.

<u>Solution</u>

Step 1: Formula. $\text{Sample Size (n)} = \frac{\sigma^2}{(\text{ME})^2}(Z_{\alpha/2})^2$

Where; $\sigma = 15$, $\text{ME} = 6.44$ and $Z_{\alpha/2} = 2.576$

Step 2: Data substitution and solving

$\text{Sample Size (n)} = \frac{(15)^2}{(6.44)^2}(2.576)^2$ ....[Work exponents]

$\text{Sample Size (n)} = \frac{225}{41.4736}(6.635776)$ ....[Simplify fraction]

$\text{Sample Size (n)} = 5.425137919(6.635776)$ ....[Solve equation]

Sample Size (n) $= \mathbf{36}$

Example 2: Given that the population standard deviation (σ) is 20, calculate the required sample size at 95% confidence level assuming;

1) A desired margin of error of 5
2) A desired margin of error of 3.22
3) A desired margin of error of 1

Solution

1) A desired margin of error of 5

Step 1: Formula. Sample Size (n) $= \frac{\sigma^2}{(\text{ME})^2}\left(\text{Z}_{\alpha/2}\right)^2$, where; $\sigma = 20$, ME $= 5$, $\text{Z}_{\alpha/2} = 1.960$

Step 2: Data substitution and solving

Sample Size (n) $= \frac{(20)^2}{(5)^2}(1.960)^2$ ....[Work exponents]

Sample Size (n) $= \frac{400}{25}(3.8416)$ ....[Simplify fraction and solve equation]

Sample Size (n) $= \mathbf{61}$

2) A desired margin of error of 3.22

Step 1: Formula. Sample Size (n) $= \frac{\sigma^2}{(\text{ME})^2}\left(\text{Z}_{\alpha/2}\right)^2$

Where; $\sigma = 20$, ME $= 3.22$ and $\text{Z}_{\alpha/2} = 1.960$

Step 2: Data substitution and solving

Sample Size (n) $= \frac{(20)^2}{(3.22)^2}(1.960)^2$ ....[Work exponents]

Sample Size (n) $= \frac{400}{10.3684}(3.8416)$ ....[Solve]

Sample Size (n) $= \mathbf{148}$

3) A desired margin of error of 1

Step 1: Formula. Sample Size (n) $= \frac{\sigma^2}{(\text{ME})^2}\left(\text{Z}_{\alpha/2}\right)^2$, where; $\sigma = 20$, ME $= 1$, $\text{Z}_{\alpha/2} = 1.960$

Step 2: Data substitution and solving

Sample Size (n) $= \frac{(20)^2}{(1)^2}(1.960)^2$ ....[Work exponents]

Sample Size (n) $= \frac{400}{1}(3.8416)$ ....[Simplify fraction]

Sample Size (n) $= 400(3.8416)$ ....[Solve equation]

Sample Size (n) $= \mathbf{1,537}$

Complementary Explanation: From the calculations, we realized that as the margin of error reduces, the sample size increases at a significant rate.

Example 3: The population standard deviation (σ) is 10. Calculate the required sample size assuming a desired margin of error of 4.56 at;

1) 90% confidence level
2) 95% confidence level
3) 99% confidence level

Solution

1) 90% confidence level ...[Rem. 90% confidence level, the confidence coefficient is 1.645]

Step 1: Formula. Sample Size (n) $= \frac{\sigma^2}{(\mathrm{ME})^2}\left(Z_{\alpha/2}\right)^2$

Where; $\sigma = 10$, ME $= 4.56$, $Z_{\alpha/2} = 1.645$

Step 2: Data substitution and solving

Sample Size (n) $= \frac{(10)^2}{(4.56)^2}(1.645)^2$ ....[Work exponents]

Sample Size (n) $= \frac{100}{20.7936}(2.706025)$ ....[Solve]

Sample Size (n) $= \mathbf{13}$

2) 95% confidence level ...[Rem. 95% confidence level, the confidence coefficient is 1.960]

Step 1: Formula. Sample Size (n) $= \frac{\sigma^2}{(\mathrm{ME})^2}\left(Z_{\alpha/2}\right)^2$

Where; $\sigma = 10$, ME $= 4.56$, $Z_{\alpha/2} = 1.960$

Step 2: Data substitution and solving

Sample Size (n) $= \frac{(10)^2}{(4.56)^2}(1.960)^2$ ....[Work exponents]

Sample Size (n) $= \frac{100}{20.7936}(3.8416)$ ....[Simplify fraction]

Sample Size (n) $= 4.809172053(3.8416)$ ....[Solve equation]

Sample Size (n) $= \mathbf{18}$

3) 99% confidence level ...[Rem. 99% confidence level, the confidence coefficient is 2.576]

Step 1: Formula. Sample Size (n) $= \frac{\sigma^2}{(\mathrm{ME})^2}\left(Z_{\alpha/2}\right)^2$

Where; $\sigma = 10$, ME $= 4.56$, $Z_{\alpha/2} = 2.576$

Step 2: Data substitution and solving

Sample Size (n) $= \frac{(10)^2}{(4.56)^2}(2.576)^2$ ....[Work exponents]

Sample Size (n) $= \frac{100}{20.7936}(6.635776)$ ....[Simplify fraction]

$\text{Sample Size (n)} = 4.809172053(6.635776)$ ....[Solve equation]

$\text{Sample Size (n)} = \mathbf{32}$

Test Your Understanding

Exercise 25: A manufacturer want to estimate the per capita number of bread consumed each month in Bamenda. In order to properly forecast the market demand, he needs the margin of error to be ± 4 items at the 90% confidence level. Considering that market standard deviation is 30, how many consumers should he survey to achieve the desired accuracy?

[Answer: Sample size $(\mathbf{n}) = \mathbf{97}$]

Exercise 26: Given that the population standard deviation (σ) is 15, calculate the required sample size at 95% confidence level assuming;

1) A desired margin of error of 5.4.................. **[Answer: Sample size $(\mathbf{n}) = \mathbf{30}$]**
2) A desired margin of error of 4.2.................. **[Answer: Sample size $(\mathbf{n}) = \mathbf{49}$]**

Exercise 27: Assume that the population standard deviation (σ) is 12.096, calculate the required sample size assuming a desired margin of error of 3.011 using

1) 95% confidence level................................ **[Answer: Sample size $(\mathbf{n}) = \mathbf{62}$]**
2) 99% confidence level. ....**[Answer: Sample size $(\mathbf{n}) = \mathbf{107}$]**

Complementary Applications and Solution

Example 1: The confidence limits of a 95% confidence level are 69.9875 (lower confidence limit) and 71.2125 (upper confidence limit). Considering that the sample size is 64, determine the sample mean ($\overline{X}$) and the population standard deviation(σ).

Solution

Step 1: Formula. Confidence Interval $= \overline{X} \pm Z_{\alpha/2}\left(\frac{\sigma}{\sqrt{n}}\right)$, where; $Z_{\alpha/2} = 1.960$ and $n = 64$

Step 2: Formulate the simultaneous equation

$\overline{X} - Z_{\alpha/2}\left(\frac{\sigma}{\sqrt{n}}\right) = 69.9875$ ....(1)

$\overline{X} + Z_{\alpha/2}\left(\frac{\sigma}{\sqrt{n}}\right) = 71.2125$ ....(2)

Step 3: Data substitution and derivation of unknown [$\overline{X}$ and σ]

$\overline{X} - 1.960\left(\frac{\sigma}{\sqrt{64}}\right) = 69.9875 = \overline{X} - \frac{1.960\,\sigma}{\sqrt{64}} = 69.9875$ ....(1)

$\overline{X} + 1.960\left(\frac{\sigma}{\sqrt{64}}\right) = 71.2125 = \overline{X} + \frac{1.960\,\sigma}{\sqrt{64}} = 71.2125$ ....(2)

Work out the root and linearized each equation

$\overline{X} - \frac{1.960\,\sigma}{8} = 69.9875 \rightarrow 8\overline{X} - 1.960\sigma = 559.9$ ....(1)

$\overline{X} + \frac{1.960\,\sigma}{8} = 71.2125 \rightarrow 8\overline{X} + 1.960\sigma = 569.7$ ....(2)

Subtract equation (1) from equation (2)

$8\overline{X} - 8\overline{X} + 1.960\sigma - (-1.960\sigma) = 569.7 - 559.9$ ....[Simplify equation]

$3.92\sigma = 9.8$ ....[Solve equation]

Population Standard Deviation $(\sigma) = \mathbf{2.5}$

Note: Since we have the value of population standard deviation, we substitute in equation to have the value of sample mean. Assume that we use equation (1).

$8\overline{X} - 1.960\sigma = 559.9$ ....[Substitute numerical value of (σ)]

$8\overline{X} - 1.960(2.5) = 559.9$ ....[Expand bracket and make $(8\overline{X})$ subject of formula]

$8\overline{X} = 564.8$ ....[Divide both sides of equation by 8]

Sample mean $(\overline{X}) = \mathbf{70.6}$

Example 2: Determine the sample mean $(\overline{X})$ and sample size(n) using the following data; confidence interval (95%), lower confidence limit (15.8630), upper confidence limit (19.9704) and population standard deviation (3.6296).

Solution

Step 1: Formula. Confidence Interval $= \overline{X} \pm Z_{\alpha/2}\left(\frac{\sigma}{\sqrt{n}}\right)$, where; $Z_{\alpha/2} = 1.960,\ \sigma = 3.6296$

Step 2: Formulate the simultaneous equation

$\overline{X} - Z_{\alpha/2}\left(\frac{\sigma}{\sqrt{n}}\right) = 15.8630$ ....(1)

$\overline{X} + Z_{\alpha/2}\left(\frac{\sigma}{\sqrt{n}}\right) = 19.9704$ ....(2)

Step 3: Data substitution and derivation of unknown [$\overline{X}$ and σ]

$\overline{X} - 1.960\left(\frac{3.6296}{\sqrt{n}}\right) = 15.8630 \equiv \overline{X} - \frac{7.114016}{\sqrt{n}} = 15.8630$ ....(1)

$\overline{X} + 1.960\left(\frac{3.6296}{\sqrt{n}}\right) = 19.9704 \equiv \overline{X} + \frac{7.114016}{\sqrt{n}} = 19.9704$ ....(2)

Add equation (1) from equation (2)

$\overline{X} + \overline{X} - \frac{7.114016}{\sqrt{n}} + \frac{7.114016}{\sqrt{n}} = 19.9704 + 15.8630$ ....[Simplify equation]

$2\overline{X} = 35.8334$ ....[Divide both sides of equation by 2]

Sample Mean $(\overline{X}) = \mathbf{17.9167}$

Note: Knowing the value of sample mean $(\overline{X})$, we substitute it in any equation (say equation 1) to get the value of sample size (n)

$\overline{X} - \frac{7.114016}{\sqrt{n}} = 15.8630$ ....[Substitute the numerical value of sample mean]

$17.9167 - \frac{7.114016}{\sqrt{n}} = 15.8630$ ....[Look like terms and multiply both sides by (-1)]

$\frac{7.114016}{\sqrt{n}} = 2.0537$ ....[Make $(\sqrt{n})$ subject of the formula]

$\sqrt{n} = 3.46399961$ ....[Square both sides of the equation]

Sample size $(n) = \mathbf{12}$

b) When the population variance is unknown

The sample size can be derived from the margin of error formula by making the sample size (n) subject of formulas as using the margin of error formula. As seen above, margin of error when the population variance is unknown is given as $\left[\text{Margin of Error (ME)} = \pm\left(\frac{S}{\sqrt{n}}\right) t_{n-1:\alpha/2}\right]$. The sample size formula derivation from the margin of error is illustrated below,

$\text{Margin of Error (ME)} = \pm\frac{S}{\sqrt{n}} t_{n-1:\alpha/2}$ ....[Multiply both sides by$(\sqrt{n})$]

$\sqrt{n}(\text{ME}) = \pm S(t_{n-1:\alpha/2})$ ....[Make $(\sqrt{n})$ subject of formula]

$\sqrt{n} = \pm\frac{S(t_{n-1:\alpha/2})}{\text{ME}}$ ....[Square both sides of the equation]

$$\text{Sample size (n)} = \pm\frac{(\mathbf{S})^2}{(\mathbf{ME})^2}\left(\mathbf{t}_{\mathbf{n-1:\alpha/2}}\right)^2$$

Example 1: The sample standard deviation (S) is 0.0246. Calculate the required sample size assuming the desired margin of error (ME) is 0.0224106 using a critical value of 2.733.

<u>**Solution**</u>

Step 1: Formula. $\text{Sample size (n)} = \pm\frac{(S)^2}{(\text{ME})^2}\left(t_{n-1:\alpha/2}\right)^2$

Where; $S = 0.0246$, $\text{ME} = 0.0224106$ and $t_{n-1:\alpha/2} = 2.733$

Step 2: Data substitution and solving

$\text{Sample size (n)} = \frac{(0.0246)^2}{(0.0224106)^2}(2.733)^2$ ....[Work exponents]

$\text{Sample size (n)} = \frac{0.00060516}{0.000502234}(7.469289)$ ....[Simplify fraction]

$\text{Sample size (n)} = 1.204936344(7.469289)$ ....[Expand bracket]

$\text{Sample size (n)} = \mathbf{9}$

Example 2: What is the sample size (n) and sample mean ($\overline{X}$) that will yield a confidence interval of 15.139 and 19.361, assuming the sample standard deviation (S) is 3.3 and the critical value is 2.861.

Solution

Step 1: Formula. Confidence Interval $= \overline{X} \pm \frac{S}{\sqrt{n}} t_{n-1:\alpha/2}$, where; $t_{n-1:\alpha/2} = 2.861, S = 3.3$

Step 2: Formulation of equations

$$\overline{X} - \frac{S}{\sqrt{n}} t_{n-1:\alpha/2} = 15.139 \quad \text{.......(1)}$$

$$\overline{X} + \frac{S}{\sqrt{n}} t_{n-1:\alpha/2} = 19.361 \quad \text{.......(2)}$$

Step 3: Data substitution and solving of sample mean ($\overline{X}$) and sample size (n)

$$\overline{X} - \frac{3.3}{\sqrt{n}}(2.861) = 15.139 \Rightarrow \overline{X} - \frac{9.4413}{\sqrt{n}} = 15.139 \quad \text{.......(1)}$$

$$\overline{X} - \frac{3.3}{\sqrt{n}}(2.861) = 19.361 \Rightarrow \overline{X} + \frac{9.4413}{\sqrt{n}} = 19.361 \quad \text{.......(2)}$$

Add equation (2) to equation (1)

$$\overline{X} + \overline{X} - \frac{9.4413}{\sqrt{n}} + \frac{9.4413}{\sqrt{n}} = 15.139 + 19.361 \quad \text{.......[Simplify equation]}$$

$$2\overline{X} = 345 \quad \text{.......[Divide both sides of equation by 2]}$$

$\text{Sample mean } (\overline{X}) = \mathbf{17.25}$

Since sample mean numerical value is known (17.25), to obtain the value of sample size, we simply substitute the value in any of the equation. If we select equation (2), sample size is derived as seen below.

$$\overline{X} + \frac{9.4413}{\sqrt{n}} = 19.361 \quad \text{......[Substitute the value of sample mean into the equation]}$$

$$17.25 + \frac{9.4413}{\sqrt{n}} = 19.361 \quad \text{.......[Take 17.25 to the right hand side of equation]}$$

$$\frac{9.4413}{\sqrt{n}} = 2.111 \quad \text{.......[Make } (\sqrt{n}) \text{ subject of the formula]}$$

$$\sqrt{n} = 4.472430128 \quad \text{.......[Square both sides of the equation]}$$

$\text{Sample size (n)} = \mathbf{20}$

Example 3: Compute the value of the sample mean ($\overline{X}$) and sample standard deviation (S) that will yield a confidence interval of 5.054 and 5.186 at 95% confidence level, assuming the sample size is 20.

Solution

Step 1: Formula. Confidence Interval $= \overline{X} \pm \frac{S}{\sqrt{n}} t_{n-1:\alpha/2}$

Where; $t_{n-1:\alpha/2} = 2.093$ and $n = 20$

Step 2: Formulation of equations

$\overline{X} - \frac{S}{\sqrt{n}} t_{n-1:\alpha/2} = 5.054$ ....(1)

$\overline{X} + \frac{S}{\sqrt{n}} t_{n-1:\alpha/2} = 5.186$ ....(2)

Step 3: Data substitution and solving of sample mean ($\overline{X}$) and sample standard deviation (S)

$\overline{X} - \frac{S}{\sqrt{20}}(2.093) = 5.054 \Rightarrow \overline{X} - \frac{2.093(S)}{\sqrt{20}} = 5.054$ ....(1)

$\overline{X} + \frac{S}{\sqrt{20}}(2.093) = 5.186 \Rightarrow \overline{X} - \frac{2.093(S)}{\sqrt{20}} = 5.186$ ....(2)

Work roots and multiply both sides of equation by the value of $(\sqrt{20})$

$4.472135955\overline{X} - 2.093(S) = 22.60217512$ ....(1)

$4.472135955\overline{X} + 2.093(S) = 23.19249706$ ....(2)

Add equation (2) to equation (1)

$8.94427191\overline{X} = 45.79467218$ ....[Make ($\overline{X}$) subject of formula]

Sample mean $(\overline{X}) = \mathbf{5.12}$

Knowing the sample mean numerical value (5.12), we can substitute in any equation to obtain the sample standard deviation value. Let use equation (1)

$4.472135955\overline{X} - 2.093(S) = 22.60217512$ ....[Substitute sample mean]

$4.472135955(5.12) - 2.093(S) = 22.60217512$ ....[Expand bracket]

$22.89733609 - 2.093(S) = 22.60217512$ ....[Collect like terms together]

$-2.093(S) = -0.295160969$........[Multiply sides of equation by (-1) .and solve equation]

Sample standard deviation $(S) = \mathbf{0.1410}$ ....[In four decimal places]

Test Your Understanding

Exercise 28: Compute the sample size needed using the following data; sample standard deviation (7.2), margin of error (2) and critical value (2.000) **[Answer: Sample size (n) = 52]**

Exercise 29: Determine the sample size (n) and sample mean ($\overline{X}$) that will yield a confidence interval of 24.88 and 51.91, assuming the sample standard deviation (S) is 18.9 and the critical value is 2.262...**[Answer: $\overline{X} = 38.395$ and $n = 10$]**

Exercise 30: Determine the sample mean ($\overline{X}$) and standard deviation (S) that will yield a confidence interval of 74.14 and 90.14 at 95% confidence level, assuming the sample size is 7

[Answer: $\overline{X} = 82.14$ and $S = 8.6410$]

2) Confidence Interval of Population Proportion

The confidence interval of the population proportion (P) derivation is based on the margin of error and the standard error of the sample proportion($S_{\hat{P}}$). In summary, confidence interval is calculated as;

$$\text{Confidence Interval} = \text{Sample Proportion}(\hat{P}) \pm \text{Margin of Error} \quad \text{.......................................(1)}$$

Note: It is worth understanding the concept of sample proportion, standard error of sample proportion and margin of error in order to determine the confidence interval value.

a) Sample Proportion $(\hat{P})$

It is defined as the fraction of the sample that has a certain characteristic and is the estimate of the population proportion (P). Sample proportion $(\hat{P})$is calculated using the formula below;

$$\text{Sample Proportion}(\hat{P}) = \frac{\text{Number of Successes (X)}}{\text{Sample Size (n)}} \quad \text{...(2)}$$

Note: The number of successes is also known as the number of members in the sample having a specified attribute.

Example 1: In a population of 57 workers, 17 are smokers. Determine the smokers sample proportion.

Solution

Step 1: Formula. $\text{Sample Proportion}(\hat{P}) = \frac{\text{Number of Successes (X)}}{\text{Sample Size (n)}}$, where; $n = 57$ and $X = 17$

Step 2: Data substitution and solving

$$\text{Sample Proportion}(\hat{P}) = \frac{\text{Number of Successes (X)}}{\text{Sample Size (n)}} \quad \text{.................................[Substitute value]}$$

Sample Proportion$(\widehat{P}) = \frac{17}{57}$ ....[Solve equation]

Sample Proportion$(\widehat{P}) = \mathbf{0.298}$ ....[In three decimal places]

Example 2: According to the class master, the class is made up of 40 males and 80 females. Determine the following;

a) Sample proportion of males
b) Sample proportion of females

Solution

a) Sample proportion of males

Step 1: Formula. Sample Proportion$(\widehat{P}) = \frac{\text{Number of Successes (X)}}{\text{Sample Size (n)}}$

Where; $N = 40 + 80 = 120$ and $X = 40$

Step 2: Data substitution and solving

Sample Proportion$(\widehat{P}) = \frac{\text{Number of Successes (X)}}{\text{Sample Size (n)}}$ ....[Substitute value]

Sample Proportion$(\widehat{P}) = \frac{40}{120}$ ....[Solve equation]

Sample Proportion$(\widehat{P}) = \mathbf{0.333}$ ....[In three decimal places]

b) Sample proportion of females

Step 1: Formula. Sample Proportion$(\widehat{P}) = \frac{\text{Number of Successes (X)}}{\text{Sample Size (n)}}$

Where; $N = 40 + 80 = 120$ and $X = 80$

Step 2: Data substitution and solving

Sample Proportion$(\widehat{P}) = \frac{\text{Number of Successes (X)}}{\text{Sample Size (n)}}$ ....[Substitute value]

Sample Proportion$(\widehat{P}) = \frac{80}{120}$ ....[Solve equation]

Sample Proportion$(\widehat{P}) = \mathbf{0.667}$ ....[In three decimal places]

Example 3: In a survey of 180 students, 55% are good in mathematics; determine the sample proportion of the students good in mathematics.

Solution

a) Method 1(Using values in percentage)

Step 1: Formula. Sample Proportion$(\widehat{P}) = \frac{\text{Number of Successes (X)}}{\text{Sample Size (n)}}$, where; $N = 100,\ X = 55$

Step 2: Data substitution and solving

Sample Proportion$(\widehat{P}) = \frac{55}{100}$ ....[Solve equation]

Sample Proportion$(\widehat{P}) = \mathbf{0.55}$

b) Method 2 (Using number of sample)

Step 1: Formula. $\text{Sample Proportion}(\widehat{P}) = \frac{\text{Number of Successes (X)}}{\text{Sample Size (n)}}$

Where; $X = 55\%(180) = 99,\ N = 180$

Step 2: Data substitution and solving

$\text{Sample Proportion}(\widehat{P}) = \frac{99}{180}$ ....[Solve equation]

$\text{Sample Proportion}(\widehat{P}) = \mathbf{0.55}$

Example 4: What is the number of successes (X) that will yield a sample proportion $(\widehat{P})$ of 0.655 given that the sample size is 58.

Solution

a) Method 1

Step 1: Formula. $\text{Sample Proportion}(\widehat{P}) = \frac{\text{Number of Successes (X)}}{\text{Sample Size (n)}}$, where; $\widehat{P} = 0.655,\ n = 58$

Step 2: Data substitution and solving

$0.655 = \frac{\text{Number of Successes (X)}}{58}$ ....[Multiply both sides of equation by 58]

$\text{Number of Successes (X)} = 0.655(58)$ ....[Expand bracket]

$\text{Number of Successes (X)} = \mathbf{38}$

b) Method 2

Step 1: Formula. $\text{Number of Successes (X)} = \widehat{P}(n)$, where; $n = 58$ and $\widehat{P} = 0.655$

Step 2: Data substitution and solving

$\text{Number of Successes (X)} = 0.655(58)$ ....[Expand bracket]

$\text{Number of Successes (X)} = \mathbf{38}$

Example 5: What is the sample size (n) that will yield a sample proportion $(\widehat{P})$ of 0.526 given that the number of successes is 10?

Solution

a) Method 1

Step 1: Formula. $\text{Sample Proportion}(\widehat{P}) = \frac{\text{Number of Successes (X)}}{\text{Sample Size (n)}}$, where; $\widehat{P} = 0.526,\ X = 10$

Step 2: Data substitution and solving

$0.526 = \frac{10}{n}$ ....[Multiply both sides of equation by (n)]

$0.526(n) = 10$ ....[Divide both sides of equation by (0.526)]

$\text{Sample Size (n)} = \mathbf{19}$

b) Method 2

Step 1: Formula. Sample Size $(\mathrm{n}) = \frac{\text{Number of Successes (X)}}{\text{Sample Proportion}(\widehat{\mathrm{P}})}$, where; $\widehat{\mathrm{P}} = 0.526$ and $\mathrm{X} = 10$

Step 2: Data substitution and solving

$\text{Sample Size } (\mathrm{n}) = \frac{10}{0.526}$ ……………………………………………[Simplify fraction]

$\text{Sample Size } (\mathrm{n}) = \mathbf{19}$

b) Standard Deviation of Sample Proportion

Standard deviation of sample proportion is also called the estimated standard error or estimated standard deviation. It is calculated as;

$$\text{Estimated Standard Error}(S_{\widehat{\mathrm{P}}}) = \sqrt{\frac{\widehat{\mathrm{P}}(1-\widehat{\mathrm{P}})}{\mathrm{n}}} \text{ ……………………………………(3)}$$

Note: The equation numerator is the produce of probability of successes $[\widehat{\mathrm{P}}]$ and probability of failure $[\widehat{\mathrm{q}} = 1 - \widehat{\mathrm{P}}]$. The equation of probability of failure is illustrated below. Remember total probability (successes plus failure) is equal to 1.

$1 = \frac{\mathrm{X}}{\mathrm{n}} + \widehat{\mathrm{q}}$ ……………………………………………[Make $(\widehat{\mathrm{q}})$ subject of the formula]

$\widehat{\mathrm{q}} = 1 - \frac{\mathrm{X}}{\mathrm{n}}$ …………………………….[Substitute X by $(\widehat{\mathrm{P}}\mathrm{n})$ since $\left(\widehat{\mathrm{P}} = \frac{\mathrm{X}}{\mathrm{n}} \equiv \mathrm{X} = \widehat{\mathrm{P}}\mathrm{n}\right)$]

$\widehat{\mathrm{q}} = 1 - \frac{\widehat{\mathrm{P}}\mathrm{n}}{\mathrm{n}}$ ………………………[Linearized equation by multiplying both sides by (n)]

$\widehat{\mathrm{q}}\mathrm{n} = \mathrm{n} - \widehat{\mathrm{P}}\mathrm{n}$ ……………………………………[Divide both sides of equation by (n)]

$\frac{\widehat{\mathrm{q}}\mathrm{n}}{\mathrm{n}} = \frac{\mathrm{n}}{\mathrm{n}} - \frac{\widehat{\mathrm{P}}\mathrm{n}}{\mathrm{n}}$ ………………………………………………[Simplify equation]

$\textbf{Probability of Non} - \textbf{Successes}(\widehat{\mathbf{q}}) = \mathbf{1} - \widehat{\mathbf{P}}$ ……………………………………(4)

From the illustration above, it is proven that $[\widehat{\mathrm{q}} = 1 - \widehat{\mathrm{P}}]$. Substituting $[\widehat{\mathrm{q}}]$ in place of $[1 - \widehat{\mathrm{P}}]$, we obtain a new equation as seen below.

$$\text{Estimated Standard Error}(S_{\widehat{\mathrm{P}}}) = \sqrt{\frac{\widehat{\mathrm{P}}\widehat{\mathrm{q}}}{\mathrm{n}}} \text{ ……………………………………(5)}$$

Note: In order to derive equation (4), we assumed that total probability equal one $[\widehat{\mathrm{q}} + \widehat{\mathrm{P}} = 1]$. This assumption can be proven mathematically as seen below.

$\text{Total probability} = \widehat{\mathrm{P}} + \widehat{\mathrm{q}}$ …………………[Substitute $(\widehat{\mathrm{P}})$ by $(1 - \widehat{\mathrm{q}})$ and $(\widehat{\mathrm{q}})$ by $(1 - \widehat{\mathrm{P}})$]

$\text{Total probability} = 1 - \widehat{\mathrm{q}} + 1 - \widehat{\mathrm{P}}$ …………[Substitute $(\widehat{\mathrm{P}})$ by $(1 - \widehat{\mathrm{q}})$ or $(\widehat{\mathrm{q}})$ by $(1 - \widehat{\mathrm{P}})$]

$\text{Total probability} = 1 - \widehat{\mathrm{q}} + 1 - (1 - \widehat{\mathrm{q}})$ ……………………………[Open bracket]

Total probability $= 1 - \hat{q} + 1 - 1 + \hat{q}$ ....[Simplify equation]

Total probability $= \mathbf{1}$ ....(6)

Example 1: In a survey of 200 students, 65% are blacks. Determine the sample standard deviation of the population proportion.

Solution

Step 1: Formula. Estimated Standard Error$(S_P) = \sqrt{\frac{\hat{P}(1-\hat{P})}{n}}$, where; $\hat{P} = 0.65$ and $n = 200$

Step 2: Data substitution and solving

Estimated Standard Error$(S_P) = \sqrt{\frac{0.65(1-0.65)}{200}}$ ....[Simplify bracket and expand bracket]

Estimated Standard Error$(S_P) = \sqrt{\frac{0.2275}{200}}$ ....[Simplify fraction]

Estimated Standard Error$(S_P) = \sqrt{0.0011375}$ ....[Work root]

Estimated Standard Error$(S_P) = \mathbf{0.0337}$ ....[In four decimal places]

Example 2: Suppose the proportion of the population in favor of a new law is 0.60. Considering that the sample size is 500, determine the estimated standard deviation.

Solution

a) **Method 1**

Step 1: Formula. Estimated Standard Error$(S_P) = \sqrt{\frac{\hat{P}(1-\hat{P})}{n}}$, where; $\hat{P} = 0.60$ and $n = 500$

Step 2: Data substitution and solving

Estimated Standard Error$(S_P) = \sqrt{\frac{0.60(1-0.60)}{500}}$ ....[Simplify bracket and expand bracket]

Estimated Standard Error$(S_P) = \sqrt{\frac{0.24}{500}}$ ....[Simplify fraction]

Estimated Standard Error$(S_P) = \sqrt{0.00048}$ ....[Work root]

Estimated Standard Error$(S_P) = \mathbf{0.0219}$ ....[In four decimal places]

b) **Method 2**

Step 1: Formula. Estimated Standard Error$(S_P) = \sqrt{\frac{\hat{P}\hat{q}}{n}}$

Where; $\hat{P} = 0.60$, $\hat{q} = 0.4$ and $n = 500$

Step 2: Data substitution and solving

Estimated Standard Error$(S_P) = \sqrt{\frac{(0.60)(0.4)}{500}}$ ....[Expand bracket]

$$\text{Estimated Standard Error}(S_P) = \sqrt{\frac{0.24}{500}}$$ ....[Simplify fraction]

$$\text{Estimated Standard Error}(S_P) = \sqrt{0.00048}$$ ....[Work root]

$$\text{Estimated Standard Error}(S_P) = \mathbf{0.0219}$$ ....[In four decimal places]

Example 3: Determine the sample standard error using the following data; $\hat{q} = 0.3$ and $n = 250$

Solution

Step 1: Formula. $\text{Estimated Standard Error}(S_P) = \sqrt{\frac{\hat{P}\hat{q}}{n}}$

Where; $\hat{P} = 0.7$, $\hat{q} = 0.3$ and $n = 250$

Step 2: Data substitution and solving

$$\text{Estimated Standard Error}(S_P) = \sqrt{\frac{(0.7)(0.3)}{250}}$$ ....[Expand bracket]

$$\text{Estimated Standard Error}(S_P) = \sqrt{\frac{0.21}{250}}$$ ....[Simplify fraction]

$$\text{Estimated Standard Error}(S_P) = \sqrt{0.00084}$$ ....[Work root]

$$\text{Estimated Standard Error}(S_P) = \mathbf{0.02898}$$ ....[In five decimal places]

Example 4: A researcher carried out a study to find out the number of students that smoke in a given school. From a randomly selected sample of 20 students he obtains the following results in the table below. Let 1 represents yes and 0 represents no.

1	0	0	1	0	1	0	0	0	0
0	1	1	0	0	1	0	0	0	1

1) Determine the value of sample proportion of students that smokes
2) What is the value of standard deviation sample proportion

Solution

1) Determine the value of sample proportion of students that smokes

Step 1: Formula. $\text{Sample Proportion}(\hat{P}) = \frac{\text{Number of Successes (X)}}{\text{Sample Size (n)}}$, where; $n = 20$ and $X = 7$

Step 2: Data substitution and solving

$$\text{Sample Proportion}(\hat{P}) = \frac{7}{20}$$ ....[Simplify fraction]

$$\text{Sample Proportion}(\hat{P}) = \mathbf{0.35 = 35\%}$$

2) **What is the value of standard deviation sample proportion**

Step 1: Formula. $\text{Estimated Standard Error}(S_P) = \sqrt{\frac{\hat{P}\hat{q}}{n}}$

Where; $\hat{P} = 0.35$, $\hat{q} = 0.65$ and $n = 20$

Step 2: Data substitution and solving

$\text{Estimated Standard Error}(S_P) = \sqrt{\frac{(0.35)(0.65)}{20}}$ ....[Expand bracket]

$\text{Estimated Standard Error}(S_P) = \sqrt{\frac{0.2275}{20}}$ ....[Simplify fraction]

$\text{Estimated Standard Error}(S_P) = \sqrt{0.011375}$ ....[Work root]

$\text{Estimated Standard Error}(S_P) = \mathbf{0.1067}$ ....[In five decimal places]

Test Your Understanding

Exercise 31: In a survey of 1,800 consumers, 810 are happy with the management style of the principal. Determine the sample proportion of the population..........**[Answer: $(\hat{P}) = 0.45$]**

Exercise 32: In a sample of 450 students, 33.5% are females. Determine the value of sample proportion of the population proportion..................................**[Answer: $(\hat{P}) = 0.335$]**

Exercise 33: What is the value of sample standard deviation of the population proportion given that $X = 750$ and $n = 1{,}000$................................ **[Answer: $(S_P) = 0.01369$]**

c) **Margin of Error**

Margin of error also called maximum error of estimate in terms of population proportion is defined as the maximum likely difference at a given significance level between the observed proportion or sample proportion $(\hat{P})$ and the true value of the population proportion. It is the product of the critical value and the standard deviation of the sample proportion.

$$\text{Margin of Error} = \pm Z_{\alpha/2}\sqrt{\frac{\hat{P}(1-\hat{P})}{n}} \quad \text{.......(1)}$$

$$\text{Margin of Error} = \pm Z_{\alpha/2}\sqrt{\frac{\hat{P}_1(1-\hat{P}_1)}{n_1} + \frac{\hat{P}_2(1-\hat{P}_2)}{n_2}} \quad \text{.......(2)}$$

Note: Equation (1) is used in situation of single population and equation (2) in used in situation of two independent population analyses.

Example 1: Determine the margin of error using the following information; $\widehat{P} = 16\%$, $n = 100$ and 5% significance level.

Solution

Step 1: Formula. Margin of Error $= \pm Z_{\alpha/2}\sqrt{\frac{\widehat{P}(1-\widehat{P})}{n}}$

Where; $\widehat{P} = 0.16$, $n = 100$ and $Z_{\alpha/2} = 1.960$

Step 2: Data substitution and solving

Margin of Error $= \pm(1.960)\sqrt{\frac{0.16(1-0.16)}{100}}$ ……………………………[Simplify numerator]

Margin of Error $= \pm(1.960)\sqrt{\frac{0.1344}{100}}$ ……………………………[Simplify fraction]

Margin of Error $= \pm(1.960)\sqrt{0.001344}$ ……………………………[Work root]

Margin of Error $= \pm(1.960)(0.036660605)$ ……………………………[Open brackets]

Margin of Error $= \pm\mathbf{0.0719}$ ……………………………[In four decimal places]

Example 2: Find the margin of error (E) given that the confidence level is 90% and the sample size is 200 of which 150 are successes.

Solution

Step 1: Formula. Margin of Error $= \pm Z_{\alpha/2}\sqrt{\frac{\widehat{P}(1-\widehat{P})}{n}}$

Where; $\widehat{P} = 0.75$, $n = 200$ and $Z_{\alpha/2} = 1.645$

Step 2: Data substitution and solving

Margin of Error(E) $= \pm(1.645)\sqrt{\frac{0.75(1-0.75)}{200}}$ ……………………[Simplify bracket and fraction]

Margin of Error(E) $= \pm(1.645)\sqrt{0.0009375}$ ……………………………[Work root]

Margin of Error(E) $= \pm(1.645)(0.030618621)$ ……………………………[Expand bracket]

Margin of Error(E) $= \pm\mathbf{0.0504}$ ……………………………[In four decimal places]

Example 3: Compute the value of margin of error (E) given that the confidence level is 99% using the following data;

	Number of successes	Sample size
Population 1	65	100
Population 2	110	200

Solution

Step 1: Formula. Margin of Error $= \pm Z_{\alpha/2}\sqrt{\frac{\widehat{P}_1(1-\widehat{P}_1)}{n_1} + \frac{\widehat{P}_2(1-\widehat{P}_2)}{n_2}}$

Where; $\widehat{P}_1 = \frac{65}{100} = 0.65$, $\widehat{P}_2 = \frac{110}{200} = 0.55$, $n_1 = 100$, $n_2 = 200$ and $Z_{\alpha/2} = 2.576$

Step 2: Data substitution and solving

$\text{Margin of Error} = \pm(2.576)\sqrt{\frac{0.65(1-0.65)}{100} + \frac{0.55(1-0.55)}{200}}$ ……………………[Simplify brackets]

$\text{Margin of Error} = \pm(2.576)\sqrt{\frac{0.2275}{100} + \frac{0.2475}{200}}$ ………………………………[Simplify fraction]

$\text{Margin of Error} = \pm(2.576)\sqrt{0.0035125}$ ……………………………………………[Solve]

$\text{Margin of Error} = \pm\mathbf{0.1527}$ ……………………………………[In four decimal places]

Test Your Understanding

Exercise 34: Determine the margin of error using the following data; $n = 10{,}000$, $X = 600$ and $\alpha = 1\%$……………………………………………**[Answer: Margin of Error(E) $= \mathbf{0.0061}$]**

Exercise 35: What is the value of margin of error given that; $\widehat{q} = 0.11$, $n = 483$ and $\alpha = 10$

[Answer: Margin of Error(E) $= \mathbf{0.0234}$]

Exercise 36: Compute the value of margin of error from the following data; $\widehat{P}_1 = 60\%$, $X_2 = 25$, $n_1 = 100$, $n_2 = 50$ and $\alpha = 5\%$……….**[Answer: Margin of Error(E) $= \mathbf{0.1686}$]**

2.1 Calculation of confidence interval of population proportion

It is worth knowing that before performing the calculation of confidence interval when dealing with population proportion, we are required to verify if the following conditions are satisfied.

a) Randomization: The sample should be a simple random sample. That is the sample is randomly selected from the population.
b) Binomial distribution conditions: Fixed number of trials and the trials should be independent. There must be two categories of outcome and the probabilities remain constant for each trial.
c) Normal distribution application condition: The product of number of successes and sample proportion and the product of number of failures and sample probability should be greater or equal to 5. That is, $(\widehat{P}n \geq 5)$ and $(\widehat{q}n \geq 5)$

Assuming the above conditions are satisfied, the formula for calculating confidence interval of population proportion is given as;

$$\text{Confidence Interval} = \widehat{P} \pm Z_{\alpha/2}\sqrt{\frac{\widehat{P}(1-\widehat{P})}{n}} \quad \text{.......................................(1)}$$

$$\text{Lower Confidence Limit} = \widehat{P} - Z_{\alpha/2}\sqrt{\frac{\widehat{P}(1-\widehat{P})}{n}} \quad \text{.......................................(1.1)}$$

$$\text{Upper Confidence Limit} = \widehat{P} + Z_{\alpha/2}\sqrt{\frac{\widehat{P}(1-\widehat{P})}{n}} \quad \text{.......................................(1.2)}$$

$$\text{Confidence Interval} = \left(\widehat{P}_1 - \widehat{P}_2\right) \pm Z_{\alpha/2}\sqrt{\frac{\widehat{P}_1(1-\widehat{P}_1)}{n_1} + \frac{\widehat{P}_2(1-\widehat{P}_2)}{n_2}} \quad \text{.....................(2)}$$

$$\text{Lower Confidence Limit} = \left(\widehat{P}_1 - \widehat{P}_2\right) - Z_{\alpha/2}\sqrt{\frac{\widehat{P}_1(1-\widehat{P}_1)}{n_1} + \frac{\widehat{P}_2(1-\widehat{P}_2)}{n_2}} \quad \text{.............(2.1)}$$

$$\text{Lower Confidence Limit} = \left(\widehat{P}_1 - \widehat{P}_2\right) + Z_{\alpha/2}\sqrt{\frac{\widehat{P}_1(1-\widehat{P}_1)}{n_1} + \frac{\widehat{P}_2(1-\widehat{P}_2)}{n_2}} \quad \text{.............(2.2)}$$

Note: Equation (1) is used in situation of single population and equation (2) in used in situation of two independent population analyses.

Example 1: The sample proportion is 52% and the sample size is 547. Determine the 99% confidence interval of the population proportion.

Solution

a) Method 1

Step 1: Formula. $\text{Confidence Interval} = \widehat{P} \pm Z_{\alpha/2}\sqrt{\frac{\widehat{P}(1-\widehat{P})}{n}}$

Where; $\widehat{P} = 0.52,\ n = 547,\ Z_{\alpha/2} = 2.576$

Step 2: Data substitution and solving

$$\text{Confidence Interval} = 0.52 \pm (2.576)\sqrt{\frac{0.52(1-0.52)}{547}} \quad \text{.........................[Simplify numerator]}$$

$$\text{Confidence Interval} = 0.52 \pm (2.576)\sqrt{\frac{0.2496}{547}} \quad \text{.................................[Simplify fraction]}$$

$$\text{Confidence Interval} = 0.52 \pm (2.576)\sqrt{0.000456307} \quad \text{.............................[Work root]}$$

$$\text{Confidence Interval} = 0.52 \pm (2.576)(0.021361346) \quad \text{.......................[Expand bracket]}$$

$$\text{Confidence Interval} = 0.52 \pm 0.055026828 \quad \text{.......................[Work out confidence limits]}$$

$$\text{Confidence Interval} = \mathbf{0.465 < P < 0.575} \quad \text{...........................[In three decimal places]}$$

b) Method 2

Step 1: Formula. Confidence Interval $= \widehat{P} \pm Z_{\alpha/2}\sqrt{\frac{\widehat{P}\hat{q}}{n}}$

Where; $\widehat{P} = 0.52, \hat{q} = 0.48, n = 547, Z_{\alpha/2} = 2.576$

Step 2: Data substitution and solving

Confidence Interval $= 0.52 \pm (2.576)\sqrt{\frac{(0.52)(0.48)}{547}}$ ....[Expand bracket]

Confidence Interval $= 0.52 \pm (2.576)\sqrt{\frac{0.2496}{547}}$ ....[Simplify fraction]

Confidence Interval $= 0.52 \pm (2.576)\sqrt{0.000456307}$........[Work root and expand bracket]

Confidence Interval $= 0.52 \pm 0.055026828$ ....[Work out confidence limits]

Confidence Interval $= \mathbf{0.465 < P < 0.575}$ ....[In three decimal places]

Step 3: Interpretation: We are 99% confident that the interval from 0.465 to 0.575 contains the true value of the population proportion (P). That is if we select many different samples of size 547 and calculate their respective confidence intervals, 99% of them would contain the value of the population proportion.

Example 2: A sample pool of 100 voters chosen at random from all voters in a given district indicates that 55% of them were in favor of a particular candidate. Find the 90% confidence limits for the population of all the voters in favor of these candidates.

Solution

Step 1: Formula. Confidence Interval $= \widehat{P} \pm Z_{\alpha/2}\sqrt{\frac{\widehat{P}\hat{q}}{n}}$

Where; $\widehat{P} = 0.55, \hat{q} = 0.45, n = 100, Z_{\alpha/2} = 1.645$

Step 2: Data substitution and solving

Confidence Interval $= 0.55 \pm (1.645)\sqrt{\frac{(0.55)(0.45)}{100}}$ ....[Expand bracket]

Confidence Interval $= 0.55 \pm (1.645)\sqrt{\frac{0.2475}{100}}$ ....[Simplify fraction]

Confidence Interval $= 0.55 \pm (1.645)\sqrt{0.002475}$ ....[Work root and expand bracket]

Confidence Interval $= 0.55 \pm 0.081837716$ ....[Work out confidence limits]

Confidence Interval $= \mathbf{0.468 < P < 0.632}$ ....[In three decimal places]

Example 3: Determine a 95% confidence interval of the population proportion using the following data;

	Sample size	Number of successes	Sample proportion
Population 1	100	90	0.9
Population 2	80	70	0.875

Solution

Step 1: Formula. Confidence Interval $= (\widehat{P}_1 - \widehat{P}_2) \pm Z_{\alpha/2}\sqrt{\frac{\widehat{P}_1(1-\widehat{P}_1)}{n_1} + \frac{\widehat{P}_2(1-\widehat{P}_2)}{n_2}}$

Where: $\widehat{P}_1 = 0.9, \widehat{P}_2 = 0.875, n_1 = 100,\ n_2 = 80$ and $Z_{\alpha/2} = 1.960$

Step 2: Data substitution and solving

Confidence Interval $= (0.9 - 0.875) \pm (1.960)\sqrt{\frac{0.9(1-0.9)}{100} + \frac{0.875(1-0.875)}{80}}$ .....[Simplify]

Confidence Interval $= (0.025) \pm (1.960)\sqrt{\frac{0.09}{100} + \frac{0.109375}{80}}$ ....[Simplify fractions]

Confidence Interval $= (0.025) \pm (1.960)\sqrt{0.002267187}$ ....[Work root]

Confidence Interval $= 0.025 \pm (1.960)(0.047614987)$ ....[Expand bracket]

Confidence Interval $= 0.025 \pm 0.093325374$ ....[Work out confidence limits]

Confidence Interval $= \mathbf{-0.068 < (P_1 - P_2) < 0.118}$ ....[In three decimal places]

Example 3: Use the given confidence interval $(0.26 < P < 0.44)$, determine the sample proportion $(\widehat{P})$ and the margin of error (E).

Solution

Step 1: Formula of confidence interval equations. Remember $\left[\text{Margin of error} = Z_{\alpha/2}\sqrt{\frac{\widehat{P}\widehat{q}}{n}}\right]$

Lower Confidence Limit $= \widehat{P} -$ Margin of Error(E) ....(1)

Upper Confidence Limit $= \widehat{P} +$ Margin of Error(E) ....(2)

Where; Lower Confidence Limit $= 0.26$ and Upper Confidence Limit $= 0.44$

Step 2: Data substitution and solving

$\widehat{P} -$ Margin of Error(E) $= 0.26$ ....(1)

$\widehat{P} +$ Margin of Error(E) $= 0.44$ ....(2)

Substract equation (1) from equation (2)

2Margin of Error(E) $= 0.18$ ....[Divide both sides of equation by (2)]

Margin of Error(E) $= \mathbf{0.09}$

Knowing the value of margin of error, we substitute the value in any of the equations to obtain the value of sample proportion $(\widehat{P})$. Let used equation (2)

$\widehat{P} + \text{Margin of Error(E)} = 0.44$ ....[Substitute the value of margin of error]

$\widehat{P} + 0.09 = 0.44$ ....[Take (0.09) to the right side of equation]

$\widehat{P} = 0.44 - 0.09$ ....[Solve equation]

$\text{Sample proportion}(\widehat{P}) = \mathbf{0.35} = \mathbf{35\%}$

Example 4: Considering that the margin of error is 1,706 and the lower confidence limit is 41,094, determine the following.

1) Upper confidence limit
2) Sample proportion

Solution

1) Upper confidence limit (UCL)

Step 1: Formula. $\text{Margin of Error(E)} = \frac{\text{Upper Confidence Limit(UCL)} - \text{Lower Confidence Limit(LCL)}}{2}$

Where; $\text{Margin of Error} = 1{,}706$ and $\text{Lower Confidence Limit(LCL)} = 41{,}094$

Step 2: Data substitution and solving

$1{,}706 = \frac{\text{Upper Confidence Limit(UCL)} - 41{,}094}{2}$ ....[Multiply both sides by (2)]

$3{,}412 = \text{Upper Confidence Limit(UCL)} - 41{,}094$ ....[Take $(-41{,}094)$ to RHS]

$\text{Upper Confidence Limit(UCL)} = \mathbf{44{,}506}$

2) Sample proportion $(\widehat{P})$

Step 1: Formula. Sample proportion $(\widehat{P}) = \frac{\text{Upper Confidence Limit(UCL)} + \text{Lower Confidence Limit(LCL)}}{2}$

Where; $\text{Upper Confidence Limit} = 44{,}506$ and $\text{Lower Confidence Limit} = 41{,}094$

Step 2: Data substitution and solving

$\text{Sample proportion }(\widehat{P}) = \frac{44{,}506 + 41{,}094}{2}$ ....[Simplify numerator]

$\text{Sample proportion }(\widehat{P}) = \frac{85{,}600}{2}$ ....[Solve equation]

$\text{Sample proportion }(\widehat{P}) = \mathbf{42{,}800}$

Test Your Undestanding

Exercise 37: A researcher observed 42 successes in 70 independent trials. Compute a 90% confidence interval for the population proportion..[**Answer:** $\mathbf{CI = 0.504 < P < 0.696}$]

Exercise 38: The advocacy group took a random sample of 1000 customers who recently purchased their product and found that 40% were happy with their purchase. Find a 95% confidence interval of the population proportion.....[**Answer:** $\mathbf{CI = 0.370 < P < 0.430}$]

Exercise 39: Determine the 95% confidence interval of a population proportion using the following data; $\widehat{P}_1 = 0.61, \widehat{P}_2 = 0.43, n_1 = 130,\ n_2 = 100$ and $Z_{\alpha/2} = 1.960$

[**Answer:** $\mathbf{Confidence\ Interval = 0.0518 < (P_1 - P_2) < 0.3082}$]

Exercise 40: Use the given confidence interval $(0.720 < P < 0.780)$, determine the sample proportion $(\widehat{P})$ and the margin of error (E). [**Answer:** $\mathbf{(E) = 0.03}$ **and** $\mathbf{(\widehat{P}) = 0.75}$]

Exercise 41: Considering that the margin of error is 0.044 and the upper confidence limit is 0.266, determine the following.

1) Upper confidence limit ....[**Answer:** $\mathbf{Lower\ Confidence\ Limit = 0.178}$]
2) Sample proportion ....[**Answer:** $\mathbf{Sample\ proportion = 0.222}$]

2.2 Determination of Sample Size

As seen under the situation of population mean, the required sample size can also be determine in the case of population proportion. The formula for sample size can be derived from the margin of error formula as seen below.

$$\text{Margin of Error} = Z_{\alpha/2}\sqrt{\frac{\widehat{P}(1-\widehat{P})}{n}} \text{ ....[Divide both sides of the equation by } (Z_{\alpha/2})]$$

$$\frac{\text{Margin of Error}}{Z_{\alpha/2}} = \sqrt{\frac{\widehat{P}(1-\widehat{P})}{n}} \text{ ....[Square both sides of the equation]}$$

$$\left(\frac{\text{Margin of Error}}{Z_{\alpha/2}}\right)^2 = \frac{\widehat{P}(1-\widehat{P})}{n} \text{ ....[Make (n) subject of formula]}$$

$$\text{Sample Size}(n) = \frac{\widehat{P}(1-\widehat{P})}{\left(\frac{\text{Margin of Error}}{Z_{\alpha/2}}\right)^2} \equiv \widehat{P}(1-\widehat{P})\left(\frac{\text{Margin of Error}}{Z_{\alpha/2}}\right)^{-2} \equiv \frac{\widehat{P}(1-\widehat{P})(Z_{\alpha/2})^2}{(\text{Margin of Error})^2} \text{ ....(1)}$$

Example 1: Determine the sample size using the following data; margin of error (0.053) significance level (0.05) and sample proportion (73%).

Solution

Step 1: Formula. $\text{Sample Size(n)} = \frac{\hat{P}(1-\hat{P})}{\left(\frac{\text{Margin of Error}}{Z_{\alpha/2}}\right)^2}$

Where; $\hat{P} = 0.73$, $Z_{\alpha/2} = 1.960$ and $E = 0.053$

Step 2: Data substitution and solving

$\text{Sample Size(n)} = \frac{0.73(1-0.73)}{\left(\frac{0.053}{1.960}\right)^2}$ ....[Simplify fraction]

$\text{Sample Size(n)} = \frac{0.73(0.27)}{(0.027040816)^2}$ ....[Work exponent and expand bracket]

$\text{Sample Size(n)} = \frac{0.1971}{0.000731205}$ ....[Simplify fraction]

$\text{Sample Size(n)} = \mathbf{270}$

Test Your Understanding

Exercise 42: Determine the sample size using the following data; margin of error (0.03) significance level (10%) and sample proportion (0.5). .**[Answer: Sample Size (n) = 752]**

CHAPTER SEVEN

HYPOTHESIS (SIGNIFICANCE) TESTING

Estimation and hypothesis testing are components of inferential statistics. Inferential statistics make use of sample statistics to draw conclusion about what should be found or observed in the population through statistical test.

7.1 Meaning of Hypothesis Testing

Hypothesis testing or significance testing is defined as a statistical (data based), scientific (proven and verifiable) and systematic (follow steps) procedure based on sample or samples evidence (information) and probability theory (significance level) used to determine whether a given hypothesis is reasonable (should not be rejected) or unreasonable (should be rejected).

Hypotheses Testing Procedures	
Critical Value Approach	P-Value Approach
1) Formulation of hypotheses 2) Determination of critical value 3) Calculation of test statistics 4) Decision making 5) Conclusion	1) Formulation of hypotheses 2) Calculation of test statistics 3) Determination of P- value 4) Decision making 5) Conclusion

Note: Hypothesis testing can be one-tailed hypothesis or two-tailed hypothesis testing and can be performed with one sample or two samples linearly independent or dependent observation. Our analysis will be limited to hypothesis testing on population mean using independent samples (paired samples excluded).

7.2 Types of Hypothesis

A hypothesis is a statement (assumption) about the value of population (parameter) that can be evaluated or verify using appropriate statistical techniques. The two main types of hypothesis include; null hypothesis and alternative hypothesis.

1) **Alternative Hypothesis** (H_1): It is the hypothesis that supports the population statistical claim. The mathematical sign of alternative hypothesis is determine from the common phrases used in making the hypothesis claim.

a) Less than sign (<): The common phrases used are; is less than, is below, is shorter than, is smaller than, is reduced from, is slower and is decreased.

b) Greater than sign (>): The common phrases used are; is greater than, is above, is higher than, is longer than, is bigger than, is faster and is increased.

c) Not equal to sign (≠): The common phrases used are; is not equal to, is different from, has changed from and is not the same as.

Note: Alternative hypothesis is by default true when the null hypothesis is proven statistically to be false and should be formulated before the null hypothesis.

2) **Null Hypothesis** (H_0)**:** It is a hypothesis that provides the opposite possibility of the alternative hypothesis or population claim. Null hypothesis uses mathematical signs such as; greater or equal to (≥), less than or equal to (≤) and equality (=). Statistically, for simplicity it is advisable to always use the equality sign no matter the mathematical sign of the alternative hypothesis. The null hypothesis assume that the population claim will not be observed and is by default true unless there is strong evidence to prove it wrong.

7.3 Hypothesis Testing for Population Mean

Hypothesis testing when dealing with single sample is, hypothesis testing is aimed at verifying whether the hypothesized population mean (K) is equal zero. When dealing with two samples situation, the objective of hypothesis testing is to verify if the two sample means are equal.

7.3.1 Hypotheses Formulation

When dealing with the hypothesis of population mean, the null hypothesis and alternative hypothesis expressions are presented in the table below.

Type of Test	One Sample Hypothesis Testing				Two Samples Hypothesis Testing		
	Alternative Hypothesis	Null Hypothesis			Alternative Hypothesis	Null Hypothesis	
2-Tailed	$H_1: \mu \neq K$	$H_0: \mu = K$	$H_0: \mu = K$		$H_1: \mu_1 \neq \mu_2$	$H_0: \mu_1 = \mu_2$	$H_0: \mu_1 = \mu_2$
1-Tailed	$H_1: \mu > K$	$H_0: \mu \leq K$	$H_0: \mu = K$		$H_1: \mu_1 > \mu_2$	$H_0: \mu_1 \leq \mu_2$	$H_0: \mu_1 = \mu_2$
1-Tailed	$H_1: \mu < K$	$H_0: \mu \geq K$	$H_0: \mu = K$		$H_1: \mu_1 < \mu_2$	$H_0: \mu_1 \geq \mu_2$	$H_0: \mu_1 = \mu_2$

Example 1: According to a doctor report, the pulse rate is different from the mean pulse rate of 80 beats per minute. Set up the null and alternative hypothesis for the statement.

Solution

Step 1: Phrases identification. The common phrase is "different from" indicating that the alternative hypothesis will have a not equal to sign ($\neq$). Null hypothesis will have an equality sign (=).

Step 2: Formulation of hypothesis

a) Null hypothesis
   1) Symbolic Presentation: $H_0: \mu = 80$
   2) Literal Presentation: The population pulse rate is 80 beats per minutes

b) Alternative hypothesis
   1) Symbolic Presentation: $H_1: \mu \neq 80$
   2) Literal Presentation: The population pulse rate is not 80 beats per minutes

Example 2: A fast food restaurant in Cameroon has launched a massive advertising campaign to increase its sales. Considering that before the campaign, the average net revenue per week is 350,000 fcfa; formulate the null hypothesis and alternative hypothesis.

Solution

Step 1: Phrases identification. The common phrase here is "to increase" indicating that the alternative hypothesis will have a greater than sign (>). Null hypothesis will have a less than or equal to sign ($\leq$).

Step 2: Formulation of hypothesis

a) Null hypothesis
   1) Symbolic Presentation: $H_0: \mu \leq 350{,}000$ or $H_0: \mu = 350{,}000$
   2) Literal Presentation: The average net revenue per week is 350,000 fcfa.

b) Alternative hypothesis
   1) Symbolic Presentation: $H_1: \mu > 350{,}000$
   2) Literal Presentation: The average net revenue per week is greater than 350,000 fcfa.

Example 3: A production company claimed that less than 20% of the good which she supplied to a super market is defective. State the hypotheses in symbols.

Solution

Step 1: Phrases identification. The common phrase here is "less than" indicating that the alternative hypothesis will have a less than sign (<). Null hypothesis will have a greater than or equal to sign (≥).

Step 2: Formulation of hypothesis

a) Null hypothesis
   1) Symbolic Presentation: $H_0: \mu \geq 0.2$ or $H_0: \mu = 0.2$
   2) Literal Presentation:

b) Alternative hypothesis
   1) Symbolic Presentation: $H_1: \mu < 0.2$
   2) Literal Presentation:

Example 4: A psychologist feels that playing soft music during a test will change the result of the test. The psychologist is not sure whether the grades will be higher or lower. Considering that in the past the mean of the scores were 73, formulate the null and alternative hypothesis.

Solution

Step 1: Phrases identification. The common phrase here is "higher or lower". The uncertainty indicates that the alternative hypothesis is neither having a greater than or less than sign (that is not equal to sign). Null hypothesis is therefore having an equality sign (=).

Step 2: Formulation of hypothesis

a) Null hypothesis
   1) Symbolic Presentation: $H_0: \mu = 73$
   2) Literal Presentation:

b) Alternative hypothesis
   1) Symbolic Presentation: $H_1: \mu \neq 73$
   2) Literal Presentation:

Example 5: A high school math teacher claims that students in her class will score higher on the math portion of the ACT than students in a colleague math class. The mean ACT math score for 49 students in her class is 22.1 and the standard deviation is 4.8. The mean ACT math score for 44 of the colleague students is 19.8 and the standard deviation is 5.4. formulate the null and alternative hypothesis.

Solution

Step 1: Phrases identification. The common phrase here is "score higher", indicates that the alternative hypothesis is neither having a greater than inequality sign (>). Null hypothesis is therefore having a less than or equal to inequality sign (≤).

Step 2: Formulation of hypothesis

a) Null hypothesis
   1) Symbolic Presentation: $H_0: \mu_1 \leq \mu_2$ or $H_0: \mu_1 = \mu_2$
   2) Literal Presentation:

b) Alternative hypothesis
   1) Symbolic Presentation: $H_1: \mu_1 > \mu_2$
   2) Literal Presentation:

Test Your Understanding

Exercise 1: A researcher reports that the average monthly salary of salesmen is more than 42,000 fcfa. State the null hypothesis and alternative hypothesis in symbols.

[Answer: $H_0: \mu \leq 42,000$ and $H_1: \mu > 42,000$]

Exercise 2: A contractor wishes to lower heating bills by using a special type of insulation in houses. Considering the mean of the monthly heating bills is 100 fcfa, formulate the null and alternative hypothesis.............................. **[Answer: $H_0: \mu \geq 100$ and $H_1: \mu < 100$]**

Exercise 3: The management of a large hospital states that the mean age of its patient has not changed from 45 years. Set up the hypotheses of this statement.

[Answer: $H_0: \mu = 45$ and $H_1: \mu \neq 45$]

7.3.2 Test Statistics

Test statistics is the mathematical procedure that helps to determine the values showing the gap between the population mean and the sample mean. It comparison with the critical value helps in determining acceptance and critical region that permit us to make decision and draw conclusion.

1) Test Statistics using Z-Test Distribution

The Z-test compares an estimator (sample mean[$\overline{X}$]) to a parameter (population mean[μ]) to determine if the difference between the means ($\overline{X} - \mu$) is statistically significant. The calculated Z-value is considered to be the sample mean value with respect to the population mean. The difference between the means is directly related to the calculated Z-value ($|\overline{X} -$

$\mu| = Z - \text{Value}$). That is the greater the difference, the larger the Z-value or Z-score and the less likely the estimate is statistically equivalent to the parameter.

The Z-test is based on the assumption that the population from which the sample or samples is drawn is independent and normally distributed. Z-test is applicable when the population mean (μ), standard deviation (σ), sample size (n) and sample mean ($\overline{X}$) values are known and when the sample size is considered to be sufficient large ($n > 30$). It is worth knowing that the Z-test does not need a degree of freedom.

a) When Population Variance is known

Generally, the Z-statistics is calculated using any of the following formulas

$$Z - \text{Statistics}(Z) = \frac{\overline{X}-\mu}{\sigma/\sqrt{n}} \quad \ldots\ldots(1)$$

$$Z - \text{Statistics}(Z) = (\overline{X} - \mu)\frac{\sqrt{n}}{\sigma} \quad \ldots\ldots(2)$$

Example 1: A researcher reports that the average monthly salary of salesmen is 100 fcfa with a standard deviation of 16 fcfa. A sample of 16 salesmen has a mean of 108 fcfa; determine the test statistics.

Solution

Hint: The population mean (μ), population standard deviation (σ), sample mean ($\overline{X}$) and sample size (n) are known. Therefore, the appropriate test statistic is the Z-statistics.

Step 1: Formula. $Z - \text{Statistics} = \frac{\overline{X}-\mu}{\sigma/\sqrt{n}}$, Where; $\overline{X} = 108$, $\mu = 100$, $\sigma = 16$ and $n = 16$

Step 2: Data substitution and solving

$Z - \text{Statistics} = \frac{108-100}{16/\sqrt{16}}$ ……[Simplify equation]

$Z - \text{Statistics} = \frac{8}{16/4}$ ……[Simplify denominator and simplify fraction]

$Z - \text{Statistics} = \mathbf{2}$ ……[Test value]

Note: The above problem can still be solved using the second formula as seen below

Step 1: Formula. $Z - \text{Statistics} = (\overline{X} - \mu)\frac{\sqrt{n}}{\sigma}$, where; $\overline{X} = 108$, $\mu = 100$, $\sigma = 16$ and $n = 16$

Step 2: Data substitution and solving

$Z - \text{Statistics} = 108 - 100 \times \frac{\sqrt{16}}{16}$ ……[Work out root]

$Z - \text{Statistics} = 8 \times \frac{4}{16}$ ……[Simplify fraction]

$Z - \text{Statistics} = 8 \times 0.25$ ……[Solve equation]

$Z - \text{Statistics} = \mathbf{2}$ ....[Test value]

Complementary Explanation: The computed Z-statistic value shows that the sample mean is exactly 2 standard deviation to the right from the population mean.

Example 2: A researcher report that the average monthly salary of salesmen is more than 42,000 fcfa. A sample of 30 salesmen has a mean of 43,260 fcfa. Considering that the standard deviation of the population of salesmen is 5,230 fcfa, calculate the test statistics

Solution

Step 1: Formula. $Z - \text{Statistics} = \frac{\overline{X}-\mu}{\sigma/\sqrt{n}}$

Where; $\overline{X} = 43{,}260$, $\mu = 42{,}000$, $\sigma = 5{,}230$ and $n = 30$

Step 2: Data substitution and solving

$Z - \text{Statistics} = \frac{43{,}260-42{,}000}{5{,}230/\sqrt{30}}$ ....[Simplify root]

$Z - \text{Statistics} = \frac{43{,}260-42{,}000}{5{,}230/5.477225575}$ ....[Simplify both numerator and denominator]

$Z - \text{Statistics} = \frac{1{,}260}{954.8629919}$ ....[Work fraction]

$Z - \text{Statistics} = \mathbf{1.3196}$ ....[Test value]

Summary: The main limitations here are that it is appropriate to use this method only when the population variance is known and the population is normally distributed.

Test Your Understanding

Exercise 4: Fast food restaurant with many outlets in Cameroon has launched a massive advertising campaign to increase its sales. Before the campaign, the average net revenue per week was 350,000 fcfa with a standard deviation of 40,000 fcfa. A random sample from 25 outlets after the advertisement campaign gives a net mean revenue of 375,000 fcfa. Determine the statistics test value... **[Answer: $Z - \text{Statistics} = 3.125$]**

Exercise 5: An IQ test is developed such that the mean quotient is 100 and the standard deviation is 12. It is given to a random sample of 50 children in one area. Assuming the average marks was 105, determine the test value....... **[Answer: $Z - \text{Statistics} = 2.9463$]**

Example 6: Calculate the test statistics from the following data; $\mu = 8$, $n = 18$, $\overline{X} = 8.6$ and $\sigma = 2$. Put answer in four decimal places.................. **[Answer: $Z - \text{Statistics} = 1.2728$]**

b) When Population Variances are known and equal

The formula applied in such a situation is given as seen below.

$$Z - \text{Statistics} = \frac{(\bar{X}_1-\bar{X}_2)-(\mu_1-\mu_2)}{\sigma\left(\frac{1}{n_1}+\frac{1}{n_2}\right)^{\frac{1}{2}}} \rightarrow \frac{(\bar{X}_1-\bar{X}_2)-(\mu_1-\mu_2)}{\sigma\left[\sqrt{\left(\frac{1}{n_1}+\frac{1}{n_2}\right)}\right]} \rightarrow \frac{(\bar{X}_1-\bar{X}_2)-(\mu_1-\mu_2)}{\sigma^2\left[\frac{1}{n_1}+\frac{1}{n_2}\right]} \text{..........................(1)}$$

Where; ($\bar{X}_1$ and $\bar{X}_2$) Represent the means of sample 1 and sample 2 respectively

(μ_1 and μ_2) Represent the means of Population 1 and population 2 respectively

Example 1: The university administration asserted that the upper class men spend more time studying than under class men. To test this assertion, two independent samples were randomly selected from two independent normal distribution populations with variance of 156.25 each and data obtained presented in the table below;

Classmen	Sample size (n)	Sample mean ($\bar{X}$)
Upperclassmen	$n_1 = 314$	$\bar{X}_1 = 198$
Underclassmen	$n_2 = 220$	$\bar{X}_2 = 176$

Solution

Step 1: Formula. $Z - \text{Statistics} = \frac{(\bar{X}_1-\bar{X}_2)-(\mu_1-\mu_2)}{\sigma\sqrt{\left(\frac{1}{n_1}+\frac{1}{n_2}\right)}}$

Where; $n_1 = 314, n_2 = 220, \bar{X}_1 = 198, \bar{X}_2 = 176, \sigma = \sqrt{156.25} = 12.5, \mu_1 = 0, \ \mu_2 = 0$

Step 2: Data substitution and solving

$$Z - \text{Statistics} - \text{Statistics} = \frac{(198-176)-(0-0)}{12.5\left[\sqrt{\frac{1}{314}+\frac{1}{220}}\right]} \text{..................[Simplify fractions and brackets]}$$

$$Z - \text{Statistics} = \frac{22}{12.5[\sqrt{0.007730167}]} \text{......................................[Work denominator root]}$$

$$Z - \text{Statistics} = \frac{22}{12.5(0.087921373)} \text{.................................[Expand denominator bracket]}$$

$$Z - \text{Statistics} = \frac{22}{1.099017169} \text{..[Solve equation]}$$

$$Z - \text{Statistics} = \mathbf{20.018} \text{...[In three decimal places]}$$

Example 2: Determine the test value from the following data; $n_1 = 9$, $n_2 = 16$, $\bar{X}_1 = 1.2$, $\bar{X}_2 = 1.7$, $\sigma = 1.4405$ and $\sigma^2 = 2.0750$.

Solution

Hint: There are two samples selection and only a population variance. This shows that the population variances of the two independent populations are equal.

Step 1: Formula. $Z - \text{Statistics} = \frac{(\bar{X}_1 - \bar{X}_2) - (\mu_1 - \mu_2)}{\sigma\left(\frac{1}{n_1} + \frac{1}{n_2}\right)^{\frac{1}{2}}}$

Where; $n_1 = 9, n_2 = 16, \bar{X}_1 = 1.2, \bar{X}_2 = 1.7, \sigma = 1.4405, \mu_1 = 0$ and $\mu_2 = 0$

Step 2: Data substitution and solving

$Z = \frac{(1.2 - 1.7) - (0 - 0)}{1.4405\left(\frac{1}{9} + \frac{1}{16}\right)^{\frac{1}{2}}}$ ....[Simplify denominator fraction and bracket]

$Z = \frac{(1.2 - 1.7) - (0 - 0)}{1.4405(0.173611111)^{\frac{1}{2}}}$ ....[Simplify numerator and work denominator exponent]

$Z = \frac{-0.5}{1.4405(0.416666666)}$ ....[Expand denominator bracket]

$Z = \frac{-0.5}{0.600208333}$ ....[Solve equation]

$Z = \mathbf{-0.833}$ ....[In three decimal places]

Test Your Understanding

Exercise 7: Determine the test value from the following data; $n_1 = 10, n_2 = 15, \bar{X}_1 = 6$ and $\bar{X}_2 = 5$. Assume the two sample have a common variance of 2.156, determine the test value.

[Answer: $Z = 1.668$]

Exercise 8: A random sample of size(n_1) 100 is taken from a normal population with variance $(\sigma_1{}^2)$ 40 and mean $(\bar{X}_1)$ 38.3. another random sample of size $80(n_2)$ is taken from a normal population with variance $(\sigma^2{}_2)$ 40 and mean $(\bar{X}_2)$ 40.1. Determine the test value from the above data..**[Answer: $Z = -1.897$]**

Exercise 9: Determine the test value of Z-value using the following information below

Sample 1			Sample 2		
$n_1 = 20$	$\bar{X}_1 = 43$	$\sigma^2{}_1 = 16$	$n_2 = 17$	$\bar{X}_2 = 40$	$\sigma^2{}_2 = 16$

[Answer: $Z = 2.274$]

c) When Population Variances known and Unequal

The formula applied in such a situation is given as seen below.

$$Z = \frac{(\bar{X}_1 - \bar{X}_2) - (\mu_1 - \mu_2)}{\left(\frac{\sigma_1{}^2}{n_1} + \frac{\sigma_2{}^2}{n_2}\right)^{\frac{1}{2}}} \rightarrow \frac{(\bar{X}_1 - \bar{X}_2) - (\mu_1 - \mu_2)}{\sqrt{\frac{\sigma_1{}^2}{n_1} + \frac{\sigma_2{}^2}{n_2}}} \quad \text{.......................(1)}$$

Example 1: Determine the test value using the following information; $n_1 = 13$, $n_2 = 8$, $\bar{X}_1 = 80.02$, $\bar{X}_2 = 79.98$, $\sigma^2{}_1 = 0.000576$ and $\sigma^2{}_2 = 0.001089$.

Solution

Step 1: Formula. $Z - \text{Statistics} = \frac{(\bar{X}_1 - \bar{X}_2) - (\mu_1 - \mu_2)}{\sqrt{\frac{\sigma_1{}^2}{n_1} + \frac{\sigma_2{}^2}{n_2}}}$

Where; $n_1 = 13$, $n_2 = 8$, $\bar{X}_1 = 80.02$, $\bar{X}_2 = 79.98$, $\sigma^2{}_1 = 0.000576$, $\sigma^2{}_2 = 0.001089$.

Step 2: Data substitution and solving

$Z - \text{Statistics} = \frac{(80.02 - 79.98) - (0 - 0)}{\sqrt{\frac{0.000576}{13} + \frac{0.001089}{8}}}$ ....[Simplify denominator root fractions]

$Z - \text{Statistics} = \frac{(80.02 - 79.98) - (0 - 0)}{\sqrt{0.000044307 + 0.000136125}}$ ....[Simplify numerator and denominator]

$Z - \text{Statistics} = \frac{0.04}{\sqrt{0.000180432}}$ ....[Solve equation]

$Z - \text{Statistics} = \mathbf{2.9779}$ ....[In four decimal places]

Exercise 2: Suppose we want to compare the average yearly income of Bamenda and Douala. It is known from experience that the variance of yearly income in Bamenda is 400 fcfa and the variance in Douala is 900 fcfa. A random sample of 20 families was taken in Bamenda, yielding an average yearly income of 470 fcfa while a random sample of 30 families was taken in Douala, yielding a mean yearly income of 520 fcfa. Determine the test statistics value.

Solution

Hint: Let the town Bamenda be represented by 1 and Douala by 2. Population variances are not equal.

Step 1: Formula. $Z - \text{Statistics} = \frac{(\bar{X}_1 - \bar{X}_2) - (\mu_1 - \mu_2)}{\sqrt{\frac{\sigma_1{}^2}{n_1} + \frac{\sigma_2{}^2}{n_2}}}$

Where; $n_1 = 20$, $n_2 = 30$, $\bar{X}_1 = 470$, $\bar{X}_2 = 520$, $\sigma^2{}_1 = 400$ and $\sigma^2{}_2 = 900$.

Step 2: Data substitution and solving

$Z - \text{Statistics} = \frac{(470 - 520) - (0 - 0)}{\sqrt{\frac{400}{20} + \frac{900}{30}}}$ ....[Simplify denominator root fractions]

$Z - \text{Statistics} = \frac{(470 - 520) - (0 - 0)}{\sqrt{20 + 30}}$ ....[Simplify numerator and denominator]

$Z - \text{Statistics} = \frac{-50}{\sqrt{50}}$ ....[Work denominator root]

$Z - \text{Statistics} = \frac{-50}{7.071067812}$ ....[Solve equation]

$Z - \text{Statistics} = \mathbf{-7.0711}$ ....[In four decimal places]

Example 3: Determine the test statistics using information from the table below.

	Sample mean ($\overline{X}$)	Population standard deviation (σ)	Sample size (n)
Town 1	82.6	1.41	35
Town 2	84	3.63	32

Solution

Step 1: Formula. $Z - \text{Statistics} = \frac{(\overline{X}_1-\overline{X}_2)-(\mu_1-\mu_2)}{\sqrt{\frac{\sigma_1{}^2}{n_1}+\frac{\sigma_2{}^2}{n_2}}}$

Where; $n_1 = 35, n_2 = 32, \overline{X}_1 = 82.6, \overline{X}_2 = 84, \sigma^2{}_1 = (\sigma)^2$ and $\sigma^2{}_2 = (\sigma)^2$

Step 2: Data substitution and solving

$Z - \text{Statistics} = \frac{(82.6-84)-(0-0)}{\sqrt{\frac{(1.41)^2}{35}+\frac{(3.63)^2}{32}}}$ ....[Work exponents]

$Z - \text{Statistics} = \frac{(82.6-84)-(0-0)}{\sqrt{\frac{1.9881}{35}+\frac{13.1769}{32}}}$ ....[Simplify denominator fractions and simplify]

$Z - \text{Statistics} = \frac{(82.6-84)-(0-0)}{\sqrt{0.468580982}}$ ....[Simplify numerator and work denominator root]

$Z - \text{Statistics} = \frac{-1.4}{0.684529752}$ ....[Solve equation]

$Z - \text{Statistics} = \mathbf{-2.0452}$ ....[In four decimal places]

Test Your Understanding

Exercise 10: A survey found that the average hotel room in Yaoundé is 88 fcfa and the average room in Limbe is 80 fcfa. Assume that the data were obtained from two samples of 50 hotels in Yaoundé and the population standard deviation is 5.1 fcfa and 50 hotels in Limbe and the standard deviation is 4.8 fcfa. Determine the test statistics value...**[Answer: Z = $\mathbf{8.0771}$]**

Example 11: Calculate the value of test statistics from the given data; $n_1 = 65$, $n_2 = 57$, $\overline{X}_1 = 16.9, \overline{X}_2 = 18.6, \sigma^2{}_1 = 1.69$ and $\sigma^2{}_2 = 1.21$....................**[Answer: Z = $\mathbf{-7.8225}$]**

Example 12: Determine the test statistics using information from the table below.

	Sample mean ($\overline{X}$)	Population standard deviation (σ)	Sample size (n)
Sample 1	45.15	7.998	13
Sample 2	42.25	8.740	12

[Answer: Z = $\mathbf{0.8632}$]

2) Test Statistics using t-Test Distribution

When the population standard deviation (σ) is unknown, the sample standard deviation (S) being an unbiased estimator or good approximation is used in its place. Sample standard deviation is derived from a population fraction which is usually not normally distributed. Secondly, the sample variance (S^2) is distributed as a Chi-square distribution, making it inappropriate to use a normal distribution Z- table to obtain its critical value. To solve this problem, we use the t-distribution.

a) When Population Variance is unknown:

The formula applied in this situation is given as seen below.

$$\text{t} - \text{Statistics} = \frac{\overline{X}-\mu}{S/\sqrt{n}} \equiv \frac{\overline{X}-\mu}{\sqrt{\frac{\Sigma(X_i-\overline{X})}{n-1}}/\sqrt{n}} \quad \text{...(1)}$$

Example 1: A sample of 9 students' marks yielded an average mark of 3.1 with estimated standard deviation of 1.0 mark. Assume the population mean mark is 4.0, what is the value of test statistics?

<u>Solution</u>

Step 1: Formula. $\text{t} - \text{Statistics(T)} = \frac{\overline{X}-\mu}{S/\sqrt{n}}$, where; $\overline{X} = 3.1$, $\mu = 4.0$, $S = 1.0$ and $n = 9$

Step 2: Data substitution and solving

$\text{t} - \text{Statistics(T)} = \frac{3.1-4.0}{1.0/\sqrt{9}}$ ....[Work denominator root and simplify fraction]

$\text{t} - \text{Statistics(T)} = \frac{3.1-4.0}{0.3333333333}$ ....[Simplify numerator]

$\text{t} - \text{Statistics(T)} = \frac{-0.9}{0.3333333333}$ ....[Solve equation]

$\text{t} - \text{Statistics(T)} = \mathbf{-2.7}$

Example 2: Determine the test statistics using the following data; $\overline{X} = 23.5$, $\mu = 22$, $S^2 = 25$ and $n = 20$.

<u>Solution</u>

Step 1: Formula. $\text{t} - \text{Statistics(T)} = \frac{\overline{X}-\mu}{S/\sqrt{n}}$, where; $\overline{X} = 23.5$, $\mu = 22$, $S = \sqrt{25} = 5$ and $n = 20$

Step 2: Data substitution and solving

$\text{t} - \text{Statistics(T)} = \frac{23.5-22}{5/\sqrt{20}}$ ....[Work denominator root and simplify fraction]

$\text{t} - \text{Statistics(T)} = \frac{23.5-22}{1.118033989}$ ....[Solve]

$\text{t} - \text{Statistics(T)} = \mathbf{1.3416}$ ....[In four decimal places]

Test Your Understanding

Exercise 13: A city health department wishes to determine if the mean bacteria count per unit volume of water at a lake beach is within the safety level of 200. A researcher collected 10 water samples of unit volume, yielding a sample mean of 194.8 and a sample variance of 172.66. ....[**Answer:** $\mathbf{t - Statistics(T) = -1.2514}$]

Exercise 14: Determine the test statistics from the following data; $\overline{X} = 2.26$, $\mu = 3.0$, $S = 0.39$ and $n = 14$. ....[**Answer:** $\mathbf{t - Statistics(T) = -7.0910}$]

b) When Variances is unknown but Equal

Remember that sample variance is given as; $S^2 = \frac{\sum(X_\iota - \overline{X})^2}{n-1}$. Considering that we are having two sample variances, we are going to have; $S_1{}^2 = \frac{\sum(X_\iota - \overline{X})^2}{n_1 - 1}$ and $S_2{}^2 = \frac{\sum(X_\iota - \overline{X})^2}{n_2 - 1}$. Assuming that the population variances are equal, it therefore means the samples variances($S^2{}_1$ and $S^2{}_2$) are both estimators of a common population variance. Therefore, we are required to sum the sample variances to obtain a common sample variance called pooled (combined) sample variance (S^2).

$$\text{Pooled Variance}(S^2) = \frac{\sum(X_\iota - \overline{X})^2{}_1}{n_1 - 1} + \frac{\sum(X_\iota - \overline{X})^2{}_2}{n_2 - 1} \text{ ....[Simplify equation]}$$

$$\text{Pooled Variance}(S^2) = \frac{\sum(X_\iota - \overline{X})^2{}_1 + \sum(X_\iota - \overline{X})^2{}_2}{n_1 + n_2 - 2} \text{ ....[Substitute the numerator with equivalent]}$$

Given that $S^2 = \frac{\sum(X_\iota - \overline{X})^2}{n-1}$, therefore, $\sum(X_\iota - \overline{X})^2 = (n-1)S^2$. Substitute in the equation, we get

$$\mathbf{Pooled\ Variance(S^2)} = \frac{\mathbf{(n_1 - 1)S_1{}^2 + (n_2 - 1)S_2{}^2}}{\mathbf{n_1 + n_2 - 2}} \text{ ....(1)}$$

Let assume a situation in which the two samples are having the same sizes [that is $(n_1 = n_2 = n)$]. Substituting the new sample size notation in equation (1), we get a new equation as seen below.

$$\text{Pooled Variance}(S^2) = \frac{(n-1)S_1{}^2 + (n-1)S_2{}^2}{n + n - 2} \text{ ....[Simplify denominator]}$$

$$\text{Pooled Variance}(S^2) = \frac{(n-1)S_1{}^2 + (n-1)S_2{}^2}{2n - 2} \text{ ....[Factories the denominator]}$$

$$\text{Pooled Variance}(S^2) = \frac{(n-1)S_1{}^2 + (n-1)S_2{}^2}{2(n-1)} \equiv \frac{(n-1)S_1{}^2}{2(n-1)} + \frac{(n-1)S_2{}^2}{2(n-1)} \text{ ....[Simplify fractions]}$$

$$\mathbf{Pooled\ Variance(S^2)} = \frac{\mathbf{S_1{}^2 + S_2{}^2}}{\mathbf{2}} \text{ ....(2)}$$

Note: The degree of freedom of equation (1) is $[df = n_1 + n_2 - 2]$ and the degree of freedom of equation (2) is $[df = 2(n-1)]$. It is worth knowing that, equation (1) is the general equation for pooled variance as it can be used in both equal and unequal sample sizes situation. The general formula for T-test statistics in this situation is given as;

$$t - \text{Statistics}(T) = \frac{(\bar{X}_1-\bar{X}_2)-(\mu_1-\mu_2)}{S\left(\frac{1}{n_1}+\frac{1}{n_2}\right)^{\frac{1}{2}}} \rightarrow \frac{(\bar{X}_1-\bar{X}_2)-(\mu_1-\mu_2)}{S\sqrt{\left(\frac{1}{n_1}+\frac{1}{n_2}\right)}} \text{ ....(2)}$$

Where; $S = \sqrt{\frac{(n-1)S_1{}^2+(n-1)S_2{}^2}{n+n-2}}$ ....[Unequal sample sizes]

$S = \sqrt{\frac{S_1{}^2+S_2{}^2}{2}}$ ....[Equal sample sizes]

Example 1: Determine the test statistics from the following data; $\bar{X}_1 = 31.75$, $\bar{X}_2 = 28.67$, $n_1 = 12$, $n_2 = 12$, $S_1{}^2 = 112.25$ and $S_2{}^2 = 66.64$.

Solution

Step 1: Formula. $T = \frac{(\bar{X}_1-\bar{X}_2)-(\mu_1-\mu_2)}{S\left[\sqrt{\left(\frac{1}{n_1}+\frac{1}{n_2}\right)}\right]}$

Where; $\bar{X}_1 = 31.75$, $\bar{X}_2 = 28.67$, $n_1 = 12$, $n_2 = 12$, $S^2 = ?$

Step 2: Determination of S^2

a) Formula. $S^2 = \frac{(n_1-1)S_1{}^2+(n_2-1)S_2{}^2}{(n_1+n_2-2)}$

Where; $n_1 = 12$, $n_2 = 12$, $S_1{}^2 = 112.25$, $S_2{}^2 = 66.64$.

b) Data substitution and solving

$S^2 = \frac{(12-1)112.25+(12-1)66.64}{(12+12-2)}$ ....[Simplify brackets]

$S^2 = \frac{(11)112.25+(11)66.64}{22}$ ....[Open brackets]

$S^2 = \frac{1,234.75+733.04}{22}$ ....[Solve equation]

$S^2 = \mathbf{89.445}$

Step 3: Data substitution and solving $[S^2 = 89.445 \therefore S = 9.457536677]$

$t - \text{Statistics}(T) = \frac{(31.75-28.67)-(0-0)}{89.445\left[\sqrt{\frac{1}{12}+\frac{1}{12}}\right]}$ ....[Simplify denominator fractions and work root]

$t - \text{Statistics}(T) = \frac{(31.75-28.67)-(0-0)}{89.445[0.40824829]}$ ....[Simplify brackets]

$t - \text{Statistics}(T) = \frac{3.08}{9.457536677[0.40824829]}$ ......[Open denominator bracket and solve equation]

$t - \text{Statistics}(T) = \mathbf{0.7977}$ ....[In four decimal places]

Example 2: Determine the test statistics using the information from the table below, assuming that the population variances are equal.

	Mean ($\bar{X}$)	Variance (S^2)	Sample size (n)
Sample 1	1,407.14	5,523.81	7
Sample 2	1,463.33	6,375.00	9

Solution

Hint: From the equation, we realized the population variances are equal and the sample sizes are not the same.

Step 1: Formula. $T = \frac{(\bar{X}_1 - \bar{X}_2) - (\mu_1 - \mu_2)}{S\left[\sqrt{\left(\frac{1}{n_1} + \frac{1}{n_2}\right)}\right]}$, where; $\bar{X}_1 = 1{,}407.14$, $\bar{X}_2 = 1{,}463.33$, $n_1 = 7$, $n_2 = 9$,

Step 2: Determination of S^2

a) Formula. $S^2 = \frac{(n_1 - 1){S_1}^2 + (n_2 - 1){S_2}^2}{(n_1 + n_2 - 2)}$

Where; $n_1 = 7$, $n_2 = 9$, ${S_1}^2 = 5{,}523.81$, ${S_2}^2 = 6{,}375.$

b) Data substitution and solving

$S^2 = \frac{(7-1)5{,}523.81 + (9-1)6{,}375.00}{(7+9-2)}$ ....[Simplify brackets]

$S^2 = \frac{(6)5{,}523.81 + (8)6{,}375.00}{14}$ ....[Open brackets]

$S^2 = \frac{33{,}142.86 + 51{,}000}{14}$ ....[Solve equation]

$S^2 = \mathbf{6{,}010}$ ....[In no decimal place]

Step 3: Data substitution and solving [$S^2 = 6{,}010 \therefore S = 77.52418977$]

$t - \text{Statistics}(T) = \frac{(1{,}407.14 - 1{,}463.33) - (0 - 0)}{77.52418977\left[\sqrt{\frac{1}{7} + \frac{1}{9}}\right]}$ ....[Simplify fractions and work root]

$t - \text{Statistics}(T) = \frac{(1{,}407.14 - 1{,}463.33) - (0 - 0)}{77.52418977[0.50395263]}$ ....[Simplify brackets]

$t - \text{Statistics}(T) = \frac{-56.19}{39.06851938}$ ....[Solve equation]

$t - \text{Statistics}(T) = \mathbf{-1.4382}$ ....[In four decimal places]

Test Your Understanding

Exercise 15: A study is done by a community group in two neighboring colleges to determine which one graduate's students with more math classes. College A samples 11 graduates and their average is 4 math classes with a standard deviation of 1.5 math classes. Collage B samples 9 graduates and their average is 3.5 math classes with a standard deviation of 1 math class. Determine the value of test statistics assuming that the population variances are equal...**[Answer: $t = 1.9013$]**

Exercise 16: Determine the statistics value using information in the table below. The population variances are equal.

Males				Female		
$n_1 = 26$	$\overline{X}_1 = 65$	$S_1 = 10.2$		$n_2 = 24$	$\overline{X}_2 = 57.5$	$S_2 = 9.7$

[Answer: $t - \text{Statistics}(T) = 2.6592$]

c) When Variances is unknown and unequal

When the population variances are unequal ($\sigma_1{}^2 \neq \sigma_2{}^2$) we are faced with heterogeneity of population variances. The samples variances($S^2{}_1$ and $S^2{}_2$) are estimators of different population variances. That is, ($S^2{}_1$) is an estimator of ($\sigma_1{}^2$) and ($S^2{}_2$) an estimator of ($\sigma_2{}^2$). Knowing that the variance of a sample mean is $\left[\text{Var}(\overline{X}) = \frac{S^2}{n}\right]$, adding two of sample mean variances gives us the equation seen below.

$$\text{Variance}(\overline{X}_1 - \overline{X}_2) = \frac{S_1{}^2}{n_1} + \frac{S_2{}^2}{n_2} \quad \text{.......................................(1)}$$

$$\text{Standard deviation}(\overline{X}_1 - \overline{X}_2) = \sqrt{\frac{S_1{}^2}{n_1} + \frac{S_2{}^2}{n_2}} \quad \text{.......................................(2)}$$

Equation (2) is also called the standard error of the difference of mean. The general formula used in such a situation to determine the test statistic is called the Welch's t-test and the degree of freedom is determine using the satterthwaite approximation equation. The Welch's t-test is a modified student t-test and is given as seen below;

$$t - \text{Statistics}(T) = \frac{(\overline{X}_1 - \overline{X}_2) - (\mu_1 - \mu_2)}{\left(\frac{S^2{}_1}{n_1} + \frac{S^2{}_2}{n_2}\right)^{\frac{1}{2}}} \rightarrow \frac{(\overline{X}_1 - \overline{X}_2) - (\mu_1 - \mu_2)}{\sqrt{\frac{S^2{}_1}{n_1} + \frac{S^2{}_2}{n_2}}} \quad \text{.......................................(3)}$$

$$\text{Degree of freedom (df)} = \nu = \frac{\left(\frac{S_1{}^2}{n_1} + \frac{S_2{}^2}{n_2}\right)^2}{\frac{\left(\frac{S_1{}^2}{n_1}\right)^2}{n_1 - 1} + \frac{\left(\frac{S_2{}^2}{n_2}\right)^2}{n_2 - 1}} \rightarrow \frac{\left(\frac{S_1{}^2}{n_1} + \frac{S_2{}^2}{n_2}\right)^2}{\frac{1}{n_1 - 1}\left(\frac{S_1{}^2}{n_2}\right)^2 + \frac{1}{n_2 - 1}\left(\frac{S_2{}^2}{n_2}\right)^2}$$

Example 1: Determine the test statistics from the following data; $\overline{X}_1 = 3{,}166.0$, $\overline{X}_2 = 2{,}240.4$, $n_1 = 4$, $n_2 = 9$, ${S_1}^2 = 6{,}328.67$ and ${S_2}^2 = 221{,}661.3$.

Solution

Step 1: Formula. $t - \text{Statistics}(T) = \frac{(\overline{X}_1 - \overline{X}_2) - (\mu_1 - \mu_2)}{\sqrt{\frac{S^2{}_1}{n_1} + \frac{S^2{}_2}{n_2}}}$

Where; $\overline{X}_1 = 3{,}166.0$, $\overline{X}_2 = 2{,}240.4$, $n_1 = 4$, $n_2 = 9$, ${S_1}^2 = 6{,}328.67$ and ${S_2}^2 = 221{,}661.3$.

Step 2: Data substitution and solving

$t - \text{Statistics}(T) = \frac{(3{,}166.0 - 2{,}240.4) - (0 - 0)}{\sqrt{\frac{6{,}328.67}{4} + \frac{221{,}661.3}{9}}}$ ....[Simplify fractions and simplify]

$t - \text{Statistics}(T) = \frac{(3{,}166.0 - 2{,}240.4) - (0 - 0)}{\sqrt{26{,}211.20083}}$ ....[Simplify brackets and work root]

$t - \text{Statistics}(T) = \frac{925.6}{161.8987364}$ ....[Solve equation]

$t - \text{Statistics}(T) = \mathbf{5.7172}$ ....[In four decimal places]

Example 3: The human resource manager of a reference hospital suspects a difference in the mean amount of sick leave taken by nurses on the day shift compared to the night shift. It is suspected that the night workers take more sick leaves on the average. A random sample of 38 day workers had a mean of $\overline{X}_1 = 10.6$ days sick leave last year the standard deviation was $S_1 = 3.3$. A random sample of 41 night workers had a mean $\overline{X}_2 = 12.9$ days sick leave last year with standard deviation $S_1 = 4.5$. Determine the test statistics value.

Solution

Step 1: Formula. $t - \text{Statistics}(T) = \frac{(\overline{X}_1 - \overline{X}_2) - (\mu_1 - \mu_2)}{\sqrt{\frac{S^2{}_1}{n_1} + \frac{S^2{}_2}{n_2}}}$

Where; $\overline{X}_1 = 10.6$, $\overline{X}_2 = 12.9$, $n_1 = 38$, $n_2 = 41$, ${S_1}^2 = (S_1)^2$ and ${S_2}^2 = (S_2)^2$

Step 2: Data substitution and solving

$t - \text{Statistics}(T) = \frac{(10.6 - 12.9) - (0 - 0)}{\sqrt{\frac{(3.3)^2}{38} + \frac{(4.5)^2}{41}}}$ ....[Work denominator exponents]

$t - \text{Statistics}(T) = \frac{(10.6 - 12.9) - (0 - 0)}{\sqrt{\frac{10.89}{38} + \frac{20.25}{41}}}$ ....[Simplify denominator fraction and simplify]

$t - \text{Statistics}(T) = \frac{(10.6 - 12.9) - (0 - 0)}{\sqrt{0.780481386}}$ ....[Simplify brackets and work root]

$t - \text{Statistics}(T) = \frac{-2.3}{0.883448576}$ ....[Solve the equation]

$t - \text{Statistics}(T) = \mathbf{-2.6034}$ ....[In four decimal places]

Example 3: A survey of family food expenditures is conducted at two major metropolitan areas. Random samples of 30 and 25 families are selected from the two areas and the following is found. Determine the t-test value.

Food Expenditure Per Month			
	Families	Mean	Sample Variance
Area 1	30	300	50
Area 2	25	250	35

Solution

Step 1: Formula. $t - \text{Statistics}(T) = \frac{(\bar{X}_1 - \bar{X}_2) - (\mu_1 - \mu_2)}{\sqrt{\frac{S^2{}_1}{n_1} + \frac{S^2{}_2}{n_2}}}$

Where; $\bar{X}_1 = 300, \bar{X}_2 = 250, n_1 = 30, n_2 = 25, S_1{}^2 = 50$ and $S_2{}^2 = 35$

Step 2: Data substitution and solving

$t - \text{Statistics}(T) = \frac{(300-250)-(0-0)}{\sqrt{\frac{50}{30}+\frac{35}{25}}}$ ...[Simplify numerator and work denominator fraction]

$t - \text{Statistics}(T) = \frac{50}{\sqrt{3.06666667}}$ ....[Work denominator root]

$t - \text{Statistics}(T) = \frac{50}{1.751190072}$ ....[Solve equation]

$t - \text{Statistics}(T) = \mathbf{28.5520}$ ....[In four decimal places]

Test Your Understanding

Exercise 17: A random sample of 130 students in Buea yields a mean mark of 27.2 and a standard deviation of 2.5. In Douala, a random sample of 155 students yields a mean mark of 38.3 and a standard deviation of 4.6. Determine the value of test statistics

[Answer: $t = -25.8354$]

Exercise 18: Determine the t-test value from the following information; $n_1 = 110, \bar{X}_1 = 77, S_1 = 15, n_2 = 85, \bar{X}_2 = 79$ and $S_2 = 21$. **[Answer: $t - \text{Statistics}(T) = -0.7436$]**

Example 19: Two factories are producing visual display units for computers. Use the information in the table below to determine the value of test statistics.

	Mean ($\bar{X}$)	Standard deviation (S)	Sample size (n)
Sample 1	0.5	3.4	125
Sample 2	19.0	2.1	180

[Answer: $t - \text{Statistics}(T) = 4.3857$]

7.3.3 Critical Values and P-Value Analysis

In hypothesis testing, the critical value is also called cutoff and when compared with the test statistic value, help in decision making (reject or not reject the null hypothesis). Generally, the null hypothesis is rejected if the absolute value of test statistics is greater than the critical value.

Our focus will be limited to the critical value of t-statistics since the critical value determination of Z-statistics has been seen under the chapter sampling and estimation. The P-value of the Z-statistics is determined the same as under the concept of normal distribution.

The calculation of critical value using t-distribution is complex than when dealing with Z-distribution, as one is required to determine the value of degree of freedom. The t-distribution is made up of two principal components; "P" component $\left[1-\alpha \text{ or } 1-\frac{\alpha}{2}\right]$ and "v" component (degree of freedom).

Example 1: Determine the critical value of $t = 0.975$ using a 5% significance level and a sample size of 30, under the two tailed alternative hypothesis condition.

Solution

Step 1: Determination of probability (P)

1) Formula. $P = 1 - \frac{\text{significance level}(\alpha)}{2}$, where; $\alpha = 5\% = 0.05$
2) Data substitution and solving

$P = 1 - \frac{0.05}{2}$ ....[Solve equation]

$P = \mathbf{0.975}$

Step 2: Determination of degree of freedom (ν)

1) Formula. $Df = \nu = n - 1$, where; $n = 30$
2) Data substitution and solving. $df = \nu = 30 - 1 = \mathbf{29}$

Step 3: Determination of critical value

p	0.75	0.90	0.95	0.975	0.99	0.995	0.9975	0.999	0.9995
$\nu = 1$	1.000	3.078	6.314	12.71	31.82	63.66	127.3	318.3	636.6
2	0.816	1.886	2.920	4.303	6.965	9.925	14.09	22.33	31.60
25	0.684	1.316	1.708	2.060	2.485	2.787	3.078	3.450	3.725
26	0.684	1.315	1.706	2.056	2.479	2.779	3.067	3.435	3.707
27	0.684	1.314	1.703	2.052	2.473	2.771	3.057	3.421	3.689
28	0.683	1.313	1.701	2.048	2.467	2.763	3.047	3.408	3.674
→ 29	0.683	1.311	1.699	2.045	2.462	2.756	3.038	3.396	3.660

Note: The critical value is at 5% significance level is 2.045

Example 2: Determine the critical value at 10% significance level under a two-tailed hypothesis testing condition using the following data; $n_1 = 6$ and $n_2 = 8$. Assume the population variances are equal.

Solution

Step 1: Determination of probability (P)

1) Formula. $P = 1 - \frac{\text{significance level}(\alpha)}{2}$, where; $\alpha = 10\% \equiv 0.1$
2) Data substitution and solving

$P = 1 - \frac{\text{significance level}(\alpha)}{2}$ ....[Substitute formula components value]

$P = 1 - \frac{0.1}{2}$ ....[Solve equation]

$P = \mathbf{0.95}$

Step 2: Determination of degree of freedom (df)

a) Formula. $df = \nu = n_1 + n_2 - 2$, where; $n_1 = 6$ and $n_2 = 8$
b) Data substitution and solving. $df = \nu = 6 + 8 - 2 = \mathbf{12}$

Step 3: Determination of critical value

p	0.75	0.90	0.95	0.975	0.99	0.995	0.9975	0.999	0.9995
$\nu = 1$	1.000	3.078	6.314	12.71	31.82	63.66	127.3	318.3	636.6
2	0.816	1.886	2.920	4.303	6.965	9.925	14.09	22.33	31.60
10	0.700	1.372	1.812	2.228	2.764	3.169	3.581	4.144	4.587
11	0.697	1.363	1.796	2.201	2.718	3.106	3.497	4.025	4.437
12	0.695	1.356	1.782	2.179	2.681	3.055	3.428	3.930	4.318
13	0.694	1.350	1.771	2.160	2.650	3.012	3.372	3.852	4.221
14	0.692	1.345	1.761	2.145	2.624	2.977	3.326	3.787	4.140

Note: The critical value is = $\pm\mathbf{1.782}$

Example 3: Determine the critical value at 1% significance level using information in the table below under the right directional hypothesis testing. Assume the population variances unequal.

	$\overline{X}$	S	n
Sample 1	75.5	9.3	29
Sample 2	88.2	15.9	25

Solution

Step 1: Determination of probability (P)

1) Formula. $P = 1 - \text{significance level}(\alpha)$, where; $\alpha = 1\% \equiv 0.01$
2) Data substitution and solving

$P = 1 - 0.01$ ....[Solve equation]

$P = \mathbf{0.99}$

Step 2: Determination of degree of freedom (df)

a) Formula. Degree of freedom (df) $= \nu = \dfrac{\left(\frac{S_1^2}{n_1}+\frac{S_2^2}{n_2}\right)^2}{\frac{\left(\frac{S_1^2}{n_1}\right)^2}{n_1-1}+\frac{\left(\frac{S_2^2}{n_2}\right)^2}{n_2-1}}$

Where; $n_1 = 29$, $n_2 = 25$, $S_1^2 = (9.3)^2 = 86.49$ and $S_2^2 = (15.9)^2 = 252.81$

b) Data substitution and solving.

Degree of freedom (df) $= \nu = \dfrac{\left(\frac{86.49}{29}+\frac{252.81}{25}\right)^2}{\frac{\left(\frac{86.49}{29}\right)^2}{29-1}+\frac{\left(\frac{252.81}{25}\right)^2}{25-1}}$ ……[Simplify fractions and brackets]

Degree of freedom (df) $= \nu = \dfrac{(13.09481379)^2}{\frac{(2.982413793)^2}{28}+\frac{(10.1124)^2}{24}}$ ………..………[Work exponents]

Degree of freedom (df) $= \nu = \dfrac{171.4741482}{\frac{8.894792033}{28}+\frac{102.2606338}{24}}$ ……….[Simplify denomination]

Degree of freedom (df) $= \nu = \dfrac{171.4741482}{4.578530886}$ ……………….....………....[Solve equation]

Degree of freedom (df) $= \nu = \mathbf{37}$

Step 3: Determination of critical value

p	0.75	0.90	0.95	0.975	0.99	0.995	0.9975	0.999	0.9995
$\nu = 1$	1.000	3.078	6.314	12.71	31.82	63.66	127.3	318.3	636.6
2	0.816	1.886	2.920	4.303	6.965	9.925	14.09	22.33	31.60
30	0.683	1.310	1.697	2.042	2.457	2.750	3.030	3.385	3.646
40	0.681	1.303	1.684	2.021	2.423	2.704	2.971	3.307	3.551
60	0.679	1.296	1.671	2.000	2.390	2.660	2.915	3.232	3.460
120	0.677	1.289	1.658	1.980	2.358	2.617	2.860	3.160	3.373
∞	0.674	1.282	1.645	1.960	2.326	2.576	2.807	3.090	3.291

Note: The critical value is = $\pm\mathbf{2.423}$

Test Your Understanding

Exercise 20: Calculate the critical value of 5% significance level using the following test type;

1) One tailed test [Left tail]……………….….. **[Answer: Critical Value = -1.645]**
2) Two-tailed test ……………………………**[Answer: Critical Value = ± 1.282]**

Exercise 21: Determine the P-Value of $Z_C = 2.00$ under the following hypothesis testing

1) One-tailed hypothesis testing ………………..….**[Answer: P – Value = 0.0225]**
2) Two-tailed hypothesis testing ……………….**[Answer: P – Value = ± 0.0456]**

Exercise 22: Determine the critical value of $t = -1.25$ using a 1% significance level and a sample size of 10, under the following hypothesis testing condition.

1) Left direction hypothesis testing ....**[Answer: The critical value = -2.821]**
2) Two-tailed hypothesis testing ....**[Answer: The critical value = ± 3.250]**

Exercise 23: Determine the critical value at 5% significance level using information in the table below under the two-tailed hypothesis testing.

	$\bar{X}$	S	n
Sample 1	51.48	11.01	21
Sample 2	41.52	17.15	23

1) Assume the population variances are unequal. ....**[Answer: ± 2.000]**
2) Assume population variances are unequal.......................... **[Answer: ± 2.021]**

7.3.4 Graphical Analysis of Hypothesis Testing

In hypothesis testing, we are going to make use of normal distribution curve. The normal distribution curve utilized here is the symmetric normal distribution curve as illustrated below.

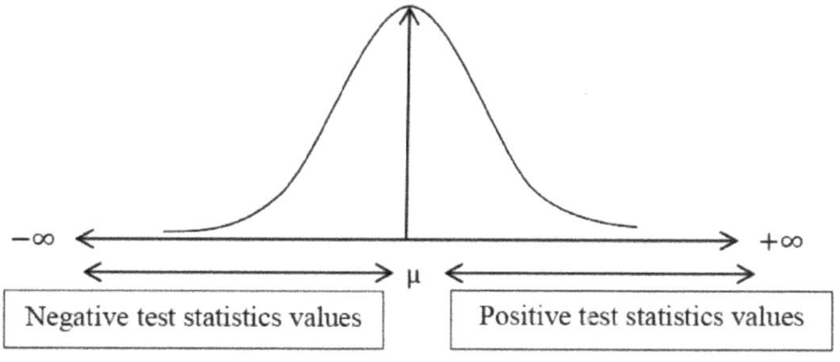

When the critical value is plotted on a symmetric normal distribution curve, it helps distinguish the critical region and the acceptance region. The critical region or rejection region is the area of the curve after the critical value. Considering the notation "C" to be the critical value, the critical region and acceptance region are illustrated below.

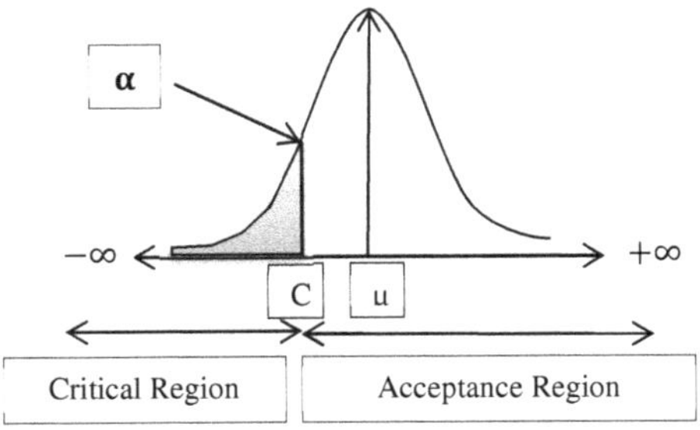

Left Tailed Hypothesis Test

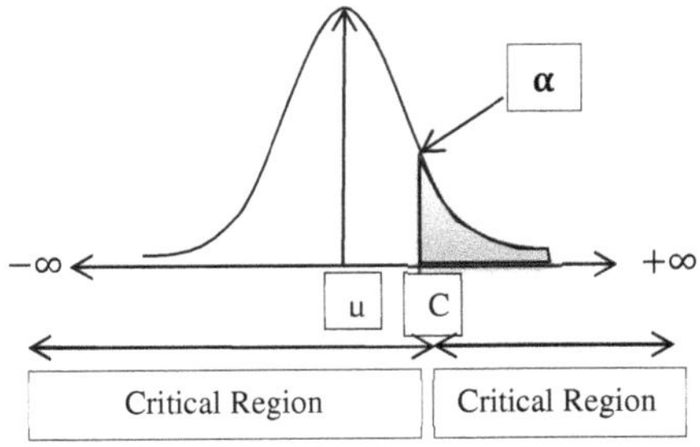

Right Tailed Hypothesis Test

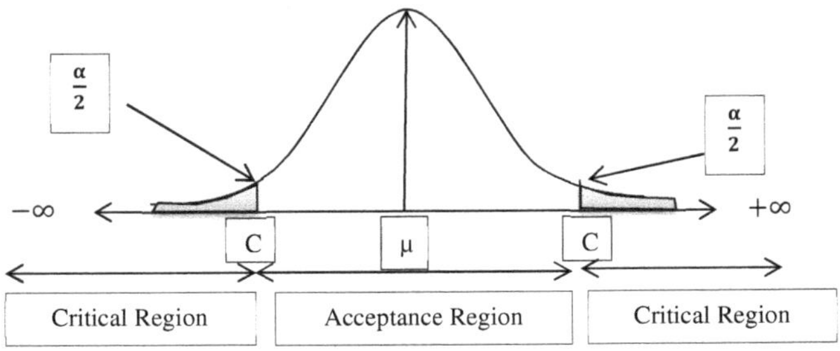

It is worth knowing that the sketch symmetric normal distribution can also be used in decision making and drawing conclusion.

The term "decision making" in hypothesis testing is the process of observing the location of test statistics value on the symmetric normal distribution curve or comparing the test statistics value with it corresponding critical value or comparing the significance level with it corresponding P-value to either reject or not reject the null hypothesis. From a sketch symmetric normal distribution table, decision making is done as follows;

1) Reject the null hypothesis if the statistics test value ($Z -$ value or $t -$ value) is greater (right-directional test) or lower (left-directional test) than the critical value. In other word when the statistics test value is located in the rejection region.
2) Don't reject the null hypothesis if the statistics test value ($Z -$ value or $t -$ value) is lower (right-directional test) or greater (left-directional test) than the critical value. In other word when the statistics test value is located in the rejection region.

The term "conclusion" in hypothesis testing is the process of using both algebraic (test statistics, critical value and P-Value) and graphical (critical and acceptance region) in making valid statement on whether or not there is enough or significant evidences at a given significance level to support the hypothesis claim made.

Application Examples of Hypothesis Test for Population Mean

Example 1: A researcher report that the average monthly salary of salesmen is more than 42,000 fcfa. A sample of 30 salesmen has a mean of 43,260 fcfa. At a significance level ($\alpha = 0.05$) test the researchers claim. The standard deviation of the population of salesmen is 5,230 fcfa.

Work Required

1) Formulate the null and alternative hypothesis
2) Find the critical values
3) Calculate the test statistics
4) Make the decision
5) Draw the conclusion

Solution

Hint: The population mean (μ) and standard deviation (σ) are unknown, the sample size equal 30, only a single sample is used, and the more than is the common phrases. Therefore, we are required to use one-sample right tailed Z-test.

1) Formulate the null and alternative hypothesis

Null hypothesis: $H_0: \mu \leq 42{,}000$

Alternative hypothesis: $H_1: \mu > 42{,}000$

2) Find the critical values

Step 1: Determine the value of P

1) Formula. $P = 1 - \text{significance level}(\alpha)$, where; $\alpha = 0.05 = 5\%$
2) Data substitution and solving

$P = 1 - \text{significance level}(\alpha)$ ……………..………[Substitute formula components value]

$P = 1 - 0.05$ ………………………...……..…..……………………....……..[Solve equation]

$P = \mathbf{0.95}$ ……………………..…………………..……..…..[P value at 5% significance level]

Step 2: Identification of critical value

Critical Values For The Normal Distribution									
P	0.75	0.90	0.95	0.975	0.99	0.995	0.9975	0.999	0.9995
Z	0.674	1.282	1.645	1.960	2.326	2.576	2.807	3.090	3.291
Note: The critical value of 5% significance level is $\mathbf{1.645}$ since it is a right tailed test									

3) **Calculate the test statistics**

Step 1: Formula. $Z = \frac{\bar{X}-\mu}{\sigma/\sqrt{n}}$, where; $\bar{X} = 43{,}260$, $\mu = 42{,}000$, $\sigma = 5{,}230$ and $n = 30$

Step 2: Data substitution and solving

$Z - \text{Statistics} = \frac{43{,}260-42{,}000}{5{,}230/\sqrt{30}}$ ....[Simplify equation]

$Z - \text{Statistics} = \frac{1{,}260}{5{,}230/5.477225575}$ ....[Solve]

$Z - \text{Statistics} = 1.320$...[In three decimal places with corresponding P-Value (0.0934)]

4) **Make the decision**

Hint: We can use the sketch of the acceptance and rejection region as well as the critical or P-value to make decision.

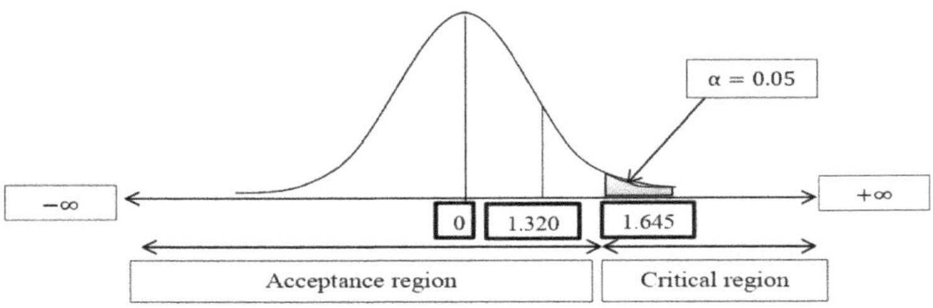

From the graph, the calculated Z-value is located at the acceptance region. Using the critical value (1.645), we realized that it is greater than the calculated Z-value (1.320). Using the P-value, we also realized that the P-value (0.0934) is greater than the significance level (0.05). Therefore, we don't reject the null hypothesis

5) **Draw the conclusion**

Since the null hypothesis ($H_0: \mu \leq 42{,}000$) is not rejected, therefore by default the alternative hypothesis ($H_1: \mu > 42{,}000$) is accepted. Therefore, there is not sufficient or enough statistical evidence at 5% that the population mean mark is greater than 42.000.

Example 2: The average mark of students in a math exam is less than 75 with a standard deviation of 8.1. To verify this claim, a random sample of 100 students we selected and yield a mean of mark of 71. Test the claim at 5% significance level.

Work Required

1) State the hypotheses in symbols
2) Find the critical values
3) Calculate the test statistics

4) Sketch the critical region and acceptance region
5) Make the decision
6) Draw the conclusion

Solution

Hint: The population mean (μ) and standard deviation (σ) are unknown, the sample size is greater than equal 30, only a single sample is used and the common phrases used is "less than". Therefore, we are required to use one-sample left tailed Z-test.

1) State the hypotheses in symbols

Null hypothesis: $H_0: \mu \geq 75$

Alternative hypothesis: $H_1: \mu < 75$

2) Find the critical values

Step 1: Determine the value of P

3) Formula. $P = 1 - \text{significance level}(\alpha)$, where; $\alpha = 5\% \equiv 0.05$
4) Data substitution and solving

$P = 1 - \text{significance level}(\alpha)$ ....[Substitute formula components value]

$P = 1 - 0.05$ ....[Solve equation]

$P = \mathbf{0.95}$

Step 2: Identification of critical value

Critical Values For The Normal Distribution									
P	0.75	0.90	0.95	0.975	0.99	0.995	0.9975	0.999	0.9995
Z	0.674	1.282	1.645	1.960	2.326	2.576	2.807	3.090	3.291
Note: The critical value of 5% significance level is $\mathbf{-1.645}$ since it is a left tailed test									

3) Calculate the test statistics

Step 1: Formula. $Z - \text{Statistics} = \frac{\overline{X}-\mu}{\sigma/\sqrt{n}}$, where; $\overline{X} = 71$, $\mu = 75$, $\sigma = 8.1$ and $n = 100$

Step 2: Data substitution and solving

$Z - \text{Statistics} = \frac{71-75}{8.1/\sqrt{100}}$ ....[Simplify equation]

$Z - \text{Statistics} = \frac{-4}{8.1/10}$ ....[Simplify denominator]

$Z - \text{Statistics} = \frac{-4}{0.81}$ ....[Work fraction]

$Z - \text{Statistics} = \mathbf{-4.938}$ ....[Z-Statistics value]

4) **Sketch the critical region and acceptance region.**

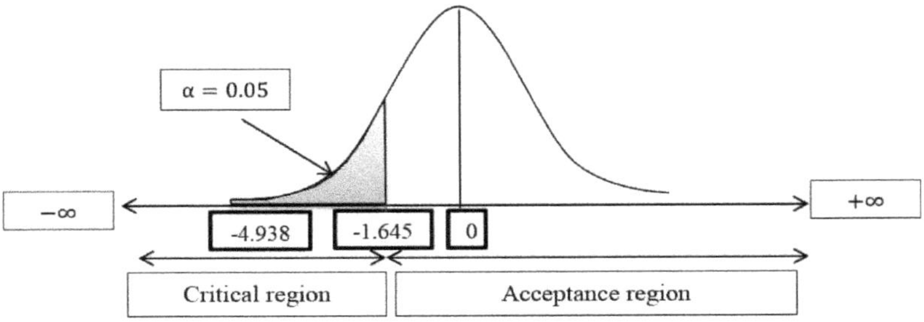

5) **Make the decision**

Comparing the critical value (-1.645) and the calculated Z-value (-4.938) we realize that the calculated value is lower than the critical value ($-4.938 < -1.645$). Secondly, looking at the sketch, we see that the calculated Z-value is located at the critical region. Therefore, the statistical decision is that we reject the null hypothesis (H_0).

6) **Draw the conclusion**

Since the null hypothesis ($H_0: \mu \geq 75$) is rejected, therefore by default the alternative hypothesis ($H_1: \mu < 75$) is accepted. We then conclude that there is sufficient statistical evidence at 5% that the population mean mark is lesser than 75.

Example 3: Use the table below and answer the following questions

	$\overline{X}$	σ	n
Sample 1	22.1	4.8	49
Sample 2	19.8	5.4	44

Work Required

1) State the hypotheses in symbols
2) Find the critical values
3) Calculate the test statistics
4) Sketch the critical region and acceptance region
5) Make the decision
6) Draw the conclusion

Solution

1) **State the hypotheses in symbols**

Null hypothesis: $H_0: \mu_1 = \mu_2$

Alternative hypothesis: $H_1: \mu_1 \neq \mu_2$

2) **Find the critical values**

Step 1: Determine the value of P

1) Formula. $P = 1 - \frac{\text{significance level}(\alpha)}{2}$, where; $\alpha = 5\% \equiv 0.05$
2) Data substitution and solving

$P = 1 - \frac{0.05}{2}$ ……………………………………………………[Solve equation]

$P = \mathbf{0.975}$

Step 2: Identification of critical value

Critical Values For The Normal Distribution									
P	0.75	0.90	0.95	0.975	0.99	0.995	0.9975	0.999	0.9995
Z	0.674	1.282	1.645	1.960	2.326	2.576	2.807	3.090	3.291
Note: The critical value of 5% significance level is ± 1.960 since it is a two tailed test									

3) **Calculate the test statistics**

Step 1: Formula. $Z = \frac{(\bar{X}_1 - \bar{X}_2) - (\mu_1 - \mu_2)}{\sqrt{\frac{\sigma_1{}^2}{n_1} + \frac{\sigma_2{}^2}{n_2}}}$

Where; $n_1 = 49$, $n_2 = 44$, $\bar{X}_1 = 22.1$, $\bar{X}_2 = 19.8$, $\sigma^2{}_1 = (4.8)^2$ and $\sigma^2{}_2 = (5.4)^2$

Step 2: Data substitution and solving

$Z = \frac{(22.1-19.8)-(0-0)}{\sqrt{\frac{(4.8)^2}{49} + \frac{(5.4)^2}{44}}}$ …………[Work denominator exponent and simplify root fractions]

$Z = \frac{(22.1-19.8)-(0-0)}{\sqrt{1.132931354}}$ …………[Simplify numerator bracket and work denominator root]

$Z = \frac{2.3}{1.064392481}$ ……………………………………………………[Solve equation]

$Z = \pm\mathbf{2.161}$ …………[In three decimal places with corresponding p-value (± 0.0154)]

4) **Sketch the critical region and acceptance region**

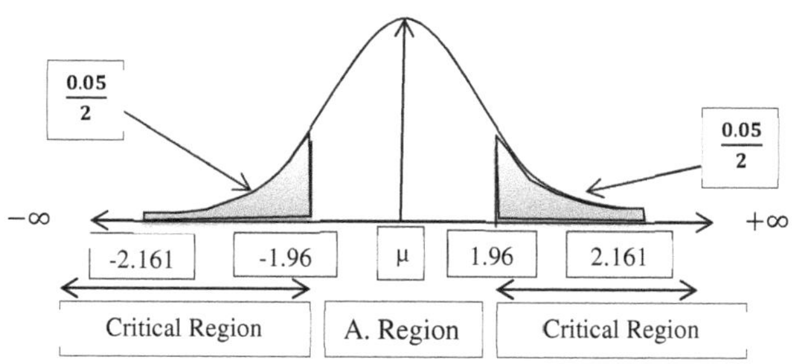

5) **Make the decision**

From the graph, the calculated Z-value (± 2.161) is found in the rejection region, that is after (± 1.960). Using the P- value approach, we see that the P- value (± 0.0154) is less than the significance level (± 0.025). Therefore, we reject the null hypothesis (H_0).

6) **Draw the conclusion**

Since the null hypothesis ($H_0: \mu_1 = \mu_2$) is rejected, therefore by default the alternative hypothesis ($H_1: \mu_1 \neq \mu_2$) is accepted. Therefore, we conclude that there is not enough evidence at 5% significance level that the population means are equal.

Example 4: Assume the population variance is equal; perform a two-tailed hypothesis test using the information in the table below at 1% significance level

	$\bar{X}$	S	n
Sample 1	85.3	2.4	18
Sample 2	95.3	3.1	17

Work Required

1) State the hypotheses in symbols
2) Calculate the test statistics
3) Sketch the critical region and acceptance region
4) Make the decision
5) Draw the conclusion

Solution

1) **State the hypotheses in symbols**

Null hypothesis: $H_0: \mu_1 = \mu_2$

Alternative hypothesis: $H_1: \mu_1 \neq \mu_2$

2) **Calculate the test statistics**

Step 1: Formula. $T = \frac{(\bar{X}_1-\bar{X}_2)-(\mu_1-\mu_2)}{S\left[\sqrt{\left(\frac{1}{n_1}+\frac{1}{n_2}\right)}\right]}$, where; $\bar{X}_1 = 85.6, \bar{X}_2 = 95.3, n_1 = 18, n_2 = 17, S^2 = ?$

Step 2: Determination of S^2

a) Formula. $S^2 = \frac{(n_1-1){S_1}^2+(n_2-1){S_2}^2}{(n_1+n_2-2)}$, where; $n_1 = 18, n_2 = 17, {S_1}^2 = 5.76, {S_2}^2 = 9.61.$

b) Data substitution and solving

$S^2 = \frac{(18-1)5.76+(17-1)9.61}{(18+17-2)}$ ....[Simplify brackets]

$S^2 = \frac{(17)5.76+(16)9.61}{(18+17-2)}$ ....[Open brackets]

$S^2 = \frac{97.92+153.76}{33}$ ....[Solve equation]

$S^2 = \mathbf{7.6267}$ ....[In four decimal places]

Step 3: Data substitution and solving [$S^2 = 7.6267 \therefore S = 2.761648059$]

$t - \text{statistics}(T) = \frac{(85.6-95.3)-(0-0)}{2.761648059\left[\sqrt{\frac{1}{18}+\frac{1}{17}}\right]}$ .....[Simplify denominator fractions and work root]

$t - \text{statistics}(T) = \frac{(85.6-95.3)-(0-0)}{2.761648059[0.33819977]}$ ....[Simplify brackets]

$t - \text{statistics}(T) = \frac{-9.7}{0.93398874}$ ....[Solve equation]

$t - \text{statistics}(T) = \mathbf{-10.3856}$ ....[In four decimal places]

Note: Degree of freedom (df) $= \nu = n_1 + n_2 - 2 \rightarrow \boldsymbol{\nu = 33}$

3) Sketch the critical region and acceptance region

Step 1: Determination of probability value (P)

1) Formula. $P = 1 - \frac{\text{significance level}(\alpha)}{2}$, where; $\alpha = 1\% \equiv 0.01$
2) Data substitution and solving

$P = 1 - \frac{0.01}{2}$ ....[Solve equation]

$P = \mathbf{0.995}$

Step 2: Determination of critical value

p	0.75	0.90	0.95	0.975	0.99	0.995	0.9975	0.999	0.9995
ν = 1	1.000	3.078	6.314	12.71	31.82	63.66	127.3	318.3	636.6
2	0.816	1.886	2.920	4.303	6.965	9.925	14.09	22.33	31.60
30	0.683	1.310	1.697	2.042	2.457	2.750	3.030	3.385	3.646
40	0.681	1.303	1.684	2.021	2.423	2.704	2.971	3.307	3.551
60	0.679	1.296	1.671	2.000	2.390	2.660	2.915	3.232	3.460
120	0.677	1.289	1.658	1.980	2.358	2.617	2.860	3.160	3.373
∞	0.674	1.282	1.645	1.960	2.326	2.576	2.807	3.090	3.291

Note: The critical value at 1% level of significance is $\pm\mathbf{2.704}$ since it is a two tailed test

Step 3: Sketching of the critical and acceptance regions

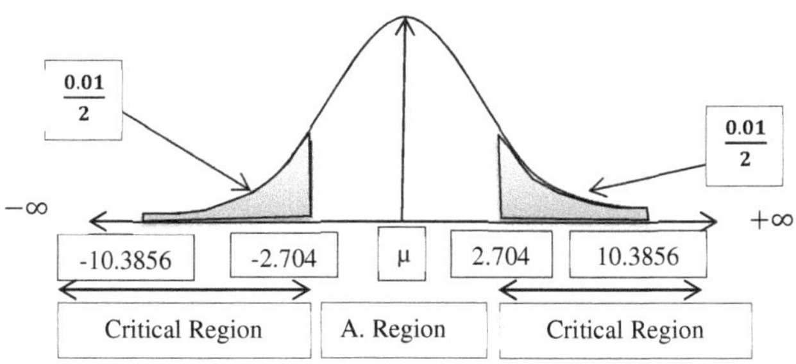

4) Make the decision

From the graph, the calculated t-value (± 10.3856) is located at the rejection region. Using the critical value approach, we see that the calculated t-value is less than the critical value (left tailed) and greater than the critical value (right tailed). Therefore, we reject the null hypothesis (H_0).

5) Draw the conclusion

Since the null hypothesis ($H_0: \mu_1 = \mu_2$) is rejected, therefore by default the alternative hypothesis ($H_1: \mu_1 \neq \mu_2$) is accepted. Therefore, there is insufficient evidence at 1% significance level that the population means are different.

Example 5: A researcher wanted to test whether or not the mean salary of male nurses was significantly different from the average salary of female nurses. Two independent samples of 7 male nurses and 9 female nurses were randomly selected and information provided in the table below.

Male nurses	1,340	1,500	1,430	1,440	1,380	1,470	1,290		
Female nurses	1,540	1,480	1,390	1,450	1,440	1,350	1,520	1,400	1,600

Assume the population variances are unequal and the populations are independent and normally distributed, test at 10% significance level whether or not there is a significance difference in the mean salaries between male nurses and female nurses.

<u>**Solution**</u>

Step 1: Formulation of the null hypothesis and alternative hypothesis

Null hypothesis: $H_0: \mu_1 = \mu_2$

Alternative hypothesis: $H_1: \mu_1 \neq \mu_2$

Step 2: Determination of needed components numerical values

Males Nurses		Female Nurses	
X	$(\mathrm{X}-\bar{\mathrm{X}})^2$	X	$(\mathrm{X}-\bar{\mathrm{X}})^2$
1,340	$(1{,}340-1{,}407.14)^2=4{,}507.78$	1,540	$(1{,}540-1{,}463.33)^2=5{,}878.29$
1,500	$(1{,}500-1{,}407.14)^2=8{,}622.98$	1,480	$(1{,}480-1{,}463.33)^2=277.89$
1,430	$(1{,}430-1{,}407.14)^2=522.58$	1,390	$(1{,}390-1{,}463.33)^2=5{,}377.29$
1,440	$(1{,}440-1{,}407.14)^2=1{,}079.78$	1,450	$(1{,}450-1{,}463.33)^2=177{,}69$
1,380	$(1{,}380-1{,}407.14)^2=736.58$	1,440	$(1{,}440-1{,}463.33)^2=544.29$
1,470	$(1{,}470-1{,}407.14)^2=3{,}951.38$	1,350	$(1{,}350-1{,}463.33)^2=12{,}843.69$
1,290	$(1{,}290-1{,}407.14)^2=13{,}721.78$	1,520	$(1{,}520-1{,}463.33)^2=3{,}211.49$
$\sum=9{,}850$	$\sum=33{,}142.86$	1,400	$(1{,}400-1{,}463.33)^2=4{,}010.69$
$\bar{\mathrm{X}}_1=1{,}407.14$		1,600	$(1{,}600-1{,}463.33)^2=18{,}678.69$
$\mathrm{S^2}_1=\frac{33{,}142.86}{7-1}=5{,}523.81$		$\sum=13{,}170$	$\sum=51{,}000.01$
$\mathrm{S}_1=\sqrt{5{,}523.81}=74.322$		$\bar{X}_2=1{,}463.33$	$\mathrm{S^2}_2=\frac{51{,}000.01}{9-1}=6{,}375.00$
		$\mathrm{S}_2=\sqrt{6{,}375.00}=79.844$	

Step 3: Determination of test statistics

Step 1: Formula. $\mathrm{T}=\frac{(\bar{\mathrm{X}}_1-\bar{\mathrm{X}}_2)-(\mu_1-\mu_2)}{\sqrt{\frac{\mathrm{S^2}_1}{\mathrm{n}_1}+\frac{\mathrm{S^2}_2}{\mathrm{n}_2}}}$, where; $\bar{\mathrm{X}}_1=1{,}407.14$, $\bar{\mathrm{X}}_2=1{,}463.33$, $\mathrm{n}_1=7$, $\mathrm{n}_2=9$, $\mathrm{S}_1{}^2=5{,}523.81$ and $\mathrm{S}_2{}^2=6{,}375.00$.

Step 2: Data substitution and solving

$$\mathrm{t-statistics(T)}=\frac{(1{,}407.14-1{,}463.33)-(0-0)}{\sqrt{\frac{5{,}523.81}{7}+\frac{6{,}375.00}{9}}}$$ ....[Simplify fractions and simplify]

$$\mathrm{t-statistics(T)}=\frac{(1{,}407.14-1{,}463.33)-(0-0)}{\sqrt{1{,}497.449048}}$$ ....[Simplify brackets and work root]

$$\mathrm{t-statistics(T)}=\frac{-56.19}{38.69688679}$$ ....[Solve equation]

$$\mathrm{t-statistics(T)}=\pm\mathbf{1.4520}$$ ....[In four decimal places]

Step 3: Determination of degree of freedom (df) and critical value

a) Formula. $\mathrm{df}=\nu=\frac{\left(\frac{\mathrm{S}_1{}^2}{\mathrm{n}_1}+\frac{\mathrm{S}_2{}^2}{\mathrm{n}_2}\right)^2}{\frac{\left(\frac{\mathrm{S}_1{}^2}{\mathrm{n}_1}\right)^2}{\mathrm{n}_1-1}+\frac{\left(\frac{\mathrm{S}_2{}^2}{\mathrm{n}_2}\right)^2}{\mathrm{n}_2-1}}$

Where; $\mathrm{n}_1=7$, $\mathrm{n}_2=9$, $\mathrm{S}_1{}^2=5{,}523.81$, $\mathrm{S}_2{}^2=6{,}375.00$.

b) Data substitution and solving

$$\text{Degree of freedom (df)} = \nu = \frac{\left(\frac{5{,}523.81}{7}+\frac{6{,}375.00}{9}\right)^2}{\frac{\left(\frac{5{,}523.81}{7}\right)^2}{7-1}+\frac{\left(\frac{6{,}375.00}{9}\right)^2}{9-1}} \text{ ....[Simplify fractions]}$$

$$\text{Degree of freedom (df)} = \nu = \frac{(1{,}497.449048)^2}{\frac{(789.1157143)^2}{6}+\frac{(708.3333333)^2}{8}} \text{ ....[Work exponents]}$$

$$\text{Degree of freedom (df)} = \nu = \frac{2{,}242{,}353.65}{\frac{622{,}703.6106}{6}+\frac{501{,}736.1111}{8}} \text{ ....[Simplify denominator]}$$

$$\text{Degree of freedom (df)} = \nu = \frac{2{,}242{,}353.65}{166{,}500.949} \text{ ....[Solve equation]}$$

$$\text{Degree of freedom (df)} = \nu = \mathbf{13}$$

Step 4: Determination of critical value

a) Determine the value of P

1) Formula. $P = 1 - \frac{\text{significance level}(\alpha)}{2}$, where; $\alpha = 10\% = 0.1$

2) Data substitution and solving

$P = 1 - \frac{0.1}{2}$ ....[Solve equation]

$P = \mathbf{0.95}$

b) Derivation of critical value

p	0.75	0.90	0.95	0.975	0.99	0.995	0.9975	0.999	0.9995
$\nu = 1$	1.000	3.078	6.314	12.71	31.82	63.66	127.3	318.3	636.6
2	0.816	1.886	2.920	4.303	6.965	9.925	14.09	22.33	31.60
10	0.700	1.372	1.812	2.228	2.764	3.169	3.581	4.144	4.587
11	0.697	1.363	1.796	2.201	2.718	3.106	3.497	4.025	4.437
12	0.695	1.356	1.782	2.179	2.681	3.055	3.428	3.930	4.318
→ 13	0.694	1.350	1.771	2.160	2.650	3.012	3.372	3.852	4.221
14	0.692	1.345	1.761	2.145	2.624	2.977	3.326	3.787	4.140

Note: The critical value $= \pm\mathbf{1.771}$

Step 5: Drawing of critical region and acceptance region

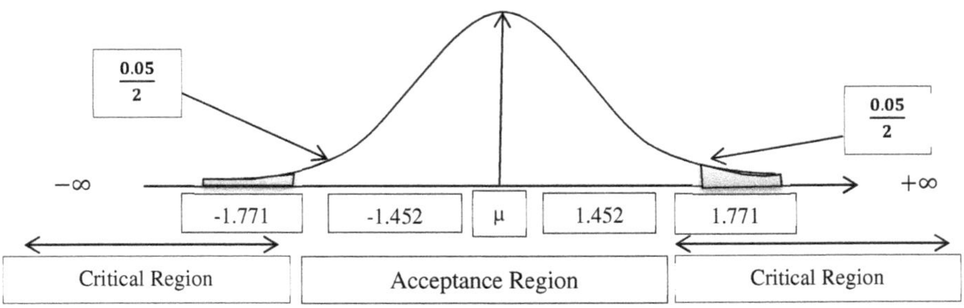

Step 5: Decision making

From the graph, the calculated t-value (± 1.452) is found in the acceptance region, that is before the critical value (± 1.771). Therefore, we don't reject the null hypothesis (H_0).

Step 6: Drawing of conclusion

Since the null hypothesis ($H_0: \mu_1 = \mu_2$) is not rejected, therefore by default the alternative hypothesis ($H_1: \mu_1 \neq \mu_2$) is not accepted. Therefore, we conclude that there is not enough evidence at 5% significance level that the population means different equal.

7.3.5 Confidence Interval and Hypothesis Testing

The concept of confidence interval and hypothesis testing shares the ability of making statistical decision. That is we are use the concept of confidence interval and hypothesis testing in deciding whether we are to reject or not reject the null hypothesis. Since confidence interval is a symmetric concept, we are going to compare it with hypothesis testing in situation of two-tailed directional test. The general rules of rejecting or not rejecting the null hypothesis using the confidence interval are;

1) Reject the null hypothesis when the confidence interval does not contain the hypothesized population mean (one-sample situation) or when the confidence interval does not contain the value zero (two-sample situation).
2) Don't reject the null hypothesis when the confidence interval contains the hypothesized population mean (one-sample situation) or when the confidence interval contains the value zero (two-sample situation).

a) When Population Variance(s) is known

The idea of confidence interval with one sample is already seen under the concept of confidence interval. In situation of two-samples, the formula for confidence interval is derived as seen below.

$$-Z_{\alpha/2} < Z < Z_{\alpha/2} \text{ ....[Substitute the formula for Z]}$$

$$-Z_{\alpha/2} < \frac{(\bar{X}_1 - \bar{X}_2) - (\mu_1 - \mu_2)}{\sqrt{\frac{\sigma_1^2}{n_1} + \frac{\sigma_2^2}{n_2}}} < Z_{\alpha/2} \text{ ....[Multiply both sides by denominator]}$$

$$-Z_{\alpha/2}\sqrt{\frac{\sigma_1^2}{n_1} + \frac{\sigma_2^2}{n_2}} < (\bar{X}_1 - \bar{X}_2) - (\mu_1 - \mu_2) < Z_{\alpha/2}\sqrt{\frac{\sigma_1^2}{n_1} + \frac{\sigma_2^2}{n_2}} \text{ ....[Subtract } (\bar{X}_1 - \bar{X}_2)\text{]}$$

$$-(\bar{X}_1 - \bar{X}_2) - Z_{\alpha/2}\sqrt{\frac{\sigma_1^2}{n_1} + \frac{\sigma_2^2}{n_2}} < -(\mu_1 - \mu_2) < -(\bar{X}_1 - \bar{X}_2) + Z_{\alpha/2}\sqrt{\frac{\sigma_1^2}{n_1} + \frac{\sigma_2^2}{n_2}}.$$

$$(\bar{X}_1 - \bar{X}_2) + Z_{\alpha/2}\sqrt{\frac{\sigma_1^2}{n_1} + \frac{\sigma_2^2}{n_2}} > (\mu_1 - \mu_2) > (\bar{X}_1 - \bar{X}_2) - Z_{\alpha/2}\sqrt{\frac{\sigma_1^2}{n_1} + \frac{\sigma_2^2}{n_2}}$$

$$CI = (\overline{X}_1 - \overline{X}_2) - Z_{\alpha/2}\sqrt{\frac{\sigma_1{}^2}{n_1} + \frac{\sigma_2{}^2}{n_2}} < (\mu_1 - \mu_2) < (\overline{X}_1 - \overline{X}_2) + Z_{\alpha/2}\sqrt{\frac{\sigma_1{}^2}{n_1} + \frac{\sigma_2{}^2}{n_2}}$$

Example 1: Perform a confidence interval test and hypothesis testing (test statistics) using the following data; $\mu = 4.0$, $n = 9$, $\overline{X} = 4.6$ and $\sigma = 1.0$. Assume a two-tailed test principle and a 99% confidence level.

Solution

1) **Confidence Interval Test**

Step 1: Formula. Confidence Interval $= \overline{X} - Z_{\alpha/2}\left(\frac{\sigma}{\sqrt{n}}\right) < \mu < \overline{X} + Z_{\alpha/2}\left(\frac{\sigma}{\sqrt{n}}\right)$

Where; $\overline{X} = 4.6$, $\sigma = 1.0$, $n = 9$, $Z_{\alpha/2} = 2.576$

Step 2: Data substitution and solving

$CI = 4.6 - 2.576\left(\frac{1.0}{\sqrt{9}}\right) < \mu < 4.6 + 2.576\left(\frac{1.0}{\sqrt{9}}\right)$ ....[Simplify brackets]

$CI = 4.6 - 2.576(0.333333333) < \mu < 4.6 + 2.576(0.333333333)$.[Expand brackets]

$CI = 4.6 - 0.858666666 < \mu < 4.6 + 0.858666666$ ....[Work out confidence limits]

Confidence Interval $= \mathbf{3.7 < \mu < 5.5}$ ....[In one decimal places]

Step 3: Decision Making: The population mean (μ) is 4.0 is within the confidence interval. Therefore, we don't reject the null hypothesis.

2) **Hypothesis Testing [Test Statistics]**

Step 1: Formula. $Z = \frac{\overline{X} - \mu}{\sigma/\sqrt{n}}$

Where; $\overline{X} = 4.6$, $\mu = 4.0$, $\sigma = 1.0$, $n = 9$ and critical value (± 2.576)

Step 2: Data substitution and solving

$Z - \text{Statistics} = \frac{4.6-4.0}{1.0/\sqrt{9}}$ ....[Work root and simplify denominator fraction]

$Z - \text{Statistics} = \frac{4.6-4.0}{0.333333333}$ ....[Simplify numerator]

$Z - \text{Statistics} = \frac{0.6}{0.333333333}$ ....[Solve equation]

$Z - \text{Statistics} = \pm\mathbf{1.8}$

Step 3: Decision Making. The Z-statistics value (± 1.8) is less than greater than the critical value (± 2.578) indicating that the Z-statistics value is located at the acceptable region. We don't reject the null hypothesis.

Example 2: Determine the confidence interval and perform a hypothesis test using a 5% significance level and applying a two-tailed test principle. Assume that the population variances are unequal.

Sample One			Sample Two		
$n = 9$	$\overline{X} = 1.2$	$\sigma = 1$	$n = 16$	$\overline{X} = 1.7$	$\sigma = 2$

Solution

1) **Confidence Interval**

Step 1: Formula. $CI = (\overline{X}_1 - \overline{X}_2) - Z_{\alpha/2}\sqrt{\frac{\sigma_1{}^2}{n_1} + \frac{\sigma_2{}^2}{n_2}} < (\mu_1 - \mu_2) < (\overline{X}_1 - \overline{X}_2) + Z_{\alpha/2}\sqrt{\frac{\sigma_1{}^2}{n_1} + \frac{\sigma_2{}^2}{n_2}}$

Where; $n_1 = 9$, $n_2 = 16$, $\overline{X}_1 = 1.2$, $\overline{X}_2 = 1.7$, $\sigma_1{}^2 = (1)^2 = 1$, $\sigma_2{}^2 = (2)^2 = 4$ and $Z_{\alpha/2} = 1.960$

Step 2: Data substitution and solving

$CI = (1.2 - 1.7) - (1.960)\sqrt{\frac{1}{9} + \frac{4}{16}} < (\mu_1 - \mu_2) < (1.2 - 1.7) + (1.960)\sqrt{\frac{1}{9} + \frac{4}{16}}$

$CI = (-0.5) - (1.960)\sqrt{0.361111111} < (\mu_1 - \mu_2) < (-0.5) + (1.960)\sqrt{0.361111111}$

$CI = (-0.5) - (1.960)(0.600925212) < (\mu_1 - \mu_2) < (-0.5) + (1.960)(0.600925212)$

$CI = -0.5 - 1.177813417 < (\mu_1 - \mu_2) < -0.5 + 1.177813417$

Confidence Interval $= \mathbf{-1.678 < (\mu_1 - \mu_2) < 0.678}$ ……[In three decimal places]

Step 3: Decision Making: The difference of the population means $(\mu_1 - \mu_2)$ is 0 and is within the confidence interval. Therefore, we don't reject the null hypothesis.

2) Hypothesis testing

Step 1: Formula. $Z - \text{Statistics} = \frac{(\overline{X}_1 - \overline{X}_2) - (\mu_1 - \mu_2)}{\sqrt{\frac{\sigma_1{}^2}{n_1} + \frac{\sigma_2{}^2}{n_2}}}$

Where; $n_1 = 9$, $n_2 = 16$, $\overline{X}_1 = 1.2$, $\overline{X}_2 = 1.7$, $\sigma_1{}^2 = (1)^2 = 1$, $\sigma_2{}^2 = (2)^2 = 4$ and $Z_{\alpha/2} = 1.960$

Step 2: Data substitution and solving

$Z - \text{Statistics} = \frac{(1.2 - 1.7) - (0 - 0)}{\sqrt{\frac{1}{9} + \frac{4}{16}}}$ ………………….....[Simplify numerator and denominator]

$Z - \text{Statistics} = \frac{-0.5 - 0}{\sqrt{0.361111111}}$ ……………………………………[Work denominator root]

$Z - \text{Statistics} = \frac{-0.5}{0.600925212}$ …………………………………………[Solve equation]

$Z - \text{Statistics} = \pm\mathbf{0.832}$ ……………………………………[In three decimal places]

Step 3: Decision Making. The Z-statistics is less than (± 0.832) is less than the critical value(± 1.960), indicating that it is located in the acceptable region. We don't reject the null hypothesis.

Test Your Understanding

Exercise 24: Perform a confidence interval test and hypothesis testing (test statistics) using the following data;$\mu = 600$, $n = 20$, $\overline{X} = 641$ and $\sigma = 100$. Assume a two-tailed test principle and a 10% significance level.

[Answer: $(\text{Confidence Interval} = 604.217 < \mu < 677.783)$ and $(Z - \text{Statistics} = \pm 1.834$ and $\text{Critical Value} = 1.645)$]. We reject the null hypothesis.

Exercise 25: Determine the confidence interval and perform a hypothesis test using a 5% significance level and applying a two-tailed test principle. Assume that the population variances are unequal.

Sample One			Sample Two		
$n = 10$	$\overline{X} = 203$	$\sigma = 3$	$n = 15$	$\overline{X} = 206$	$\sigma = 5$

[Answer: $(Cl = -6.140, < (\mu_1 - \mu_2) < 0.140)$ and $(Z = \pm 1.873$ and $\text{Critical Value} = 1.960)$]. We don't reject the null hypothesis.

b) When Population Variance(s) is Unknown

When dealing with unknown population variance or variances, the formula for confidence interval with two-sample vary. This variation is due to the implication of degree of freedom. The derivation of confidence interval formula in this situation is similar to the situation of known variances seen above. The confidence interval formula for two-sample in situation of heterogeneous (equation 1) and homogenous (equation 2) population variances is given as seen below;

$$CI = (\overline{X}_1 - \overline{X}_2) - (t_{df:\,\alpha/2})\sqrt{\frac{S_1^2}{n_1} + \frac{S_2^2}{n_2}} < (\mu_1 - \mu_2) < (\overline{X}_1 - \overline{X}_2) + (t_{df:\,\alpha/2})\sqrt{\frac{S_1^2}{n_1} + \frac{S_2^2}{n_2}} \quad .....(1)$$

$$CI = (\overline{X}_1 - \overline{X}_2) - (t_{df:\,\alpha/2})S\sqrt{\frac{1}{n_1} + \frac{1}{n_2}} < (\mu_1 - \mu_2) < (\overline{X}_1 - \overline{X}_2) + (t_{df:\,\alpha/2})S\sqrt{\frac{1}{n_1} + \frac{1}{n_2}} \quad .....(2)$$

Example 1: Duracell manufactures batteries that the CEO claims will last an average of 300 hours under normal use. A researcher randomly selected 20 batteries from the production line and tested these batteries. The tested batteries had a mean life span of 270 hours with a standard deviation of 50 hours. Using a 5% significance level, do we have enough evidence to suggest that the claim of an average lifetime of 300 hours is false? Apply any of the following technique

1) Confidence interval
2) Hypothesis testing method [Perform only the test statistics]

Solution

Hint: The question is a two tailed single and two sample problem. Since the population variances are unknown and unequal, the t-test of unequal variance is the appropriate test to perform.

1) **Confidence interval**

Step 1: Formula. Confidence Interval $= \overline{X} - \frac{S}{\sqrt{n}} t_{n-1:\alpha/2} < \mu < \overline{X} + \frac{S}{\sqrt{n}} t_{n-1:\alpha/2}$

Where; $\overline{X} = 270$, $S = 50$, $n = 20$ and $t_{n-1:\alpha/2} = 2.093$ [Since $5\% \alpha \cong 95\%$ Confidence level]

Step 2: Data substitution and solving

$CI = 270 - \frac{50}{\sqrt{20}}(2.093) < \mu < 270 + \frac{50}{\sqrt{20}}(2.093)$ ....[Work roots]

$CI = 270 - \frac{50}{4.472135955}(2.093) < \mu < 270 + \frac{50}{4.472135955}(2.093)$ ....[Simplify fraction]

$CI = 270 - 11.18033989(2.093) < \mu < 270 + 11.18033989(2.093)$

Confidence Interval $= \mathbf{246.510 < \mu < 293.400}$ ....[In three decimal places]

Step 3: Decision Making: The population mean (μ) is 300 is above the upper confidence limit. That is the population mean is not within the confidence interval. Therefore, we reject the null hypothesis.

2) **Hypothesis testing method [Perform only the test statistics]**

Step 1: Formula. $T = \frac{\overline{X} - \mu}{S/\sqrt{n}}$, where; $\overline{X} = 207$, $\mu = 300$, $S = 50$ and $n = 20$, critical value (± 2.093)

Step 2: Data substitution and solving

$t - \text{statistics} = \frac{207-300}{50/\sqrt{20}}$ ....[Work root and simplify denominator]

$t - \text{statistics} = \frac{207-300}{11.18033989}$ ....[Simplify numerator]

$t - \text{statistics} = \frac{-93}{11.18033989}$ ....[Solve equation]

$t - \text{statistics} = \mathbf{\pm 8.318}$ ....[In three decimal places]

Step 3: Decision Making. The t-statistics value (± 8.318) is greater than the critical value (± 2.093) indicating that the t-statistics value is located at the rejection region. We reject the null hypothesis.

Example 2: A researcher claims that the mean amount of time boys and girls ages t through 11 spend playing each day is the same. An experiment is done; data is collected, resulting in the table below:

	Sample size (n)	Sample mean ($\bar{X}$)	Sample standard deviation (S)
Girls	9	2 hour	$\sqrt{0.75}$
Boys	16	3.2 hours	1.00

Is there a difference in the average amount of time boys and girls ages 7 through 11 spend to play each day? Assume a 0.05 significance level, answer the question using;

1) Confidence interval
2) Hypothesis testing [Test statistics]

Solution

Hint: The question is a two-tailed and two sample problem. We are required to apply the t-statistics since the population variance is unknown and unequal.

1) **Confidence Interval**

Step 1:Formula. $CI = (\bar{X}_1 - \bar{X}_2) - (t_{df:\alpha/2})\sqrt{\frac{S_1^2}{n_1} + \frac{S_2^2}{n_2}} < (\mu_1 - \mu_2) < (\bar{X}_1 - \bar{X}_2) + (t_{df:\alpha/2})\sqrt{\frac{S_1^2}{n_1} + \frac{S_2^2}{n_2}}$

Where; $\bar{X}_1 = 2$, $\bar{X}_2 = 3.2$, $n_1 = 9$, $n_2 = 16$, $S_1^2 = (\sqrt{0.75})^2 = 0.75$, $S_2^2 = (1)^2 = 1$, $df = (\nu) = 19$ and Critical value $= 2.093$

Step 2: Data substitution and solving

$$CI = (2 - 3.2) - (2.093)\sqrt{\frac{0.75}{9} + \frac{1}{16}} < (\mu_1 - \mu_2) < (2 - 3.2) + t_{n-1\alpha/2}\sqrt{\frac{0.75}{9} + \frac{1}{16}}$$

$$CI = (-1.2) - (2.093)\sqrt{0.145833333} < (\mu_1 - \mu_2) < (-1.2) + (2.093)\sqrt{0.145833333}$$

$$CI = (-1.2) - (2.093)(0.381881307) < (\mu_1 - \mu_2) < (-1.2) + (2.093)(0.381881307)$$

$$CI = -1.2 - 0.799277577 < (\mu_1 - \mu_2) < 1.2 + 0.799277577$$

Confidence Interval $= \mathbf{-1.999 < (\mu_1 - \mu_2) < -0.400}$ ....[In three decimal places]

Step 3: Decision Making: The difference of the population means ($\mu_1 - \mu_2$) is 0 and is not within the confidence interval. Therefore, we reject the null hypothesis.

2) **Hypothesis testing [Test statistics].** Let girls be denoted by 1 and boys denoted by 3

Step 1: Formula. $\text{t} - \text{Statistics} = \frac{(\bar{X}_1-\bar{X}_2)-(\mu_1-\mu_2)}{\sqrt{\frac{S^2{}_1}{n_1}+\frac{S^2{}_2}{n_2}}}$,

Where; $\bar{X}_1 = 2, \bar{X}_2 = 3.2, n_1 = 9, n_2 = 16, S_1{}^2 = \left(\sqrt{0.75}\right)^2 = 0.75,\ S_2{}^2 = (1)^2 = 1,$

$\text{df} = (\nu) = 19$ and $\text{Critical value} = 2.093$

Step 2: Data substitution and solving

$\text{t} - \text{Statistics} = \frac{(2-3.2)-(0-0)}{\sqrt{\frac{0.75}{9}+\frac{1}{16}}}$ ....[Simplify denominator fractions]

$\text{t} - \text{Statistics} = \frac{(2-3.2)-(0-0)}{\sqrt{0.083333333+0.0625}}$ ....[Simplify numerator and denominator]

$\text{t} - \text{Statistics} = \frac{-1.2}{\sqrt{0.145833333}}$ ....[Work denominator root and solve equation]

$\text{t} - \text{Statistics} = \pm\mathbf{3.142}$ ....[In three decimal places]

Step 3: Decision Making. The t-statistics value (±3.142) is greater than the critical value(±2.093) indicating that the t-statistics value is located at the rejection region. We reject the null hypothesis.

Test Your Understanding

Exercise 26: Perform a confidence interval test and hypothesis testing (test statistics) using the following data;$\mu = 5,\ n = 5,\ \bar{X} = 3.871$ and $S = 0.679$. Assume a two-tailed test principle and a 1% significance level.

[Answer: ($\textbf{Confidence Interval} = \mathbf{2.473} < \mu < \mathbf{5.270}$) and ($\textbf{t} - \textbf{Statistics} = \pm\mathbf{3.718}$ and $\textbf{Critical Value} = \mathbf{4.604}$)]. We don't reject the null hypothesis.

Exercise 27: Determine the confidence interval and perform a hypothesis test using a 5% significance level and applying a two-tailed test principle. Assume that the population variances are equal.

Sample One			Sample Two		
$n = 42$	$\bar{X} = 5.9$	$S^2 = 16.81$	$n = 47$	$\bar{X} = 4.1$	$S^2 = 13.69$

[Answer: ($\textbf{Confidence Interval} = \mathbf{0.153} < (\mu_1 - \mu_2) < \mathbf{3.447}$) and ($\textbf{t} - \textbf{Statistics} = \pm\mathbf{2.177}$ and $\textbf{Critical Value} = \pm\mathbf{1.980}$)]. We reject the null hypothesis.

7.4 Hypothesis Testing of Population Proportion

Hypothesis test when dealing with population proportion follows the same steps as when dealing with population mean. The main difference is found in hypothesis formulation (μ changed to P) and determination of test statistics. The summary of hypothesis formulation under one and two population proportion is given in the table below.

	One Sample Hypothesis Testing				Two Samples Hypothesis Testing		
	Alternative Hypothesis	Null Hypothesis			Alternative Hypothesis	Null Hypothesis	
2-Tailed	$H_1: P \neq P_0$	$H_0: P = P_0$	$H_0: P = P_0$		$H_1: P_1 \neq P_2$	$H_0: P_1 = P_2$	$H_0: P_1 = P_2$
1-Tailed	$H_1: P > P_0$	$H_0: P \leq P_0$	$H_0: P = P_0$		$H_1: P_1 > P_2$	$H_0: P_1 \leq P_2$	$H_0: P_1 = P_2$
1-Tailed	$H_1: P < P_0$	$H_0: P \geq P_0$	$H_0: P = P_0$		$H_1: P_1 < P_2$	$H_0: P_1 \geq P_2$	$H_0: P_1 = P_2$

It is worth knowing that the Z-value is used when dealing with population proportion hypothesis testing. In order to apply the Z-statistics, the binomial condition should be satisfied and the expected value must be greater than five $[n\hat{P} > 5]$. When the expected value is less than five $[n\hat{P} < 5]$, we make use of the Z-approximation. The Z-value or test statistics is calculated using the formulas below.

$$Z - \text{Statistics} = \frac{\hat{P} - P_0}{\sqrt{\frac{P_0(1-P_0)}{n}}} \quad \ldots\ldots\ldots\ldots(1)$$

$$Z - \text{Statistics} = \frac{(\hat{P}_1 - \hat{P}_2) - (P_1 - P_2)}{\sqrt{\frac{\hat{P}_1(1-\hat{P}_1)}{n_1} + \frac{\hat{P}_2(1-\hat{P}_2)}{n_2}}} \quad \ldots\ldots\ldots\ldots(2)$$

$$Z - \text{Statistics} = \frac{(\hat{P}_1 - \hat{P}_2) - (P_1 - P_2)}{\sqrt{\frac{\hat{P}_c(1-\hat{P}_c)}{n_1} + \frac{\hat{P}_c(1-\hat{P}_c)}{n_2}}} \quad \ldots\ldots\ldots\ldots(3)$$

$$Z - \text{Statistics} = \frac{(\hat{P}_1 - \hat{P}_2) - (P_1 - P_2)}{\sqrt{\hat{P}_c\hat{q}_c\left(\frac{1}{n_1} + \frac{1}{n_2}\right)}} \quad \ldots\ldots\ldots\ldots(4)$$

Where: $\hat{P}_c = \frac{(X_1 + X_2)}{(n_1 + n_2)}$ and $\hat{P}_c \neq \frac{X_1}{n_1} + \frac{X_2}{n_2}$ and $\hat{q}_c = 1 - \hat{P}_c$ ….[Pooled sample proportion]

$(\hat{P})$ represents the sample proportion

(P_0) Represents the population proportion

(n) Represents sample size

Note: Equation (1) is used in hypothesis test when dealing with single population proportion and equations (2), (3) and (4) is used in hypothesis test when dealing with two independent population proportion. Since formulas components derivation have already been seen in under confidence interval of population proportion, we will move directly to test statistics calculation and hypothesis testing examples.

Example 1: A researcher claims that at least 15% of smokers fail to eat any fruits and vegetables at least 3 days a week. Is there sufficient evidence to reject his claim if is discover that 17 of the 200 smokers in a sample eat no fruits and vegetables at least 3 days a week? Assume a 5% significance level.

Solution

Step 1: Formulation of hypotheses

Null hypothesis is given as $H_0: P \geq P_0$

Alternative hypothesis is given as $H_1: P < P_0$

Step 2: Determination of Test statistics

a) Formula. $Z - \text{Statistics} = \frac{\hat{P} - P_0}{\sqrt{\frac{P_0(1-P_0)}{n}}}$

Where; $\hat{P} = 0.085$, $P_0 = 15\% = 0.15$ and $n = 200$

b) Data substitution and solving

$Z - \text{Statistics} = \frac{0.085 - 0.15}{\sqrt{\frac{0.15(1-0.15)}{200}}}$ ....[Simplify brackets and fractions]

$Z - \text{Statistics} = \frac{-0.065}{\sqrt{0.0006375}}$ ....[Work root]

$Z - \text{Statistics} = \frac{-0.065}{0.025248762}$ ....[Solve equation]

$Z - \text{Statistics} = \mathbf{-2.274}$ ....[In three decimal places]

Note: Since $Z = -2.274$, therefore, the P-Value equals 0.0115. Remember $P(Z < -2.274) = P(Z > 2.274)$ and $P(Z > 2.274) = 1 - \Phi(2.274)$. The critical value at 95% confidence level is (-1.645).

Step 2: Decision making. Comparing the P-Value (0.0115) and the significance level (0.05), we realized that the P-Value is less than the significance level $(0.0115 < 0.05)$. Therefore, we reject the null hypothesis.

Step 3: Conclusion: There is enough evidence at 95% confidence level or 5% significance level to support that claim that the proportion of at least 15% of smokers fail to eat any fruits and vegetables at least 3 days a week.

Example 2: In a survey of 1245 male students, 361 said they smoke at least one pack of cigarettes a day and in a survey of 1065 female students, 341 said they smoke at least one pack a day. Calculate the test statistics.

Solution

a) Method 1

Step 1: Formula. $Z - \text{Statistics} = \frac{(\widehat{P}_1-\widehat{P}_2)-(P_1-P_2)}{\sqrt{\frac{\widehat{P}_1(1-\widehat{P}_1)}{n_1}+\frac{\widehat{P}_2(1-\widehat{P}_2)}{n_2}}}$

Where; $\widehat{P}_1 = 0.289959839$, $n_1 = 1{,}245$, $\widehat{P}_2 = 0.320187793$ and $n_2 = 1{,}065$

Step 2: Data substitution and solving

$Z - \text{Statistics} = \frac{(0.289959839-0.320187793)-(0-0)}{\sqrt{\frac{0.289959839(1-0.289959839)}{1{,}245}+\frac{0.320187793(1-0.320187793)}{1{,}065}}}$ ....[Simplify brackets]

$Z - \text{Statistics} = \frac{-0.030227954-0}{\sqrt{\frac{0.20588313}{1{,}245}+\frac{0.21766757}{1{,}065}}}$ ....[Simplify fraction]

$Z - \text{Statistics} = \frac{-0.030227954}{\sqrt{0.00036975}}$ ....[Work denominator root]

$Z - \text{Statistics} = \frac{-0.030227954}{0.019228901}$ ....[Simplify fraction]

$Z - \text{Statistics} = \mathbf{-1.572}$ ....[In three decimal places]

b) Method 2

Step 1: Formula. $Z - \text{Statistics} = \frac{(\widehat{P}_1-\widehat{P}_2)-(P_1-P_2)}{\sqrt{\widehat{P}_c\widehat{q}_c\left(\frac{1}{n_1}+\frac{1}{n_2}\right)}}$

Where; $\widehat{P}_1 = 0.289959839$, $n_1 = 1{,}245$, $\widehat{P}_2 = 0.320187793$, $n_2 = 1{,}065$, $\widehat{P}_c = \frac{(361+341)}{(1{,}245+1{,}065)} = \frac{702}{2{,}310} = 0.303896103$ and $\widehat{q}_c = 0.696103896$

Step 2: Data substitution and solving

$Z - \text{Statistics} = \frac{(0.289959839-0.320187793)-(0-0)}{\sqrt{(0.303896103)(0.696103896)\left(\frac{1}{1{,}245}+\frac{1}{1{,}065}\right)}}$ ....[Simplify brackets]

$Z - \text{Statistics} = \frac{-0.030227954}{\sqrt{0.211543261(0.001742179)}}$ ....[Simplify denomination]

$Z - \text{Statistics} = \frac{-0.030227954}{\sqrt{0.000368546}}$ ....[Work denominator root]

$Z - \text{Statistics} = \frac{-0.030227954}{0.019197563}$ ....[Solve equation]

$Z - \text{Statistics} = \mathbf{-1.575}$ ....[In three decimal places]

Example 3: In a sample of 200 surgeons, 15% thought the government should control health care. In a sample of 200 general practitioners, 21% felt the same way. At $\alpha = 0.01$, is there a difference in the proportions?

Solution

Step 1: Formulation of hypotheses

Null hypothesis is given as $H_0: P_1 = P_2$

Alternative hypothesis is given as $H_1: P_1 \neq P_2$

Step 2: Determination of Test statistics

a) Formula. $|Z - \text{Statistics}| = \frac{(\hat{P}_1 - \hat{P}_2) - (P_1 - P_2)}{\sqrt{\frac{\hat{P}_1(1-\hat{P}_1)}{n_1} + \frac{\hat{P}_2(1-\hat{P}_2)}{n_2}}}$

Where; $\hat{P}_1 = 0.15$, $n_1 = 200$, $\hat{P}_2 = 0.21$ and $n_2 = 200$ and Critical value $= \pm 2.576$

b) Data substitution and solving

$Z - \text{Statistics} = \frac{(0.15-0.21)-(0-0)}{\sqrt{\frac{0.15(1-0.15)}{200} + \frac{0.21(1-0.21)}{200}}}$ ....[Simplify brackets and fractions]

$Z - \text{Statistics} = \frac{0.06-0}{\sqrt{0.0006375+0.0008295}}$ ....[Work root]

$Z - \text{Statistics} = \frac{0.06}{0.038301436}$ ....[Solve equation]

$Z - \text{Statistics} = \pm \mathbf{1.567}$ ....[In three decimal places]

Step 3: Decision making. The critical value at 1% significance level or 99% confidence level is 2.576. The absolute value of the Z-statistics is less than the critical value($|1.567| < 2.576$), therefore, we don't reject the null hypothesis.

Step 4: Conclusion. There is not enough evidence at 1% significance level that the there is a difference in the proportions.

Test Your Understanding

Exercise 28: Given that $n_1 = 190$, $n_2 = 514$, $X_1 = 135$ and $X_2 = 293$. Determine the value of pooled sample proportion. Leave your answer in four decimal places... **[Answer: 0.6080]**

Exercise 29: Determine the Z-value from the following information; $n_1 = 250$, $X_1 = 101$, $n_2 = 250$ and $X_2 = 75$. Leave answer in three decimal places.....**[Answer: $Z = 2.449$]**

Exercise 30: Independent random samples of ($n_1 = 140$) and ($n_1 = 140$) observations were randomly selected from binomial populations 1 and 2, respectively. Sample 1 had 74 successes, and sample 2 had 81 successes. Determine the value of test statistics and critical value [Given $\alpha = 5\%$]**[Answer: Test Statistics(Z) $= \pm 0.843$ and Critical value = 1.960]**

Exercise 31: Two types of phone operating system are being tested to determine if there is a difference in the proportions of system failures (crashes). Fifteen out of a random sample of

150 phones with OS_1 had system failures within the first eight hours of operation. Nine out of another random sample of 150 phones with OS_2 had system failures within the first eight hours of operation. OS_2 is believed to be more stable (have fewer crashes) than OS_1. Complete a hypothesis test at the $\alpha = 0{:}05$ significance level. [Assume a two tailed test]

[Answer: Z − value(1.280) < Critical value (1.960), we dont reject the null hypothesis]

7.5 Hypothesis Decision Making Errors

Since hypothesis testing is based on sample data, it is possible to make error in drawing decision. The two possible errors made during decision making are; Type I and Type II errors. Another important concept to examine is the power of hypothesis testing.

7.5.1 Type I Error

It occurs when the null hypothesis (H_0) is rejected by a statistical test under a given significance level (α) when the null hypothesis was true. The probability of Type I error occurrence is equal to alpha (α). Therefore, alpha (α) or significance level is the probability of rejecting the null hypothesis (H_0) when it is true or when it should not be rejected. The alpha value of 5% can be interpreted as there is 5% chance that when the null hypothesis is true, it will be erroneously (falsely) rejected or that there is 5% chance you would observe the outcome (claim) with the null hypothesis being true. Type I error probability can be expressed in a summarized form as;

$$P(\text{Type I Error}) = P(\text{Reject } H_0/H_0 \text{ is True}) = \alpha \quad \text{.......(1)}$$

Graphically, Alpha (α) is defined as the area under the symmetric normal distribution curve after the critical value. The chance of Type I error occurrence is directly related to the level of significance. That is higher alpha (α) means higher probability of making Type I error.

7.5.2 Type II Error

It occurs when the null hypothesis (H_0) is not rejected by a statistical test at a given significance level (α) when it should have been. The probability of Type II error occurrence is equal to beta (β). Literally, bate (β) is defined as the probability of accepting the alternative hypothesis (H_1) when it is actually false or should not have been accepted. Type II error probability can be expressed in a summarized form as;

$$P(\text{Type II Error}) = P(\text{Fail to reject } H_0/H_0 \text{ is False}) = \beta \quad \text{.......(2)}$$

Note: Since total probability equal one, mathematically, beta equals the difference between total probability (1) and alpha (α), that is$[\beta = 1 - \alpha]$. Therefore, the probability of not making a Type II error (Λ) is calculated as total probability (1) minus probability of making Type II error (β). That is$[\Lambda = 1 - \beta]$.

7.5.3 Power of Hypothesis Testing

The Power of hypothesis testing is defined as the probability of rejecting null hypothesis when null is false. That is power is the probability of correctly rejecting the null hypothesis or the probability of avoiding a type II error. The power of a hypothesis testing can be increased by increasing the sample size and significance level. It is expressed as;

$\text{Power} = \text{P}(\text{Reject } H_0/H_0 \text{ is False}) = 1 - \beta$ ....(3)

Example 1: Assume the probability of making a Type II error is 0.16; determine the power of the hypothesis test.

Solution

Step 1: Formula. $\text{Power} = \text{P}(\text{Reject } H_0/H_0 \text{ is False}) = 1 - \beta$, where; $\beta = 0.16$

Step 2: Data substitution and solving

$\text{Power} = 1 - \beta$ ....[Substitute component numerical values]

$\text{Power} = 1 - 0.16$ ....[Solve equation]

$\text{Power} = \mathbf{0.84} = \mathbf{84\%}$

The three concepts of Type I, Type II and Power of hypothesis testing can be summarized in a tabular form as seen below

	Accept H_0	Reject H_0
H_0 is true	Correct decision ($P = 1 - \alpha$)	Type I Error ($P = 1 - \beta$)
H_1 is true	Type II Error ($P = \alpha$)	Correct decision ($P = \beta$)

Conclusively, probability of making Type I error is inversely related to the probability of making type II error, showing that alpha (α) and beta (β) are not statistically independent. That is an increase in one is by default a decrease in the other. Note that both probabilities are conditional probabilities.

CHAPTER EIGHT

PROJECT MANAGEMENT

Henry Gantt

A project is defined as a composition of related activities that are directed towards the accomplishment of a pre-determined objective. Projects differ in sizes (based on size and money required) and complexity (technology and labour skills required). Construction of house, roads and bridges are examples of large and complex projects.

Management is the process of planning, controlling, coordinating and allocating resources appropriate towards the accomplishment of an objective or set goals.

8.1 Meaning of Project Management

Project management is defined as the overall planning and co-ordination of a project from conception to completion. Project management is also defined as the scientific and systematic process of planning, scheduling and controlling of a number of interrelated activities or tasks with the use of limited resources (labour, machine, money and time). The five main processes of project management are illustrated below.

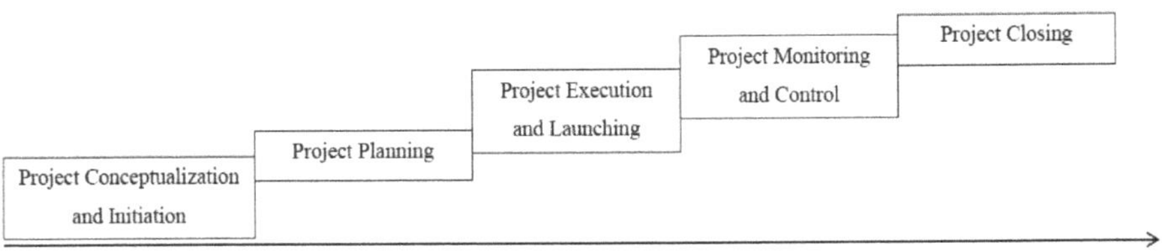

Project Management Processes Direction

1) Conceptualization/Initiation: It is the start of a project and involves the determination of project value and feasibility. Project value here implies the justifying the need of the project in relation to the society (project market) and stakeholders or sponsor expectation (project return on investment). Project feasibility here implies the evaluation of project objective and goals, project duration and project cost. Project objective should be; specific, measureable, achievable, important, result oriented and time bound.
2) Project Planning: It involves the breakdown of main objective (stated in process one) to sub-objectives, identification of tasks/activities necessary to achieve and task

duration (scheduling) and resources to accompany these activities. Planning also involves the establishment of activities teams, communication chain and determination of possible project risks. Project planning reduces and/or eliminates poor, overambitious and unsustainable planning.

3) Project Launching and Execution: Here, the theoretical or paper work of project is made practical. Here, project managers and activities team leaders and members must matter what need to be done, how it should be done, who needs to do what and when what is to be done needs to be completed.
4) Project Monitoring and Controlling: It involves the analyzing and evaluating of project progress against project plain (time, resource utilization and desired quality). The process of resource reallocation, project crashing and project review is performed in this stage.
5) Project Closing: Here, outstanding contracts with suppliers, consultants and other third parties providers are closed. All project and administrative documents are reviewed and stored and project reports as well as troubleshooting and maintenance plan are produced and recommendation suggested to project owners.

8.2 Network Diagram Analysis

Network diagram is a diagram showing sequential link of activities from one event to another. It shows project completion paths and provides project manager the ability to identify problematic from non-problematic path and assist them for proper and rational activity duration adjustment. Network diagram is made up of activities and events with their respective durations.

8.2.1 Network Diagram Activity

Activity is defined as any individual operation which utilizes resources (human and material) and has an end and a beginning duration. Activity is also called task or job and is represented by an arrow. Activity is sub-divided into several types based on two criteria; resource utilization and activity position.

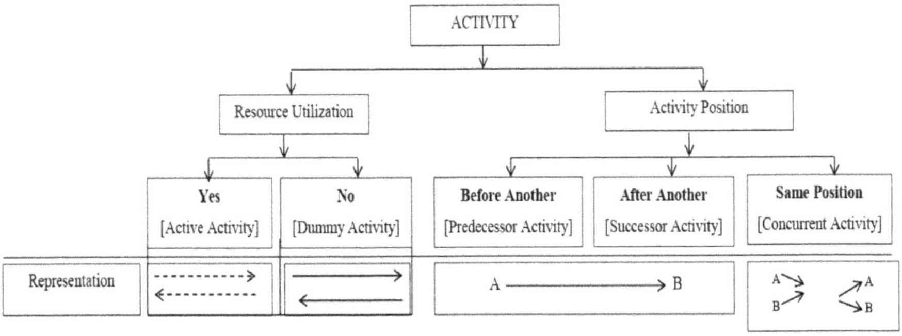

1) Active Activity: These are activities that utilize project resources and whose completion time is greater than zero (0). Active activity can be predecessor, successor and concurrent in nature.
2) Dummy (Non-Reactive) Activity: Dummy activities do not consume resources and are having duration equal to zero (0). Dummy activity is use to link suspended activities to a common event and suspended events to a common event as well as link concurrent activities.
3) Predecessor (Former) Activity: These are activities that must be completed before the start of another activity. That is activities that must be completed immediately prior to the start of another activity. Predecessor activity can be active or dummy in nature.
4) Successor (Current) Activity: These are activities that cannot start until the completion of activities before them. That is activities that cannot be started until one or more of other activities are completed.

A, 5 ⟶ B, 10 ⟶ C, 4

Note: Activity A is a predecessor activity for activity B and activity B is a predecessor activity for activity C. activity C is a successor activity of activity B and activity B is a successor activity for activity A. activity C is not a successor activity for activity A and activity A is not a predecessor activity for activity C.

5) Concurrent (Co-operating) Activity: These are activities which can be accomplished together or at the same time but which may have the same or different completion duration.

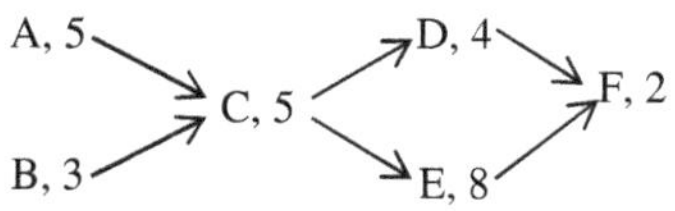

Figure 1

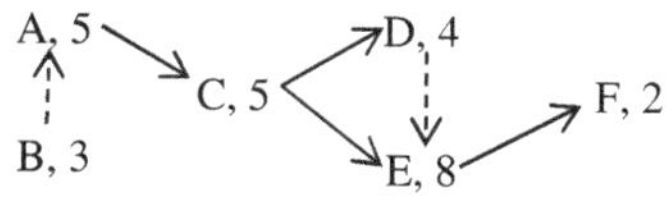

Figure 2

Note: Activity A and B as well as D and E are concurrent activities. Figure 2 is identical to figure but differ in that it uses dummy activities to link the concurrent activities. When linking concurrent activities, we link the activity with the smaller duration to the activity with the larger duration using incomplete arrows as seen above.

Note: Activities are symbolized using letters and the length of the arrow representing the activity is of no significance and has no relation to activity duration. Project activities can be represented using latters or numbers (Fulkerson rule).

Fulkerson Numbering Rule

Activity	(1,2)	(2,3)
Duration	4	6

Activity	1 – 2	2 – 3
Duration	4	6

Note: Here the number represents events not actual activities. Activities are placed in-between the numbers.

Activity	B	C
Duration	4	6
Predecessor	A	C

8.2.2 Network Diagram Event

An event represents the starting and completion or end point of a project activity. An event is usually represented by a circle or rectangle and is also called node or connector. Events can also be active or dummy in nature. Dummy events is used to link suspended multiple events to a common starting or ending event and does not utilize any project resources. The number of event predecessor activities and/or successor activities helps to distinguish events into three main types.

1) Merge Event: It shows situation in which two or more (multiple) activity are completed at the same time. Remember the activities maybe the same or differ in duration.
2) Burst Event: It shows a situation where two or more (multiple) activities start from a common event.
3) Mixed Event: It shows a situation where multiple activities end and leave a given event. It is a combination of merge event and burst event.

Merge Event	Burst Event	Mixed Event
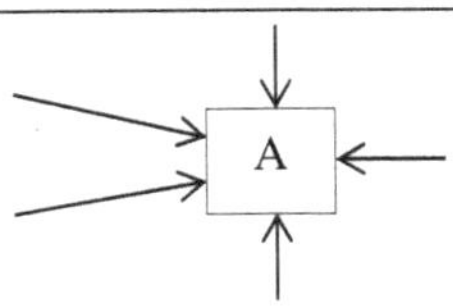	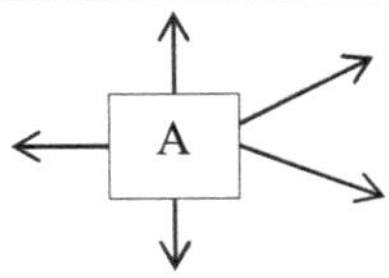	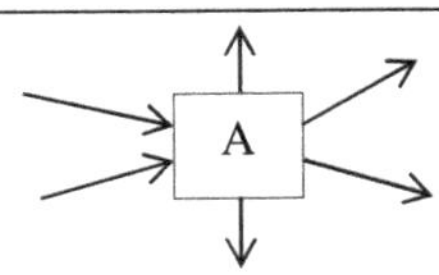

Example 1: Draw a network diagram from the following table

Activity	A, B	C	D,E,F	G	H,I
Proceeding Activity		A	B	C,D	F

Solution

Hint: Activity A and B have no predecessor activities. Therefore, they are suspended and should be tied or link by a dummy start event.

Using Non-Linear Arrows	Using Linear Arrow
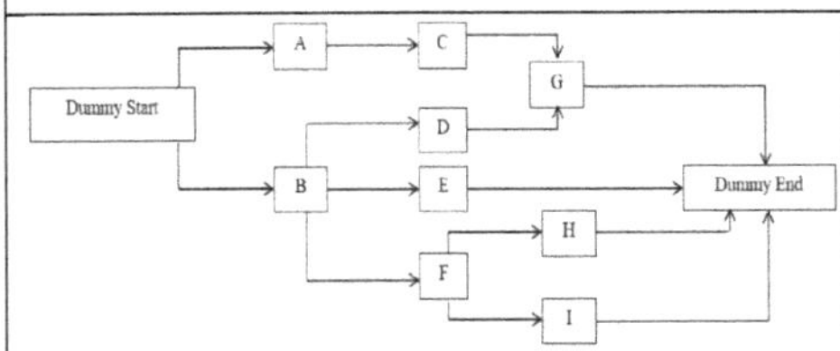	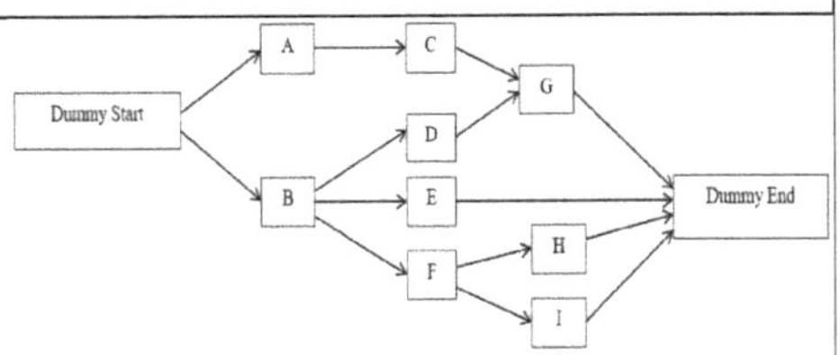

Note: From the diagram, we realized that activity G, H, E and I are suspended. Therefore, we tied or link them to a common dummy end event.

Example 2: From the project activities below, draw the network diagram and identify the project completion paths.

Activities	1 – 2	2 – 3	2 – 4	3 – 4	4 – 5	5 – 6

Solution

Hint: The numbers represent events and not activities. The first numbers are the predecessor events and the second number the successor events. The activity is represented along the arrow.

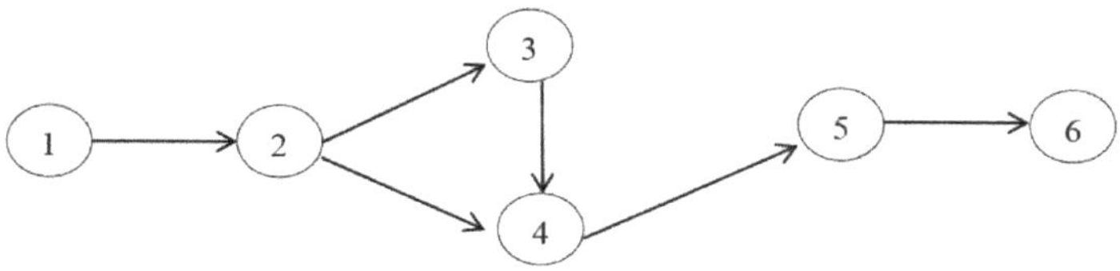

Note: The project completion paths are; [1, 2, 3, 4, 5 and 6] and [1, 2, 4, 5 and 6]

Example 3: Draw a network diagram and identify the project completion paths.

Activity	A	B	C	D	E	F
Duration	6	9	8	7	10	12
Predecessor			A,B	A,B	D	C,E

Solution

Hint: Activities A and B are not having a predecessor activity. Therefore, they are considered suspended and we are required to use a dummy event to link or tied them.

<table>
<tr><td>Using dummy and non-dummy activity</td><td>Using only active activity</td></tr>
<tr><td>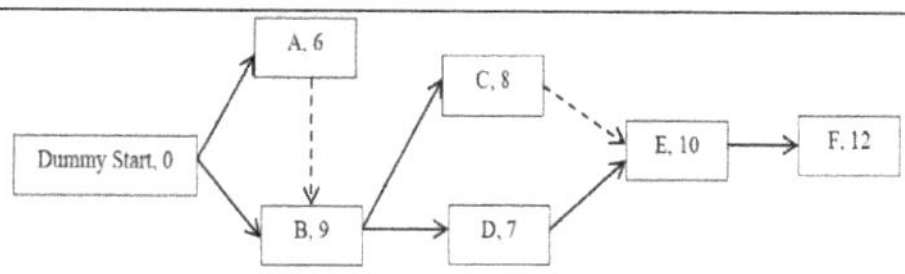
</td><td>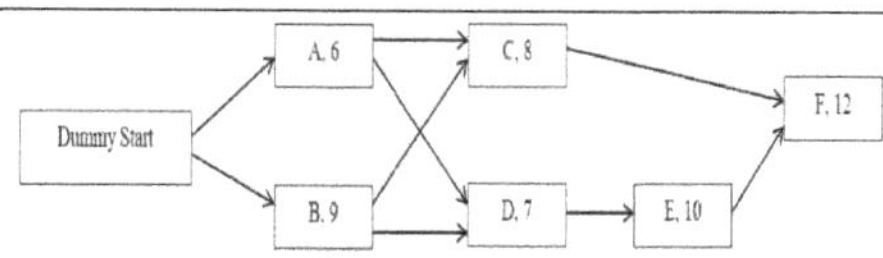
</td></tr>
<tr><td colspan="2">Completion Paths: (Dummy,ACF), (Dummy,ADEF), (Dummy,BCF) and (Dummy, B,D,E,F)</td></tr>
</table>

Example 4: Draw the network diagram and inset the activities duration using information from the table below.

Activity	(1, 2)	(1, 3)	(1, 4)	(2, 4)	(2, 5)	(3, 6)	(4, 6)	(5, 7)	(6, 7)
Duration	4	12	10	8	6	8	10	0	4

Solution

Hint: Event 5 and 7 are link by an activity with zero duration. Zero duration here is equivalent to dummy activity. Therefore, we are going to use a dummy activity arrow to link the events. Event 5 to event 7 is occupied by an activity with zero duration. Therefore, these events will be linked by a broken arrow indicating dummy activity.

Using Linear Arrows	Using Non-Linear Arrows
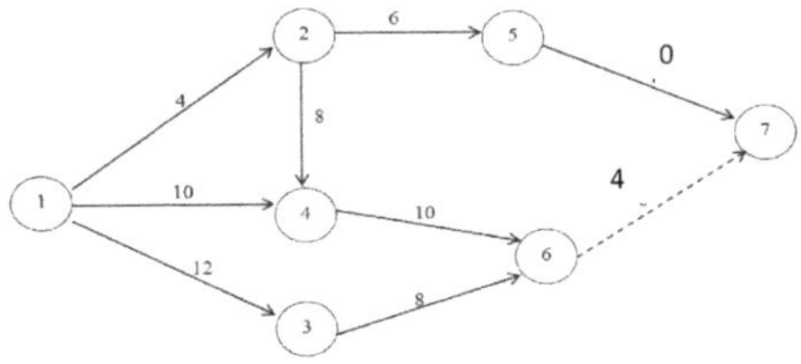	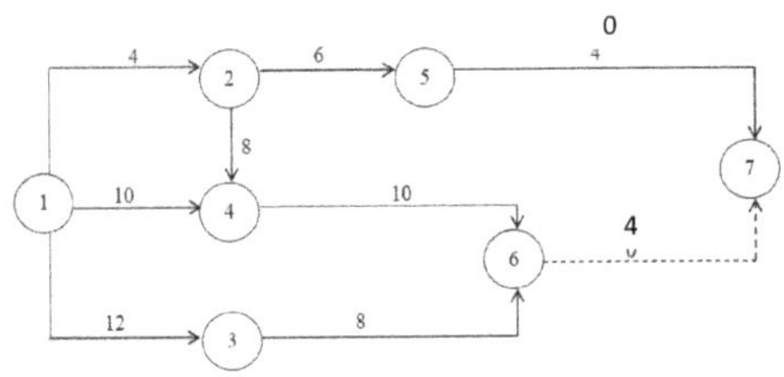

Test Your Understanding

Exercise 1: Sketch a network diagram using the following tables below

Table 1

Activity	A	B	C	D	E	F
Duration	9	7	5	8	6	9
Predecessor			A	A,B	C	D,E

Table 2

Activity	A	B	C	D	E	F	G	H	I
Duration	5	2	5	4	2	4	3	2	6
Predecessor	D	G,H	B		G,H	E,I		D	A

Table 3

Activity	(1,2)	(1,3)	(1,4)	(2,4)	(3,4)	(4,5)
Duration	9	8	15	5	10	2

Table 4

Activity	1 – 2	2 – 3	2 – 4	2 – 5	3 – 4	4 – 5	5 – 6
Duration	3	6	9	7	8	5	3

Answers……………………………………………………………..[See Appendix 1]

8.2.3 Network Diagram Time

Network diagram provides different project completion paths and helps in distinguishing critical from non-critical project completion paths. In order to determine the critical path, we are required to compute activities slack or float time. Slack time determination is possible only after the calculation of activities or events earliest and latest time.

1) **Earliest Time:** It is calculated using the forward technique. That is from the starting activity or event to the ending activity or event.

   a) Fulkerson Technique: Earliest time is also called event earliest occurrence time denoted "E". The earliest time of the first event is by default zero. The formula for earliest time is given as;

      $\text{Current Earliest Time } (E_n) = E_{n-1} + D_n$ ....(1)

      Where; E_{n-1} = Predecessor event Earliest Time and D_n = Event activity duration . **Note:** In concurrent event situation, the earliest time of an events is the highest current earliest time.

   b) Non-Fulkerson Technique: Earliest time is sub-divided into earliest start time (ES) and earliest finish time (EF) and the earliest start time is calculated before the earliest finish time.

Earliest Start Time (ES)	Earliest Finish Time (EF)
a) The earliest start time (ES) of the first activity is by default zero. b) The earliest start time of other activities, it the highest earliest finish time of the activity predecessor activity.	a) Earliest finish time (EF) of an activity is the sum of the activity's earliest start time and duration. That is; $EF_n = ES_n + D_n$......................(2)

Note: The manner of placing the earliest time varies. The placement technique utilized in this document is illustrated below.

Fulkerson Technique	Non-Fulkerson Technique
Earliest Time (E) Activity (Slack)	Earliest Start Time (ES) | Earliest Finish Time (EF) Activity, Duration [Slack]

Example 1: Draw a network diagram using information in the table below and determine the activities earliest start time (ES) and earliest finish time (EF) .

Activity	A	B	C	D	E	F
Duration (Days)	5	3	3	4	3	5
Predecessor			A	A,B	C	D,E

Solution

a) Graphical Method

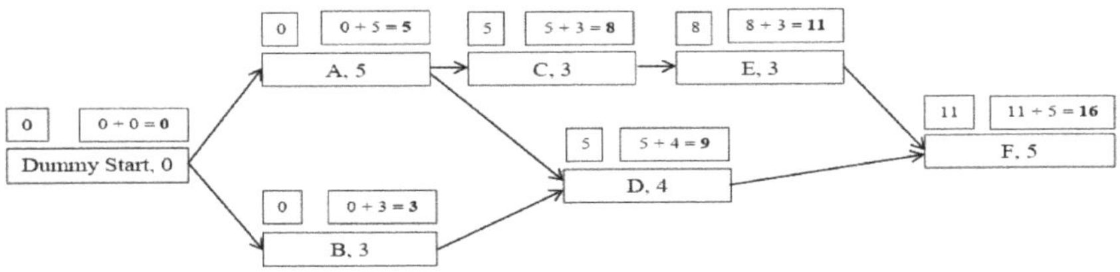

Complementary Explanation: The predecessor activities of activity "D" are activities "A" and "B" with earliest finish time 5 and 3 days respectively. The highest earliest finish time of activity "D" predecessor activities is 5 days which by default becomes the earliest start time for activity "D". The predecessor activities of "F" are activities "E" and "D" with earliest finish time 11 and 9 days respectively. The highest earliest finish time is 11 days and is considered the earliest start time for activity "F".

b) Tabular Method

Activity		Predecessor activity	Earliest Starting Time [ES]	Earliest Finishing Time [EF]
	Duration		[ES = Predecessor highest EF]	[EF = ES plus Duration]
A	5	Dummy	**0** [Since dummy time is zero]	$0 + 5 = \mathbf{5}$
B	3	Dummy	**0** [Since dummy time is zero]	$0 + 3 = \mathbf{3}$
C	3	A	**5** [Since A EF is 5]	$5 + 3 = \mathbf{8}$
D	4	A,B	**5** [Since $A(EF; 5) > B(EF; 3)$]	$5 + 4 = \mathbf{9}$
E	3	C	**8** [Since C EF is 8]	$8 + 3 = \mathbf{11}$
F	5	D,E	**11** [Since $E(EF; 11) > D(EF; 9)$]	$11 + 5 = \mathbf{16}$

Example 2: A project consists of the following activities. Their sequence and duration (days) are given in the table below. Draw a network diagram and determine the events earliest time (E).

Activity	1 – 2	1 – 3	2 – 5	2 – 7	3 – 4	3 – 6	4 – 5	5 – 6	5 – 7	6 – 7	7 – 8
Duration	20	24	16	24	12	10	16	16	20	12	14

Solution

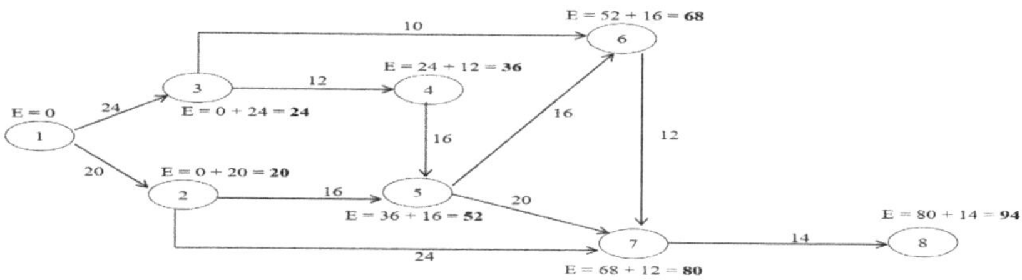

Complementary Explanation: Event 5 is having two predecessor events; event 2 and event 4. To get event 5 earliest time, we add the predecessor event earliest time with their respective activity duration and consider the highest as the earliest time of event 5. Applying this, event 4 value is $[36 + 16 = 52]$ and event 2 value is$[20 + 16 = 26]$, with 52 days being the highest value and by default the earliest time of event 5. Event 7 have three predecessor events, that is; event 2, event 5 event and event 6 with values$[20 + 24 = \mathbf{44}]$, $[52 + 20 = \mathbf{72}]$ and $[68 + 12 = \mathbf{80}]$ respectively. Event 7 earliest time is 80 days since it is the highest value.

Test Your Understanding

Exercise 2: Draw a network diagram using information in the table below and determine the activities earliest time.

Table 1

Activity	A	B	C	D	E	F	G	H	I	J	K
Duration	5	1	2	5	2	2	1	4	10	1	1
Predecessor			B	C	C,D	D	F	F	G,H	I	J

Table 2

Activity	(1,2)	(1,3)	(1,4)	(2,6)	(3,7)	(3,5)	(4,5)	(5,9)	(6,8)	(7,8)	(8.9)
Duration	2	2	1	4	5	8	3	5	1	4	3

Answer..[See Appendix 1]

2) **Latest Time:** It is calculated using the backward technique,. That is from the last activity or event to the first activity or event.

   a) Fulkerson Technique: Latest time is also called event latest occurrence time denoted "L". The latest time of the last event is by default the last event earliest time. The formula for earliest time is given as;

   $$\text{Current Latest Time } (L_n) = L_{n-1} - D_n \quad \ldots\ldots\ldots\ldots\ldots\ldots\ldots\ldots(3)$$

   Where; L_{n-1} = Successor event Latest Time and D_n = Event activity duration .

   Note: In concurrent event situation, the latest time of an events is the lowest current latest time.

   b) Non-Fulkerson Technique: Latest time is sub-divided into latest start time (LS) and latest finish time (LF) and the latest finish time (LF) is calculated before the latest start time (LS).

Latest Finish Time (LF)	Latest Start Time (LS)
a) The latest finish time (LF) of the last activity is by default the last activity earliest finish time[$LF_{Last} = EF_{last}$]. b) The latest finish time of other activities, it the lowest latest start time of the activity successor activity.	a) Latest start time (LS) of an activity is the difference of the activity's latest finish time and duration. That is; $LS_n = LF_n - D_n$........................(4)

Note: The manner of placing the earliest time varies. The placement technique utilized in this document is illustrated below.

Fulkerson Technique	Non-Fulkerson Technique
Latest Time (L) Earliest Time (E) Activity (Slack)	Earliest Start Time (ES) | Earliest Finish Time (EF) Activity, Duration [Slack] Latest Start Time (LS) | Latest Finish Time (LE)

Example 1: Draw a network diagram using information in the table below and determine the activities latest times.

Activity	A	B	C	D	E	F
Duration	6	9	8	7	10	12
Predecessor			A,B	A,B	D	C,E

Solution

a) Graphical Method

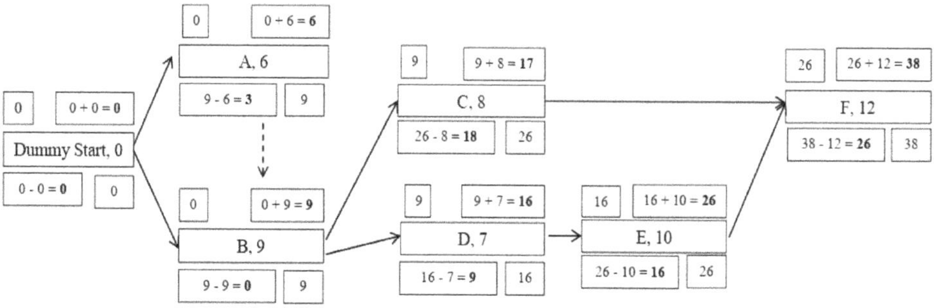

Complementary Explanation: Activity "B" is having two successor activities, that is activity "D" and "C" with latest start time 9 days and 18 days respectively. We realized that 9 days is the smallest values and hence considered the latest finish time of activity "B". Dummy activity is having two successor activities, that is activity "A" and "B" with latest start time 3 days and zero days. The latest finish time of the dummy activity is zero since it is the smallest successor value.

b) Tabular Method

Activity		Predecessor	ES	EF		LS	LF	
A	6	Dummy	0	6	↓	**9** [Since $D(LF:9) < C(LF:18)$]	$9 - 6 = \mathbf{3}$	↑
B	9	Dummy	0	9		**9** [Since $D(LF:9) < C(LF:18)$]	$9 - 9 = \mathbf{0}$	
C	8	A,B	9	17		**26** [Since C is successor of F]	$26 - 8 = \mathbf{18}$	
D	7	A,B	9	16		**16** [Since D is successor of E]	$16 - 7 = \mathbf{9}$	
E	10	D	16	26		**26** [Since E is successor of F]	$26 - 10 = \mathbf{16}$	
F	12	C,E	26	38		**38**	$38 - 12 = \mathbf{26}$	

Example 2: Draw a network diagram using information in the table below and determine the activities latest time.

Activity	1-2	1-3	2-3	2-5	3-4	3-6	4-5	4-6	5-6	6-7
Duration (Days)	15	15	3	5	8	12	1	14	3	14

Solution

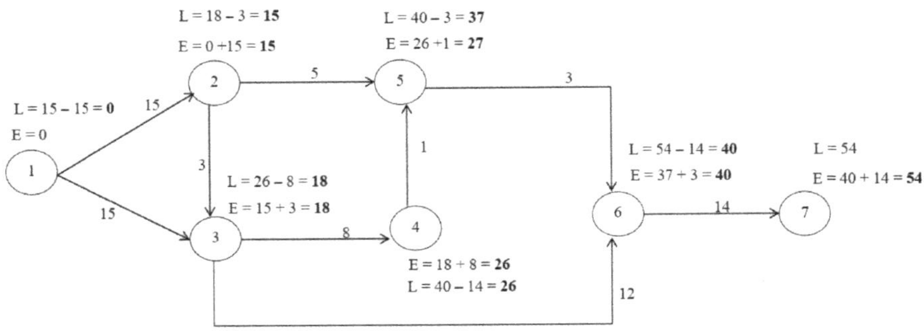

Complementary Explanation: Event "3" is having two successor events, that is event "6" and event "4" with event latest occurrence time 40 days and 26 days respectively. Subtracting each event with their respective activity gives, event 6 value $[40 - 12 = \mathbf{28}]$ and event 4 value $[26 - 8 = \mathbf{18}]$. Event "3" latest occurrence time is 18 days since it is the smallest. Event 2 is having two successor events (3 and 5) with values $[18 - 3 = \mathbf{15}]$ and $[37 - 5 = \mathbf{32}]$. Therefore, event 2 latest occurrence time is 15 days. Event 1 is also having two successor events (2 and 3) with values $[15 - 15 = \mathbf{0}]$ and $[18 - 15 = \mathbf{3}]$ respectively. Event 1 latest occurrence time is 0 day since zero is the smallest value.

Test Your Understanding

Exercise 3: Draw a network diagram using information in the table below and determine the activities latest time(s).

Table 1

Activity	A	B	C	D	E	F	G	H	I
Duration	3	5	7	2	5	2	6	2	10
Predecessor			A	A	A	E	D,F	B,C	G,H

Table 2

Activity	(1,2)	(1,3)	(1,4)	(2,4)	(3,4)	(3,5)	(4,6)	(4,7)	(5,7)	(6,7)
Duration	6	4	9	2	7	8	5	10	4	8

Answers ....[See Appendix 1]

3) **The Slack Time (ST):** It is the left over time after the completion of an activity or event. Activity or event with zero slack or float time is called critical activity or event

and the sequence of critical activities or events is called critical path. Critical path is usually the longest path and its duration equals the duration of the project. It is calculated using the following formula;

$$\text{Slack time} = \text{LS} - \text{ES} = \text{LF} - \text{EF} \qquad (5)$$

$$\text{Slack time} = \text{L} - \text{E} \qquad (6)$$

Example 1: Draw a network diagram using information in the table below and determine the activities slack time.

Activity	A	B	C	D	E
Duration	3	5	7	2	8
Predecessor			A	B	C,D

Solution

a) Graphical Method

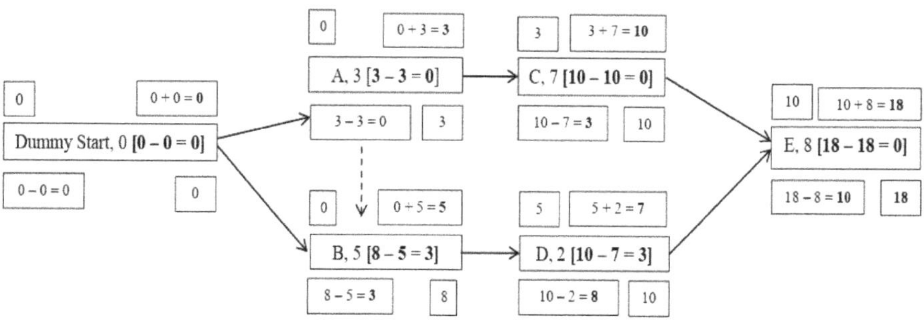

b) Tabular Method

Activity		Predecessor							Slack
A	3	Dummy	0	$0+3=\mathbf{3}$		3	$3-3=\mathbf{0}$		$3-3=\mathbf{0}$
B	5	Dummy	0	$0+5=\mathbf{5}$		8	$8-5=\mathbf{3}$		$8-5=\mathbf{3}$
C	7	A	3	$3+7=\mathbf{10}$		10	$10-7=\mathbf{3}$		$10-10=\mathbf{0}$
D	2	B	5	$5+2=\mathbf{7}$		10	$10-2=\mathbf{8}$		$10-7=\mathbf{3}$
E	8	C,D	10	$10+8=\mathbf{18}$		18	$18-8=\mathbf{10}$		$18-18=\mathbf{0}$

Example 2: Draw a network diagram using information in the table below and determine the activities slack time.

Activity	A	B	C	D	E	F	G
Duration	6	5	3	2	5	9	5
Predecessor		A	A	B	B	D,E	C,F

Solution

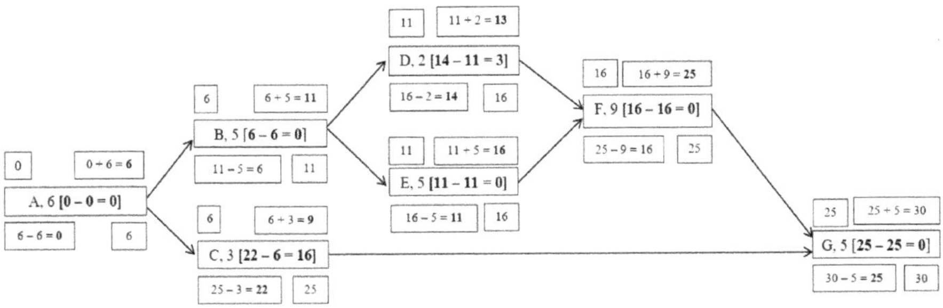

Example 3: Draw a network diagram using information in the table below and determine the activities slack time.

Activity	(0,1)	(1,2)	(1,3)	(2,4)	(2,5)	(3,4)	(3,6)	(4,7)	(5,7)	(6,7)
Duration	2	8	10	6	3	3	7	5	2	8

Solution

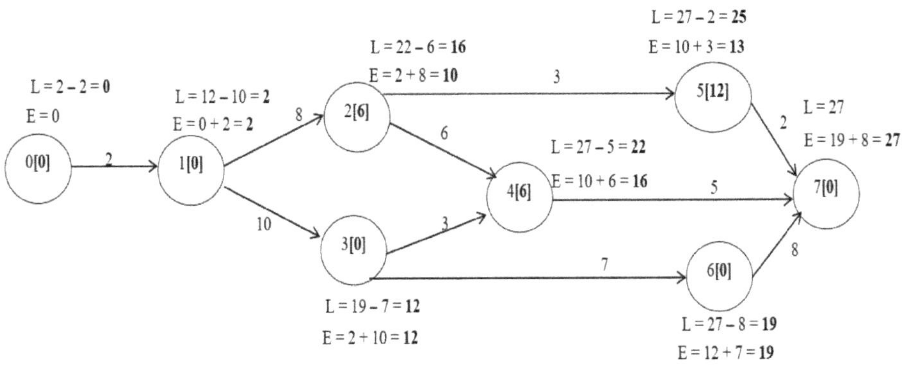

Example 4: Draw a network diagram using information in the table below and determine the activities slack time.

Activity	1 – 2	1 – 3	1 – 4	2 – 5	3 – 5	4 – 6	5 – 6
Duration	4	8	6	2	12	10	14

Solution

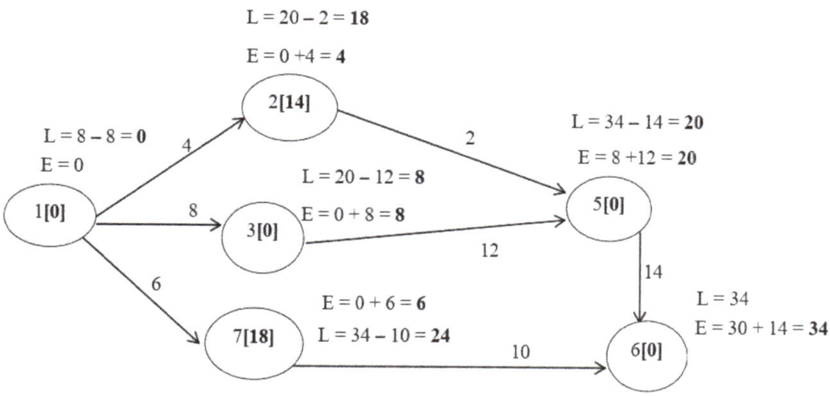

Test Your Understanding

Exercise 4: Draw a network diagram using information in the table below and determine the activities slack time.

Table 1

Activity	A	B	C	D	E	F
Duration (Da s)	5	6	5	3	7	3
Predecessor		A	A	B	C	D,E

Table 2

Activity	1 – 2	1 – 3	1 – 4	2 – 6	3 – 5	5 – 6	4 – 6
Duration (Days)	4	2	8	6	4	1	1

Answers...[See Appendix 1]

8.3 Project Planning Methods or Techniques

Morgan R Walker | James E. Kelley Jr

The three major methods or techniques of project planning are the Gantt chart (developed by Henry L. Gantt), program evaluation and review technique (PERT) and critical path method (CPM) developed by Morgan Walker and James Kelley. Our study will be limited to program evaluation and review technique (PERT) and critical path method (CPM)

8.3.1 The Critical Path Method (CPM)

The critical path method was developed by Morgan R. Walker and James E. Kelley Jr. The critical path method is having as main objective the identification of activities (critical activity) whose delay is likely to influence the project completion duration. The critical path method is based on the certainty of activity time estimation by project managers.

Example 1: Use the information in the table below and answer the following questions

Activities	A	B	C	D	E	F	G	H
Immediate predecessors		A	B	C	A	C,E	E	F,G
Duration	4	4	4	2	6	6	6	4

Work required

1) Draw a network diagram of the project
2) Determine the critical path and justify your answer.

<u>**Solution**</u>

1) Draw a network diagram of the project

Using the dummy activity technique	Using the Non-dummy activity technique
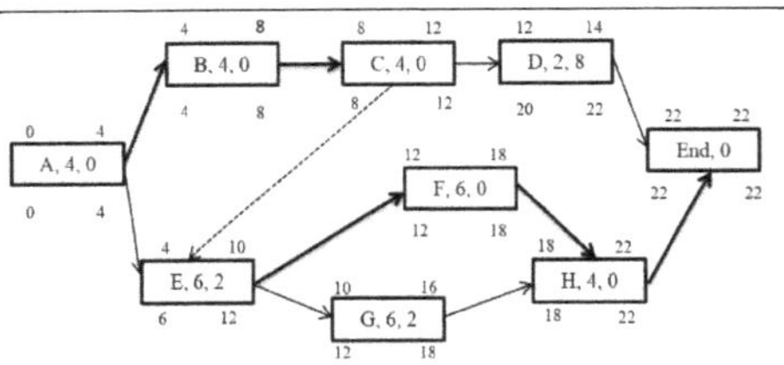	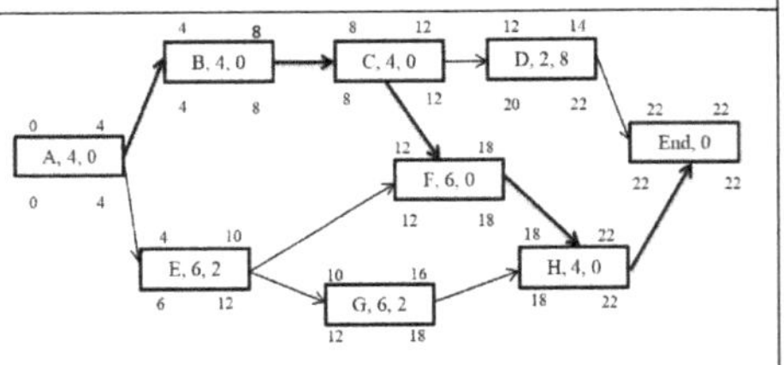

2) Determine the critical path and justify your answer.

From the network diagram above, we realize that the critical activities are; A, B, C, F, H and End. Therefore, the critical path is A, B, C, F, H and End. This path is justifiable as the sum of its activities duration $(4 + 4 + 4 + 6 + 4 + 0 = 22)$ equals the duration of the project (22 weeks).

Example 2: The activities and durations (weeks) of a small project are represented in the table below. Draw the network diagram and determine the project completion critical path

Activity	(1,2)	(1,3)	(1,4)	(2,6)	(3,7)	(3,5)	(4,5)	(5,9)	(6,8)	(7,8)	(8.9)
Duration	2	2	1	4	5	8	3	5	1	4	3

Solution

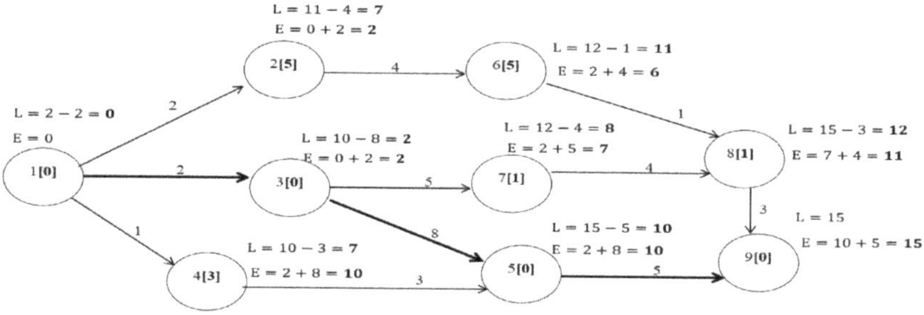

The project completion critical path is $[1 \rightarrow 3 \rightarrow 5 \rightarrow 9]$ and the critical path duration is 15 weeks, that is$[2 + 8 + 5 = 15]$. This path is the critical path because the events along the path are having zero slack or float time. Alternative project completion paths include;$[1 \rightarrow 4 \rightarrow 5 \rightarrow 9]$ with duration 9 weeks, $[1 \rightarrow 3 \rightarrow 7 \rightarrow 8 \rightarrow 9]$ with duration 14 weeks and $[1 \rightarrow 2 \rightarrow 6 \rightarrow 8 \rightarrow 9]$ with duration 10 weeks.

Example 3: Draw the network diagram and determine the critical path using the table below

Activity	A	B	C	D	E	F	G
Dependency			A	B	C	D	E,F
Duration (Days)	3	6	4	2	8	4	2

Solution

Method 1[Using Active Activity]

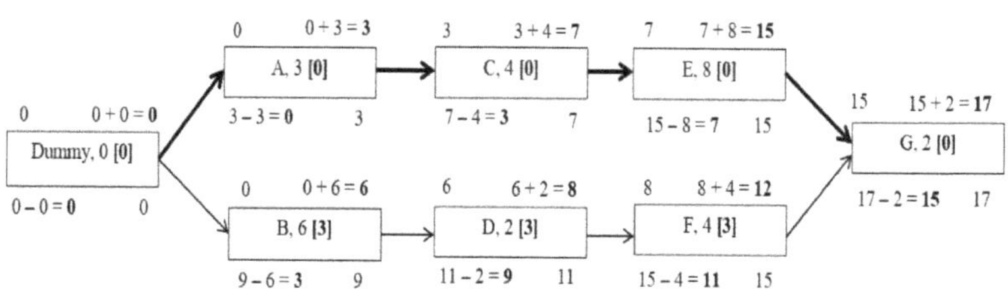

Method 2 [Using Dummy Activity]

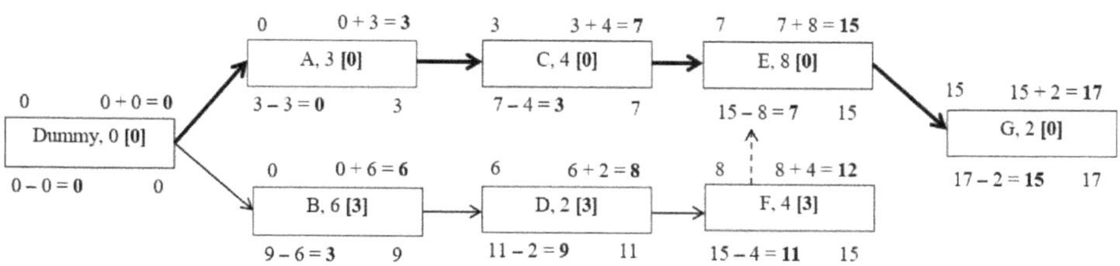

Note: The project completion critical path is [Dummy, A, C, E, G] with duration 17 days. An alternative project completion path is [Dummy, B, D, F, G] with duration 14 days.

Example 4: The activities and durations (months) of a small project are represented in the table below.

Activity	1-2	2-3	2-4	3-5	4-6	4-7	5-8	6-8	7-9	8-10	9-10
Duration	2	3	4	2	4	3	6	6	5	4	4

Work required

1) Draw a network diagram
2) Determine the critical path and justify your answer

Solution

1) Draw a network diagram

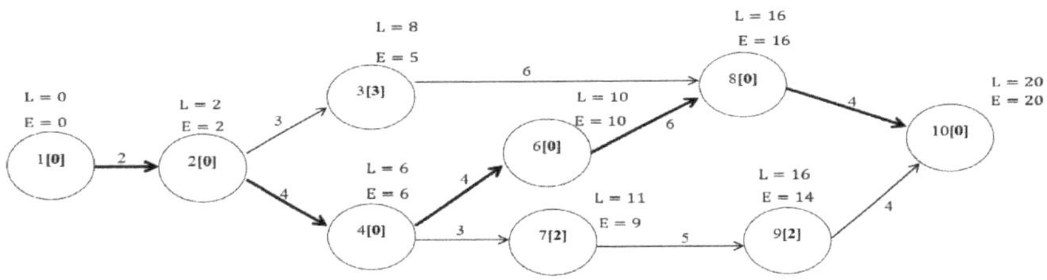

2) Determine the critical path and justify your answer.

The project completion critical path is [1 → 2 → 4 → 6 → 8 → 10] with duration 20 months. Alternative project completion paths are; [1 → 2 → 3 → 5 → 6 → 10] with duration 17 months and [1 → 2 → 4 → 7 → 9 → 10] with duration 18 months.

Example 4: Draw a network diagram and determine the critical path using the information on the table below.

Activity	A	B	C	D	E	F	G	H
Predecessors		A	A	B,C	B,C	E	D,F	G
Duration (Weeks)	5	1	2	3	2	4	2	6

Solution

Method 1 ....[Using Active Activity]

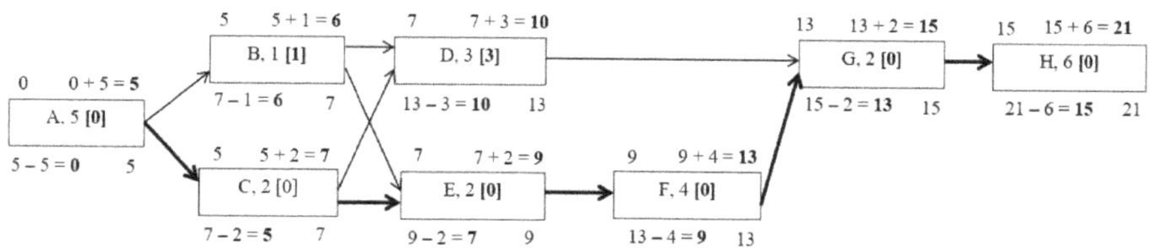

Method 2 ....[Using Dummy Avtivity]

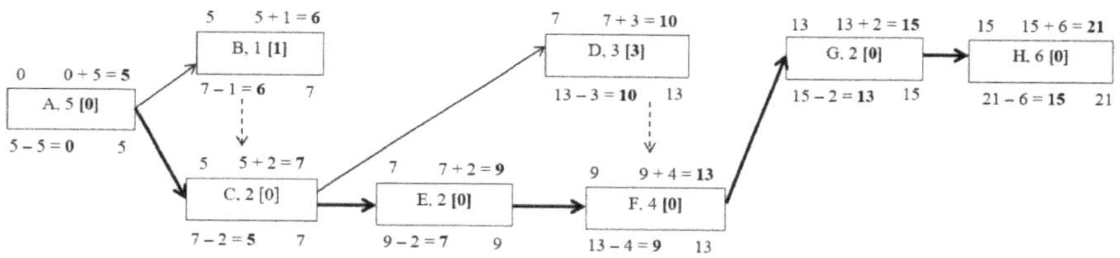

Note: The project completion critical path is [A, C, E, F, G, H] with duration 21 weeks. Alternative project completion paths are [A, B, D, G, H] with duration 17 weeks, [A, B, E, F, G, H] with duration 20 weeks and [A, C, D, G, H] with duration 18 weeks.

Test Your Understanding

Exercise 5: From the tables below, draw a network diagram and identify the project completion critical path with justification.

Table 1

Activity	A	B	C	D	E	F	G
Immediate predecessors			A,B	C	C	C	D,E,F
Duration (Days)	5	6	2	1	3	4	5

Table 2

Activity	A	B	C	D	E
Immediate predecessor			A, B	A, B	D
Duration (Weeks)	2	3	2	2	3

Exercise 6: From the tables below, draw a network diagram and identify the project completion critical path with justification.

Table 1

Activity	(1,2)	(1,3)	(2,3)	(2,4)	(2,5)	(3,6)	(4,5)	(5,6)
Duration (Days)	3	4	2	6	7	4	2	5

Table 2

Activity	1-2	2-4	1-3	3-4	1-4	2-5	4-7	3-6	5-7	6-8	7-8
Duration (Weeks)	7	8	8	6	6	16	19	24	9	7	8

Answers...[See Appendix]

8.3.2 Program Evaluation and Review Technique (PERT)

Program Evaluation and Review Technique (PERT) is an alternative project management tool to critical path method (CPM) used to schedule, organize, and coordinate tasks within a project. The PERT was developed primarily to simplify the planning and scheduling of larger and complex project by the U.S Navy Special Project (U.S Navy's Polaris nuclear submarine project). It is worth knowing that the PERT is used in conjunction with the critical path method but is based on the uncertainty of estimated time. Due to the uncertainty, the PERT analysis makes use of three times and consider the mean as the estimated time of an activity.

1) **Activity Expected Duration**

As seen above, a distinguishing feature of PERT is its ability to deal with uncertainty in activity completion time. The three main time estimation of activities based on PERT analysis includes;

1) Optimistic time (a): It is the shortest time in which the activity can be completed if the condition is excellent (ideal or very good)
2) Most likely time (m): It is the length of time it will take to accomplish the task/activity in normal (usual, regular) condition. It is the completion time with the highest probability and lies between the optimistic and pessimistic time estimate.
3) Pessimistic time (b): It is the longest or maximum possible time it could take to accomplish an activity if the condition is adverse (unfavorable or hostile or abnormal).

The three estimate times are used to determine the expected or average or mean time. The mean time is equivalent to duration time under the critical path method (CPM). The expected time of an activity completion is calculated using the formula below.

$$\text{Expected Time (te)} = \frac{a+4[m]+b}{6} \quad \text{..(1)}$$

Note: Equation (1) can still be expressed in an alternative from as illustrated below.

$$\text{Expected Time (te)} = \frac{a+4[m]+b}{6} \quad \text{....................................[Segment fraction]}$$

$$\text{Expected Time (te)} = \frac{a}{6} + \frac{4m}{6} + \frac{b}{6} \quad \text{....................[Simplify individual fraction]}$$

$$\text{Expected Time (te)} = \frac{a}{6} + \frac{2m}{3} + \frac{b}{6} \quad \text{..................[Factorize denomination LCM]}$$

$$\text{Expected Time (te)} = \frac{1}{3}\left(\frac{a}{6} + 2m + \frac{b}{6}\right) \quad \text{.............[Re-arranged bracket elements]}$$

$$\text{Expected Time (te)} = \frac{1}{3}\left(2m + \frac{a}{6} + \frac{b}{6}\right) \quad \text{...............................[Simplify bracket]}$$

$$\text{Expected Time (te)} = \frac{1}{3}\left(2m + \frac{a+b}{6}\right) \quad \text{..(2)}$$

Example 1: The times and activity of a project is given in the table below, determine the expected time of each of the activities in the table below

Activity	Optimistic Time	Most Likely Time	Pessimistic Time	Preceding Activities
A	4	7	13	
B	3	6	9	
C	2	4	12	A
D	2	3	10	B
E	1	3	11	B
F	4	6	8	C,D
G	1	5	15	E

Solution

Step 1: Formula. $\text{Expected Time(te)} = \frac{\text{Optimistic(a)} + 4[\text{Most Likely}+(m)]+\text{Pessimistic(b)}}{6}$

Step 2: Data substitution and solving

Activity	Estimated Time			Preceding	**Expected Time**	
	Optimistic	Most Likely	Pessimistic		**Working**	**Values**
A	4	7	13		$[4+4(7)+13]/6$	7.5
B	3	6	9		$[3+4(6)+9]/6$	6
C	2	4	12	A	$[2+4(4)+12]/6$	5
D	2	3	10	B	$[2+4(3)+10]/6$	4
E	1	3	11	B	$[1+4(3)+11]/6$	4
F	4	6	8	C,D	$[4+4(6)+8]/6$	6
G	1	5	15	E	$[1+4(5)+15]/6$	6

Example 2: The activities and estimated times of a small project is given in the table below. Find the expected time of the following activities.

Activity	$1-2$	$1-3$	$1-4$	$2-5$	$3-5$	$4-6$	$5-6$
Optimistic	1	1	2	1	2	2	3
Most Likely	1	4	2	1	5	5	6
Pessimistic	7	7	8	1	14	8	15

Solution

Step 1: Formula. $\text{Expected Time}(te) = \frac{\text{Optimistic(a) +4[Most Likely+(m)]+Pessimistic(b)}}{6}$

Step 2: Data substitution and solving

Activity	Estimated Time			**Expected Time**	
	Optimistic	Most Likely	Pessimistic	**Working**	**Value**
$1-2$	1	1	7	$[1+4(1)+7]/6$	2
$1-3$	1	4	7	$[1+4(4)+7]/6$	4
$1-4$	2	2	8	$[2+4(2)+8]/6$	3
$2-5$	1	1	1	$[1+4(1)+1]/6$	1
$3-5$	2	5	14	$[2+4(5)+14]/6$	6
$4-6$	2	5	8	$[2+4(5)+8]/6$	5
$5-6$	3	6	15	$[3+4(6)+15]/6$	7

Example 3: Calculate the missing values in the table below

Activity	Optimistic (a)	Most likely (m)	Pessimistic (b)	Expected Time (te)
A	4		10	7
B	7	23		21
C		14	17	14
D	10	22	28	
E	7		27	21
F	22	29	30	

Solution

Calculation of optimistic Time of activity C

Step 1: Formula. $\text{Optimistic Time(a)} = 6\ (\text{te}) - 4\text{m} - \text{b}$, where; $\text{te} = 14$, $\text{m} = 14$ and $\text{b} = 17$

Step 2: Data substitution and solving

$\text{Optimistic Time(a)} = 6(14) - 4(14) - 17$ ....[Expand brackets]

$\text{Optimistic Time(a)} = 84 - 56 - 17$ ....[Solve equation]

$\text{Optimistic Time(a)} = 11$

Calculation of most likely time

Step 1: Formula. $\text{Most Likely Time(m)} = [6\ (\text{te}) - \text{b} - \text{a}]/4$

Step 2: Data substitution and solving

Activity A	Activity E
Where; $\text{te} = 7$, $\text{a} = 4$, $\text{b} = 10$	Where; $\text{te} = 21$, $\text{a} = 7$, $\text{b} = 27$
$\text{Most Likely Time(m)} = [6\ (7) - 10 - 4]/4$ $\text{Most Likely Time(m)} = [42 - 10 - 4]/4$ $\text{Most Likely Time(m)} = 28/4$ $\text{Most Likely Time(m)} = \mathbf{7}$	$\text{Most Likely Time(m)} = [6\ (21) - 27 - 7]/4$ $\text{Most Likely Time(m)} = [126 - 27 - 7]/4$ $\text{Most Likely Time(m)} = 92/4$ $\text{Most Likely Time(m)} = \mathbf{23}$

Calculation of pessimistic time of activity B

Step 1: Formula. $\text{Pessimistic Time(b)} = 6\ (\text{te}) - 4\text{m} - \text{a}$, where; $\text{te} = 21$, $\text{a} = 7$, $\text{M} = 23$

Step 2: Data substitution and solving

$$\text{Pessimistic Time(b)} = 6\,(21) - 4(23) - 7 \text{ ....[Expand brackets]}$$

$$\text{Pessimistic Time(b)} = 126 - 92 - 7 \text{ ....[Solve equation]}$$

$$\text{Pessimistic Time(b)} = \mathbf{27}$$

Calculation of expected time

Step 1: Formula. $\text{Expected Time (te)} = [a + 4m + b]/6$

Step 2: Data substitution and solving

Activity D	Activity F
Where; $a = 10, m = 22, b = 28$	Where; $a = 22, m = 29, b = 30$
$\text{Expected Time (te)} = [10 + 4(22) + 28]/6$ $\text{Expected Time (te)} = [10 + 88 + 28]/6$ $\text{Expected Time (te)} = 126/6$ $\text{Expected Time (te)} = \mathbf{21}$	$\text{Expected Time (te)} = [22 + 4(29) + 30]/6$ $\text{Expected Time (te)} = [22 + 116 + 30]/6$ $\text{Expected Time (te)} = 168/6$ $\text{Expected Time (te)} = \mathbf{28}$

Activity	Optimistic (a)	Most likely (m)	Pessimistic (b)	Expected Time (te)
A	4	**7**	10	7
B	7	23	**27**	21
C	**11**	14	17	14
D	10	22	28	**21**
E	7	**23**	27	21
F	22	29	30	**28**

Test Your Understanding

Exercise 7: Determine the expected time of each of the activities in the following tables below

Table 1

Activity	Optimistic Time (a)	Most Likely Time (m)	Pessimistic Time (b)
A	1	2	3
B	4	3	8
C	6	9	18
D	4	4	10
E	21	4	5

Table 2

Activity	Optimistic Time	Most Likely Time	Pessimistic Time
1 – 2	3	24	9
1 – 3	2	20	8
2 – 4	6	48	18
3 – 5	4	20	6

Exercise 8: Calculate the missing values in the table below

Activity	Optimistic (a)	Most likely (m)	Pessimistic (b)	Expected Time (te)
	4	5		6
B	2	3	4	
C		8	22	10
D	4		8	6
E	3	4	5	
F	2	4		4
G	2	3	4	
H		7	15	8

Answer...**[See Appendix 1]**

2) Network Diagram

Network drawing in PERT analysis is the same as the case of critical path method (CPM). The difference is that in PERT analysis, we are required to determine the expected time from the estimated times and use the expected time as activities duration.

Example 1: Draw a network and determine the various project completion paths and duration.

Activity	Estimated Time (Days)			Predecessor
	Optimistic (a)	Most likely (m)	Pessimistic (b)	
A	1	1	7	
B	1	4	7	
C	2	2	8	
D	1	1	1	A
E	2	5	14	B
F	2	5	8	C
G	3	6	15	D,E
H	1	2	3	F,G

Solution

Step 1: Determination of activities expected time (Duration)

a) Formula. $\text{Expected Time(te)} = \frac{\text{Optimistic(a)} + 4[\text{Most Likely(m)}] + \text{Pessimistic(b)}}{6}$

b) Data substitution and solving of individual activity expected time

Activity	**Estimated Time**			**Expected Time**		**Predecessor**
	(a)	(m)	(b)	Working	**Value**	
A	1	1	7	$1 + 4(1) + 7/6$	**2**	
B	1	4	7	$1 + 4(4) + 7/6$	**4**	
C	2	2	8	$2 + 4(2) + 8/6$	**3**	
D	1	1	1	$1 + 4(1) + 1/6$	**1**	**A**
E	2	5	14	$2 + 4(5) + 14/6$	**6**	**B**
F	2	5	8	$2 + 4(5) + 8/6$	**5**	**C**
G	3	6	15	$3 + 4(6) + 15/6$	**7**	**D,E**
H	1	2	3	$1 + 4(2) + 3/6$	**2**	**F,G**

Step 2: Drawing of network diagram and determination of completion paths and duration

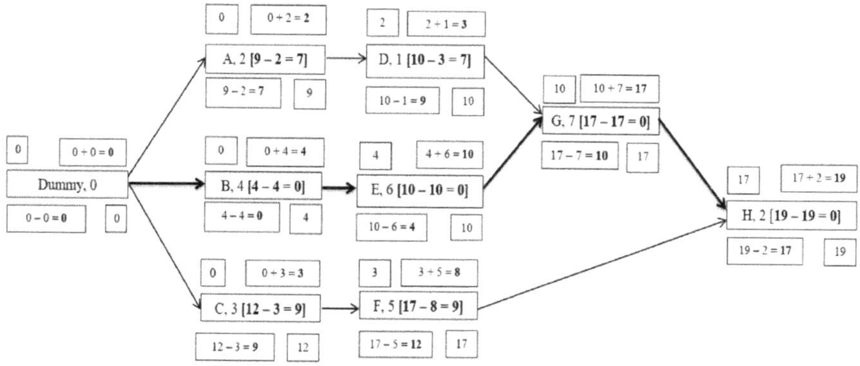

Project Completion Paths	ADGH	**BEGH (Critical path)**	CFH
Duration	12 Days	**19 Days**	10 Days

Example 2: Draw a network diagram and determine the project critical path and duration

Activity	Estimated Time			Predecessor
	Optimistic (a)	Most Likely (m)	Pessimistic (b)	
A	4	5	12	
B	2	3	4	A
C	6	8	22	B
D	4	6	8	C
E	3	4	5	C
F	2	4	6	E
G	2	3	4	D,F

Solution

Step 1: Determination of activities expected time (Duration)

a) Formula. $\text{Expected Time(te)} = \frac{\text{Optimistic(a)} + 4[\text{Most Likely}+(\text{m})]+\text{Pessimistic(b)}}{6}$

b) Data substitution and solving of individual activity expected time

Activity	Estimated Time			Estimated Time		Predecessor
	(a)	(m)	(b)	Working	Value	
A	4	5	12	$4 + 4(5) + 12/6$	**6**	
B	2	3	4	$2 + 4(3) + 4/6$	**3**	**A**
C	6	8	22	$6 + 4(8) + 22/6$	**10**	**B**
D	4	6	8	$4 + 4(6) + 8/6$	**6**	**C**
E	3	4	5	$3 + 4(4) + 5/6$	**4**	**C**
F	2	4	6	$2 + 4(4) + 6/6$	**4**	**E**
G	2	3	4	$2 + 4(3) + 4/6$	**3**	**D,F**

Step 2: Drawing of network and determination of project completion paths and duration

a) Graphical Method

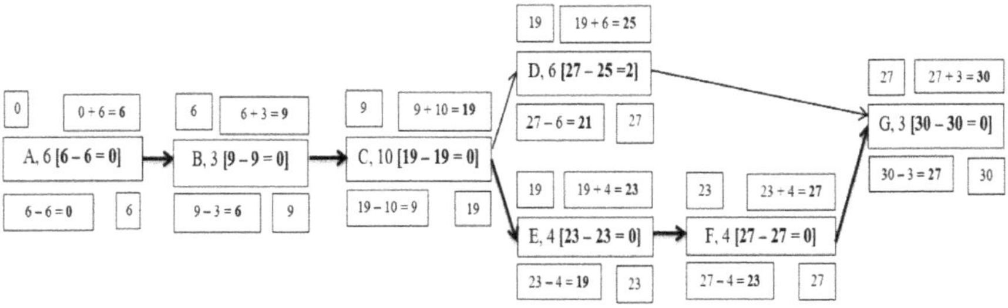

b) Tabular Method

Activity	Estimated Time			Estimated Time	Predecessor Activities	Earliest Time		Latest Time		Slack Time
	(a)	(m)	(b)	Value		**ES**	**EF**	**LF**	**LS**	**LS - ES**
A	4	5	12	6	[Dummy]	0	6	6	0	**0**
B	2	3	4	3	A	6	9	9	6	**0**
C	6	8	22	10	B	9	19	19	9	**0**
D	4	6	8	6	C	19	25	27	21	2
E	3	4	5	4	C	19	23	23	19	**0**
F	2	4	6	4	E	23	27	27	23	**0**
G	2	3	4	3	D,F	27	30	30	27	**0**
[Critical Path = A → B → C → E → F → G and Duration = 30 Days]										

Example 3: Draw a network diagram and determine the critical path using information from the table below.

Activity	Optimistic Time	Most Likely Time	Pessimistic Time
1 − 2	1	1	7
1 − 3	1	4	7
1 − 4	2	2	8
2 − 5	1	1	1
3 − 5	2	5	14
4 − 6	2	5	8
5 − 6	3	6	15

Solution

Step 1: Calculation of activities expected time

Activity	Optimistic Time	Most Likely Time	Pessimistic Time	**Expected Time**
1 − 2	1	1	7	**2**
1 − 3	1	4	7	**4**
1 − 4	2	2	8	**3**
2 − 5	1	1	1	**1**
3 − 5	2	5	14	**6**
4 − 6	2	5	8	**5**
5 − 6	3	6	15	**7**

Step 2: Network drawing and identification of project completion critical path

Graphical Method

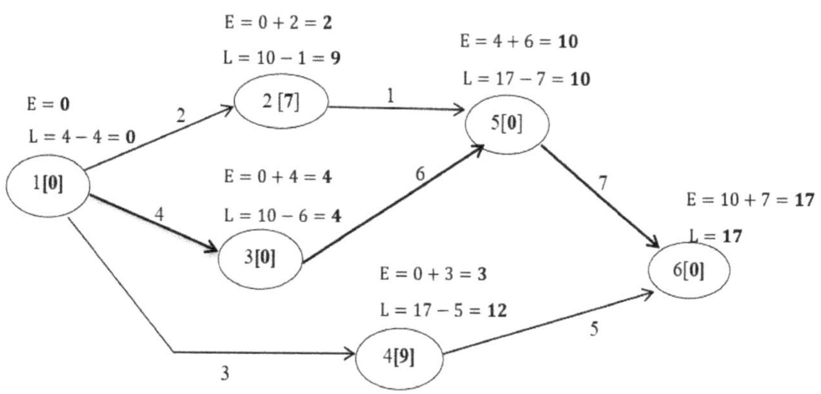

Note: The project critical path is; $1 \rightarrow 3 \rightarrow 5 \rightarrow 6$ with duration $4 + 6 + 7 =$ **17 Days**

Example 4: Draw a network diagram and determine the critical path using information from the table below. [Use the tabular method]

Activity	A	B	C	D	E	F	G	H	I	J
Expected Time	3	5	3	4	8	2	4	2	5	3
Predecessor			B	A,C	D	C	F	F	B	H,E,G

Solution

Activity	Expected Time	Predecessor Activities	Earliest Time			Latest Time			Slack Time
			ES	**EF**		**LF**	**LS**		**LF - EF**
A	3	Dummy	0	3	↓	8	5	↑	5
B	5	Dummy	0	5		5	0		0
C	3	B	5	8		8	5		0
D	4	A,C	8	12		12	8		0
E	8	D	12	20		20	12		0
F	2	C	8	10		16	14		6
G	4	F	10	14		20	16		6
H	2	F	10	12		20	18		8
I	5	B	5	10		23	18		13
J	3	H,E,G	20	23		23	20		0
Interpretation: The critical path is given as; **Dummy → B → C → D → E → J → Dummy**									

Example 5: Draw the network diagram and identify the possible project completion path and their respective duration.

Activity	$(1,2)$	$(2,3)$	$(2,4)$	$(3,4)$	$(3,5)$	$(5,6)$	$(3,6)$	$(4,6)$
Optimistic	3	6	5	3	1	2	4	2
Most Likely	6	12	11	9	4	5	19	5
Pessimistic	15	30	17	27	7	8	28	14

Solution

Step 1: Determination of activities expected time

Activity	Estimated Time			Expected Time	
	Optimistic	Most Likely	Pessimistic	Working	Value
$(1,2)$	3	6	15	$[3+4(6)+15]/6$	7
$(2,3)$	6	12	30	$[6+4(12)+30]/6$	14
$(2,4)$	5	11	17	$[5+4(11)+17]/6$	11
$(3,4)$	3	9	27	$[3+4(9)+27]/6$	11
$(3,5)$	1	4	7	$[1+4(4)+7]/6$	4
$(5,6)$	2	5	8	$[2+4(5)+8]/6$	5
$(3,6)$	4	19	28	$[4+4(19)+28]/6$	18
$(4,6)$	2	5	14	$[2+4(5)+14]/6$	6

Step 2: Drawing of network diagram and identification of completion path and duration

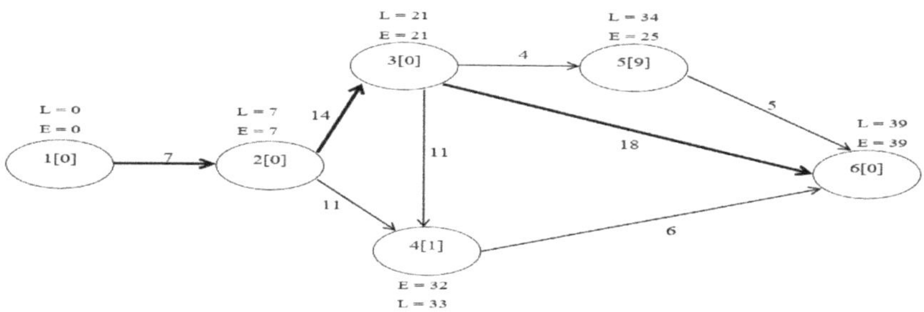

Project Completion Paths	1,2,3,5,6	1,2,3,6 [Critical Path]	1,2,3,4,6	1,2,4,6
Duration	30 Day	39 Days	38 Days	24 Day

Test Your Understanding

Exercise 9: Determine the different project completion paths and their duration (Days)

Activity	Predecessor	Optimistic Time	Most Likely Time	Pessimistic Time
A		2	5	8
B	A	2	3	4
C	A	6	8	10
D	A	2	4	6
E	B	2	6	10
F	C	6	7	8
G	D,E,F	6	8	10

Answer			
Project Completion Paths	ABEG	ACFG	ADG
Duration	22 Days	28 Days	17 Days

Exercise 10: Determine the critical path and its duration using information in the table below

Activity	A	B	C	D	E	F	G	H
Expected Time (weeks)	2	3	4	1	2	2	4	3
Predecessor Activity		A	A	C	C	E	D,F	C

[Answer: Critical path ($A \rightarrow C \rightarrow E \rightarrow F \rightarrow G$) and Duration (14 weeks)]

Exercise 11: The time estimates (in days) for the activities of two projects are given in the tables below. Determine the critical path and critical path duration.

Table 1

Activity	1 – 2	1 – 3	1 – 4	2 – 5	3 – 5	4 – 6	5 – 6
Optimistic Duration	1	1	2	1	2	2	3
Most Likely Duration	1	4	2	1	5	5	6
Pessimistic Duration	7	7	8	1	14	8	15

[Answer: Critical path ($1 \rightarrow 3 \rightarrow 5 \rightarrow 6$) and Duration (17 days)]

Table 2

Activity	$(1,2)$	$(1,3)$	$(2,4)$	$(3,4)$	$(4,5)$	$(2,5)$	$(3,5)$
Optimistic Time	6	5	4	4	4	4	2
Most Likely Time	9	8	7	7	10	7	5
Pessimistic Time	18	17	22	16	22	10	8

[Answer: Critical Path = $1 \to 2 \to 4 \to 5$ and duration = 30 Days]

3) Probability of Project Completion

Due to curiosity, it is logical for managers to determine the probability of completing a project at a given time. To determine the probability, we are required to obtain the project completion duration variance, which is the sum of critical path activities duration variances (when a pre-determine project variance is not given). It is worth knowing that the probability of completing a project at a certain date follows a normal probability distribution. Therefore, our analysis in this section will be limited to project duration variance and project duration standard deviation. The calculation of probability of project completion will be seen under the chapter "normal probability distribution".

a) Activity Duration Variance: Variance measures the difference between the expected time and actual time of an activity. As the variance of an activity duration increases, the estimate of activity duration is less accurate. The formula for calculating an activity duration variance is given as;

$$\text{Activity Duration Variance}(\sigma^2) = \left(\frac{b-a}{6}\right)^2 \quad \text{...(1)}$$

Note: It is worth knowing that equation (1) can be written as a fraction as seen below

$$\text{Activity Duration Variance}(\sigma^2) = \left(\frac{b-a}{6}\right)^2 \quad \text{..................[Remember}\left(\left(\frac{a-b}{m}\right)^n = \frac{(a-b)^n}{m^n}\right)\text{]}$$

$$\text{Activity Duration Variance}(\sigma^2) = \frac{(b-a)^2}{6^2} \quad \text{....................[Work denominator exponent]}$$

$$\text{Activity Duration Variance}(\sigma^2) = \frac{(b-a)^2}{36} \quad \text{...(2)}$$

Example 1: Determine the variance of activates in the table below

Activity	Optimistic time (a)	Most likely time (m)	Pessimistic time (b)
A	1	1	7
B	1	4	7
C	2	2	8
D	1	1	1
E	2	5	14
F	2	5	8
G	3	6	15

Solution

Step 1: Formula. Activity Duration Variance$(\sigma^2) = \frac{(b-a)^2}{36}$

Step 2: Data substitution and solving

Activity	**Estimated Time**			**Variance**	
	(a)	(m)	(b)	Working	Value
A	1	1	7	$(7-1)^2/36 = 36/36$	1
B	1	4	7	$(7-1)^2/36 = 36/36$	1
C	2	2	8	$(8-2)^2/36 = 36/36$	1
D	1	1	1	$(1-1)^2/36 = 0/36$	0
E	2	5	14	$(14-2)^2/36 = 144/36$	4
F	2	5	8	$(8-2)^2/36 = 36/36$	1
G	3	6	15	$(15-3)^2/36 = 144/36$	4

b) Activity Duration Standard Deviation: Standard deviation is defined as the square root of variance. Therefore, the formula for calculating activity duration standard deviation is derived as seen below.

Activity Standard Deviation$(\sigma) = \sqrt{\frac{(b-a)^2}{36}}$ ....[Apply surd division principle]

Activity Standard Deviation$(\sigma) = \frac{\sqrt{(b-a)^2}}{\sqrt{36}}$ ......[Square numerator and denominator]

Activity Standard Deviation$(\sigma) = \frac{(b-a)^2}{36}$ ....[Simplify fraction]

Activity Standard Deviation$(\sigma) = \frac{b-a}{6}$ ....(3)

Example 1: Determine the standard deviation of activities in the table below

Activity	Optimistic time (a)	Most likely time (m)	Pessimistic time (b)
A	1	5	3
B	1	7	4
C	1	5	3
D	5	11	8
E	2	6	4
F	5	7	6
G	4	6	5
H	1	5	3

Solution

Step 1: Formula. Activity Standard Deviation$(\sigma) = \frac{b-a}{6}$

Step 2: Data substitution and solving

Activity	Estimated Time			Standard Deviation	
	(a)	(m)	(b)	Working	Values
A	1	5	3	$(3-1)/6$	$1/3$
B	1	7	4	$(4-1)/6$	$1/2$
C	1	5	3	$(3-1)/6$	$1/3$
D	5	11	8	$(8-5)/6$	$1/2$
E	2	6	4	$(4-2)/6$	$1/3$
F	5	7	6	$(6-5)/6$	$1/6$
G	4	6	5	$(5-4)/6$	$1/6$
H	1	5	3	$(3-1)/6$	$1/3$

Test Your Understanding

Exercise 12: Determine the variance and standard deviation of activities in the table below

Activity	A	B	C	D	E	F	G
Optimistic	7	15	7	9	2	14	2
Most likely	10	18	8	12	24	18	3
Pessimistic	12	20	9	17	26	20	7

Exercise 13: Fill the empty spaces in the table below

Activity	Predecessor Activity	Optimistic Time	Most Likely Time	Pessimistic Time	Variance	Standard Deviation
A			6	15	4	2
B		2	5	14	4	2
C	A	6	1	30		4
D	A		5	8	1	1
E	B,C	5	11		4	2
F	D,E	3	6	15	4	

[Answer..See Appendix 1]

8.4 Project Crashing Analysis

Project Crashing is the method of shortening or reducing project completion duration. To crash a project, we are required to identify the project completion critical path and crash all activities belong to the critical path. Project crashing shows the relationship between time and cost (time-cost trade off) and helps in determining the minimum and optimum project completion duration and cost. Project crashing is based on the assumption that activities are performed quickly when more resources are allocated towards them. Project crashing is induced by project manager and/or customer. A customer induced project crashing by providing incentive to contractor for early project completion. Project contractor perform project crashing for the following reasons illustrated below.

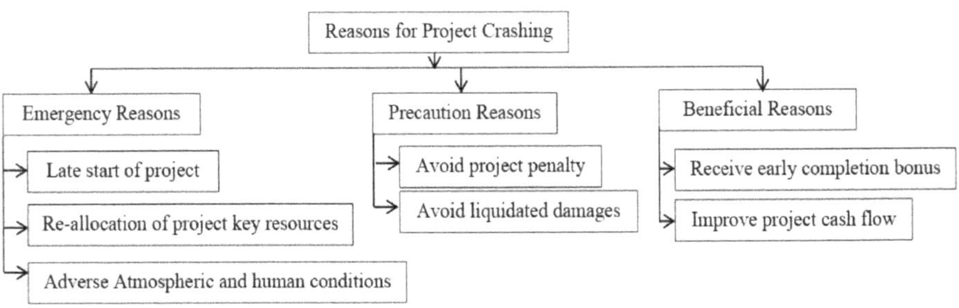

Note: Avoid liquidated damage is the amount of money that both parties in a contract agree upon if a contract is breached or if a party takes legal action. Breaching a contract means situation a party fails to honor or respect the terms or obligations accepted during contract signing. To crash a project, we are required to determine project activities extra cost, possible reduction time and crash cost per unit time (cost slope).

8.4.1 Crash Cost per Unit Time of Activities

Remember that the object of project crashing is to reduce project initial completion time. To do this, project managers are required to increase project resources directed toward the activities to be crashed. The time reduction produces an additional cost that when expressed in per unit time is called crash cost per unit of activities, or cost slope or incremental cost or marginal cost. Activity cost slope indicates the additional cost incurred per unit of time saved in reducing the duration of an activity. It is worth knowing that activity cost is sub-divided into crash cost and normal cost and activity time is also sub-divided into crash time and normal time. The linear expression of cost and time relationship in project crashing is illustrated below.

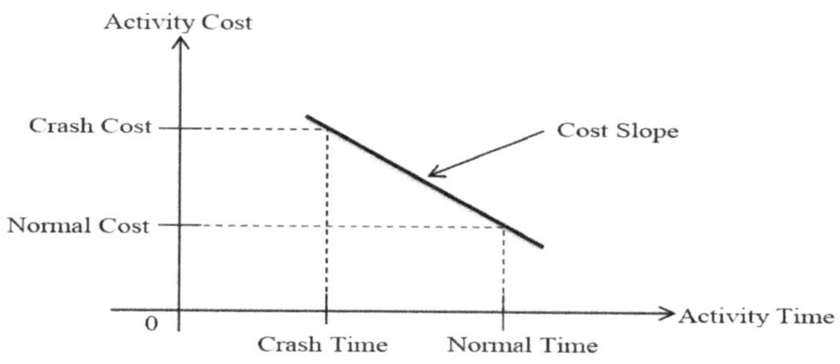

Activity normal time is the time required to complete an activity with crashing. Activity crash time is the minimum time required to complete an activity as a result of crashing. Activity normal cost is the direct cost (labour, equipment, material and subcontractors cost) required to complete an activity under normal time situation. Activity crash cost is the direct cost required to complete an activity under a crash time situation. Cost slope is calculated using the formula below.

$$\text{Cost Slope} = \frac{\text{Crash Cost} - \text{Normal Cost}}{\text{Normal Time} - \text{Crash Time}} \quad \ldots\ldots(2)$$

Where; Crash Cost − Normal Cost = Extra Cost = Change in Cost

Normal Time − Crash Time = Possible Reduction Time = Change in Time

$$\text{Cost Slope} = \frac{\text{Extra Cost}}{\text{Possible Reduction Time}} \quad \ldots\ldots(3)$$

Note: Normal time is by default greater than crash time and normal cost is by default greater than crash cost. Normal time is also called maximum time and crash time minimum time. Crash cost is also called maximum cost and normal cost minimum cost.

Example 1: An activity takes 60 days to complete at a normal cost of 13,500 fcfa and the activity is still possible to be completed in 45 days with an additional cost of 18,000 fcfa. What is the incremental cost of the activity?

Solution

Step 1: Formula. $\text{Incremental Cost} = \frac{\text{Crash Cost} - \text{Normal Cost}}{\text{Normal Time} - \text{Crash Time}}$,

Where; $\text{Crash Cost} = 18{,}000$, $\text{Normal Cost} = 13{,}500$, $\text{Normal Time} = 60$, $\text{Crash Time} = 45$

Step 2: Data substitution and solving

$\text{Incremental Cost} = \frac{18{,}000 - 13{,}500}{60 - 45}$ ....[Simplify numerator and denominator]

$\text{Incremental Cost} = \frac{4{,}500}{15}$ ....[Solve fraction]

$\text{Incremental Cost} = \mathbf{300\ fcfa}$

Step 3: Interpretation: A reduction of a day will cost 300 fcfa extra.

Example 2: The cost and time of project activities is given in the table below. Determine the activities incremental cost.

Activity	Duration (Days)		Cost (FCFA)	
	Normal	Crash	Normal	Crash
A	120	100	12,000	14,000
B	20	15	1,800	2,800
C	40	30	16,000	22,000
D	30	20	1,400	2,000
E	50	40	3,600	4,800
F	60	45	13,500	18,000

Solution

Step 1: Formula. Incremental Cost $= \frac{\text{Crash Cost} - \text{Normal Cost}}{\text{Normal Time} - \text{Crash Time}}$

Step 2: Data substitution and solving

Activity	Duration (Days)		Cost (FCFA)		**Cost Slope**		**Rank**
	Normal	Crash	Normal	Crash	**Working**	**Value**	
A	120	100	12,000	14,000	$\frac{14{,}000-12{,}000}{120-100}$	100	2
B	20	15	1,800	2,800	$\frac{2{,}800-1{,}800}{20-15}$	200	4
C	40	30	16,000	22,000	$\frac{22{,}000-16{,}000}{40-30}$	600	6
D	30	20	1,400	2,000	$\frac{2{,}000-1{,}400}{30-20}$	60	1
E	50	40	3,600	4,800	$\frac{4{,}800-3{,}600}{50-40}$	120	3
F	60	45	13,500	18,000	$\frac{18{,}000-13{,}500}{60-45}$	300	5

Example 3: The cost and time of small project activities is presented in the table below. Compute the activities cost slope values.

Activity	1 – 2	1 – 3	1 – 4	2 – 5	3 – 2	3 – 4	4 – 5
Normal Time (Day)	15	6	9	16	8	6	13
Normal Cost (fcfa)	500	800	800	850	1,120	1,200	1,600
Crash Time (Day)	11	3	5	12	5	3	8
Crash Cost (fcfa)	900	860	910	865	1,230	1,380	1,850

Solution

Step 1: Formula. Cost Slope $= \frac{\text{Extra Cost}}{\text{Possible Reduction Time}}$

Step 2: Data substitution and solving

Activity	Extra Cost [Crash Cost – Normal Cost]	Possible Reduction [Normal Time – Crash Time]	Activity Cost Slope $\frac{\text{Extra Cost}}{\text{Possible Reduction Time}}$
1 – 2	$900 - 500 = \mathbf{400}$	$15 - 11 = \mathbf{4}$	$400/4 = \mathbf{100}$
1 – 3	$860 - 800 = \mathbf{60}$	$6 - 3 = \mathbf{3}$	$60/3 = \mathbf{20}$
1 – 4	$910 - 800 = \mathbf{110}$	$9 - 5 = \mathbf{4}$	$110/4 = \mathbf{27.5}$

2 – 5	865 – 850 = **15**	16 – 12 = **4**	15/4 = **3.75**
3 – 2	1,230 – 1,120 = **110**	8 – 5 = **3**	110/3 = **36.6⁺**
3 – 4	1,380 – 1,200 = **180**	6 – 3 = **3**	180/3 = **60**
4 – 5	1,850 – 1,600 = **250**	13 – 8 = **5**	250/5 = **50**

Example 4: The cost and time information of a project activities ate given in the table below. Compute the cost slope for each of the activities. Cost is in fcfa and duration in days.

Activity	Optimistic Time	Most Likely Time	Pessimistic Time	Normal Cost	Crash Time	Crash Cost
1 – 2	1	5	3	5,000	1	9,000
2 – 3	1	7	4	8,000	3	14,000
2 – 4	1	5	3	4,000	2	6,000
2 – 5	5	11	8	5,000	7	6,000
3 – 6	2	6	4	3,000	2	5,000
4 – 6	5	7	6	2,000	4	3,600
5 – 7	4	6	5	10,000	4	14,000
6 – 7	1	5	3	7,000	1	10,600

Solution

Hint: In order to determine the cost slope values, we are required the extra cost (difference between crash cost and normal cost) and possible reduction time (difference between expected time and crash time). There our first step will be the determination of expected time.

Step 1: Formula. $\text{Cost Slope} = \frac{\text{Extra Cost}}{\text{Possible Reduction Time}} = \frac{\text{Crash Cost} - \text{Normal Cost}}{\text{Expected Time} - \text{Crash Time}}$

Step 2: Determination of expected time or duration

Activity	Optimistic Time (a)	Most Likely Time (m)	Pessimistic Time (b)	Expected Time $\left[\text{Expected Time(te)} = \frac{a + 4(m) + b}{6}\right]$
1 – 2	1	5	3	$[1 + 4(5) + 3]/6 = 4$
2 – 3	1	7	4	$[1 + 4(7) + 4]/6 = 5.5 \cong 6$
2 – 4	1	5	3	$[1 + 4(5) + 3]/6 = 4$
2 – 5	5	11	8	$[5 + 4(11) + 8]/6 = 9.5 \cong 10$
3 – 6	2	6	4	$[2 + 4(6) + 4]/6 = 5$
4 – 6	5	7	6	$[5 + 4(7) + 6]/6 = 6.5 \cong 7$
5 – 7	4	6	5	$[3 + 4(6) + 5]/6 = 5.5 \cong 6$
6 – 7	1	5	3	$[1 + 4(5) + 3]/6 = 4$

Step 3: Data substitution and solving

Activity	Expected Time	Normal Cost	Crash Time	Crash Cost	Extra Cost	Possible Reduction	Cost Slope
1 – 2	4	5,000	1	9,000	4,000	3	1,333
2 – 3	6	8,000	3	14,000	6,000	3	2,000
2 – 4	4	4,000	2	6,000	2,000	2	1,000
2 – 5	10	5,000	7	6,000	1,000	3	333
3 – 6	5	3,000	2	5,000	2,000	3	667
4 – 6	7	2,000	4	3,600	1,600	3	533
5 – 7	6	10,000	4	14,000	4,000	2	2,000
6 – 7	4	7,000	1	10,600	3,600	3	1,200

Test Your Understanding

Exercise 14: Determine the extra cost and possible reduction time for each activity

Activity	Normal		Crash	
	Duration (Days)	Cost (fcfa)	Duration (Days)	Cost (fcfa)
A	4	8,000	2	9,000
B	8	16,000	4	20,000
C	4	12,000	3	13,000
D	6	34,000	2	35,000

Exercise 15: Determine the cost slope value of the project activities in the following tables

Table 1

Activity	Duration (Weeks)		Cost (fcfa)	
	Normal	Crash	Normal	Crash
1 – 2	6	2	42.000	44,000
1 – 3	5	3	16,000	16,500
2 – 4	7	4	66,000	72,000
3 – 4	4	1	2,000	5,000

Table 2

Activity	Predecessor Activity	Estimated Duration			Cost		Crash Time
		Optimistic Time	Most Likely Time	Pessimistic Time	Normal	Crash	
A		1	1	7	8,000	10,000	4
B		1	4	7	2,500	3,000	2
C		2	2	8	5,000	6,000	1
D	A	1	1	1	1,000	1,000	1
E	B	2	5	14	9,000	12,000	3
F	C	2	5	8	5,000	20,000	2
G	D,E	3	6	15	7,500	10,000	5
H	F,G	1	2	3	9,000	14,000	1

Answer……………………………………………………………………[See appendix]

8.4.2 Activity Crashing Selection

The values of activities cost slope provide vital information for activity crashing selection ordering or preference. The following ideas are worth knowing when selecting activities for crashing.

1) Activity Selection preference: First select activity on the critical path with the smallest crash cost per unit time (cost slope).
2) Activity Crashing Scope: Crash the activity selected to the maximum units permissible. The maximum unit permissible is the possible reduction time of the activity. It is worth knowing that possible reduction time of activities at the end of crashing process must and/or may be zero and time reduction can be done in block or per unit time.

Note: Activity crashing can create new (alternative) critical paths leading to a situation of multiple project completion paths. In multiple critical paths situation, crashing should be performed in all the critical paths simultaneously. At the end of project crashing, we should be able to distinguish three project completion times [normal project completion duration, minimum project completion duration and optimum project completion duration].

1) Normal project completion duration is the first or original project completion critical path duration or project duration before the application of crashing process.
2) Minimum project completion duration is the smallest project completion path duration after the application of crashing process.
3) Optimum project completion duration is the project completion duration after the application of crashing process with the smallest project completion cost.

Example 1: The cost and time information of a small farm project is given in the table below. Draw the network and classify the critical path activities in crashing preference

Activity	Predecessor	Duration [Days]		Cost [fcfa]	
		Normal	Crash	Normal	Crash
A		7	6	15,000	18,000
B	A	12	9	11,000	14,000
C	A	22	21	18,500	19,000
D	B	11	10	8,000	9,000
E	C,D	6	5	4,000	4,500

Solution

Step 1: Drawing of network and identification of critical path and duration

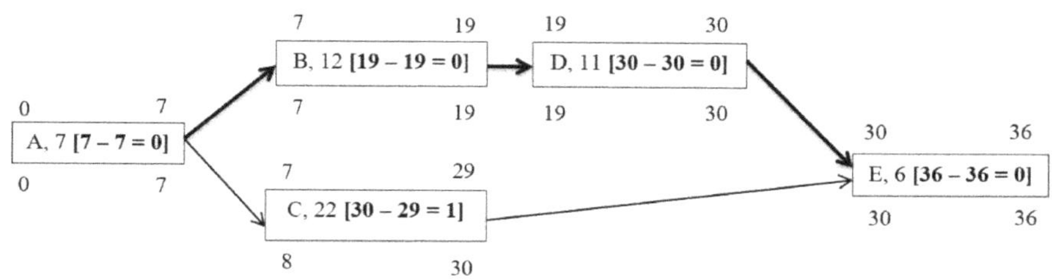

Note: The critical path is given as; ABDE and duration is 36 days.

Step 2: Determination of activities cost slope and crashing classification

1) Formula. $\text{Cost Slope} = \frac{\text{Extra Cost}}{\text{Possible Reduction Time}}$
2) Data substitution and solving

Activity	A	B	C	D	E
Extra cost	3000	3000	500	1000	500
Possible reduction Time	1	3	1	1	1
Cost slope	3000	1000	500	1000	500
Activity Crashing Classification	**4**	**2**		**3**	**1**

Explanation: Activity E is having the smallest cost slope, making it the first activity to be crash. Activity B and D are having the same cost slope value but different possible reduction time. We use to the possible reduction time to decide on which activity to be crash. It is more logical to crash the activity with the highest possible reduction time, making activity B second and activity D third crashing activity. Activity A is the critical activity with the highest cost slope, making it the last crashing activity. Assuming a non-multiple critical paths situation, activity C is not crashed as it does not belong to the critical path.

Example 2: From the cost and time information of a project of seven activities is presented in the table below.

Activity	Maximum Time	Minimum Cost	Minimum Time	Maximum Cost	Predecessor
A	15	30	12	39	
B	20	40	17	49	A
C	15	10	14	15	A
D	5	10	3	20	B
E	3	5	2	16	B
F	7	8	6	10	C
G	17	30	13	38	D,E,F

Work Required

1) Draw the network diagram and identify the different project completion paths and their respective durations.
2) Crash the project and identify the normal project completion duration and minimum project completion duration.

Solution

1) Draw the network diagram and identify the different project completion paths and their respective durations.

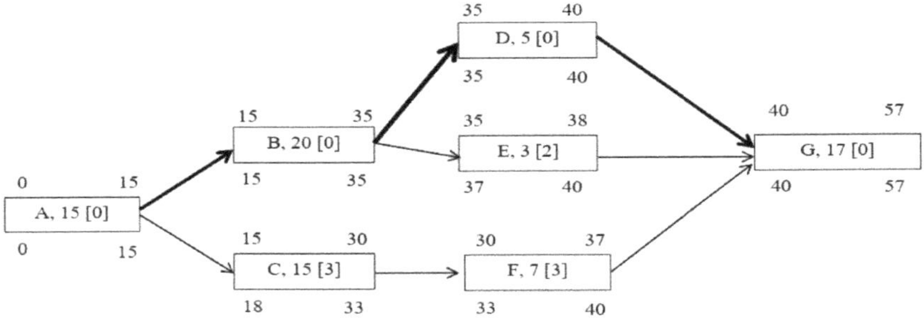

Project Paths	ABDG	ABEG	ACFG
Duration	$15 + 20 + 5 + 17 =$ **57**	$15 + 20 + 3 + 17 =$ **55**	$15 + 15 + 7 + 17 =$ **54**

2) Crash the project and identify the normal project completion duration and minimum project completion duration.

Hint: The minimum cost is also called normal cost and maximum cost is also known as crash cost. Maximum time is equivalent to normal time and minimum time is also called crash time.

Step 1: Calculation of activities cost slope or activities cost coefficient

1) Formula. $\text{Cost Slope} = \frac{\text{Extra Cost}}{\text{Possible Reduction Time}}$
2) Data substitution and solving

Activity	A	B	C	D	E	F	G
Extra Cost	9	9	5	10	11	2	8
Possible Reduction Time	3	3	1	2	1	1	4
Cost Slope	3	3	5	5	11	2	2

Step 2: Crashing of project

Hint: The number of crashing is related to the number of activities in the original or first project critical path. Crashing process ends when all the activities in the first critical path are crashed. Here, we are going to have four crashing processes.

First Crashing Process: Here, we have only a critical path (ABDG) and the critical activity with the smallest cost slope is G with duration 4 days. Since activity G is related to all completion paths, we reduce 4 days from each completion path.

Project Completion Path	ABD<u>G</u>	ABE<u>G</u>	ACF<u>G</u>
New Duration	$57 - 4 =$ **53**	$55 - 4 =$ **51**	$54 - 4 =$ **50**

Complementary Explanation: Activity G initial duration is 17 days. Removing 4 days from it gives a new duration of 13 days. The new network with this adjustment is illustrated below.

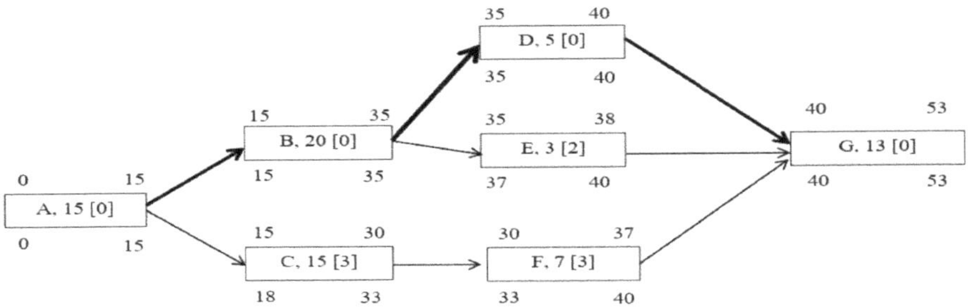

Second Crashing Process: ABDG is still the only critical path as it is having the highest duration. Activity A and B are having same cost slope and duration. Therefore any of them can be selected for crashing. Let's select activity A, we reduce 3 days from each project completion path since A is related to all project completion path.

Project Completion Path	ABDG	ABEG	ACFG
New Duration	53 − 3 = **50**	51 − 3 = **48**	50 − 3 = **47**

Complementary Explanation: Let consider Activity "B" is selected; its initial duration is 20 days. Removing 3 days from it gives a new duration of 17 days. The new network with this adjustment is illustrated as seen below.

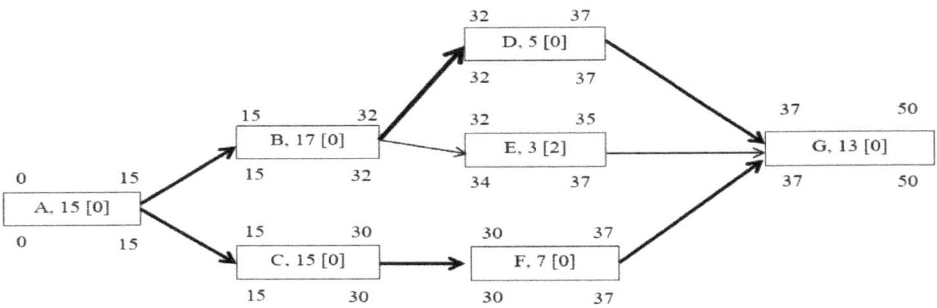

Third Crashing Process: Activity B is now crashed. Here, we reduce 3 days in project completion paths (ABDG) and (ABEG) only. Project completion path (ACFG) is not reduced since activity B is not related to it.

Project Completion Path	ABDG	ABEG	ACFG
New Duration	50 − 3 = **47**	48 − 3 = **45**	**47**

Complementary Explanation: Now select Activity "A" and its initial duration is 15 days. Removing 3 days from it gives a new duration of 12 days. The new network with this adjustment is illustrated below.

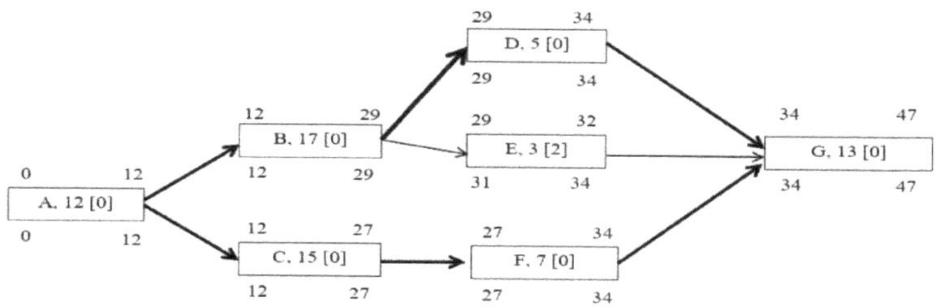

Fourth Crashing Process: From the third crashing table, we realized that project completion paths (ABDG) and (ACFG) are having the same and highest project completion duration (47 days). Since the paths are not having a common activity, we identify from each path the activity with the smallest cost slope and consider the crashing activity. In (ABDG) is activity D and (ACFG) is activity F. completion path (ABEG) is not included as it is not a critical path and have no common activity with the critical paths (ABDG) and (ACFG).

Project Completion Path	ABDG	ABEG	ACFG
New Duration	$47 - 2 = \mathbf{45}$	**45**	$47 - 1 = \mathbf{46}$

Complementary Explanation: Activity "D" with initial duration 5 days is reduced by 1 day giving 4 days and activity "F" with initial duration 7 days is reduced by 1 day giving 6 days. The new network with this adjustment is illustrated as seen below.

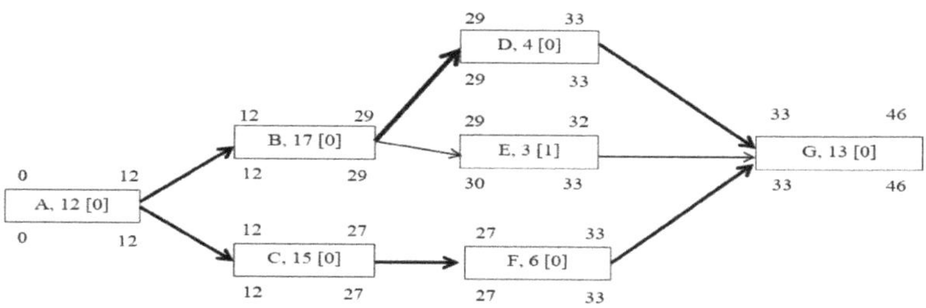

Step 3: Crashing Interpretation. The normal project completion duration is 57 days and the minimum project completion duration is 45 days. The optimum project completion duration cannot be determined at this level since total project completion cost values are not given.

Complementary Explanation: Since all activities in the original project completion critical paths (ABDG) are crashed, we end the crashing process. The general crashing process can be summarized in the summary crashing table as seen below.

Completion Paths	Crashing Process					Critical Paths Evolution Analysis	
	Pre-crashing	1st	2nd	3rd	4th	Crashing	Paths
ABDG	**57**	**53**	**50**	**47**	**45**	1st	ABDG
ABEG	55	51	48	45	45	2nd	ABDG
ACFG	54	50	47	47	46	3rd	ABDG and ACFG
						4th	ACFG

Example 3: The time/duration and cost information of project activities is presented in the table below.

Activity	Predecessor	Duration (Days)		Cost (fcfa)	
		Normal	Crash	Normal	Crash
A		4	3	8,000	9,000
B	A	5	3	16,000	20,000
C	A	4	3	12,000	13,000
D	B	6	5	34,000	35,000
E	C	6	4	42,000	44,000
F	D	5	4	16,000	16,500
G	E	7	4	66,000	72,000
H	F,G	4	3	2,000	5,000

Solution

Step 1: Drawing of project network and identification of completion paths

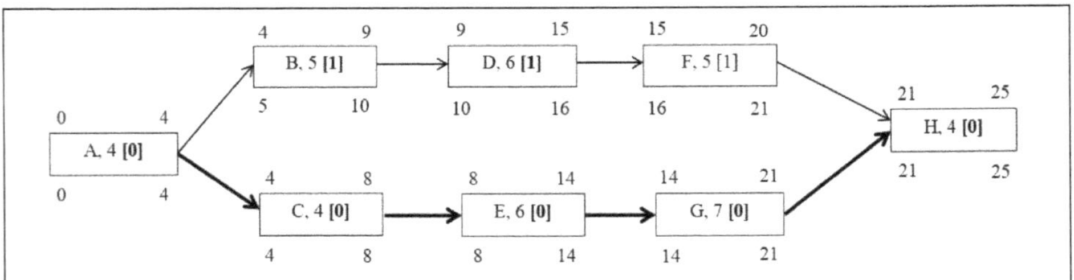

Project Completion Path	Critical path is ACEGH with duration [4 + 4 + 6 + 7 + 4 = 25 Days]
	Non-critical path is ABDFH with duration [4 + 5 + 6 + 5 + 4 = 24 Days]

Step 2: Determination of activities cost slope

a) Formula. $\text{Activity Cost Slope} = \frac{\text{Extra Cost}}{\text{Possible Reduction Time}}$

b) Data substitution and solving

Activity	A	B	C	D	E	F	G	H
Extra Cost	1,000	4,000	1,000	1,000	2,000	500	6,000	3,000
Possible Reduction	1	2	1	1	2	1	3	1
Cost Slope	1,000	2,000	1,000	1,000	1,000	500	2,000	3,000

Step 3: Project crashing

Hint: Since a specific crashing limit is given, we are required to use the individual time period crashing method. Here, we are not required to crash all critical path activities but we are required to crash the critical path duration by three (3) days.

First Crashing: From the critical path activities, we can see that activities A, C and E are having the same cost slope value. Therefore, any of the activities can be crashed.

Completion Paths	Crashing A	Crashing C	Crashing E
ACEGH	$25 - 1 = \mathbf{24}$	$25 - 1 = \mathbf{24}$	$25 - 1 = \mathbf{24}$
ABDFH	$24 - 1 = \mathbf{23}$	24	24
Possible Reduction Balance	$1 - 1 = \mathbf{0}$	$1 - 1 = \mathbf{0}$	$2 - 1 = \mathbf{1}$

Second Crashing: After the first crashing, the project schedule of project activities is now given as seen below.

Crashing A	Activity	A	B	C	D	E	F	G	H
	Predecessor		A	A	B	C	D	E	F,G
	Duration	4 – 1 = **3**	5	4	6	6	5	7	4
Crashing C	Activity	A	B	C	D	E	F	G	H
	Predecessor		A	A	B	C	D	E	F,G
	Duration	4	5	4 – 1 = **3**	6	6	5	7	4
Crashing E	Activity	A	B	C	D	E	F	G	H
	Predecessor		A	A	B	C	D	E	F, G
	Duration	4	5	4	6	6 – 1 = **5**	5	7	4

Note. The network diagram of the following crashing possibilities in the table above is illustrated below.

Assuming activity "A" was crashed	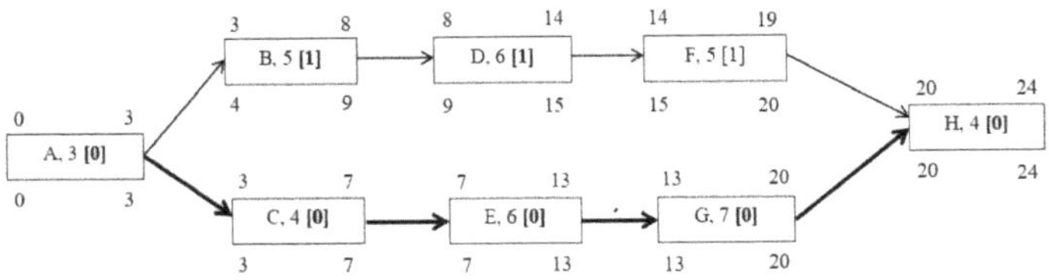
Assuming activity "C" was crashed	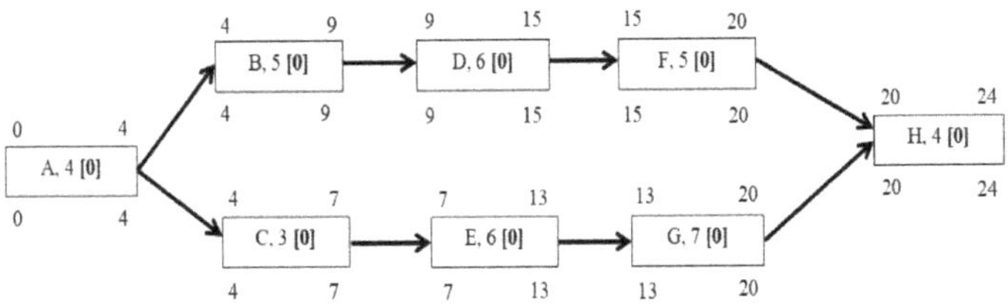
Assuming activity "E" was crashed	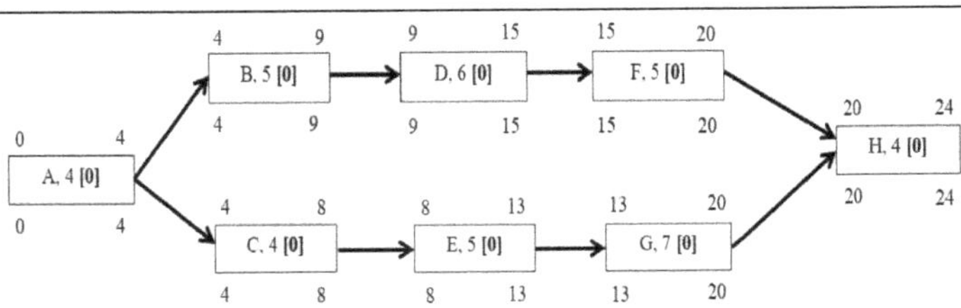

From the above illustration, we realized that there exist three possibilities, that is assuming activity A was crashed, assuming activity C was crashed and assuming activity E was crashed. To reduce work complexity, we consider the situation that A was crashed. Here, activity A cannot be crashed further since it possible reduction time is now zero. Therefore, we can crash activity C or activity E by one day.

Crashing C	Activity	A	B	C	D	E	F	G	H
	Predecessor		A	A	B	C	D	E	F,G
	Duration	3	5	4 – 1 = **3**	6	6	5	7	4
Crashing E	Activity	A	B	C	D	E	F	G	H
	Predecessor		A	A	B	C	D	E	F,G
	Duration	3	5	4	6	6 – 1 = **5**	5	7	4

Note. The network diagram of the following crashing possibilities in the table above is illustrated below.

Assuming activity "C" was crashed	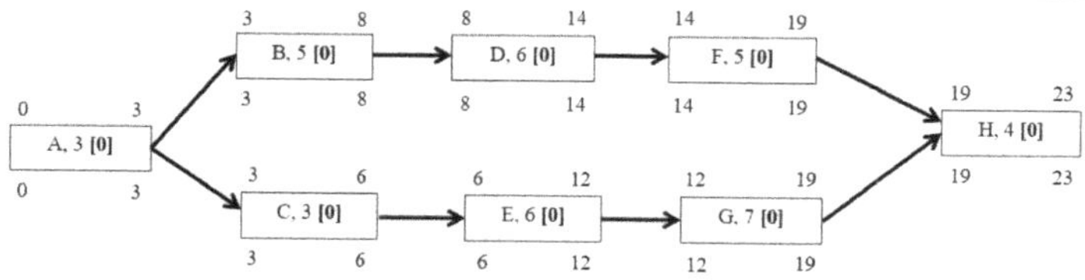
Assuming activity "E" was crashed	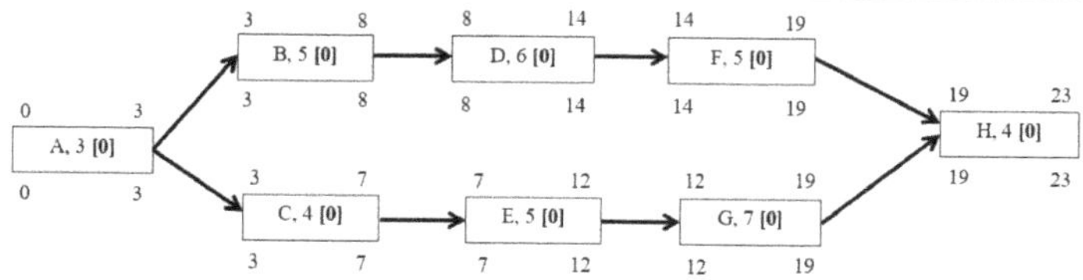

Third Crashing: From the above, we realized that we had two crashing possibilities, that crashing activity "C" or activity "E"

Assuming activity "C" was crashed; crashing activity "C" generates two critical paths, that is the original critical path (ACEGH) and the alternative critical path (ABDFH). In the original critical path, activities "A" and "C" can't be crashed any further. Activity "E" is therefore crashed by 1 day. In the alternative critical path, activity "A" can't be crashed any further, therefore activity "F" is crashed by 1 day.

Assuming activity "E" was crashed, crashing activity E produces two critical paths, that is the original critical path (ACEGH) and the alternative critical path (ABDFH). In the original critical path, we crash activity E by 1 day and in the alternative critical path, we crash activity F by 1 day.

After crashing the two critical paths, our new project schedule and network diagram is given as seen below.

Crashing activities E and F		Activity	A	B	C	D	E	F	G	H
		Predecessor		A	A	B	C	D	E	F,G
		Duration	3	5	3	6	6 – 1 = **5**	5 – 1 = **4**	7	4
Crashing activities E and F		Activity	A	B	C	D	E	F	G	H
		Predecessor		A	A	B	C	D	E	F,G
		Duration	3	5	4	6	5 – 1 = **4**	5 – 1 = **4**	7	4

Assuming activity “C” was crashed

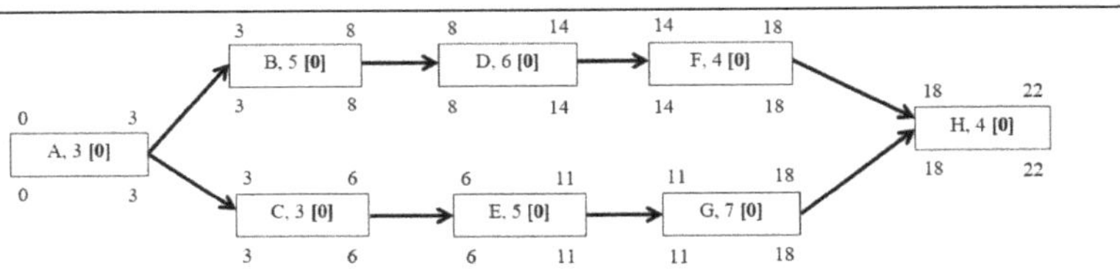

Assuming activity “E” was crashed

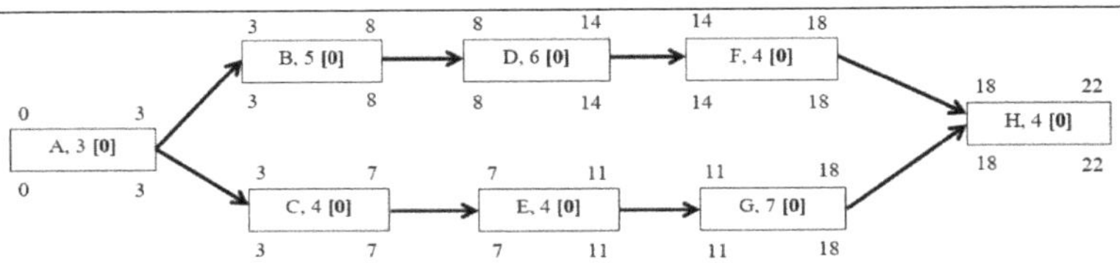

Note: The new project completion duration is 22 days

Test Your Understanding

Exercise 16: The cost and duration of a project is given in the tables below. Determine the normal and minimum project completion duration.

Table 1

Activity	Normal		Crash		Predecessor
	Duration	Cost	Duration	Cost	
A	3	5	2	16	
B	7	8	6	10	A
C	17	30	13	38	A
D	8	15	6	25	B,C
E	0	0	0	0	C,D
F	16	10	14	12	D,E

[Answer: Normal Duration = 44 Days and Minimum Duration = 25 Days]

Table 2

Activities	Normal time	Crash time	Normal cost	Crash cost
1 – 2	7	6	15,000	18,000
2 – 3	12	9	11,000	14,000
2 – 4	22	21	18,500	19,000
3 – 4	11	10	8,000	9,000
4 – 5	6	5	4,000	4,500

[Answer: Normal Duration = 35 Days and Minimum Duration = 33 Days. The minimum duration is 33 days because above this duration, the alternative critical path duration id greater than the original critical path duration]

8.4.3 Project Completion Cost

Project completion cost is the sum of direct cost and indirect cost. Direct cost or normal includes cost of cost of labour, equipment, material and subcontractors cost. Indirect cost involves necessary costs of doing work which cannot be related to a particular activity.

$$\text{Project Total Cost} = \text{Direct Cost} + \text{Indirect Cost} \quad \ldots\ldots\ldots\ldots\ldots\ldots\ldots\ldots\ldots\ldots\ldots\ldots(4)$$

$$\text{Where; Direct Cost} = \sum \text{Activities Normal Cost}$$

$$\text{Indirect Cost} = \text{Project Duration} \times \text{Indirect Cost Per Time}$$

Note: Indirect cost is constant and is given (certain). Cost slope cost varies as its value depends on the activity being crashed and is calculated. Given that crashing changes project cost, the formula for calculating a project cost after a given crashing process is given as;

$$\text{New Project Total Cost} = \text{Previous Project Cost} - \text{Indirect Cost} + \text{Cost Slope} \quad \ldots\ldots(5)$$

At the end of crashing process, three different project cost can be determined. That is normal project completion cost, minimum project completion cost and optimal project completion cost.

1) Normal project completion cost: It is the project total cost before the application of crashing or crashing critical path activities.
2) Minimum project completion cost: It is the project total cost associated to the minimum project completion time.
3) Optimum project completion cost: It is the lowest project total cost after the application of project crashing. Optimum project completion cost can be normal project or minimum project completion cost or can be different from both.

Note: In a situation where the indirect cost per time period is not given, total project completion cost equal sum of activities normal cost.

Example 1: The table below shows the data of a project. Consider that there is a 200 fcfa per day charge for variable overhead.

Activity	Predecessor	Normal		Crash	
		Time	Cost	Time	Cost
A		5	200	3	400
B		4	100	4	100
C	A	2	500	1	800
D	B	1	50	1	50
E	B	5	150	3	300
F	B	5	300	4	350
G	C,D	4	200	4	200
H	F	3	300	2	500

Work required

1) Draw the project network, identify the critical path, critical path duration and calculate the total cost of the project.
2) Find the cost of completing the project in the shortest or minimum time

Solution

1) Draw the project network, identify the critical path, critical path duration and calculate the total cost of the project.

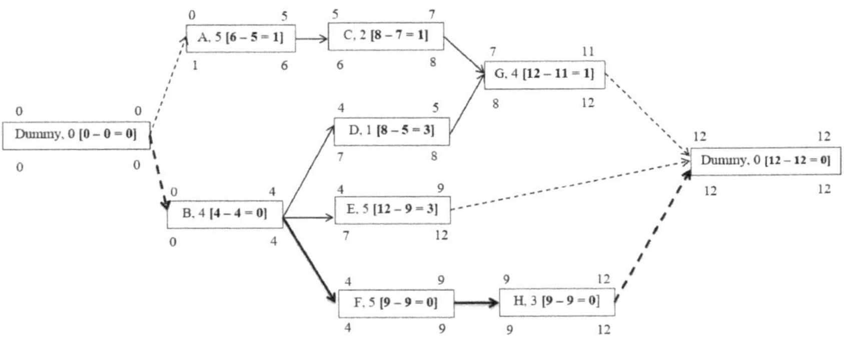

Note: The critical path is BFH and the duration is 12 days. Project total cost is the sum of the indirect cost and direct cost of the project.

Step 1: Formula. $\text{Project Total Cost} = \text{Direct Cost} + \text{Indirect Cost}$

Step 2: Determination of direct and indirect cost

Calculation of Direct or Normal Cost

1) Formula. $\text{Project Direct Cost} = \sum \text{Activities Normal Cost}$
2) Data substitution and solving

$\text{Direct Cost} = 200 + 100 + 500 + 50 + 150 + 300 + 200 + 300$ ....[Sum values]

$\text{Direct Cost} = \mathbf{1,800\ fcfa}$ ....[**Project Direct Cost**]

Calculation of Indirect or Overhead Cost

1) Formula. $\text{Indirect Cost} = \text{Project Duration} \times \text{Indirect Cost Per Time}$

Where; $\text{Project Duration} = 12\ \text{Days}$ and $\text{Indirect Cost Per Time} = 200\ \text{fcfa}$

2) Data substitution and solving

$\text{Indirect Cost} = 12 \times 200$ ....[Multiply values]

$\text{Indirect Cost} = \mathbf{2,400\ fcfa}$

Step 3: Data substitution and solving

$\text{Project Total Cost} = 1{,}800 + 2{,}400$ ....[Sum values]

$\text{Project Total Cost} = \mathbf{4,200\ fcfa}$

2) Find the cost of completing the project in the shortest time

Hint: Remember the critical path is BFH.

Step 1: Calculation of activities cost slope

1) Formula. $\text{Cost Slope} = \frac{\text{Extra Cost}}{\text{Possible Duration}}$,where; $\text{Extra Cost} = \text{Crash Cost} - \text{Normal Cost}$ and $\text{Possible Reduction} = \text{Normal Duration} - \text{Crash Duration}$
2) Data substitution and solving

Activity	A	B	C	D	E	F	G	H
Extra Cost	200	0	300	0	150	50	0	200
Possible Reduction	2	0	1	0	2	1	0	1
Cost Slope	100	0	300	0	75	50	0	200

Step 2: Determination of new project cost after crashing

1) Formula. $\text{New Project Cost} = \text{Previous Project Cost} - \text{Indirect Cost} + \text{Cost Slope}$
2) Project completion path and durations

Completion path	BFH (Critical path)	ACG	BDG	BE
Duration (Days)	12	11	9	9

3) Crashing analysis [Focus should be on the original critical path]

Hint: Crashing stops when there is no possible reduction in the original critical path. In a situation of multiple critical path creation during crashing, reduction should be done simultaneously. The activity with the lowest cost slope should be crashed first.

First Crashing: From the cost slope table above, the activity with the lowest cost slope belonging to the critical path is activity F (50).

Method 1

1) Formula. $\text{New Project Cost} = \text{Previous Project Cost} - \text{Indirect Cost} + \text{Cost Slope}$

   $\text{Previous Project Cost} = 4{,}200$, $\text{Indirect Cost} = 200$ and $\text{Cost Slope} = 50$

2) Data substitution and solving

   $\text{New Project Cost} = 4{,}200 - 200 + 50$ ....[Sum values]

   $\text{New Project Cost} = \mathbf{4050}$ **..................................[BFH new duration is 11 days]**

Method 2

1) Formula. $\text{New Project Cost} = \text{Project Direct Cost} + \text{Project Indirect Cost}$
2) Determination of unknown [Project Direct Cost and Project Indirect Cost].

   Project Direct Cost

   a) Formula. $\text{Project Direct Cost} = \text{Previous Project cost} + \text{Crashing Cost}$

      Where; $\text{Previous Project cost} = 1{,}800$ and $\text{Crashing Cost} = 50$

   b) Data substitution and solving

      $\text{Project Direct Cost} = 1{,}800 + 50$ ....[Sum values]

      $\text{Project Direct Cost} = \mathbf{1{,}850}$ **...............................[Project Direct Cost]**

   Project Indirect Cost

   a) Formula. $\text{Project Indirect Cost} = \text{Project Duration} \times \text{Indirect Cost per Time}$

      Where; $\text{Project Duration} = 11$ and $\text{Crashing Cost} = 200$

   b) Data substitution and solving

      $\text{Project Indirect Cost} = 11 \times 200$ ....[Multiply values]

      $\text{Project Indirect Costt} = \mathbf{2{,}200}$ **...........................[Project Indirect Cost]**

3) Data substitution and solving

   $\text{Project Direct Cost} = \text{Previous Project cost} + \text{Crashing Cost}$ [Put numerical values]

   $\text{New Project Cost} = 1{,}850 + 2{,}200$ ....[Sum values]

   $\text{New Project Cost} = \mathbf{4{,}050}$ **...........................[Project cost after first crashing]**

Completion path	BFH (Critical path)			ACG (Critical path)			BDG	BE
Duration (Days)	11			11			9	9
Activity	A	**B**	C	D	E	**F**	G	H
Possible reduction	2	**0**	1	0	2	**0**	0	1
Note: Not all activities (H) in the original critical path possible duration reduction are zero								

Second Crashing: The two project completion path with the highest duration are BFH (11 days) and ACG (days). Therefore, we are having two critical paths and hence applied simultaneous duration reduction.

In path BFH, activity H duration is reduced since activity B cannot be reduced and H is the last lowest cost slope activity. Activity H cost slope is 200 fcfa

In path ACG, activity A duration is reduced since G cannot be reduced and the cost slope of C is greater than the cost slope of A. Activity A cost slope is 100 fcfa.

Since, both path are reduced simultaneously, they share a common indirect cost (That is 200).

1) Formula. $\text{New Project Cost} = \text{Previous Project Cost} - \text{Indirect Cost} + \text{Cost Slope}$

   $\text{Previous Project Cost} = 4{,}050$, $\text{Indirect Cost} = 200$ and $\text{Cost Slope} = 200 + 100$

2) Data substitution and solving

   $\text{New Project Cost} = 4{,}050 - 200 + 200 + 100$ ....[Sum values]

   $\text{New Project Cost} = \mathbf{4,150}$ **...............[BFH and ACG new duration are 10 days]**

Completion path	BFH (Critical path)			ACG (Critical path)			BDG	BE
Duration (Days)	10			10			9	9
Activity	A	**B**	C	D	E	**F**	G	**H**
Possible reduction	1	**0**	1	0	2	**0**	0	**0**
Note: All activities in the original critical path possible duration reduction are zero								

Step 3: Crashing Summary Table

Completion paths	1st Crashing	2nd Crashing	3rd Crashing
BFH	12	11	10
ACG	11	11	10
BDG	9	9	9
BE	9	9	9
Project Total Cost	**4,200 fcfa**	**4,050 fcfa**	**4,150 fcfa**

Interpretation: The minimum or shortest time to complete the project is 10 days at cost of 4,150 fcfa. The optimum duration of completing the project is 11 days as it has the lowest project completion cost (4,050 fcfa).

From the above calculations, we are also study the relationship between direct cost and duration as well as indirect cost and duration.

Direct Cost Analysis

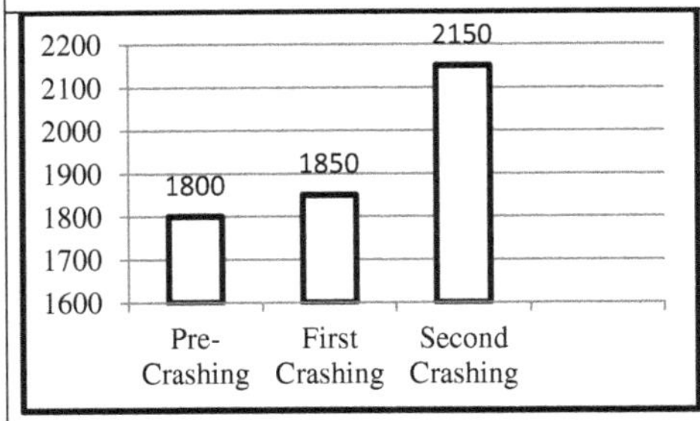

Indirect Cost Analysis

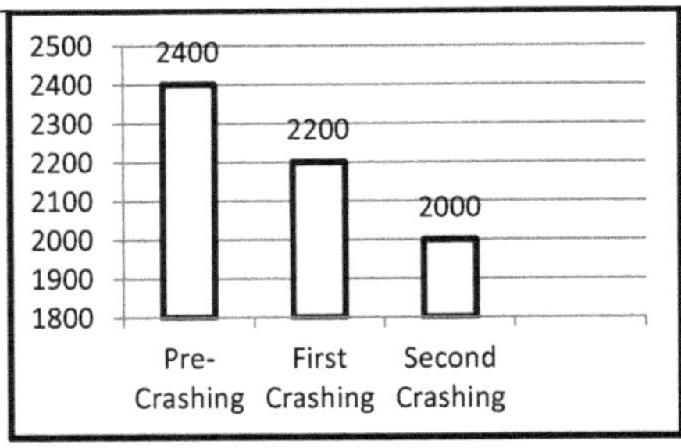

From the graphs above, we realize the direct cost of a project increases as project is been crashed while the indirect cost reduces as project is being crashed. Therefore, direct cost is negatively related to project duration and indirect cost is positively related to project duration.

Example 2: The project time and cost of project activities is given in the table below.

Activity	Predecessor	Time (weeks)		Cost (fcfa)	
		Normal	Crash	Normal	Crash
A		6	4	10,000	14,000
B		4	3	5,000	8,000
C	A	3	2	4,000	5,000
D	B	8	3	1,000	6,000
E	B	14	4	9,000	13,000
F	C,D	8	4	7,000	8,000

Considering indirect cost of 1,000 fcfa per week, answer the following questions.

1) Determine the minimum project duration and corresponding cost
2) Determine optimum project duration and corresponding cost if any.

Solution

Step 1: Drawing of network diagram and determination of project completion paths

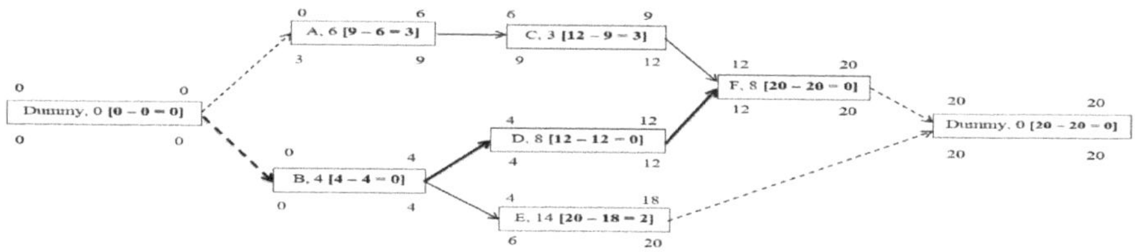

Project completion path	Duration
BDF (Critical path)	$4 + 8 + 8 = 20$ Weeks
BCF	$6 + 3 + 8 = 17$ Weeks
BE	$4 + 14 = 18$ Weeks
Project Total Cost $= 36,000 + [20 \times 1,000] = 56,000$ **fcfa**	

Step 2: Calculation of project activities cost slope

1) Formula. $\text{Cost Slope} = \frac{\text{Extra Cost}}{\text{Possible Duration}}$,where; $\text{Extra Cost} = \text{Crash Cost} - \text{Normal Cost}$ and $\text{Possible Reduction} = \text{Normal Duration} - \text{Crash Duration}$
2) Data substitution and solving

Activity	A	B	C	D	E	F
Extra Cost	4,000	3,000	1,000	5,000	4,000	1,000
Possible Reduction	2	1	1	5	10	4
Cost Slope	2,000	3,000	1,000	1,000	400	250

Step 3: Crashing and derivation of crashing result summary

1) Formula. $\text{New Project Cost} = \text{Previous Project Cost} - \text{Indirect Cost} + \text{Cost Slope}$
2) Project completion path and durations

Completion path	BDF (Critical path)	BCF	BE
Duration (Days)	20	17	18

3) Crashing analysis [Focus should be on the original critical path]

First Crashing: From the cost slope table above, the activity with the lowest cost slope belonging to the critical path is activity F (250). Since activity F lies on both critical paths, activity F will be reduced by the same amount (4).

1) Formula. New Project Cost = Previous Project Cost − Indirect Cost + Cost Slope

   Previous Project Cost = 56,000, Indirect Cost = 1,000 and Cost Slope = 250

2) Data substitution and solving

   New Project Cost = 56,000 − 1,000 + 250 ....[Sum values]

   New Project Cost = **55,250** **.......................[BDF new duration is 16 days]**

Completion path	BDF(Critical path)		BCF		BE	
Duration (Days)	16		13		18	
Activity	A	B	C	D	E	**F**
Possible reduction	2	1	1	5	10	**0**
Note: Not all activities (B,D) in the original critical path possible duration reduction are zero						

Second Crashing: The second activity in the original critical path with the lowest cost slope is activity D (1,000) and the possible reduction is 5 weeks.

1) Formula. New Project Cost = Previous Project Cost − Indirect Cost + Cost Slope

   Previous Project Cost = 55,250, Indirect Cost = 1,000 and Cost Slope = 1,000

2) Data substitution and solving

   New Project Cost = 55,250 − 1,000 + 1,000 ....[Sum values]

   New Project Cost = **55,250** **.........................[BDF new duration is 11 days]**

Completion path	BDF(Critical path)		BCF		BE	
Duration (Days)	11		13		18	
Activity	A	B	C	**D**	E	**F**
Possible reduction	2	1	1	**0**	10	**0**
Note: Not all activities (B) in the original critical path possible duration reduction are zero						

Third Crashing: The next activity in the original critical path with the lowest cost slope is activity B (1,000) and the possible reduction is 1 day.

1) Formula. New Project Cost = Previous Project Cost − Indirect Cost + Cost Slope

   Previous Project Cost = 55,250, Indirect Cost = 1,000 and Cost Slope = 3,000

2) Data substitution and solving

   New Project Cost = 55,250 − 1,000 + 3,000 ....[Sum values]

   New Project Cost = **57,250** **...............................[BDF new duration is 10 days]**

Completion path	BDF(Critical path)		BCF		BE	
Duration (Days)	10		12		17	
Activity	A	**B**	C	**D**	E	**F**
Possible reduction	2	**0**	1	**0**	10	**0**
Note: All activities in the original critical path possible duration reduction are zero						

Step 3: Crashing Summary Table

Completion paths	1st Crashing	2nd Crashing	3rd Crashing
BDF	16	11	10
BCF	13	13	12
BE	18	18	17
Project Total Cost	**55,250 fcfa**	**55,250 fcfa**	**57,250 fcfa**

Interpretation: The minimum or shortest time to complete the project is 10 days at cost of 57,250 fcfa. The optimum duration of completing the project is 16 or 11 days as it has the lowest project completion cost (55,250 fcfa).

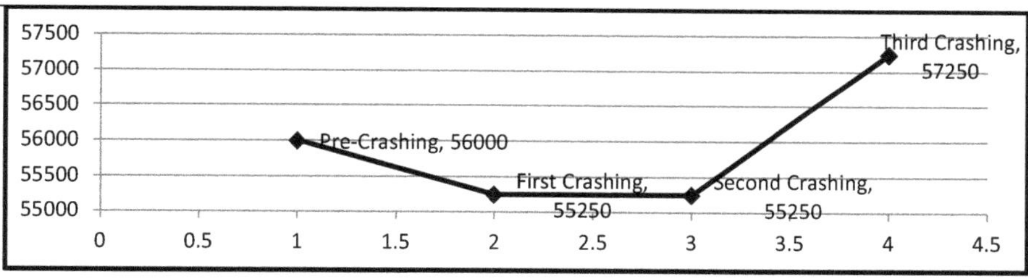

Example 3: A small project is having seven activities. The relevant data about these activities is given below

Activity	Predecessor	Normal Duration	Crash Duration	Normal Cost	Crash Cost
A		7	5	500	900
B	A	4	2	400	400
C	A	5	5	500	500
D	A	6	4	800	800
E	B,C	7	4	700	700
F	C,D	5	2	800	800
G	E,F	6	4	800	800

Work Required

1) Draw the project network and identify the completion paths and their duration
2) Determine the normal, minimum and optimum duration of the project completion and their corresponding cost.

<u>**Solution**</u>

1) Draw the project network and identify the completion paths and their duration

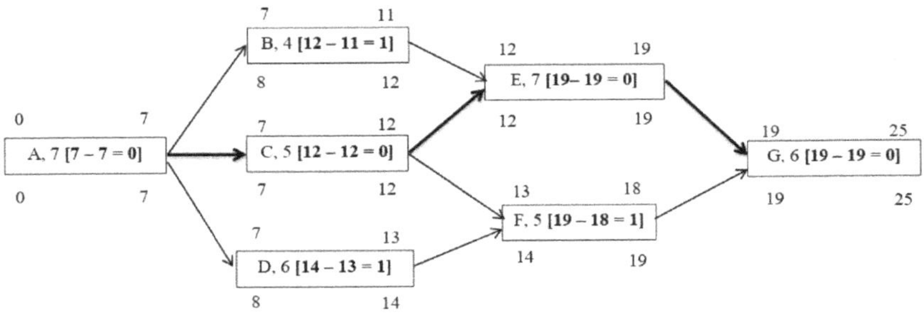

Project Completion Path	Duration (Days)
ACEG (Critical path)	$7+5+7+6=\mathbf{25}$
ABEG	$7+4+7+6=\mathbf{24}$
ACFG	$7+5+5+6=\mathbf{23}$
ADFG	$7+6+5+6=\mathbf{24}$

2) Determine the normal, minimum and optimum duration of the project completion and their corresponding cost.

Step 1: Determination of activities cost slope and project total cost

Activity	A	B	C	D	E	F	G
Extra Cost	400	200	0	200	300	600	800
Possible Reduction	2	2	0	2	3	3	2
Cost Slope	200	100	0	100	100	200	400
Note: Project Normal Total cost equal project total cost since indirect cost is not given. **Project Total Cost** $= \mathbf{500+400+500+800+700+800+800=4500}$ **fcfa**							

Step 2: Crashing project activities

First Crashing: From the cost slope table above, the activity with the lowest cost slope belonging to the critical path is activity E (100).

1) Formula. New Project Cost = Previous Project Cost − Indirect Cost + Cost Slope

   Previous Project Cost = 4,500, Indirect Cost = 0 and Cost Slope = 100

2) Data substitution and solving

   New Project Cost = 4,500 − 0 + 100 ....[Sum values]

   New Project Cost = **4,600** ....**[ACEG new duration is 22 days]**

Completion path	ACEG (Critical path)			ABEG	ACFG		ADFG
Duration (Days)	22			21	23		24
Activity	A	B	C	D	**E**	F	G
Possible reduction	2	2	0	2	**0**	3	2
Note: Not all activities in the original critical path possible duration reduction are zero							

Second Crashing: The activity with the lowest cost slope belonging to the critical path is activity after activity E is activity A (200).

1) Formula. New Project Cost = Previous Project Cost − Indirect Cost + Cost Slope

   Previous Project Cost = 4,600, Indirect Cost = 0 and Cost Slope = 200

2) Data substitution and solving

   New Project Cost = 4,600 − 0 + 200 ....[Sum values]

   New Project Cost = **4800** ....**[ACEG new duration is 20 days]**

Completion path	ACEG (Critical path)			ABEG	ACFG		ADFG
Duration (Days)	20			19	21		22
Activity	**A**	B	C	D	**E**	F	G
Possible reduction	**0**	2	0	2	**0**	3	2
Note: Not all activities in the original critical path possible duration reduction are zero							

Third Crashing: The activity with the lowest cost slope belonging to the critical path is activity after activity A is activity G (400).

1) Formula. New Project Cost = Previous Project Cost − Indirect Cost + Cost Slope

   Previous Project Cost = 4,800, Indirect Cost = 0 and Cost Slope = 400

2) Data substitution and solving

   New Project Cost = 4,800 − 0 + 400 ....[Sum values]

   New Project Cost = **5,200** ....**[ACEG new duration is 18 days]**

Completion path	ACEG (Critical path)			ABEG	ACFG		ADFG
Duration (Days)	18			17	19		20
Activity	**A**	B	C	D	**E**	F	**G**
Possible reduction	**0**	2	0	2	**0**	3	**0**
Note: All activities in the original critical path possible duration reduction are zero							

Step 3: Crashing result summary and determination of durations and their respective cost

Completion paths	Pre-Crashing	1st Crashing	2nd Crashing	3rd Crashing
ACEG	25	22	20	18
ABEG	24	21	19	17
ACFG	23	23	21	19
ADFG	24	24	22	20
Project Total Cost	**4,500 fcfa**	**4,600 fcfa**	**4,800 fcfa**	**5,200 fcfa**

Interpretation: The normal duration is 25 days with project completion cost 4,500 fcfa. The minimum or shortest time is 18 days with project completion cost 5,200 fcfa. The optimum duration of is 25 days with completion cost 4,500 fcfa. Therefore, the normal duration is the optimal duration indicating that crashing this project is not profitable.

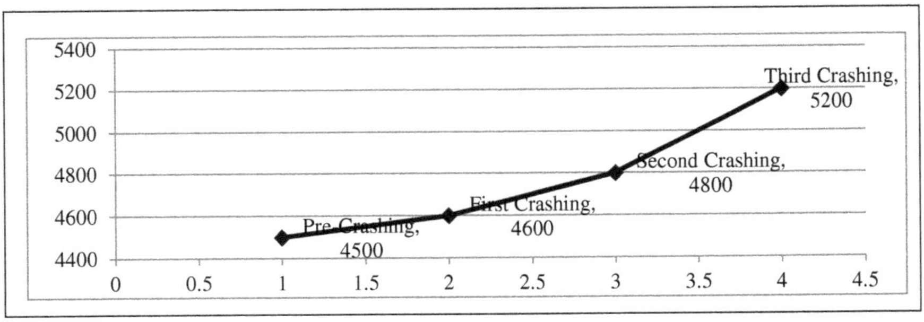

Example 5: A project is composed of event activities as per the details given below. Duration is measured in days and cost in fcfa. Indirect cost per day of the period is 500 fcfa.

Activity	Normal duration	Crash duration	Normal cost	Crash cost
1 – 2	4	3	1,500	2,000
1 – 3	2	2	1,000	1,000
1 – 4	5	4	1,875	2,250
2 – 3	7	5	1,000	1,500
2 – 5	7	6	2,000	2,500
3 – 5	2	1	1,250	1,625
4 – 5	5	4	1,500	2,125

Work required

1) Draw the project network, identify the critical path and critical path duration
2) Fine the minimum duration and optimum duration and their resultant cost of the project

Solution

1) Draw the project network, identify the critical path and critical path duration

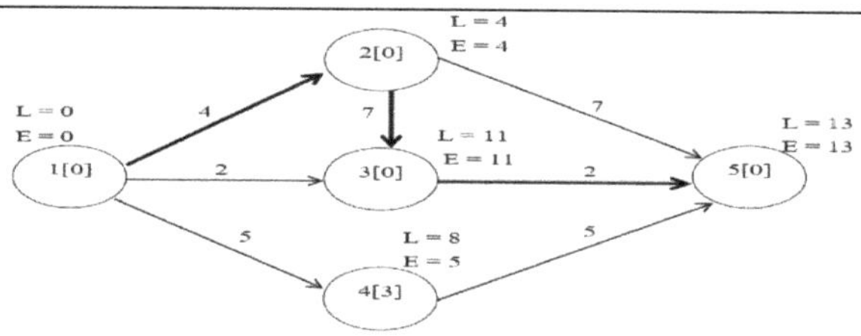

Note: The critical path is $[1 \to 2 \to 3 \to 5]$ and critical path duration is $[4 + 7 + 2 = 13 \text{ Days}]$

Note: The original project completion paths before crashing is given as illustrated below

Project Paths	$1 \to 2 \to 5$	$1 \to 2 \to 3 \to 5$	$1 \to 3 \to 5$	$1 \to 4 \to 5$
Duration	11 Days	13 Days	4 Days	10 Days
Project Cost $= 10{,}125 + (13 \times 500) = 16{,}625$ fcfa				

2) Fine the minimum duration and optimum duration and their resultant cost of the project

Step 1: Determination of activities cost slope values

Activity	$1-2$	$1-3$	$1-4$	$2-3$	$2-5$	$3-5$	$4-5$
Extra Cost	500	0	375	500	500	402	625
Possible Reduction Time	1	0	1	2	1	1	1
Activity Cost Slope	500	0	375	250	500	402	625

Step 2: Application of crashing process

First Crashing: Here, we have a single critical path $(1 \to 2 \to 3 \to 5)$ with duration 13 days. The crashing table is given as seen below.

Critical Path	Activities	Cost Slope	Possible Reduction		Normal Time	
			Before	After	Before	After
$1 \to 2 \to 3 \to 5$	$1 \to 2$	500	1	1	4	4
	$\mathbf{2 \to 3}$	**250**	**2**	$\mathbf{2 - 1 = 1}$	**7**	$\mathbf{7 - 1 = 6}$
	$3 \to 5$	402	1	1	2	2
Project Completion Cost $= 16{,}625 - 500 + 250 = \mathbf{16{,}375}$ **fcfa**						

Second crashing: The new project schedule after the first crashing is different due to the 1 day reduction. This new schedule is given as seen below.

Activity	$1 \to 2$	$1 \to 3$	$1 \to 4$	$2 \to 3$	$2 \to 5$	$3 \to 5$	$4 \to 5$
Actual Time	4	2	5	6	7	2	5

From the new project schedule table, we can draw a new network diagram as illustrated below

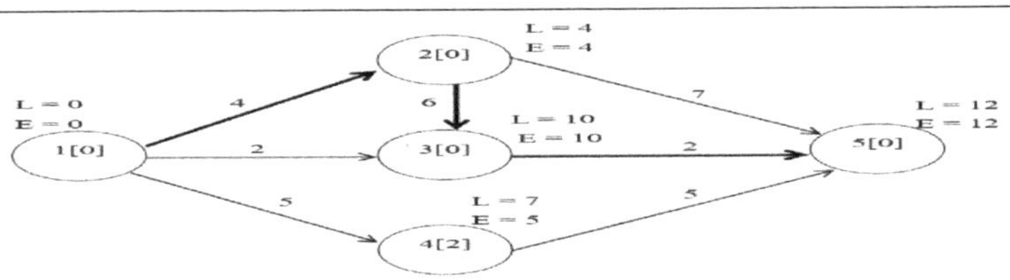

Note: The critical path is $[1 \to 2 \to 3 \to 5]$ and critical path duration is $[4 + 6 + 2 = 12 \text{ Days}]$

From the network diagram, we realized that the critical path is the same. Event $(2 \to 3)$ is crashed by 1 day since it is having the smallest cost slope value. The crashing table is given as seen below.

Critical Path	Activities	Cost Slope	Possible Reduction		Normal Time	
			Before	After	Before	After
$1 \to 2 \to 3 \to 5$	$1 \to 2$	500	1	1	4	4
	$2 \to 3$	**250**	**1**	**$1 - 1 = 0$**	**6**	**$6 - 1 = 5$**
	$3 \to 5$	402	1	1	2	2
Project Completion Cost $= 16{,}375 - 500 + 250 =$ **$16{,}125$ fcfa**						

Third crashing: The new project schedule after the second crashing is given as seen below

Activity	$1 \to 2$	$1 \to 3$	$1 \to 4$	$2 \to 3$	$2 \to 5$	$3 \to 5$	$4 \to 5$
Actual Time	4	2	5	5	7	2	5

From the new project schedule table, we can draw a new network diagram as illustrated below

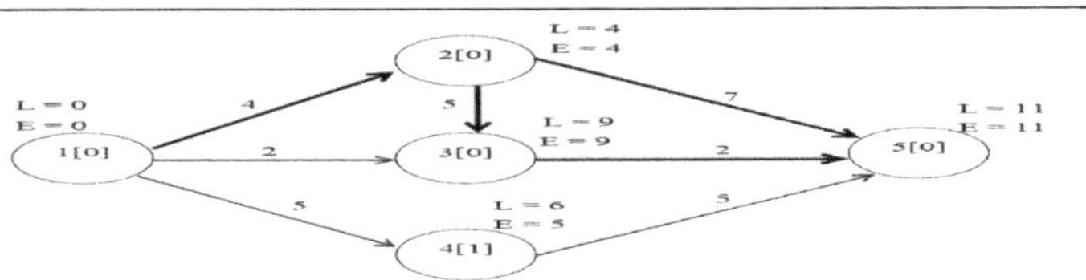

Original critical path is $[1 \to 2 \to 3 \to 5]$ and critical path duration is $[4 + 5 + 2 = 11 \text{ Days}]$

Additional critical path is $[1 \to 2 \to 5]$ and critical path duration is $[4 + 7 = 11 \text{ Days}]$

From the network diagram, we realized that we have two critical paths. In the original critical path, event $(2 \rightarrow 3)$ is not crashed as it possible reduction value is now zero. Event $(3 \rightarrow 5)$ is crashed as it is the alternative event with the smallest cost slope value. In the additional critical path, any event can be crashed since they have the same cost slope value. Let assume event $(2 \rightarrow 5)$ is crashed; the crashing table is given below.

Critical Path	Activities	Cost Slope	Possible Reduction		Normal Time	
			Before	After	Before	After
$1 \rightarrow 2 \rightarrow 3 \rightarrow 5$	$1 \rightarrow 2$	500	1	1	4	4
	$2 \rightarrow 3$	250	1	0	6	5
	$\mathbf{3 \rightarrow 5}$	**402**	**1**	$\mathbf{1 - 1 = 0}$	**2**	$\mathbf{2 - 1 = 1}$
$1 \rightarrow 2 \rightarrow 5$	$1 \rightarrow 2$	500	1	1	4	4
	$\mathbf{2 \rightarrow 5}$	**500**	**1**	$\mathbf{1 - 1 = 0}$	7	$7 - 1 = 6$
Project Completion Cost $= 16{,}125 - 500 + (402 + 500) = \mathbf{16{,}527\ fcfa}$						

Fourth crashing: The new project schedule after the third crashing is given as seen below

Activity	$1 \rightarrow 2$	$1 \rightarrow 3$	$1 \rightarrow 4$	$2 \rightarrow 3$	$2 \rightarrow 5$	$3 \rightarrow 5$	$4 \rightarrow 5$
Actual Time	4	2	5	5	6	1	5

From the new project schedule table, we can draw a new network diagram as illustrated below

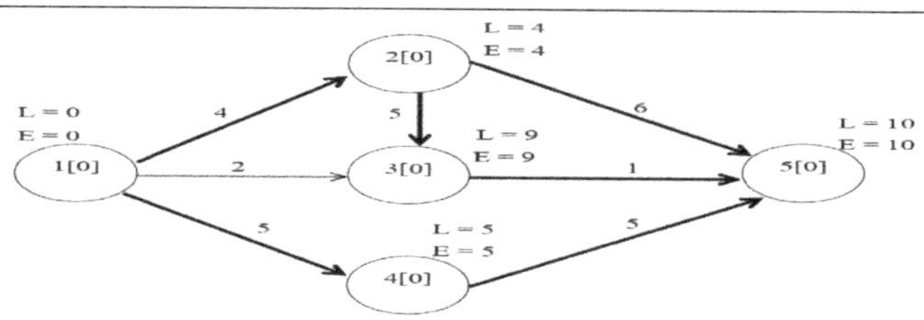

Original critical path is $[1 \rightarrow 2 \rightarrow 3 \rightarrow 5]$ and critical path duration is $[4 + 5 + 1 = 10$ Days$]$
First Additional critical path is $[1 \rightarrow 2 \rightarrow 5]$ and critical path duration is $[4 + 6 = 10$ Days$]$
Second Additional critical path is $[1 \rightarrow 4 \rightarrow 5]$ and critical path duration is $[5 + 5 = 10$ Days$]$

From the network diagram, the original critical path, events $(2 \rightarrow 3)$ and $(3 \rightarrow 5)$ are not crashed due to the fact that their possible reduction value are zero. Event$(1 \rightarrow 2)$ is the only possible event to be crashed. In the first additional critical path, event $(2 \rightarrow 5)$ is not crashed as it possible reduction time is zero. Event $(1 \rightarrow 2)$ is the only alternative event to be reduced.

In the second additional critical path, event $(1 \rightarrow 4)$ is crashed as it is having the smallest cost slope value.

Critical Path	Activities	Cost	Possible Reduction		Normal Time	
		Slope	Before	After	Before	After
$1 \rightarrow 2 \rightarrow 3 \rightarrow 5$	**$1 \rightarrow 2$**	**500**	**1**	**$1 - 1 = 0$**	**4**	**$4 - 1 = 3$**
	$2 \rightarrow 3$	250	1	0	5	5
	$3 \rightarrow 5$	402	1	0	1	1
$1 \rightarrow 2 \rightarrow 5$	$1 \rightarrow 2$	500	1	1	4	4
	$2 \rightarrow 5$	500	1	0	6	6
$1 \rightarrow 4 \rightarrow 5$	**$1 \rightarrow 4$**	**375**	**1**	**$1 - 1 = 0$**	**5**	**$5 - 1 = 4$**
	$4 \rightarrow 5$	625	1	1	5	5
Project Completion Cost $= 16{,}527 - 500 + (500 + 500 + 375) = \mathbf{17{,}402\ fcfa}$						

Step 3: Interpretation. The critical activities of the original critical path are all having possible reduction value of zero. This shows that we should stop the crashing process.

	Duration	Cost
Normal project analysis		16,625 fcfa
Minimum project analysis		17,402 fcfa
Optimum project analysis		16, 125 fcfa

Test Your Understanding

Exercise 17: Activity data for a small work is given below. Considering that indirect cost of project is 1,400 fcfa per day.

Activity	Predecessor	Duration (Days)		Cost (fcfa)	
		Normal	Crash	Normal	Crash
P		5	5	5,000	5,000
Q	P	8	4	6,000	18,000
R	P	6	5	3,000	4,500
S	Q	2	2	1,000	1,000
T	Q	6	2	5,000	10,000
U	R	5	4	2,000	3,000
V	S,T	7	5	18,000	20,000
W	R,T	5	3	1,000	4,000
X	U,V,W	8	8	15,000	15,000

1) Identify the project completion paths and their respective durations
2) Determine the normal, minimum and optimum duration and their respective cost.

[Answer..See appendix]

Exercise 18: The table below gives estimates of time and cost for activities involved in completing a contract offered to o a construction company. Duration is measured in days and cost in fcfa.

Activity	Predecessor	Normal		Crash	
		Duration	Cost	Duration	Cost
A		12	10,000	8	14,000
B		10	5,000	10	5,000
C	A	0	0	0	0
D	A	6	4,000	4	5,000
E	B,C	16	9,000	14	12,000
F	D	16	3,200	8	8,000

1) Identify the project completion paths and their respective durations.
2) Determine the normal, minimum and optimum duration and their respective cost.

[Answer..See appendix]

Exercise 19: The time and cost information of a small project is represented in the table below. Determine the normal, optimal and minimum project duration and cost.

Activity	Optimistic Time	Most Likely Time	Pessimistic Time	Crash Time	Normal Cost	Crash Cost
1 – 2	1	3	5	1	5,000	9,000
2 – 3	1	4	7	3	8,000	14,000
2 – 4	1	3	5	2	4,000	6,000
2 – 5	5	8	11	7	5,000	6,000
3 – 6	2	4	6	2	3,000	5,000
4 – 6	5	6	7	4	2,000	3,600
5 – 7	4	5	6	4	10,000	14,000
6 – 7	1	3	5	1	7,000	10,600

Answer		
	Duration	Project Cost
Normal analysis	16	44,000 fcfa
Optimum analysis	16	44,000 fcfa
Minimum analysis	12	53,800 fcfa

CHAPTER NINE

DECISION MAKING

Decision theory is an analytic and systematic approach to the study of decision making and a decision making is a cognitive process of selecting between two or more courses of action. All good decisions are based on logic (reason), makes use of all available data and possible alternatives and quantitative approach.

9. 1 Types of Decision-Making Environments

Generally, the decision making environment is sub-divided into two; decision making with certainty and decision making with uncertainty.

1) Decision making with certainty: The decision maker knows without doubt what are the decision alternatives, what states of nature are associated with each alternative and the outcomes of each decision alternatives. The decision maker has accurate, measurable and reliable information to know the outcome of decision before it is made.
2) Decision making with uncertainty: Decision making with uncertainty is sub-divided into two situations; non-probability situation and probability situation.
    a) Non-probability Situation: It is a decision making environment in which the decision maker knows the possible outcomes but does not know the probability of the outcomes occurrence. The payoff table or opportunity loss table is not assign probabilities value to the given events. It is also called decision making under uncertainty.
    b) Probability Situation: It is a decision making environment in which the decision maker knows both the possible outcomes and their probability of occurrence. The payoff table or opportunity loss table is assign probabilities value to the given events.

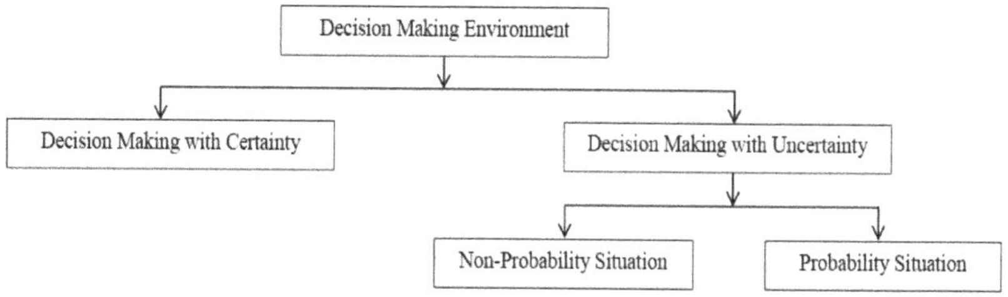

Note: Our focus will be more on decision making with uncertainty; non-probability situation and probability situation.

9.2 The Concept of Payoff Table

A payoff table is a table that represents a range of possible state of nature and with (non-probability situation) or without (probability situation) their probabilities and a variety of possible act. That is, a payoff table contains each possible event that can occur for each alternative course of action and a value or payoff for each combination of an event and course of action.

1) Act. These are decisions (actions, strategies, responds) available to a decision maker (the person responsible to take decision) from which he/she is expected to select the best (optimal) to achieve the pre-determine objective. Let's denoted it (A_i) and where (i) ranges from 1 to (m)
2) States of Nature: These are occurrence (economic, political, and socio-cultural) which affects the achievement of the objectives. States of nature are mutually exclusive in nature (cannot happen at the same time) and in which the decision maker have little or no control over. It is also called events, outcomes and will be denoted (E_i) and where (i) ranges from 1 to (n)
3) Payoff: These are revenue $(+)$ or cost $(-)$ associated with any action (A_m) with a particular sates of nature(E_n). It is also called consequence or rewards and let it be denoted(C_{mn}).

N/B: Generally, a payoff table is of two types; payoff table for non-probabilistic uncertainty and payoff table for probabilistic uncertainty. From the payoff table, we can derive the payoff matrix.

9.2.1 Payoff Table for Non-Probabilistic Uncertainty

Non-probability uncertainty payoff table is also called non-deterministic uncertainty payoff table or decision making in situation of uncertainty payoff table. The payoff table is not assign probabilities value to events. A typical illustration of a payoff table is given below

States of Nature	Action Alternatives			
	A_1	A_2	$\cdots$	A_m
E_1	C_{11}	C_{12}	$\cdots$	C_{1m}
E_2	C_{21}	C_{22}	$\cdots$	C_{2m}
$\vdots$	$\vdots$	$\vdots$	$\vdots$	$\vdots$
E_n	C_{n1}	C_{n2}	$\cdots$	C_{nm}

Matrix Dimension: [(m by n) or (m × n)]

		State of Nature			
		E_1	E_2	$\cdots$	E_n
Decisions Alternatives	A_1	C_{11}	C_{12}	$\cdots$	C_{1n}
	A_2	C_{21}	C_{22}	$\cdots$	C_{2n}
	$\vdots$	$\vdots$	$\vdots$	$\vdots$	$\vdots$
	A_m	C_{m1}	C_{m2}	$\cdots$	C_{mn}

Matrix Dimension: [(n by m) or (n × m)]

9.2.2 Payoff Table for Probabilistic Uncertainty

Probability uncertainty payoff table is also called decision making under risk payoff table. The payoff table is given probabilities value to events. A typical illustration of a payoff table is given below.

States of Nature	Probabilities	Action Alternatives			
		A_1	A_2	$\cdots$	A_m
E_1	p_1	C_{11}	C_{12}	$\cdots$	C_{1m}
E_2	p_2	C_{21}	C_{22}	$\cdots$	C_{2m}
$\vdots$	$\vdots$	$\vdots$	$\vdots$	$\vdots$	$\vdots$
E_n	p_n	C_{n1}	C_{n2}	$\cdots$	C_{nm}

Matrix Dimension: [(m by n) or (m × n)]

		State of Nature			
Decisions Alternatives		E_1	E_2	$\cdots$	E_n
		p_1	p_2	$\cdots$	p_n
	A_1	C_{11}	C_{12}	$\cdots$	C_{1n}
	A_2	C_{21}	C_{22}	$\cdots$	C_{2n}
	$\vdots$	$\vdots$	$\vdots$	$\vdots$	$\vdots$
	A_m	C_{m1}	C_{m2}	$\cdots$	C_{mn}

Matrix Dimension: [(n by m) or (n × m)]

Note: Another important type table is the opportunity loss table. The structure of the opportunity loss table or regret table is the same as the payoff table but differ in the payoff value derivation. The opportunity loss table will be explained below.

Example 1: A decision maker is faced with the following investment decision alternatives; real estate and agriculture and states of nature; high demand, moderate demand and low demand. Derive a draft payoff table.

Solution

Step 1: Identification

1) Decision alternatives: Real estate and agriculture
2) States of nature: High demand, moderate demand and low demand

Step 2: Drawing of payoff table

First Presentation

Decision alternatives (A_i)	States of Nature (E_i)		
	High demand (E_1)	Moderate demand (E_2)	Low demand (E_3)
Real Estate (A_1)			
Agriculture (A_2)			

Matrix Dimension: [(3 by 2) or (3 × 2)]

Second Presentation

States of Nature (E_i)	Decision alternatives (A_i)	
	Real Estate (A_1)	Agriculture (A_2)
High demand (E_1)		
Moderate demand (E_2)		
Low demand (E_3)		

Matrix Dimension: [(2 by 3) or (2 × 3)]

Example 2: A manager is faced with no growth and rapid growth as state of nature with probability of occurrence 30% and 70% respectively. Given that the investment decision alternatives are bonds and shares, draw a draft payoff table.

Solution

Step 1: Identification

1) Decision alternatives: Bonds and shares
2) States of nature and probability: No growth (30% = 0.3) and rapid growth (70% = 0.7)

Step 2: Drawing of payoff table

First Presentation

States of Nature (E_i)	Probability	Action alternatives (A_i)	
		Bonds (A_1)	Shares (A_2)
No growth (E_1)	30% = 0.3		
Rapid growth (E_2)	70% = 0.7		

States of Nature (E_i)	Action alternatives (A_i)	
	Bonds (A_1)	Shares (A_2)
No growth ($E_1 = 0.3$)		
Rapid growth ($E_2 = 0.7$)		

Matrix Dimension: [(2 by 2) or (2 × 2)]

Second Presentation

Decision alternatives (A_i)	States of Nature (E_i)	
	No growth ($E_1 = 0.3$)	Rapid growth ($E_2 = 0.7$)
Bonds (A_1)		
Shares (A_2)		

Decision alternatives (A_i)	States of Nature (E_i)	
	No growth (E_1)	Rapid growth (E_2)
	30% = 0.3	70% = 0.7
Bonds (A_1)		
Shares (A_2)		

Matrix Dimension: [(2 by 2) or (2 × 2)]

Example 3: A decision market is faced with favourable market and unfavourable market as states of nature. Construct a payoff table using the data below.

1) Favourable market: Large plant produces 200 FCFA and small plant produces 100 FCFA.
2) Unfavorable market: Large plant produces 180 FCFA and small plant produces 20 FCFA.

Solution

Step 1: Identification

1) Decision alternatives: Large plant and small plant
2) States of nature: Favourable market and unfavourable market
3) Payoff or reward:

$$\begin{bmatrix} \text{Large plant produces 200 FCFA and small plant produces 100 FCFA} \\ \text{Large plant produces 180 FCFA and small plant produces 20 FCFA} \end{bmatrix}$$

Step 2: Drawing of payoff table

First Presentation

Decision alternatives (A_i)	States of Nature (E_i)	
	Favourable Market (E_1)	Unfavourable Market (E_2)
Large Plant (A_1)	200	180
Small Plant (A_2)	100	20

Matrix Dimension: $[(2 \text{ by } 2) \text{ or } (2 \times 2)]$

Second Presentation

States of Nature (E_i)	Action alternatives (A_i)	
	Large Plant (A_1)	Small Plant (A_2)
Favourable Market (E_1)	200	100
Unfavourable Market (E_2)	180	20

Matrix Dimension: $[(2 \text{ by } 2) \text{ or } (2 \times 2)]$

Example 4: A driver is faced with fuel decrease and fuel increase as state of nature with probability of occurrence 0.4 and 0.6 respectively. Construct a payoff table using the data below.

1) Small car: Fuel decrease (-225) and fuel increase (425).
2) Medium car: Fuel decrease (125) and fuel increase (-150).
3) Large car: Fuel decrease (350) and fuel increase (-400).

Solution

Step 1: Identification

1) Decision alternatives: Small car, medium car and large car
2) States of nature: Fuel increase and fuel decrease
3) Payoff or reward: $\begin{bmatrix} \text{Small car: Fuel decrease } (-225) \text{ and fuel increase } (425) \\ \text{Medium car: Fuel decrease } (125) \text{ and fuel increase } (-150) \\ \text{Large car: Fuel decrease } (350) \text{ and fuel increase } (-400) \end{bmatrix}$

Step 2: Drawing of payoff table

First Presentation

Decision alternatives (A_i)	States of Nature (E_i)	
	Fuel decrease (E_1)	Fuel increase (E_2)
	$0.4 = 40\%$	$0.6 = 60\%$
Small car (A_1)	-225	425
Medium car (A_2)	125	-150
Large car (A_3)	350	-400

Matrix Dimension: $[(2 \text{ by } 3) \text{ or } (2 \times 3)]$

Second Presentation

States of Nature (E_i)	Probability	Action alternatives (A_i)		
		Small car (A_1)	Medium car (A_2)	Large car (A_3)
Fuel decrease (E_1)	$0.4 = 40\%$	-225	125	350
Fuel increase (E_2)	$0.6 = 60\%$	425	-150	-400

Matrix Dimension: $[(3 \text{ by } 2) \text{ or } (3 \times 2)]$

Test Your Understanding

Exercise 1: The general manager of a company is faced with; don't produce, produce few and produce many as decision alternatives. Construct a payoff table using the data below.

1) Not receptive: Don't produce (-50), produce few (-200) and produce many (-600).
2) Receptive: Don't produce (-50), produce few (300) and produce many (100).
3) Very receptive: Don't produce (-50), produce few (400) and produce many $(1{,}000)$.

Exercise 2: A man is faced with no expansion, add on and build a new facility as action alternatives. Construct a payoff table using the data below.

1) Less (30%): No expansion (-30), add on (-400) and build a new facility $(-2{,}100)$.
2) No change (10%): No expansion (20), add on (-280) and build a new facility $(-1{,}450)$.
3) Moderate increase (40%): No expansion (30), add on (100) and build a new facility (-50).
4) Large increase (20%): No expansion (60), add on (200) and build a new facility (550).

[Answers:.. See Appendix]

9.3 Decision Making Under Uncertainty

The major criteria for decision making under uncertainty to be examined includes; maximax criterion, maximin criterion, criterion of realism, Laplace criterion and minimax regret criterion.

9.3.1 Maximax Criterion

The term maximax is an abbreviation of the phrase 'maximum of the maximum' and is also called the optimistic criterion. It consists of identifying the most favourable (highest value) consequence in each decision from the payoff table and finally choosing the highest favourable consequence. The decision corresponding to this highest favourable consequence is considered the best decision.

Example 1: Let consider three decisions and four states of nature data as seen in the given below.

	E_1	E_2	E_3	E_4
A_1	20	25	40	100
A_2	5	30	50	125
A_3	40	50	75	0

Solution

Step 1: Condition. Select the action with the highest favourable consequence

Step 2: Application of condition

Original Table					Working Table	
	E_1	E_2	E_3	E_4	Actions Favourable Consequence	Highest Favourable Consequence
A_1	20	25	40	**100**	$A_1 = E_4 = 100$	
A_2	5	30	50	**125**	$A_2 = E_4 = 125$	$A_2 = E_4 = \mathbf{125}$
A_3	40	50	**75**	0	$A_3 = E_3 = 75$	

N/B: The best decision is decision A_2. This is because it has the highest favourable consequence (125). Hence, the decision preference will be given as $[A_2(125) > A_1(100) > A_3(75)]$.

Example 2: A vendor at a local baseball stadium must determine whether to sell ice cream or soft drinks at today's game. The vendor believes that the profit made will depend on the weather. The payoff table (in FCFA) is as follows:

	Actions	
Event	Sell Soft Drinks (A_1)	Sell Ice Cream (A_2)
Cool weather (E_1)	50	30
Warm weather (E_2)	60	90

From the payoff table above, determine the optional action based on the maximax criterion.

Solution

Step 1: Condition. Select the action with the highest favourable consequence

Step 2: Application of condition

	Actions	
Event	Sell Soft Drinks (A_1)	Sell Ice Cream (A_2)
Cool weather (E_1)	50	30
Warm weather (E_2)	**60**	**90**
Action Favourable consequence	$E_2 = 60$	$E_2 = 90$
Highest Favourable Consequence		$E_2 = \mathbf{90}$

N/B: The best action is A_2. This is because the action is having the highest favourable consequence (90). The action preference is given as $[A_2(90) > A_1(60)]$.

Test your understanding

Exercise 3: Determine the payoff of each action and identify the optimal decision using the maximax criterion.

Decision Alternatives	States of Nature	
	Low (E_1)	High (E_2)
Do nothing (A_1)	10	−25
Expand (A_2)	40	30
Subcontract (A_3)	16	50

[Answer: $A_1 = 10$, $A_2 = 40$, $A_3 = 50$ and Optimal decision $= A_3(50)$]

Exercise 4: An investor has a certain amount of money available to invest now. Three alternative investments are available. The estimated profits ($) of each investment under each economic condition are indicated in the following payoff table:

Events	Decisions (Investment Selection)		
	A_1	A_2	A_3
Economy declines (E_1)	500	−2,000	−7,000
No change (E_2)	1,000	2,000	−1,000
Economy expands (E_3)	2,000	5,000	20,000

From the payoff table above, determine the optional action based on the maximax criterion.

[Answer: $A_1 = 2,000$, $A_2 = 5,000$, $A_3 = 2,000$ and Optimal decision $= A_2(5,000)$]

9.3.2 Maximin Criterion

Maximin means 'Maximum of the Minimum' and is also called the pessimistic criterion or Wald criterion. It consists of identifying the most unfavorable (lowest value) consequence in each decision and choosing the highest unfavorable consequence. The decision corresponding to this highest unfavorable consequence is considered the optimal decision.

Example 1: Using the payoff table below, determine the optimal action to take.

	Events	
Actions	New Business (E_1)	No New Business (E_2)
Lease new equipment (A_1)	210	200
Retain old equipment (A_2)	−600	400

Solution

Step 1: Condition. Select the action with the highest unfavourable consequence

Step 2: Application of condition

	Events		Working Table	
Actions	New Business (E_1)	No New Business (E_2)	Action unfavourable consequence	Highest Unfavourable Consequence
Lease new equipment (A_1)	210	200	$E_2 = 200$	$E_2 = \mathbf{200}$
Retain old equipment (A_2)	−600	400	$E_1 = -600$	

N/B: The best action is A_1. The action is having the highest unfavourable consequence (200). The action preference can be given as $[A_1(200) > A_2(-600)]$.

Example 2: The profit payoff table of a company is given below. Determine the optimal action using the following criterions.

	High Demand (E_1)	Low Demand (E_2)
Low Production (A_1)	20,000	5,000
High Production (A_2)	12,000	9,000

1) The maximax criterion
2) The maximin criterion

Solution

1) **The maximax criterion**

Step 1: Condition. Select the action with the highest most favourable consequence

Step 2: Application of condition

Original Table			Working Table	
	E_1	E_2	Actions Favourable Consequence	Highest Favourable Consequence
A_1	20,000	5,000	$A_1 = E_1 = 20{,}000$	$A_1 = E_1 = \mathbf{20,000}$
A_2	12,000	9,000	$A_2 = E_1 = 12{,}000$	

N/B: The best decision is decision A_1 (Low production). This it because it is the decision with the highest favourable consequence (20,000). The decision preference is given as $[A_1(20{,}000) > A_2(12{,}000)]$.

2) **The maximin criterion**

Step 1: Condition. Select the action with the highest unfavorable consequence

Step 2: Application of condition

	E_1	E_2	Action Unfavourable Consequence	Highest Unfavourable Consequence
A_1	20,000	5,000	$E_2 = 5{,}000$	
A_2	12,000	9,000	$E_2 = 9{,}000$	$E_2 = \mathbf{9{,}000}$

N/B: The best decision is A_2 (High production). The action is having the highest unfavourable consequence (9,000). Hence the action preference is given as $[A_2(9{,}000) > A_1(5{,}000)]$.

Note: From the above calculation, we realize that the best action differs with each criterion. The best action is A_1 with maximax criterion and A_2 with maximin criterion.

Example 3: Use the payoff table for auto insurance below and determine the optimal decision using the following criterion.

Decision	States of Nature	
	No Accident (E_1)	Accident (E_2)
Purchase Insurance (A_1)	50	100
Don't Purchase Insurance (A_2)	200	125

1) The maximax criterion
2) The maximin criterion

Solution

1) **The maximax criterion**

Step 1: Condition. Select the action with the highest most favourable consequence

Step 2: Application of condition

	E_1	E_2	Action Favourable Consequence	Highest Favourable Consequence
A_1	50	100	$E_2 = 100$	
A_2	200	125	$E_1 = 200$	$E_2 = 200$

N/B: The optimal decision is A_2 (Don't purchase insurance). The decision is having the highest favourable consequence (200). The decision preference is given as $[A_2(200) > A_1(100)]$.

2) **The maximin criterion**

Step 1: Condition. Select the action with the highest unfavorable consequence

Step 2: Application of condition

	E_1	E_2	Action Unfavourable Consequence	Highest Unfavourable Consequence
A_1	50	100	$E_1 = 50$	
A_2	200	125	$E_2 = 125$	$E_2 = 125$

N/B: The optimal decision is A_2 (Don't purchase insurance). The decision is having the highest unfavourable consequence (125). The decision preference is given as $[A_2(125) > A_1(50)]$.

Note: The best decision is the same for both maximax criterion and maximin criterion. Comparing this result with that of example (2) above, we can conclude that it is not a general principle that both criterion will yield different or the same choice as to what is the optimal decision or action.

Test Your Understanding

Exercise 5: What is the optimal decision to be taken using the maximin criterion

	Moderate (E_1)	High (E_2)	Very High (E_2)
Reassign staff (A_1)	500	600	850
New staff (A_2)	600	620	600
Redesign collection (A_3)	400	500	900

[Answer: $A_2 = 600$]

Exercise 6: Using the payoff table below, determine the optimal decision using the following,

	Actions		
Events	House (A_1)	Shopping Center (A_2)	Lease (A_3)
Stable (E_1)	50	300	500
Increase (E_2)	10	100	200

1) Maximax criterion...**[Answer: $A_3 = 500$]**
2) Maximin criterion..**[Answer: $A_3 = 200$]**

9.3.3 Minimax Regret Criterion

Minimax means 'Minimum of the Maximum' and minimax regret criterion is also called Savage criterion. To take decision using the minimax regret criterion, we are required to derive the regret matrix from the payoff table and form the regret matrix. Regret is the difference between the optimal payoff and the actual reward received. The following steps are recommended.

1) Identify the highest value in each consequence column and subtract the other values of the column from the highest value. Let's use the table below as an illustration.

	E_1	E_2	E_3	E_4
A_1	20	25	40	100
A_2	5	30	50	125
A_3	40	50	75	0

From the table, the highest consequence column values are 40 for consequent (E_1), 50 for consequent (E_2), 75 for consequent (E_3) and 125 for consequent (E_4). After this identification process, we perform column subtraction as seen below.

	E_1	E_2	E_3	E_4	Pre-Regret Matrix
A_1	$40 - 20 = \mathbf{20}$	$50 - 25 = \mathbf{25}$	$75 - 40 = \mathbf{35}$	$125 - 100 = \mathbf{25}$	$\begin{bmatrix} 20 & 25 & 35 & 25 \\ 35 & 20 & 25 & 0 \\ 0 & 0 & 0 & 125 \end{bmatrix}$
A_2	$40 - 5 = \mathbf{35}$	$50 - 30 = \mathbf{20}$	$75 - 50 = \mathbf{25}$	$125 - 125 = \mathbf{0}$	
A_3	$40 - 40 = \mathbf{0}$	$50 - 50 = \mathbf{0}$	$75 - 75 = \mathbf{0}$	$125 - 0 = \mathbf{125}$	

N/B: The table above can be summarized and distinguished from the payoff table as seen below.

Payoff Table

	E_1	E_2	E_3	E_4
A_1	20	25	40	100
A_2	5	30	50	125
A_3	40	50	75	0

Regret Table

	E_1	E_2	E_3	E_4
A_1	20	25	35	25
A_2	35	20	25	0
A_3	0	0	0	125

2) From the regret table in each action, identify the highest regret (consequence) values. From these values, select the lowest value and its corresponding action and optimal action.

	E_1	E_2	E_3	E_4	Highest Actions Regrets	Regret Matrix
A_1	$40 - 20 = \mathbf{20}$	$50 - 25 = \mathbf{25}$	$75 - 40 = \mathbf{35}$	$125 - 100 = \mathbf{25}$	$A_1 = E_3 = 35$	$\begin{bmatrix} 35 \\ 35 \\ 125 \end{bmatrix}$
A_2	$40 - 5 = \mathbf{35}$	$50 - 30 = \mathbf{20}$	$75 - 50 = \mathbf{25}$	$125 - 125 = \mathbf{0}$	$A_2 = E_1 = 35$	
A_3	$40 - 40 = \mathbf{0}$	$50 - 50 = \mathbf{0}$	$75 - 75 = \mathbf{0}$	$125 - 0 = \mathbf{125}$	$A_3 = E_4 = 125$	

From the regret matrix, the lowest value is 35. Therefore, the decision maker is indifferent between action A_1 and action A_2.

Example 1: Determine the regret matrix using the information in the payoff table below

	E_1	E_2	E_3
A_1	200	-180	10
A_2	100	-20	40

Solution

Step 1: Determination of pre-regret matrix

Hint: The highest value of column (E_1) is 200, in column (E_2) is -20 and in column (E_3) is 40.

	E_1	E_2	E_3	Pre-Regret Matrix
A_1	$200 - 200 = 0$	$-20 - (-180) = 160$	$40 - 10 = 30$	$\begin{bmatrix} 0 & 160 & 30 \\ 100 & 0 & 0 \end{bmatrix}$
A_2	$200 - 100 = 100$	$-20 - (-20) = 0$	$40 - 40 = 0$	

Step 2: Determination of regret matrix

	E_1	E_2	E_3	Highest Action Regret	Regret Matrix
A_1	$200 - 200 = 0$	$-20 - (-180) = \mathbf{160}$	$40 - 10 = 30$	160	$\begin{bmatrix} 160 \\ 100 \end{bmatrix}$
A_2	$200 - 100 = \mathbf{100}$	$-20 - (-20) = 0$	$40 - 40 = 0$	100	

Example 2: Determine the optimal action using the payoff table below by applying the maximin regret criterion.

State of Nature	Action alternatives		
	(A_1)	(A_2)	(A_3)
(E_1)	20	40	60
(E_2)	15	-10	-15
(E_3)	35	25	-20

Solution

Step 1: Condition. Select the action with the lowest (minimum) regret matrix value

Step 2: Determination of pre-regret matrix

Hint: The highest value of row (E_1) is 60, in row (E_2) is 15 and in row (E_3) is 35.

State of Nature	Action alternatives			Pre-regret Matrix
	(A_1)	(A_2)	(A_3)	
(E_1)	$60 - 20 = 40$	$60 - 40 = 20$	$60 - 60 = 0$	$\begin{bmatrix} 40 & 20 & 0 \\ 0 & 25 & 30 \\ 0 & 10 & 55 \end{bmatrix}$
(E_2)	$15 - 15 = 0$	$15 - (-10) = 25$	$15 - (-15) = 30$	
(E_3)	$35 - 35 = 0$	$35 - 25 = 10$	$35 - (-20) = 55$	

N/B: The original table is different from the working. This difference is given below

Original Table				Working Table			
State of Nature	Action alternatives			State of Nature	Action alternatives		
	(A_1)	(A_2)	(A_3)		(A_1)	(A_2)	(A_3)
(E_1)	20	40	60	(E_1)	40	20	0
(E_2)	15	−10	−15	(E_2)	0	25	30
(E_3)	35	25	−20	(E_3)	0	10	55

Step 3: Data substitution and solving

State of Nature	Action alternatives			Pre-regret Matrix	Regret Matrix
	(A_1)	(A_2)	(A_3)		
(E_1)	$60 - 20 = 40$	$60 - 40 = 20$	$60 - 60 = 0$	$\begin{bmatrix} 40 & 20 & 0 \\ 0 & 25 & 30 \\ 0 & 10 & 55 \end{bmatrix}$	$\begin{bmatrix} 40 \\ 25 \\ 55 \end{bmatrix}$
(E_2)	$15 - 15 = 0$	$15 - (-10) = 25$	$15 - (-15) = 30$		
(E_3)	$35 - 35 = 0$	$35 - 25 = 10$	$35 - (-20) = 55$		
Highest Action Regret	$E_1 = 40$	$E_2 = \mathbf{25}$	$E_3 = 55$		

N/B: The optimal action is A_2. The action is having the highest regret matrix value. the action preference is given as $[A_2(25) > A_1(40) > A_3(55)]$

Example 3: A company has an opportunity to computerize its records department and the existing personnel have job security under union agreement. The cost of the three alternative programs for the changeover depends upon the attitude of the union and is estimated as follows:

	Antagonist (E_1)	Passive (E_2)	Enthusiastic (E_3)
General (A_1)	780	900	1,020
Selective (A_2)	756	1,056	936
Hire New (A_3)	732	912	1,092

Determine the optional action to be taken using the payoff table below under the following criterion.

1) The maximax criterion
2) The maximin criterion
3) The minimax regret criterion

<u>**Solution**</u>

1) **The maximax criterion**

Step 1: Condition. Select the action with the highest most favourable consequence

Step 2: Application of condition

	Antagonist (E_1)	Passive (E_2)	Enthusiastic (E_3)	Action Favourable Consequence	Highest Unfavourable Consequence
General (A_1)	780	900	**1,020**	$E_3 = 1{,}020$	
Selective (A_2)	756	**1,056**	936	$E_2 = 1{,}056$	
Hire New (A_3)	732	912	**1,092**	$E_3 = 1{,}092$	$E_3 = \mathbf{1{,}092}$

N/B: The optimal action is A_3. The action is having the highest favourable consequence (1,092). The action preference can be given as $[A_3(1{,}092) > A_2(1{,}056) > A_1(1{,}020)]$.

2) The maximin criterion

Step 1: Condition. Select the action with the highest unfavorable consequence

Step 2: Application of condition

	Antagonist (E_1)	Passive (E_2)	Enthusiastic (E_3)	Action Unfavourable Consequence	Highest Unfavourable Consequence
General (A_1)	**780**	900	1,020	$E_1 = 780$	$E_1 = \mathbf{780}$
Selective (A_2)	**756**	1,056	936	$E_1 = 756$	
Hire New (A_3)	**732**	912	1,092	$E_1 = 732$	

N/B: The optimal action is A_1. The action is having the highest unfavourable consequence (780). The decision preference can be given as $[A_1(780) > A_2(756) > A_3(732)]$.

3) The minimax regret criterion

Step 1: Condition. Select the action with the lowest regret matrix value

Step 2: Determination of pre-regret matrix

Hint: The highest value of column (E_1) is 780, in column (E_2) is 1,056 and in column (E_3) is 1,092.

	Antagonist (E_1)	Passive (E_2)	Enthusiastic (E_3)
General (A_1)	$780 - 780 = 0$	$1{,}056 - 900 = 156$	$1{,}092 - 1{,}020 = 72$
Selective (A_2)	$780 - 756 = 24$	$1{,}056 - 1{,}056 = 0$	$1{,}092 - 936 = 156$
Hire New (A_3)	$780 - 732 = 48$	$1{,}056 - 912 = 144$	$1{,}092 - 1{,}092 = 0$

N/B: The original table is different from the working. This difference is given below

Original Table

	Antagonist (E_1)	Passive (E_2)	Enthusiastic (E_3)
General (A_1)	780	900	1,020
Selective (A_2)	756	1,056	936
Hire New (A_3)	732	912	1,092

Working Table

	Antagonist (E_1)	Passive (E_2)	Enthusiastic (E_3)
General (A_1)	0	156	72
Selective (A_2)	24	0	156
Hire New (A_3)	48	144	0

Step 3: Data substitution and solving

	Antagonist (E_1)	Passive (E_2)	Enthusiastic (E_3)	Pre-Regret Matrix	Highest Action Regret	Regret Matrix
General (A_1)	0	156	72	$\begin{bmatrix} 0 & 156 & 72 \\ 24 & 0 & 156 \\ 48 & 144 & 0 \end{bmatrix}$	$E_2 = 156$	$\begin{bmatrix} 156 \\ 156 \\ 144 \end{bmatrix}$
Selective (A_2)	24	0	156		$E_3 = 156$	
Hire New (A_3)	48	144	0		$E_2 = 144$	

N/B: The optimal action is A_3. The action is having the highest regret matrix value. the action preference is given as $[A_3(144) > A_1(156) > A_2(156)$ or $A_3(144) > A_2(156) > A_1(156)]$

Test Your Understanding

Exercise 7: Derive the opportunity loss table using the payoff table below

States of Nature	Action (Purchase) Alternatives		
	Apartment building (A_1)	Office building (A_2)	Warehouse (A_3)
Good economic condition (E_1)	5	8	10
Poor economic condition (E_2)	6	6	7
Best economic condition (E_3)	10	7	5

[Answer: ....See Appendix]

Exercise 8: Determine the optimal decision from the opportunity loss table below using the minimax regret criterion.

	States of Nature			
Action Alternatives	E_1	E_2	E_3	E_4
A_1	3	0	0	5
A_2	0	0	6	4
A_3	6	0	2	0

[Answer: Optimal decision is $A_1 = 5$]

Exercise 9: An agricultural company wants to decide which commodity it should stock to get maximum profit. The estimated profit or losses of the three commodities are given below.

	Decision alternatives		
Events	Rice (A_1)	Wheat (A_2)	Maize (A_3)
Excess (E_1)	100	40	40
Normal (E_2)	-40	-30	80
Deficient (E_3)	40	10	-10

Determine the optional decision to be taken using the following criterion.

1) The maximax criterion..**[Answer: Rice (A_1) = 100]**
2) The maximin criterion...**[Answer: Rice (A_1) = −40]**
3) The minimax regret criterion ....**[Answer: Maize (A_3) = 60]**

9.3.4 Laplace Criterion

The Laplace criterion is based on the principle of insufficient reason which states that 'In the absence of any prior knowledge, we assume that the states of nature have equal probability of occurrence'. The decision role is based on the expected payoff value and the optimal decision is the decision with the highest expected payoff value. The equal likely probability is calculated using the formula below.

$$\text{Equal Likely Probability} = \frac{1}{\text{Total Number of Events}} \qquad \text{.................................(1)}$$

Example 1: Use the payoff table below and answer the following questions

States of Nature	Actions		
	A_1	A_2	A_3
E_1	200	120	250
E_2	250	150	300
E_3	300	200	220

1) Compute the equal likely probability
2) Determine the optimal action using the Laplace criterion

<u>Solution</u>

1) Compute the equal likely probability

Step 1: Formula. $\text{Equal Likely Probability} = \frac{1}{\text{Total Number of Events}}$

Where; $\text{Total No of Events} = 3$

Step 2: Data substitution and solving

$$\text{Equal Likely Probability} = \frac{1}{3} \qquad \text{.............................[Equal likely probability]}$$

2) Determine the optimal action using the Laplace criterion

Step 1: Condition. Select action with the highest expected payoff value

Step 2: Data substitution and solving

States of Nature	Actions		
	A_1	A_2	A_3
$E_1\left(\frac{1}{3}\right)$	$\left(\frac{1}{3} \times 200\right) = 66.67$	$\left(\frac{1}{3} \times 120\right) = 40$	$\left(\frac{1}{3} \times 250\right) = 83.33$
$E_2\left(\frac{1}{3}\right)$	$\left(\frac{1}{3} \times 250\right) = 83.33$	$\left(\frac{1}{3} \times 150\right) = 50$	$\left(\frac{1}{3} \times 300\right) = 100$
$E_3\left(\frac{1}{3}\right)$	$\left(\frac{1}{3} \times 300\right) = 100$	$\left(\frac{1}{3} \times 200\right) = 66.67$	$\left(\frac{1}{3} \times 220\right) = 78.33$
Expected Payoff Value	$\sum = 66.67 + 83.33 + 100 = 250$	$\sum = 40 + 50 + 66.67 = 156.67$	$\sum = 83.33 + 100 + 78.33 = 261.66$

N/B: The optimal action is A_3 with expected payoff value of 261.66. The action preference is given as $[A_3(261.66) > A_1(250) > A_2(156.67)]$.

Example 2: Determine the optional decision from the payoff table below using the Laplace criterion and maximin regret criterion.

Decision Alternatives	States of Nature	
	Favourable (E_1)	Unfavourable (E_2)
Large plant (A_1)	200	-180
Small Plant (A_2)	100	-20

Solution

1) **Optimal decision using Laplace criterion**.........[Equal Likely Probability $= \frac{1}{2}$]

Decision Alternatives	States of Nature		Expected Payoff Value
	Favourable $\left(E_1 = \frac{1}{2}\right)$	Unfavourable $\left(E_2 = \frac{1}{2}\right)$	
Large plant (A_1)	$\left(\frac{1}{2} \times 200\right) = 100$	$\left(\frac{1}{2} \times -180\right) = -90$	$\Sigma = 100 + (-90) = 10$
Small Plant (A_2)	$\left(\frac{1}{2} \times 100\right) = 50$	$\left(\frac{1}{2} \times -20\right) = -10$	$\Sigma = 50 + (-10) = \mathbf{40}$

N/B: The optimal decision is A_2 with expected payoff value of 40. The decision preference is given as $[A_2(40) > A_1(10)]$.

2) **Optimal decision using maximin regret criterion**

Step 1: Condition. Select decision with the highest expected payoff value

N/B: It is assumed that we already know how to derive the regret table and pre-regret matrix. If performed properly, we will obtain the table below.

Original Table

Decision Alternatives	States of Nature	
	Favourable (E_1)	Unfavourable (E_2)
Large plant (A_1)	200	-180
Small Plant (A_2)	100	-20

Working Table

Decision Alternatives	States of Nature	
	Favourable (E_1)	Unfavourable (E_2)
Large plant (A_1)	0	160
Small Plant (A_2)	100	0

Step 2: Data substitution and solving

Decision Alternatives	States of Nature		Action Highest Regret
	Favourable (E_1)	Unfavourable (E_2)	
Large plant (A_1)	0	160	$E_2 = 160$
Small Plant (A_2)	100	0	$E_1 = \mathbf{100}$

N/B: The optimal decision is A_2 (Small plant) with regret value of 100. The decision preference is given as $[A_2(100) > A_1(160)]$.

Test your understanding

Exercise 10: Compute the expected payoff value of the following actions in the payoff table below and identify the optimal action.

Actions	States of Nature		
	E_1	E_2	E_3
A_1	2,475	496	−4,122
A_2	1,299	112	−2,659
A_3	123	−273	−1,196

[Answer: $A_1 = -383.67, A_2 = -416 , A_1 = -448.67$ and Optimal $= A_1 = -383.67$]

Exercise 11: Determine the optimal action using the payoff table below under the following criteria.

States of Nature	Actions (Investment)		
	Shares (A_1)	Bonds (A_2)	Savings (A_3)
High growth (E_1)	10	65	4
Moderate growth (E_2)	8	6	1
Low growth (E_3)	6	5	5
No growth (E_4)	4	8	10

1) Laplace criterion..**[Answer: $(A_2) =$ Bonds $= 21$]**
2) Maximax criterion..**[Answer: $(A_2) =$ Bonds $= 65$]**
3) Maximin criterion..**[Answer: $(A_1) =$ Shares $= 6$]**

9.3.5 Criterion of Realism

It is also called Harwicz alpha criterion and is a combination of maximax and maximin. It makes use of the coefficient of optimism denoted alpha (α) and coefficient of pessimism denoted $(1 - \alpha)$. The coefficient of optimism (α) value ranges from 0 (total pessimism) to 1 (total optimism). The decision role is based on the value of (D_i) and the action with the highest (D_i) value is seen as the optimal decision. The formula for calculating a given action (A_i) is given below.

$$D_{(A_i)} = \alpha\left[\text{Max Value}_{(A_i)}\right] + [1 - \alpha]\text{Min Value}_{(A_i)} \quad \text{.............................(1)}$$

N/B: When the coefficient of optimism is equal to one ($\alpha = 1$), criterion of realism is transformed to maximax (decision maker is optimistic) and when the coefficient of optimism is equal to zero one ($\alpha = 0$), criterion of realism is transformed to maximin (decision maker is pessimistic). The coefficient of optimism ($0 \leq \alpha \leq 1$) is subjective.

Example 1: Determine the optimal decision from the payoff table below using the criterion of realism. Assume the coefficient of optimism (α) is 60%.

Actions	States of Nature		
	Good (E_1)	Fair (E_2)	Poor (E_3)
Product A (A_1)	35	15	5
Product B (A_2)	50	20	-3

Solution

Step 1: Condition. Select action with the highest (D_i) as the optimal action

Step 2: Data substitution and solving ...$\{D_{(A_i)} = \alpha[\text{Max Value}_{(A_i)}] + [1 - \alpha]\text{Min Value}_{(A_i)}\}$

Actions	Max value	Min value	Working
Product A (A_1)	35	5	$D_{(A_1)} = 0.6[35] + [1 - 0.6]5 = 21 + 2 = 23$
Product B (A_2)	50	-3	$D_{(A_2)} = 0.6[50] + [1 - 0.6](-3) = 30 - 1.2 = \mathbf{28.8}$

N/B: The optimal action is product B ($A_2 = 28.8$). The action preference is given as seen below $[A_2(28.8) > A_1(23)]$

Example 2: Determine the optimal decision from the payoff table below using the following criterions,

Decisions	States of Nature		
	E_1	E_2	E_3
A_1	50	800	1,300
A_2	-20	880	1,480
A_3	-250	800	150

1) Laplace criterion
2) Criterion of realism ($\alpha = 0.5$)
3) Maximin regret criterion

Solution

1) Laplace criterion......................................[Equal Likely Probability = $\frac{1}{3}$]

Step 1: Condition. Select action with the highest expected payoff value

Step 2: Data substitution and solving

Decisions	States of Nature			Expected payoff value
	$E_1\left(\frac{1}{3}\right)$	$E_2\left(\frac{1}{3}\right)$	$E_3\left(\frac{1}{3}\right)$	
A_1	$\left(\frac{1}{3}\times 50\right) = 16.67$	$\left(\frac{1}{3}\times 800\right) = 266.67$	$\left(\frac{1}{3}\times 1{,}300\right) = 433.33$	$\Sigma = 16.67 + 266.67 + 433.33 = 716.67$
A_2	$\left(\frac{1}{3}\times -20\right) = -6.67$	$\left(\frac{1}{3}\times 880\right) = 293.33$	$\left(\frac{1}{3}\times 1{,}480\right) = 493.33$	$\Sigma = -6.67 + 293.33 + 493.33 = \mathbf{779.99}$
A_3	$\left(\frac{1}{3}\times -250\right) = -83.33$	$\left(\frac{1}{3}\times 800\right) = 266.67$	$\left(\frac{1}{3}\times 150\right) = 50$	$\Sigma = -83.33 + 266.67 + 50 = 233.34$

N/B: The optimal action is A_2 with expected payoff value of 779.99. The action preference is given as $[A_2(779.99) > A_1(716.67) > A_3(233.34)]$.

2) Criterion of realism ($\alpha = 0.5$)

Step 1: Condition. Select action with the highest (D_i) as the optimal action

Step 2: Data substitution and solving ...$\{D_{(A_i)} = \alpha[\text{Max Value}_{(A_i)}] + [1-\alpha]\text{Min Value}_{(A_i)}\}$

Decisions	Max Value	Min Value	Working Table
A_1	1,300	50	$D_{(A_i)} = 0.5[1{,}300] + [1 - 0.5]50 = 650 + 25 = 675$
A_2	1,480	−20	$D_{(A_i)} = 0.5[1{,}480] + [1 - 0.5](-20) = 740 + (-10) = \mathbf{730}$
A_3	800	−250	$D_{(A_i)} = 0.5[800] + [1 - 0.5](-250) = 400 + (-125) = 275$

N/B: The optimal action is product B ($A_2 = 730$). The action preference is given as seen below $[A_2(730) > A_1(675) > A_3(275)]$

3) Maximin regret criterion

Step 1: Condition. Select decision with the highest expected payoff value

N/B: It is assumed that we already know how to derive the regret table and pre-regret matrix. If performed properly, we obtain the table below.

Original Table

Decisions	States of Nature		
	E_1	E_2	E_3
A_1	50	800	1,300
A_2	−20	880	1,480
A_3	−250	800	150

Working Table

Decisions	States of Nature		
	E_1	E_2	E_3
A_1	0	80	180
A_2	70	0	0
A_3	300	80	1,330

Step 2: Data substitution and solving

Decisions	States of Nature			Decision Highest Regret
	E_1	E_2	E_3	
A_1	0	80	180	180
A_2	70	0	0	70
A_3	300	80	1,330	1,330

N/B: The optimal decision is A_2 with regret value of 70. The decision preference is given as $[A_2(70) > A_1(180) > A_3(1{,}330)]$.

Test Your Understanding

Exercise 12: Compute the (D_i) of the decisions and identify the optimal decisions from the payoff table using the criterion of realism.

Actions	States of Nature	
	Boom (E_1)	Slump (E_2)
Product A (A_1)	50	60
Product B (A_2)	20	80
Product B (A_3)	40	70

[Answer; $D_{(A_1)} = 54$, $D_{(A_2)} = 44$, $D_{(A_3)} = 52$ and Optimal decision $D_{(A_1)} = 54$]

Exercise 13: Determine the optimal action using the payoff table below under the following criterions.

States of Nature	Actions (Investment)	
	Sell cola (A_1)	Sell coffee (A_2)
Cold weather (E_1)	15	5
Warm weather (E_2)	1	4

1) Maximax criterion...**[Answer: A_1(Sell cola) $= 15$]**
2) Maximin criterion...**[Answer: A_2(Sell coffee) $= 4$]**
3) Laplace criterion...**[Answer: A_1(Sell cola) $= 8$]**
4) Criterion of realism ($\alpha = 0.7$)..........................**[Answer: A_1(Sell cola) $= 10.8$]**

9.4 Decision Making Under Risk

Major criteria of decision making under risk includes; expected monetary value (EMV), expected regret value (ERV) and expected value of perfect information (EVPI). Decision making under risk can be computed using the algebraic method (payoff or regret table) and/or the graphical method (decision tree).

A decision tree is a sequence of branches (indicating acts) and sub-branches (indicating states of nature). A decision tree starts with a decision node (represented by a square), followed by a chance node (represented by a circle) and terminates with an end point (includes the states of nature probabilities and payoff). A typical illustration of decision tree is given below.

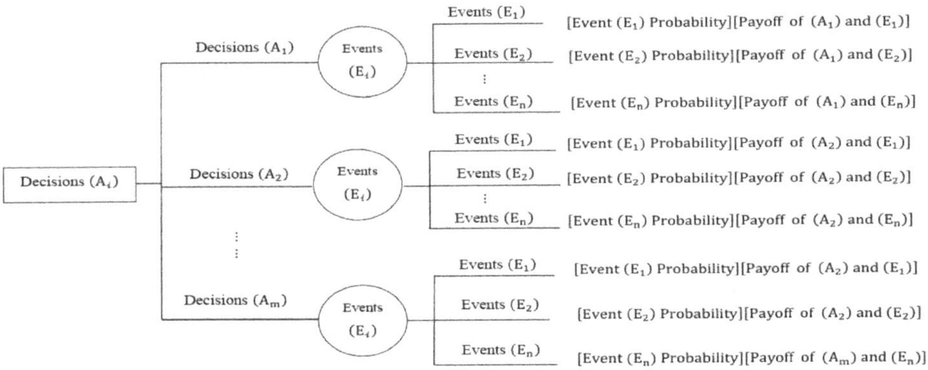

9.4.1 Expected Monetary Value (EMV)

The total expected monetary value is derived by multiplying the payoff of each action at a time with the probability of the corresponding states of nature and the sum the results.

An Action Expected Monetary Value $_{(n)} = p_n A_n$ ....(1)

Total Expected Monetary Value $= \sum[p_i A_i]$ ....(2)

N/B: The decision role of expected monetary value criterion is that we chose the alternative or decision that maximizes the expected monetary value of the payoff.

Example 1: An individual is faced with the scenario below. Compute the total expected monetary value.

Best case provides a 15% probability of making 200,000 FCFA

Worst case provides a 25% probability of making 15,000 FCFA

Most likely case provides a 60% probability of making 45,000 FCFA.

Solution

Step 1: Formula. Total Expected Monetary Value $= \sum[p_i A_i]$

Step 2: Data substitution and solving

Scenarios	Probabilities	Outcomes	Working
Best case	15%	200,000	$0.15 \times 200{,}000 = 30{,}000$
Worst case	25%	15,000	$0.25 \times 15{,}000 = 3{,}750$
Most likely case	60%	45,000	$0.6 \times 45{,}000 = 27{,}000$
			$\sum = 30{,}000 + 3{,}750 + 27{,}000 = \mathbf{60,750}$
N/B: The total expected monetary value is 60,750			

Example 2: Compute the expected monetary value of the different actions using the payoff table below.

Decision Alternatives	States of Nature	
	Pass (E_1)	Fail (E_2)
	40%	60%
Corn (A_1)	500	-250
Peanuts (A_2)	35	60
Soybeans (A_3)	50	50

Solution

Step 1: Formula. Expected Monetary Value $_{(n)} = p_n A_n$

Step 2: Data substitution and solving

	E_1	E_2	Expected Monetary Value
	40%	60%	
A_1	$500 \times 0.4 = 200$	$-250 \times 0.6 = -150$	$\sum = 200 + (-150) = 50$
A_2	$35 \times 0.4 = 14$	$60 \times 0.6 = 36$	$\sum = 14 + 36 = 50$
A_3	$50 \times 0.4 = 20$	$50 \times 0.6 = 30$	$\sum = 20 + 30 = 50$

N/B: $\text{Action}(A_1) = 50$ FCFA, $\text{Action}(A_2) = 50$ FCFA and $\text{Action}(A_3) = 50$ FCFA

Example 3: For the following payoff table, the probability of event 1 is 0.70, the probability of event 2 is 0.20 and the probability of event 3 is 0.10. Determine the expected monetary value of the different actions and identify the optimal action.

Events	Actions		
	A_1	A_2	A_3
E_1	0	6	12
E_2	30	6	12
E_3	60	36	12

Solution

Hint: The above payoff table can be re-written with the different probabilities as seen below

		Actions		
Events	Probabilities	A_1	A_2	A_3
E_1	0.70	0	6	12
E_2	0.20	30	6	12
E_3	0.10	60	36	12

a) Tabular Method

Step 1: Formula. Expected Monetary Value $_{(n)} = p_n A_n$

Step 2: Data substitution and solving

		Actions		
Nature of State	Probabilities	A_1	A_2	A_3
E_1	0.70	$0 \times 0.70 = 0$	$6 \times 0.70 = 4.2$	$12 \times 0.70 = 8.4$
E_2	0.20	$30 \times 0.20 = 6$	$6 \times 0.20 = 1.2$	$12 \times 0.20 = 2.4$
E_3	0.10	$60 \times 0.10 = 6$	$36 \times 0.10 = 3.6$	$12 \times 0.10 = 1.2$
Expected Monetary Value		$\sum = 0 + 6 + 6 = \mathbf{12}$	$\sum = 4.2 + 1.2 + 3.6 = \mathbf{9}$	$\sum = 8.4 + 2.4 + 1.2 = \mathbf{12}$

N/B: The decision maker is indifference between action (A_1) and action (A_3). This is because both actions have the same and highest values (12).

b) Decision tree method

Step 1: Formula. Expected Monetary Value $_{(n)} = p_n A_n$

Step 2: Data substitution and solving

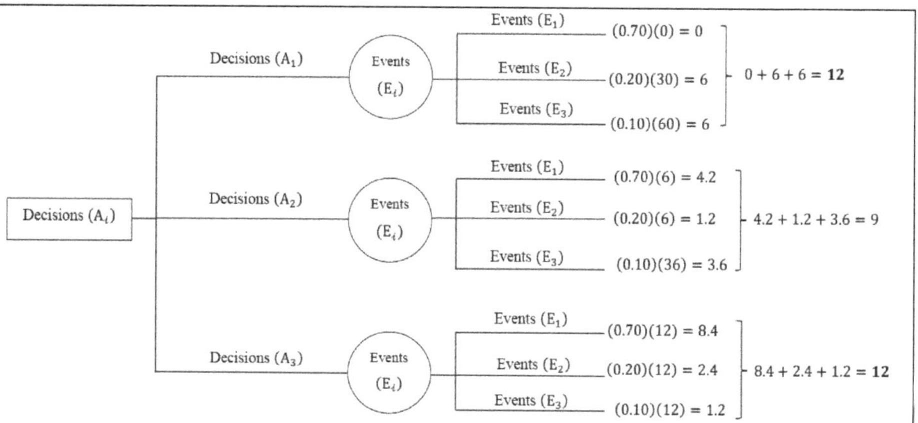

N/B: The decision maker is indifference between action (A_1) and action (A_3). This is because both actions have the same and highest values (12).

Test Your Understanding

Exercise 14: A sales person is paid commission on sales. If the following sales commission has the given probability;

10,000 probability 25%

90,000 probability 40%

100,000 probability 35%

Calculate the person expected monetary value.................................**[Answer: 73,500 FCFA]**

Exercise 15: Compute the expected monetary value of the different decisions (A_1, A_2, A_3) in the payoff table below.

Decision Alternatives	States of Nature		
	Strong Economy (E_1)	Stable Economy (E_2)	Weak Economy (E_3)
	20%	35%	45%
Large Factory (A_1)	100	55	−25
Average Factory (A_2)	46	25	15
Small Factory (A_3)	20	20	20

[Answer: A_1 = 28 FCFA, A_2 = 24.7 FCFA and A_3 = 20 FCFA]

Exercise 16: Calculate the expected monetary value for all possible decisions and hence determine the optimal decision.

		Actions		
Nature of State	Probabilities	A_1	A_2	A_3
E_1	55%	800	400	250
E_2	30%	400	300	250
E_3	15%	$-1,000$	0	250

[Answer: $A_1 = 410$ FCFA, $A_2 = 310$ FCFA, $A_3 = 250$ FCFA and Optimal Decision $= A_1(410)$]

9.4.2 Expected Regret Value (ERV)

The expected regret value (ERV) is also called expected opportunity loss (EOL). The decision role here is that we select the decision that minimizes expected loss (smallest expected regret value or expected opportunity loss value). We make use of the regret table to determine the expected regret value.

Example 1: Transform the payoff table below to regret table.

		Actions		
Nature of State	Probabilities	Motel (A_1)	Restaurant (A_2)	Theater (A_3)
Shortage (E_1)	0.2	350,000	326,000	334,000
Stable (E_2)	0.4	350,000	341,000	349,000
Theater (E_3)	0.4	350,000	356,000	364,000

Solution

		Actions		
Nature of State	Probabilities	A_1	A_2	A_3
E_1	0.2	350,000 – 350,000 = 0	350,000 – 326,000 = 24,000	350,000 – 334,000 = 16,000
E_2	0.4	369,000 – 350,000 = 19,000	369,000 – 341,000 = 28,000	369,000 – 369,000 = 0
E_3	0.4	364,000 – 350,000 = 14,000	364,000 – 364,000 = 0	364,000 – 356,000 = 8,000

N/B: The expected monetary value table and expected regret value table is given below

Expected Monetary Value

		Actions		
Nature of State	Probabilities	A_1	A_2	A_3
E_1	0.2	350,000	326,000	334,000
E_2	0.4	350,000	341,000	369,000
E_3	0.4	350,000	364,000	356,000

Expected Regret Value

		Actions		
Nature of State	Probabilities	A_1	A_2	A_3
E_1	0.2	0	24,000	16,000
E_2	0.4	19,000	28,000	0
E_3	0.4	14,000	0	8,000

Example 2: Determine the best action from the payoff table below using the expected opportunity loss (EOL) or expected regret value (ERV).

Decisions	States of Nature			
	E_1	E_2	E_3	E_4
	15%	25%	40%	20%
A_1	20	25	40	100
A_2	5	30	50	125
A_3	40	50	75	0

Solution

Step 1: Condition. Select the minimum value among the expected opportunity loss values.

Step 2: Derivation of expected regret table

Working Table

	E_1	E_2	E_2	E_4
	15%	25%	40%	20%
A_1	$40 - 20 = 20$	$50 - 25 = 25$	$75 - 40 = 35$	$125 - 100 = 25$
A_2	$40 - 5 = 35$	$50 - 30 = 20$	$75 - 50 = 25$	$125 - 125 = 0$
A_3	$40 - 40 = 0$	$50 - 50 = 0$	$75 - 75 = 0$	$125 - 0 = 125$

Table to be used

	E_1	E_2	E_3	E_4
	15%	25%	40%	20%
A_1	20	25	35	25
A_2	35	20	25	0
A_3	0	0	0	125

Step 3: Data substitution and solving

	E_1	E_2	E_3	E_4	Expected Opportunity Loss (EOL)
	15%	25%	40%	20%	$\Sigma = 15\% + 25\% + 40\% + 20\% = 100\%$
A_1	$0.15 \times 20 = 3$	$0.25 \times 25 = 6.25$	$0.4 \times 35 = 14$	$0.2 \times 25 = 5$	$\Sigma = 3 + 6.25 + 14 + 5 = 28.25$
A_2	$0.15 \times 35 = 5.25$	$0.25 \times 20 = 5$	$0.4 \times 25 = 10$	$0.2 \times 0 = 0$	$\Sigma = 5.25 + 5 + 10 + 0 = 20.25$
A_3	$0.15 \times 0 = 0$	$0.25 \times 0 = 0$	$0.4 \times 0 = 0$	$0.2 \times 125 = 25$	$\Sigma = 0 + 0 + 0 + 25 = 25$

N/B: The best action is action (A_2) as it has the smallest EOL value (20.25). The preference of action is given as $[A_2(20.25) > A_3(25) > A_1(28.25)]$.

Example 3: Using the payoff table below, identify the best action using the following criterion

		Actions		
Nature of State	Probabilities	Widget (A_1)	Hummer (A_2)	Nimnot (A_3)
Favourable (E_1)	0.3	500	0	−500
Stable (E_2)	0.5	490	1,000	500
Unfavourable (E_3)	0.2	480	500	1,500

1) Expected monetary value (EMV)
2) Expected regret value (ERV)

Solution

1) Expected monetary value (EMV)

Step 1: Condition. Select the maximum value among the expected monetary values.

Step 2: Data substitution and solving

		Actions		
Nature of State	Probabilities	A_1	A_2	A_3
E_1	0.3	$0.3 \times 500 = 150$	$0.3 \times 0 = 0$	$0.3 \times (-500) = -150$
E_2	0.5	$0.5 \times 490 = 245$	$0.5 \times 1{,}000 = 500$	$0.5 \times 500 = 250$
E_3	0.2	$0.2 \times 480 = 96$	$0.2 \times 500 = 100$	$0.2 \times 1{,}500 = 300$
Expected Monetary Value		$\sum = 150 + 245 + 96 = \mathbf{491}$	$\sum = 0 + 500 + 100 = \mathbf{600}$	$\sum = -150 + 250 + 300 = \mathbf{400}$

N/B: The best action is (A_2) as it has the greatest value (600). The action preference is given as $[A_2(600) > A_1(491) > A_3(400)]$.

2) Expected regret value (ERV)

Step 1: Condition. Select the minimum value among the expected regret values.

Step 2: Derivation of the regret table

		Actions		
Nature of State	Probabilities	A_1	A_2	A_3
E_1	0.3	$500 - 500 = 0$	$500 - 0 = 500$	$500 - (-500) = 1{,}000$
E_2	0.5	$1{,}000 - 490 = 510$	$1{,}000 - 1{,}000 = 0$	$1{,}000 - 500 = 500$
E_3	0.2	$1{,}500 - 480 = 1{,}020$	$1{,}500 - 500 = 1{,}000$	$1{,}500 - 1{,}500 = 0$

N/B: The payoff table and the regret table are given below

Payoff Table

		Actions		
Nature of State	Probabilities	A_1	A_2	A_3
E_1	0.3	500	0	−500
E_2	0.5	490	1,000	500
E_3	0.2	480	500	1,500

Regret Table

		Actions		
Nature of State	Probabilities	A_1	A_2	A_3
E_1	0.3	0	500	1,000
E_2	0.5	510	0	500
E_3	0.2	1,020	1,000	0

Step 3: Data substitution and solving

a) Tabula method

Nature of State	Probabilities	Actions		
		A_1	A_2	A_3
E_1	0.3	$0.3 \times 0 = 0$	$0.3 \times 500 = 150$	$0.3 \times 1{,}000 = 300$
E_2	0.5	$0.5 \times 510 = 255$	$0.5 \times 0 = 0$	$0.5 \times 500 = 250$
E_3	0.2	$0.2 \times 1{,}020 = 204$	$0.2 \times 1{,}000 = 200$	$0.2 \times 0 = 0$
Expected Regret Value		$\Sigma = 0 + 255 + 204 = \mathbf{459}$	$\Sigma = 150 + 0 + 200 = \mathbf{350}$	$\Sigma = 300 + 250 + 0 = 550$

N/B: The best action is (A_2) as it has the smallest value (350). The action preference is given as $[A_2(350) > A_1(459) > A_3(550)]$.

b) Decision tree method

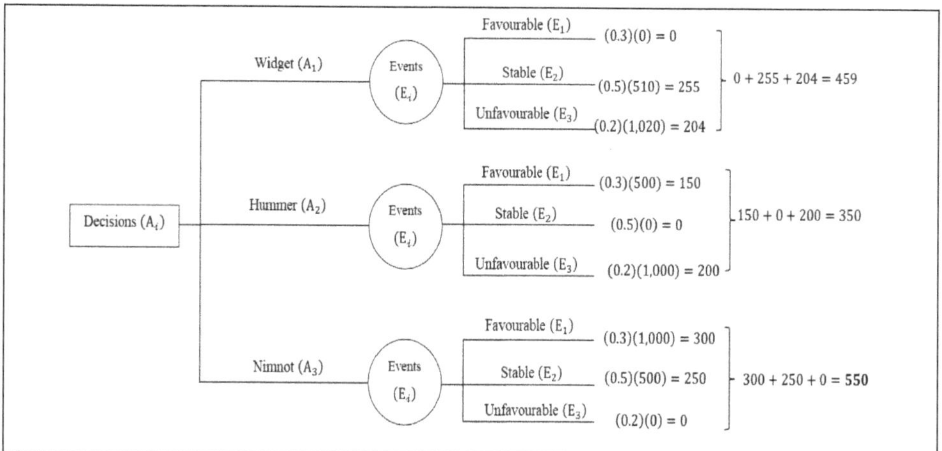

N/B: The best action is (A_2) as it has the smallest value (350). The action preference is given as $[A_2(350) > A_1(459) > A_3(550)]$.

Note: The relationship between the expected monetary value (EMV) and the expected regret value (ERV) is illustrated below.

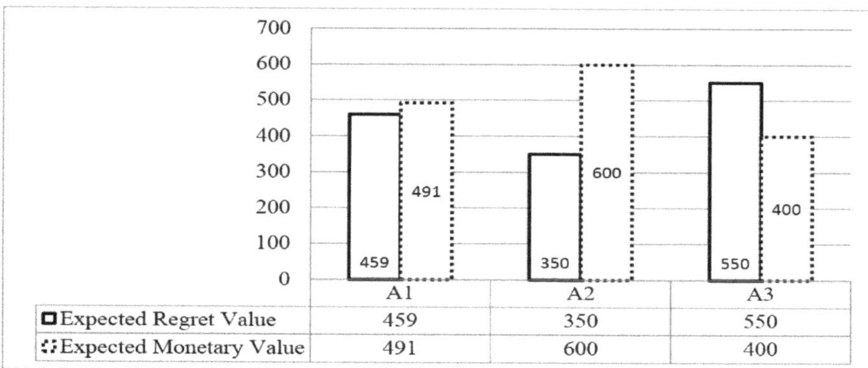

From the illustration above, we realized that the expected monetary values and expected regret values are inversely related. The best action is one with the highest expected monetary value and lowest expected regret value.

Test Your Understanding

Exercise 17: Transform the payoff table below to regret table.

Decisions	States of Nature		
	E_1	E_2	E_3
	0.25	**0.5**	**0.25**
A_1	12	-6	24
A_2	36	12	48
A_3	-3	60	30

[Answer:..See Appendix]

Exercise 18: Using the payoff table below, identify the best action using the following criterion.

Decisions	Good (E_1)	Recession (E_2)
	0.35	0.65
Bellhop (A_1)	750,000	125,000
Management (A_2)	875,000	125,000

1) Expected monetary value (EMV).......**[Answer: Management (A_2) $= \mathbf{387,500}$]**
2) Expected regret value (ERV) ....**[Answer: Management (A_2) $= 0$]**

Exercise 19: Using the payoff table below, identify the best action using the following criterion.

		Actions		
Nature of State	Probabilities	A_1	A_2	A_3
E_1	0.3	12	36	-3
E_2	0.5	-6	12	60
E_3	0.2	24	48	30

1) Expected monetary value (EMV) ....**[Answer: $A_3 = \mathbf{35.1}$]**
2) Expected regret value (ERV) ....**[Answer: $A_3 = \mathbf{15.3}$]**

9.4.3 The Expected Value of Perfect Information (EVPI)

The expected value of perfect information is the maximum amount a decision maker would pay for additional information resulting in a decision better than one made without perfect information. It places a limit as what a decision maker should pay for additional information. It is the difference between the expected value with perfect information (EVWPI) and maximum expected monetary value (EMV).

The Expected Value of Perfect Information (EVPI) = EVwPI − Max EMV ……………..(1)

N/B: To determine the expected value with perfect information (EVwPI), we identify the maximum payoff value of each states of nature and multiply with its corresponding probability and sum the values.

Example 1: Compute the expected value with perfect information (EVwPI), using the payoff table below.

States of Nature		Decision alternatives		
	Probability	A_1	A_2	A_3
E_1	0.2	30,000	25,000	22,000
E_2	0.5	20,000	35,000	20,000
E_3	0.3	40,000	30,000	35,000

Solution

Step 1: Formula. Expected Value with Perfect Information (EVwPI) $= \sum(P_i E_{(i)Max})$

Step 2: Data substitution and solving

	States of Nature		
	E_1	E_1	E_1
Probability	0.2	0.5	0.3
Maximum Payoff	30,000	35,000	40,000
Solving	$0.2 \times 30{,}000 =$ 6,000	$0.5 \times 35{,}000 =$ 17,500	$0.3 \times 40{,}000 =$ 12,000
EVwPI = 6,000 + 17,500 + 12,000 = **35,500 FCFA**			

Example 2: Calculate the expected value of perfect information (EVPI) using the payoff table below.

Actions	States of Nature		
	E_1 (0.4)	E_2 (0.2)	E_3 (0.4)
A_1	750	150	100
A_2	600	300	100

Solution

Step 1: Formula. The Expected Value of Perfect Information (EVPI) $=$ EVwPI $-$ Max EMV

Step 2: Determination of maximum expected monetary value $\left(EMV_{(Max)}\right)$

1) Formula. Expected Monetary Value $_{(n)} = p_n A_n$
2) Data substitution and solving

Actions	States of Nature			EMV
	E_1 (0.4)	E_2 (0.2)	E_3 (0.4)	
A_1	$0.4 \times 750 = 300$	$0.2 \times 150 = 30$	$0.4 \times 100 = 40$	$300 + 30 + 40 = 370$
A_2	$0.4 \times 600 = 240$	$0.2 \times 300 = 60$	$0.4 \times 100 = 40$	$240 + 60 + 40 = 340$
N/B: The maximum expected monetary value is **370**				

Step 3: Determination of expected value with perfect information or expected pay off

1) Formula. Expected Value with Perfect Information (EVwPI) $= \sum\left(P_i E_{(i)Max}\right)$
2) Data substitution and solving

	States of Nature		
	E_1	E_1	E_1
Probability	0.4	0.2	0.4
Maximum Payoff	750	300	100
Solving	$0.4 \times 750 = 300$	$0.2 \times 300 = 60$	$0.4 \times 100 = 40$
Expected Payoff $= 300 + 60 + 40 =$ **400 FCFA**			

Step 4: Data substitution and solving

Expected Value with Perfect Information (EVPI) $= 400 - 370$ ....[Solve equation]

Expected Value with Perfect Information (EVPI) $=$ **30 FCFA**

Interpretation: The value 30 FCFA means the decision maker should pay a maximum 30 FCFA for any additional information.

Example 3: Use the payoff table below and determine optimal decision

States of Nature		Decision alternatives		
	Probability	Don't Plant (A_1)	Small Tree Farm (A_2)	Large Tree Farm (A_3)
Decline (E_1)	0.35	2,000	600	1,200
Same (E_2)	0.4	600	500	540
Increase (E_3)	0.25	60	600	300

1) Determine the optimal decision using the expected monetary value (EMV) method
2) Determine the optimal decision using the expected opportunity loss (EOL) method
3) Compute the expected value of perfect information (EVPI)

Solution

1) Determine the optimal decision using the expected monetary value (EMV) method

States of Nature		Decision alternatives		
	Probability	A_1	A_2	A_3
E_1	0.35	$0.35 \times 2{,}000 = 700$	$0.35 \times 600 = 210$	$0.35 \times 1{,}200 = 420$
E_2	0.4	$0.4 \times 600 = 240$	$0.4 \times 500 = 200$	$0.4 \times 540 = 216$
E_3	0.25	$0.25 \times 60 = 15$	$0.25 \times 600 = 150$	$0.25 \times 300 = 75$
EMV		$700 + 240 + 15 = \mathbf{955}$	$210 + 200 + 150 = \mathbf{560}$	$420 + 216 + 75 = \mathbf{711}$
N/B: The optimal decision is $A_1 = 955$ and the decision preference is $[A_1(955) > A_3(711) > A_2(560)]$				

2) Determine the optimal decision using the expected opportunity loss (EOL)

States of Nature		Decision alternatives		
	Probability	A_1	A_2	A_3
E_1	0.35	$0.35 \times 0 = 0$	$0.35 \times 1{,}400 = 490$	$0.35 \times 800 = 280$
E_2	0.4	$0.4 \times 0 = 0$	$0.4 \times 100 = 40$	$0.4 \times 60 = 24$
E_3	0.25	$0.25 \times 540 = 135$	$0.25 \times 0 = 0$	$0.25 \times 300 = 75$
EOL		$0 + 0 + 135 = \mathbf{135}$	$490 + 40 + 0 = \mathbf{530}$	$280 + 24 + 75 = \mathbf{379}$
N/B: The optimal decision is $A_1 = \mathbf{135}$ and the decision preference is $[A_1(135) > A_3(379) > A_2(530)]$				

N/B: The relationship between the expected monetary value (EMV) and expected opportunity loss (EOL) is indirect. At the optimal decision(A_1), the expected monetary value is highest and the expected opportunity loss is lowest as illustrated below.

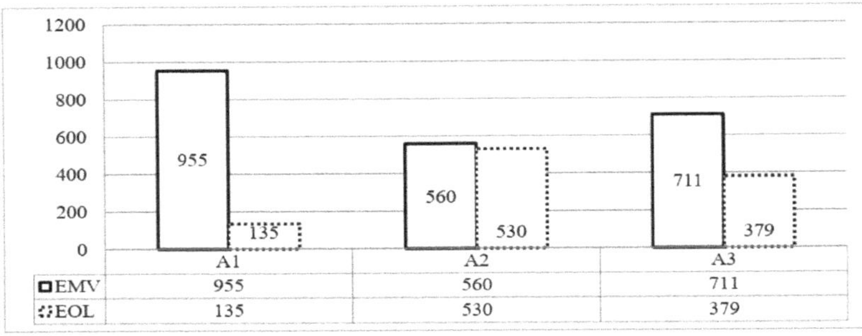

From the illustration above, we realized that the optimal decision (A_1) is having the highest expected monetary value (EMV) and lowest expected opportunity loss (EOL). From this, we can conclude that expected monetary value is inversely related to expected opportunity loss.

3) Compute the expected value of perfect information (EVPI)

Hint: Part (1) already gives us the expected monetary values and consequently the maximum expected monetary value (955). From the payoff table, we can derive the working table below.

	States of Nature		
	E_1	E_2	E_3
Probability	0.35	0.4	0.25
Maximum payoff	2,000	600	1,200

Step 1: Formula. The Expected Value of Perfect Information (EVPI) = EVwPI − Max EMV

Step 2: Determination of expected value with perfect information or expected payoff value

1) Formula. Expected Value with Perfect Information (EVwPI) = $\sum(P_i E_{(i)Max})$
2) Data substitution and solving

$EVwPI = (0.35 \times 2{,}000) + (0.4 \times 600) + (0.25 \times 1{,}200)$ ...,.........[Work brackets]

$EVwPI = 700 + 240 + 300$ ....[Solve equation]

Expected Value with Perfect Information (EVwPI) = 1,240 FCFA

Step 3: Data substitution and solving

Expected Value of Perfect Information (EVPI) = 1,240 − 955 ....[Solve equation]

Expected Value of Perfect Information (EVPI) = **285 FCFA**

Interpretation: The maximum amount a decision maker should pay for any additional information is 285 FCFA.

Test Your Understanding

Exercise 20: Compute the expected value of perfect information (EVPI) given that the maximum expected monetary value (Max EMV) is 192.5 FCFA and the expected value with perfect information (EVwPI) is 240 FCFA..............................**[Answer: 47.5 FCFA]**

Exercise 21: Calculate the expected value of perfect information (EVPI) using payoff table and expected monetary value data below.

Decision Alternatives	States of Nature			
	E_1 (0.4)	E_2 (0.3)	E_3 (0.3)	EMV
A_1	950	1,050	1,150	1,040
A_2	850	1,100	1,350	1,075
A_3	700	1,000	1,300	970

[Answer: 0 FCFA]

Exercise 22: Determine the optimal action using the payoff table below under the following criteria.

States of Nature		Action Alternatives		
	Probability	A_1	A_2	A_3
E_1	0.6	2,000	1,200	2,500
E_2	0.4	2,500	1,500	3,000

1) Equal likelihood criterio

   [Answer: $A_3(2,750) > A_1(2,250) > A_2(1,350)$ and Optimal A_3]

2) Harwicz alpha criterion

   [Answer: $A_3(2,825) > A_1(2,325) > A_2(1,395)$ and Optimal A_3]

3) EMV...............**[Answer: $A_3(2,700) > A_1(2,200) > A_2(1,320)$ and Optimal A_3]**
4) EOL.........................**[Answer: $A_2(180) > A_1(300) > A_3(300)$ and Optimal A_3]**
5) Compute the expected value of perfect information....................**[Answer: 0 FCFA]**

Exercise 23: Given that the expected value for perfect information (EVPI) is 6. Calculate the maximum expected monetary value using the table below.

	States of Nature		
	E_1	E_2	E_3
Probability	0.3	0.6	0.1
Maximum payoff	250	25	10

[Answer: 85 FCFA]

CHAPTER TEN

CHI-SQUARE TEST

A chi-square distribution is a non-negative continuous probability distribution written as $(\mathcal{X}^2)$ with one parameter denoted $(\mathcal{V})$ called degree of freedom. The two major chi-square test of interest here is the test of independence and the test of goodness of fit (through the contingency table).

10.1 Chi-Square Test of Goodness of fit

Chi-square test of goodness of fit is used to test whether a frequency distribution obtained experimentally (observed values) fit an expected frequency distribution (expected values). It uses a sample to determine whether a frequency distribution of the population conforms to a particular probability distribution that is believed to follow. To perform a chi-square goodness of fit test, the following steps are worth respected.

1) **Hypothesis:** Assume we are testing for the goodness of fit of two categorical variables; the two major hypotheses are given below.
   a) Null Hypothesis (H_0): The observed frequency is equal to the expected frequency. That is, there is no significant difference between the observed and expected value.
   b) Alternative Hypothesis (H_1): The observed frequency is not equal to the expected frequency. That is, there is a significance difference between the observed and expected value.

   Note: The null hypothesis and alternative hypothesis can also be started based on the frequency distribution. This will be seen when solving examples.
2) **Statistics**: To compute the chi-square value$(\mathcal{X}^2)$, we are required to have a significance level(α). The general formula is given as seen below.

$$\text{Chi Square } (\mathcal{X}^2) = \sum\left[\frac{(O_i - E_i)^2}{E_i}\right] \sim {\mathcal{X}^2}^{(\alpha)}_{(df)} \quad \ldots\ldots\ldots\ldots\ldots\ldots\ldots\ldots(1)$$

Where: $(\mathbf{O}_i)$ represents observed frequency, $(\mathbf{E}_i)$ represent expected frequency $(\mathbf{df})$ represent the degree of freedom, $(\boldsymbol{\alpha})$ represent the significance level

Note: Expected frequency less than 5 should be combined with another expected frequency to yield a value greater than 5. The combination should be with preceding or succeeding value(s). The formula of degree of freedom and expected frequency varies with the nature of distribution as seen below.

Distribution	Total Number of Restriction	Degree of Freedom
Uniform Distribution	1	$K-1$
Binomial Distribution	2	$K-2$
Poisson Distribution	2	$K-2$
Normal Distribution	3	$K-3$

3) **Decision Rule:** To make decision and conclusion, we are required to derive the critical value and use the significance level. The decision rule is given as seen below.
   a) Reject (H_0) if the calculated chi-square value is greater than the critical value.
   b) Don't reject (H_0) if the calculated chi-square value is less than the critical value.

10.1.1 Uniform Distribution

The uniform distribution is having a parameter (mean). The mean is equal to the expected frequency and is the same or uniform to all the scores (elements). The mean value is calculated using the formula below.

$$\text{Mean}(\mu) = \text{Expected Frequency } (E_i) = \frac{\text{Sum of Frequency}(\sum f_i)}{\text{Number of Elements}(n)} \quad \ldots\ldots\ldots\ldots\ldots\ldots\ldots\ldots\ldots\ldots(1)$$

Example 1: A normal die (6-sides) is thrown 60 times and we record the number of each time. The data in the table below represents the outcome of the 60 tosses. Compute the expected frequencies.

Number of face up (Score)	1	2	3	4	5	6
Counts (Frequency)	5	8	9	8	10	20

Solution

Step 1: Formula. $\text{Expected Frequency}(E_i) = \frac{\text{Sum of Frequency}(\sum f_i)}{\text{Number of Elements}(n)}$, where; $n = 6$

Step 2: Data substitution and solving

$$\text{Expected Frequency}(E_i) = \frac{5+8+9+8+10+20}{6} \quad \ldots\ldots\ldots\ldots\ldots\ldots\ldots\ldots\text{[Sum numerator]}$$

$$\text{Expected Frequency}(E_i) = \frac{60}{6} \quad \ldots\ldots\ldots\ldots\ldots\ldots\ldots\ldots\ldots\text{[Solve equation]}$$

$$\text{Expected Frequency}(E_i) = \mathbf{10}$$

Step 3: Presentation of the Chi-square table [Horizontal expression]

Number of face up	1	2	3	4	5	6
Observed (O_i)	5	8	9	8	10	20
Expected (E_i)	10	10	10	10	10	10

Example 2: Joe has a die which has face number 1 to 6. He got the following scores represented in the table below. Calculate the chi-square value. Assume a 5% significance level.

Scores	1	2	3	4	5	6
Frequency	17	20	29	20	18	16

Solution

Step 1: Formula. Chi Square $(\mathcal{X}^2) = \sum\left[\frac{(O_i-E_i)^2}{E_i}\right] \sim \mathcal{X}^{2(\alpha)}{}_{(k-1)}$

Where; $\alpha = 0.05$, $k = 6$, $E_i = 20$

Step 2: Data substitution and solving...[Chi-Square Table]

Scores	O_i	E_i	$O_i - E_i$	$(O_i - E_i)^2$	$\frac{(O_i - E_i)^2}{E_i}$
1	17	20	$17 - 20 = -3$	$-3^2 = 9$	$9/20 = 0.45$
2	20	20	$20 - 20 = 0$	$0^2 = 0$	$0/20 = 0$
3	29	20	$29 - 20 = 9$	$9^2 = 81$	$81/20 = 4.05$
4	20	20	$20 - 20 = 0$	$0^2 = 0$	$0/20 = 0$
5	18	20	$18 - 20 = -2$	$-2^2 = 4$	$4/20 = 0.2$
6	16	20	$16 - 20 = -4$	$-4^2 = 16$	$16/20 = 0.8$
					$\sum = \mathbf{5.5}$
The calculated chi-square ($\mathcal{X}^2$) value is 5.5					

Example 3: The computed chi-square value is 14.618, the significance level is 5% and the number of category is 5. Determine the critical value and interpret the result.

Solution

Step 1: Derivation of critical value..............$\left[\chi^{2(\alpha)}{}_{(k-1)} = \chi^{2(0.05)}{}_{(5-1)} = \chi^{2(0.05)}{}_{(4)}\right]$

$\alpha =$	0.995	0.99	0.975	0.95	0.90	0.10	0.05	0.025	0.01	0.005
v = 1	---	---	---	---	0.02	2.71	3.84	5.02	6.63	7.88
2	0.01	0.02	0.05	0.10	0.21	4.61	5.99	7.38	9.21	10.60
3	0.07	0.11	0.22	0.35	0.58	6.25	7.81	9.35	11.34	12.84
4	0.21	0.30	0.48	0.71	1.06	7.78	9.49	11.14	13.28	14.86
5	0.41	0.55	0.83	1.15	1.61	9.24	11.07	12.83	15.09	16.75

The Critical value is **9.49**

Step 2: Interpretation: The calculated chi-square value is greater than the critical value (14.618 > 9.49). We reject the null hypothesis. That is, the observed frequency is not equal to the expected frequency or the distribution is not uniform.

Test Your Understanding

Exercise 1: Using the data in the table below, compute the following. Assume $\alpha = 10\%$

Score	1	2	3	4	5	6	7	8
Frequency	7	10	11	9	12	10	14	7

1) The expected frequency...**[Answer: 10 for all scores]**
2) The critical value..**[Answer: 18.48]**

Exercise 2: The following table contains data on the number of customers a shop has on each day of the week. Assume $\alpha = 0.05$, compute the following.

Scores	1	2	3	4	5	6
Frequency	78	87	87	76	85	87

1) The chi-square value...**[Answer: 1.5041 in 4dp]**
2) The critical value..**[Answer: 11.07]**
3) The conclusion ....**[Answer: Don't reject H_0]**

10.1.2 Poisson Distribution

The Poisson distribution is having one parameter (λ) usually expressed as[$X \sim Po(\lambda)$]. The value of lamda (λ) is equal to the sample mean($\mu = \lambda$). The last score probability is derived by subtracting the sum of other probabilities (probabilities above the last score) from one.

Example 1: Determine the expected frequencies of the scores in the table below. Assume the value of $\lambda = 2.214$.

Scores	0	1	2	3	4	5	6
Frequency	6	13	26	14	7	4	0

Solution

Step 1: Formula. Expected Values$(E_i) = [P(X = i) \times \sum f_i]$

Step 2: Determination of scores probability $[P(X = i)]$

1) Formula. $P(X = i) = e^{-\lambda}\left(\frac{\lambda^i}{i!}\right)$, where; $\lambda = 2.214$ and $i = 0, 1, 2, 3, 4$ and 5
2) Data substitution and solving...........................[Remember $\mathbf{e} = \mathbf{2.718281828}$]

$$P(X = 0) = 2.718281828^{-2.214}\left(\frac{2.214^0}{0!}\right) = 0.109262722\left(\frac{1}{1}\right) = 0.109262722$$

$$P(X = 1) = 2.718281828^{-2.214}\left(\frac{2.214^1}{1!}\right) = 0.109262722\left(\frac{2.214}{1}\right) = 0.241907667$$

$$P(X = 2) = 2.718281828^{-2.214}\left(\frac{2.214^2}{2!}\right) = 0.109262722\left(\frac{4.901796}{2}\right) = 0.267791787$$

$$P(X = 3) = 2.718281828^{-2.214}\left(\frac{2.214^3}{3!}\right) = 0.109262722\left(\frac{10.85257634}{6}\right) = 0.197630339$$

$$P(X = 4) = 2.718281828^{-2.214}\left(\frac{2.214^4}{4!}\right) = 0.109262722\left(\frac{24.02760403}{24}\right) = 0.109388392$$

$$P(X = 5) = 2.718281828^{-2.214}\left(\frac{2.214^5}{5!}\right) = 0.109262722\left(\frac{53.19711531}{120}\right) = 0.04843718$$

$$P(X \geq 6) = 1 - P(X > 6) = 1 - 0.974418087 = 0.025581913$$

Step 3: Data substitution and solving

Scores	0	1	2	3	4	5	6	Total
Frequency	6	13	26	14	7	4	0	70
$P(X = i)$	0.109262722	0.241907667	0.267791787	0.197630339	0.109388392	0.04843718	0.025581913	1
$E_i = [P(X = i) \times \sum f_i]$	7.648	16.934	18.745	13.834	7.657	3.391	1.791	70

N/B: The expected frequency of score 5 (3.391) and score 6 (1.791) are lesser than 5. We combine two expected frequencies$(3.391 + 1.791 = 5.182)$. The value obtain (5.182) is greater than 5 solving the problem. The working table is given below.

Scores	0	1	2	3	4	5+	Total
Frequency	6	13	26	14	7	4	70
$P(X = i)$	0.109262722	0.241907667	0.267791787	0.197630339	0.109388392	0.074019093	1
$E_i = [P(X = i) \times \sum f_i]$	7.648	16.934	18.745	13.834	7.657	5.182	70

N/B: The value of K = **6**

Example 2: Calculate the expected frequency of the following number of malfunctions classes. Assume the value of $\lambda = 1.25$

Number of malfunctions (X_i)	0	1	2	3	4	5
Number of days (f_i)	77	90	55	30	5	3

Solution

Step 1: Formula. Expected Values$(E_i) = [P(X = i) \times \sum f_i]$

Step 2: Determination of number of malfunctions probability

1) Formula. $P(X = i) = e^{-\lambda}\left(\frac{\lambda^i}{i!}\right)$, where; $\lambda = 1.25$ and $i = 0, 1, 2, 3, 4$ and 5
2) Data substitution and solving......................[Remember $\mathbf{e = 2.718281828}$]

$P(X = 0) = 2.718281828^{-1.25}\left(\frac{1.25^0}{0!}\right) = 0.286504796\left(\frac{1}{1}\right) = 0.286504796$

$P(X = 1) = 2.718281828^{-1.25}\left(\frac{1.25^1}{1!}\right) = 0.286504796\left(\frac{1.25}{1}\right) = 0.358130995$

$P(X = 2) = 2.718281828^{-1.25}\left(\frac{1.25^2}{2!}\right) = 0.286504796\left(\frac{1.5625}{2}\right) = 0.223831871$

$P(X = 3) = 2.718281828^{-1.25}\left(\frac{1.25^3}{3!}\right) = 0.286504796\left(\frac{1.953125}{6}\right) = 0.09326379$

$P(X = 4) = 2.718281828^{-1.25}\left(\frac{1.25^4}{4!}\right) = 0.286504796\left(\frac{2.44140625}{24}\right) = 0.029144774$

$P(X \geq 5) = 1 - P(X >) = 1 - (0.990876226) = 0.009123774$

Step 3: Data substitution and solving..................................[In three decimal places]

Number of malfunctions (X_i)	0	1	2	3	4	5	Total
Number of days (f_i)	77	90	55	30	5	3	260
$P(X = i)$	0.286504796	0.358130995	0.223831871	0.09326379	0.029144774	0.009123774	1
$E_i = [P(X = i) \times \sum f_i]$	74.491	93.114	58.196	24.249	7.578	2.372	260

N/B: The expected frequency of class 5 (2.372) is lesser than 5. Combining class 5 and class 4 solve the problem$[7.578 + 2.372 = 9.95]$. The working table is given below.

Number of malfunctions (X_i)	0	1	2	3	4+	Total
Number of days (f_i)	77	90	55	30	8	260
$P(X = i)$	0.286504796	0.358130995	0.223831871	0.09326379	0.038268548	1
$E_i = [P(X = i) \times \sum f_i]$	74.491	93.114	58.196	24.249	9.95	260

N/B: The value of K here is **5**

Example 3: A manufacturer produces high quality aluminum sheets for use in high stressed aircraft wings. A random sample of 100 sheets is inspected and the number of faults per sheet recorded is given below.

Number of faults per sheet	0	1	2	3	4
Frequency of occurrence	50	24	14	8	4

Solution

Step 1: Formula. $\text{Expected Values}(E_i) = [P(X = i) \times (\sum f_i)]$

Step 2: Determination of mean or average of an event per unit (λ)

1) Formula. $\text{Average} = \frac{\sum(X_i \times f_i)}{\text{Sum of Frequencies } (\sum f_i)}$
2) Data substitution and solving

$\text{Mean of an Event per Unit}(\lambda) = \frac{(50\times0)+(24\times1)+(14\times2)+(8\times3)+(4\times4)}{100}$.....[Simplify numerator]

$\text{Mean of an Event per Unit}(\lambda) = \frac{92}{100}$ ....[Solve equation]

$\text{Mean of an Event per Unit}(\lambda) = \mathbf{0.92}$

Step 3: Determination of number of fault per sheet probability............**[N/B: $\boldsymbol{\lambda = 0.92}$]**

1) Formula. $P(X = i) = e^{-\lambda}\left(\frac{\lambda^i}{i!}\right)$, where; $\lambda = 0.92$ and $i = 0, 1, 2, 3$ and 4
2) Data substitution and solving.......................[Remember $\mathbf{e = 2.718281828}$]

$$P(X = 0) = 2.718281828^{-0.92}\left(\frac{0.92^0}{0!}\right) = 0.398519041\left(\frac{1}{1}\right) = 0.398519041$$

$$P(X = 1) = 2.718281828^{-0.92}\left(\frac{0.92^1}{1!}\right) = 0.398519041\left(\frac{0.92}{1}\right) = 0.366637517$$

$$P(X = 2) = 2.718281828^{-0.92}\left(\frac{0.92^2}{2!}\right) = 0.398519041\left(\frac{0.8464}{2}\right) = 0.168653258$$

$$P(X = 3) = 2.718281828^{-0.92}\left(\frac{0.92^3}{3!}\right) = 0.398519041\left(\frac{0.778688}{6}\right) = 0.051720332$$

$$P(X \geq 4) = 1 - P(X > 4) = 1 - 0.985530148 = 0.014469852$$

Step 4: Data substitution and solving.......................................[In three decimal places]

Number of faults per sheet	0	1	2	3+	Total
Frequency of occurrence	50	24	14	12	100
$P(X = i)$	0.398519041	0.366637517	0.168653258	0.066190184	1
$E_i = [P(X = i) \times \sum f_i]$	39.852	36.664	16.865	6.619	100

Example 4: The number of telephone calls made to a counseling service is thought to be modeled by the Poisson distribution. Using a 5% significance level, answer the following questions.

Number of calls per hour	0	1	2	3	4	5	6
Frequency	6	13	26	14	7	4	0
Expected value	7.65	16.93	18.74	13.84	7.66	3.39	1.79

1) State the hypotheses
2) Compute the chi-square value
3) Determine the critical value and make conclusion

Solution

1) State the hypotheses

Null Hypothesis(H_0): The number of calls follows a Poisson distribution.

Alternative Hypothesis(H_1): The number of calls does not follow a Poisson distribution.

2) Compute the chi-square value

Step 1: Formula. Chi Square $(\mathcal{X}^2) = \sum\left[\frac{(O_i - E_i)^2}{E_i}\right] \sim \mathcal{X}^{2(\alpha)}{}_{(k-2)}$, where; $\alpha = 0.05$

Step 2: Data substitution and solving

Number of calls per hour	0	1	2	3	4	5+	Total
Frequency	6	13	26	14	7	4	70
Expected value	7.65	16.93	18.74	13.84	7.66	5.18	70

$$\mathcal{X}^2 = \frac{(6-7.65)^2}{7.65} + \frac{(13-16.93)^2}{16.93} + \frac{(26-18.74)^2}{18.74} + \frac{(14-13.84)^2}{13.84} + \frac{(7-7.66)^2}{7.66} + \frac{(4-5.18)^2}{5.18}$$

$$\mathcal{X}^2 = \frac{2.7225}{7.65} + \frac{15.4449}{16.93} + \frac{52.7076}{18.74} + \frac{0.0256}{13.84} + \frac{0.4356}{7.66} + \frac{1.3924}{5.18} + \frac{3.2041}{1.79}$$

$$\mathcal{X}^2 = 0.355882352 + 0.912279976 + 2.812572038 + 0.00184971 + 0.05686684 + 0.268803088$$

Chi Square $(\mathcal{X}^2) = \mathbf{4.4083}$ ....[In four decimal places]

3) Determine the critical value and make conclusion

$$\left[\mathcal{X}^{2(\alpha)}{}_{(k-2)} = \mathcal{X}^{2(0.05)}{}_{(6-2)} = \mathcal{X}^{2(\alpha)}{}_{(4)}\right]$$

α =	0.995	0.99	0.975	0.95	0.90	0.10	0.05	0.025	0.01	0.005
v = 1	---	---	---	---	0.02	2.71	3.84	5.02	6.63	7.88
2	0.01	0.02	0.05	0.10	0.21	4.61	5.99	7.38	9.21	10.60
3	0.07	0.11	0.22	0.35	0.58	6.25	7.81	9.35	11.34	12.84
4	0.21	0.30	0.48	0.71	1.06	7.78	9.49	11.14	13.28	14.86
5	0.41	0.55	0.83	1.15	1.61	9.24	11.07	12.83	15.09	16.75

N/B: The critical value is 9.49 and it is greater than the statistic value [4.4083 < 9.49].

Conclusion: Since [4.4083 < 9.49], we don't reject the null hypothesis.

Test Your Understanding

Exercise 3: Determine the value of lamda (λ) using the data in the table below.

Scores	0	1	2	3	4	5	6
Frequency	31	34	20	9	4	2	0

[Answer: $\lambda = 127/100 = 1.27$]

Exercise 4: Compute the following using data in the table below

Score	0	1	2	3	4	5
Frequency	273	361	263	78	21	4

1) The value of lamda (λ)..............................**[Answer: $\lambda = 1,225/1,000 = 1.225$]**
2) Expected frequency of scores.......................................**[Answer: See Appendix]**
3) The degree of freedom (df).....................................**[Answer: df $= 6 - 2 = 4$]**

Exercise 5: The number of emails arriving at a service per minute is claimed to follow a Poisson distribution. To test this claim, the number of emails arriving in 70 randomly chosen 1-minute interval is recorded. The table below summarizes the result.

Number of emails	0	1	2	3	≥ 4
Frequency	13	22	23	12	0

Assume $\alpha = 5\%$, calculate the following

1) The value of lamda (λ)........................**[Answer: 1.486 in three decimal places]**
2) The expected frequency ....**[Answer: See Appendix]**
3) The chi-square value...**[Answer: 2.445]**
4) The critical value...**[Answer: 5.99]**

Exercise 6: The chi-square statistic for a Poisson distribution is 0.823. Assume $\alpha = 5\%$, and df = 3 calculate the critical value and make conclusion.....**[Answer: 7.81. Don't reject H_o]**

10.1.3 Binomial Distribution

Binomial distribution is having two parameters (n and p) usually expressed as[$X \sim Bin(np)$ or $X \sim B(np)$]. The population mean is the product of the parameters [$\mu = np$]

and the probability of event success of occurrence is the quotient of the population mean and number of classes[$p = \mu/n$].

Example 1: Compute the following using the data in the table below

Scores (X)	0	1	2	3	4	5
Frequency (f)	34	24	19	14	9	0

1) The probability of event success (p)
2) The expected frequency of the scores.

Solution

1) The probability of event success (p)

Step 1: Formula. $\text{Probability of Event Success (p)} = \frac{\text{Sample Mean }(\mu)}{\text{Number of Elements(n)}}$, where; $n = 5$

Step 2: Determination of sample mean (μ)

1) Formula. $\text{Sample Mean}(\mu) = \frac{\sum(X_i \times f_i)}{\text{Sum of Frequency }(\sum f_i)}$, where; $(\sum f_i) = 100$

2) Data substitution and solving

$$\text{Sample Mean}(\mu) = \frac{(0\times34)+(1\times24)+(2\times19)+(3\times14)+(4\times9)\times(5\times0)}{100}$$.[Simplify numerator]

$$\text{Sample Mean}(\mu) = \frac{0+24+38+42+36+0}{100}$$ ....[Solve equation]

$$\text{Sample Mean}(\mu) = 1.4$$

Step 3: Data substitution and solving

$$\text{Probability of Event Success (p)} = \frac{1.4}{5}$$ ....[Solve equation]

$$\text{Probability of Event Success (p)} = \mathbf{0.28}$$ ....[$q = 1 - p = 1 - 0.28 = 0.72$]

2) The expected frequency of the scores.

Step 1: Formula. $\text{Expected Values}(E_i) = [P(X = i) \times (\sum f_i)]$

Step 2: Determination of scores probabilities

1) Formula. $P(X = i) = \frac{n!}{i!\,(n-i)!}(p^i \times q^{n-i})$

Where; $p = 0.28$, $q = 0.72$ and $i = 0, 1, 2, 3, 4$ and 5

2) Data substitution and solving..............................[Remember $\mathbf{e} = \mathbf{2.718281828}$]

$$P(X = 0) = \frac{5!}{0!\,(5-0)!}(0.28^0 \times 0.72^{5-0}) = \frac{120}{120}(0.193491763) = 0.193491763$$

$$P(X = 1) = \frac{5!}{1!\,(5-1)!}(0.28^1 \times 0.72^{5-1}) = \frac{120}{24}(0.075246796) = 0.376233984$$

$$P(X = 2) = \frac{5!}{2!\,(5-2)!}(0.28^2 \times 0.72^{5-2}) = \frac{120}{12}(0.029262643) = 0.292626432$$

$$P(X = 3) = \frac{5!}{3!\,(5-3)!}(0.28^3 \times 0.72^{5-3}) = \frac{120}{12}(0.011379916) = 0.113799168$$

$$P(X = 4) = \frac{5!}{4!\,(5-4)!}(0.28^4 \times 0.72^{5-4}) = \frac{120}{24}(0.004425523) = 0.022127616$$

$$P(X = 5) = \frac{5!}{5!\,(5-5)!}(0.28^5 \times 0.72^{5-5}) = \frac{120}{120}(0.001721036) = 0.001721036$$

Step 3: Data substitution and solving

Original Table

Scores (X)	0	1	2	3	4	5	Total
Frequency (f)	34	24	19	14	9	0	100
$P(X = i)$	0.193491763	0.376233984	0.292626432	0.113799168	0.022127616	0.001721036	1
$E_i = [P(X = i) \times (\sum f_i)]$	19.349	37.623	29.263	11.380	2.213	0.172	100

Working Table

Scores (X)	0	1	2	3,4,5	Total
Frequency (f)	34	24	19	23	100
$P(X = i)$	0.193491763	0.376233984	0.292626432	0.13764782	1
$E_i = [P(X = i) \times (\sum f_i)]$	19.349	37.623	29.263	13.765	100

Example 2: An egg packaging firm has introduced a new box for its eggs. Each box holds six eggs and unfortunately, it finds that the new box tends to mark the eggs. Data on the number of eggs marked in 100 boxes are collected and presented below. Assume $\alpha = 10\%$.

Number of marked eggs	0	1	2	3	4	5	6
Number of boxes	3	3	27	29	10	7	21

1) Compute the chi-square value
2) Determine the critical value

<u>Solution</u>

1) **Compute the chi-square value**$[X \sim Bin(6, 0.575), \text{that is}, p = 0.575, q = 0.425, n = 6]$

N/B: It is assumed that the derivation of expected frequency values and working table is understood by the student. The result if done properly is represented below.

Original Table

Number of marked eggs	0	1	2	3	4	5	6	Total
Number of boxes	3	3	27	29	10	7	21	100
$P(X = i)$	0.005892961	0.047836979	0.161801546	0.291877299	0.296169613	0.160280025	0.036141574	1
$E_i = [P(X = i) \times (\sum f_i)]$	0.589	4.784	16.180	29.188	29.617	16.028	3.614	100

Working Table						
Number of marked eggs	0,1	2	3	4	5,6	Total
Number of boxes	6	27	29	10	28	100
$P(X = i)$	0.05372994	0.161801546	0.291877299	0.296169613	0.196421599	1
$E_i = [P(X = i) \times (\sum f_i)]$	5.373	16.180	29.188	29.617	19.642	100

Step 1: Formula. Chi Square $(\mathcal{X}^2) = \sum\left[\frac{(O_i - E_i)^2}{E_i}\right] \sim \mathcal{X}^{2(\alpha)}{}_{(k-2)}$, where; $\alpha = 0.1$

Step 2: Data substitution and solving

$$\mathcal{X}^2 = \frac{(6-5.373)^2}{5.373} + \frac{(27-16.180)^2}{16.180} + \frac{(29-29.188)^2}{29.188} + \frac{(10-29.617)^2}{29.617} + \frac{(28-19.642)^2}{19.642} \text{.........[Simplify]}$$

$$\mathcal{X}^2 = \frac{0.393129}{5.373} + \frac{117.0724}{16.180} + \frac{0.035344}{29.188} + \frac{384.826689}{29.617} + \frac{69.856164}{19.642} \text{.................[Solve equation]}$$

Chi Square $(\mathcal{X}^2) = \mathbf{23.860}$ ....[In three decimal places]

2) **Determine the critical value**.................. $\left[\mathcal{X}^{2(\alpha)}{}_{(k-2)} = \mathcal{X}^{2(0.1)}{}_{(6-2)} = \mathcal{X}^{2(0.1)}{}_{(4)}\right]$

α =	0.995	0.99	0.975	0.95	0.90	0.10	0.05	0.025	0.01	0.005
v = 1	---	---	---	---	0.02	2.71	3.84	5.02	6.63	7.88
2	0.01	0.02	0.05	0.10	0.21	4.61	5.99	7.38	9.21	10.60
3	0.07	0.11	0.22	0.35	0.58	6.25	7.81	9.35	11.34	12.84
4	0.21	0.30	0.48	0.71	1.06	7.78	9.49	11.14	13.28	14.86
5	0.41	0.55	0.83	1.15	1.61	9.24	11.07	12.83	15.09	16.75

N/B: The critical value is 7.78 and is lesser than the chi-square calculated value (23.860)

Example 3: A medical researcher wants to decide whether a common medical condition runs in families (genetics). He selected 200 sets of 6 closely related people at random and determines how many people in each have the condition. The results are given as follows. Perform a chi-square test of goodness of fit.

No in set with the condition	0	1	2	3	4	5	6
Frequency	15	40	68	47	24	5	1

Solution

Step 1: Hypothesis Formulation

Null Hypothesis (H_0): The common medical condition runs in families

Alternative Hypothesis (H_1): The common medical condition does not run in families

Step 2: Statistics

N/B: The pre-calculation gives the following results; $p = \frac{(444/200)}{6} = 0.37$ and $q = 1 - 0.37 = 0.63$. The working table is presented below

Original Table								
N̲o in set with the condition	0	1	2	3	4	5	6	Total
Frequency	15	40	68	47	24	5	1	200
$P(X = i)$	0.062523502	0.220320912	0.323487054	0.253312613	0.111578175	0.026212015	0.00256726	1
$E_i = [P(X = i) \times (\sum f_i)]$	12.505	44.064	64.697	50.663	22.316	5.242	0.513	200

Working Table							
N̲o in set with the condition	0	1	2	3	4	5,6	Total
Frequency	15	40	68	47	24	6	200
$P(X = i)$	0.062523502	0.220320912	0.323487054	0.253312613	0.111578175	0.028779275	1
$E_i = [P(X = i) \times (\sum f_i)]$	12.505	44.064	64.697	50.663	22.316	5.755	200

1) Formula. Chi Square $(\mathcal{X}^2) = \sum\left[\frac{(O_i - E_i)^2}{E_i}\right] \sim \mathcal{X}^{2(\alpha)}{}_{(k-2)}$, where; $\alpha = 0.05$

2) Data substitution and solving

$$\mathcal{X}^2 = \frac{(15-12.505)^2}{12.505} + \frac{(40-44.064)^2}{44.064} + \frac{(68-64.697)^2}{64.697} + \frac{(47-50.663)^2}{50.663} + \frac{(24-22.316)^2}{22.316} + \frac{(6-5.755)^2}{5.755}$$

$$\mathcal{X}^2 = \frac{6.225025}{12.505} + \frac{16.516096}{44.064} + \frac{10.909809}{64.697} + \frac{13.417569}{50.663} + \frac{2.835856}{22.316} + \frac{0.060025}{5.755}$$

Chi Square $(\mathcal{X}^2) = \mathbf{1.444}$ ……………………………………[In three decimal places]

Step 3: Decision rule and conclusion……………… $\left[\mathcal{X}^{2(\alpha)}{}_{(k-2)} = \mathcal{X}^{2(0.05)}{}_{(6-2)} = \mathcal{X}^{2(0.05)}{}_{(4)}\right]$

α =	0.995	0.99	0.975	0.95	0.90	0.10	0.05	0.025	0.01	0.005
v = 1	---	---	---	---	0.02	2.71	3.84	5.02	6.63	7.88
2	0.01	0.02	0.05	0.10	0.21	4.61	5.99	7.38	9.21	10.60
3	0.07	0.11	0.22	0.35	0.58	6.25	7.81	9.35	11.34	12.84
4	0.21	0.30	0.48	0.71	1.06	7.78	9.49	11.14	13.28	14.86
5	0.41	0.55	0.83	1.15	1.61	9.24	11.07	12.83	15.09	16.75

N/B: The statistical value (1.444) is lesser than the critical value (9.49). Hence, we don't reject the null hypothesis [H_0].

Test Your Understanding

Exercise 7: Determine the expected frequency value of the following scores

Number of failing standard	0	1	2	3	4
Number of weeks	35	31	10	4	0

1) Compute the probability of success (p)……………………………….[**Answer: 0.197**]
2) Determine the expected frequency values…………………….**[Answer: See Appendix]**

Exercise 8: The chi-square statistic for a binomial distribution is 12.274. Assume the significance level is 5% and the degree of freedom is 10, determine the critical value...**[Answer: 18.31]**

Exercise 9: Compute the chi-square statistics and the critical value using the data in the table below. Assume $\alpha = 10\%$.

Scores	0	1	2	3
Observed values	144	91	32	13
Expected values	139.048	97.328	34.076	9.548

[Answer: Chi Square = 1.96 and Critical Value = 2.71]

10.1.4 Normal Distribution

A normal distribution is having two parameters, the mean (μ) and variance (σ^2) and is expressed as [$X \sim N(\mu, \sigma^2)$]. Note that the concept of normal distribution will be greatly applicable in this section. To perform a chi-square goodness of fit test, we are required to calculate the mean and standard deviation, class probability which with the sum of frequency is used to obtain the expected frequency values of classes. The following formulas are remembering.

$$\text{Mean}(\mu) = \frac{\Sigma(f_i X_i)}{\Sigma f_i} \quad \text{...(1)}$$

$$\text{Standard Deviation}(\sigma) = \sqrt{\frac{\Sigma f_i x_i^2}{\Sigma f_i} - \left(\frac{\Sigma f_i x_i}{\Sigma f_i}\right)^2} \quad \text{..(2)}$$

$$\text{Standardized Normal Variable}(Z) = \frac{x - \mu}{\sigma} \quad \text{...(3)}$$

Example 1: Determine the normal distribution parameters using the data in the table below

Classes	Frequency
$26 \leq X < 28$	7
$28 \leq X < 30$	22
$30 \leq X < 32$	36
$32 \leq X < 34$	45
$34 \leq X < 36$	33
$36 \leq X < 38$	28
$38 \leq X < 40$	4

Solution

1) Determination of mean (μ)

Step 1: Formula. $\text{Mean}(\mu) = \frac{\sum(f_i X_i)}{\sum f_i}$

Step 2: Determination of unknown components

Classes	Frequency	Mid-Point $\left[X = \frac{UCL+LCL}{2}\right]$	$[f_i X_i]$
$26 \le X < 28$	7	$X_1 = \frac{26+28}{2} = \frac{54}{2} = 27$	$7 \times 27 = 189$
$28 \le X < 30$	27	$X_2 = \frac{28+30}{2} = \frac{58}{2} = 29$	$27 \times 29 = 783$
$30 \le X < 32$	36	$X_3 = \frac{30+32}{2} = \frac{62}{2} = 31$	$36 \times 31 = 1{,}116$
$32 \le X < 34$	45	$X_4 = \frac{32+34}{2} = \frac{66}{2} = 33$	$45 \times 33 = 1{,}485$
$34 \le X < 36$	33	$X_5 = \frac{34+36}{2} = \frac{70}{2} = 35$	$33 \times 35 = 1{,}155$
$36 \le X < 38$	28	$X_6 = \frac{36+38}{2} = \frac{74}{2} = 37$	$28 \times 37 = 1{,}036$
$38 \le X < 40$	4	$X_7 = \frac{38+40}{2} = \frac{78}{2} = 39$	$4 \times 39 = 156$
	$\sum f_i = 180$		$\sum(f_i \times X_i) = 5{,}920$

Step 3: Data substitution and solving

$\text{Mean}(\mu) = \frac{5{,}920}{180}$ ....[Solve equation]

$\text{Mean}(\mu) = \mathbf{32.889}$ ....[In three decimal places]

2) Determination of standard deviation (σ)

Step 1: Formula. $\text{Standard Deviation}(\sigma) = \sqrt{\frac{\sum f_i {x_i}^2}{\sum f_i} - \left(\frac{\sum f_i x_i}{\sum f_i}\right)^2}$

Step 2: Determination of unknown components

Classes	Frequency	Mid-Point (x)	$[f_i x_i]$	$(f_i x_i)^2$
$26 \le X < 28$	7	$x_1 = 27$	189	$189^2 = 35{,}721$
$28 \le X < 30$	27	$x_2 = 29$	783	$783^2 = 613{,}089$
$30 \le X < 32$	36	$x_3 = 31$	1,116	$1{,}116^2 = 1{,}245{,}456$
$32 \le X < 34$	45	$x_4 = 33$	1,485	$1{,}485^2 = 2{,}205{,}225$
$34 \le X < 36$	33	$x_5 = 35$	1,155	$1{,}155^2 = 1{,}334{,}025$
$36 \le X < 38$	28	$x_6 = 37$	1,036	$1{,}036^2 = 1{,}073{,}296$
$38 \le X < 40$	4	$x_7 = 39$	156	$156^2 = 24{,}336$
	$\sum = 180$		$\sum = 5{,}920$	$\sum f_i {x_i}^2 = 6{,}531{,}148$

Step 3: Data substitution and solving

$$\text{Standard Deviation}(\sigma) = \sqrt{\frac{6,531,148}{180} - \left(\frac{5,920}{180}\right)^2} \text{ ......[Simplify fraction and work power]}$$

$$\text{Standard Deviation}(\sigma) = \sqrt{36,284.15556 - 1,081.679012} \text{ ...[Simplify and work root]}$$

$$\text{Standard Deviation}(\sigma) = \mathbf{187.623} \text{ ....[In three decimal places]}$$

Example 2: Given that mean is 5.08 and variance is 3.29, determine the classes probability and classes expected frequency.

Classes	Frequency
$X < 2$	1
$2 < X \leq 3$	4
$3 < X \leq 4$	12
$4 < X \leq 5$	18
$5 < X \leq 6$	11
$6 < X \leq 7$	5
$7 < X \leq 8$	4
$8 < X \leq 9$	2
$9 < X \leq 10$	2
$10 < X$	1

Solution

1) Determination of classes probabilities

Classes	Class Probability	
	$P(a < X \leq b) = \Phi\left[\frac{b-\mu}{\sigma}\right] - \Phi\left[\frac{a-\mu}{\sigma}\right]$ ....(1) $P(X > a) = 1 - \Phi\left[\frac{a-\mu}{\sigma}\right]$ ....(2)	$[\Phi(b) - \Phi(-a) = \Phi(b) + \Phi(a) - 1]$ ....(1) $[\Phi(-b) - \Phi(-a) = \Phi(a) - \Phi(b)]$ ....(2)
$X < 2$	$P(X < 2) = \Phi\left[\frac{2-5.08}{1.81}\right] = \Phi[-1.702]$	$1 - \Phi[1.702] = 1 - 0.9556 = \mathbf{0.0444}$
$2 < X \leq 3$	$P(2 < X \leq 3) = \Phi\left[\frac{3-5.08}{1.81}\right] - \Phi\left[\frac{2-5.08}{1.81}\right] = \Phi[-1.149] - \Phi[-1.702]$	$\Phi[1.702] - \Phi[1.149] = 0.9556 - 0.8747 = \mathbf{0.0809}$
$3 < X \leq 4$	$P(3 < X \leq 4) = \Phi\left[\frac{4-5.08}{1.81}\right] - \Phi\left[\frac{3-5.08}{1.81}\right] = \Phi[-0.597] - \Phi[-1.149]$	$\Phi[1.149] - \Phi[0.597] = 0.8747 - 0.7248 = \mathbf{0.1499}$
$4 < X \leq 5$	$P(4 < X \leq 5) = \Phi\left[\frac{5-5.08}{1.81}\right] - \Phi\left[\frac{4-5.08}{1.81}\right] = \Phi[-0.044] - \Phi[-0.597]$	$\Phi[0.597] - \Phi[0.044] = 0.7248 - 0.5176 = \mathbf{0.2072}$
$5 < X \leq 6$	$P(5 < X \leq 6) = \Phi\left[\frac{6-5.08}{1.81}\right] - \Phi\left[\frac{5-5.08}{1.81}\right] = \Phi[0.508] - \Phi[-0.044]$	$\Phi[0.508] + \Phi[0.044] - 1 = 0.6942 + 0.5176 - 1 = \mathbf{0.2118}$
$6 < X \leq 7$	$P(6 < X \leq 7) = \Phi\left[\frac{7-5.08}{1.81}\right] - \Phi\left[\frac{6-5.08}{1.81}\right] = \Phi[1.061] - \Phi[0.508]$	$\Phi[1.061] - \Phi[0.508] = 0.8556 - 0.6942 = \mathbf{0.1614}$
$7 < X \leq 8$	$P(7 < X \leq 8) = \Phi\left[\frac{8-5.08}{1.81}\right] - \Phi\left[\frac{7-5.08}{1.81}\right] = \Phi[1.613] - \Phi[1.061]$	$\Phi[1.613] - \Phi[1.061] = 0.9466 - 0.8556 = \mathbf{0.091}$
$8 < X \leq 9$	$P(8 < X \leq 9) = \Phi\left[\frac{9-5.08}{1.81}\right] - \Phi\left[\frac{8-5.08}{1.81}\right] = \Phi[2.166] - \Phi[1.613]$	$\Phi[2.166] - \Phi[1.613] = 0.9848 - 0.9466 = \mathbf{0.0382}$
$9 < X \leq 10$	$P(9 < X \leq 10) = \Phi\left[\frac{10-5.08}{1.81}\right] - \Phi\left[\frac{9-5.08}{1.81}\right] = \Phi[2.718] - \Phi[2.166]$	$\Phi[2.718] - \Phi[2.166] = 0.9967 - 0.9848 = \mathbf{0.0119}$
$10 < X$	$P(X > 10) = 1 - \Phi\left[\frac{10-5.08}{1.81}\right] = 1 - \Phi[2.718]$	$1 - \Phi[2.718] = 1 - 0.9967 = \mathbf{0.0033}$

2) **Determination of expected frequencies**

Step 1: Formula. $\text{Expected Values}(E_i) = [P(X = i) \times (\sum f_i)]$, where; $\sum f_i = 60$

Step 2: Data substitution and solving

Class	Class Probabilities	Observed Frequency	Expected Frequency
$X < 2$	0.0444	1	$0.0444 \times 60 = 2.664$
$2 < X \leq 3$	0.0809	4	$0.0809 \times 60 = 4.854$
$3 < X \leq 4$	0.1499	12	$0.1499 \times 60 = 8.994$
$4 < X \leq 5$	0.2072	18	$0.2072 \times 60 = 12.432$
$5 < X \leq 6$	0.2118	11	$0.2118 \times 60 = 12.708$
$6 < X \leq 7$	0.1614	5	$0.1614 \times 60 = 9.684$
$7 < X \leq 8$	0.091	4	$0.091 \times 60 = 5.46$
$8 < X \leq 9$	0.0382	2	$0.0382 \times 60 = \mathbf{2.292}$
$9 < X \leq 10$	0.0119	2	$0.0119 \times 60 = \mathbf{0.714}$
$10 < X$	0.0033	1	$0.0033 \times 60 = \mathbf{0.198}$
	$\sum = 1$	$\sum = 60$	$\sum = 60$

N/B: We add up all expected frequencies lesser than 5. After doing this, we obtain a new table as seen below.

Class	Class Probabilities	Observed Frequency	Expected Frequency
$X \leq 3$	0.1253	5	$0.1253 \times 60 = 7.518$
$3 < X \leq 4$	0.1499	12	$0.1499 \times 60 = 8.994$
$4 < X \leq 5$	0.2072	18	$0.2072 \times 60 = 12.432$
$5 < X \leq 6$	0.2118	11	$0.2118 \times 60 = 12.708$
$6 < X \leq 7$	0.1614	5	$0.1614 \times 60 = 9.684$
$7 < X \leq 8$	0.091	4	$0.091 \times 60 = 5.46$
$8 < X$	0.0534	5	$0.0534 \times 60 = 3.204$
	$\sum = 1$	$\sum = 60$	$\sum = 60$

Example 3: Determine the expected frequency of the classes using information in the table below. Assume mean is 0.20 and standard deviation is 0.05

Classes	Frequency
$X = 0.143$	11
$0.143 \leq X < 0.166$	10
$0.166 \leq X < 0.184$	19
$0.184 \leq X < 0.200$	10
$0.200 \leq X < 0.216$	16
$0.216 \leq X < 0.234$	17
$0.234 \leq X < 0.258$	6
$0.258 \leq X$	11

Solution

Step 1: Formula. Expected Values$(E_i) = [P(X = i) \times (\sum f_i)]$, where; $\sum f_i = 100$

Step 2: Determination of class's probabilities $[P(X = i)]$

Classes	Classes probability	
$X = 0.143$	$\Phi\left[\frac{0.143-0.20}{0.05}\right] = \Phi[-1.14]$	$1 - \Phi[1.14] = 1 - 0.8729 = 0.1271$
$0.143 \leq X < 0.166$	$\Phi\left[\frac{0.166-0.20}{0.05}\right] - \Phi\left[\frac{0.143-0.20}{0.05}\right] = \Phi[-0.68] - \Phi[-1.14]$	$\Phi[1.14] - \Phi[-0.68] = 0.8729 - 0.7517 = 0.1212$
$0.166 \leq X < 0.184$	$\Phi\left[\frac{0.184-0.20}{0.05}\right] - \Phi\left[\frac{0.166-0.20}{0.05}\right] = \Phi[-0.32] - \Phi[-0.68]$	$\Phi[0.68] - \Phi[0.32] = 0.7517 - 0.6255 = 0.1262$
$0.184 \leq X < 0.200$	$\Phi\left[\frac{0.200-0.20}{0.05}\right] - \Phi\left[\frac{0.184-0.20}{0.05}\right] = \Phi[0] - \Phi[-0.32]$	$\Phi[0] + \Phi[0.32] - 1 = 0.5000 + 0.6255 - 1 = 0.1255$
$0.200 \leq X < 0.216$	$\Phi\left[\frac{0.216-0.20}{0.05}\right] - \Phi\left[\frac{0.200-0.20}{0.05}\right] = \Phi[0.32] - \Phi[0]$	$\Phi[0.32] - \Phi[0] = 0.6255 - 0.5000 = 0.1255$
$0.216 \leq X < 0.234$	$\Phi\left[\frac{0.234-0.20}{0.05}\right] - \Phi\left[\frac{0.216-0.20}{0.05}\right] = \Phi[0.68] - \Phi[0.32]$	$\Phi[0.68] - \Phi[0.32] = 0.7517 - 0.6255 = 0.1262$
$0.234 \leq X < 0.258$	$\Phi\left[\frac{0.258-0.20}{0.05}\right] - \Phi\left[\frac{0.234-0.20}{0.05}\right] = \Phi[1.16] - \Phi[0.68]$	$\Phi[1.16] - \Phi[0.68] = 0.8770 - 0.7517 = 0.1253$
$0.258 \leq X$	$1 - \Phi\left[\frac{0.258-0.20}{0.05}\right] = 1 - \Phi[1.16]$	$1 - \Phi[1.16] = 1 - 0.8770 = 0.123$

Step 2: Data substitution and solving

Classes	Observed	Probability	Expected Frequency
$X = 0.143$	11	0.1271	$0.1271 \times 100 = 12.71$
$0.143 \leq X < 0.166$	10	0.1212	$0.1212 \times 100 = 12.12$
$0.166 \leq X < 0.184$	19	0.1262	$0.1262 \times 100 = 12.62$
$0.184 \leq X < 0.200$	10	0.1255	$0.1255 \times 100 = 12.55$
$0.200 \leq X < 0.216$	16	0.1255	$0.1255 \times 100 = 12.55$
$0.216 \leq X < 0.234$	17	0.1262	$0.1262 \times 100 = 12.62$
$0.234 \leq X < 0.258$	6	0.1253	$0.1253 \times 100 = 12.53$
$0.258 \leq X$	11	0.123	$0.123 \times 100 = 12.3$
	$\sum = 100$	$\sum = 1$	$\sum = 100$

Example 4: Compute the chi-square value and the critical value. The significance level is given to be 5 percent.

Class	Frequency	Class Probability
$0 < X \leq 20$	11	0.267
$20 < X \leq 40$	21	0.196
$40 < X \leq 60$	19	0.143
$60 < X \leq 80$	9	0.106
$80 < X \leq 100$	4	0.077
$100 < X \leq 120$	3	0.056
$120 < X \leq 140$	5	0.041
$140 < X \leq 160$	4	0.053
$160 <$	4	0.061

Solution

1) **Determination of chi-square**

Step 1: Formula. Chi Square $(\mathcal{X}^2) = \sum\left[\frac{(O_i - E_i)^2}{E_i}\right] \sim \mathcal{X}^{2(\alpha)}{}_{(k-2)}$, where; $\alpha = 5\% = 0.05$

Step 2: Determination of expected Frequency

1) Formula. Expected Values$(E_i) = [P(X = i) \times (\sum f_i)]$, where; $\sum f_i = 80$
2) Data substitution and solving

Class	Frequency	Class Probability	Expected Frequency
$0 < X \leq 20$	11	0.267	$0.267 \times 80 = 21.36$
$20 < X \leq 40$	21	0.196	$0.196 \times 80 = 15.68$
$40 < X \leq 60$	19	0.143	$0.143 \times 80 = 11.44$
$60 < X \leq 80$	9	0.106	$0.106 \times 80 = 8.48$
$80 < X \leq 100$	4	0.077	$0.077 \times 80 = 6.16$
$100 < X \leq 120$	3	0.056	$0.056 \times 80 = 4.48$
$120 < X \leq 140$	5	0.041	$0.041 \times 80 = 3.28$
$140 < X \leq 160$	4	0.053	$0.053 \times 80 = 4.24$
$160 <$	4	0.061	$0.061 \times 80 = 4.88$

Step 3: Data substitution and solving

Class	Observed (O_i)	Expected (E_i)	$(O_i - E_i)^2$	$\frac{(O_i - E_i)^2}{E_i}$
$0 < X \le 20$	11	21.36	$(11 - 21.36)^2 = 107.3296$	$\frac{107.3296}{21.36} = 5.024794007$
$20 < X \le 40$	21	15.68	$(21 - 15.68)^2 = 28.3024$	$\frac{28.3024}{15.68} = 1.805$
$40 < X \le 60$	19	11.44	$(19 - 11.44)^2 = 57.1536$	$\frac{57.1536}{11.44} = 4.995944056$
$60 < X \le 80$	9	8.48	$(9 - 8.48)^2 = 0.2704$	$\frac{0.2704}{8.48} = 0.031886792$
$80 < X \le 100$	4	6.16	$(4 - 6.16)^2 = 4.6656$	$\frac{4.6656}{6.16} = 0.757402597$
$100 < X \le 120$	3	4.48	$(3 - 4.48)^2 = 2.1904$	$\frac{2.1904}{4.48} = 0.488928571$
$120 < X \le 140$	5	3.28	$(5 - 3.28)^2 = 2.9584$	$\frac{2.9584}{3.28} = 0.901951219$
$140 < X \le 160$	4	4.24	$(4 - 4.24)^2 = 0.0576$	$\frac{0.0576}{4.24} = 0.013584905$
$160 <$	4	4.88	$(4 - 4.88)^2 = 0.7744$	$\frac{0.7744}{4.88} = 0.158688524$
	$\Sigma = 80$	$\Sigma = 80$		$\Sigma = $ **14.17818067**

N/B: The calculated chi-square value is **14.1782** in four decimal places

2) **Determination of critical value**............ $\left[\chi^{2(\alpha)}{}_{(k-2)} = \chi^{2(0.05)}{}_{(9-3)} = \chi^{2(0.05)}{}_{(6)}\right]$

$\alpha =$	0.995	0.99	0.975	0.95	0.90	0.10	0.05	0.025	0.01	0.005
6	0.68	0.87	1.24	1.64	2.20	10.64	12.59	14.45	16.81	18.55
7	0.99	1.24	1.69	2.17	2.83	12.02	14.07	16.01	18.48	20.28
8	1.34	1.65	2.18	2.73	3.49	13.36	15.51	17.53	20.09	21.96
9	1.73	2.09	2.70	3.33	4.17	14.68	16.92	19.02	21.67	23.59
10	2.16	2.56	3.25	3.94	4.87	15.99	18.31	20.48	23.21	25.19

N/B: The critical value is **12.59**

Example 4: The calculated chi-square value is 8.27 and the number of classes is 7. Given that the significance level is 5%, determine the critical value and make conclusion.

Solution

Step 1: Determination of critical value............. $\left[\chi^{2(\alpha)}{}_{(k-2)} = \chi^{2(0.05)}{}_{(7-3)} = \chi^{2(0.05)}{}_{(4)}\right]$

$\alpha =$	0.995	0.99	0.975	0.95	0.90	0.10	0.05	0.025	0.01	0.005
v = 1	---	---	---	---	0.02	2.71	3.84	5.02	6.63	7.88
2	0.01	0.02	0.05	0.10	0.21	4.61	5.99	7.38	9.21	10.60
3	0.07	0.11	0.22	0.35	0.58	6.25	7.81	9.35	11.34	12.84
4	0.21	0.30	0.48	0.71	1.06	7.78	9.49	11.14	13.28	14.86
5	0.41	0.55	0.83	1.15	1.61	9.24	11.07	12.83	15.09	16.75

N/B: The critical value is 9.49

Step 2: Decision rule and conclusion

The calculated chi-square value (8.27) is lesser than the critical value (9.49). Hence, we don't reject the null hypothesis.

Test Your Understanding

Exercise 10: Using the normal distribution table below, with a mean (μ) 33 and standard deviation (σ) 2.91, determine the following

Classes	Frequency
$26 \le X < 28$	7
$28 \le X < 30$	22
$30 \le X < 32$	36
$32 \le X < 34$	45
$34 \le X < 36$	33
$36 \le X < 38$	28
$38 \le X < 40$	4

1) Class probabilities..**[See appendix]**
2) Expected frequency ....**[See appendix]**

Exercise 11: Compute the chi-square vale and critical value using the table below. Assume the significance level is 10% and the degree of freedom is 5.

Classes	Observed Frequency (O_i)	Expected Frequency (E_i)
$X = 0.143$	11	12.71
$0.143 \le X < 0.166$	10	12.12
$0.166 \le X < 0.184$	19	12.62
$0.184 \le X < 0.200$	10	12.55
$0.200 \le X < 0.216$	16	12.55
$0.216 \le X < 0.234$	17	12.62
$0.234 \le X < 0.258$	6	12.53
$0.258 \le X$	11	12.3

[Answer: Chi Square = 10.3535 and Critical Value = 9.24]

Exercise 12: Given that the computed chi-square value is 8.483, significance level is 5% and the degree of freedom is 3, find the critical value and interpret the result

[Answer: 7.815, Reject H_0]

10.2 Chi-Square Test of Independence

Apart of the chi-square test of independence, other methods of testing for independence between two categorical variables include the G-test and Fisher's Exact Test. Chi-square test and G-test are applied to any size of contingency table and are more accurate with large sample size while Fisher's Exact Test is only applied to a 2 by 2 contingency table.

10.2.1 Contingency Table

A contingency table is a tabular method of presenting the frequencies of the outcome from an experiment in which the observations in the sample are categorized according to two criteria. In a contingency table, each cell of the table gives the number of occurrences for a particular combination of categories. A table representing categorical variables without the row and column sum is called a data table. To derive a contingency table, we add a final column giving the row sums and a final row giving the column sum. The sum of the final column and the sum of the final row both must be equal to the number of samples.

Our focus here will be on a two by two $(2 * 2)$ contingency table. In a two by two contingency table, the categorical variables are having on two categories. Using two variables (X and Y), a sample of two by two contingency table is illustrated below.

Var. X \ Var. Y	Y_1	Y_2	Total
X_1	n_{11}	n_{12}	$n_{1\cdot} = n_{11} + n_{12}$
X_2	n_{21}	n_{22}	$n_{2\cdot} = n_{21} + n_{22}$
Total	$n_{\cdot 1} = n_{11} + n_{21}$	$n_{\cdot 2} = n_{12} + n_{22}$	$n_{\cdot\cdot} = n_{1\cdot} + n_2$ OR $n_{\cdot\cdot} = n_{\cdot 1} + n_{\cdot 2}$

Example 1: The mathematic test result of a class of 80 students is given as follows; 15 males and 12 females passed the exam and 13 males and 40 females failed the exam. Construct a data table placing gender (male and female) on the row and performance (passed and failed) on the column.

Solution

Gender \ Performance	Passed	Failed
Male	15	13
Female	12	40

Example 2: Construct a contingency table using the data table below

	Right Handed	Left Handed
Male	43	20
Female	12	17

Solution

Hint: To transform the data table to a contingency table, we calculate the sum of each categories and the grand table.

	Right Handed	Left Handed	Total
Male	43	20	$43 + 20 = \mathbf{63}$
Female	12	17	$12 + 17 = \mathbf{29}$
Total	$43 + 12 = \mathbf{55}$	$20 + 17 = \mathbf{37}$	$55 + 37 = \mathbf{92}$ OR $63 + 29 = \mathbf{92}$

Test Your Understanding

Exercise 13: In a sample of 167, 73 from the 85 of the smokers had been divorced and of the non-smokers, only 43 of 82 had been divorced. Construct a data table.

[**Answer: See Appendix**]

Exercise 14: Construct a contingency table using the data table below

	Spoiled	Unspoiled
Unfumigated	8	16
Fumigated	2	14

[Answer: ....See Appendix]

10.2.2 Chi-Square test of Independence

From a given contingency table, to perform a chi-square test of independence, the following states should be respected.

1) **Hypothesis:** Assume we are testing for the independence between two categorical variables (A and B) ,the two major hypothesis of chi-square test of independence is given below.

a) Null Hypothesis (H_0): Categorical variable (A) and categorical variable (B) are independent. That is, there is no relationship between the categorical variables. This indicates that the value of one variable does not help in predicting the value of the other variable.

b) Alternative Hypothesis (H_1): Categorical variable (A) and categorical variable (B) are not independent. That is, there is relationship between the categorical variables. This indicates that the value of one variable do help in predicting the value of the other variable.

2) **Statistics**: To compute the chi-square value($\mathcal{X}^2$), we are required to have a significance level(α). The general formula is given as seen below.

$$\text{Chi Square } (\mathcal{X}^2) = \sum\left[\frac{(O_{ij}-E_{ij})^2}{E_{ij}}\right] \sim \mathcal{X}^{2(\alpha)}{}_{(r-1)(c-1)} \quad \text{.........................(1)}$$

Where: O_{ij} represent the observed values (Values in the data table)

E_{ij} represent the expected values (Calculated)

$(r-1)(c-1)$ represent the degree of freedom (df)

(α) represent the significance level (Given)

(r) represent number of rows and (c) number of columns

N/B: The expected value on row (i) and column (j) given as (E_{ij}) is the quotient between the product of the sum of rows and sum of columns and the total sum.

$$\text{Expected Value}(E_{ij}) = \frac{\text{Sum of Row } i\ (n_{i*}) \times \text{Sum of Column } j\ (n_{*j})}{\text{Total Size } (n_{**})} \quad \text{..................(2)}$$

3) **Decision Rule**

a) Reject (H_0) if the calculated chi-square value is greater than the critical value

b) Don't reject (H_0) if the calculated chi-square value is less than the critical value

Example 1: A survey of 70 workers was conducted regarding their education (Collage and University) and level of job satisfaction (Low and High). The results are presented below.

	Low	High	Total
College	18	20	38
University	11	21	32
Total	29	41	70

Work Required

1) State the hypothesis
2) Compute the expected values

Solution

1) **State the hypothesis**
   a) Null hypothesis (H_0): The level of education and the level of satisfaction are independent.
   b) Alternative hypothesis (H_1): The level of education and the level of satisfaction are not independent.
2) **Compute the expected values**

Step 1: Formula. Expected Value$(E_{ij}) = \frac{\text{Sum of Row } i\ (n_{i*}) \times \text{Sum of Column } j\ (n_{*j})}{\text{Total Size } (n_{**})}$

Where; Total Size $(n_{**}) = 70$

Step 2: Data substitutionn and solving

	Low	High	Total
College	$\frac{38\times29}{70} = 16.15714286$	$\frac{38\times41}{70} = 22.25714286$	38
University	$\frac{32\times29}{70} = 13.25714286$	$\frac{32\times41}{70} = 18.74285714$	32
Total	29	41	70

Example 2: A 2 by 2 (2*2) contingence table is having a computed chi-square table of 6.20. using a 5% significance level, determine the critical value.

Solution

Step 1: Derivation of critical value [Significance Level = α = 5% = 0.05]

a) Formula. Chi Square $(\mathcal{X}^2) = \sum\left[\frac{(O_{ij}-E_{ij})^2}{E_{ij}}\right] \sim \mathcal{X}^{2(\alpha)}{}_{(r-1)(c-1)}$, where; α = 5% = 0.05,

$r = 2, c = 2,\ df = v = (2-1)(2-1) = 1$ and $\mathcal{X}^2 = \sum\left[\frac{(O_{ij}-E_{ij})^2}{E_{ij}}\right] = 6.20$

b) Tabular derivation of critical value

α =	0.995	0.99	0.975	0.95	0.90	0.10	0.05	0.025	0.01	0.005
v = 1	---	---	---	---	0.02	2.71	3.84	5.02	6.63	7.88
2	0.01	0.02	0.05	0.10	0.21	4.61	5.99	7.38	9.21	10.60
3	0.07	0.11	0.22	0.35	0.58	6.25	7.81	9.35	11.34	12.84
4	0.21	0.30	0.48	0.71	1.06	7.78	9.49	11.14	13.28	14.86
5	0.41	0.55	0.83	1.15	1.61	9.24	11.07	12.83	15.09	16.75

The Critical value is $\left[\mathcal{X}^{2(\alpha)}{}_{(r-1)(c-1)} = \mathcal{X}^{2(0.05)}{}_{(2-1)(2-1)} = \mathbf{3.84}\right]$

Step 2: Interpretation: The calculated chi-square value is greater than the critical value (6.20 > 3.84). This indicate that the two categorical variables are not independent.

Example 3: A survey of students was conducted regarding their gender (male and female) and their performance (success and failure). Compute a chi-square test of independence using the data table below.

	Success	Failure
Male	10	9
Female	19	12

Solution

Step 1: Hypothesis

a) Null hypothesis (H_0): Gender and performance are independent.

b) Alternative hypothesis (H_1): Gender and performance are not independent.

Step 2: Statistics

1) Formula. Chi Square $(\mathcal{X}^2) = \sum\left[\frac{(O_{ij}-E_{ij})^2}{E_{ij}}\right] \sim \mathcal{X}^{2(\alpha)}{}_{(r-1)(c-1)}$

Where; $\alpha = 5\% = 0.05$, $r = 2$ and $c = 2$

2) Derivation of contingency table and working table

$$\text{Expected Value}(E_{ij}) = \frac{\text{Sum of Row } i\ (n_{i*}) \times \text{Sum of Column } j\ (n_{*j})}{\text{Total Size } (n_{**})}$$

Contingency Table

	Success	Failure	Total
Male	10	9	19
Female	19	12	31
Total	29	21	50

Working Table

	Success	Failure	Total
Male	$\frac{29\times19}{50} = \mathbf{11.02}$	$\frac{21\times19}{50} = \mathbf{7.98}$	19
Female	$\frac{29\times31}{50} = \mathbf{17.98}$	$\frac{21\times31}{50} = \mathbf{13.02}$	31
Total	29	21	50

3) Data Substitution and solving

a) Method 1

$\mathcal{X}^2 = \frac{(10-11.02)^2}{11.02} + \frac{(9-7.98)^2}{7.98} + \frac{(19-17.98)^2}{17.98} + \frac{(12-13.02)^2}{13.02}$ ....[Work numerator exponents]

$\mathcal{X}^2 = \frac{1.0404}{11.02} + \frac{1.0404}{7.98} + \frac{1.0404}{17.98} + \frac{1.0404}{13.02}$ ....[Simply fractions]

$\mathcal{X}^2 = 0.094410162 + 0.130375939 + 0.057864293 + 0.079907834$.[Sum values]

Chi Square $(\mathcal{X}^2) = \mathbf{0.36}$ ....[In two decimal places]

b) Method 2...[Tabula method]

Number	Observed values (O_{ij})	Expected values (E_{ij})	$O_{ij} - E_{ij}$	$(O_{ij} - E_{ij})^2$	$\frac{(O_{ij} - E_{ij})^2}{E_{ij}}$
1	10	11.02	-1.02	1.0404	0.094410163
2	9	7.98	1.02	1.0404	0.130375939
3	19	17.98	1.02	1.0404	0.057864293
4	12	13.02	-1.02	1.0404	0.079907834
					$\sum = \mathbf{0.36}$ **in 2dp**

4) Determination of critical value and interpretation.... $\left[\chi^{2(0.05)}{}_{(2-1)(2-1)} = \chi^{2(0.05)}{}_{(1)}\right]$

$\alpha =$	0.995	0.99	0.975	0.95	0.90	0.10	0.05	0.025	0.01	0.005
v = 1	---	---	---	---	0.02	2.71	3.84	5.02	6.63	7.88
2	0.01	0.02	0.05	0.10	0.21	4.61	5.99	7.38	9.21	10.60
3	0.07	0.11	0.22	0.35	0.58	6.25	7.81	9.35	11.34	12.84

The critical value is given as $\left[\chi^{2(0.05)}{}_{(2-1)(2-1)} = \chi^{2(0.05)}{}_{(1)} = \mathbf{3.84}\right]$

N/B: The computed chi-square value is greater than the critical value $(0.36 > 3.84)$. This indicate that the gender and performance are not independent.

<u>est Your Understanding</u>

Exercise 15: Derive the expected values of the data table below

	Happy	Sad
Male	107	289
Female	291	81

[Answer: ....See Appendix]

Exercise 16: A sample of 40 students is used to record personality (extroverts and introverts) and colour preference (blue and red). Using the data in the table below, is there a relationship between personality and colour preference? Assume the significance level is 10%.

	Blue	Red
Extroverted	5	20
Introverted	10	5

[Answer: $\chi^2 = 8.711$, Critical value =2.71, degree of freedom = 1. Reject the H_0]

CHAPTER ELEVEN

CONTROL CHART

W. A. Shewhats

The control chart creation is credited to Dr. Walters Andrew Shewhats in 1924. It is a graphic display of process stability (consistency or fall within control limits) or instability over time. Control Chart is having as main objective to achieve and maintain process stability, as process are having variations resulting from common causes and from special causes. Control chart is sub-divided into; variables control charts and attributes control charts.

A control chart is segmented by lines called control limits. Control limits represent the limits of variation that should be expected from a process in a state of statistical control. Control limits shows variation from the central line. Our analysis will be limited to a type of variable control charts called mean control chart.

11.1 Mean Control Chart

A mean control chart is also known as Shewhart mean chart. A mean control chart is used to monitor changes in the average values of mean measurement over time. In a typical situation, data are collected in at least 20 subgroups or samples of 3 to 6 measurements. A typical mean control chart is made up of central line, warning limits, action limits and subgroup mean line.

The warning limits are located at a distance of ($\pm$) two times the standard deviation from the central line ($CL = \pm 2\sigma$) and in a normal distribution situation, about 95% of the result is within this limit. The action limits are located at a distance of ($\pm$) three times the standard deviation from the central line ($CL = \pm 3\sigma$) and in a normal distribution situation, about 99.7% of the result is within this limit.

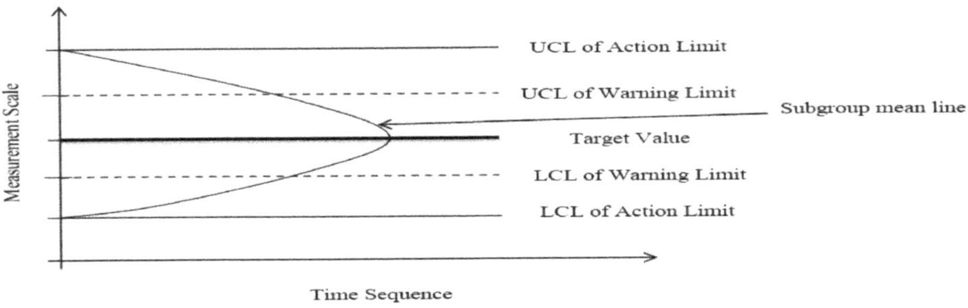

From the graph above, we realized that the action upper control limit is greater than the warning upper control limit and the warning lower control limit is greater than the action lower control limit. To construct a mean control chart, the following concepts are worth knowing.

11.1.1 Subgroup mean and subgroup Range

The subgroup mean is the sum of observation is a given subgroup divided by the number of observation that makes the subgroup. The subgroup range is derived by subtracting the minimum observation value from the maximum observation value.

$$\text{Subgroup Mean}(\bar{X}_i) = \frac{\sum X_i}{n} \qquad (1)$$

$$\text{Subgroup Range } (R_i) = X_{i(\text{Max})} - X_{i(\text{Min})} \qquad (2)$$

Example 1: Determine the subgroup mean and subgroup range using the data below.

Subgroups	X_1	X_2	X_3	X_4	X_5
1	41	41	46	44	43
2	42	41	42	41	45
3	41	40	44	43	48
4	43	46	47	49	42
5	47	43	49	44	44

<u>**Solution**</u>

Step 1: Formula: Subgroup $\text{Mean}(\overline{X}_i) = \frac{\sum X_i}{n}$

$$\text{Subgroup Range } (R_i) = X_{i(\text{Max})} - X_{i(\text{Min})}$$

Step 2: Data substitution and solving………………………………………………..…..**[n = 5]**

Original Table						Subgroup (Sample)	
Subgroups	X_1	X_2	X_3	X_4	X_5	$\text{Mean}(\overline{X}_i)$	Range (R_i)
1	**41**	41	**46**	44	43	$\frac{41+41+46+44+43}{5} = \mathbf{43.0}$	$46 - 41 = \mathbf{5}$
2	42	41	42	**41**	**45**	$\frac{42+41+42+41+45}{5} = \mathbf{42.2}$	$45 - 41 = \mathbf{4}$
3	41	**40**	44	43	**48**	$\frac{41+40+44+43+48}{5} = \mathbf{43.2}$	$48 - 40 = \mathbf{8}$
4	43	46	47	**49**	**42**	$\frac{43+46+47+49+42}{5} = \mathbf{45.4}$	$49 - 42 = \mathbf{7}$
5	47	**43**	**49**	44	44	$\frac{47+43+49+44+44}{5} = \mathbf{45.4}$	$49 - 43 = \mathbf{6}$
						$\sum = 219.2$	$\sum = 30$

11.1.2 Grand Mean and Mean Range

The grand mean is the sum of subgroup mean divided by the number of subgroup. The mean of all subgroup range is the sum of subgroups ranges divided by the number of subgroups. The grand mean value is also known as the target value and is used to derive the central line.

$$\text{Grand Mean}(\overline{\overline{X}}_i) = \frac{\sum \overline{X}_i}{N} \quad \text{……………………………………………………(1)}$$

$$\text{Mean of all Subgroup Range}(\overline{R}) = \frac{\sum R_i}{N} \quad \text{…………………………………………(2)}$$

Example 1: The sum of the mean of subgroup is 219.2, the sum of subgroup range is 30 and the number of observation is 6. Compute the grand mean and mean of all the subgroup range values.

<u>**Solution**</u>

a) **Calculation of grand mean**

Step 1: Formula. $\text{Grand Mean}(\overline{\overline{X}}_i) = \frac{\sum \overline{X}_i}{N}$, where; $\sum \overline{X}_i = 219.2$ and N = 6

Step 2: Data substitution and solving

$$\text{Grand Mean}(\overline{\overline{X}}_i) = \frac{219.2}{6} \quad \text{…………………………………………[Solve equation]}$$

$$\text{Grand Mean}(\overline{\overline{X}}_i) = \mathbf{36.53} \quad \text{……………………………[Central line or target value]}$$

b) Calculation of mean of all the subgroup range

Step 1: Formula. Mean of all Subgroup Range$(\overline{R}) = \frac{\sum R_i}{N}$, where; $\sum \overline{X}_i = 30$ and N = 6

Step 2: Data substitution and solving

Mean of all Subgroup Range$(\overline{R}) = \frac{30}{6}$ ....[Solve equation]

Mean of all Subgroup Range$(\overline{R}) = \mathbf{5}$

Example 2: Compute the grand mean and mean of all subgroup range using the subgroup mean and subgroup range values given below. Assume N is 4.

Samples	1	2	3	4	5	6	7	8
Mean	8.33	8.63	8.25	8.15	8.30	8.40	8.53	8.25
Range	1.5	3.2	1.5	1.6	1.6	0.6	2.4	1.2

Solution

Step 1: Formula. Grand Mean$(\overline{\overline{X}}_i) = \frac{\sum \overline{X}_i}{N}$

Mean Subgroup Range$(\overline{R}) = \frac{\sum R_i}{N}$, where; N = 4

Samples	1	2	3	4	5	6	7	8	**Total**
Mean	8.33	8.63	8.25	8.15	8.30	8.40	8.53	8.25	$\sum \overline{X}_i = \mathbf{66.84}$
Range	1.5	3.2	1.5	1.6	1.6	0.6	2.4	1.2	$\sum R_i = \mathbf{13.6}$

Step 2: Data substitution and solving

Grand Mean	Mean of all Subgroup
Grand Mean$(\overline{\overline{X}}_i) = \frac{66.84}{5}$ ....[Solve] Grand Mean$(\overline{\overline{X}}_i) = \mathbf{13.368}$	Mean Subgroup Range$(\overline{R}) = \frac{13.6}{4}$ ....[Solve] Mean Subgroup Range$(\overline{R}) = \mathbf{3.4}$

Test Your Understanding

Exercise 1: Compute the grand mean and the mean of all subgroup range given that, $\sum \overline{X}_i = 61.5$, N = 5 and $\sum R_i = 2.6$. ....**[Answer: $\overline{\overline{X}}_i = 12.3$ and $\overline{R} = 0.52$]**

Exercise 2: Compute the grand mean and mean of all subgroup range using the subgroup mean and subgroup range values given below.

Samples	1	2	3	4	5	6	7	8	9	10
X_1	42	64	53	62	26	27	16	17	48	41
X_2	57	76	71	31	54	37	54	44	72	59
X_3	36	52	41	17	62	69	32	46	76	80
X_4	8	40	56	44	51	61	45	49	64	68

[Answer:.. See Appendix]

11.1.3 Mean Control Charts Limits

The control limits are located above (upper limit) and below (lower limit) the central line or target value (grand mean value).

$$\text{Warning Control Limits} = \bar{\bar{X}} \pm 2\hat{\sigma}_{\bar{X}} \quad \text{..(1)}$$

$$\text{Upper Control Limit(UCL)} = \bar{\bar{X}} + 2\hat{\sigma}_{\bar{X}} = \bar{\bar{X}} + 2\left[\frac{1}{d_{2_{(n)}}} \times \frac{\bar{R}}{\sqrt{n}}\right] \text{..........................(1.1)}$$

$$\text{Lower Control Limit(LCL)} = \bar{\bar{X}} - 2\hat{\sigma}_{\bar{X}} = \bar{\bar{X}} + 2\left[\frac{1}{d_{2_{(n)}}} \times \frac{\bar{R}}{\sqrt{n}}\right] \text{..........................(1.2)}$$

$$\text{Action Control Limits} = \bar{\bar{X}} \pm A_{2_{(n)}}\bar{R} \text{ (OR) Action Control Limits} = \bar{\bar{X}} \pm 3\hat{\sigma}_{\bar{X}} \text{ ....(2)}$$

$$\text{UCL} = \bar{\bar{X}} + A_{2_{(n)}}\bar{R} \text{ (OR) UCL} = \bar{\bar{X}} + 3\hat{\sigma}_{\bar{X}} = \bar{\bar{X}} + 3\left[\frac{1}{d_{2_{(n)}}} \times \frac{\bar{R}}{\sqrt{n}}\right] \text{..........................(2.1)}$$

$$\text{LCL} = \bar{\bar{X}} - A_{2_{(n)}}\bar{R} \text{ (OR) LCL} = \bar{\bar{X}} - 3\hat{\sigma}_{\bar{X}} = \bar{\bar{X}} + 3\left[\frac{1}{d_{2_{(n)}}} \times \frac{\bar{R}}{\sqrt{n}}\right] \text{..........................(2.2)}$$

N/B: $(\hat{\sigma}_{\bar{X}})$ is the estimate of $(\sigma_{\bar{X}})$ and value of $\left(d_{2_{(n)}}\right)$ and $\left(A_{2_{(n)}}\right)$ are constants and their respective values are derived from the control chart constant table seen below.

n	c_4	d_2	A_2	D_3	D_4	$D_{.001}$	$D_{.999}$
2	0.7979	1.128	1.880	0.000	3.267		
3	0.8862	1.693	1.023	0.000	2.575		
4	0.9213	2.059	0.729	0.000	2.282	0.199	5.309
5	0.9400	2.326	0.577	0.000	2.115	0.367	5.484
6	0.9515	2.534	0.483	0.000	2.004	0.535	5.619
7	0.9594	2.704	0.419	0.076	1.924	0.691	5.730

Table 1: Control Chart Constant Table

Example 1: Given that; $\bar{\bar{X}} = 2.514$, $\bar{R} = 0.77$ and $n = 5$, calculate the values of the warning limits and action limits.

Solution

a) Calculation of warning limits

Step 1: Formula. Warning Control Limits = $\bar{\bar{X}} \pm 2\hat{\sigma}_{\bar{X}}$

Step 2: Data substitution and solving……………………………………[$\boldsymbol{d_{2_{(n)}} = d_{2_{(5)}} = 2.326}$]

Upper Control Limit $\left[\bar{\bar{X}} + 2\left[\frac{1}{d_{2_{(n)}}} \times \frac{\bar{R}}{\sqrt{n}}\right]\right]$	Lower Control Limit $\left[\bar{\bar{X}} - 2\left[\frac{1}{d_{2_{(n)}}} \times \frac{\bar{R}}{\sqrt{n}}\right]\right]$
$UCL = 2.514 + 2\left[\frac{1}{2.326} \times \frac{0.77}{\sqrt{5}}\right]$ ..[Work Root]	$LCL = 2.514 - 2\left[\frac{1}{2.326} \times \frac{0.77}{\sqrt{5}}\right]$.[Work Root]
$UCL = 2.514 + 2\left[\frac{1}{2.326} \times \frac{0.77}{2.236067978}\right]$	$LCL = 2.514 - 2\left[\frac{1}{2.326} \times \frac{0.77}{2.236067978}\right]$
$UCL = 2.514 + 0.296091545$ ………[Solve]	$LCL = 2.514 - 0.296091545$ ……[Solve]
$UCL = \mathbf{2.81}$ ………………………[In 2 dp]	$LCL = \mathbf{2.22}$ ……………………[In 2 dp]

b) Calculation of action limits

Step 1: Formula. Action Control Limits = $\bar{\bar{X}} \pm A_{2_{(n)}}\bar{R}$

Step 2: Data substitution and solving……………………………………[$\boldsymbol{A_{2_{(n)}} = A_{2_{(5)}} = 0.5768}$]

Upper Control Limit = $\bar{\bar{X}} + A_{2_{(n)}}\bar{R}$	Lower Control Limit = $\bar{\bar{X}} - A_{2_{(n)}}\bar{R}$
$UCL = 2.514 + 0.5768\ (0.77)$	$LCL = 2.514 - 0.5768\ (0.77)$
$UCL = 2.514 + 0.444136$ …………..[Solve]	$LCL = 2.514 - 0.444136$ …………..[Solve]
$UCL = \mathbf{2.96}$ ……………………….[In 2 dp]	$LCL = \mathbf{2.07}$ ……………………..[In 2 dp]

N/B: The calculated values of warning limits and action limits are illustrated graphically below

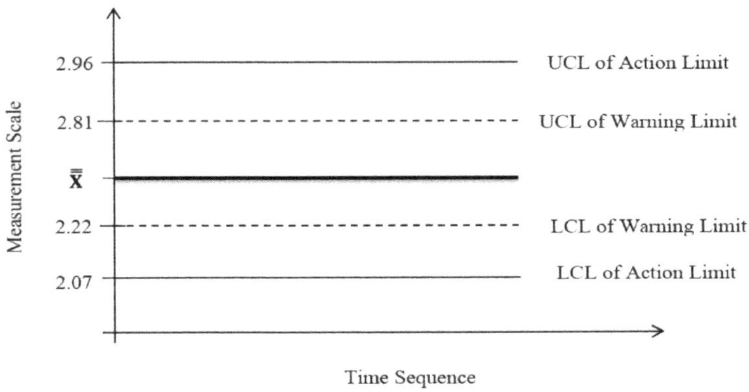

NOTE: From the semi-mean control chart above, we realized that the upper limit of the action limit is greater than the upper limit of the warning limit and the lower limit of the warning limit is greater than the lower limit of the action limit.

Example 2: Draw a mean semi-control chart using the table below

Subgroups	X_1	X_2	X_3	X_4	X_5
1	2.7	2.3	2.6	2.4	2.7
2	2.6	2.4	2.6	2.3	2.8
3	2.3	2.3	2.4	2.5	2.4
4	2.8	2.3	2.4	2.6	2.7
5	2.6	2.5	2.6	2.1	2.8

Solution

Step 1: Determination of grand mean and mean of all subgroup range

1) Formula. Grand Mean$(\overline{\overline{X}}_i) = \frac{\sum \overline{X}_i}{N}$

Mean of all Subgroup Range$(\overline{R}) = \frac{\sum R_i}{N}$, where = 5

2) Data substitution and solving

Subgroups	X_1	X_2	X_3	X_4	X_5	Subgroup Mean $\left[\overline{X}_i = \frac{\sum X_i}{n}\right]$	Subgroup Range $\left[R_i = X_{i(Max)} - X_{i(Min)}\right]$
1	2.7	2.3	2.6	2.4	2.7	2.54	0.4
2	2.6	2.4	2.6	2.3	2.8	2.54	0.5
3	2.3	2.3	2.4	2.5	2.4	2.38	0.2
4	2.8	2.3	2.4	2.6	2.7	2.56	0.5
5	2.6	2.5	2.6	2.1	2.8	2.52	0.7
						$\sum = \mathbf{12.54}$	$\sum = \mathbf{2.3}$
Grand Mean$(\overline{\overline{X}}_i) = \frac{\sum \overline{X}_i}{N} = \frac{12.54}{5} = \mathbf{2.508}$					Mean of all Subgroup Range$(\overline{R}) = \frac{\sum R_i}{N} = \frac{2.3}{5} = \mathbf{0.46}$		

Step 2: Determination of warning limits and action limits

a) Calculation of warning limits

Step 1: Formula. Warning Control Limits = $\overline{\overline{X}} \pm 2\hat{\sigma}_{\overline{X}}$

Step 2: Data substitution and solving.....................................$[\boldsymbol{d_{2_{(n)}}} = \boldsymbol{d_{2_{(5)}}} = \mathbf{2.326}]$

Upper Control Limit $\left[\overline{\overline{X}} + 2\left[\frac{1}{d_{2_{(n)}}} \times \frac{\overline{R}}{\sqrt{n}}\right]\right]$	Lower Control Limit $\left[\overline{\overline{X}} - 2\left[\frac{1}{d_{2_{(n)}}} \times \frac{\overline{R}}{\sqrt{n}}\right]\right]$
$UCL = 2.508 + 2\left[\frac{1}{2.326} \times \frac{0.46}{\sqrt{5}}\right]$ ..[Work Root]	$LCL = 2.508 - 2\left[\frac{1}{2.326} \times \frac{0.46}{\sqrt{5}}\right]$ ..[Work Root]
$UCL = 2.508 + 2\left[\frac{1}{2.326} \times \frac{0.46}{2.236067978}\right]$	$LCL = 2.508 - 2\left[\frac{1}{2.326} \times \frac{0.46}{2.236067978}\right]$
$UCL = 2.508 + 0.176885858$ ......[Solve]	$LCL = 2.508 - 0.296091545$ ......[Solve]
$UCL = \mathbf{2.68}$ ....[In 2 dp]	$LCL = \mathbf{2.33}$ ....[In 2 dp]

b) Calculation of action limits

Step 1: Formula. Action Control Limits $= \bar{\bar{X}} \pm A_{2_{(n)}}\bar{R}$

Step 2: Data substitution and solving..................................$[\mathbf{A_{2_{(n)}} = A_{2_{(5)}} = 0.5768}]$

Upper Control Limit $= \bar{\bar{X}} + A_{2_{(n)}}\bar{R}$	Lower Control Limit $= \bar{\bar{X}} - A_{2_{(n)}}\bar{R}$
$UCL = 2.508 + 0.5768\ (0.46)$ $UCL = 2.508 + 0.265328$ ....[Solve] $UCL = \mathbf{2.77}$ ....[In 2 dp]	$LCL = 2.508 - 0.5768\ (0.46)$ $LCL = 2.508 - 0.265328$ ....[Solve] $LCL = \mathbf{2.24}$ ....[In 2 dp]

Step 3: Drawing of semi mean control chart

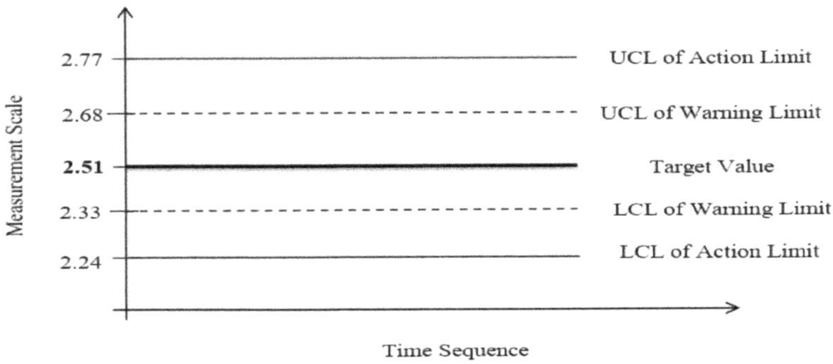

11.1.3 Subgroup Mean Plotting

A complete mean control chart is one having all the limits line and the subgroup mean line. After calculating and plotting the warning and action control limits, we are required to plot the subgroup mean values.

Example 1: The value of $\bar{\bar{X}} = 15.40$, $\bar{R} = 1.8$ and n = 5. The subgroup mean values are given below. Construct a complete mean control chart.

Subgroup	1	2	3	4	5	6	7	8	9
Mean	15.36	15.04	15.82	15.36	15.98	15.34	15.52	15.58	14.56

Solution

Step 1: Determination of warning and action limits

a) Calculation of warning limits

Step 1: Formula. Warning Control Limits $= \bar{\bar{X}} \pm 2\hat{\sigma}_{\bar{X}}$

Step 2: Data substitution and solving......................................$[d_{2_{(n)}} = d_{2_{(5)}} = \mathbf{2.326}]$

Upper Control Limit $\left[\bar{\bar{X}} + 2\left[\frac{1}{d_{2_{(n)}}} \times \frac{\bar{R}}{\sqrt{n}}\right]\right]$	Lower Control Limit $\left[\bar{\bar{X}} - 2\left[\frac{1}{d_{2_{(n)}}} \times \frac{\bar{R}}{\sqrt{n}}\right]\right]$
$UCL = 15.40 + 2\left[\frac{1}{2.326} \times \frac{1.8}{\sqrt{5}}\right]$ ..[Work Root]	$LCL = 15.40 - 2\left[\frac{1}{2.326} \times \frac{1.8}{\sqrt{5}}\right]$.[Work Root]
$UCL = 15.40 + 2\left[\frac{1}{2.326} \times \frac{1.8}{2.236067978}\right]$	$LCL = 15.40 - 2\left[\frac{1}{2.326} \times \frac{1.8}{2.236067978}\right]$
$UCL = 15.40 + 0.692162056$ ......[Solve]	$LCL = 15.40 - 0.692162056$ ......[Solve]
$UCL = \mathbf{16.09}$ ....[In 2 dp]	$LCL = \mathbf{14.71}$ ....[In 2 dp]

b) Calculation of action limits

Step 1: Formula. Action Control Limits $= \bar{\bar{X}} \pm A_{2_{(n)}}\bar{R}$

Step 2: Data substitution and solving.......................................$[\mathbf{A}_{2_{(n)}} = \mathbf{A}_{2_{(5)}} = \mathbf{0.5768}]$

Upper Control Limit $= \bar{\bar{X}} + A_{2_{(n)}}\bar{R}$	Lower Control Limit $= \bar{\bar{X}} - A_{2_{(n)}}\bar{R}$
$UCL = 15.40 + 0.5768\ (1.8)$	$UCL = 15.40 - 0.5768\ (1.8)$
$UCL = 15.40 + 1.03824$ ....[Solve]	$UCL = 15.40 - 1.03824$ ....[Solve]
$UCL = 16.43$ ....[In 2 dp]	$UCL = 14.36$ ....[In 2 dp]

Step 3: Drawing of a complete mean control chart

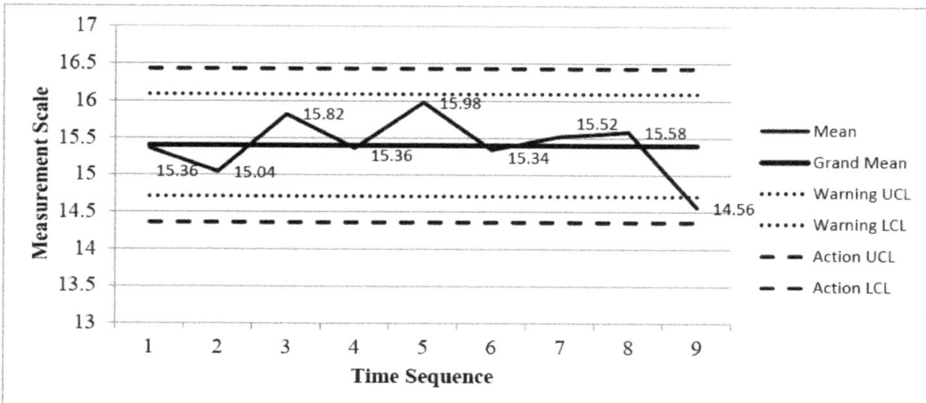

N/B: The total number of observation is 9 (15.36, 15.04, 15.82, 15.36, 15.98, 15.34, 15.52, 15.58 and 14.56). The total percentage of observations that are within the warning limits is 88.89% and the total percentage of observations that are within the action limit is 100%. No observation is out of the limits.

Example 2: Construct a mean control chart using the table.

Samples	1	2	3	4	5	6	7
X_1	209.0	214.5	204.5	217.5	211.0	224.0	210.0
X_2	211.0	210.0	209.0	216.0	220.0	220.0	208.0
X_3	213.5	212.0	198.5	217.0	224.0	224.0	210.0
X_4	205.0	203.5	203.0	214.0	218.5	218.5	220.0
X_5	210.0	214.0	213.5	209.5	210.0	210.0	211.0

Test Your Understanding

Exercise 3: The grand mean is 48.4, the mean of all sample ranges is 5.1 and the sample size is 4. Compute the warning control limits action control limits.

[Answer: $UCL_{Action} = 52.1$, $LCL_{Action} = 44.7$, $UCL_{Warning} = 50.9$ and $LCL_{Warning} = 45.9$]

Exercise 4: Given that grand mean is 61.5, mean of all subgroup range is 2.6 and number of subgroup is 4. Construct a mean control chart....................**[Answer: See Appendix]**

11.1.4 Interpretation of Control Chart

Dr. Walter A. Shewhart developed eight rules commonly called Shewhart Rules or Western Electric Rules to interpret a control chart. These rules act as criteria for identifying the presence of special cause (unexpected causes) variation in a process (unnatural pattern). Our interpretation will be limit to the identification of special cause variation in a process.

A process experiencing only common cause variation will have all the subgroup mean values within the action control limits. A process experiencing special cause variation will have some of the subgroup mean values out of the action control limits.

To apply these rules, a control chart is sub-divided into zones (A, B, and C). The warning control chart is sub-divided into two, that is $(\pm 2\sigma)$ and $(\pm 1\sigma)$ as seen below.

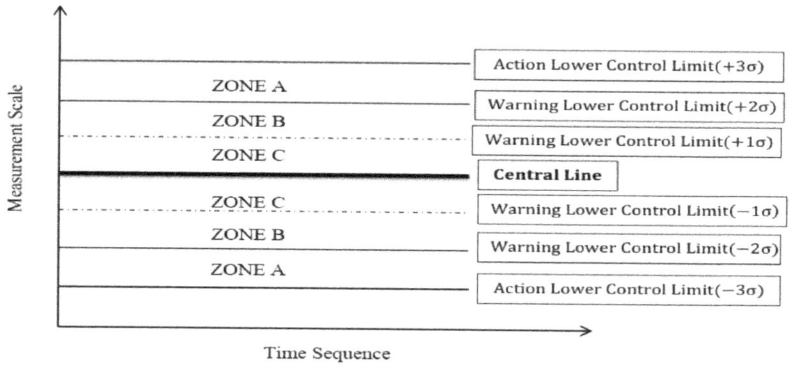

Figure 1: The Mean control chart with different zones

Example 1: The grand mean is 275, the standard deviation is 43 and the sample size is 4. Illustrate the A, B, and C zones.

<u>Solution</u>

Step 1: Formula. Control Limits = $\bar{\bar{X}} \pm Y\left(\frac{\sigma}{\sqrt{n}}\right)$

Where; Y ranges from 1, 2 and 3, $\bar{\bar{X}} = 275$, $\sigma = 43$ and n = 4

Step 2: Data substitution and solving

		Upper Control Limit	Lower Control Limit
Action Limits	Y = 3	$275 + 3\left(\frac{43}{\sqrt{4}}\right) = \mathbf{339.5}$	$275 - 3\left(\frac{43}{\sqrt{4}}\right) = \mathbf{210.5}$
Warning Limits	Y = 2	$275 + 2\left(\frac{43}{\sqrt{4}}\right) = \mathbf{318.0}$	$275 - 2\left(\frac{43}{\sqrt{4}}\right) = \mathbf{232.0}$
	Y = 1	$275 + 1\left(\frac{43}{\sqrt{4}}\right) = \mathbf{296.5}$	$275 - 1\left(\frac{43}{\sqrt{4}}\right) = \mathbf{253.5}$

Step 3: Illustration of A, B and C zones

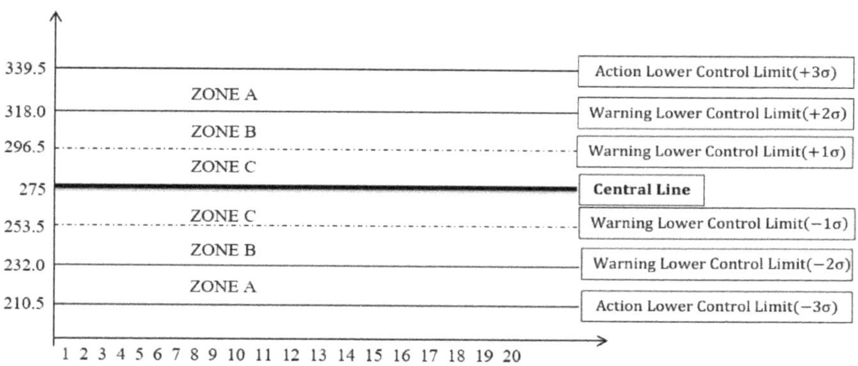

Example 3: The grand mean is 34.088, the action upper control limit is 35.6 and the action lower control limit is 32.57. Using the subgroup mean values below, construct and interpret a mean control chart.

Subgroups	Mean	Subgroups	Mean
1	34.05	11	33.27
2	34.40	12	33.71
3	33.59	13	34.03
4	35.96	14	34.58
5	34.70	15	34.02
6	33.51	16	33.97
7	33.79	17	34.05
8	34.04	18	34.04
9	34.52	19	33.73
10	33.75	20	34.05

<u>Solution</u>

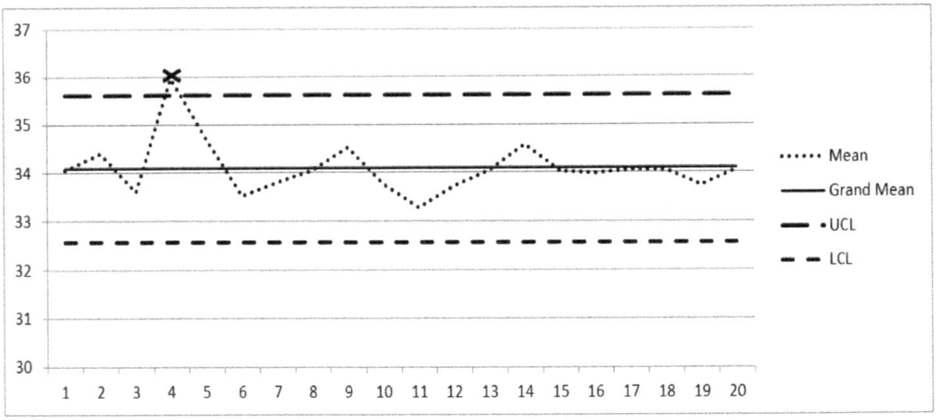

Note: A subgroup mean value (Marked by a cross) is above the distance of 3 times standard deviation from the grand mean value. This shows the presence of s special cause variation.

Example 4: The grand mean is 11.5 and the estimated standard deviation is 0.2. Construct a mean control chart using the data sets below.

Samples	Data A	Data B	Data C	Samples	Data A	Data B	Data C
1	11.602	11.627	11.495	11	11.664	11.383	11.534
2	11.547	11.613	11.475	12	11.823	11.715	11.624
3	11.312	11.493	11.465	13	11.629	11.485	11.629
4	11.449	11.602	11.497	14	11.602	11.509	11.575
5	11.401	11.360	11.573	15	11.756	11.429	11.730
6	11.608	11.374	11.563	16	11.707	11.477	11.680
7	11.471	11.592	11.321	17	11.612	11.570	11.729
8	11.453	11.458	11.533	18	11.628	11.623	11.704
9	11.446	11.552	11.486	19	11.603	11.472	12.052
10	11.522	11.463	11.502	20	11.816	11.531	11.905

Solution

Step 1: Formula. Control Limits = $\overline{\overline{X}} \pm Y\widehat{\sigma}_{\overline{X}}$

Where; Y ranges from 1, 2 and 3 and $\overline{\overline{X}} = 11.5$, $\widehat{\sigma}_{\overline{X}} = 0.2$

Step 2: Data substitution and solving

		Upper Control Limit	Lower Control Limit
Action Limits	Y = 3	$11.5 + 3(0.2) = 12.1$	$11.5 - 3(0.2) = 10.9$
Warning Limits	Y = 2	$11.5 + 2(0.2) = 11.9$	$11.5 - 2(0.2) = 11.1$
	Y = 1	$11.5 + 1(0.2) = 11.7$	$11.5 - 1(0.2) = 11.3$

Step 3: Construction of mean control charts

1) **Data A mean control chart**

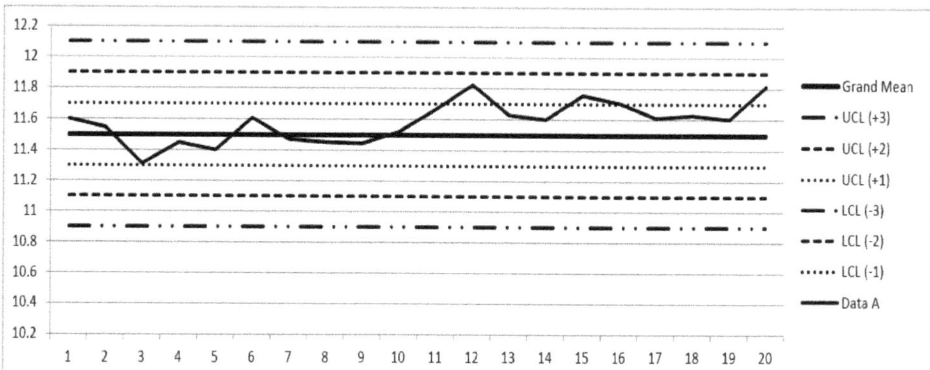

Note: The subgroup means are all within the distance of 2 times standard deviation from the grand mean value. That is, the variation is as a result of common causes and process is under control.

2) Data B mean control chart

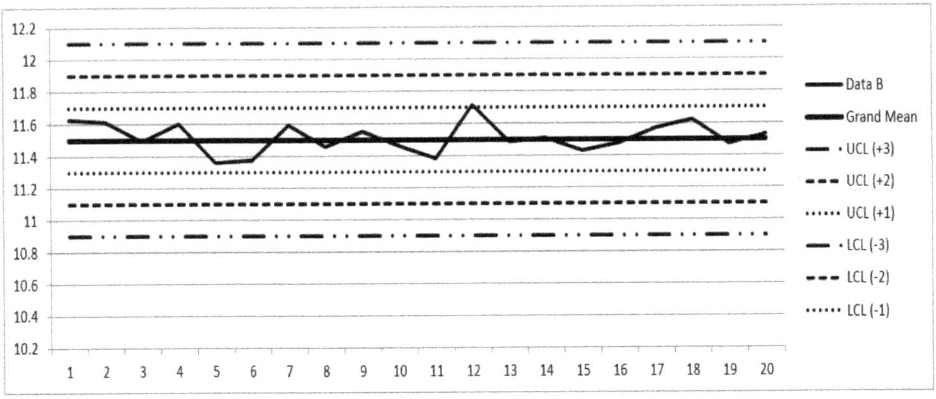

Note: The subgroup means are all within the distance of 1 times standard deviation from the grand mean value. This indicates that the variation is as a result of common causes and process is under control.

3) Data C mean control chart

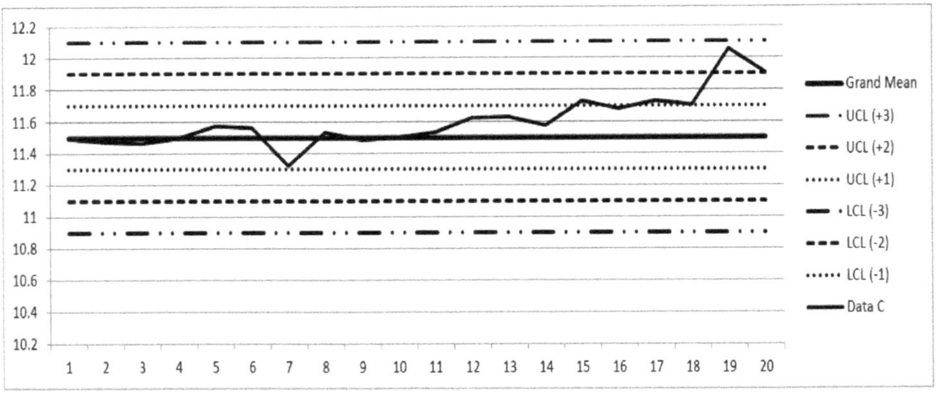

Note: The subgroup means are all within the distance of 3 times standard deviation from the grand mean value. This shows that the variation is as a result of common causes and process is under control.

Test Your Understanding

Exercise 5: Construct and interpret the mean control chart using the subgroup mean values below.

Samples	1	2	3	4	5	6	7	8
Mean	2.325	2.625	2.25	2.15	2.3	2.4	2.525	2.25

		Upper Control Limit	Lower Control Limit
Action Limits	$\pm 3\sigma$	3.59	1.11
	$\pm 2\sigma$	3.18	1.52
Warning Limits	$\pm 1\sigma$	2.76	1.94

[Answer:...See Appendix]

Example 6: Interpret the mean control chart below and justify your answer

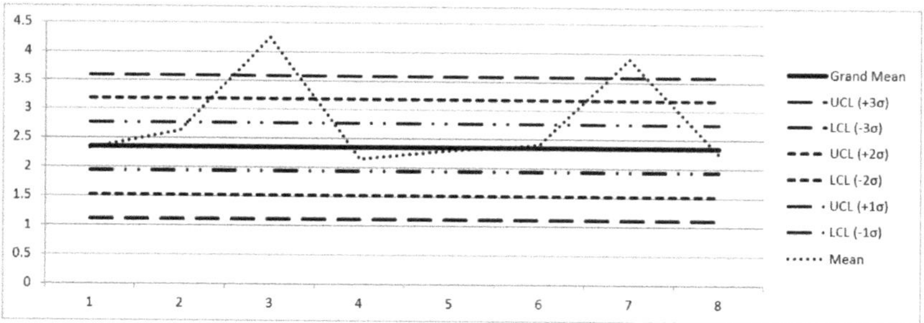

[Answer: The existence of special cause variation as some mean values are above the control limits]

APPENDIX 1 [Answers to Exercises]

Chapter 1 [Linear Correlation]

Exercise 1

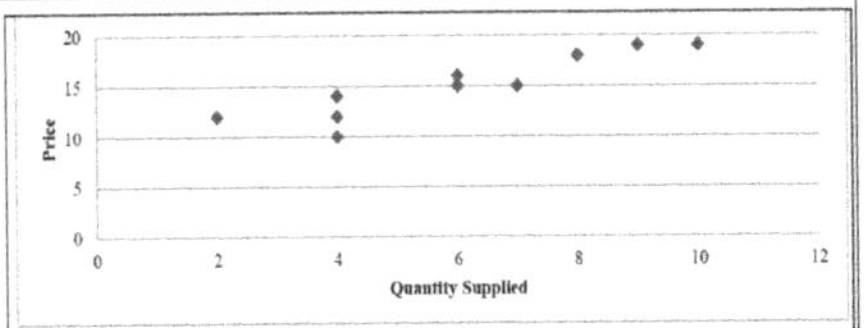

Interpretation: The upward shows that the relationship between price and quantity demanded is positive.

Exercise 2

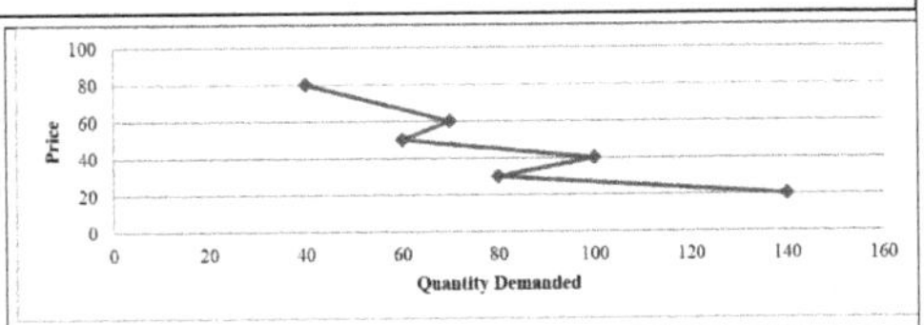

Interpretation: The down ward direction shows that price and quantity demanded are positively related.

Chapter Two [Time Series Data]

Exercise 3

Years	2000	2001	2002	2003	2004	2005	2006	2007
Workers' wages	20	40	55	70	80	100	150	155
5 years moving average			**53**	**69**	**91**	**111**		

Exercise 4

Year	2000	2001	2002	2003	2004	2005	2006
Salary	16	50	22	59	63	46	43
4 years moving average			**85.25**	**96**	**100.25**		
Centered moving average			**42.625**	**48**	**50.125**		

Exercise 5

Years (X)	1	2	3	4	5	6	7
Quantity of cocoa (Y)	320	334	329	344	358	347	383
2 years moving average		**658.5**	**668**	**687.5**	**703.5**	**717.5**	
3 years moving average		**327.7**	**335.7**	**343.7**	**349.7**	**362.7**	

Exercise 6 (2)

Number of crime committed (X_i)	1	3	3	5	8
Money spend on security (Y_i)	8	6		4	2
$\hat{Y}$	**7.47**	**5.83**	**5.83**	**4.19**	**1.73**

Exercise 8 (1)

Years (X)	2000	2001	2002	2003	2004	2005
Quantity of Irish (Y)	7	10	13	15	20	28
$\hat{Y}$	**5.7**	**9.6**	**13.5**	**17.4**	**21.3**	**25.2**

Exercise 9

1)

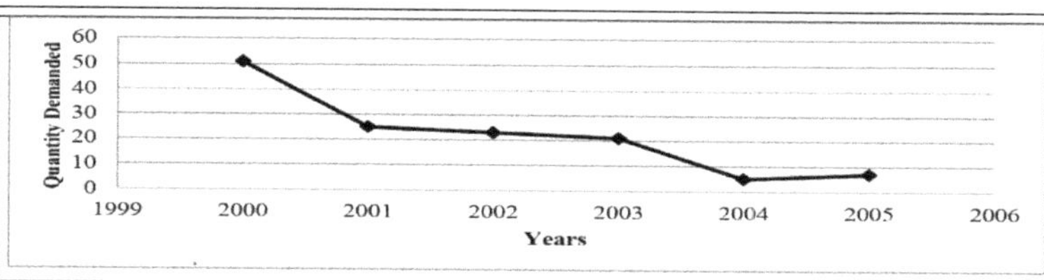

Interpretation: The downward movement of the line shows a negative relationship between years and quantity demanded

2)

a) Mayer method.. $[\hat{Y}_t = 34.33 - 0.67\ X_i]$

b)

Years	2000	2001	2002	2003	2004	2005
3 Years moving average		33	23	16	11	

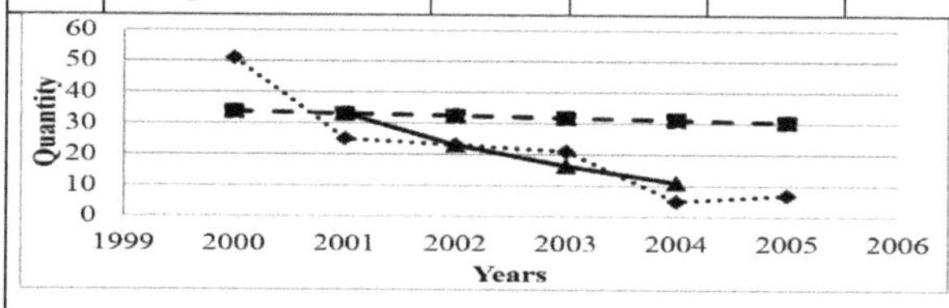

Actual Value ....

Mayer Value - - - - - - - - - - - - -

Moving Average Value ______________

Exercise 10

1)

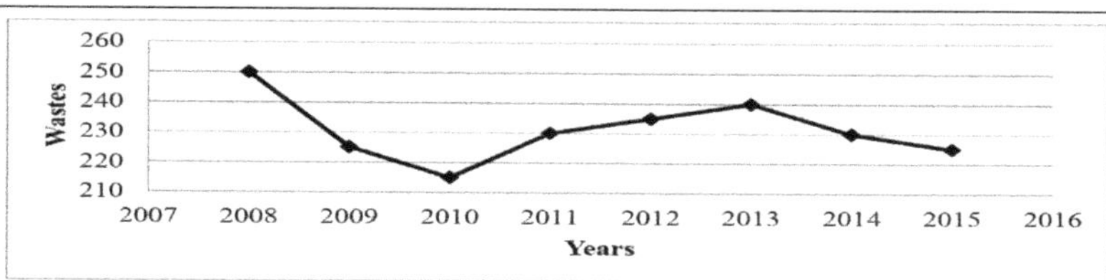

2)

$\hat{Y} = 232.02 - 0.17X_t$...[In two decimal places]

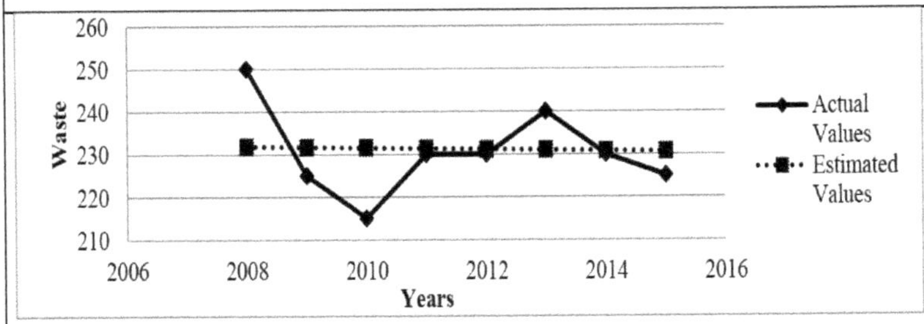

Exercise 11

Years	Q_1	Q_2	Q_3	Q_4
Quarter Mean	308	388.2	364	340
Total Mean	$308 + 388.2 + 364 + 340/4 = 350.05$			

Exercise 12

				Seasonality Coefficient (S_i^*)	
	2001	2002	Quarter mean (S_i)	Additive	Multiplicative [in 4 pd]
Q_1	240	470	355	$355 - 395.125 = -40.125$	$355/395.125 = 0.8984$
Q_2	330	531	430.5	$430.5 - 395.125 = 35.375$	$430.5/395.125 = 1.0895$
Q_3	320	500	410	$410 - 395.125 = 14.875$	$410/395.125 = 1.0376$
Q_4	290	480	385	$385 - 395.125 = -10.125$	$385/395.125 = 0.9743$
			Total Mean($\bar{S}_i$) =395.125	$\Sigma = 0$	$\Sigma = 4$

Exercise 13

				Seasonality Coefficient(S_i^*)		Deseasonalized Value(Y_t^*)	
		Observed Values (Y_t)	Quarter Mean(S_i)	Additive	Multiplicative	Additive	Multiplicative
2009	Q_1	97.9	97.65	−9.5125	0.91123294	107.4125	107.4369
	Q_2	102.7	102.65	−4.5125	0.957891053	107.2125	107.2147
	Q_3	112.9	114.3	7.1375	1.066604456	105.7625	105.8499
	Q_4	113.8	114.05	6.8875	1.06427155	106.9125	106.9276
2010	Q_1	97.4	97.65	−9.5125	0.91123294	106.9125	106.8881
	Q_2	102.6	102.65	−4.5125	0.957891053	107.1125	107.1103
	Q_3	115.7	114.3	7.1375	1.066604456	108.5625	108.4751
	Q_4	114.3	114.05	6.8875	1.06427155	107.4125	107.3974
			$\bar{S}_i = \frac{428.65}{4} = 107.1625$				

Exercise 14

Years		Quantity	2-Years Moving Average Forecast	
			Formula	Working
2000	Y_1	18		
2001	Y_2	13		
2002	Y_3	16	$F_{(2002)} = (Y_1 + Y_2)/n$	$(18 + 13)/2 = 15.5$
2003	Y_4	11	$F_{(2003)} = (Y_2 + Y_3)/n$	$(13 + 16)/2 = 14.5$
2004	Y_5	17	$F_{(2004)} = (Y_3 + Y_4)/n$	$(16 + 11)/2 = 13.5$
2005			$F_{(2005)} = (Y_4 + Y_5)/n$	$(11 + 17)/2 = 14$

Exercise 15

Years		Demand	3-Years Moving Average Forecast		Forecast Error
			Formula	Working	$[e_t = Y_t - F_t]$
1	Y_1	24			
2	Y_2	13			
3	Y_3	20			
4	Y_4	12	$F_4 = (Y_1 + Y_2 + Y_3)/n$	$(24 + 13 + 20)/3 = 19$	$e_4 = 12 - 19 = -7$
5	Y_5	19	$F_5 = (Y_2 + Y_3 + Y_4)/n$	$(13 + 20 + 12)/3 = 15$	$e_5 = 19 - 15 = 4$
6	Y_6	23	$F_6 = (Y_3 + Y_4 + Y_5)/n$	$(20 + 12 + 19)/3 = 17$	$e_6 = 23 - 17 = 6$

Exercise 16

Years		Quantity	2-Years Moving Average Forecast	Forecast Error
Expression	Representation			$[e_t = Y_t - F_t]$
2010	Y_1	17		
2011	Y_2	21		
2012	Y_3	19	$F_{(2012)} = \frac{[(1\times17)+(2\times21)]}{1+2} = 19.667$	$e_{(2012)} = 19 - 19.667 = -0.667$
2013	Y_4	23	$F_{(2013)} = \frac{[(1\times21)+(2\times19)]}{1+2} = 19.667$	$e_{(2013)} = 23 - 19.667 = 3.333$
2014	Y_5	18	$F_{(2014)} = \frac{[(1\times19)+(2\times23)]}{1+2} = 21.667$	$e_{(2014)} = 18 - 21.667 = -3.667$
2015	Y_6	16	$F_{(2015)} = \frac{[(1\times23)+(2\times18)]}{1+2} = 19.667$	$e_{(2015)} = 16 - 19.667 = -3.667$
2016			$F_{(2016)} = \frac{[(1\times18)+(2\times16)]}{1+2} = 16.667$	

Exercise 19

Years	Q_1	Q_2	Q_3	Q_4
Quarter Forecast	$Q_1 = 54.33 + 8.5X_t$	$Q_2 = 83.33 + 12X_t$	$Q_3 = 100.67 + 13.5X_t$	$Q_4 = 33.33 + 8.5X_t$
Annual Forecast $[2025 = X_t = 10]$	$\hat{Y}_{(2025)} = [54.33 + 8.5(10)] + [83.33 + 12(10)] + [100.67 + 13.5(10)] + [33.33 + 8.5(10)]$			
	$\hat{Y}_{(2025)} = 139.33 + 203.33 + 235.67 + 118.33 =$ **696.66 ≅ 697 Units**			

Exercise 20

Years	Demand (Y_t)	Working	Level
2012	17,496	$L_1 = Y_1 = 17{,}496$	17,496
2013	18,965	$L_2 = 0.29(18{,}965) + (1 - 0.29)17{,}496$	17,922
2014	12,535	$L_3 = 0.29(12{,}535) + (1 - 0.29)17{,}922$	16,360
2015	14,781	$L_4 = 0.29(14{,}781) + (1 - 0.29)16{,}360$	15,902
2016	16,722	$L_5 = 0.29(16{,}722) + (1 - 0.29)15{,}902$	16,140
2017	15,858	$L_6 = 0.29(15{,}858) + (1 - 0.29)16{,}140$	16,058

Exercise 21

Years	Supply	Level ($\alpha = 0.2$) $[L_t = \alpha Y_t + (1 - \alpha)L_{t-1}]$	Forecast $[F_{t+1} = L_t]$
2013	80	$L_1 = Y_1 = 80$	
2014	82	$L_2 = 0.2(82) + (1 - 0.2)80 = 80.4$	80
2015	84	$L_3 = 0.2(84) + (1 - 0.2)80.4 = 81.12$	80.4
2016	83	$L_4 = 0.2(83) + (1 - 0.2)81.12 = 81.496$	81.12
2017	83	$L_5 = 0.2(83) + (1 - 0.2)81.496 = 81.7968$	81.496
2018			81.7968

Exercise 23

Years	Sales	Forecast	Forecast Error
2001	18		
2002	**13**	18.00	−5.00
2003	16	15.50	**0.50**
2004	11	**16.67**	−4.67
2005	17	14.50	2.50
2006	14	**14.998**	**−0.998**

Exercise 24

Years	Production (Y_t)	Level ($\alpha = 0.6$) $[L_t = \alpha Y_t + (1-\alpha)(L_{t-1} + T_{t-1})]$	Trend ($\beta = 0.4$) $[T_t = \beta(L_t - L_{t-1}) + (1-\beta)T_{t-1}]$
2015	205	$L_1 = Y_1 = 205$	$L_1 = 7$ ....[Given]
2016	212	$L_2 = 0.6(212) + (1-0.6)(205+7) = 212$	$T_2 = 0.4(212-205) + (1-0.4)7 = 7$
2017	218	$L_3 = 0.6(218) + (1-0.6)(212+7) = 218.4$	$T_3 = 0.4(218.4-212) + (1-0.4)7 = 6.76$
2018	224	$L_4 = 0.6(224) + (1-0.6)(218.4+6.76) = 224.464$	$T_4 = 0.4(224.464-218.4) + (1-0.4)6.76 = 6.4816$
2020			

Years	Production (Y_t)	Level ($\alpha = 0.6$)	Trend ($\beta = 0.4$)	Forecast (F_{t+1})
2015	205	205	7	
2016	212	212	7	$205 + 7 = 212$
2017	218	218.4	6.76	$212 + 7 = 219$
2018	224	224.464	6.4816	$218.4 + 6.76 = 225.16$
2020				$224.464 + 6.4816 = 230.9456$

Chapter Three [Probability]

Exercise 7 (a)

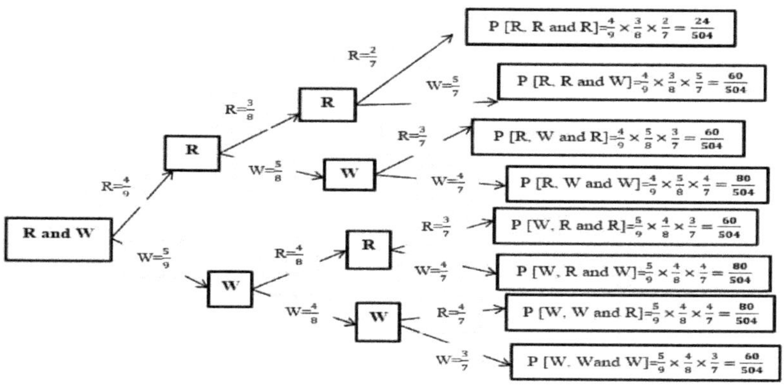

Chapter Four [Further Analysis of Probability]

Exercise 1

Table 1

Scores	5	10	15	20	25	30	35	40	45	50
Frequency	0.2	0.1	0.08	0.12	0.15	0.03	0.07	0.05	0.04	0.16

Table 2

Marks	1	2	3	4	5	Total
Frequency	0.3	0.15	0.2	0.1	0.25	1

Table 3

Scores	1	2	3	4	5	Total
Number of students	25	10	**20**	15	**30**	100
Probability	0.25	**0.1**	0.2	0.15	0.3	1

Exercise 6

a)

Ages of students (X)	16	18	19	20	21	30	Total
Number of students (f)	1	4	9	3	2	1	20
Probability$[P(X = x)] = \frac{f(X_i)}{\Sigma f}$	0.05	0.2	0.45	0.15	0.1	0.05	1

b) $E(X) = \mathbf{19.55}$

Chapter Five [Special Probability Distribution]

Exercise 4

1)

X	0	1	2	3	4	5	Total
$P(x = r)$	0.32768	0.4096	0.2048	0.0512	0.0064	0.00032	1

2)

X	0	1	2	3	4	5
$P(x = r)$	0.32768	0.73728	0.94208	0.99328	0.99968	1

Chapter Eight [Project Management]

Exercise 1

Table 1

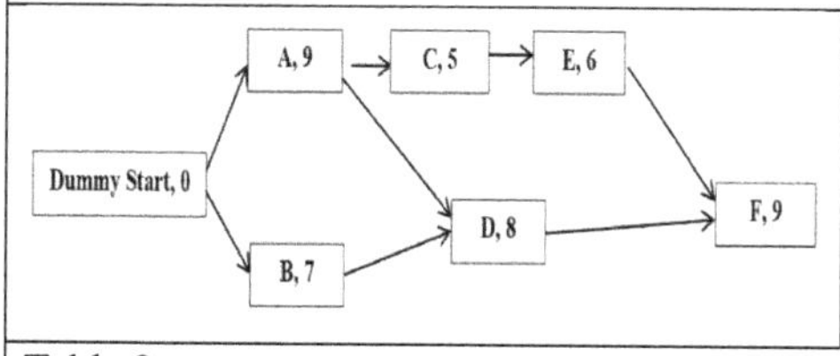

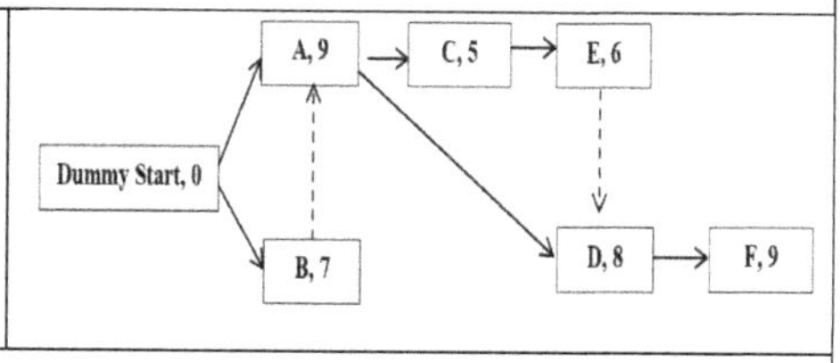

Table 2

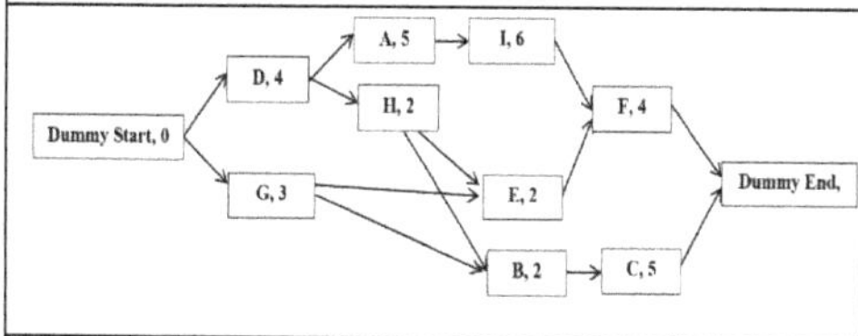

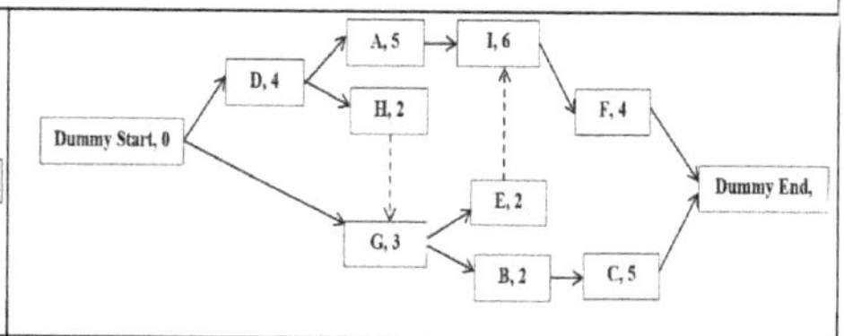

Table 3

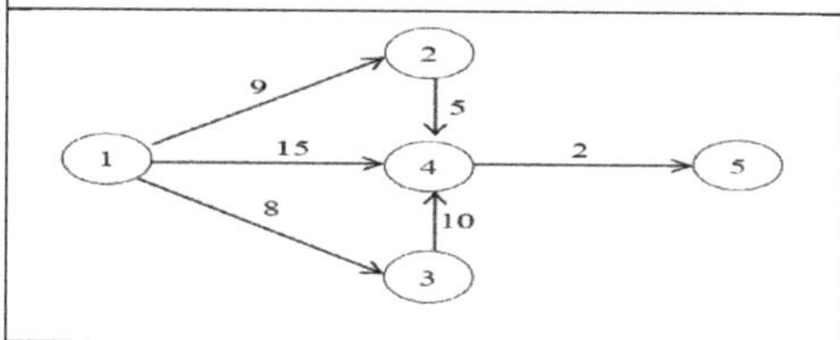

Table 4

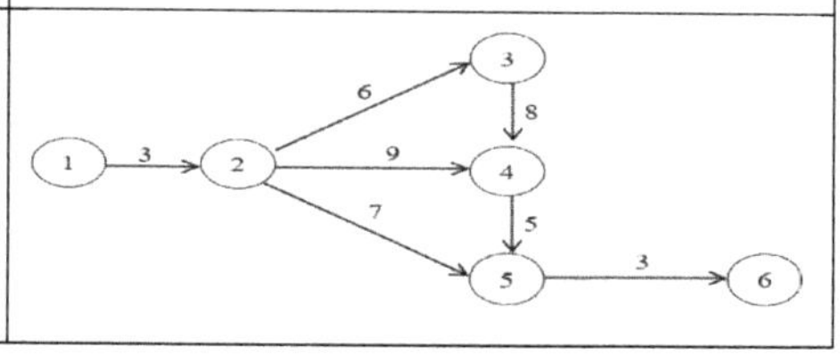

Exercise 2

Table 1

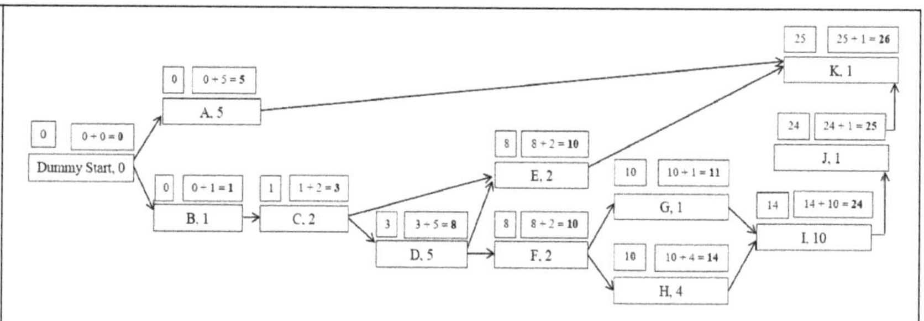

Table 2

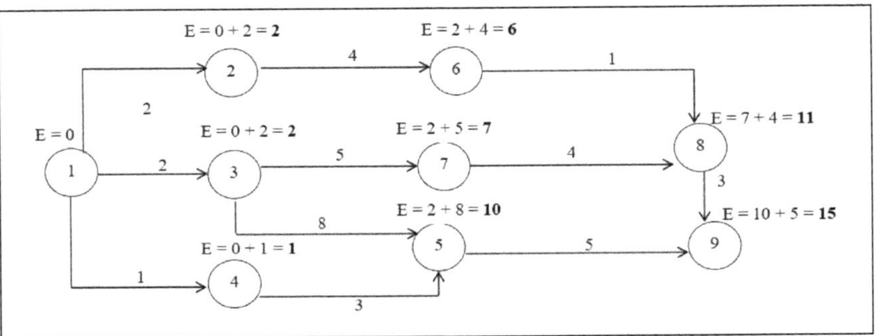

Exercise 3

Table 1

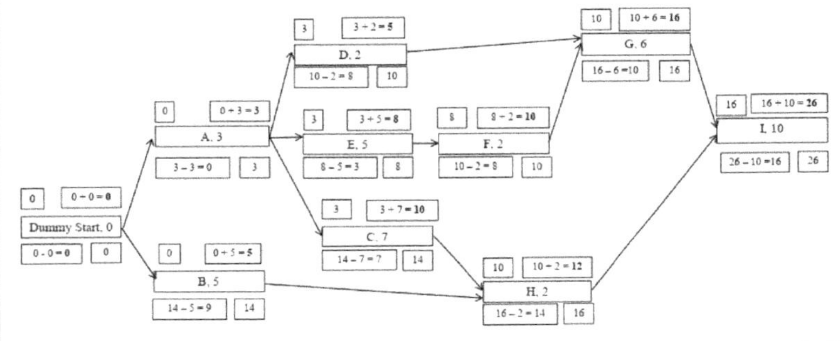

Table 2

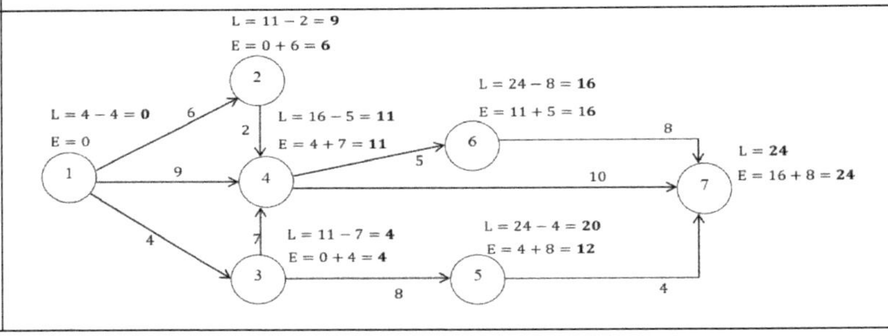

Exercise 4

Table 1

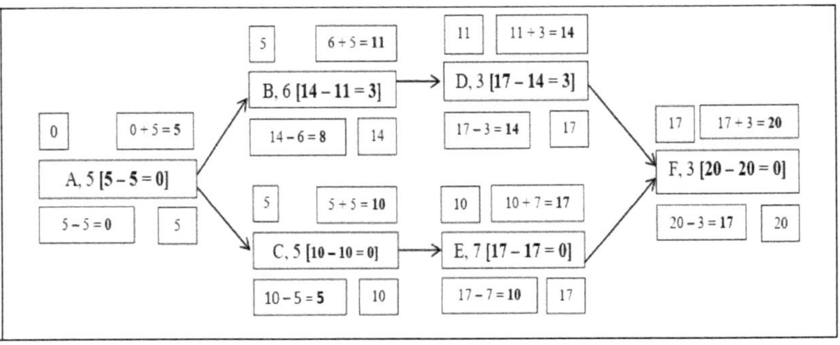

Table 2	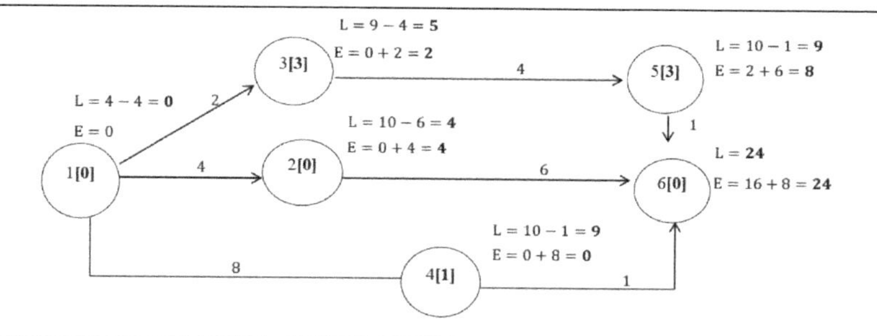

Exercise 5

Table 1	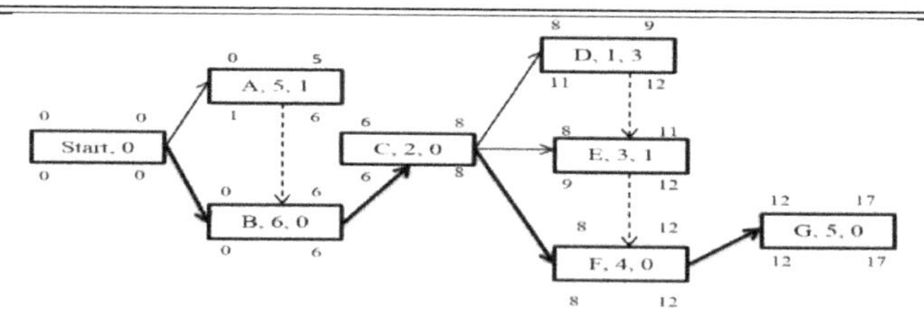 **Note:** The critical path is start, B, C, F, and G. The critical path duration or project duration is 17 days
Table 2	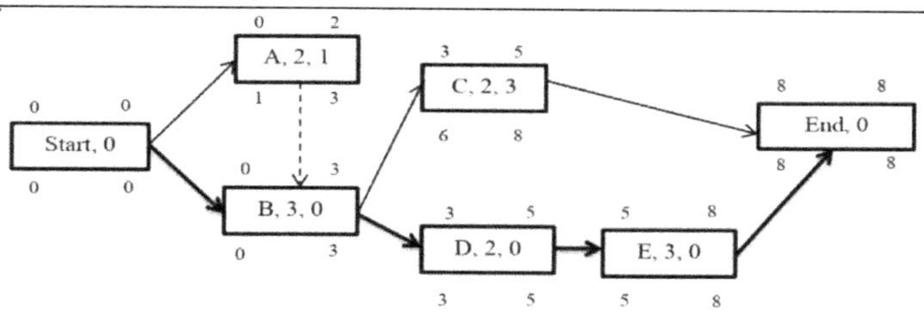 **Note**: The critical path is [Start, B, D, E and End] and the critical path duration is 8 weeks

Exercise 6

Table 1	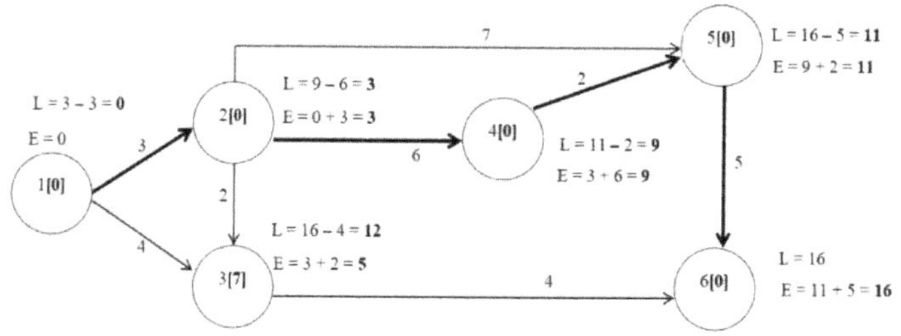 **Note:** The project completion critical path is [1 → 2 → 4 → 5 → 6] and duration is 16 days

Table 2	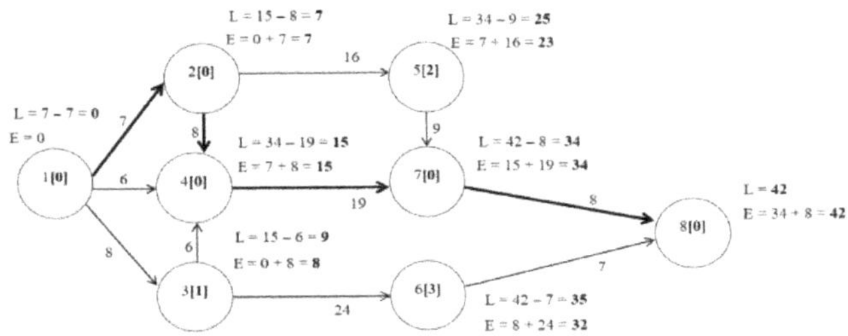 **Note:** The project completion critical path is [1 → 2 → 4 → 7 → 8] and duration is 42 weeks

Exercise 7

Table 1

Activity	A	B	C	D	E
Expected Time	2	4	10	5	7

Table 2

Activity	1 – 2	1 – 3	2 – 4	3 – 5
Expected Time	6	5	12	5

Exercise 8

Activity	Optimistic (a)	Most likely (m)	Pessimistic (b)	Expected Time (te)
A	4	5	**12**	6
B	2	3	4	**3**
C	**6**	8	22	10
D	4	**6**	8	6
E	3	4	5	**4**
F	2	4	**6**	4
G	2	3	4	**3**
H	**5**	7	15	8

Exercise 12

Activity	A	B	C	D	E	F	G
Variance	25/36	25/36	1/9	16/9	1	1	25/36
Standard Deviation	5/6	5/6	1/3	4/3	1	1	5/6

Exercise 13

Activity	Predecessor Activity	Optimistic Time	Most-Likely Time	Pessimistic Time	Variance	Standard Deviation
A		**3**	6	15	4	2
B		2	5	14	4	2
C	A	6	1	30	**16**	4
D	A	**2**	5	8	1	1
E	B,C	5	11	**7**	4	2
F	D,E	3	6	15	4	**2**

Exercise 14

Activity	A	B	C	D
Extra Cost	1,000	4,000	1,000	1,000
Possible Reduction Time	2	4	1	4

Exercise 15

Table 1

Answer				
Activity	1 – 2	1 – 3	2 – 4	3 – 4
Cost slope Value	500	250	2,000	1,000

Table

Answer								
Activity	A	B	C	D	E	F	G	H
Cost Slope	1.000	250	500	0	1,000	5,000	1,250	5,000

Exercise 17

1)

Project Completion Paths	PQTVX	PQSVX	PQTWX	PRWX	PRUX
Duration	34	30	32	24	24

Note: PQTVX is the critical path

2)

	Duration	Cost
Normal Analysis	34 Days	103,600 fcfa
Minimum Analysis	24 Days	104,650 fcfa
Optimum Analysis	28 Days	103,050 fcfa

Exercise 18

1)	Project Completion Path	ADF	ACE	BE
	Duration	34 Days	28 Days	26 Days
	Note: The critical path is ADF			

		Duration	Cost
2)	Normal Analysis	34 Days	31,200 fcfa
	Minimum Analysis	20 Days	33,300 fcfa
	Optimum Analysis	34 Days	31, 200 fcfa

Chapter nine [Decision Making]

Exercise 1

States of Nature	Decision Alternatives		
	Don't Produce (A_1)	Produce Few (A_2)	Produce Many (A_3)
Not receptive (E_1)	−50	−200	−600
Receptive (E_2)	−50	300	100
Very receptive (E_3)	−50	400	1,000

Exercise 2

States of Nature	Probability	Decision Alternatives		
		No Expansion (A_1)	Add on (A_2)	Build a New Facility (A_3)
Less (E_1)	0.3	−30	−400	−2,100
No Change (E_2)	0.1	20	−280	−1,450
Moderate Increase (E_3)	0.4	30	100	−50
Large Increase (E_4)	0.2	60	200	550

Exercise 7

States of Nature	Action (Purchase) Alternatives			Pre-regret Matrix
	Apartment building (A_1)	Office building (A_2)	Warehouse (A_3)	
Good economic condition (E_1)	$10 - 5 = 5$	$10 - 8 = 2$	$10 - 10 = 0$	$\begin{bmatrix} 5 & 2 & 0 \\ 1 & 1 & 0 \\ 0 & 3 & 5 \end{bmatrix}$
Poor economic condition (E_2)	$7 - 6 = 1$	$7 - 6 = 1$	$7 - 7 = 0$	
Best economic condition (E_3)	$10 - 10 = 0$	$10 - 7 = 3$	$10 - 5 = 5$	

Exercise 17

Original Table

Decisions	States of Nature		
	E_1	E_2	E_3
	0.25	**0.5**	**0.25**
A_1	12	−6	24
A_2	36	12	48
A_3	−3	60	30

Working Table

Decisions	States of Nature		
	E_1	E_2	E_3
	0.25	**0.5**	**0.25**
A_1	24	66	24
A_2	0	48	0
A_3	39	0	18

Chapter Ten [Chi-Square]

Exercise 4 (2)

Score	0	1	2	3	4	5	Total
Frequency	273	361	263	78	21	4	1,000
$P(X = i)$	0.2937577	0.359853183	0.220410074	0.09000078	0.027562739	0.008415524	1
$E_i = [P(X = i) \times (\sum f_i)]$	293.758	359.853	220.410	90.000	27.563	8.415	1,000

Exercise 5 (2)

Original Table						
Number of emails	0	1	2	3	4	Total
Frequency	13	22	23	12	0	70
$P(X = i)$	0.226275951	0.336246064	0.249830825	0.123749535	0.063897625	1
$E_i = [P(X = i) \times (\sum f_i)]$	15.839	23.537	17.488	8.662	4.473	70

Working Table					
Number of emails	0	1	2	3,4	Total
Frequency	13	22	23	12	70
$P(X = i)$	0.226275951	0.336246064	0.249830825	0.18764716	1
$E_i = [P(X = i) \times (\sum f_i)]$	15.839	23.537	17.488	13.135	70

Exercise 7 (2)

Nº of failing standard	Nº of weeks	Probabilities	Expected Frequency
0	35	$P(X = 0) = \frac{4!}{0!\,(4-i)!}(0.197^0 \times 0.803^{4-0}) = 0.415778646$	$0.415778646 \times 80 = 33.2623$
1	31	$P(X = 1) = \frac{4!}{1!\,(4-1)!}(0.197^1 \times 0.803^{4-1}) = 0.408011922$	$0.408011922 \times 80 = 32.6410$
2	10	$P(X = 2) = \frac{4!}{2!\,(4-2)!}(0.197^2 \times 0.803^{4-2}) = 0.150146354$	$0.150146354 \times 80 = 12.0117$
3	4	$P(X = 3) = \frac{4!}{3!\,(4-3)!}(0.197^3 \times 0.803^{4-4}) = 0.024556938$	$0.024556938 \times 80 = 1.9646$
4	0	$P(X = 4) = \frac{4!}{4!\,(4-4)!}(0.197^4 \times 0.803^{4-4}) = 0.001506138$	$0.001506138 \times 80 = 0.1205$
	$\sum = 80$	$\sum = 1$	$\sum = 80$

Exercise 10

1)

Classes	Frequency	Probability	
$X < 26$	0	$\Phi\left[\frac{26-33}{2.91}\right] = \Phi[-2.405]$	$1 - \Phi[2.405] = 1 - 0.9919 = 0.0081$
$26 \leq X < 28$	7	$\Phi\left[\frac{28-33}{2.91}\right] - \Phi\left[\frac{26-33}{2.91}\right] = \Phi[-1.718] - \Phi[-2.405]$	$\Phi[2.405] - \Phi[1.718] = 0.9919 - 0.9571 = 0.0348$
$28 \leq X < 30$	22	$\Phi\left[\frac{30-33}{2.91}\right] - \Phi\left[\frac{28-33}{2.91}\right] = \Phi[-1.031] - \Phi[-1.718]$	$\Phi[1.718] - \Phi[1.031] = 0.9571 - 0.8487 = 0.1084$
$30 \leq X < 32$	36	$\Phi\left[\frac{32-33}{2.91}\right] - \Phi\left[\frac{30-33}{2.91}\right] = \Phi[-0.344] - \Phi[-1.031]$	$\Phi[1.031] - \Phi[0.344] = 0.8487 - 0.6346 = 0.2141$
$32 \leq X < 34$	45	$\Phi\left[\frac{34-33}{2.91}\right] - \Phi\left[\frac{32-33}{2.91}\right] = \Phi[0.344] - \Phi[-0.344]$	$\Phi[0.344] + \Phi[0.344] - 1 = 0.6346 + 0.6346 - 1 = 0.2692$
$34 \leq X < 36$	33	$\Phi\left[\frac{36-33}{2.91}\right] - \Phi\left[\frac{34-33}{2.91}\right] = \Phi[1.031] - \Phi[0.344]$	$\Phi[1.031] - \Phi[0.344] = 0.8487 - 0.6346 = 0.2141$
$36 \leq X < 38$	28	$\Phi\left[\frac{38-33}{2.91}\right] - \Phi\left[\frac{36-33}{2.91}\right] = \Phi[1.718] - \Phi[1.031]$	$\Phi[1.718] - \Phi[1.031] = 0.9571 - 0.8487 = 0.1084$
$38 \leq X < 40$	4	$\Phi\left[\frac{40-33}{2.91}\right] - \Phi\left[\frac{38-33}{2.91}\right] = \Phi[2.405] - \Phi[1.718]$	$\Phi[2.405] - \Phi[1.718] = 0.9919 - 0.9571 = 0.0348$
$40 \leq X$	0	$1 - \Phi\left[\frac{40-33}{2.91}\right] = 1 - \Phi[2.405]$	$1 - \Phi[2.405] = 1 - 0.9919 = 0.0081$

2)

Table 1

Classes	Frequency	Probability	Expected Frequency
$X < 26$	0	0.0081	$0.0081 \times 175 = 1.4175$
$26 \leq X < 28$	7	0.0348	$0.0348 \times 175 = 6.09$
$28 \leq X < 30$	22	0.1084	$0.1084 \times 175 = 18.97$
$30 \leq X < 32$	36	0.2141	$0.2141 \times 175 = 37.4675$
$32 \leq X < 34$	45	0.2692	$0.2692 \times 175 = 47.11$
$34 \leq X < 36$	33	0.2141	$0.2141 \times 175 = 37.4675$
$36 \leq X < 38$	28	0.1084	$0.1084 \times 175 = 18.97$
$38 \leq X < 40$	4	0.0348	$0.0348 \times 175 = 6.09$
$40 \leq X$	0	0.0081	$0.0081 \times 175 = 1.4175$
	$\sum = 175$	$\sum = 1$	$\sum = 175$

Table 2

Classes	Frequency	Probability	Expected Frequency
$X < 28$	7	0.0429	$0.0429 \times 175 = 7.5075$
$28 \leq X < 30$	22	0.1084	$0.1084 \times 175 = 18.97$
$30 \leq X < 32$	36	0.2141	$0.2141 \times 175 = 37.4675$
$32 \leq X < 34$	45	0.2692	$0.2692 \times 175 = 47.11$
$34 \leq X < 36$	33	0.2141	$0.2141 \times 175 = 37.4675$
$36 \leq X < 38$	28	0.1084	$0.1084 \times 175 = 18.97$
$38 \leq X$	4	0.0429	$0.0429 \times 175 = 7.5075$
	$\sum = 175$	$\sum = 1$	$\sum = 175$

Exercise 13

	Divorced	Non-Divorced
Smokers	73	12
Non-Smokers	43	39

Exercise 14

	Spoiled	Unspoiled	Total
Unfumigated	8	16	24
Fumigated	2	14	16
Total	10	30	

Exercise 15

Data Table

	Happy	Sad
Male	107	289
Female	291	81

Contingency Table

	Happy	Sad	Total
Male	107	289	396
Female	291	81	372
Total	398	370	768

Expected Value Table

	Happy	Sad
Male	205.21875	190.78125
Female	192.78125	179.21875

Chapter Eleven [Control Chart]

Exercise 2

Samples	1	2	3	4	5	6	7	8	9	10	
X_1	42	64	53	62	26	27	16	17	48	41	
X_2	57	76	71	31	54	37	54	44	72	59	
X_3	36	52	41	17	62	69	32	46	76	80	
X_4	8	40	56	44	51	61	45	49	64	68	
Grand Mean ($\overline{X}_i$)	35.75	58	55.25	38.5	48.25	48.5	36.75	39	65	62	$\sum \overline{X}_i = \mathbf{487}$
Mean Range (R_i)	49	36	30	45	36	42	38	32	28	39	$\sum R_i = \mathbf{375}$
Grand Mean($\overline{\overline{X}}_i$) $= \frac{487}{10} = \mathbf{48.7}$				Mean of all Subgroup Range($\overline{R}$) $= \frac{375}{10} = \mathbf{37.5}$							

Exercise 4

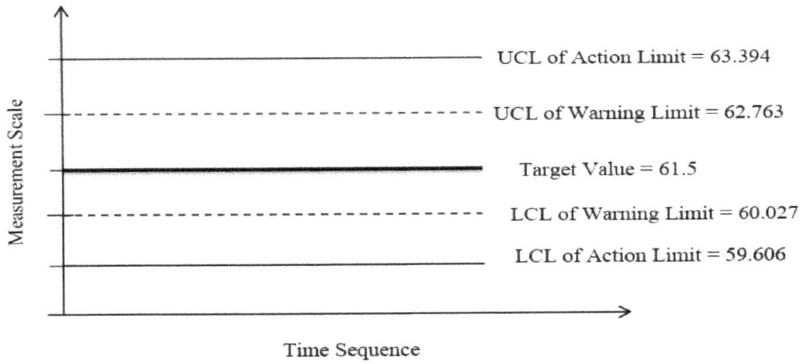

Exercise 5

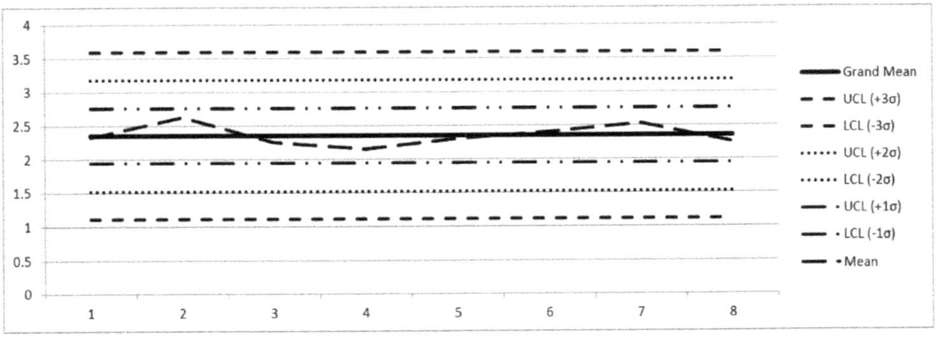

APPENDIX 2 [Statistical Tables]

THE NORMAL DISTRIBUTION FUNCTION

If Z has a normal distribution with mean 0 and variance 1, then, for each value of z, the table gives the value of $\Phi(z)$, where

$$\Phi(z) = P(Z \leqslant z).$$

For negative values of z, use $\Phi(-z) = 1 - \Phi(z)$.

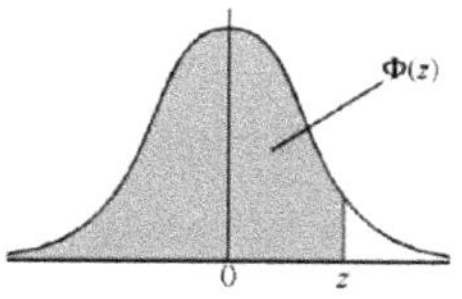

z	0	1	2	3	4	5	6	7	8	9	1	2	3	4	5	6	7	8	9
															ADD				
0.0	0.5000	0.5040	0.5080	0.5120	0.5160	0.5199	0.5239	0.5279	0.5319	0.5359	4	8	12	16	20	24	28	32	36
0.1	0.5398	0.5438	0.5478	0.5517	0.5557	0.5596	0.5636	0.5675	0.5714	0.5753	4	8	12	16	20	24	28	32	36
0.2	0.5793	0.5832	0.5871	0.5910	0.5948	0.5987	0.6026	0.6064	0.6103	0.6141	4	8	12	15	19	23	27	31	35
0.3	0.6179	0.6217	0.6255	0.6293	0.6331	0.6368	0.6406	0.6443	0.6480	0.6517	4	7	11	15	19	22	26	30	34
0.4	0.6554	0.6591	0.6628	0.6664	0.6700	0.6736	0.6772	0.6808	0.6844	0.6879	4	7	11	14	18	22	25	29	32
0.5	0.6915	0.6950	0.6985	0.7019	0.7054	0.7088	0.7123	0.7157	0.7190	0.7224	3	7	10	14	17	20	24	27	31
0.6	0.7257	0.7291	0.7324	0.7357	0.7389	0.7422	0.7454	0.7486	0.7517	0.7549	3	7	10	13	16	19	23	26	29
0.7	0.7580	0.7611	0.7642	0.7673	0.7704	0.7734	0.7764	0.7794	0.7823	0.7852	3	6	9	12	15	18	21	24	27
0.8	0.7881	0.7910	0.7939	0.7967	0.7995	0.8023	0.8051	0.8078	0.8106	0.8133	3	5	8	11	14	16	19	22	25
0.9	0.8159	0.8186	0.8212	0.8238	0.8264	0.8289	0.8315	0.8340	0.8365	0.8389	3	5	8	10	13	15	18	20	23
1.0	0.8413	0.8438	0.8461	0.8485	0.8508	0.8531	0.8554	0.8577	0.8599	0.8621	2	5	7	9	12	14	16	19	21
1.1	0.8643	0.8665	0.8686	0.8708	0.8729	0.8749	0.8770	0.8790	0.8810	0.8830	2	4	6	8	10	12	14	16	18
1.2	0.8849	0.8869	0.8888	0.8907	0.8925	0.8944	0.8962	0.8980	0.8997	0.9015	2	4	6	7	9	11	13	15	17
1.3	0.9032	0.9049	0.9066	0.9082	0.9099	0.9115	0.9131	0.9147	0.9162	0.9177	2	3	5	6	8	10	11	13	14
1.4	0.9192	0.9207	0.9222	0.9236	0.9251	0.9265	0.9279	0.9292	0.9306	0.9319	1	3	4	6	7	8	10	11	13
1.5	0.9332	0.9345	0.9357	0.9370	0.9382	0.9394	0.9406	0.9418	0.9429	0.9441	1	2	4	5	6	7	8	10	11
1.6	0.9452	0.9463	0.9474	0.9484	0.9495	0.9505	0.9515	0.9525	0.9535	0.9545	1	2	3	4	5	6	7	8	9
1.7	0.9554	0.9564	0.9573	0.9582	0.9591	0.9599	0.9608	0.9616	0.9625	0.9633	1	2	3	4	4	5	6	7	8
1.8	0.9641	0.9649	0.9656	0.9664	0.9671	0.9678	0.9686	0.9693	0.9699	0.9706	1	1	2	3	4	4	5	6	6
1.9	0.9713	0.9719	0.9726	0.9732	0.9738	0.9744	0.9750	0.9756	0.9761	0.9767	1	1	2	2	3	4	4	5	5
2.0	0.9772	0.9778	0.9783	0.9788	0.9793	0.9798	0.9803	0.9808	0.9812	0.9817	0	1	1	2	2	3	3	4	4
2.1	0.9821	0.9826	0.9830	0.9834	0.9838	0.9842	0.9846	0.9850	0.9854	0.9857	0	1	1	2	2	2	3	3	4
2.2	0.9861	0.9864	0.9868	0.9871	0.9875	0.9878	0.9881	0.9884	0.9887	0.9890	0	1	1	1	2	2	2	3	3
2.3	0.9893	0.9896	0.9898	0.9901	0.9904	0.9906	0.9909	0.9911	0.9913	0.9916	0	1	1	1	1	2	2	2	2
2.4	0.9918	0.9920	0.9922	0.9925	0.9927	0.9929	0.9931	0.9932	0.9934	0.9936	0	0	1	1	1	1	1	2	2
2.5	0.9938	0.9940	0.9941	0.9943	0.9945	0.9946	0.9948	0.9949	0.9951	0.9952	0	0	0	1	1	1	1	1	1
2.6	0.9953	0.9955	0.9956	0.9957	0.9959	0.9960	0.9961	0.9962	0.9963	0.9964	0	0	0	0	1	1	1	1	1
2.7	0.9965	0.9966	0.9967	0.9968	0.9969	0.9970	0.9971	0.9972	0.9973	0.9974	0	0	0	0	0	1	1	1	1
2.8	0.9974	0.9975	0.9976	0.9977	0.9977	0.9978	0.9979	0.9979	0.9980	0.9981	0	0	0	0	0	0	0	1	1
2.9	0.9981	0.9982	0.9982	0.9983	0.9984	0.9984	0.9985	0.9985	0.9986	0.9986	0	0	0	0	0	0	0	0	0

Critical values for the normal distribution

If Z has a normal distribution with mean 0 and variance 1, then, for each value of p, the table gives the value of z such that

$$P(Z \leqslant z) = p.$$

p	0.75	0.90	0.95	0.975	0.99	0.995	0.9975	0.999	0.9995
z	0.674	1.282	1.645	1.960	2.326	2.576	2.807	3.090	3.291

TABLES

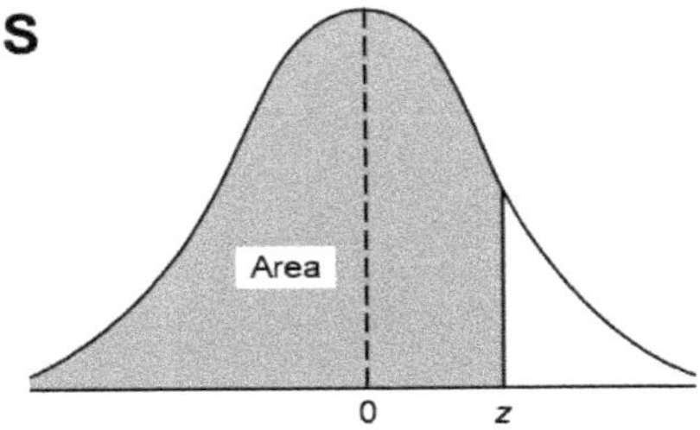

Table 1 The normal curve

(a) Area under the normal curve

z	0.00	0.01	0.02	0.03	0.04	0.05	0.06	0.07	0.08	0.09
−3.4	0.0003	0.0003	0.0003	0.0003	0.0003	0.0003	0.0003	0.0003	0.0003	0.0002
−3.3	0.0005	0.0005	0.0005	0.0004	0.0004	0.0004	0.0004	0.0004	0.0004	0.0003
−3.2	0.0007	0.0007	0.0006	0.0006	0.0006	0.0006	0.0006	0.0005	0.0005	0.0005
−3.1	0.0010	0.0009	0.0009	0.0009	0.0008	0.0008	0.0008	0.0008	0.0007	0.0007
−3.0	0.0013	0.0013	0.0013	0.0012	0.0012	0.0011	0.0011	0.0011	0.0010	0.0010
−2.9	0.0019	0.0018	0.0017	0.0017	0.0016	0.0016	0.0015	0.0015	0.0014	0.0014
−2.8	0.0026	0.0025	0.0024	0.0023	0.0023	0.0022	0.0021	0.0021	0.0020	0.0019
−2.7	0.0035	0.0034	0.0033	0.0032	0.0031	0.0030	0.0029	0.0028	0.0027	0.0026
−2.6	0.0047	0.0045	0.0044	0.0043	0.0041	0.0040	0.0039	0.0038	0.0037	0.0036
−2.5	0.0062	0.0060	0.0059	0.0057	0.0055	0.0054	0.0052	0.0051	0.0049	0.0048
−2.4	0.0082	0.0080	0.0078	0.0075	0.0073	0.0071	0.0069	0.0068	0.0066	0.0064
−2.3	0.0107	0.0104	0.0102	0.0099	0.0096	0.0094	0.0091	0.0089	0.0087	0.0084
−2.2	0.0139	0.0136	0.0132	0.0129	0.0124	0.0122	0.0119	0.0116	0.0113	0.0110
−2.1	0.0179	0.0174	0.0170	0.0166	0.0162	0.0158	0.0154	0.0150	0.0146	0.0143
−2.0	0.0228	0.0222	0.0217	0.0212	0.0207	0.0202	0.0197	0.0192	0.0188	0.0183
−1.9	0.0287	0.0281	0.0274	0.0268	0.0262	0.0256	0.0250	0.0244	0.0239	0.0233
−1.8	0.0359	0.0352	0.0344	0.0336	0.0329	0.0322	0.0314	0.0307	0.0301	0.0294
−1.7	0.0446	0.0436	0.0427	0.0418	0.0409	0.0401	0.0392	0.0384	0.0375	0.0367
−1.6	0.0548	0.0537	0.0526	0.0516	0.0505	0.0495	0.0485	0.0475	0.0465	0.0455
−1.5	0.0668	0.0655	0.0643	0.0630	0.0618	0.0606	0.0594	0.0582	0.0571	0.0559
−1.4	0.0808	0.0793	0.0778	0.0764	0.0749	0.0735	0.0722	0.0708	0.0694	0.0681
−1.3	0.0968	0.0951	0.0934	0.0918	0.0901	0.0885	0.0869	0.0853	0.0838	0.0823
−1.2	0.1151	0.1131	0.1112	0.1093	0.1075	0.1056	0.1038	0.1020	0.1003	0.0985
−1.1	0.1357	0.1335	0.1314	0.1292	0.1271	0.1251	0.1230	0.1210	0.1190	0.1170
−1.0	0.1587	0.1562	0.1539	0.1515	0.1492	0.1469	0.1446	0.1423	0.1401	0.1379
−0.9	0.1841	0.1814	0.1788	0.1762	0.1736	0.1711	0.1685	0.1660	0.1635	0.1611
−0.8	0.2119	0.2090	0.2061	0.2033	0.2005	0.1977	0.1949	0.1922	0.1894	0.1867
−0.7	0.2420	0.2389	0.2358	0.2327	0.2296	0.2266	0.2236	0.2206	0.2177	0.2148
−0.6	0.2743	0.2709	0.2676	0.2643	0.2611	0.2578	0.2546	0.2514	0.2483	0.2451
−0.5	0.3085	0.3050	0.3015	0.2981	0.2946	0.2912	0.2877	0.2843	0.2810	0.2776
−0.4	0.3446	0.3409	0.3372	0.3336	0.3300	0.3264	0.3228	0.3192	0.3156	0.3121
−0.3	0.3821	0.3783	0.3745	0.3707	0.3669	0.3632	0.3594	0.3557	0.3520	0.3483
−0.2	0.4207	0.4168	0.4129	0.4090	0.4052	0.4013	0.3974	0.3936	0.3897	0.3859
−0.1	0.4602	0.4562	0.4522	0.4483	0.4443	0.4404	0.4364	0.4325	0.4286	0.4247
−0.0	0.5000	0.4960	0.4920	0.4880	0.4840	0.4801	0.4761	0.4721	0.4681	0.4641

CRITICAL VALUES FOR THE *t*-DISTRIBUTION

If T has a t-distribution with ν degrees of freedom, then, for each pair of values of p and ν, the table gives the value of t such that:

$P(T \leqslant t) = p.$

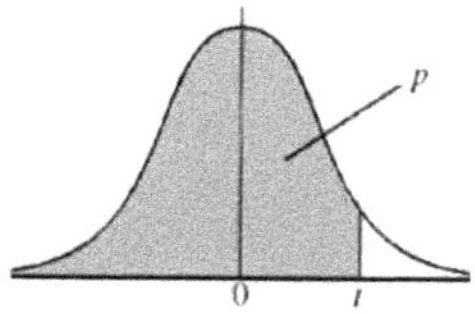

p	0.75	0.90	0.95	0.975	0.99	0.995	0.9975	0.999	0.9995
$\nu = 1$	1.000	3.078	6.314	12.71	31.82	63.66	127.3	318.3	636.6
2	0.816	1.886	2.920	4.303	6.965	9.925	14.09	22.33	31.60
3	0.765	1.638	2.353	3.182	4.541	5.841	7.453	10.21	12.92
4	0.741	1.533	2.132	2.776	3.747	4.604	5.598	7.173	8.610
5	0.727	1.476	2.015	2.571	3.365	4.032	4.773	5.894	6.869
6	0.718	1.440	1.943	2.447	3.143	3.707	4.317	5.208	5.959
7	0.711	1.415	1.895	2.365	2.998	3.499	4.029	4.785	5.408
8	0.706	1.397	1.860	2.306	2.896	3.355	3.833	4.501	5.041
9	0.703	1.383	1.833	2.262	2.821	3.250	3.690	4.297	4.781
10	0.700	1.372	1.812	2.228	2.764	3.169	3.581	4.144	4.587
11	0.697	1.363	1.796	2.201	2.718	3.106	3.497	4.025	4.437
12	0.695	1.356	1.782	2.179	2.681	3.055	3.428	3.930	4.318
13	0.694	1.350	1.771	2.160	2.650	3.012	3.372	3.852	4.221
14	0.692	1.345	1.761	2.145	2.624	2.977	3.326	3.787	4.140
15	0.691	1.341	1.753	2.131	2.602	2.947	3.286	3.733	4.073
16	0.690	1.337	1.746	2.120	2.583	2.921	3.252	3.686	4.015
17	0.689	1.333	1.740	2.110	2.567	2.898	3.222	3.646	3.965
18	0.688	1.330	1.734	2.101	2.552	2.878	3.197	3.610	3.922
19	0.688	1.328	1.729	2.093	2.539	2.861	3.174	3.579	3.883
20	0.687	1.325	1.725	2.086	2.528	2.845	3.153	3.552	3.850
21	0.686	1.323	1.721	2.080	2.518	2.831	3.135	3.527	3.819
22	0.686	1.321	1.717	2.074	2.508	2.819	3.119	3.505	3.792
23	0.685	1.319	1.714	2.069	2.500	2.807	3.104	3.485	3.768
24	0.685	1.318	1.711	2.064	2.492	2.797	3.091	3.467	3.745
25	0.684	1.316	1.708	2.060	2.485	2.787	3.078	3.450	3.725
26	0.684	1.315	1.706	2.056	2.479	2.779	3.067	3.435	3.707
27	0.684	1.314	1.703	2.052	2.473	2.771	3.057	3.421	3.689
28	0.683	1.313	1.701	2.048	2.467	2.763	3.047	3.408	3.674
29	0.683	1.311	1.699	2.045	2.462	2.756	3.038	3.396	3.660
30	0.683	1.310	1.697	2.042	2.457	2.750	3.030	3.385	3.646
40	0.681	1.303	1.684	2.021	2.423	2.704	2.971	3.307	3.551
60	0.679	1.296	1.671	2.000	2.390	2.660	2.915	3.232	3.460
120	0.677	1.289	1.658	1.980	2.358	2.617	2.860	3.160	3.373
∞	0.674	1.282	1.645	1.960	2.326	2.576	2.807	3.090	3.291

Table 3 Critical values of the *F*-distribution

Level of significance $\alpha = 0.05$

ν_2 \ ν_1	1	2	3	4	5	6	7	8	9
1	161.4	199.5	215.7	224.6	230.2	234.0	236.8	238.9	240.5
2	18.51	19.00	19.16	19.25	19.30	19.33	19.35	19.37	19.38
3	10.13	9.55	9.28	9.12	9.01	8.94	8.89	8.85	8.81
4	7.71	6.94	6.59	6.39	6.26	6.16	6.09	6.04	6.00
5	6.61	5.79	5.41	5.19	5.05	4.95	4.88	4.82	4.77
6	5.99	5.14	4.76	4.53	4.39	4.28	4.21	4.15	4.10
7	5.59	4.74	4.35	4.12	3.97	3.87	3.79	3.73	3.68
8	5.32	4.46	4.07	3.84	3.69	3.58	3.50	3.44	3.39
9	5.12	4.26	3.86	3.63	3.48	3.37	3.29	3.23	3.18
10	4.96	4.10	3.71	3.48	3.33	3.22	3.14	3.07	3.02
11	4.84	3.98	3.59	3.36	3.20	3.09	3.01	2.95	2.90
12	4.75	3.89	3.49	3.26	3.11	3.00	2.91	2.85	2.80
13	4.67	3.81	3.41	3.18	3.03	2.92	2.83	2.77	2.71
14	4.60	3.74	3.34	3.11	2.96	2.85	2.76	2.70	2.65
15	4.54	3.68	3.29	3.06	2.90	2.79	2.71	2.64	2.59
16	4.49	3.63	3.24	3.01	2.85	2.74	2.66	2.59	2.54
17	4.45	3.59	3.20	2.96	2.81	2.70	2.61	2.55	2.49
18	4.41	3.55	3.16	2.93	2.77	2.66	2.58	2.51	2.46
19	4.38	3.52	3.13	2.90	2.74	2.63	2.54	2.48	2.42
20	4.35	3.49	3.10	2.87	2.71	2.60	2.51	2.45	2.39
21	4.32	3.47	3.07	2.84	2.68	2.57	2.49	2.42	2.37
22	4.30	3.44	3.05	2.82	2.66	2.55	2.46	2.40	2.34
23	4.28	3.42	3.03	2.80	2.64	2.53	2.44	2.37	2.32
24	4.26	3.40	3.01	2.78	2.62	2.51	2.42	2.36	2.30
25	4.24	3.39	2.99	2.76	2.60	2.49	2.40	2.34	2.28
26	4.23	3.37	2.98	2.74	2.59	2.47	2.39	2.32	2.27
27	4.21	3.35	2.96	2.73	2.57	2.46	2.37	2.31	2.25
28	4.20	3.34	2.95	2.71	2.56	2.45	2.36	2.29	2.24
29	4.18	3.33	2.93	2.70	2.55	2.43	2.35	2.28	2.22
30	4.17	3.32	2.92	2.69	2.53	2.42	2.33	2.27	2.21
40	4.08	3.23	2.84	2.61	2.45	2.34	2.25	2.18	2.12
60	4.00	3.15	2.76	2.53	2.37	2.25	2.17	2.10	2.04
120	3.92	3.07	2.68	2.45	2.29	2.17	2.09	2.02	1.96
∞	3.84	3.00	2.60	2.37	2.21	2.10	2.01	1.94	1.88

Table 3 continued

Level of significance $\alpha = 0.05$

ν_2 \ ν_1	10	12	15	20	24	30	40	60	120	∞
1	241.9	243.9	245.9	248.0	249.1	250.1	251.1	252.2	253.3	254.3
2	19.40	19.41	19.43	19.45	19.45	19.46	19.47	19.48	19.49	19.50
3	8.79	8.74	8.70	8.66	8.64	8.62	8.59	8.57	8.55	8.53
4	5.96	5.91	5.86	5.80	5.77	5.75	5.72	5.69	5.66	5.63
5	4.74	4.68	4.62	4.56	4.53	4.50	4.46	4.43	4.40	4.36
6	4.06	4.00	3.94	3.87	3.84	3.81	3.77	3.74	3.70	3.67
7	3.64	3.57	3.51	3.44	3.41	3.38	3.34	3.30	3.27	3.23
8	3.35	3.28	3.22	3.15	3.12	3.08	3.04	3.01	2.97	2.93
9	3.14	3.07	3.01	2.94	2.90	2.86	2.83	2.79	2.75	2.71
10	2.98	2.91	2.85	2.77	2.74	2.70	2.66	2.62	2.58	2.54
11	2.85	2.79	2.72	2.65	2.61	2.57	2.53	2.49	2.45	2.40
12	2.75	2.69	2.62	2.54	2.51	2.47	2.43	2.38	2.34	2.30
13	2.67	2.60	2.53	2.46	2.42	2.38	2.34	2.30	2.25	2.21
14	2.60	2.53	2.46	2.39	2.35	2.31	2.27	2.22	2.18	2.13
15	2.54	2.48	2.40	2.33	2.29	2.25	2.20	2.16	2.11	2.07
16	2.49	2.42	2.35	2.28	2.24	2.19	2.15	2.11	2.06	2.01
17	2.45	2.38	2.31	2.23	2.19	2.15	2.10	2.06	2.01	1.96
18	2.41	2.34	2.27	2.19	2.15	2.11	2.06	2.02	1.97	1.92
19	2.38	2.31	2.23	2.16	2.11	2.07	2.03	1.98	1.93	1.88
20	2.35	2.28	2.20	2.12	2.08	2.04	1.99	1.95	1.90	1.84
21	2.32	2.25	2.18	2.10	2.05	2.01	1.96	1.92	1.87	1.81
22	2.30	2.23	2.15	2.07	2.03	1.98	1.94	1.89	1.84	1.78
23	2.27	2.20	2.13	2.05	2.01	1.96	1.91	1.86	1.81	1.76
24	2.25	2.18	2.11	2.03	1.98	1.94	1.89	1.84	1.79	1.73
25	2.24	2.16	2.09	2.01	1.96	1.92	1.87	1.82	1.77	1.71
26	2.22	2.15	2.07	1.99	1.95	1.90	1.85	1.80	1.75	1.69
27	2.20	2.13	2.06	1.97	1.93	1.88	1.84	1.79	1.73	1.67
28	2.19	2.12	2.04	1.96	1.91	1.87	1.82	1.77	1.71	1.65
29	2.18	2.10	2.03	1.94	1.90	1.85	1.81	1.75	1.70	1.64
30	2.16	2.09	2.01	1.93	1.89	1.84	1.79	1.74	1.68	1.62
40	2.08	2.00	1.92	1.84	1.79	1.74	1.69	1.64	1.58	1.51
60	1.99	1.92	1.84	1.75	1.70	1.65	1.59	1.53	1.47	1.39
120	1.91	1.83	1.75	1.66	1.61	1.55	1.50	1.43	1.35	1.25
∞	1.83	1.75	1.67	1.57	1.52	1.46	1.39	1.32	1.22	1.00

Table 3 continued

Level of significance $\alpha = 0.01$

ν_2 \ ν_1	1	2	3	4	5	6	7	8	9
1	4052	4999	5403	5625	5764	5859	5928	5981	6022
2	98.50	99.00	99.17	99.25	99.30	99.33	99.36	99.37	99.39
3	34.12	30.82	29.46	28.71	28.24	27.91	27.67	27.49	27.35
4	21.20	18.00	16.69	15.98	15.52	15.21	14.98	14.80	14.66
5	16.26	13.27	12.06	11.39	10.97	10.67	10.46	10.29	10.16
6	13.75	10.92	9.78	9.15	8.75	8.47	8.26	8.10	7.98
7	12.25	9.55	8.45	7.85	7.46	7.19	6.99	6.84	6.72
8	11.26	8.65	7.59	7.01	6.63	6.37	6.18	6.03	5.91
9	10.56	8.02	6.99	6.42	6.06	5.80	5.61	5.47	5.35
10	10.04	7.56	6.55	5.99	5.64	5.39	5.20	5.06	4.94
11	9.65	7.21	6.22	5.67	5.32	5.07	4.89	4.74	4.63
12	9.33	6.93	5.95	5.41	5.06	4.82	4.64	4.50	4.39
13	9.07	6.70	5.74	5.21	4.86	4.62	4.44	4.30	4.19
14	8.86	6.51	5.56	5.04	4.69	4.46	4.28	4.14	4.03
15	8.68	6.36	5.42	4.89	4.56	4.32	4.14	4.00	3.89
16	8.53	6.23	5.29	4.77	4.44	4.20	4.03	3.89	3.78
17	8.40	6.11	5.18	4.67	4.34	4.10	3.93	3.79	3.68
18	8.29	6.01	5.09	4.58	4.25	4.01	3.84	3.71	3.60
19	8.18	5.93	5.01	4.50	4.17	3.94	3.77	3.63	3.52
20	8.10	5.85	4.94	4.43	4.10	3.87	3.70	3.56	3.46
21	8.02	5.78	4.87	4.37	4.04	3.81	3.64	3.51	3.40
22	7.95	5.72	4.82	4.31	3.99	3.76	3.59	3.45	3.35
23	7.88	5.66	4.76	4.26	3.94	3.71	3.54	3.41	3.30
24	7.82	5.61	4.72	4.22	3.90	3.67	3.50	3.36	3.26
25	7.77	5.57	4.68	4.18	3.85	3.63	3.46	3.32	3.22
26	7.72	5.53	4.64	4.14	3.82	3.59	3.42	3.29	3.18
27	7.68	5.49	4.60	4.11	3.78	3.56	3.39	3.26	3.15
28	7.64	5.45	4.57	4.07	3.75	3.53	3.36	3.23	3.12
29	7.60	5.42	4.54	4.04	3.73	3.50	3.33	3.20	3.09
30	7.56	5.39	4.51	4.02	3.70	3.47	3.30	3.17	3.07
40	7.31	5.18	4.31	3.83	3.51	3.29	3.12	2.99	2.89
60	7.08	4.98	4.13	3.65	3.34	3.12	2.95	2.82	2.72
120	6.85	4.79	3.95	3.48	3.17	2.96	2.79	2.66	2.56
∞	6.63	4.61	3.78	3.32	3.02	2.80	2.64	2.51	2.41

Table 3 continued

Level of significance $\alpha = 0.01$

ν_2 \ ν_1	10	12	15	20	24	30	40	60	120	∞
1	6056	6106	6157	6209	6235	6261	6287	6313	6339	6366
2	99.40	99.42	99.43	99.45	99.46	99.47	99.47	99.48	99.49	99.50
3	27.23	27.05	26.87	26.69	26.60	26.50	26.41	26.32	26.22	26.13
4	14.55	14.37	14.20	14.02	13.39	13.84	13.75	13.65	13.56	13.46
5	10.05	9.89	9.72	9.55	9.47	9.38	9.29	9.20	9.11	9.02
6	7.87	7.72	7.56	7.40	7.31	7.23	7.14	7.06	6.97	6.88
7	6.62	6.47	6.31	6.16	6.07	5.99	5.91	5.82	5.74	5.65
8	5.81	5.67	5.52	5.36	5.28	5.20	5.12	5.03	4.95	4.86
9	5.26	5.11	4.96	4.81	4.73	4.65	4.57	4.48	4.40	4.31
10	4.85	4.71	4.56	4.41	4.33	4.25	4.17	4.08	4.00	3.91
11	4.54	4.40	4.25	4.10	4.02	3.94	3.86	3.78	3.69	3.60
12	4.30	4.16	4.01	3.86	3.78	3.70	3.62	3.54	3.45	3.36
13	4.10	3.96	3.82	3.66	3.59	3.51	3.43	3.34	3.25	3.17
14	3.94	3.80	3.66	3.51	3.43	3.35	3.27	3.18	3.09	3.00
15	3.80	3.67	3.52	3.37	3.29	3.21	3.13	3.05	2.96	2.87
16	3.69	3.55	3.41	3.26	3.18	3.10	3.02	2.93	2.84	2.75
17	3.59	3.46	3.31	3.16	3.08	3.00	2.92	2.83	2.75	2.65
18	3.51	3.37	3.23	3.08	3.00	2.92	2.84	2.75	2.66	2.57
19	3.43	3.30	3.15	3.00	2.92	2.84	2.76	2.67	2.58	2.49
20	3.37	3.23	3.09	2.94	2.86	2.78	2.69	2.61	2.52	2.42
21	3.31	3.17	3.03	2.88	2.80	2.72	2.64	2.55	2.46	2.36
22	3.26	3.12	2.98	2.83	2.75	2.67	2.58	2.50	2.40	2.31
23	3.21	3.07	2.93	2.78	2.70	2.62	2.54	2.45	2.35	2.26
24	3.17	3.03	2.89	2.74	2.66	2.58	2.49	2.40	2.31	2.21
25	3.13	2.99	2.85	2.70	2.62	2.54	2.45	2.36	2.27	2.17
26	3.09	2.96	2.81	2.66	2.58	2.50	2.42	2.33	2.23	2.13
27	3.06	2.93	2.78	2.63	2.55	2.47	2.38	2.29	2.20	2.10
28	3.03	2.90	2.75	2.60	2.52	2.44	2.35	2.26	2.17	2.06
29	3.00	2.87	2.73	2.57	2.49	2.41	2.33	2.23	2.14	2.03
30	2.98	2.84	2.70	2.55	2.47	2.39	2.30	2.21	2.11	2.01
40	2.80	2.66	2.52	2.37	2.29	2.20	2.11	2.02	1.92	1.80
60	2.63	2.50	2.35	2.20	2.12	2.03	1.94	1.84	1.73	1.60
120	2.47	2.34	2.19	2.03	1.95	1.86	1.76	1.66	1.53	1.38
∞	2.32	2.18	2.04	1.88	1.79	1.70	1.59	1.47	1.32	1.00

Source: Pearson and Hartley, 1970

Table 5 Critical values for the χ^2-distribution

Columns a denote the lower boundaries or the left-sided critical values.
Columns b denote the upper boundaries or the right-sided critical values.

	Level of significance α							
Two-sided	0.20		0.10		0.05		0.01	
One-sided	0.10		0.05		0.025		0.005	
ν	a	b	a	b	a	b	a	b
1	0.016	2.71	39.10^{-4}	3.84	98.10^{-5}	5.02	16.10^{-5}	6.63
2	0.21	4.61	0.10	5.99	0.05	7.38	0.02	9.21
3	0.58	6.25	0.35	7.81	0.22	9.35	0.11	11.34
4	1.06	7.78	0.71	9.49	0.48	11.14	0.30	13.28
5	1.61	9.24	1.15	11.07	0.83	12.83	0.55	15.09
6	2.20	10.64	1.64	12.59	1.24	14.45	0.87	16.81
7	2.83	12.02	2.17	14.07	1.69	16.01	1.24	18.48
8	3.49	13.36	2.73	15.51	2.18	17.53	1.65	20.09
9	4.17	14.68	3.33	16.92	2.70	19.02	2.09	21.67
10	4.87	15.99	3.94	18.31	3.25	20.48	2.56	23.21
11	5.58	17.28	4.57	19.68	3.82	21.92	3.05	24.73
12	6.30	18.55	5.23	21.03	4.40	23.34	3.57	26.22
13	7.04	19.81	5.89	22.36	5.01	24.74	4.11	27.69
14	7.79	21.06	6.57	23.68	5.63	26.12	4.66	29.14
15	8.55	22.31	7.26	25.00	6.26	27.49	5.23	30.58
16	9.31	23.54	7.96	26.30	6.91	28.85	5.81	32.00
17	10.09	24.77	8.67	27.59	7.56	30.19	6.41	33.41
18	10.86	25.99	9.39	28.87	8.23	31.53	7.01	34.81
19	11.65	27.20	10.12	30.14	8.91	32.85	7.63	36.19
20	12.44	28.41	10.85	31.41	9.59	34.17	8.26	37.57
21	13.24	29.62	11.59	32.67	10.28	35.48	8.90	38.93
22	14.04	30.81	12.34	33.92	10.98	36.78	9.54	40.29
23	14.85	32.01	13.09	35.17	11.69	38.08	10.20	41.64
24	15.66	33.20	13.85	36.42	12.40	39.36	10.86	42.98
25	16.47	34.38	14.61	37.65	13.12	40.65	11.52	44.31
26	17.29	35.56	15.38	38.89	13.84	41.92	12.20	45.64
27	18.11	36.74	16.15	40.11	14.57	43.19	12.88	46.96
28	18.94	37.92	16.93	41.34	15.31	44.46	13.56	48.28
29	19.77	39.09	17.71	42.56	16.05	45.72	14.26	49.59
30	20.60	40.26	18.49	43.77	16.79	46.98	14.95	50.89
40	29.05	51.81	26.51	55.76	24.43	59.34	22.16	63.69
50	37.69	63.17	34.76	67.50	32.36	71.42	29.71	76.15
60	46.46	74.40	43.19	79.08	40.48	83.30	37.48	88.38
70	55.33	85.53	51.74	90.53	48.76	95.02	45.44	100.43
80	64.28	96.58	60.39	101.88	57.15	106.63	53.54	112.33
90	73.29	107.57	69.13	113.15	65.65	118.14	61.75	124.12
100	82.36	118.50	77.93	124.34	74.22	129.56	70.06	135.81

REFERENCES

Andren T. (2007). Econometrics. Ventus publishing APS. ISBN: 978-87-7681-235-5.

Atanga N. A. (2008). Advanced Level Mechanics and Probability. Revised Edition

Casado, D. (2015). Statistical Inference. *Statistics*, *35*, 37.

Crawshaw, J., & Chambers, J. (2001). *A concise course in advanced level statistics: with worked examples*. Nelson Thornes.

Creel, M. (2002). Graduate Econometrics Lecture Notes.

Dunn, O. J., & Clark, V. A. (2009). *Basic statistics: a primer for the biomedical sciences*. John Wiley & Sons.

Durrett, R. (2019). *Probability: theory and examples* (Vol. 49). Cambridge university press.

H Greene, W. (2002). Econometric analysis.

Hong, Y. (2011). Advanced Econometrics.

Hsu, H. P. (1997). *Schaum's outline of theory and problems of probability, random variables, and random processes*. McGraw-Hill.

Mason L. R. (1988). Mathematics for Business and Commerce. 4th Edition, Business Publication INC. ISBN 0 – 256 – 05921 – 7.

Podgorski K. (2009). Lecture Notes on Statistical Inference. Department of Mathematics and Statistics; University of Limerick, Ireland.

Reddy, T. A. (2011). *Applied data analysis and modeling for energy engineers and scientists*. Springer Science & Business Media.

Ross, S. M. (2004). *Introduction to probability and statistics for engineers and scientists*. Elsevier.

Sahoo, P. (2013). Probability and mathematical statistics. *University of Louisville*.

Salvatore D. & Reagle D. (2002). Theory and Problems of Statistics and Econometrics. Second edition. Copyright by McGraw-Hill Companies, Inc. ISBN: 0-07-134852-2.

Shao, J. (2006). *Mathematical statistics: exercises and solutions*. Springer Science & Business Media.

Soong, T. T. (2004). *Fundamentals of probability and statistics for engineers*. John Wiley & Sons.

Vohra, R. V. (2004). *Advanced mathematical economics*. Routledge.

Xie, T. (2012). A Sample Lecture Notes for Undergraduate Econometrics.

www.ingramcontent.com/pod-product-compliance
Ingram Content Group UK Ltd.
Pitfield, Milton Keynes, MK11 3LW, UK
UKHW020659041026
15590UKWH00001B/363

9 781639 027286